Masters of the
"Humdrum" Mystery

Masters of the "Humdrum" Mystery

*Cecil John Charles Street,
Freeman Wills Crofts,
Alfred Walter Stewart and the
British Detective Novel, 1920–1961*

CURTIS EVANS

McFarland & Company, Inc., Publishers
Jefferson, North Carolina, and London

LIBRARY OF CONGRESS CATALOGUING-IN-PUBLICATION DATA

Evans, Curtis J., 1965–
Masters of the "humdrum" mystery : Cecil John Charles Street,
Freeman Wills Crofts, Alfred Walter Stewart and the British
detective novel, 1920–1961 / Curtis Evans.
        p.   cm.

ISBN 978-0-7864-7024-2
softcover : acid free paper ∞

1. Detective and mystery stories, English — History and criticism. 2. Street, Cecil J.C. (Cecil John Charles), 1884–1964 — Criticism and interpretation. 3. Crofts, Freeman Wills, 1879–1957 — Criticism and interpretation. 4. Connington, J.J., 1880–1947 — Criticism and interpretation. 5. Science in literature. 6. Detective and mystery stories, English — Appreciation. I. Title. II. Title: British detective novel, 1920–1961.
PR830.D4E93   2012
823'.087209091—dc23   2012014497

BRITISH LIBRARY CATALOGUING DATA ARE AVAILABLE

© 2012 Curtis Evans. All rights reserved

No part of this book may be reproduced or transmitted in any form or by any means, electronic or mechanical, including photocopying or recording, or by any information storage and retrieval system, without permission in writing from the publisher.

Front cover images: © 2012 Shutterstock

Manufactured in the United States of America

*McFarland & Company, Inc., Publishers
Box 611, Jefferson, North Carolina 28640
www.mcfarlandpub.com*

This book is dedicated to
Jacques Barzun, who catalogued crime;
Douglas Greene, who explained miracles; and
Bill Pronzini, who kept gun in cheek.

Table of Contents

Preface   1
Introduction: Mere Puzzles?   5

CHAPTER ONE
"The Masters": Cecil John Charles Street, Freeman Wills Crofts, and Alfred Walter Stewart   15

CHAPTER TWO
Cecil John Charles Street (John Rhode/Miles Burton) (1884–1964): Public Brain Tester No. 1   45

CHAPTER THREE
Freeman Wills Crofts (1879–1957): The Greatest Puritan of Them All   146

CHAPTER FOUR
Alfred Walter Stewart (J.J. Connington) (1880–1947): Survival of the Fittest   193

Appendix I: Notable Criminous Works by Cecil John Charles Street   247
Appendix II: Notable Criminous Works by Freeman Wills Crofts   250
Appendix III: Round Robin Writer: Freeman Wills Crofts' Contributions to The Floating Admiral *(1931) and* Double Death *(1939)*   252
Appendix IV: Notable Genre Works by Alfred Walter Stewart   255
Chapter Notes   257
Bibliography   281
Index   291

Preface

MORE THAN TWENTY YEARS AGO, in the spring of 1989, Chinese students protested tyranny in Tiananmen Square and I encountered John Dickson Carr in the mystery section of a basement Chicago bookstore. The event in which I was concerned obviously was a much less important one, yet it resulted in the book you are reading today. I encountered three paperback reprint John Dickson Carr novels, to be precise — two with prefaces from the dean of American mystery genre scholars and future Carr biographer Douglas G. Greene — tales with the evocative titles *Hag's Nook*, *The Burning Court* and *The Judas Window*. Suddenly in my early twenties I realized there was more to classical fair play puzzle detective fiction than the myriad Agatha Christie novels I had read in the late 1970s and early 1980s as an adolescent, more even than the novels I had read in the mid–'80s by Christie's sister "Crime Queens," Dorothy L. Sayers, Margery Allingham and Ngaio Marsh. By the time I entered graduate school the next year, I had discovered both Bill Pronzini's and Marcia Muller's mammoth *1001 Midnights* and Jacques Barzun's and Wendell Hertig Taylor's gargantuan *A Catalogue of Crime*, and with them additional highly praised fair play detective novelists: Cecil John Charles Street, Freeman Wills Crofts, J.J. Connington, Henry Wade. Searching the used bookstores of Baton Rouge — Caliban's was a particularly rich repository — I was able to find no Conningtons at all but I did happen on some Wade titles reprinted in an enterprising Harper & Row series (Harper Perennials), a couple Street books (also Harper Perennials) and some Crofts novels in old Penguin editions from the 1960s. Yet my appetite was scarcely satiated. Cecil (I would later learn he went by John) Street, for example, had written something like 140 novels, mostly true tales of detection. What in the world had happened to them all? Why had they been swept from the bookshelves — swept, indeed, from the shelves of mystery genre history?

I had other things to concern me in the 1990s (for example, getting a Ph.D. in American history), but by the late 1990s I had found that the internet afforded wonderful opportunities for locating books by undeservedly forgotten "Golden Age" mystery authors. Such sites as AbeBooks and the online auction site eBay were then gold mines for even the most demanding and discriminating fans of classical mystery fiction. As I amassed my personal collection of Streets, Crofts, Conningtons, Wades and other writers (and began book dealing myself), I realized how much of the history of the detective fiction of the Golden Age was lost in genre studies focusing so determinedly and relentlessly on contrasting four British Crime Queens (Christie, Sayers, Allingham, Marsh) with the male hard-boiled authors of the United States (most famously Dashiell Hammett and Raymond Chandler).

How had this state of affairs come into being? As readers of this book will soon see, much of the responsibility must rest with a crime writer I genuinely admire, Julian Symons (1912–1994), and the hugely influential mystery genre survey that he originally penned in 1972, *Bloody Murder*. Determined to cut the fair play puzzle detective novel down to size and to elevate in stature the "crime novel" (with which he himself was mostly associated), Symons cast numerous Golden Age writers into literary perdition as "Humdrums": writers who had some limited talent for puzzle construction, but no finer qualities whatsoever, making them essentially unreadable, in his view. Some of the writers Symons damned as Humdrums by no conceivable measure belonged there (for example, Henry Wade, one of the most accomplished Golden Age pioneers of the crime and police procedural novels). And while Street, Crofts and Connington admittedly focused more on the puzzle than purely literary stylings, their books to me clearly were vastly more interesting, both as puzzles and as social documents—sometimes even purely as novels—than Symons allowed.

The flood of academic studies following *Bloody Murder* in the last forty years has compounded the injustice originally inflicted by Julian Symons, though from a different motivating force. Symons' authoritative "Humdrums" paradigm well served mystery genre scholars bent on bifurcating the history of the genre into a "masculine" hard-boiled style prevalent in the United States and a "feminine" cozy or domestic style ascendant in Great Britain. Only one British woman writer, Margaret Cole (one-half of the mystery writing and political theorizing team of G.D.H. and Margaret Cole), ever was included by Symons in the Humdrum ranks, meaning that on the whole the "Humdrums" were an overwhelmingly male body that could be conveniently snipped from gynocentric mystery genre studies. Returning once important male British mystery writers to the history of the Golden Age detective novel may complicate the narrative that mystery genre scholars have laboriously constructed over the last forty years, but sometimes truth requires complication. Literary history cannot always be so nicely and neatly compartmentalized.

Other male Golden Age English detective novelists deserve greater attention as well—as do, indeed, female authors who were not part of the elect group of "Crime Queens." John Dickson Carr, H.C. Bailey, Michael Innes, Nicholas Blake, Anthony Berkeley Cox, Milward Kennedy, Henry Wade, R. Austin Freeman (a pre–Golden age writer who also published fiction all though the Golden Age), Anthony Gilbert (pseudonym of a woman), E.C.R. Lorac (ditto) and Gladys Mitchell are some of the writers who have been unjustly neglected in genre studies focusing mostly on the Crime Queens (similarly, American Golden Age mystery writers who did not write in the hard-boiled style tend to be overlooked in genre studies today). Yet the so-called Humdum writers are a deserving group in their own right. For one thing, they have been the most persistently and undeservedly defamed of English mystery writers from the Golden Age period. Elementary fairness calls for a more in-depth look at their written record. Secondly, as a group they offer a picture of the genre as it existed between the two world wars that is strikingly different in many ways from what we customarily get in academic studies. Focusing mostly on the Crime Queens Christie, Sayers, Allingham and Marsh has produced often interesting but unfortunately overly sweeping assessments of the English Golden Age detective novel as "feminized" and culturally/politically High Tory (agrarian and backward-looking) in nature. The Humdrum writers John Street (an army officer and electrical engineer), Freeman Wills Crofts (a railway engineer) and J.J. Connington (a chemistry professor) often varied considerably in their social/political outlooks from the Crime Queens. Aesthetically they differed from the Crime Queens as well, exhibiting less of an interest in the arts and social manners and a greater interest in business and industry, science and material detail. While Agatha Christie and Dorothy L. Sayers admitted the influence on their work of nineteenth century mystery novels by, respectively, Anna Katharine Green (*The Leavenworth Case*) and Wilkie Collins (*The Moonstone*), the Humdrums followed in the footsteps of Arthur Conan Doyle's closest rival, R. Austin Freeman, creator of the great scientific detective, Dr. John Thorndyke. Their emphasis on material detail and technical and scientific soundness has lost favor in the modern world of the crime novel, which prefers morbid psychology, physical violence and emotional exhibition; yet the Humdrum approach once had many admirers. To fully understand the world of Golden Age detective fiction, we must disinter and analyze the long-buried works (familiar today mostly to collectors) by such neglected prominent writers from the period as the Humdrums.

As I expect the Introduction will demonstrate, I am conversant with academic literature on the subject of Golden Age detective fiction and I have been influenced by certain fine academic studies, such as Alison Light's pathbreaking *Forever England: Femininity, Literature and Conservatism between the Wars* (1991), with its illuminating chapter on Agatha Christie and persuasive thesis concerning "conservative modernity," and Merja Makinen's *Agatha Christie: Investigating Femininity* (2006), which brilliantly develops and expands Professor Light's arguments. Yet because of the pervasive academic neglect of male writers of English Golden Age detective fiction, particularly the Humdrums, to a great extent I have been plowing a virgin field. What I have found especially helpful is (1) tracking down and reading the books themselves (no easy task), (2) working with primary sources such as newspapers, magazines, journals, diaries and letters from the 1920s through the 1950s to recover the material culture of the detective fiction genre in those decades, and (3) absorbing certain works outside the narrower ambit of the modern academic monograph, such as H. Douglas Thomson's *Masters of Mystery* (1931), an overlooked — one might say criminally overlooked — analysis of detective fiction; Jacques Barzun's and Wendell Hertig Taylor's magisterial *A Catalogue of Crime* (1971/1989); Bill Pronzini's and Marcia Muller's fascinating *1001 Midnights* (1986); Bill Pronzini's hilarious and learned study of "alternative" classics of crime fiction, *Gun in Cheek* (1982); and Douglas G. Greene's classic 1995 biography of one of the great masters of Golden Age fair play puzzle detective fiction, John Dickson Carr. Not only did these books personally inspire me with their erudition and accessible writing, they took me into the world of the Golden Age detective novel in a way many theory-driven academic monographs do not seem able to do. My dedication page speaks to the debt I owe these writers. Bill and Doug in particular must be singled out here for the continual encouragement they offered me over the years, when I myself on occasion had become dejected with the project's prospects.

My list of acknowledgments necessarily is considerably longer, for many additional individuals helped this book along its journey from inception to publication. Heidi Truty, Head of Public Services/Archivist of the Marion E. Wade Center, Wheaton College, was unfailingly helpful in facilitating my work with the Dorothy L. Sayers papers located at that institution. Jonathan Betts, Senior Specialist in horology at the Royal Observatory, Greenwich, was extremely generous in making available for my perusal his copies of the correspondence between Alfred Walter Stewart (J.J. Connington) and Rupert Thomas

Gould. That great Golden Age researcher Tony Medawar has been quite kind and supportive, as has Peter Lovesey, Detection Club member and distinguished crime writer in the classical tradition.

A long line of correspondents must be mentioned for information kindly imparted to me: Irene Stewart, daughter of Alfred Walter Stewart (J.J. Connington); Edward Aubrey-Fletcher, youngest child of Henry Lancelot Aubrey-Fletcher (Henry Wade); Josephine Pullein-Thompson, daughter of Joanna Cannan; Paula Simpson, friend of John Street when he lived in the village of Swanton Novers during the 1940s; Juanita Hadwin for the information on Swanton Novers on her website and her introduction of me to her cousin Paula Simpson; Martin Roundell-Greene, who discovered John Street's career as an electrical engineer; Tony Kremer, local historian of Yalding, Kent, who provided me with information on Street's years in the village of Laddingford and with photographs of Street and his house; Patrick Mileham of Street's alma mater, Wellington College; Mark Terry, owner of the fantastically informative Facsimile Dust Jackets L.L.C. website; and bookseller Mark Sutcliffe and his *Two Brothers*.

Numerous net friends must be mentioned also. Jon Jermey's GAdetection site on yahoo served as an incubator for this project, with its countless group discussions about detective fiction from a lively host of learned and talented people, including (among others) Xavier Lechard (At the Villa Rose), Henrique Vallé, Nick Fuller, Jeffrey Marks, Kevin Killian, Les Blatt (classicmysteries.net), John Norris (Pretty Sinister Books), Mike Grost (mikegrost.com), Carola Dunn, Patrick Ohl (At the Scene of the Crime) and "Tom-Cat" (Detection by Moonlight). Great thanks must go as well to Sam Karnick of The American Culture (at stkarnick.com), Steve Lewis of Mystery*File and Geoff Bradley, editor of *CADS: Crime and Detective Stories*, for publishing my essays and articles over the last several years and for their moral support of my book projects. Also from mysteryfile, that stimulating contributor David Vineyard should be mentioned. The discerning collector Anita Hoffman made available to me a couple exceedingly rare Miles Burton books — one of which, the delightful *To Catch a Thief* (1934), found its way into the John Street section at several points. The advice of Ralph Spurrier (of Post Mortem Books) and Tom Schantz (of Rue Morgue Press) on certain matters was pertinent and timely. David Lane provided the delightful and unexpected photograph of his relative Eileen Street holding the feline that likely was the model for Belisarius, the murder witness in *The Cat Jumps* (1946).

Determined as I was to carry out this project, sometimes I began to wonder whether those who assured me that "it couldn't be done" were right. Many more people, however, advised me that it could be done and I listened to them. Fortunately, *they* were the ones who were right.

Spoilers

In some cases thorough illustration of the plotting ability and the themes of the authors discussed in this book require divulging aspects of mystery solutions, or "spoilers." Points in the book where this occurs will be marked by the headings [**SPOILER ALERT**] at the beginning of the spoiler and [**END SPOILER ALERT**] at its termination.

Introduction
Mere Puzzles?

Reviewing John Curran's *Agatha Christie's Secret Notebooks* (2009), an exhaustive structural analysis of the Queen of Crime's copious surviving working notes, Agatha Christie biographer Laura Thompson complained that the effect of Curran's book was "to make Christie seem like not much more than the sum of her plots ... a mere devisor of puzzles." In an earlier article that touched in part on the *Secret Notebooks*, Thompson asserted that to treat Christie simply as an ingenious puzzle maker was, in her view, essentially an act of denigration. "Her critics have called Christie a purveyor of mere puzzles, of 'animated algebra,'" wrote Thompson. "Yet if she were only that, it is impossible her books could have endured as they have. [Christie] had an intrinsic wisdom — a grasp of human nature — that informed the geometry of her plots and made them profoundly, morally satisfying." This idea expressed by Laura Thompson, that writing puzzles—*mere* puzzles — is an inherently less worthy endeavor for a detective novelist than revealing to one's readers one's morally satisfying intrinsic wisdom, hardly is held by Thompson alone. Indeed, Thompson's opinion is the dominant critical view of crime fiction today, and has been so for decades. Thompson's 2007 biography of Christie constituted a bid by the author to persuade critics and book reviewers to take the Queen of Crime more seriously, not as a purveyor of puzzles (though these puzzles are commonly seen as the greatest such devised in the history of the genre), but as a mainstream author with sober things to say about the human condition. Thompson's effort to place Christie in the pantheon of noteworthy, serious writers deserving of respectful critical treatment met with little success in the eyes of the mass media, however. Reviewers of her biography predictably proved resistant to the idea that Christie could be seen as anything more than a mere puzzler. *London Observer* columnist Rachel Cooke, for example, was openly mirthful at the very notion that one could take Christie seriously as a writer: "Thompson quotes the novels ... reverentially, as if they were Wharton or Eliot, not the result of the hack-work that meant Christie could write one and sometimes two novels a year for five decades. She repeatedly tells you how brilliant this or that book is — and what she admires is not Christie's way with riddles, but the stuff nobody else can find in her books: insight, motivation, deep emotion." Expressing similar skepticism in her review in the *London Telegraph*, Jessica Mann, herself a mystery novelist, bluntly deemed Thompson's assertion that

Christie's "perfect geometric puzzles" also are "perfectly distilled meditations upon human nature" to be "over the top." Yet another reviewer, the *Times Literary Supplement*'s Lindsay Duguid, questioned whether even Christie's clever puzzle plotting could salvage what Duguid found to be the Queen of Crime's intolerably banal writing. "[R]eading [Christie's detective novels] brings one hard up against the realities of leaden exchanges and flat, repetitious description," Duguid wrote dismissively. "One can hardly bear to read on." Duguid derisively termed Christie's beloved tales of detection "anti-novels."[1]

Despite such critical scoffing, Agatha Christie readers for nine decades now, delighted by the ingenuity of those critically derided puzzles, have proven more than able to bear reading on; and Christie detective novels still are enthusiastically devoured today, over thirty-five years after the death of the author, while new Hercule Poirot and Miss Marple films adapted from those novels continue to appear on television (though sometimes in free adaptations that give Christie fans more pain than pleasure). Additionally, a coterie of British detection writers who, like Christie, first appeared in the span of years known as the Golden Age of detective fiction (a period, from roughly 1920 to 1940, when a "fair play" puzzle with a solution potentially deducible by the reader was generally considered an integral part of a detective novel), remains in print today, most notably Christie's sister Crime Queens, Dorothy L. Sayers, Margery Allingham and Ngaio Marsh.[2] However, another group of impressive Golden Age detective novelists — a group once eagerly read and celebrated, like Agatha Christie always has been, for skill in puzzle construction — today is mostly forgotten by all but book collectors and classical mystery enthusiasts and specialists: the so-called "Humdrums." Though these "Humdrum" detective novelists most often are dismissed by the modern critics who deign to take even momentary notice of them as hack purveyors of "mere puzzles," unworthy of serious attention, these authors actually merit sound scholarly investigation, on account of their intrinsic merit as mystery writers as well as for the light they shed on both the mystery genre itself and English social history in the decades from the 1920s to the 1950s.

The term "Humdrum"—that damning appellation for a particular band of once widely-esteemed Golden Age detective novelists — was popularized by an influential post–Golden Age mystery critic and crime writer, Julian Symons (1912–1994), whose genre survey, *Bloody Murder* (1972, reprinted in 1985 and 1993), remains a cornerstone of mystery criticism. Rather than seeing the period between World War I and World War II — when considerable emphasis in mystery literature was laid on crafting fairly clued puzzles for the reader to solve — as a "Golden Age" from which modern crime writers had declined, Symons viewed the period as an eccentric detour off the main road of aesthetic development in the mystery genre, from the Victorian era's "sensation novel" (a serious novel where shocking and sensational events, encompassing crime and sometimes murder, play a great role) to the modern age's "crime novel" (a novel about crime, usually murder, ideally including realistic police procedure, social observation and psychological penetration). Though he recognized her limitations as a literary writer, Symons had genuine admiration for Christie as a detective novelist, deeming her a clever designer of puzzles who was capable as well of composing sprightly narratives. Yet of the writers he labeled Humdrums, Symons declared peremptorily that he could "no longer read [their work] with any pleasure." Symons asserted that most of these Humdrum writers "came late to writing fiction" and that few of them "had much talent for it." While they doubtlessly "had some skill in constructing puzzles," Symons grudgingly allowed, Humdrums had "nothing more" than that to offer readers — and that alone was not enough.[3]

Although it was with *Bloody Murder* that Julian Symons cemented the notion of a *passé* Humdrum school of detective fiction in the minds of modern mystery critics and readers, he had written in disparaging terms about this group of writers before *Bloody Murder* first appeared in 1972. In a 1959 crime fiction review column in the *Sunday Times*, Symons, noting the death of detective novelist Freeman Wills Crofts, crowned Crofts' countryman and contemporary John Rhode (a pseudonym of Cecil John Charles Street) as Britain's now reigning "master of the humdrum." Four years later, in his first general survey of the mystery genre, "The Detective Story in Britain" (a pamphlet published for The British Council and the National Book League), Symons did not specifically use the term "Humdrum" to identify a particular group of, in his view, dull detection authors, but he clearly had the word or something quite like it in mind when he wrote of Golden Age mystery novelists who "produced books which had almost invariably been plotted with a slide rule, but were written without style or savour." In these works, Symons asserted, "plot ... was all," while "wit, characterisation and consideration of the psychology of the people involved in the books" counted for "nothing." In Symons' view, the determined adherence of these authors to restrictive rules laid down for the writing of fair play detective fiction in the 1920s trapped them in a sterile, artistically constricted environment that could yield only lifeless sub-literature.[4]

Julian Symons made his disdain for Humdrums clear enough in his critical writings, but he was less clear about just which writers actually comprised this group. In "The Detective Story in Britain," Symons cited as specific examples of the inferior writers he had in mind Freeman Wills Crofts, spouses G.D.H. and Margaret Cole, E.R. Punshon, J.J. Connington (pseudonym of Alfred Walter Stewart) and Ronald Knox, adding that these individuals stood "among a host of writers now almost forgotten." Ten years later, in *Bloody Murder*, Symons recalled as notable Humdrums three of these "now almost forgotten" writers, John Rhode, R.A.J. Walling and J.S. Fletcher; while he dropped from the list Punshon and Connington and transferred Knox to another category, "Farceurs." Crofts and the Coles held their places, the former being given the dubious distinction of being the best of this dull lot. In a later edition of *Bloody Murder*, Symons added to the list Sir Henry Lancelot Aubrey-Fletcher, who wrote as Henry Wade.[5] Later critics have followed Symons in noting the existence of a group of Golden Age Humdrum writers, yet the exact membership roll of this group has remained imprecise to this day.

Most often Freeman Wills Crofts, John Street, Alfred Walter Stewart, Henry Lancelot Aubrey-Fletcher and G.D.H. and Margaret Cole are mentioned as humdrum writers, with Crofts being treated as the leading figure among them. In this study I focus on three writers — railway engineer and devout low church Anglican Freeman Wills Crofts; army artillerist, military intelligence officer and electrical engineer Major Cecil John Charles Street; and Scots-Irish chemistry professor Alfred Walter Stewart — as the greatest exponents of the true Humdrum school (Aubrey-Fletcher and the Coles, who are not really properly considered Humdrums at all, I deal with in a separate study). I aim to demonstrate that this school of mystery fiction has been unjustly disparaged by Julian Symons and the many critics who have adopted his views.[6]

What really distinguishes "Humdrums" as a discrete group of writers? As we have seen, Julian Symons essentially identified Humdrums as individuals who "came late to writing fiction" and placed greater emphasis on puzzle construction and adherence to fair play detection than on characterization and stylish writing. This is fair enough as far as it goes, though in my view Symons insufficiently values the great technical sophistication of the plots in the best works of these authors. All three of the foremost Humdrums — Crofts, Street and Stewart — were men of professional backgrounds who brought considerable workplace expertise to their writing of detective fiction, producing some of the finest works in the classical, puzzle-oriented style of the Golden Age of the British detective novel. At their peak, they were among the most popular and critically-esteemed British detective novelists. Indicative of the one-time standing of Crofts, Street and Stewart is that they — like the great (and much better studied) Crime Queens Agatha Christie and Dorothy L. Sayers — were all founding members of the Detection Club, a social body consisting of the elite of Golden Age British detective novelists.

This trio of writers has been neglected in genre studies for too long. With the exception of Jacques Barzun's and Wendell Hertig Taylor's monumental defense of the classical Golden Age puzzle novel, *A Catalogue of Crime* (originally published in 1971, a year before the appearance of *Bloody Murder*), critical works on the genre in the last forty years overwhelmingly have aped Symons' approach to the Humdrums, treating these authors as writers of little account and giving them at best only sporadic, most often dismissive, mentions in surveys. In my view, this approach is mistaken. Not only are the works of these so-called Humdrum authors of note for having once been among the most well-received and widely read detective fiction of the period, but they stand as useful correctives to genre historians, who too often have reached over-broad conclusions about the purported "feminization" and conservatism of the British detective novel in the Golden Age based on interpretations of the books of only a small number of writers from the era, commonly the Crime Queens Christie, Sayers, Allingham and Marsh.[7]

In *Bloody Murder* Julian Symons admits to having omitted discussion of once highly-regarded work by "many Golden Age writers" on the ground that he had examined in detail "the most notable practitioners ... and the period can properly be judged by them." More recent genre surveys have offered coverage of Golden Age authors that is even further truncated than that found in *Bloody Murder*. For example, in his *Watteau's Shepherds: The Detective Novel in Britain, 1914–1940*, Leroy Lad Panek cavalierly dubs the Humdrums an irrelevant "group of hangers-on" and immediately dismisses them from his consideration.[8] I dissent from the view that the works of so many writers from this period can be thus cast aside. Just as the modern-day British Crime Queens, P.D. James and Ruth Rendell, cannot be said to stand for all crime writers of more recent times, the Golden Age Crime Queens (plus the occasional attendant male or two) cannot justly be said to have stood for all the British detective novelists of their day. In point of fact, the writers who are the subjects of this book differed in significant ways from the today much better known and studied Crime Queens.

The most obvious difference between the Humdrums and the Crime Queens is the simple biological fact that the Humdrums were men rather than women. As the reputation of the Crime Queens relative to that of other British detective novelists (a great many of whom were male) rose after World War II, critics came increasingly to see classical British mystery, in contrast with the American "hardboiled" private detective novel of Dashiell

Hammett and Raymond Chandler, as a feminine demesne. This tendency has accelerated with the proliferation of feminist studies in academia over the last several decades. While laudably correcting a previous tendency by many male critics toward unjustly dismissive attitudes concerning female-authored mystery fiction, these studies have helped foster an unfortunate neglect of male British Golden Age detective novelists.

Today many studies either entirely omit male British mystery authors of the Golden Age or too hastily dismiss them. For example, when setting the Golden Age context for British detective fiction in her 2007 popular biography of Agatha Christie, author Laura Thompson finds it necessary to mention only Christie's sister Crime Queens, Dorothy L. Sayers, Margery Allingham and Ngaio Marsh, completely ignoring male writers of the period. Thompson even concludes that Christie "was probably the least feminine of any of the writers of classic detective fiction"—an assertion that surely would have come as a surprise to John Street, Freeman Wills Crofts and Alfred Walter Stewart. Similarly, genre scholar Erin A. Smith asserts that the "best-selling and most critically acclaimed British mystery authors of the 1920s and '30s were disproportionately women" (just what is meant by "disproportionately" is not explained). "There were some successful male authors of classical detective fiction between the wars," Professor Smith allows; yet she also asserts that British women mystery novelists "were so prominent" in the genre "that the occupation of mystery writing could seem as 'feminine' as teaching or nursing." Encapsulating the currently ascendant critical view, Susan Rowland concludes in her 2010 essay, "The 'Classical' Model of the Golden Age" (which omits all but one of the Humdrum authors and misinterprets the remaining one, Freeman Wills Crofts, based on a reading of merely one of his thirty-three detective novels): "All in all, the golden age form is a feminized one."[9]

Admittedly British mystery writing of the Golden Age, as portrayed by most genre critics and scholars today, does indeed appear to have been as feminine an occupation as, say, nursing; but, as any mystery reader should know, appearances can deceive and red herrings abound. From my research I have concluded that certainly a majority of British writers of Golden Age detective fiction were men; and among these men were some of the most popular and highly-regarded mystery writers of the period, including the Humdrum authors. Over the years the traces of these writers may have become obscured, like rug-covered bloodstains on the parquet flooring in a country house mystery, yet they remained under concealment, awaiting dramatic discovery by curious scholar "detectives."

Besides being male, the Humdrums also differ from the Crime Queens in their occupational backgrounds. In their writing they made use of significantly different real world vocational experiences, particularly an intense familiarity with science and technology. A survey of the Crime Queens reveals a paucity of such vocational experiences on their part. Agatha Christie was the daughter of an American expatriate living on inherited income. She herself had no professional background, with the exception of some volunteer dispensing work during World War I, until she became a successful writer. Dorothy L. Sayers, the daughter of a country clergyman, attended Somerville College, Oxford, where she studied modern languages and medieval literature. She later worked nine years in the advertising business, experience she used in her detective novel *Murder Must Advertise* (1933). Margery Allingham, the daughter of a newspaper serialist, began writing professionally by the age of nineteen. Ngaio Marsh, daughter of a bank clerk, produced Shakespearean plays in addition to writing her series of detective novels. Conversely, the Humdrums came to fiction writing from well-established technical/scientific vocational backgrounds: John Street, an English army artillerist, intelligence officer and electrical engineer; Freeman Wills Crofts, a North Ireland railway engineer; and Alfred Walter Stewart, a chemistry professor who taught at Queen's College, Belfast and the University of Glasgow.[10]

Naturally enough, the vocational experiences of Humdrum authors influenced their writing, making it diverse from that of the Crime Queens. This divergence of professional backgrounds among British Golden Age writers and its diversifying effect on the genre fiction they produced is a point typically missed in discussions of Golden Age detective fiction that draw mostly on the Crime Queens for evidence. For example, Erin A. Smith claims that "classical English detective fiction, murders aside, trafficked in remarkably feminine currencies — emotion, private life, domestic spaces." Leaving aside the question of the merit in the view that emotion, private life and domestic spaces invariably are "remarkably feminine currencies," it will become readily apparent to readers of this study that Humdrum works often trafficked in more stereotypically masculine currencies, such as the very public spaces in which businessmen and the police performed their professional functions. To note the single most extreme instance known to me of a Humdrum British Golden Age detective novelist trafficking in remarkably "masculine" currencies, in *Mystery on Southampton Water*, a 1934 Freeman Wills Crofts novel concerning industrial espionage and multiple murder involving feuding cement companies (we are a very long way from country houses here), the author rather strikingly goes so far as to entirely omit female characters from his tale.[11]

The error in which too narrow a focus on the Golden Age Crime Queens can result is apparent as well in P.D. James' "autobiographical fragment," *Time to Be in Earnest* (1999), in which the modern-day British Crime Queen asserts that Golden Age detective novelists "had very little knowledge of and even less apparent interest in forensic medicine." P.D. James offers in proof of her assertion the point that "many of the most eminent [Golden Age writers] were women with no scientific training" and concomitantly little interest in realistically portraying science in their fiction. These "many" eminent women writers James cites turn out to be three of the four usual Crime Queen suspects, Dorothy L. Sayers, Margery Allingham, and Ngaio Marsh (Agatha Christie qualified as a dispenser during World War I, gaining wide knowledge about drugs and poisons which she put to ingenious murderous use in her tales). James' reliance on three women writers as her evidentiary basis leads again to an overly sweeping generalization about the Golden Age, for the Humdrum writers she fails to consider in her analysis of the period tended to be scrupulous in dealing with precisely those points of technical accuracy she chides Golden Age writers for ignoring.[12]

The critical focus on the Crime Queens has led to a general consensus that not only was the Golden Age British detective novel an essentially "feminine" genre, but that it also was politically and socially conservative as well as classist and racist, being riddled with disdain and condescension toward the English working class, foreigners and ethnic and racial minorities. Three of the Crime Queens, Dorothy L. Sayers, Margery Allingham and Ngaio Marsh, created aristocratic gentleman sleuths who often carry out their investigations in milieus deemed outrageously snobbish by hostile critics of the classical form of the mystery genre. Moreover, while Agatha Christie's most famous Golden Age detective, Hercule Poirot, was a solidly bourgeois Belgian émigré (middle class and *foreign*, no less!), Christie often has been accused of a snobbish treatment of servants in her work, on account of such notorious passages as this reflection from the bright young heroine of her 1925 mystery, *The Secret of Chimneys*: "I certainly knew her face quite well—in that vague way one does know governesses and companions.... It's awful, but I never really look at them properly. Do you?"[13]

Drawing largely on the works of the Crime Queens, genre critics typically portray the world of the British Golden Age detective novel as a unitary one that is, to quote P.D. James in *Talking about Detective Fiction*, "middle-class, hierarchical, rural, peaceable." On this matter critics have been heavily influenced by poet and voracious detective fiction reader W.H. Auden's 1948 essay, "The Guilty Vicarage." In this essay Auden discusses his preferred sort of detective story, that in which murder takes place in a placid English village. Murder disrupts the orderly life of the village, Auden explains, until the detective arrives "to restore the state of grace" that, Eden-like, previously existed there. Although Auden in actuality was writing only about his preferred sort of detective story ("I find it very difficult ... to read one not set in rural England," he admits), his essay all too often has been taken as a generalized description of all British detective fiction from the Golden Age, leading once again to the drawing of misleadingly sweeping conclusions about the genre in this period.[14]

More conservative critics, like Auden himself as well as P.D. James, have taken a benign perspective of this purported portrayal in Golden Age detective novels of an Edenic, rigidly stratified, pastoral world. Indeed, P.D. James, who was born in 1920, argues that these works essentially portrayed, without overmuch exaggeration, a place that actually existed for many individuals during the years when she grew into adulthood:

> [I]t was an England I knew, a cohesive world, overwhelmingly white and united by a common belief in a religious and moral code based on the Judeo-Christian inheritance ... and buttressed by social and political institutions which ... were accepted as necessary to the well-being of the state: the monarchy, the Empire, the Church, the criminal justice system, the City, the ancient universities. It was an ordered society in which virtue was regarded as normal, crime an aberration, and in which there was small sympathy for the criminal.... [T]he 1930s were years of remarkable freedom from domestic crime.... It was therefore possible to live in a country town or village and feel almost entirely secure. We can read an Agatha Christie novel set in what seems a mythical village, in which the inhabitants are happily reconciled to their allotted rank and station, and we feel that this is an exaggerated, romanticized or idealized world. It isn't, not altogether.[15]

To be sure, most critics, likely viewing the genre from a more left perspective than P.D. James, are far less sympathetic than she concerning the social and political biases that they perceive in the Golden Age British mystery. "The social order in [British Golden Age] stories was as fixed and mechanical as that of the Incas," damningly declares Julian Symons in *Bloody Murder*. Rather grudgingly Symons allows that Golden Age British mystery writers were not "*openly* [emphasis added] anti–Semitic or anti–Radical," yet he adds that "they were overwhelmingly conservative in feeling." For his part, Colin Watson, author of *Snobbery with Violence*, another seventies-era, politically left history of Golden

Age British mystery and thriller fiction, wrote even more caustically of the works of the period than Symons, asserting that in their books between-the-wars genre writers consistently adopted the views of an obtuse English middle class that saw "working class people as envious, unreasonable and vicious, but too stupid, fortunately, to constitute a real menace in any political sense." According to Watson, the placid English village temporarily disturbed by murder in these tales (memorably dubbed by him "Mayhem Parva") was emphatically a false creation, "a sort of museum of nostalgia" for the social and political structure of a vanished Edwardian England. A more tempered statement of this view can be found in two highly influential leftist academic studies of mystery fiction from the same era, Stephen Knight's *Form and Ideology in Crime Fiction* (1980) and Dennis Porter's *The Pursuit of Crime: Art and Ideology in Detective Fiction* (1981). Both men implicitly treat their narrow and thinly sourced interpretations of Agatha Christie's detective fiction as broadly applicable to the Golden Age British mystery genre as a whole. "The world of the [Agatha] Christie novel," insists Knight, "is a dream of bourgeois rural living without the heights, depths or conflicts of real social activity. It is a projection of the dreams of those anxious middle-class people who would like a life where change, disorder and work are all equally absent." Porter likewise stresses the alleged backward-looking, pastoral conservatism of Christie's mystery fiction. The Crime Queen's novels, Porter declares, "projected the vision of a mythic England of cottage and manor house, churchyards and country lanes, where only solvable crimes posed a threat to age-old ways of life."[16]

However accurate a view of the Crime Queens this may be (it has been persuasively challenged by other scholars and in my own opinion is not entirely merited), in my view Humdrum authors treated various sociocultural issues in a more nuanced and unpredictable manner than critics and reviewers typically have allowed of British mystery writers in the Golden Age. In her study of Agatha Christie, Merja Makinen has astutely pointed out that political conservatism does "not necessarily rule out a questioning and even subversive attitude" toward particular generally accepted cultural and political norms. While it is true that the Humdrums, like the majority of Golden Age British detective novelists, can be classified to some extent as "conservative," nevertheless they are not the High Tory, gentry-worshiping caricatures too often found in genre surveys. Although John Street came of genteel origins, he was a political Liberal who despised hidebound social structures and in his writing sympathetically depicted energetic men of humble backgrounds rising in both urban and rural business environments through their hard work. Similarly, Freeman Wills Crofts through his novels made his unassuming, petit bourgeois policeman, Inspector French, one of the most famous fictional English detectives of the Golden Age. Also notably, John Street vigorously condemned anti–Semitism, while Freeman Wills Crofts, a strong believer in the Social Gospel, after the onset of the Depression became extremely critical of big business and private greed. To be sure, the post–World War II writings of Street and Crofts, which were produced at a time when an ascendant Labour government was pushing through ambitious and controversial left-of-center political reform, are more reactionary in tone than their earlier works; yet those earlier works are much more varied than critics typically have allowed of mystery genre fiction in the Golden Age. Even Alfred Walter Stewart, the most consistently conservative of these authors, is notable for the acerbically cynical and unsentimental view he takes of much of humanity in his J.J. Connington tales. English society, as portrayed in books by the Humdrums, often is far less closed, comfortable, stratified and stable than one would expect from a reading of most genre critics. In short, greater familiarity with writings by these neglected authors gives us a significantly better balanced understanding of the Golden Age of British mystery fiction.[17]

For scholars of mystery genre history, the treatment of gender issues by the Humdrums also has interest, despite the fact that the Humdrums were uniformly male. John Street, who in his own personal life defied social strictures of his day by living with one woman while he was married to another, created some dynamic and rebellious female characters that do not conform to gender-bound conventions of the time. Boundaries, whether professional or sexual, sometimes are transgressed by these daring women. To be sure, Freeman Wills Crofts and Alfred Walter Stewart offer more traditional treatments of female characters, yet these treatments are of interest in their own right; and they receive attention as well.[18]

While an ever-increasing number of studies of Golden Age detective fiction have appeared since the trailblazing publications of Jacques Barzun's and Wendell Hertig Taylor's *A Catalogue of Crime* and Julian Symons' *Bloody Murder* nearly forty years ago, few of these studies have attempted to follow Barzun and Taylor and integrate the so-called Humdrum detective novelists into their analyses by taking serious, informed looks at their work. Rather, they have echoed Symons' dismissal of the efforts of Humdrum authors as "mere puzzles," unworthy of serious critical consideration. Yet works by this particular group of writers once were seen by many critics as supreme examples of the mystery art form, and they were quite popular with readers. Moreover, these books remain prized by admirers of Golden Age detective fiction even today. It must be said, with respect, that there was more to the Golden Age than the four Queens of Crime, important as these women clearly are in the history of the genre. "To read the detective novels of these four women," notes P.D. James of the Golden Age Crime Queens, "is to learn more about the England in which they lived than most popular social histories can provide."[19] Beyond doubt one can glean valuable historical detail from the books of the Crime Queens, yet one can do so as well from the books of other popular Golden Age detective novelists, most certainly including the Humdrums. Detailed study of "Humdrum" detective novels and stories is justified because it shines light on neglected works and because it informs understanding of both the genre as a whole and of the time and place in which that genre thrived. In the Golden Age's country house of mystery, there in truth were many mansions, some of which, having stood for decades sadly shuttered and neglected, now receive a long overdue airing.

CHAPTER ONE

"The Masters"
Cecil John Charles Street, Freeman Wills Crofts, and Alfred Walter Stewart

WITH THE PASSING OF FREEMAN WILLS CROFTS in 1957, Major Cecil John Charles Street with facetious ceremony was crowned in print two years later by author and *Sunday Times* crime fiction reviewer Julian Symons as Britain's reigning "master of the humdrum." Fifteen years later, in his influential study of crime and detective fiction, *Bloody Murder*, Symons classified a group of Golden Age detective novelists under the heading "Humdrum," a pejorative title for fiction writers who essentially, it seemed, had not much business writing fiction in the first place. "Most of them came late to writing fiction, and few had much talent for it," pronounces Symons of these authors. "They had some skill in constructing puzzles, nothing more."[1] Julian Symons' words set the final negative critical seal on this group of once-admired genre writers, whose reputations already had been declining since the end of World War II. Today, they are of interest only to more informed Golden Age mystery enthusiasts and collectors, a great change from the decades between World War I and World War II, when their works issued forth from the presses year after year to numerous eager readers around the globe. The decline in critical and popular status of this group of authors reflects the more general decline of the puzzle-oriented detective novel, commonly regarded as the signature achievement of the Golden Age of British mystery and today most strongly associated with the still widely-selling works of Agatha Christie. Yet, like the works of Agatha Christie, the works of the Humdrums, despite being castigated as "mere puzzles," have lasting merit both as intelligent, ingenious entertainment and as social history; and they deserve reappraisal.

Just who were the "Humdrum" British detective novelists? Though credited with coining the term *Humdrum*, Julian Symons was, as discussed in the Introduction, inconsistent over the years when listing the authors who in his view actually comprised this group. Nor did Symons provide any reasons for the classification of any particular Humdrum writer as such, with the exception of Freeman Wills Crofts, the sole listed Humdrum whose work Symons ever discussed in any detailed way (in *Bloody Murder* Symons informs readers that "Crofts was not just a typical, but also the best, representative" of the Humdrum school). Additionally, Symons muddies the critical waters in later editions of *Bloody*

Murder by casually adding to his Humdrum list writers whom he did not personally enjoy. For example, Australian mystery novelist Arthur Upfield, who as a local color crime writer still claims a following, was actually, we learn from *Bloody Murder*, part of a new wave of thirties Humdrums. So too, it seems, was Gladys Mitchell, currently undergoing something of a revival. Responding to "friends and less friendly critics" vexed over *Bloody Murder*'s dismissal of Mitchell as one of "very many Golden Age writers whose work was once highly regarded" but did not merit modern-day consideration, Symons in *Bloody Murder*'s second edition tackled "half a dozen" of Mitchell's books (he actually lists only four, all from the 1940s, over a decade after Mitchell began writing) and found himself "defeated by what appeared to be an average Humdrum," one particularly to be faulted for her "lengthy examination" of "tediously fanciful aspects of English life." Yet a modest examination of Mitchell's earlier work makes clear that she is a lively and witty writer, more properly belonging in Symons' "Farceur" category of detective novelists. Moreover, Mitchell tales like *Speedy Death*, with its depiction of Freudian psychology and aberrant country house sexual behavior; *St. Peter's Finger*, with its sober examination of convent life; *Come Away, Death*, with its exploration of the world of Greek myth; and *The Rising of the Moon*, with its compelling evocation of adolescence, are worlds away from the sort of conventional puzzle-making Symons decries in *Bloody Murder*.[2] For Symons to apply the label Humdrum this carelessly means essentially that "Humdrum" as defined by Symons is simply a writer Symons himself happened to find dull — not a very useful classification.

Still, despite this lack of system in Symons' application of the term "Humdrum," it is clear that with his use of the term in *Bloody Murder* Symons is meaning to describe a discrete group of Golden Age detective fiction writers: those who "came late to writing fiction" (presumably from other occupational backgrounds besides writing) and placed greater emphasis on puzzle construction and "fair play" detection than on rounded characterization and evocative composition. A trio of important British Golden Age detection authors best fit this classification: Major Cecil John Charles Street, who published detective fiction under the pseudonyms John Rhode, Miles Burton and Cecil Waye; Freeman Wills Crofts; and Alfred Walter Stewart, who published detective fiction under the name J.J. Connington. Each man had established a distinguished career in another field before he began writing fiction; Street as an officer in the British Royal Artillery and the MI7b and the electrical engineer of a pioneering English power company, Crofts as a railway engineer in Ulster, and Stewart as a Professor of Chemistry at Queen's University, Belfast. These professional backgrounds gave these three men skills of great value in the Golden Age of the detective novel, a time when technical and scientific accuracy and authenticity were highly prized by many readers of mystery fiction. Crofts is well-known for having put his familiarity with railway timetables to use in numerous novels, but he also had experience with business organization and shipping that he employed in his works. Stewart, an individual of historical significance in the study of chemistry, had a vast well of scientific knowledge to draw upon for his detective novels. Finally, Major Street, an accomplished artillery and intelligence officer and electrical engineer, was an astonishing scientific and technical jack-of-all-trades with expertise in mechanics, chemistry, cryptography, physics, geology and geography.

In *Shifting Gears: Technology, Literature, Culture in Modernist America* (1987), Cecelia Tichi documents the important but overlooked influence of the engineering profession in early twentieth-century American literary culture. "As engineers made their presence felt in the American scene," Tichi writes, "they began to figure prominently in imaginative literature." Yet she noted that scholars had "failed to recognize the engineer's presence or to notice the embodiment of engineering values either in popular or enduring literature." As "the exponent of efficiency and the slayer of that dragon, waste," Tichi explains, the engineer in an "age of pervasive machine technology ... was a messianic figure, or at least a priestly one. His values — efficiency, organization, production, functional and elegant design — enabled Americans once again to expect national salvation."[3] We will see that the engineers John Street and Freeman Wills Crofts and the scientist J.J. Connington brought those same values — efficiency, organization, production, functional and elegant design — to the British detective novel; and that in doing so they attracted an appreciative audience of readers in the post–World War I years, when individuals yearned for a more rationalized order to set a fallen world aright.

Unfortunately for the long-term literary reputations of these authors, their undoubted technical skills have less impressed most post–Golden Age critics, who generally have found little to laud in mere puzzles. Some of them have even written dismissively of the very significance of the puzzle in the Golden Age. "The detective fiction of pure ratiocination has never been genuinely popular," declares genre scholar Dennis Porter in an oft-cited 1981 academic study, *The Pursuit of Crime*. "In order to appeal to the broader public, [the detective story] needed the vital admixture of action or manners, violence or satire." Another prominent genre scholar, Leroy Lad Panek, concurs with Porter in his downplaying of the significance of the puzzle in Golden Age detective fiction. "Successful writers flouted the [puzzle] rule with abandon," insists Panek in *An Introduction to the Detective Story* (1987), "and the public loved it." Yet, to the contrary, in the heyday of the Golden Age the Humdrums Street, Crofts and Stewart won considerable praise from critics and attracted a devoted readership with books graced with sound and ingenious puzzle plots. Reflecting the common view at the time, H. Douglas Thomson, author of the first major book-length study of the genre, *Masters of Mystery* (1931), therein defined the detective story as "a puzzle to be solved, the plot consisting of a logical deduction of the solution from the existing data." Though modern-day genre critics tend to see the detective novel, so defined, as sub-literature not meriting the attention of intelligent readers, many Golden Age critics, including even "highbrows," praised the genre as a worthy, though lesser, literary form. In 1926 — some years before the rise of the host of self-consciously literary Crime Queens and Detection Dons in the late 1930s — Oxford tutor and literary critic E.M. Wrong wrote approvingly of the detective story as "fit and proper reading for evenings and holidays" and noted significantly that "its most devoted adherents are found principally among the highly educated." Barrister and historian Philip Guedalla fully concurred with Wrong's opinion, famously dubbing detective stories "the natural recreation for noble minds." For her part, Oxford-educated mystery novelist and critic Dorothy L. Sayers found "remarkable" the strength of the fascination of detective stories for "intellectually-minded" readers.[4] Works by Street, Crofts and Connington, which placed puzzles at the center of the narratives, most certainly were not seen as exceptions to Wrong's, Guedalla's and Sayers' pronouncements. Year after year in the Golden Age critics praised detective novels by these three men as among the cream of the mystery crop and readers devotedly borrowed their books from rental libraries.

John Street's novels (particularly those by "John Rhode") often were singled out by reviewers for their cognitively stimulating mechanical and scientific ingenuity. One reviewer in 1937 went so far as to designate Street's John Rhode as "Public Brain Tester No. 1," while the previous year another opined of Street's Miles Burton that "most serious detective-story connoisseurs would never miss reading any of his stories." Other reviewers in the strongest terms concurred in these assessments. "The name 'John Rhode' has come to stand for definite achievement among the ranks of writers of detective stories," declared one. "Some critics give him first place in the field, and the most cautious reader will probably place him amongst the first three authors." Yet another avowed that "Mr. Rhode is one of the best living writers of mystery stories, and his powers of ingenious invention and craftsmanlike construction seem well-nigh inexhaustible." Even Crime Queen Dorothy L. Sayers, who would soon call for detective novelists to become less puzzle-focused and more literary by emulating the nineteenth century novel of manners, freely conceded Rhode's strengths as a detective novelist. In a John Rhode tale, Sayers noted in one of her 1930s *Sunday Times* book reviews, readers were sure to find "a sound plot, a well-knit process of reasoning, and a solidly satisfying solution with no loose ends or careless errors of fact." Similarly, Anthony Berkeley Cox, another mystery writer who himself challenged pure puzzle orthodoxy in his own crime fiction (particularly under his pseudonym Francis Iles), in his *Daily Telegraph* column declared that "John Rhode never lets you down. A carefully worked out plot, precise detection, with no logical flaws or jumping to conclusions, and enough of character and atmosphere to carry the thing along; these, one is always sure of receiving from him." Perhaps not altogether surprisingly, Rhode's publishers emphatically agreed with Sayers and Cox. Dodd, Mead and Company, John Rhode's American publishers, boasted to readers in 1940 that Rhode's latest novel, *Death on the Boat Train*, was "for connoisseurs," with its "chief fascination" lying "in the diabolical ingenuity and intricacy of its surprising plot." A few years earlier, the Collins Crime Club, publisher in England of Street's John Rhode novels from 1931 to 1945, had adopted the same stance, boasting of Street's unerring accuracy in his treatment of technology, math and science. "Whether it is a matter of road distances, railway time tables, the reactions of chemicals, the technicalities peculiar to firearms, John Rhode cannot be caught out on a point of detail," Collins confidently declared. The publisher also flattered the intelligence of current and prospective Rhode readers by informing them that Rhode's books "appeal mostly to those who like a really intricate problem, the details of which can be mapped out on paper. Often one will need a map, ruler and compass." To strengthen the equation of Rhode's books with challenging math and science problems, Collins added that "some of Mr. Rhode's books have been illustrated by diagrams." Julian Symons and temperamentally like-minded critics have referred disdainfully to the maps, plans, diagrams and timetables in detective stories of this period, but to many intelligent readers of this time, such stuff was the mental warp and woof of the detective novel.[5]

Opposite: Endpaper maps in Freeman Wills Crofts, *Death on the Way* (1932), and John Rhode, *Dead Men at the Folly* (1932). Genre histories typically stress that Golden Age detective novels take place in closed settings — preferably country houses — yet in fact comparatively few of the novels of John Street and Freeman Wills Crofts were confined to landed estates. The endpaper maps to these two 1932 detective novels indicate just how porous the settings actually are. The criminal investigators in these novels are tasked with finding their way around modern railroads and highways, not ancient country house corridors.

WHITNESS
to Bournemouth
"Serque"
PEG 180
170
Park
Contractors' Yard
Spinney
160
Viaduct
Chine
150
Tunnel
Hills
140
Rocky Shelf
Hills
Main Road
Hills
130
Southern Railway
to London
Main Road
90
100
110
120
20
30
40
50
60
70
80
New Deviation
Browne's Bay
Cannan's Cutting
PEG 10
0
Downey's Point
Bridge 982
Existing Line
REDCHURCH
from Lydmouth
ENGLISH CHANNEL
ENGLISH CHANNEL

TO LONDON
Priory
East Hensley
Mr. Turnour's
Charlton Candover
Charlton Junction
Line
Breen Ridge
A
Elverton Bridge
CHARLTON MONTAGUE
B
Folly
Transmission
Manor
Elverton
R. Breen
From Exeter
C
Hinton Varley
Varley Cross
Pucklebury
Kirdford

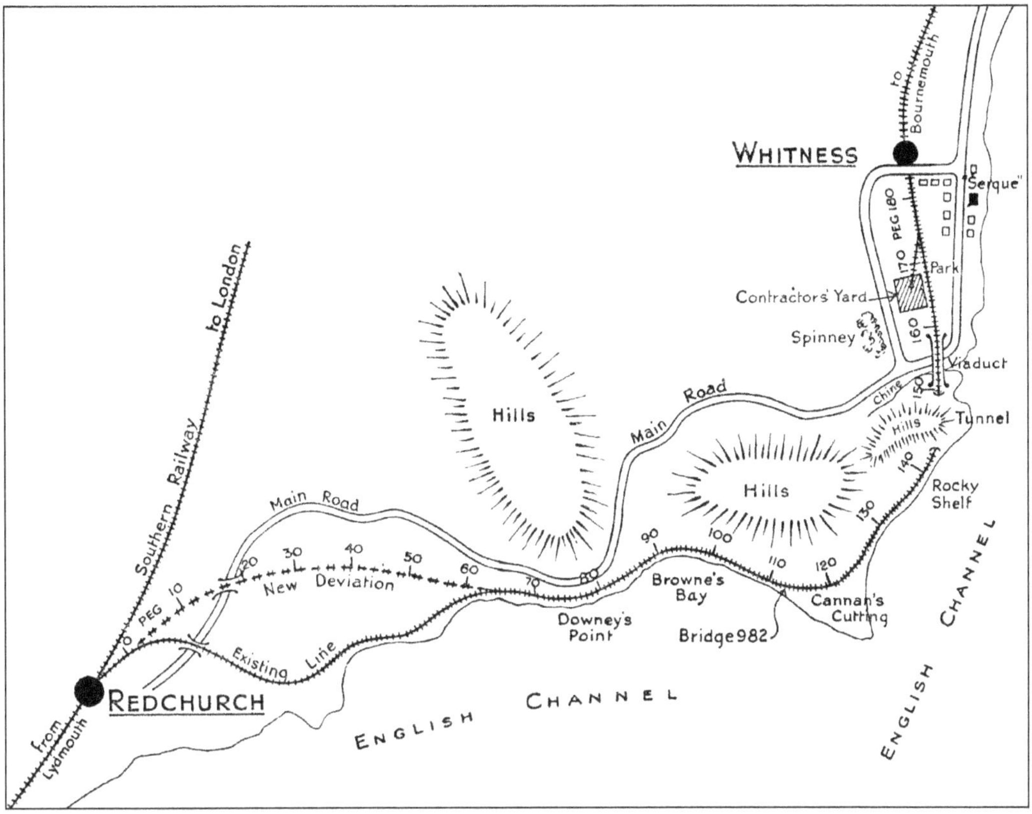

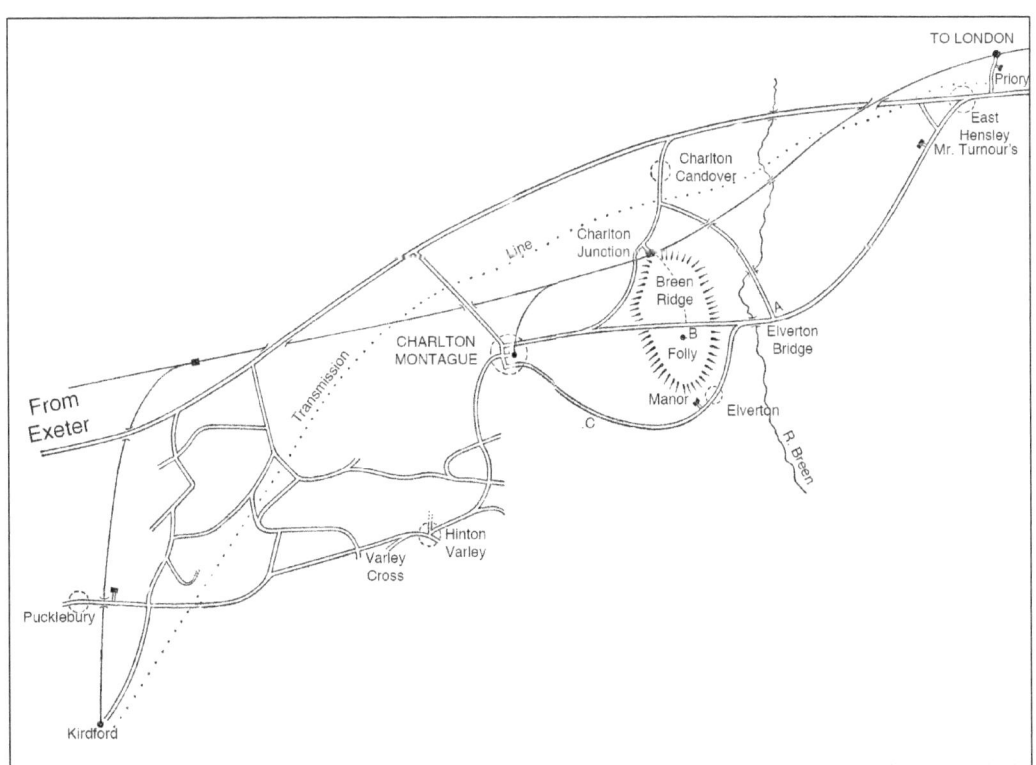

Just as critics warmly embraced John Street's tales of detection, they enthusiastically welcomed works by Freeman Wills Crofts and Alfred Walter Stewart. Indeed, many critics between the wars considered Freeman Wills Crofts—who had preceded both Street and Stewart in the publication of a detective novel by several years and had an undisputed genre milestone, *The Cask* (1920), to his credit—the leading light not just among the three men but arguably among all currently writing mystery authors. In the 1920s high culture priest T.S. Eliot, an avid detective fiction reader, classed Crofts with R. Austin Freeman, a still-active contemporary of Arthur Conan Doyle, as the two greatest living detective novelists. Of Crofts, Ivor Brown, drama critic and Oxford graduate in the Classics, humbly declared: "Before his invention, mine eyes dazzle." Speaking on the BBC, novelist, book collector and literary historian Michael Sadleir pronounced that to minds capable of appreciating "logical reasoning," Crofts' "type of puzzle fiction" was "enthralling." Writer and Oxford University Press editor Charles Williams wrote of Crofts' detective novels that they had "a neatness of pattern, an economy of means, an ordered development, a final resolution" that were all most "pleasing to the instructed reader." He deemed Crofts' *The Hog's Back Mystery* (1933) "in the highest flight of detective aeroplanes" and predicted that it would "delight" even "the crudest reader" while inducing a state of "catastrophic" euphoria in the more refined. American fans of mystery concurred with these extremely favorable judgments from their British brethren. A 1928 reviewer for the *New York Times Book Review*, for example, strongly praised Crofts' ability in his new novel, *The Sea Mystery*, to construct a brain-teasing, technically superb and logically airtight plot. "Inspector

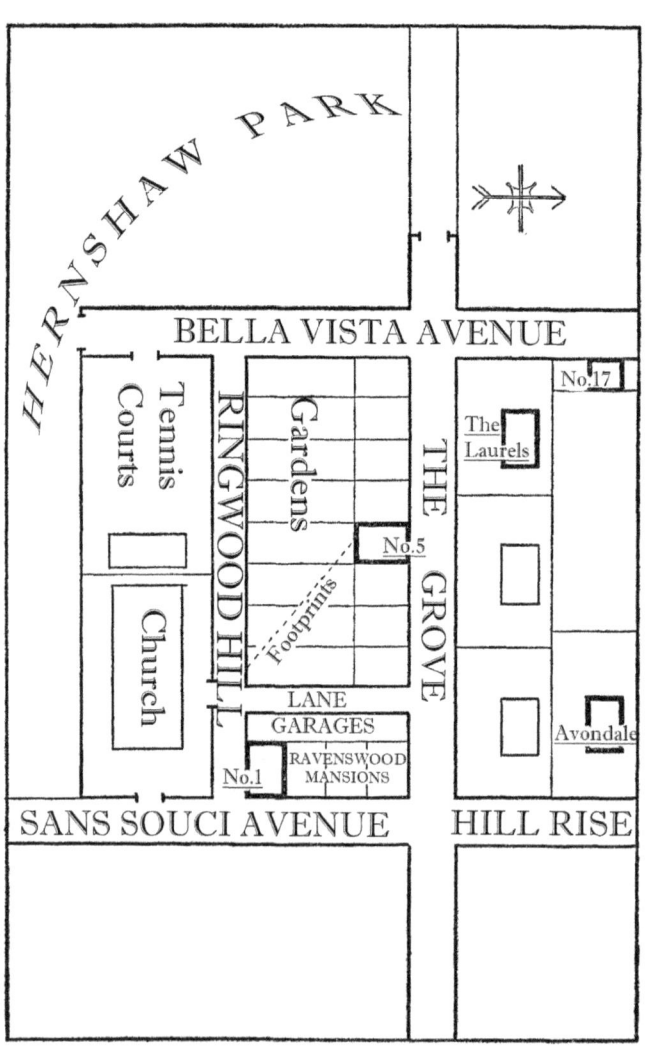

Frontis Map in J.J. Connington, *The Tau Cross Mystery* (*In Whose Dim Shadow*) (1935). Although J.J. Connington relied more than Street and Crofts on country house settings, this 1935 novel is solidly suburban, as the map demonstrates.

French's first task is to discover how the body happened to be in that particular spot," noted the fascinated reviewer. "By studying the tides, [French] discovers not only when but where it was thrown into the water, and from that point on he proceeds by logical steps until he has discovered the identity of the murdered man and arrests the murderer. The crime has been most ingeniously planned and executed."[6]

Nor were Alfred Walter Stewart's puzzle-oriented J.J. Connington tales lacking vocal admirers. Little, Brown and Company, the American publishers of the Connington detective novels, left no doubt in its promotional material but that cleverly and carefully wrought murder problems were the main attractions of their man's books. With Connington's 1930 train mystery, *The Two Tickets Puzzle*, for instance, Little, Brown and Company attempted to lure readers with the following boasts about the book, placed prominently in large type on the back of its eye-catching, art deco illustrated jacket:

- An honest detective story.
- All the clues given.
- Clever reasoning from the clues but no superhuman brain stuff.
- No mass of evidence unearthed at the last moment.
- No freak solutions.
- A minimum of horrors.
- A police detective could read this book and not be annoyed by the procedure.

Charles Williams concurred with Little, Brown's estimation of Connington merits, writing in his review of *The Two Tickets Puzzle* that "Mr. Connington's method is deservedly famous. He generally starts with his simple murder — a body under the seat of a railway compartment, say, as here — and proceeds by pure lucidity of action and thought to a complete and exciting finish. He has little color and no pyrotechnics, but he has accuracy, coolness, neatness and speed. His known quantities are always credible, and his unknown never incredible."[7]

Golden Age critics responded most favorably to the Connington "method." No less a figure than the hugely influential American hard-boiled crime writer Dashiell Hammett, often cited significantly by genre critics as no great devotee of the traditional British detective novel, conceded that Connington's *The Case with Nine Solutions* (1928) was "quite readable" and "quite satisfactorily" elucidated; while other sophisticated reviewers voiced similarly positive appraisals, some verging on gushing. The indisputably highbrow icon T.S. Eliot, for example, with "pleasure" informed readers of his *Monthly Criterion* that Connington's *Murder in the Maze* (1927) "is a really first-rate detective story" that placed the author "in the front rank of detective story writers." A year later, English journalist and barrister H.C. Harwood went Eliot several better when he opined that the chemist-turned-novelist's *Mystery at Lynden Sands* (1928) "may just fail of being the detective story of the century." Highlighting the criteria by which many readers at this time judged detective novels, Harwood noted that "the intricate detail is lucidly presented, and the ratiocination, though it taxes, does not overwhelm the intellect." Reviewing *The Case with Nine Solutions* (1928) the same year, an anonymous critic for the *Times Literary Supplement* found that Connington's "particular strength lies in his respect for the readers' intelligence." *The Case with Nine Solutions* was "a very well-constructed story, and piece after piece is added till the reader shuts the book with a mind satisfied and replete."[8]

J.J. Connington, *The Two Ticket Puzzle* (1930). The publishers of this 1930 Connington tale wanted readers to rest assured that it was an honest, fair play detective story (courtesy Mark Terry).

Many reviewers sampled amply from the myriad delights available at the Humdrum's mental buffet, reading and enjoying works by all three authors. Roger Pippett, mystery fiction reviewer for the Labor organ the London *Daily Herald* and future friend and publisher of famed American novelist Richard Wright, savored such works as Rhode's *Shot at Dawn*, Crofts' *Mystery in the Channel* and Connington's *The Sweepstake Murders*. Crofts' *Mystery in the Channel* Pippett placed with the author's famed *The Cask* as "one of the classics of modern detective fiction"; while even a tale he did not enjoy as much, *Sudden Death*, still delighted Pippett's mental palate with the "heaven-sent" inspiration of the "thumbprint on the shining little brass tap of a fatal gas-fire." Avowed the delighted Pippett: "Mr. Crofts tells you everything about that tap — everything! He actually draws a sketch of it for you! But, even so, I doubt whether you'll see what he wants you to see." With Connington's *Sweepstake Murders*, Pippett found that the author had maintained his high level with a "characteristically intricate and workmanlike problem." Pippett's most favored Humdrum chef, however, was John Rhode, whose 1930s concoctions he consistently relished. In 1931, for example, Pippett declared Rhode "the man to watch" in detective fiction, while three years later he deemed Rhode "one of our soundest and most satisfying detective-story specialists." The next year, 1935, Pippett was pleased to report to *Herald* readers that the master was "still at the top of his inimitable form."[9]

Prominent American humorist and rather unjustly forgotten mystery fiction reviewer Will Cuppy was another notable glutton for Humdrum detective tales, for he possessed a mammoth appetite for the sort of rich material detail these authors provided in their works. Cuppy, best known for his humorous sketches on natural and human history, some of which were gathered in the bestselling posthumous collection, *The Decline and Fall of Practically Everybody*, himself was an insatiable fact hoarder who before commencing writing any book would amass hundreds upon hundreds of index cards of data on the subject he was to address. "Cuppy felt that he must know his subject as thoroughly as was humanly possible before going to work on it," recalled a friend. It is no wonder that such an individual appreciated Humdrum detective novels, which are nothing if not detail-laden. In a long review of Crofts' *Crime at Guildford* (*The Crime at Nornes* in the United States), for example, Cuppy humorously conceded the flaws in Crofts' "pedestrian" writing style, but he nevertheless clearly was enthralled by the "amazing amount of new material" turned up by Crofts' intrepid Inspector French in the course of the tale. Cuppy had no doubt that readers of *Crime at Guildford* would be kept mentally engaged by the author's "authoritative comments about chemical analysis, medical jurisprudence, a rope, some alibis, the contents of a yellow box, a passport and a tiny but important bit of film — more properties than you generally get in a couple of thrillers, and all to the point." Of Connington's *In Whose Dim Shadow* (published in the United States as *The Tau Cross Mystery*), a nearly dazzled Cuppy assured his readers: "Here's another one you shouldn't miss if you like an abundance of clews and many other aids to armchair sleuthing." Cuppy proceeded to list the tantalizing series of discoveries made on the murder scene by a succession of policemen:

> Police Constable Danbury finds a body in a dismantled flat ... together with an extra pair of shoes, a handkerchief soaked in gore and an overturned paint pot. Inspector Chesilton goes him one better by spotting the fact that the corpse wears rubber gloves. Enter Chief Constable Sir Clinton Driffield, who turns up a small bludgeon, a crumpled piece of brown paper and a little gold ornament in the shape of a Tau cross. With all these aids, Sir Clinton can hardly fail, especially as he's letter perfect on "The Golden Bough," can quote Sir Thomas Browne's "Garden of Cyrus," and can speak any language — we mean, he's smart.[10]

Will Cuppy seems to have read every Rhode/Burton book by the prolific John Street that was published in the United States, and to have enjoyed them all. "We have long felt that the Dr. Priestley tales should be in every home," avowed Cuppy fervidly in 1935. "For meaty, full-bodied detective stories, crammed with fundamental brainwork and adorned with all manner of merit," he added in 1936, "you'll hardly find such another as John Rhode. When you've finished 'Death at Breakfast,' for instance, you feel as though you'd read at least a half dozen books, and good ones, too; there's none of that thin quality in Mr. Rhode, yet there's nothing in his tales that doesn't belong." Reviewing *The Corpse in the Car* in 1935, Cuppy enthusiastically avowed that Rhode "simply dazes his readers with experiments in toxicology, taxidermy, embroidery, metallurgy and scattering, winding up with a brilliant apprehension of the fiend." Similarly, reviewing *Shot at Dawn* in the same year, Cuppy advised his own readers: "If you crave an abundance of scientific detectivism, with enough detailed measurements and other minutiae to keep your brain at high pressure for a whole evening, better grab this latest Dr. Priestly tale." Cuppy also praised books written by Street under the Miles Burton pseudonym, stating of *Death in the Tunnel*, for example, that it was a fascinating problem tale that suffered not one whit from its absence of love interest (a once much lamented element in detective fiction that reached its Golden Age apex the previous year with the publication of Dorothy L. Sayers'

Gaudy Night). *Death in the Tunnel* Cuppy found "a swell baffler of the old-fashioned, leisurely, logical, all-wool kind, with no straining for a new kind of mystery and no heroine." The tale was "a fine buy if you can do without love for an hour and a half," added the reviewer, a confirmed bachelor.[11]

That the books of the Humdrums were valued precisely for the rich mental feasts (without indigestible emotional entanglements) that they provided readers is at odds with the view of most post–Golden Age genre critics that Humdrum detective novels are markedly inferior to the more consciously literary mystery tales of such writers as Crime Queens Dorothy L. Sayers, Margery Allingham and Ngaio Marsh and Detection Dons Michael Innes and Nicholas Blake. In a section of his *The Bedside Companion to Crime* ironically titled "The Duller the Better," mystery writer and critic H.R.F. Keating writes dismissively that Humdrum works were popular in the Golden Age simply because they were nicely dull and predictable, making them the pre–World War II equivalent of "anodyne, samey television" performing "the vital task of keeping us just awake in the evenings." In her recent short genre survey, *Talking about Detective Fiction*, modern day Crime Queen P.D. James with similar dismissiveness deems the interest in a detective novel's puzzle to be merely "quasi-intellectual." To James, puzzle-oriented tales (certainly including those of the Humdrums but also those as well of Agatha Christie) clearly are less intellectually respectable than a Dorothy L. Sayers novel such as *Gaudy Night*, which deals with a rash of poison pen letters and assorted outrages committed at a women's college at Oxford and addresses such serious matters as the proper balance for a woman between one's career and one's private emotional life. James deems *Gaudy Night*, in contrast with puzzle-oriented tales by Humdrum authors, a "novel of social realism and serious purpose" and thus a far worthier affair altogether. In James' view the ingenious puzzle plots of the sort associated with Agatha Christie and the Humdrums actually detract from, rather than enhance, a detective novel. "We have largely outgrown ... ingenuity," declares James of modern crime writers like herself, "realism and credibility" having mostly supplanted mere cleverness in the crime novel of the twenty-first century.[12]

In the Golden Age of the detective novel, particularly the earlier years, such a view as that expressed by James in 2009—that ingenuity is something to be "outgrown"— would have seemed absurd to many readers and critics, and they would have challenged the assertion that the detective novel was merely "quasi-intellectual." In truth, many intellectuals viewed puzzle-oriented mysteries as perfectly legitimate intellectual entertainment. Moreover, they believed the focus in the detective novel should remain firmly fixed on the puzzle, rather than shift to such things as extended descriptions of settings and emotional relationships among characters. The stance taken by such modern-day critics as Symons, Keating and James more reflects the polarization between the sciences and the humanities famously described over a half century ago by British scientist and novelist C.P. Snow in his 1959 Rede Lecture, "The Two Cultures," than it does any objective artistic "truth." Critics dismissive of the intellectual merit of Humdrum detective novelists in relation to other, more "literary" mystery writers implicitly are privileging authorial emphasis on the humanities and the emotions over that on logic, math and science. In contrast with such modern-day critics, however, many Golden Age readers reversed these values, figuratively awarding ribbons of merit to works of detective fiction notable for the convincing and creative application of the sterner disciplines.

H.R.F. Keating and P.D. James merely implied, without stating directly, that readers of Humdrum mysteries were, intellectually, not quite up to snuff. Julian Symons, however, makes this implicit point more explicit in the first edition of *Bloody Murder*. Scoffing at Jacques Barzun's assertion that Humdrum works are "dependable as entertainment and respectable as literature," Symons sharply retorted: "It is politicians and not literary critics who have respected such works."[13] Certainly many may feel that one cannot get much more insulting than to compare a person's taste in literature to that of a politician's, but, in any event, Symons' claim is something less than true.

Many of the more august literary critics of the genre, such as Jacques Barzun, Dorothy L. Sayers, E.M. Wrong and H. Douglas Thomson, respected the works of the Humdrums, to say nothing of numerous lesser newspaper and journal reviewers, as well as lay readers of eminence, such as the respected mainstream novelists Sheila Kaye-Smith (1887–1956) and Joanna Cannan (1898–1961). Shelia Kaye-Smith abominated the detective novels of Sayers, Allingham and Marsh (with their "glamour boy" aristocrat investigators, as she derided them), much preferring John Rhode tales. "Mr. Rhode has devised more brilliant and unusual ways of getting rid of unwanted members of the human race than any other writer I know," an admiring Kaye-Smith wrote in her retrospective volume, *All the Books of My Life*, published the year of her death in 1956. Similarly, Joanna Cannan, who herself wrote a small body of acclaimed detective fiction, enjoyed reading John Rhode novels. Cannan goes so far as to favorably reference John Rhode's Great Detective Dr. Priestley in two of her own mysteries, *Death at the Dog* (1941) and *And Be a Villain* (1958). Cannan's daughter Josephine Pullein-Thompson recalls that her mother "admired Dorothy Sayers' writing, but couldn't take [Lord Peter]Wimsey and she grew tired of [Agatha Christie's] [Hercule] Poirot." In addition to John Rhode books, the personal mystery library of Cannan and her husband also included works by Freeman Wills Crofts.[14]

To cite another example, teacher, philately expert and author of mystery criticism Peter Ibbotson (born 1918) fondly recalled whiling away his time with "John Rhode paperbacks on late 1930s "term train journeys between home and school or university"; and his youthful admiration for this Humdrum author, as in the case of Sheila Kaye-Smith and Joanna Cannan, lasted him his whole life. Admittedly, the press on both sides of the Atlantic during the 1920s and 1930s repeatedly declared that eminent politicians devoured detective novels in their down time (in a particular case Symons likely had in mind, Stanley Baldwin, a conservative British prime minister in the 1920s and 1930s intensely disliked by many intellectuals, was said to be "addicted to detective fiction"). Yet whatever one thinks of the mental capacities of politicians, it also is true that many indisputably intelligent people — even high artistic intellectuals like T.S. Eliot — savored the delights of Humdrum detection. Genre critics have often noted Eliot's high praise for *The Moonstone*, the landmark mystery tale by the Victorian author Wilkie Collins, yet very few critics have similarly noted Eliot's encomia for the Humdrum detective novels of Freeman Wills Crofts.[15]

To be sure, a good number of these intelligent puzzle-oriented detective fiction fans likely were mathematicians, scientists, engineers and businessmen, whose taste literary critics naturally would view more dubiously than the taste of, say, literary critics. For example, Alfred Lucas (1867–1945), forensic scientist and consulting chemist to the Egyptian Department of Antiquities in Cairo, was a great devotee of detective fiction of the

"Humdrum" sort and numbered both R. Austin Freeman and John Street among his personal friends (Street's John Rhode short story "The Elusive Bullet" was modeled after a real life case Lucas had helped solve). Illustrating this division between two antipathetic sorts of occupational cultures, the arts and the sciences, is a humorous anecdote by poet and art critic Sir Herbert Read, in which Read told of a mystery-fiend friend, one Winterton, his former math tutor at the University of Leeds, who insatiably read detective novels, but had no interest in the higher arts. "Something of an amateur geologist and an expert climber," writes Read of Winterton, "his brain fits neatly into a square box and he has a healthy contempt for literature. As for art, besides his pipe-rack the only thing to be seen on his walls is a print of Durer's 'Melancolia.' But like many of his kind he has an insatiable appetite for detective fiction." Read always deferred to Winterton on this subject. "I have my own opinions [of detective fiction]," he noted wryly, "but they are merely literary."[16]

The preponderance of such persons as Read's Winterton in the readership of Humdrum detective novels is suggested by a dedicatory note to a conventional, puzzle-oriented 1923 detective novel authored by American Charles J. Dutton, a Unitarian minister and one-time state historian of Pennsylvania. Noting that at this time, the dawn of the Golden Age, some dubious critics were wondering who actually read mystery stories, Dutton hastened to demonstrate the respectability of the genre by listing the names and occupations of a half-dozen intelligent friends who happily confessed to the "crime." The six individuals, all male, claimed the following vocations: physician, inventor, professor of mechanical engineering, steel sales agent, journalist and Pennsylvania Railroad executive.[17]

An impressive cohort of detection readers from math and science fields can be glimpsed in the 1937 membership roll of Princeton University's "University League Book Club, Detective Group." Members of this faculty organization, which was devoted to reading thirty British and American detective novels and story collections between November 1, 1937, and May 30, 1938 (a rate of one a week), included professors of chemical engineering (Joseph C. Elgin and Richard H. Wilhelm), physics (William Francis Magie), mathematics (John Gale Hun), geology (Joseph A. Cushman) and archaeology (E. Baldwin Smith), as well as those from humanities-oriented fields, such as English (R.K. Root), classics and religion (Henry Snyder Gehman), Byzantine art (George Rowley) and Indo-Germanic philology (Harold H. Bender). The group's secretary, Nancy Hough Smith, wife of E. Baldwin Smith and daughter of one of the most respected federal judges of the first-quarter of the twentieth century, Charles Merrill Hough, herself graduated from Bryn Mawr in 1925 with a major in biology and chemistry and, after her prominent husband's death in 1956, served for fifteen years as assistant editor of the *American Journal of Archaeology*. Of the thirty mysteries that members of this group were slated to read in the coming seven months, nineteen were British detective novels and story collections, including not only works by Crime Queens Margery Allingham and Agatha Christie, but a Humdrum trifecta of Crofts' *Found Floating*, Connington's *A Minor Operation* and Rhode's *Death Sits on the Board*.[18]

Some Golden Age readers of mystery fiction doubtlessly were more attracted by the math and science and the intensive focus on plot in Humdrum detective novels rather than by the genteel detectives, love story elements, conspicuous dropping of literary quotations and other elements that became increasingly associated in the 1930s with the "sophisticated" works of such authors as Sayers, Allingham, Marsh, Innes and Blake. Sheila Kaye-Smith may have been more blunt than most such readers when she declared that she had "rejoiced when Miss [sic] Sayers turned from crime to theology," but no doubt some other Humdrum fans, dismayed at the ever more "literary" turn Sayers' mysteries had taken in the 1930s (particularly with *The Nine Tailors*, 1934; *Gaudy Night*, 1935; and *Busman's Honeymoon*, 1937), shared Kaye-Smith's sentiment. For his part, Gilbert Norwood, the esteemed Director of Classical Studies at University College, University of Toronto, admitted that Sayers wrote "better novels than Freeman Wills Crofts, better mysteries than (say) Galsworthy"—but where did that get one, he asked rhetorically. With works like *Gaudy Night*, Sayers certainly was not producing "better *detective* novels than Freeman Wills Crofts." Nor were these works "good enough" as straight novels to provide an adequate substitute interest for detection that in Sayers' hands had "dwindled" to the point of triviality.[19]

Reviews in the 1930s and 1940s from the *Saturday Review of Literature* and the *New Yorker* often similarly evince weariness with the literary school of British detection. In 1937, "Judge Lynch," the mystery reviewer for the *Saturday Review of Literature*, perused both Miles Burton's *The Clue of the Fourteen Keys (Death at the Club)* and Margery Allingham's *Dancers in Mourning* and preferred the former tale. "First class, moves gallantly to surprise climax," Lynch raved of the Burton book, while he sighed of *Dancers in Mourning* that it was bursting with "overwriting a la Dorothy Sayers." Of two Michael Innes detective novels, the *New Yorker* sourly noted that "[Inspector Appleby] can trade Latin quotations with the best of them ... recommended for those with a pedantic turn of mind" (*The Weight of the Evidence*, 1943) and "designed for readers who like their detectives urbane, not to say precious (*Appleby's End*, 1945)." Concerning the highly-regarded *The Moving Toyshop* (1946) by Edmund Crispin, a recent Oxford graduate with a BA in modern languages and a late entrant to the ranks of literarily erudite British mystery writers, the *New Yorker* expressed hope that "Mr. Crispin would relax in his efforts to wrest Dorothy Sayers' scholarly laurels away from her." Conversely, though in the 1940s the *New Yorker* admitted books by Crofts and Street were "leisurely" compared with those by new wave British mystery writers like Innes and Crispin, it praised Crofts and Street mysteries for plots that stayed to the presumed point of a detective novel, detection: "Pure detection in the old-fashioned way ... may prove tedious to youngsters, but it's sound reading for those slightly grey about the temples" (John Rhode, *Dead on the Track*, 1943); "technically brilliant" (John Rhode, *The Fourth Bomb*, 1942); "very neatly plotted" (John Rhode, *The Links of the Chain/The Paper Bag*, 1948); "very good" (Freeman Wills Crofts, *Double Tragedy/The Affair at Little Wokeham*, 1943); "ingenious" (Freeman Wills Crofts, *Enemy Unseen*, 1945).[20]

Many Golden Age traditionalists likely had been weaned as mystery readers not only on the celebrated adventures of Arthur Conan Doyle's Sherlock Holmes but on those of R. Austin Freeman's great scientific detective, Dr. John Thorndyke. The latter author, R. Austin Freeman, justifiably can be labeled the Humdrum Founding Father. All three of the true Humdrums—Street, Crofts and Stewart—read Freeman as younger men, and the older author clearly was a significant influence both on Street, who employed devices obviously drawn from Freeman tales in several of his own novels, and Stewart, who wrote in the 1930s that he considered Freeman beyond question the mystery genre's premier detective novelist, in a class by himself. Sheila Kaye-Smith held Freeman in similar esteem. Kaye-Smith discovered both the Holmes and Thorndyke stories during World War I, when she was "staying unhappily at a cheap and battered club in Maida Vale, trying to warm my heart at the ashes of an extinguished love affair." She recalled during this time reading works by both authors while sitting "alone at tea," and being "surprised to find how interesting and how comforting they were." Eventually Kaye-Smith "came to prefer Freeman" over Doyle and she went on to read everything Freeman wrote. In her view Freeman's "extraordinary lucidity and directness, and the width of his interests, among which however medicine predominated, made up for Doyle's superiority in presenting life and character."[21]

Sheila Kaye-Smith's words may well have described the views of those Golden Age readers who preferred a tale by Rhode or Crofts or Connington over one by Dorothy L. Sayers (particularly by the mid–1930s, after Sayers had begun downplaying the puzzle aspect of her detective fiction in favor of the exploration of social manners). Speculating in her recent survey, *Talking about Detective Fiction*, on the nature of the popularity of Dorothy L. Sayers' mysteries during the Golden Age, P.D. James places greater emphasis on literary trappings than on plots, arguing that those trappings offered soothing psychic comforts to readers troubled by the tumultuous times in which they lived:

> Readers of Dorothy L. Sayers, traveling home to mortgaged Metroland or worried by the threat of unemployment and the storm clouds over Europe, must have entered with relief into Lord Peter's flat with the fire burning, shedding its light on the bronze chrysanthemums, the comfortable chairs and the grand piano, while Bunter deferentially offers them a glass of expensive sherry or vintage wine and Lord Peter entertains them by playing Scarlatti.[22]

What people enjoyed most about mystery fiction such as Sayers,' so this argument runs, was not so much the mental stimulation of trying to solve any intricate murder problem that Lord Peter Wimsey might confront, but rather the vicarious immersion in the warm, scented bath of leisured luxury and old money culture that this charming, aristocratic detective enjoyed. No doubt this is an accurate statement of the feelings of many of Sayers' readers. Yet what the Sheila Kaye-Smiths of the mystery reading world primarily wanted from a detective novel was not a fanciful lord tinkling the ivories with the strains of a Scarlatti sonata or exchanging clever repartee with his love interest and eventual wife, the brilliantly talented mystery novelist Harriet Vane, but rather a no-nonsense, safely celibate detective sternly employing all his faculties in the solving of a challenging murder problem solidly grounded in accurate mathematical and scientific fact.[23]

Sir Herbert Read's old math tutor Winterton vigorously expressed just such a traditionalist view in the discussion, detailed by Read, that the two men had about a new crop of 1937 crime tales, including Sayers' final Lord Peter novel, *Busman's Honeymoon*, which Winterton not so cordially loathed:

> "...[A]ll this love interest [in Sayers' detective novels] is so much padding. I am prepared to admit that women make admirable writers of crime stories.... But they should leave the serious business of love to men. Good God, do you remember what [Lord Peter] calls his long-limbed, honey-skinned and bone-shaking wife?
>
> "I seem to recollect 'Heart's desire.'"
>
> "Worse! 'Domina!' [*Busman's Honeymoon*] is 446 pages long. Somewhere embedded in its pulpy thickness is the material for a short. And not a very good short at that."

Winterton's fulmination over the sundry literary provocations of *Busman's Honeymoon* climaxed when the conversation turned to characterization:

> "... I distrust this itch for introducing characterization into detective fiction."
>
> "You must find much to object to then in *Busman's Honeymoon*. The oh-so-determined-to-be-passionate-lovers, the dear old Dickensian Bunter, the poetic Superintendent, the country cottage by Beverley Nichols..."
>
> But [Winterton] would not let me finish. He fixed me from behind his steel-rimmed spectacles and uttered his final judgment: "I can stand most things for the sake of a teasing problem; I have endured an incredible dose of the facetious Whimsey [*sic*] and the bland Bunter; but that there should be added to these a general atmosphere of lubricious coyness..."
>
> "But there are some pretty quotations to give it a face," I interrupted.
>
> "The last depravity!" he cried. "Why should my corpse be garnished with parsley from the *Young Maiden's Garden of Verses?*"

Winterton suggested to his friend Read that if he wanted a mystery in the "right tradition," he should try Josephine Bell's debut detective novel, *Murder in Hospital*. "Shakespeare and Aldous Huxley are never once mentioned," he avowed.[24]

To be sure, even at the height of the Golden Age, by no means all voices sang with Kaye-Smith and Winterton in this Humdrum chorus. A major literary critic who early on dissented from the view that detective fiction of the pure puzzle sort could be considered worthy reading material, even as mere down time diversion, was the English novelist Arnold Bennett. In his weekly book review column in the *Weekly Standard*, which ran from 1926 to 1931 (the year of his death), the famous author on occasion took time to denounce the detective fiction craze. Bennett disliked most modern detective novels, seeing them, in contrast with earlier works of mystery by such nineteenth century authors as Wilkie Collins and Emile Gaboriau, as puzzle-fixated pseudo-literature; yet Bennett's particular disdain for Humdrum authors should be noted, because his view of these writers ultimately carried the day. Indeed, many of Julian Symons' influential opinions in *Bloody Murder* bookend disdainful sentiments Bennett had voiced over forty years earlier, during the Humdrum heyday. Upon finishing Connington's *The Case with Nine Solutions*—a work praised for its sound construction and "respect for the readers' intelligence," it will be recalled—Bennett reported withcringly:

> I cannot say that I was particularly interested.... The human repercussions of the story simply are not handled.... The book is inhuman. If a jig-saw puzzle has emotional quality, then *The Case with Nine Solutions* has emotional quality. If not, not. The story is flat; it has no contours. And the writing is as flat as the story. I do not deny that the thing can be read. It has some attraction, but no attraction of emotion. It has employed the invention of the author, not his imagination. A tragedy is not a tragedy until it moves you. This book has four tragedies, and you do not care twopence.[25]

Bennett cared not twopence whether his intellect had been engaged when his emotions had not been touched.

The next year, a year before his death, Bennett took Freeman Wills Crofts to task for dullness and drab writing. Of Crofts' *Sir John Magill's Last Journey* (which, the author and critic noted, had been praised on the wireless "in terms extremely warm" by "a perhaps high-brow critic of undeniable taste, erudition and prestige"—probably Michael Sadleir), Bennett complained:

It lacks liveliness. Mr. Crofts is very slow off the mark. He seems to disdain the common business of interesting his reader page by page.... [He] will not, or cannot, divert his reader. He refuses all compromises with the poor man. He does not even care twopence about his mere writing, which, if not repellent, is certainly not attractive. He will calmly and negligently commit incredible sins of composition. Hardly could I believe my eyes when I saw Mr. Crofts describing a meal as "fortifying the inner man"! Does not Mr. Crofts know better than this, or doesn't he care? If he doesn't know, he ought to know, and if, knowing, he doesn't care, he ought to care."[26]

Arnold Bennett died before the Humdrums were humbled and emotion vanquished ratiocination in the detective novel, but his views could be heard even in the pronouncements of certain prestigious members of the Detection Club, that ostensibly purist holy of holies to which not only Agatha Christie and Dorothy L. Sayers, but Street, Crofts and Stewart had belonged since its creation in 1930. The Detection Club, founded as a social organization by most of the finest British detection writers of the period, originally sought to mark an aesthetic boundary in mystery fiction between the highbrow, cerebral detective novels produced by Detection Club members and the lowbrow, sensationalist thrillers associated with such authors as the egregiously prolific Edgar Wallace, at the time the bestselling author in Britain; Sax Rohmer (pseudonym of Arthur Henry Sarsfield Ward), creator of the diabolically cunning Oriental criminal mastermind, Dr. Fu Manchu; and Sapper (pseudonym of H.C. McNeile), whose renowned fictional hero, Bulldog Drummond, battled Germans and Bolshies with altogether excessive gusto. Tellingly, the Club required prospective members to take an oath in which they promised to observe a "seemly moderation" in the use of such stock thriller devices as "Gangs, Conspiracies, Death-Rays, Ghosts, Hypnotism, Trap-Doors, Chinamen, Super-Criminals and Lunatics" and to foreswear "utterly and forever" resort to "Mysterious Poisons unknown to Science."[27]

No doubt much of this purportedly solemn oath-taking business was tongue-in-cheek, yet there was some serious artistic design in back of it all. The keystone of the Detection Club oath was that part in which the prospective member promised to fairly present to the reader all the clues used by the detective in solving the mystery. "No longer did crude sensationalism dominate the form," writes Douglas G. Greene of mystery literature in the Golden Age. "The emphasis was now on the intellectual challenge implicit in the fair play principle." Without "fair play," the intellectual, ratiocinative aspect of the detective novel was destroyed, and it ceased to be a detective novel, becoming instead either a mystery (where a problem is presented, but due to the withholding of clues on the part of the author the reader has no chance of solving the problem by means of logical deduction) or a thriller (where no pretense is made of providing a problem to be solved, the reader instead being taken by the author on a thrill ride of criminal occurrences, usually involving a ruthless international gang led by a nefarious criminal mastermind). It was precisely the demanding artistic technique of the fair play convention, wrote H. Douglas Thomson in 1931 (the year after the founding of the Detection Club), that justified "the consideration of the detective story as an independent genre." Reflecting the thriller-exclusionist thinking that lay behind the creation of the Detection Club oath, Thomson insisted that "the detective story must be first and foremost a problem. The main ingredient must be logic." In Thomson's view, there was "quite enough excitement in a problem without calling in the aid of death, crape and firing squads."[28]

In the course of a review of John Rhode's *Peril at Cranbury Hall* (1930), another critic took time out to explain in enlightening detail the essential difference between the true detective novel as represented by Rhode and the thriller as represented by Edgar Wallace. The former was commendably cerebral, the latter crudely sensationalistic:

> Mr. Rhode and Mr. Austin Freeman have revolted against the school of fiction headed by Mr. Edgar Wallace. Mr. Wallace and his followers rely, for their effects, on sensationalism, and the fact that a detective is the mainspring of their stories does not mean that there is any obligation for deduction on the part of the reader. Plots are unraveled with facility, apparently without effort on the part of the hero-detective, and certainly without effort on the part of the reader. Mr. Wallace has written some very entertaining tales; but his greatest admirer could not claim that he made his public think. With Mr. Rhode, the process of detection is a collection of facts, carefully fitted together, with the reader's intelligent understanding, carrying him from clue to clue, until he is neck to neck with the author in the discovery of the criminal. He is always careful to put all his known facts on the table, and the reader has just as much chance of following the trail as the author's character. If there is any art in the detective story, Mr. Rhode undoubtedly employs the rules of that art.[29]

Despite the fact that the Detection Club oath, in congruence with the thinking of many critics and lay readers of the time, elevated fair play detection as the very pinnacle of the mystery writer's art, the Club's own founding membership included dissidents within its ranks. The very year the Club was founded, as Arnold Bennett was damning Freeman Wills Crofts for fortifying his detective's inner man and boring at least one reader, Club member Anthony Berkeley Cox began explicitly expounding genre heresy. Cox certainly held no brief for the bare white knuckles thriller; yet, he came to see the fair play puzzle convention as something that shackled the artistic potential of the mystery novel, preventing genre writers from exploring the twisting labyrinths of criminal psychology, which in his view were vastly more tantalizing to the intelligent mind than any mere whodunit conundrum could ever be. By the time of the founding of the Detection Club, Cox was one of the most prominent British detective novelists, yet already for several years (under the pen name "Anthony Berkeley") he had been tugging the beards, so to speak, of what he saw as the hoary, grimly orthodox fans of classical puzzle fiction. Cox introduced his most famous series detective, the insouciant, young Roger Sheringham, in *The Layton Court Mystery* in 1925. In a move subversive of a basic premise of the classical detective novel — that the detective solves his case through his detection — Cox in the Sheringham novels often depicts his detective enthusiastically racing down what turn out to be false trails and reaching thumpingly wrong solutions.[30]

While *Layton Court* itself is a traditional country house affair, with Sheringham actually solving the case, Cox's mystery from the following year, *The Wychford Poisoning Case*, is a different kettle of red herring. Sheringham here reaches the wrong conclusion, making rather a fool of himself in the process, but even more notable, in their challenge to detection orthodoxy, are the sentiments espoused in the novel by both the author and his detective. Cox dedicated *Wychford*, which he significantly subtitled *A Problem in Criminology* (as opposed to one in detection), to E.M. Delafield, best known today for her humorous, lightly satirical *Provincial Lady* book series, but at the time of *Wychford*'s publication the author of the recent *Messalina of the Suburbs*, a fictional rendering of the notorious 1923 Thompson-Bywaters murder case, which had fascinated both Delafield and Cox. "I hope you will recognize the attempt I have made to substitute for the usual crime puzzle of fiction those psychological values which are (as we have so often agreed) the basis of the universal interest in the far more absorbing criminological dramas of real life," Cox wrote Delafield in the dedicatory preface. In similar fashion, the garrulous Roger Sheringham lectures at length throughout *Wychford* on the superiority of real life crime drama over bookish murder puzzles. "Ordinary detective yarns bore me," announces Sheringham at one point, "because all they set out to do is show who committed the crime; what I care about is why the crime was committed.... [T]he real interest in a murder case in actual life ... is not the crime puzzle of the carefully manufactured detective story, but the human element which led the, quite possibly, very ordinary crime to be committed at all." Sheringham goes on to pronounce that because of their inherent "psychological values," the real life, human "dramas of the Central Criminal Court are more interesting than any detective story ever written."[31]

Wychford proves of interest primarily for this extraneous philosophizing, for it disappoints both as a detective novel and as an exercise in criminal psychology (Cox's "psychology," expressed through Sheringham, often is embarrassingly puerile in this novel). Cox continued on his merry, subversive way, however. In the next Sheringham opus, 1927's *Roger Sheringham and the Vane Mystery*, the over-confident amateur detective pronounces another classically imaginative, airy-fairy murder solution, only to have it brought crashing down to earth by his attendant policeman, Chief Inspector Moreseby. "Do you know what's the matter with you, sir?" the author with heavy irony has Moreseby explain to the dejected amateur detective, "You've been reading too many of those detective stories."[32] Bloodied but unbowed — indeed, rather irritatingly chirpy — Sheringham appeared the next year in *The Silk Stocking Murders* (1928), eager as ever to speculate lengthily, if absurdly, on the conundra of criminal psychology. Perhaps surprisingly to Anthony Berkeley readers by this time, he even correctly solves the case. However, Cox for good measure rounded out the decade of the 1920s with yet another ratiocinative debacle for Sheringham, this time in a novel, *The Poisoned Chocolates Case*, which is still sometimes mentioned in surveys, unlike other Anthony Berkeley tales.

What distinguishes *The Poisoned Chocolates Case* is that the murder case is presented to a round table of amateur detectives, each of whom successively "solves" it, only to be successively proven wrong, until the very last person, the diffident, self-effacing Ambrose Chitterwick, is reached. Then Mr. Chitterwick, the least likely detective of them all, actually does solve the case. Julian Symons pronounced *The Poisoned Chocolates Case* "one of the most stunning trick stories in the history of detective fiction," but what is most striking about the tale from the vantage point of this study is the way it systematically undermines the concept of truth in detective fiction.[33] If the same set of facts can be twisted some half-dozen times to reach seemingly plausible, but in reality false, solutions each time, one might ask after reading *The Poisoned Chocolates Case*: is not any "solution" in a detective story something simply imposed arbitrarily on the reader by the author? Is not the game, in other words, by its very nature, rigged?

After becoming one of the founding members of the Detection Club in 1930, Cox only became bolder in his novelistic challenges to the puzzle status quo. In the preface to his novel *The Second Shot*, published that same year, Cox declared provocatively that "the days of the old crime-puzzle, pure and simple, relying entirely upon the plot and without any added attractions of character, style, or even humor, are in the hands of the auditor." The future of the genre, Cox believed, lay with novels with merely "a detective or crime interest," ones that would hold readers "less by mathematical than by psychological ties." Even the most ordinary real life murders had enticing complications "of emotion, drama, psychology, and adventure," which the "conventional detective story," beset by its rigid conventions, was incapable of conveying. Yet despite the bravado of its preface, *The Second Shot* is a rather conventional tale, its most original point echoing an Agatha Christie novel. The next year, however, Cox put into practice what he preached with his publication, under the pseudonym Francis Iles, of *Malice Aforethought*, a so-called "inverted mystery" in which the interest is not the mental one of trying to solve a murder puzzle though logical deduction, but the emotional one of watching a person commit murder and try to evade the machinery of justice. Cox was not the first person to write such a book — indeed, Joanna Cannan had published just such an inverted murder mystery, *No Walls of Jasper*, the year before — but Cox published *Malice Aforethought* to a fanfare of publicity (due in part to speculation stoked by his publisher that the Francis Iles pseudonym hid a great serious author) and made a tremendous impression on writers, critics and public alike. Moreover, on the heels of *Malice Aforethought* Cox as Iles published a second unconventional mystery novel, *Before the Fact*, in which the focus this time was on the emotional state of a woman believing her husband is planning to murder her. The cumulative impact of these two books was to produce cracks in the Humdrum artistic edifice, ultimately helping to bring about its collapse.[34]

In addition to publishing his dramatically subversive Francis Iles novels, Cox continued in the 1930s to produce more subtly iconoclastic Sheringham novels under the Anthony Berkeley name. One of the most entertaining Sheringham tales, *Top Storey Murder* (1931), sees Sheringham again coming up with a brilliant, but incorrect, solution. More significant, in terms of their iconoclasm, are the last two Sheringham novels, *Jumping Jenny* (1933) and *Panic Party* (1934), both of which shift the narrative emphasis away from detection more toward what would later come to be termed "psychological suspense." In his preface to *Panic Party*, Cox explained that fellow Detection Club member Milward Kennedy once had challenged him "to write a book in which the only interest should be the detection." Cox impudently retorted that he had "no hesitation in refusing to do anything so tedious." Instead, the puckish author announced, he would take "the greatest pleasure" in presenting a book to Kennedy "which is precisely the opposite, which breaks every rule of the austere Club to which we both belong, and which will probably earn my expulsion from its membership."[35]

Far from expelling the heretic in their midst, other members of the Detection Club joined Cox in his deviancy. Of the nine non-founding authors admitted to the Detection Club before the end of World War II (all from 1933 to 1937), only two, E.R. Punshon and Christopher Bush, have been associated with the Humdrum "school" (accurately or not); and four others, Anthony Gilbert, Gladys Mitchell, Margery Allingham and Nicholas Blake, chafed at the limitations of the rules and sought to shift the balance of interest in the detective novel more in favor of richer characterization and writing. Of active founding members, three others besides Cox — Henry Wade (Henry Lancelot Aubrey-Fletcher), Milward Kennedy (Milward Rodon Kennedy Burge) and, most importantly, Dorothy L. Sayers — began drifting away from the traditional puzzle form.

Although written with an appreciation for style and theme, the first six novels of Henry Wade, published between 1926 and 1932, are relatively orthodox in their emphasis on fair play puzzles. Beginning in 1933 with *Mist on the Saltings*, however, we see a clear break with the past in Wade's work, with greater interest being shown in realistic character development and police procedure, often at the expense of the puzzles. One novel, *Heir Presumptive* (1935), even is in inverted form, in the manner of Iles, while two others, *The High Sheriff* (1937) and *Released for Death* (1938), are more "crime novels" than tales of detection. Another pair of tales, *Bury Him Darkly* (1936) and *Lonely Magdalen* (1940), are pioneering works in their use of detailed, realistic police procedure.

Milward Kennedy's works show a similar progression to Wade's, from relatively orthodox puzzle plot novels from 1928 to 1932 to a series of attempts to break from the limitations of the form: two novels, *Bull's Eye* (1933) and *Corpse in Cold Storage* (1934), featuring a lively con artist rogue in the role of detective; a semi-inverted village satire, *Poison in the Parish* (1935); *Sic Transit Gloria* (1936), a recounting of "a few days in the life of a man whose friend dies" that is more a psychological study than a conventional puzzle; and *I'll Be Judge, I'll Be Jury* (1937), a dark inverted mystery, far closer in spirit to the world of the crime novel as envisioned by Julian Symons than that of Humdrum detective novels. In *Sic Transit Gloria*, Kennedy, evidently having caught the preface bug from the incorrigible Anthony Berkeley Cox, declared to his publisher, Victor Gollancz, a deliberate missionary intent: "You and I are both lovers of the detective novel, and believe that it has a place in literature. For my part I believe too that if the detective novel becomes too stereotyped, if its "rules" are applied too rigidly, the genre may be destroyed.... *Sic Transit Gloria* may infect others with the desire to experiment."[36]

Milward Kennedy's more unorthodox crime tales failed to create the literary contagion he had so hopefully envisioned, but there is no question but that Dorothy L. Sayers hugely impacted the genre with her 1930s bid to transform the detective tale into what she called "the novel of character and manners." While such notable Sayers critics as Edmund Wilson, Raymond Chandler, Graham Greene and more recently Julian Symons have cast doubt — to put it rather mildly — on Sayers' success in this area ("there is a breathtaking gap here between intention and achievement," pronounces Symons witheringly), it seems safe to say that most genre critics of the last forty years have been far more positive about Sayers' effort. "To her admirers," writes P.D. James (among whom James herself clearly numbers), Sayers "is the writer who did more than any other to make the detective story intellectually respectable, and to change it from an ingenious but lifeless sub-literary puzzle into a specialized branch of fiction with serious claims to be judged as a novel." Whether one sides with admirers like James or detractors like Symons on the question of the quality of Sayers' later fictional works, the fact that Sayers had a tremendous influence on the mystery genre in the 1930s is, for any fair-minded observer, undeniable. Her critical writings on the genre won her considerable attention from intellectuals, while her last two Lord Peter tales in particular became significant sellers on both sides of the Atlantic, all of which served to make her an enviable example of critical and popular success that other mystery genre writers on both sides of the Atlantic naturally sought to emulate.[37]

The dramatic artistic transformation Sayers personally underwent between 1928 and 1936 can be followed in her influential introductions to the first and second series of Gollancz's *Great Short Stories of Detection, Mystery and Horror* (1928, 1931) and to the Everyman's Library *Tales of Detection* (1936), as well as in her mystery reviews from 1933 to 1935 in the *Sunday Times* and her own detective novels. In her earliest criticism Sayers rejected the idea that the detective novelist could scale the highest peaks of Literary Art. To be sure, she opined in 1928, that severest form of mystery story, the "pure analytical exercise" detective novel, could justly be deemed "a highly finished work of art, within its highly artificial limits." Indeed, Sayers impressively pronounced, the detective story "possesses an Aristotelian perfection of beginning, middle, and end. A definite single problem is set, worked out, and solved.... It has the rounded (though limited) perfection of a triolet." She warned that the farther the detective story "escapes from pure analysis, the more difficulty it has in achieving artistic unity."[38]

Nevertheless, in Sayers' view the detective story as she thus defined it could never "attain the highest level of literary achievement." Effectively conceding the sort of criticism Arnold Bennett made of Connington's *The Case with Nine Solutions* ("the human repercussions of the story simply are not handled"), Sayers expounded on the inherent artistic limitations of the detective story: "Though it deals with the most desperate effects of rage, jealousy, and revenge, it rarely touches the heights and depths of human passion. It presents us only with the *fait accompli*, and looks upon death and mutilation with a dispassionate eye.... The victim is shown rather as a subject for the dissecting-table than as a husband and father." But what Bennett diagnosed as a catastrophic breakdown in any literary form — the artistically fatal curtailment of genuine human emotion — Sayers believed to be a necessary condition of successful detective fiction. "A too violent emotion flung into the glittering mechanism of the detective story jars the movement by disturbing its delicate balance," she warned. "[I]t is better to err in the direction of too little feeling than too much." One emotion in particular, love, was "better left out," Sayers concluded. While she allowed that a very few works — Wilkie Collins' *The Moonstone*, E.C. Bentley's *Trent's Last Case* and A.E.W. Mason's *The House of the Arrow*— had managed the feat of maintaining a "strong detective interest" while simultaneously erecting "the convincing psychological structure of the novel of character," Sayers maintained that these were "unusual instances" that would be difficult for others to emulate. She seemed daunted as to the possibility of "allowing real human beings into a detective-story," as Arnold Bennett was uncompromisingly demanding. "At some point or other," Sayers contended, acutely stating the problem that was to vex detective novelists of her generation, either real human beings and their emotions "make hay of the detective interest, or the detective interest gets hold of [those real human beings] and makes their emotions look like pasteboard."[39]

Sayers defended the detective story as a lesser literary art, but she also considered it, as did Street, Crofts and Stewart, a damnably difficult craft: "It is obvious that the job of writing detective-stories is by no means growing easier. The reader must be given every clue.... How can we at the same time show the reader everything and yet legitimately obfuscate him as to its meaning?" At the same time, Sayers speculated near the end of her essay that "a new and less rigid formula" might well develop, one that would link the detective story "more closely to the novel of manners." Though rather an aside in her 1928 essay, this thought gradually took hold of Sayers over the course of the 1930s and found expression in both her literary criticism and her fiction. In the end, she succeeded in helping to shatter the very literary aesthetic of the detective story that she had laboriously constructed in 1928, taking down with it the artistic reputations of Street, Crofts, Stewart and anyone else with the bad fortune to incur the label "Humdrum."[40]

In her relatively brief 1931 introduction to the second series of *Great Stories of*

Detection, Mystery and Horror, Sayers has less of note to say on weighty literary matters concerning the detective story; yet she includes some significant commentary, indicating that her view of the "pure analytical exercise" as a "highly finished work of art" was in flux. Implicitly comparing the works Symons later dubbed Humdrum with "the more modern tales," Sayers contrasted the "flatness and lack of distinction" sometimes found in the former with "the genuine attempt to create real atmosphere" in the latter. In these "modern" works Sayers found evident "a genuine eagerness to bring the detective-story into line with the traditions of the English novel and to make it increasingly a real part of literature." Here Sayers obviously is moving closer to Symons' side of the argument with Barzun as to whether Humdrum detective tales rightly could be considered "respectable as literature." Tellingly, Sayers found room in her short essay to quote a long excerpt from what she called the "manifesto" of Anthony Berkeley Cox in *The Second Shot*. Sayers speculated that in the struggle over the proper nature of the detective story, popular opinion was on the side of "reformers" like Cox.[41]

By 1936, when Sayers penned the last of these critical essays, the author herself had wholeheartedly joined the movement "to bring the detective story into line with the traditions of the English novel," as evidenced by both her 1933–1935 mystery fiction review columns in the *Sunday Times* (where she often preached the cause of the "manners" mystery) and her own detective novels, particularly *The Nine Tailors* (1934) and the controversial *Gaudy Night* (1935) — though in fact this trend in her fictional work can be detected as early as 1930, with the publication of *Strong Poison*, which introduced Harriet Vane, a serious love interest for Lord Peter Wimsey, and *The Documents in the Case*, a sober portrayal of a rather meanly sordid suburban crime of passion. While her earlier works from the 1920s are more distinguished for their clever problems and light humor, Sayers' 1930s novels, with the exception of 1931's *The Five Red Herrings* (a railway timetable novel in the manner of Freeman Wills Crofts), clearly aim at more serious treatments of characters and settings. Especially in her last three novels, formal detective problems pale in significance compared to purely "literary" elements: the portrayal of an idealized, organic English village in *Tailors*; the question of women's education in *Gaudy Night*; the marriage of Lord Peter and Harriet in *Busman's Honeymoon*. Though the latter two works, *Gaudy Night* and *Busman's Honeymoon*, had detractors among highbrow haters of detective fiction *en masse* as well as among mystery fiend traditionalists, both were highly praised by many critics and sold impressively in both Britain and the United States, providing Sayers the dual pleasures of substantial monetary remuneration and a personal sense of artistic vindication.[42]

Now unquestionably the most public face of British detective fiction and in addition endowed with an intellectual prestige (as the leading exponent of the crime novel of manners) that no other British mystery writer could claim, Sayers in 1936 could casually dismiss as mere craft the once seemingly important matter of mystery plot construction. "Any competent craftsmen could hammer together a problem of this kind," she airily pronounced. Consequently, the genre had come to be "neglected by the genuine literary artists." Only a few great souls, like E.C. Bentley and A.E.W. Mason, "remembered that they were novelists and strove hard to keep the detective story in touch with life." By use of the passive voice rather avoiding her own culpability in the elevation of craft over art with her 1928 essay, Sayers complained: "It became axiomatic that the great romantic emotions were out of place in detective fiction, so that we observed the extraordinary phenomenon of a whole literature based upon a hypothesis of crime and violence and yet abstaining from any serious treatment of the sins and passions — particularly the sexual passions — which commonly form the motives for violent crime." Detective stories had to change and give "serious artistic treatment of the psychological elements," Sayers warned, or the genre would die. "No kind of fiction can survive for very long cut off from the great interests of humanity and from the main stream of contemporary literature," she avowed; yet too many writers of detective stories feared attempting "profound treatment of the larger emotions" and continued gingerly "to handle their characters as mere chess-pieces endowed with conventional attributes."[43] In eight years, Sayers had come full circle. In 1928 she feared the mess of human passions could wreck the delicate and intricate machinery of the Aristotelian rational detective novel; by 1936 she believed it was only those human passions that could save it, precisely by making it human, though she admitted that writers had not yet discovered how best to combine puzzle and human elements to create a truly literary detective novel.

Two additional members of the Detection Club who expressed impatience with Humdrum authors in the thirties were Margaret Cole and Nicholas Blake. Margaret Cole was the wife of the famous socialist academic, G.D.H. Cole, and joint author with him of detective novels ironically dubbed "Humdrum" by Julian Symons; while "Nicholas Blake" was the Communist poet Cecil Day Lewis, who wrote detective novels under the Blake pseudonym. Both writers occasionally reviewed mysteries in the *Spectator*. In a 1931 column where she praised Francis Iles' *Malice Aforethought* (Mr. Francis Iles ... knows how to write and to sketch a character"), Cole wrote dismissively of the works of Freeman Wills Crofts, making clear that the appeal of his timetable mysteries, where the detective laboriously breaks down elaborate alibis to catch the murderer, was lost on her. Crofts' characters, she declared, "are not characters at all; they are — to use a biological metaphor — extremely simple structures provided with name-labels and impregnable alibis." Voicing the concerns of others in the thirties who were finding dulled the once "glittering mechanism" of the purely analytical detective novel, she continued: "There are a limited number of possible variants of the pure puzzle ... when one has read a sufficient number, unless one possesses the type of mind that goes on solving crosswords forever and ever, one becomes jaded and demands some additional flavouring to the puzzle-dish." Later in the decade, new detective novelist Nicholas Blake expressed similar reservations in the *Spectator*. In a review of John Rhode's *Mystery at Olympia* (1935), Blake complained: "He has relied more and more upon the ingenuity of his plots — and highly ingenious they are — to hold our interest.... But the characters are ciphers, and the dialogue as desiccated as the question and answer of an official form." The next year, in praising Crofts' *The Loss of the "Jane Vosper*," Blake could not forbear adding what became the *cri de couer* of the Julian Symons school of mystery criticism: "I cannot help feeling that the author relies too much on pure detection."[44]

It is worth noting, however, that Sayers and Milward Kennedy, both of whom reviewed mysteries for the august *Sunday Times* in the 1930s, continued to read and enjoy Humdrum detective fiction, despite their exclamations of impatience with the traditional form. Certainly Dorothy L. Sayers never completely lost that part of herself which delighted in confronting a mystery puzzle. Until her death in 1957, she continued to participate in the Detection Club and to read detective novels, enjoying the puzzle elements.[45] Even in her 1936 essay, where her propagandizing for the mystery novel of manners reached its apex, Sayers made clear that she still respected the puzzle novel as an intellectual exercise. Indeed, when she complained that the detective novel in general had become "over-intellectualized," tantalizing the brain but leaving the heart unmoved, she was tacitly acknowledging that such works had some value to intellectuals, if only as leisure-time mental stimulus.

Sayers' detective fiction reviews in the *Sunday Times* indicate that despite calling for aesthetic reform in the genre in the 1930s, she simultaneously continued to enjoy a good puzzle novel as much as any mystery-friendly, classically-educated British intellectual of the time. In early 1934, for example, in a review of *The 12.30 from Croydon*, she waxed biblically that Freeman Wills Crofts had in 1920 with the publication of *The Cask* "devised a formula and became thereby the only begetter of a numerous and distinguished detective progeny." It was the Anglo-Irish former railroad engineer who had "first made police routine fascinating and distilled romance from the pages of a Bradshaw." Admittedly Sayers expressed a wish that "the various personages" in *12.30 from Croydon* might "be a little more strongly characterized," but she nevertheless affirmed that "the story, as a story, is highly successful." Later that year Sayers wrote of Connington's *The Ha-Ha Case* that the author "has given us a sound and interesting plot, very carefully and ingeniously worked out." The charmed reviewer even went so far as to praise the novelist's characterization and to note the book's "admirable" map-illustrated dust jacket, very handy for reference.[46]

John Street's John Rhode and Miles Burton novels came in for praise from Sayers as well, though the Burton novels struck her as rather too leisurely paced. In another pair of reviews from 1934, the Crime Queen found Rhode's *Poison for One* "as usual, sound, pleasantly-written and entertaining," while she was tickled at being utterly bamboozled by the central plot gimmick in his *Shot at Dawn*, writing with mock indignation over "the perfectly heartless manner in which he led my innocence up the garden.... Fair? Yes, of course it was fair: that is what makes it so galling." Sayers noted that she did "guess who fired the fatal shot, though at a disgracefully late point in the story." Of one of Rhode's 1935 contributions, *The Corpse in the Car*, a wickedly delighted Sayers informed her readers: "Mr. John Rhode has found a grand new way of eliminating people.... Happily, the murder-method is one that requires a special set of circumstances to make it feasible: otherwise one might expect to find the countryside peppered with the corpses of tiresome old ladies and gentlemen, now that we know the way to get rid of them."[47]

After Dorothy L. Sayers left the *Sunday Times* as crime fiction reviewer in 1935, she was succeeded by Milward Kennedy, who by this time shared her professed view that the detective novel needed to become more literary to survive as a genre. Yet Kennedy, like Sayers, continued to enjoy reading the Humdrum masters. In a 1936 review of Crofts' *The Loss of the "Jane Vosper,"* Kennedy declared flatly that "Mr. Crofts pretends to little grace of style or fullness of characterization." Yet Kennedy believe that Crofts had a "gift": the ability "to interest the reader in a pedestrian account of the search for a needle in a haystack." *The Loss of the "Jane Vosper"* was "perhaps his most astonishing performance." Kennedy similarly wrote with admiration of Connington's *A Minor Operation*. The novel proved "that the murder-plot is capable of as many variations as the love-story, and that

[Connington] has very few superiors in its construction." Like Sayers, Kennedy qualified his praise of Street's Miles Burton, but with John Rhode he tended to be more favorable, deeming as he did Rhode's detective Dr. Priestley "one of the chief exponents of logical deduction." What made Rhode's books significant in Kennedy's eyes was not his characters (though he noted that when he so wished Rhode could present them "very adequately") but his plot mechanics, which the critic resoundingly declared "outstanding." John Rhode "must hold the record for the invention of ingenious ways of taking human life," he reflected admiringly. Kennedy seemed most pleased with Rhode's *Death on the Board* (1937), a cleverly contrived tale of creative and gruesome multiple murders. "John Rhode, always prodigal of murder, has never been more prodigal or more ingenious," he wrote, in a pronouncement that was promptly snapped up for publicity purposes by Rhode's publishers. Indeed, so charmed with *Death on the Board* was Kennedy that he even declared that the characters in the novel were "distinct and life-like"—no small accomplishment for a Humdrum.[48]

Nicholas Blake, a leading light of the fiery Young Turks of mystery, proved capable as well, in his *Spectator* reviews, of praising a writer "following in the austere path of Freeman Wills Crofts," in this case John Streets' Miles Burton. With Burton's *Murder of a Chemist* (1936) Blake was quite enamored, despite the fact that he saw Burton as "a pillar of orthodoxy" who gave the reader "crime, the whole crime, and nothing but the crime." Blake deemed *Murder of a Chemist* "quite the best book" by Burton that he had read, with Burton's detectives, Inspector Arnold and Desmond Merrion making "a good team" and demonstrating "tenacity and acumen." As much as he liked *Murder of a Chemist*, he found *Where Is Barbara Prentice?* from the same year even better: "Paying greater attention to character and background," Blake pronounced, "[Miles Burton] has written his best book." Although Blake, like Sayers in 1936, desired that detective stories become more literary in style, he was wary, like Sayers in 1928, of attempts to write detection on what he termed "a full reality basis." Such experiments he found "dangerous" for mystery novelists, "because very few writers can hope to attain the breadth and subtlety of understanding necessary for the creation of a 'real' murderer, a 'real' victim, and the real relationship between them." Blake would firmly establish himself in 1938 as one of these dangerous experimenters with his path-breaking *The Beast Must Die*, but for now, at least, he continued to find intellectual comfort in the pages of Humdrum works.[49]

Despite enjoying some considerable praise from high places in the 1930s, Humdrums found themselves outstripped in the British school of detection on the one hand by the livelier traditionalists Agatha Christie and John Dickson Carr—respectively the mistress of misdirection and the lord of the locked room mystery—and on the other hand by such "reformers" as Margery Allingham, Ngaio Marsh, Michael Innes and Nicholas Blake, who had followed the exhortations of Sayers, Kennedy and Cox and published detective novels with greater emphasis on elegant writing and rounded characterization. Over the thirties and into the forties reviews of Humdrum works in the major English newspapers and journals offered increasingly muted praise of the Humdrums, using damningly lukewarm words like "workmanlike," "competent," "painstaking" and "methodical," while a new Blake, Allingham or Marsh, on the other hand, was lavishly acclaimed as stylish, sophisticated and utterly engrossing, something even "people who don't like detective stories" (that ever-elusive consumer demographic) might appreciate. To these reviewers, if detective novels could be seen as literary desserts, works by writers like Blake, Allingham and Marsh were smooth and light ices, delightful to the palate of the mind, while the tomes of Crofts, Street and Connington, chock full of material clues, increasingly seemed like heavy, sticky and nearly indigestible suet puddings.

This aesthetic shift, which was becoming prevalent on both sides of the Atlantic, received one of its most significant articulations in an article, "The Golden Age of English Detection," by the Oxford-educated British Communist intellectual John Strachey, that appeared in the *Saturday Review of Literature* in 1939. In the first application of the term "Golden Age" to between-the-wars detective fiction that is known to me, Strachey pronounced: "[T]his is, perhaps, the Golden Age of the English detective story writers. Here suddenly we come to a branch of literature — if you can call it that — that is genuinely flourishing," Strachey waxed enthusiastically. "Here are a dozen or so authors at work, turning out books which you find that your friends have read and are eager to discuss.... I have myself little doubt that some of these detective novels are far better jobs, on any account, than are nine tenths of the more pretentious and ambitious highbrow novels." Though dismissive of Dorothy L. Sayers, who, he declared, "has now almost ceased to be a first-rate detective story writer and has become an exceedingly snobbish popular novelist," Strachey also evinced little affection for Freeman Wills Crofts, dismissing him as a writer who gravely devoted his "bleak attention to the mechanics of the detective story," determinedly refusing "to have anything to do with literary frivols."[50] Strachey cited three newer detective fiction writers, Margery Allingham, Michael Innes and Nicholas Blake, as the leading lights blazing a promising new path for their genre.

What Strachey most appreciated in the work of these three younger authors was not those bleak "mechanics of detection" so assiduously oiled by Crofts, but the "literary frivols" neglected by the former railway engineer. Allingham's *The Fashion in Shrouds*, for example, was notable for "really good social observation of a certain set which exists within the English plutocracy." Similarly, Strachey proudly asserted, "in the hands ... of two young intellectuals, Mr. Michael Innes and Mr. Nicholas Blake," the British detective novel was reaching new heights of literary "sophistication." Innes' *Hamlet, Revenge!* "though full of technical flaws as a detective story" seemed to Strachey "a work which any young writer, in whatever field, could regard with most justifiable pride." As for Nicolas Blake, the pseudonym of "the radical novelist and poet" C. Day Lewis, his tale *The Beast Must Die* was not simply a brilliant mystery story but "an admirable novel."[51]

With their more "literary" detective novels, Allingham, Innes and Blake — along with another up-and-comer (and future Crime Queen), the New Zealand resident Ngaio Marsh — increasingly garnered the lion's share of critical attention among British detection writers from prestige reviewers in both Britain and the United States in the late 1930s. Such praise naturally caught the attention of readers as well. While traditionalists objected to the "literary frivols" in the work of these writers, others were delighted with the new approach. For example, the hugely influential Canadian literary critic and theorist Northrop Frye, a great fan of mystery fiction, confessed in his diary in 1942, "I don't really quite understand why I like reading [detective stories]"; but he ultimately concluded that what he liked in them were not the puzzles, which he could never solve anyway, but, rather, what he called the literary "overtones." If an author provided such things in a detective novel as "a good style, some traces of wit & characterization, [and] a sense of atmosphere,"

Frye avowed, seemingly reflecting an increasingly common attitude among readers, then as far as he was concerned "a lot of the professional intricacies of the game can go to hell."[52]

Reviewers for the *Spectator* and *New Statesman and Nation* illustrate the increasingly ho-hum attitude toward Humdrum authors in some higher-browed literary quarters. Future noted publisher and man of letters Rupert Hart-Davis occasionally reviewed detective fiction for the *Spectator* in the 1930s. Hart-Davis was a young man at this time who tipped over the sacred cows of mystery with youthful abandon, one of his favorite targets being the novels of Freeman Wills Crofts. In a 1937 review of *Found Floating*, he took time to pay the Humdrum master a paragraph of tribute, with his tongue very much in his cheek:

> Last, and far, far slowest, comes Mr. Freeman Wills Crofts. In *Found Floating*, as in most of his books, are to be found all the [literary] vices ... and yet with him one would not have it otherwise. His Bellmanism ("What I say three times is true"); his excruciating love scenes ("I love you, Runciman," she answered, "but until this terrible shadow has cleared away I cannot marry you"); the flat lollop of the writing; all have their own particular attraction.... *Found Floating* will not bear detailed description, but lovers of Inspector French ... will enjoy it immensely. He has as much snap as a wet biscuit, and he'd never set the Thames on fire, though if anyone else did, he'd track the culprit down, if it took him a thousand pages.

Two years later, Hart-Davis still found digesting Crofts a challenge. In 1939 *Fatal Venture* contained, it seemed, yet "another unsweetened slab of Inspector French's interminable activity." Reflected the critic of the tediously tenacious Inspector French: "One cannot avoid feeling some affection for this gigantic bore; he is like a tame elephant that never forgets."[53]

John Street came in for similar mocking treatment from *Spectator* critics, though not at such pitiless length. One crime fiction reviewer, E.B.C. Jones — the pseudonym of novelist Emily Beatrix Coursolles Jones — noted in 1937 of Street's "John Rhode" that he belonged "at the Crofts end of the scale [of detective fiction]." Jones complained that members of the Crofts school wrote "the slightly laborious kind of story which tells you every time a door is shut or a cigarette-case opened. You are forced to read closely for fear of missing a clue, but the act of reading is not one of pure pleasure." In the 1940s, wartime reviewer John Fairfield noted of *They Watched by Night* (1941): "The puzzle is scrupulously fair, and unrolls with the customary deliberation till the time comes for Dr. Priestley to shy the *Encyclopaedia Britannica* at the reader's head." Of *Night Exercise*, from the next year, Fairfield found a puzzle "elaborate, ingenious and fairly worked out in full view of the reader," but he added that that same reader might "find himself murmuring the song popularised a little time ago by a colored singer, 'Lord you made the night too long.'"[54]

Ralph Partridge took similar delight in firing an occasional squib at a lumbering Humdrum. Partridge, known today for his membership in the Bloomsbury Group and his odd, quasi ménage-à-trois relationship with writer Lytton Strachey and painter Dora Carrington (depicted in the 1995 Emma Thompson film *Carrington*), colorfully reviewed mystery fiction for the *New Statesman and Nation* for twenty-eight years, until his death in 1960. He seemed to dislike most of what he read in those three decades, finding very few authors indeed who were capable of springing true surprises on him in the manner of his beloved mystery idol, Agatha Christie. Crofts, Street and Connington he evidently could not resist teasing, with Crofts being his favored target: "Mr. Wills Crofts," Partridge mocked in 1936, "is like the roast beef of old England. He provides the wholesome diet on which our national character depends." Criticizing dull passages in another author's work the same year, Partridge observed: "Only Mr. Wills Crofts can do such tedious work well, and *he* can only do it because he loves it so." The impish reviewer stamped *Fear Comes to Chalfont* (1942) "an admirable specimen" of "the same plain, nourishing stodge" that Crofts supplied "year in, year out." Readers surely would derive "glutinous gratification ... from wallowing every inch of the way to the solution." Of John Rhode's *Death in the Hopfields* (1937), Partridge revealed helpfully to his readers that the title "sums up the contents of the book to perfection.... I recommend the book to people who would like to know about hops." Partridge made a similar joke the next year, noting of Connington's *Truth Comes Limping* that the title "is a cruelly accurate description of its plot."[55]

Humdrum stock dropped rapidly after World War II. Alfred Walter Stewart died in 1947, and only one of his mystery titles was reprinted in a paperback edition after his death. Freeman Wills Crofts' health declined precipitously in the early 1950s, leaving him struggling to publish what turned out to be his last book, *Anything to Declare?* which he finally managed the year of his death in 1957. In a sort of symbolic shutting of the door on the past, American publishers declined to publish the tale, though it was the mystery swan song by the man who with *The Cask* had helped launch the Golden Age back in 1920. Under his two most prominent pseudonyms, Major Street stolidly soldiered on alone, throughout the fifties continuing to publish, at an astonishing rate of three or four books a year, mostly uninspired and indifferently-reviewed detective novels.

To many reviewers in what Julian Symons termed an era of "reaction against the pre–[World War II] Superman detective" brilliant amateur sleuths like Street's Lancelot Priestley and Desmond Merrion increasingly came to seem like silly anachronisms. A striking example of this phenomenon can be found in Australia's *Adelaide Mail* in the late 1940s and early 1950s crime fiction reviews of A.R. McElwain. The outspoken McElwain repeatedly railed (not too strong a word) against Rhode's police detective at this time, Superintendent Jimmy Waghorn, for constantly depending on the brilliant Dr. Priestley to solve all his murder cases for him. "Priestley ... is the pompous old bore at whose feet these many years has sat the docile Superintendent Jimmy Waghorn of the Yard," wrote McElwain sneeringly. "What has puzzled me all these years is why, if old Priestley is so darned smart, he doesn't totter from his London home and ... go to the scene of the crime, take charge from Waghorn, and get the thing over with."[56]

Unbowed by such critical blasts, Street stayed in the game until his own failing health ended his forty-five year writing career in 1961. With John Street's death three years later, what might be termed the Humdrum Era officially passed, though in truth it had died artistically many years earlier, surviving only on the diminished patronage of loyal but aging readers on both sides of the Atlantic who continued, in the age of Ian Fleming, Mickey Spillane and Patricia Highsmith and their Cold War spies, tough private eyes and simmering psychotics, to yearn for solidly-constructed, true-blue detective stories, ones that actually contained some measure of honest detection, no matter how "humdrum."[57] By the 1960s only Freeman Wills Crofts remained in print, some dozen of his novels having been republished in Penguin paperback editions in Britain. John Street and J.J. Connington seemed completely forgotten.

In 1971, seven years after John Street's death, professors Jacques Barzun and Wendell Hertig Taylor made a significant effort to revive the Humdrums' critical reputation with the publication of *A Catalogue of Crime*, an 831-page tome with listings for 2,304 "novels of detection, crime, mystery and espionage." For thirty years Professor Barzun had sporadically penned short, eloquent defenses of the puzzle, or ratiocinative, element in detective fiction, and the *Catalogue* reflected his decades of persuasive advocacy. Just over a half-century removed from Freeman Wills Crofts' keystone humdrum work, *The Cask*, Barzun and Taylor's *Catalogue* defended old masters like Crofts, Street and Connington, urging that, "despite their many awkwardnesses and lavish use of cardboard," these authors were well worth reading for ingenious "situations and lethal means, and the even greater skill of their detection." That the professorial pair had devoted some considerable time to reading Humdrum authors is apparent from the numerous entries made in the *Catalogue* for their books: 36 for Burton and 57 for Rhode (so that Street's books alone totaled 93 entries); 25 for Crofts and 22 for Connington. Barzun and Taylor singled out for particular praise Major Street, who they found had demonstrated in his best books "adroit and straightforward" storytelling and "a gift of characterization ... slight, but not wholly absent."[58]

Praise from Barzun and Taylor spurred a very modest revival of the works of John Street. In the 1970s and 1980s five Burton and two Rhode titles were reprinted, the Rhodes in American paperback editions by Harper & Row. Even the late H.R.F. Keating, whose judgment of Street's work over the years often seemed dismissive, found kind words for the author in his introduction to the 1985 Collins Crime Club edition of *The Claverton Mystery*, praising the book's "ingeniously conceived mystery" and its sleuth, Dr. Priestley, as a true "Great Detective" of the genre. The interest of collectors of Golden Age detective fiction in Street's work markedly increased during this period, with, for example, a tatty, ex-library copy of one of Street's rarest books, the Miles Burton title *Death of Two Brothers* (1941), astonishingly selling in 2004 for over 797 pounds (nearly 1,500 U.S. dollars) on the online auction site eBay.[59]

Freeman Wills Crofts' entire body of detective fiction was reprinted in paperback in 2000, surely in part on the strength of recollections of the old sixties Penguin editions and of Symons' influential (if backhanded) praise of the railway engineer turned author as the best of the Humdrums. Additionally, three J.J. Connington detective novels were reprinted in 2012. Both authors remain, like Street, highly valued by collectors, with first editions listed by booksellers for hundreds of dollars in the case of Connington or even thousands of dollars in the case of Crofts.

Aficionados of Golden Age detective fiction decry the critical neglect of Humdrum authors in favor of the Crime Queens and Detection Dons, but on the whole they, like Barzun and Taylor before them, have been unsuccessful in altering this state of literary affairs. Critical opinion largely has followed Julian Symons is his dismissal of Humdrum works. Three recent 2005 academic surveys of the detective fiction genre fail to discuss Humdrum authors in sections on the Golden Age detective novel, with only Crofts rating even a passing mention by name, and that in just one of the works. A wide-ranging study from the previous year (reissued in an expanded edition in 2010), Stephen Knight's *Crime Fiction 1800–2000: Detection, Death, Diversity*, omits any reference to Connington while devoting a single small paragraph to Crofts ("the epitome of what Symons calls the humdrum") and all of one sentence to John Street ("possibly the plainest of them all," but at least "an efficient plotter").[60] Focus on Golden Age British detective novelists in these works, as in others before and after them, remains devoted to a small band of at most a bare dozen or so writers (most typically the "literary" Dorothy L. Sayers, Margery Allingham, Ngaio Marsh, Gladys Mitchell, Francis Iles, Nicholas Blake, Michael Innes, H.C. Bailey and Cyril Hare and the puzzlers Agatha Christie and John Dickson Carr), with the four Crime Queens getting by far the most attention.

It is time for a serious, in-depth analysis and assessment of Humdrum detective novelists, writers once widely read and highly regarded, however dismissed and forgotten today. My reading of the books of these authors, which includes non-criminous works as well as the thirty-three Crofts crime novels, the twenty-four Connington crime novels and 140 of Street's staggering 143 crime novels (nearly 200 books total), has convinced me that not only are Barzun and Taylor correct in their assessment that Humdrum efforts frequently do have merit and have been undeservingly neglected, but also that these works importantly provide us with a fuller picture of the sociocultural views of the generation of detective fiction writers (and presumably readers) that matured between the two world wars. Focusing mostly on the period works of the Crime Queens, as most studies do, is understandable, as works by these writers are undeniably significant as well as — in contrast with Humdrum books — accessible for purchase in cheap paperback or eBook editions or for borrowing from libraries (ironically, even the Crofts reprints of a decade ago are themselves now out-of-print and highly collectible); yet such a narrow focus seriously truncates our understanding of the genre. "Humdrum" detective fiction authors are a distinctive group of writers and they deserve discrete analysis.

Chapter Two

Cecil John Charles Street (*John Rhode/Miles Burton*) (1884–1964)
Public Brain Tester No. 1

Part One: John Street, Man of Mystery

Major Cecil John Charles Street receives little recognition today in mystery genre studies, outside of an occasional stray reference to his status as a member of the British "Humdrum" school. Yet during the Golden Age of detective fiction, Major John Street was one of the best-known writers of classical, puzzle-oriented mystery tales. Particularly under his most famous pseudonym, John Rhode, Street was admired for his fiendishly clever yet credible murder methods. If Street's good friend and fellow detective novelist, John Dickson Carr, was the Golden Age's lord of the locked room mystery, Street was the period's undisputed master of murder means. The means of murder employed by Street, especially in his John Rhode tales, typically involve the creative application of science and engineering, in the manner of Street's pre–Golden Age predecessor, R. Austin Freeman, creator of the greatest rival of Sherlock Holmes, the medical jurist Dr. John Thorndyke. Indeed, the series detective in the John Rhode tales, Dr. Lancelot Priestley, clearly is, in the words of a rare genre scholar who has read some John Rhode works, "the most direct Golden Age heir" of Freeman's Dr. Thorndyke and other original scientific methodological detectives.

Cecil John Charles Street. Author of 143 mystery novels, John Street arguably was the most prolific spinner of true tales of detection in the history of the genre (by Howard Coster, 1930, © National Portrait Gallery, London).

John Rhode: "Public Brain-Tester No. 1." This reviewer's memorable title for John Street's pseudonym, John Rhode, was soon picked up for publicity purposes by the Collins Crime Club (courtesy Mark Sutcliffe).

Two. Cecil John Charles Street (1884–1964)

For Golden Age readers interested in credible scientific detection of material facts, Street's "John Rhode" was the preeminent mystery author of his generation. As one delighted contemporary critic put it, among British mystery writers John Rhode was "Public Brain Tester No. 1."[1]

As merited as this title may be, there is more to John Street than his punning John Rhode pseudonym. In 1930, five years after Street as Rhode had introduced Dr. Priestley to the mystery world, the author successfully launched another popular and long running series of detective novels, these under a second pseudonym, Miles Burton. The Miles Burton tales, which feature Desmond Merrion, one of the Golden Age's more significant gentleman amateur detectives, are worthy of study in their own right. While admittedly overshadowed by the often more scientifically and mechanically minded John Rhode, Miles Burton became, like his pseudonymous predecessor, a significant name in British Golden Age mystery, one unjustly forgotten today.

Taken together, the many books that appeared under the John Rhode and Miles Burton pseudonyms offer interesting contrasts with the conventional "country house" stereotype of the English Golden Age detective novel. Perhaps most notably, Street in his work often rejects the reactionary pastoralism associated with the British Golden Age mystery. Street is markedly more interested in technology and the workings of modern business than many of his better-known contemporaries in the genre, like the Crime Queens. He also is less inclined than authors such as Dorothy L. Sayers, Margery Allingham and Ngaio Marsh to romanticize England's traditional power elite, the landed gentry. Moreover, Street breaks from stereotype in the attitude he displays toward a number of other matters, such as class, sex, gender, anti–Semitism and state authority. Additionally, Street helped pioneer the study of "true crime" as a major contributor to the historiography of the 1860 Constance Kent case, one of England's most notorious murders (recently the subject of a bestselling book, *The Suspicions of Mr. Whicher*).

Not only is Street's writing of interest for its frequent parting from Golden Age stereotype, it is better writing than it has been made out to be by Street's critics, most notably Julian Symons. Symons reviewed crime novels in the 1950s, giving him his greatest exposure as a reader to Street in the years when the author had already published over one hundred mystery novels and resultantly had lost much of his spark as a tale teller. But in Street's best years, from the 1920s into the 1940s, his works often boasted not only fascinating plot ideas but also more narrative drive and humor than has been recognized by modern critics. Moreover, Street's character drawing has merit. In Desmond Merrion Street created an enjoyable series detective, while in Dr. Priestley he created a talismanic one. I believe that, as Barzun and Taylor urge in *A Catalogue of Crime*, Street is one of the major figures of the Golden Age of British detective fiction. In terms of consistent plotting ingenuity — the keystone in the aesthetic arch of the Golden Age — Street ranks among masters of the genre like Dorothy L. Sayers and John Dickson Carr. It is true that the Major's characters tend, like Agatha Christie's, to remain stock and that his writing is deliberate and unadorned, but as a writer Street is not without a distinct spark of vitality lacking in his more famous Humdrum contemporary Freeman Wills Crofts. Doubtlessly Street wrote far too many books, particularly in the 1950s. The large number of extremely dull books he wrote in that decade — works typically with only the merest flickers of originality and life in them — certainly did much to lend force to the Humdrum appellation bestowed on him by Julian Symons and others who followed Symons. Yet any writer deserves to be remembered for his best books; and one of the goals of this study is to guide readers to John Street's many fine works.

For decades John Street, the man behind John Rhode and Miles Burton, has been even more obscure than his pseudonyms (for example, only in July 2011 did the citizens of Gibraltar awake to the fact that Street is a native son). Yet perhaps this should not be surprising, for during his professional life as a popular author, Street himself was something of a man of mystery. After Street's death in 1964, the author of his *Sunday Times* obituary (likely Bruce Montgomery, who wrote mysteries as "Edmund Crispin") reflected that because of the Major's "reticences"—which "were such that all who met him could not fail to respect them"—"John Street was not an easy man to know." Writing of "John Rhode" two decades earlier, genre historian Howard Haycraft deemed the author "one of the most secretive of all writers of detective fiction."[2] Recent research by me (as well as Tony Medawar and Martin Roundell Greene) has pierced this veil of reticence and uncovered aspects of a life that in many ways appears as interesting as those of the characters found in mysteries and thrillers.

It turns out that John Street had an impressive family background and an accomplished (and sometimes controversial) military and business career. The son of a distinguished British Army general and a descendant from a long line of landed gentry through his mother, Street was born in Gibraltar, where his father was in service, in 1884. The younger Street himself entered the army after graduating from Wellington College (a school briefly attended some fifteen years later by George Orwell) and the Royal Military Academy, Woolwich. Commissioned into the Royal Artillery at Portsmouth in 1903, Street three years later transferred from the Regular Army into the Special Reserves and the same year, 1906, married Hyacinth Maud Kirwan, daughter of Major John Denis Kirwan, also of the Royal Artillery. (Though the Street-Kirwan union later that year produced a daughter, Verena Hyacinth Iris, who would die in 1932, it was not a successful one, for at some point the couple separated. By the 1930s — probably earlier — Street was living with Eileen Annette Waller; the pair would marry in 1949, shortly after the death of Street's first wife.) Street spent several of the remaining eight years before the outbreak of the First World War in the southern coastal town of Lyme Regis as a shareholder in and the chief engineer of the pioneering Lyme Regis Electric Light & Power Company, Ltd. He and his wife (their daughter in 1911 was residing with Street's mother in a flat in London's luxurious Hyde Park Mansions) lived with a staff of cook, parlor maid and housemaid at Summerhill, a mansion that later became home to one of England's most famous (or infamous) progressive schools. The master of Summerhill was listed as having "private means." When war came, Street was called back to military service, and he performed with distinction as a Captain in the Royal Garrison Artillery, Special Reserve, getting wounded three times and receiving the Military Cross. Between April 21 and November 13, 1918, Street, now a Major, headed the MI7b, a branch of British Military Intelligence devoted to the production of press propaganda and the study of foreign presses. He later served as an Information Officer at the Headquarters of the British Administration in Ireland, Dublin Castle, controversially becoming between 1919 and 1921 what one Irish authority has termed "the senior British propagandist in Dublin Castle during the Black and Tan War [or Irish War of Independence]."[3]

The first phase of John Street's writing career stemmed directly from his activities in the British army as an artillery and intelligence officer. *With the Guns* and *The Making of a Gunner*, both published in 1916, concern his experiences the previous year as a Forward Observation Officer in the Royal Artillery (both works were credited to "F.O.O."), while *The Worldly Hope* (1917, also by "F.O.O.") is a clearly semi-autobiographical war novel about an officer in the Royal Garrison Artillery during World War I. Another six books, published between 1921 and 1924, deal with contemporary power politics in Ireland, France, Germany, Hungary and Czechoslovakia. Between 1925 and 1930, Street would pen two more political works, as well as translate from the original French biographies of the Marquis de Vauban, the seventeenth-century French Marshall and fortification designer, and Captain James Cook. The decisive development in Street's writing was seen in 1924, however: the publication, in addition to *East of Prague* and *The Treachery of France*, of two thrillers, *A.S.F.* and *The Double Florin* (the thrillers under the pseudonym John Rhode, an obvious play on his name, John Street). With the appearance the next year of his first Dr. Priestley detective novel, *The Paddington Mystery*, Street's career as a mystery writer became firmly established.

Over the next thirty-five years John Street would produce, primarily under two pseudonyms, John Rhode and Miles Burton, 143 mystery novels (mostly classical tales of detection), an average rate of four a year. Street and his post–World War I companion

The Orchards, Laddingford, Kent. Located in a Kentish village, The Orchards was John's and Eileen's home for much of the 1930s. Originally much of the area around the house was wooded, hence the name. Here Street wrote his Kent-set tale, *Death in the Hopfields* (1937), and worked with his friend John Dickson Carr on their jointly-credited detective novel, *Drop to His Death/Fatal Descent* (1939) (courtesy Anthony Kremer).

(later wife), Eileen Waller, enjoyed a comfortable life together, residing variously over the years at attractive older homes in at least half a dozen different villages in southern and central England (the most years were spent in Laddingford, Kent and Swanton Novers, Norfolk) and taking occasional cruises in the Mediterranean, Baltic and Caribbean Seas. Though Street and Eileen led a peripatetic life, Street enjoyed taking a role in village affairs, and he generously supported local institutions and activities of whatever village in which the couple was currently residing. In addition to his local public activities and of course his voluminous writing, the Major, as Street was known, would as well invariably spend an hour every day lifting a glass at the local public house (the Chequers in Laddingford, the Bell in Swanton Novers). Not surprisingly, solidly grounded village and pub settings play a significant role in his fictional works.

In 1930 Street became one of the founding members of England's Detection Club, and he remained active in the group for two decades, traveling to London for meetings and dinners, at which he established a reputation with the prewar membership for considerable conviviality. His greatest friends in the Club, John Dickson Carr and Lucy Beatrice Malleson (who wrote as Anthony Gilbert) remembered him warmly. By 1950 he ceased attending meetings, though he kept up his astounding rate of novel production for the entire decade. Only his drastically deteriorating health halted the great flow of Major Street's words in 1961.

John Street's earliest writings, his memoirs of his World War I experiences, *With the*

The Chequers, Laddingford, Kent. The Chequers was one of John Street's favorite fictional pub names, including in *Death in the Hopfields*, which just happens to be set in Kent. Pubs are a hugely important element in Street's books generally (courtesy Anthony Kremer).

Guns and its sequel *The Making of a Gunner*, revealed a strong personality — precise, authoritative and conservative, yet also wryly humorous — that would resurface in his detective stories. Those familiar only with Street as an author of putatively dry as dust "Humdrum" mysteries, no doubt would be surprised to learn that reviewers of *With the Guns* and *The Making of a Gunner* praised the young veteran's war accounts as "intensely vivid" and lacking even "one dull page." Indeed, no less a critical source than the *Sunday Times* found *With the Guns* "certainly one of the very best books which the war has produced." Particularly striking qualities of both memoirs (given Street's later reputation) are the flashes of mirth that can be glimpsed within them. A review of a modern reprint of *With the Guns* justly admires the work for its author's "excellent style of writing" and "warm sense of humor."[4]

John Street before John Rhode. John Street — presumably in his thirties, before he became "John Rhode."

Within the pages of his memoirs, Street often is amusingly self-deprecating. In recounting his failed ambition to keep a war diary, for example, the author exhibits a wry modesty about his grandiose wartime dream of literary renown (this modesty later would characterize his attitude to his mystery writing as well). "On the eve of sailing with the Battery" to France, Street recalled,

> I searched the shops until I found a really convenient little book that I made up my mind I would carry in my haversack, to be duly filled at my unemployed moments with vivid accounts of all the wonderful things that I was sure were about to happen to me. My only doubt was whether there would be enough room in which to recount them. I reflected with pride how in years to come my descendants would pore over the well-thumbed volume, how they would read history in the making, how they would draw mental pictures of their illustrious ancestor leading his Battery into action, seated upon the driving seat of a three-ton motor-lorry, brandishing his prismatic compass, the very indication of martial ardor. It was a beautiful dream that might have been realized but for one single unlucky incident. In the final bustle of departure, I left the little book behind.[5]

All turned out well enough, however, for Street soon realized that circumstances would not allow him the leisure to compose "passages that should breathe the very spirit of war" and that, in any event, he "had competitors in the descriptive art who far outshone me." Tasked with censoring letters written by members of his battery, Street found himself extremely impressed with the ingenuity of one eloquent gunner, who managed to keep up a correspondence with "an apparently limitless acquaintance among the fair sex" by making use of several sheets of carbon paper to produce multiple copies of the same letter, and then sending one copy to each woman.[6]

Writing of the training of recruits at a depot in Britain before his battery shipped out, Street humorously recalls the day "when the Welsh invasion took place with all its attendant horrors." A flood of hundreds of south Welsh recruits sent dismayed officers scrambling to learn "the true pronunciations of such jaw-breaking names as Ynysybwl,

Cwmaman, and Llanddawryth," as well as to identify specific individuals in a mass of men with seemingly "only half a dozen surnames between [sic] them, Jones, Evans, Lewis, and a few others." Street recalled with particular sympathy the officer charged with paying out different sums of money to the battery's twenty-two Welshmen named John Evans, all of whom had "discarded all recollection of their [regimental] numbers."[7]

Reminiscent of his later praise of the famous Czechoslovakian political leader Thomas Masaryk for standing against majority opinion in his pursuit of legal justice for a member of a despised minority during the Polna ritual murder trials (see below), Street mocks zealous civilians in the early days of the war who victimized a harmless member of a foreign ethnicity. Local police in the town where his depot was located were "worse bitten with the epidemic spy-fever than anybody else in the town," Street recalled. "We were inclined to laugh at them, but the arm of the law is long and patient.... They had their eyes upon their man, and could bide their time.... [U]pon the very morning when our declaration of war upon Turkey was announced, they proudly brought before the astonished C.O. the local Turkish Bath attendant." Despite being informed by the obviously benign old gentleman that he had been born in Jerusalem some seventy years earlier and had migrated to England at the age of five, Street's battery was obliged to keep him under detention until an official release could be obtained from on high. During his few days in captivity, the initially distraught man — he at first had feared he would be put to death — came to enjoy his new state. Street revealed that their prisoner "could always be found sitting over the guard room fire telling wholly imaginary stories of his native land to an appreciative audience of recruits." Even after his release was secured, he continued to make daily visits to his former captors, regaling them with a series of Arabian Nights tales that were, alas, "not always quite drawing room."[8]

Major Street's accounts of army life in *With the Guns* and *The Making of a Gunner* also are "not always quite drawing room." For example, in a chapter in the former book devoted to the subject of field observation, Street finds occasion to relay a mildly racy anecdote from his own training days:

> Well do I remember many years ago forming one of a class of young officers under instruction in the use of the "observation of fire instrument," which consists of a telescope fearfully and wonderfully mounted on a gigantic tripod.... Our instructor, a highly capable but choleric major (Majors always were apt to be petulant, I thought, in those days), had spent the best part of a warm June morning explaining the use of the cumbrous toy, until the whole class were sick at heart. At last he sent one of our number some distance away with orders to observe and report upon some object in the distance out to sea, the while he discoursed to the remainder. The minutes slipped by, and no word came from the keeper of the lonely vigil. "Go and see what the dam! fool is up to, sergeant-major," said our instructor. Anon the sergeant-major returned, with a face as impassive as the metal of the instrument itself. "Well?" rapped out the major. "If you please, sir, Mr. Robinson is a-studying observation of the ladies bathing-place!"[9]

A sense of humor, Street wrote, helped him retain his equanimity in wartime. "War is such a desperately serious business, [and] has such a terrible effect upon one's nerves and temper if one broods over it too long," he reflected, "that it is obviously up to someone to treat the whole thing in an irresponsible spirit." Street relished the moments of humor he could find amidst the tragedies of war. Like many a soldier before and after him, he took especial pleasure in mocking that favorite target of wartime caricature, the army staff officer who rarely exposes himself to fire — at least intentionally:

One day, I was stretching my legs in the road outside [my observation post], when a staff officer, somewhat of a *rara avis* in so advanced a spot, came by, evidently having lost his way. Now a staff officer was once defined to me by a very distinguished regimental officer as "a being whose natural common sense was buried forever beneath the vast mountain of his own ignorance." This magnificent gentleman — he had probably been a distinguished grocer, the pride of the local volunteers, before the war — informed me that observation was impossible from where I then was, and, indicating a ruin, the remains of whose roof could just be seen above the hedges, expressed his intention of surveying the country from its more favorable eminence. Bowing before his superior wisdom, I saluted and we parted, he to pursue the even tenor of his knowledge, I to my seat behind the window to watch the fun, knowing his objective was about half a mile behind the German lines. With an unholy delight, I saw him blunder into our trenches, exchange a hurried word with an officer who came forward to meet him, and then beat a precipitate retreat pursued by a most audible titter that ran swiftly along the line.[10]

This anecdote of Street's reveals not merely the major's distaste for staff officers, but also suggests a certain feeling of class superiority on his part (the sneer at "the distinguished grocer, the pride of the local volunteers"). Nevertheless, thorough familiarity with Street's life and writing makes clear that he valued a man's own personal accomplishments over his family heritage. To be sure, John Street himself came from one of the more privileged backgrounds among British Golden Age mystery writers, though this was another subject about which Street remained modestly circumspect in later years. Street's parents were Major General John Alfred Street, CB (1822–1889) and Caroline Bill (c. 1850), a daughter of Charles Horsfall Bill (1818–1908), originally of Storthes Hall in Yorkshire, where the Bills had been prominent landowners since the sixteenth century. Caroline Bill Street married somewhat late, in 1881, and gave birth to her only child, Cecil John Charles, when she was around thirty-five. Her much older husband, who had retired from the army at the age of sixty-two shortly after his son was born, died suddenly at the family home, Uplands, in Woking, Surrey, when the boy was but five years old. Two years later, in 1891, both Caroline and young John were living with Charles Horsfall Bill at Firlands, also in Woking.[11]

Life at Firlands would appear to have been quite comfortable. A staff of seven, including a cook, a parlor maid, two housemaids, a kitchen maid, a groom and an "indoor boy," serviced the household. Over a half-century later, in a John Rhode detective novel, *Men Die at Cyprus Lodge* (1943), Street's genteel police detective, Jimmy Waghorn, while exploring a reputedly haunted nineteenth-century house where the latest of several mysterious deaths has recently occurred, comes across something that vividly recalls to his mind an image from his childhood days: "a long board, fixed just above the kitchen door, with a couple of bent and broken cranks still fitted to it." Jimmy recognizes the purpose of the bell board immediately: "[A]n exactly similar board had existed in the house where he had been born. The board had carried a row of bells, each hung on a spring and connected by a wire to a pull in one of the other rooms of the house. It had been great fun to tug at one of these pulls, to hear the clanging, and then run to the board and watch the bell swinging on its spring until it came slowly to rest." One can easily imagine the young John Street delighting in testing a servants' bell board in the kitchen at Firlands, perhaps to the exasperation of an indoor staff trying to go about its daily business without the distraction of an energetic, mechanically-minded little boy.[12]

Street's interest in all things mechanical and scientific, evident in his adult vocations as an army artillerist and a civilian electrical engineer, became the signature feature of his detective novels, where one finds men (invariably they are men) of mechanical and/or scientific genius treated with respect for that genius, whatever the social class from which these men have emerged. This is not to say that Street found social distinctions insignificant factors in making the measure of a man. Throughout his writing life he remained dismissive of working class men lured by the siren song of socialism, like the "new gunner" he describes in *The Making of a Gunner*, who had been taught "enough to convince him that all men were born equal, except himself, who was better than them all, and not enough to show him that true supremacy comes only from devotion to duty and the ideals of a gentleman." In the factory where he had labored in peacetime, this new gunner had proven "a thoroughly good, skilled workman"; sadly, he also had swallowed "improperly digested doctrines of an impossible socialism," making him a prickly character for army officers to handle when he entered the wartime ranks. Despite this unfortunate ideological contamination, the new gunner was, Street conceded, "comparatively well-educated and undoubtedly quick at absorbing knowledge"; and he had successfully trained as a telephonist, "a branch of specialization most important to a gunner." Eventually the zealous socialist even brought himself "to say 'sir' when delivering a message to an officer," though this particular concession came more "by the ridicule of his comrades than by any other agency."[13]

Street implicitly contrasted the rough-hewn former factory worker with a brilliant and polished colonial civil servant who, serving in World War I as a temporary officer, had died of wounds earlier in the year, "an officer temporarily and a gentleman permanently in the full sense of the word." Of this gentleman, Street wrote glowingly that he was "one of the most fully educated men" he had known. A graduate from "one of the leading Public Schools," the temporary officer possessed a "natural cleverness and application" that had given him "every advantage" in the struggles of life. During war he excelled as much as he had in peacetime. Particularly impressive to Street was the temporary officer's "aptitude for absorbing the scientific side of his profession."[14] As will be seen in his later mystery novels, birth counted for Street, but what mattered most to him was what a man had done with the advantages life had bestowed upon him.

Just as John Street disdained leftist political sentiment, he also was dismissive of what he saw as other Utopian notions, such as pacifism. Street appears throughout the pages of his war memoirs as a highly competent, strongly-opinionated and unsentimental professional soldier of the British imperial era. Today this is an image not necessarily seen as a white and shining one. For example, one recent writer, Brendan Clifford, has condemned Street's F.O.O. books as bellicose statements "designed to show what a glorious thing a war for world dominance is." Yet more harshly, Clifford, after considering Street's political writings of the decade of the 1920s along with the earlier F.O.O. works, goes so far as to suggest that Street's political thought constitutes "what is generally thought of as Nazism"—a heavy charge to lay against the author, and one I find overwrought.[15]

To be sure, Street in his memoirs declines judging war in moral terms, preferring instead to adopt what he sees as a "realistic" view of human motivations. While conceding that warfare of course had "its sorrows, its pathos," Street nevertheless uncompromisingly declares it "a necessary condition of human existence on the planet." For what he viewed as idealists' high-minded cant about abstract principles of right and wrong, Street had little time: "let us rid our minds of the hypocrisy that nations go to war upon questions of right, and realize that they do so when it is expedient for their welfare." Street saw the current world conflict in Darwinian terms as the latest episode in a natural "struggle for existence between two great races, ourselves and the Germans." Often Street refers to war as "the Great Game," recalling later Golden Age references to "the rules of the game" in that other theater of death where Street would prominently figure, detective fiction.[16]

Ninety years of further experience with warfare, of games without rules, has caused many to doubt Street's martial certitudes, if not to find them repugnant, but to equate them with Nazisim seems to me unfair. Unquestionably, Street's political works evince a generally conservative world outlook, but it is the conservatism of a typical twentieth-century British imperialist, not a Nazi. Clifford strains hard to attribute a Hitlerian racial prejudice, particularly anti–Semitism, to Street, but he does not convince. To be sure, in his writings Street betrays a not altogether surprising ethnocentrism, particularly when discussing cases of subject colonial peoples causing inconvenience to the Empire. Most notoriously, Street's *Rhineland and Ruhr* (1923) sees him condemning the French occupation of the coal-rich Ruhr region of Germany, partly on the grounds that the French employed "colored troops" (Moroccans, Algerians and Senegambians) in the occupation. Street decried such troops as "unfitted from every aspect of decency and propriety, for employment as the garrison of a highly civilized district inhabited by a white population." Though widely held in Britain at the time (by people on both the right and the left of the political spectrum), this sentiment obviously is sure to offend today.[17]

Yet Street's views are more accurately characterized as examples of ethnic and national chauvinism rather than racism, in that they seem informed by notions of European, particularly English, cultural superiority rather than a belief that non–Western ethnic groups and races are inherently inferior. On the question of native Africans "mixing on equal terms with white men and women," for example, Street concluded that "for this privilege the African races are not yet educationally or culturally equipped," a conclusion that implies a belief on his part that they one day could become so equipped, as beneficiaries of the "white man's burden." Such rhetoric, admittedly condescending, would seem to share more in common with popular interpretations of Rudyard Kipling than with Adolf Hitler. In this context it is worth noting Street's patriotic assertion that French colonial African troops had "not yet approached the standards of discipline and behavior maintained by [British colonial African] troops."[18]

The charge of anti–Semitism, often thrown against British writers of detective novels and thrillers of the between-the-wars period, seems particularly unfair in Street's case, given his laudatory 1928 and 1930 biographies of, respectively, Rufus Isaacs, first Marquess of Reading, and Czech president Thomas Masaryk. Lord Reading was an Anglo-Jewish Liberal politician prominent in British affairs in the first third of the twentieth century, while President Masaryk had famously intervened three decades earlier on behalf of Leopold Hilsner, a Jewish man sentenced to death for the so-called Polna ritual murders of two young Czech women. In his Masaryk biography Street joins his subject in noting the manifest absurdity of Hilsner's convictions, predicated on the popular belief that Hilsner had done the young women to death in order to obtain their blood "for some form of Jewish sacrifice." Casting for an explanation of this outrageous affair, Street concludes without quibble that it was to be found in "a wild and unreasoning anti–Semitic fury" on the part of the Czech public. The ritual murder belief he dismisses as a "fantastic legend" and "mediaeval superstition." Street approvingly notes that Masaryk, a "realist," understood that the Czech people, "in adhering to belief in such fairy stories, were making themselves the laughing-stock of Europe and seriously belying any claims they might have to superior culture." Crediting Masaryk with achieving the commutation of Hilsner's death sentence in 1901, Street praises the Czech statesman for demonstrating that "patriotism did not consist in blind agreement with the opinions of the majority, but in striving to lead the national thought into reasonable and truthful channels."[19] Like John Rhode's implacable amateur detective Dr. Priestley, the brilliant intellectual Masaryk had proven stubbornly determined to find the truth in a famous murder case, even when that determination meant inconveniencing a legal authority committed to its own fallacious theory.

Just as notable as Street's high regard for the racially progressive Masaryk is his great admiration for Rufus Isaacs (this latter attitude, it is worth noting, sets him apart from other writers of the era later charged with anti–Semitism, including G.K. Chesterton, Hillaire Belloc and Rudyard Kipling). When Street published his biography of Isaacs in 1928, the Marquess was an elder statesman of British politics, with a distinguished career behind him that included service as Attorney General, Lord Chief Justice and Viceroy of India. Yet there remained a black spot on his record, namely the Marconi Scandal of 1912. The genesis of this scandal was Isaacs' purchase of shares in the American Marconi Company [AMC] in 1912. Managed by Isaacs' brother Godfrey, AMC was a subsidiary of the Marconi Company, which had numerous other subsidiaries in various countries, including the English Marconi Company, which had recently been awarded a contract with the British government, in which Isaacs served. Stirred by attacks on Isaacs' stock transaction made in *The Eye-Witness*, a journal founded by Hillare Belloc and edited by G.K. Chesterton's brother, Cecil, the feeling spread among certain sections of the English public that Isaacs had been involved in *something* underhanded. Eventually, a parliamentary inquiry resulted, in which Isaccs was exonerated of corruption charges, leading to outrage in some quarters over this supposed whitewash. In his posthumously published autobiography, G.K. Chesterton — whose brother Cecil had done much to agitate the "scandal" and thereby been embroiled in a libel suit brought by Rufus Isaac's brother over the aspersions Cecil had cast — dramatically pronounced the Marconi affair "one of the turning points in the whole history of England and the world," even going so far as to divide all world history into the "Pre-Marconi and Post-Marconi days." Even the more restrained Rudyard Kipling, who never became personally involved in the Marconi matter like the Chesterton brothers did, was inspired by the affair to write the poem "Gehazi," in which the duplicitous and disgraced Old Testament servant of Elisha proxies for the reviled Rufus Isaacs:

> Stand up, Stand up, Gehazi,
> Draw close thy robe and go.
> Gehazi, Judge in Israel,
> A leper white as snow![20]

John Street's assessment of the Marconi Scandal was more measured than those offered by the Chestertons and Kipling. Of Isaac's actions, Street admitted no more than that the Attorney General had been guilty of an "error of judgment." "The public," he concluded phlegmatically, "is loath to accept the simple and obvious explanation of a politician's action. It prefers to search beneath the surface for some complicated motive which could exist only in the imagination." As for the matter of anti–Semitism, Street conceded that Isaacs' public success as a Jew aroused in bigots "bitterness," "anger," and "blind jealousies"; yet he proudly insisted that "the England which had granted [Isaacs] his pathway to success, because of the man who he was, cared for none of these things." Street himself saw Isaacs as an abundantly admirable public servant, someone who steered a steady course over his life between what Street viewed as the stubbornly reactionary policies of the Tories and the demagogic populism of the Laborites and the more vociferous Liberals, as exemplified by David Lloyd George.[21]

Part Two: John Rhode

After several years of postwar non-fiction writing addressing weighty historical matters and current political affairs, John Street penned two mystery thriller novels in 1924, under the punning pseudonym "John Rhode." For whatever reason Street took this literary course (perhaps Street had begun cohabiting with Eileen Waller and desired additional income), it signaled a seismic shift in the author's writing life, from that of a relatively unheralded commentator on European politics and history to one of Britain's best-known crime fiction authors of the Golden Age period. Having in his fortieth year discovered a marked talent for mystery mongering (foreshadowed, perhaps, by his propaganda work in Ireland), the Major made the most of that talent, publishing 143 detective novels and thrillers over the next thirty-eight years. With justification, Street has been called "one of the most prolific of true detective novelists." His peak year of production, 1933, saw the author publishing seven novels, three each under his pseudonyms John Rhode and Miles Burton and one under his short-lived pen name, Cecil Waye, as well as making a long contribution to *Ask a Policeman*, a Detection Club joint novel. Like the famously productive thriller writer, Edgar Wallace, Street resorted, at least by 1949, to the use of a Dictaphone in composing novels. Concerning Street's enormous output, fellow Humdrum mystery author Freeman Wills Crofts that year informed a correspondent that Street "reels [his books] off into a dictaphone, and I understand ... he is so good at it, that the subsequent typescript requires little revision."[22] Such productivity naturally has given rise to charges of hackery on Street's part; yet although many of Street's novels admittedly are routine — particularly those he wrote later in his life — a score or more of the Major's works stand as classics of Golden Age detective fiction.

Street began his mystery-writing career rather modestly in 1924, publishing merely two novels, the thrillers *A.S.F.* and *The Double Florin*. Of the two books, the first, *A.S.F.*, is the superior work, retaining considerable naive charm today. *A Catalogue of Crime* rightly designated *A.S.F.* "something of a period piece to be cherished." As its less subtle American title, *The White Menace*, suggests, *A.S.F.* concerns illicit cocaine trafficking in twenties England. In classic Edgar Wallace thriller tradition, a nefarious "master brain" is behind the whole deadly business, which has spread its tentacles into the highest reaches of English society, entwining such notable victims as the "world-famous" medievalist Professor Hallinstone and Sir Henry Hebblewhite, M.P. and owner of the Hebblewhite Paper Mills. Sir Henry, ruefully aware of the temptation the stimulant of cocaine holds for powerful, restless brains such as his, puts his finger on the danger the drug poses for English society: "There have always been cocaine-takers, and there probably always will be. The trouble is that the habit is spreading at a fearful pace, and that an entirely new class is taking to it. In the old days it was mainly confined to the idle neurotics, and the harm it did them was not of much importance to the community. Now it's spreading to a vastly more important class."[23]

While preparing to expose what he knows of the secretive organization, including its A.S.F. distribution code, Sir Henry is diabolically and fatally dispatched. The ultimate unmasking is left to young Frank Clements, an assistant to the Home Secretary, Sir William Westwood, but only after a devilish attempt has been made to gas him in a hothouse full of coca plants. **[SPOILER ALERT]** Again according to Edgar Wallace tradition, the "master brain" of the cocaine ring turns out to be a lofty personage naturally considered above suspicion (but immediately suspected by any modern-day reader), Sir William Westwood's elder brother, Richard. With heavy irony, Richard Westwood's own daughter, the captivatingly exotic, half-French Therese, turns out to be the latest in the deadly drug's string of victims. In high-flown, melodramatic, Victorian rhetoric not previously employed in the novel, Richard Westwood bitterly confesses all to his brother:

> "That you should achieve your present position was just one of those malicious strokes of Fate which endows men's actions with a grim humor. How often have I not contemplated it. One brother the head of a conspiracy to defeat the law, the other the head of the organization equipped to enforce it! And if in the unwitting contest the latter prevailed, ruin for both, ruin for both!... The days of the great cocaine enterprise are over, and it has no further vengeance to take, except on those responsible for it. We cannot escape. Even beyond the reach of men's hands the curse we fostered clings to us."[24] **[END SPOILER ALERT]**

Frank Clements, who had once been attracted to the now fatally languishing Therese, fortunately has the charming and plucky Betty Plimsoll to turn to in this tragic hour. Though only the daughter of a modest antique dealer, Betty had been "educated far beyond the shop," her father having sent her to a "first-class school." Even after learning that Betty's father is a "gaol-bird" who had been extorted into an unwilling participation in the cocaine business, Frank still desires her hand in marriage, something he makes clear in the same stilted language used by Richard Westwood: "'What does all the distant past matter?' he said eagerly. 'Let us begin again from now, and go out together, you and I, to meet the morning. Let all the long wasted years pass with the night to leave us nothing but the sunshine of happiness. Betty, dear, come to me, I want you!'"[25]

Aside from its final two chapters, which are weighed down by such leaden passages as those quoted above, *A.S.F.* is an appealing specimen of the twenties thriller. Street's other thriller from 1924, *The Double Florin*, is a more muddled and less entertaining novel, though its political matter retains some interest today for the cultural historian. Like Sapper's *Bulldog Drummond* (1920) and Agatha Christie's *The Secret Adversary* (1922), both of which slightly preceded it, *The Double Florin* concerns a shadowy Bolshevist conspiracy to induce labor instability in England, bringing about the demise of world capitalism and constitutional government. As the enigmatic Dr. Quixano explains to the novel's "clean-limbed young Englishman" hero, Lord Robert Mountmichael (merely "Mike" to his friends), England is the initial target of the conspiracy "because an outbreak of Bolshevism in England would be the first stage in the collapse of the social system of the whole world." Dr. Quixano enlists Mike in the service of L.I.D.O. (*Ligue Internationale pour la Defense de l'Ordre*), an organization of international financiers formed to counter the activities of "the powers of disorder." [**SPOILER ALERT**] The pair eventually discover that the conspiracy is directed by England's own Professor Sanderson, the formidable, world-renowned mathematician ("the man had an international reputation for daring speculation in the most abstruse mathematical fields ... he was prone to sarcasm at the expense of any rival who dared to question his theories"), aided by his sinister Chinese manservant, Ah-Ling; a Jewish pawnbroker, Mr. Hirschbein; and a Bolshevistic working-class firebrand known simply as the Orator. Sanderson's lovely daughter, Joan, naturally is ignorant of her father's nefarious activities, only learning the appalling truth in the course of her falling in love with Lord Robert Mountmichael.[26]

Professor Sanderson, it is revealed, is himself not motivated by Marxist ideology, but rather by an intense desire to order society according to the dictates of pure reason (his own): "'Is it not logical that the most highly developed intellect should rule the universe as the brain rules the body?... I shall produce an intellectual despotism, in which mathematical laws, impervious to good and evil, to sentimental considerations of mercy or lenience, will alone operate.'" Though reminded by his adversaries that England stands for "religion, order, good government," the monomaniacal professor remains intent on carrying out his disruptive plans. In the end, he is stymied only by the Orator, who has learned the aim of his leader is "not the emancipation of the oppressed," but his own elevation to absolute power. The Orator, a "sincere fanatic," fatally shoots the professor, talks down the impending strike by informing strikers "that the day of the millennium had not yet dawned," and finally, heartbroken, kills himself.[27]

The vision of the world expressed in Street's early thrillers matches that found in the more serious, overtly political works that the Major wrote under his own name. England and its capitalist system of ordered liberty stands as a bulwark against world Bolshevism. Yet, despite his admiration for natural leaders of society like industrialist Sir Henry Hebblewhite and that "clean-limbed young Englishman" Lord Robert Mountmichael, Street recognizes in *The Double Florin* that there exists an authoritarian threat within the elite as well, from hubristic intellectuals who would cast aside constitutional considerations and create a despotism of remorseless logic [**END SPOILER ALERT**].

Street's early thrillers also are significant in their sympathetic presentation of the business class, including international financiers, something atypical of the genre in the twenties. As Leroy Panek notes, British thriller writers since William LeQueux (1864–1927) had developed a consistent theme attributing "both international and domestic strife to the machinations of evil foreign capitalists." Frequently these evil foreign capitalists are caricatured cosmopolitan Jews.[28] In his two debut novels from 1924, Major Street views capitalists more benignly. *A.S.F.*'s heroic Sir Henry Hebblewhite rose to prominence not as a member of England's traditional landed gentry, but as a paper mill owner. More significantly, included among the membership of *The Double Florin's* L.I.D.O., an organization upon which the security and stability of the world depends, are such heads of great international financial houses as M. de Fauricourt of France, Homer D. Rogers of the United States and Dr. Gottlieb Baumgartner of Austria. Surely the presence of the presumably Jewish Baumgartner on the side of Street's angels mitigates the presence of the pawnbroker Mr. Hirschbein on the side of his devils.

Further significance is found in *The Double Florin* when it is realized that in Professor Sanderson, we have the genesis of Street's most famous fictional creation, his amateur detective Doctor Priestley, who debuted the next year in *The Paddington Mystery*. Between *The Double Florin* and *The Paddington Mystery* lay another novel, an ill-advised and best-forgotten love story involving Portuguese gun-running titled *The Alarm*.[29] Though *The Paddington Mystery*, which appeared a few months later in 1925, also has an undistinguished plot, it was justifiably chosen a genre cornerstone by Ellery Queen because it introduced Lancelot Priestley to readers of detective novels.

Like Professor Sanderson in *The Double Florin*, Lancelot Priestley is a disputatious retired professor of mathematics (at the time of 1933's *The Claverton Mystery*, Priestley is fifty-seven years old, which would make him, rather improbably, under fifty when he debuts in 1925). While Sanderson takes his passion for logic to extreme ends, the equally contentious Priestley contents himself with flinging at intellectual adversaries the occasional "bomb in the shape of a highly controversial thesis in some ultra-scientific journal." Priestley similarly is a widower with a lovely daughter, his wife having expired some years ago, possibly from "a surfeit of logarithms."[30] Priestley's name likely was suggested by Joseph Priestley, the eighteenth century theologian and natural philosopher who wrote *The History and Present State of Electricity* (1767), a work with which Street, an electrical engineer, was likely familiar. Both Priestley's first and last names suggest a virtuous quester for truth.

In *The Paddington Mystery*, April Priestley, the Professor's daughter, had formerly been casually engaged to Harold Merefield (pronounced "Merryfield"), a son of a former schoolfellow and lifelong friend of the Professor; and when Harold finds himself embroiled in a murder case after discovering a corpse in his bed, Dr. Priestley intervenes to rescue the innocent Harold. Priestley of course succeeds in discovering the true killer, which leaves the way open, at the novel's end, for the reconciliation and impending marriage of Harold and April. The mystery plot itself is disappointing; and without a strong plot to moor the tale, the reader is left drifting with only a tedious love story to moor his interest, as Harold and April make their predictable way from estrangement to reengagement. Harold Merefield is an amiable young chap, not the usual stolid prig in such tales, but a man who has enjoyed his share of dissipation in life (indeed, when he first glimpses a body in his bed he speculates to himself that it might be a lax-virtued lady friend come to reconcile with him and is disappointed to find his prospective bedmate is a man). Unfortunately, April Priestley is one of those tiresomely ultra-modern society women of twenties fiction who, like several characters in Agatha Christie novels of this decade, finds it necessary to react flippantly to everything under the sun, as illustrated by her arch manner of conversing with her formidable and erudite father:

"What an inquisitive old darling it is!"

"I'll stop at home if you like, and do problems with you. We'll evaluate X plus Y to the power of N or something thrilling like that, every evening for an hour after dinner. Won't that be fun?"

"Proceed, Professor Sherlock Priestley!"[31]

Thankfully, Street, evidently deciding that his forte as a writer lay in puzzle plotting rather than the devising of romantic relationships, soon banished the tryingly facetious April to literary exile, giving her only a passing reference in his second Priestley novel, *Dr. Priestley's Quest* (she is making a round of visits in the country), and then not ever mentioning her again, except for a stray sentence in 1953's *By Registered Post*. On the other hand, Harold — now presumably Priestley's son-in-law — finds employment (some might

Dr. Priestley, Great Detective. Found on the dust jacket of the English edition of *Tragedy at the Unicorn* (1928) is the definitive artistic rendering of John Rhode's Great Detective, Dr. Priestley, one of the most impressive criminal investigators in the genre.

say enslavement) for the entire series as the professor's private secretary and plays a significant role in the earlier tales (he even narrates *Dr. Priestley's Quest* and *The Ellerby Case*). Priestley increasingly becomes a sort of thinking machine with a compulsion for solving murder puzzles as well as mathematical and scientific problems. Over the 1930s he becomes even more acidulous and less ambulatory, preferring to remain ensconced in his house in Westbourne Terrace, leaving direct investigations of crime to others, namely Scotland Yard inspectors Hanslet (introduced in *The Paddington Mystery*) and Waghorn (introduced ten years later in *Hendon's First Case*). Yet Priestley remains a distinctive character to the end: an acerbic retired academic with a guilty passion for abstract crime problems and an at times unconcealed contempt for the continued incompetence and illogic of the police (and, indeed, the whole human race in general). His admonishment of the hapless Hanslet (later Waghorn too) for sinful indulgence in conjecture is a welcome staple of the Priestley tales:

> "May I ask, sir, what impression you formed as to Vincent's veracity?" enquired Hanslet.
> "I have spent the greater part of my life in schooling myself to avoid making impressions," replied the Professor in a tone of irritation. "The balance of probability is that he was telling me the truth, if that is what you mean."
> *The Ellerby Case* (1927)
>
> "Have you formed any theory, Professor?" asked Hanslet quickly.
> "If I had I should not express it," replied Dr. Priestley. "Theory founded upon conjecture is valueless."
> *The Davidson Case* (1929)
>
> "Have you any idea what you expect to find at Clandown Towers, Professor? [Hanslet] asked abruptly.
> Dr. Priestley gazed at him pityingly though his spectacles. "You reveal a frame of mind which is, I regret to say, fatal to any form of scientific investigation," he replied severely.
> *The Corpse in the Car* (1935)[32]

Concerning the crime problems brought to his door, Priestley frequently pronounces that it is the problem alone that interests him. Once he has achieved a solution to a problem through a process of logical deduction, the crime itself ceases to be of concern. It is for the agencies of law enforcement to deal with the fate of the criminal. "You know how I regard these matters, Davidson," lectures the professor in *The Davidson Case*. "I regard them as problems, which do not concern me except in the solution. Once they are solved, the fate of the criminal is a matter of complete indifference to me." Far from morally condemning criminals, Priestley praises the occasional exceptionally intelligent villain, in contrast to the sour commentaries he delivers on the mental capacities of the police. For example, of the fiendishly clever murderer of Priestley's friend Sir Noel Ellerby, who has only just missed successfully luring the investigating Priestley and Harold to their own horrific deaths by drowning, the professor praisefully comments: "A most ingenious scheme, to my mind. I think that the murderer of Ellerby is one of the very few criminals I have heard of who really uses his reasoning faculties."[33]

The half-dozen Priestley novels that followed *The Paddington Mystery* in the 1920s show marked improvement in terms of plotting and pacing. Published just a year after *Paddington* in 1926, *Dr. Priestley's Quest* is the first major John Rhode detective novel. The first words spoken by Dr. Priestley in *Quest* effectively convey this memorable character that readers of John Rhode novels would follow for the next thirty-five years: "Your eyes are younger than mine, Harold.... Perhaps you will be good enough to examine this document of Mr. Heatherdale's and describe it to us. But facts, mind, facts! Conjecture is all very well, but in a case like this it may prove misleading."[34] In style and tone *Quest* owes a rather obvious debt to Arthur Conan Doyle's Sherlock Holmes tales, but it launches Priestley and his Watson, Harold, on an interesting case involving the murders of the two Heatherdale brothers. Though the plot is not as complex as those found in many later Rhode works, Priestley is highly active and there is ample ratiocination on his part, with no narrative *longueurs* and no tedious love interest.

In *Dr. Priestley's Quest* Street still refers to Dr. Priestley as a mathematician and the tales revolves around Priestley's application of principles of logic rather than science. In the next John Rhode novel, *The Ellerby Case* (1927), the author first demonstrates what was to become his signature contribution to the mystery novel, his ingenious employment of scientific and mechanical murder means. When Dr. Priestley and Harold Merefield investigate the death of Priestley's friend Sir Noel Ellerby, the professor and his secretary are plunged into their most dangerous case. Several diabolically clever attempts are made in the course of the novel to slay Dr. Priestley himself, including murder through the agency of a green hedgehog — something surely unique within the genre! Sounding a note of praise that would be heard many more times, an admiring reviewer for the *Evening Standard* asked of the episode of the green hedgehog: "Could there possibly be a more ingenious method of committing a murder?" Another reviewer avowed of the tale that its death traps made it "vibrant with excitement."[35]

With such tales as *Dr. Priestley's Quest* and *The Ellerby Case* to his credit, John Street joined the ranks of the first-tier British detective novelists, becoming in 1930 a founding member of the Detection Club as well as one of the leading authors in the Collins Crime Club, the great British detective fiction publisher. For the United States market, Street in 1927 contracted with the noted Dodd, Mead and Company to publish his books, beginning with *The Ellerby Case*. Street was given a fifty pound advance (about $250) on this novel and promised a royalty of ten percent on all copies sold up to 5,000 and a royalty of fifteen percent on all copies sold over 5,000. Editors at Dodd, Mead expressed enthusiasm about Street's work during the rest of the decade. *Tragedy at the Unicorn* was deemed "quite up to his other books," while *The House on Tollard Ridge* drew an assurance that Dodd, Mead was "anxious to continue as Mr. Rhode's publishers." After a weekend reading of *The Murders in Praed Street*, an editor wrote enthusiastically, "We can say at once that we want it." Later that year, *Murder at Bratton Grange* (*The Davidson Case*) created "an excellent impression" with the publishers.[36]

Reflecting these favorable comments, the 1930 John Rhode contract with Dodd, Mead increased the author's royalty rate (to 12.5 percent up to 2,500 copies and 15 percent for copies over 2,500) and heightened his advance to $600. If we assume that Street received a similar amount for his Miles Burton mysteries, then the author would have realized, in present day dollars, nearly $30,000 a year from American advances during that decade. Were similar terms obtained in Britain — where, unlike in the United States, all the Miles Burton books were published — the $30,000 annual figure would increase to about $70,000. Moreover, because Street's $600 advance per book title published was the equivalent of his royalty on 2,400 copies of a title sold, it is likely that Street made more than the amount advanced on each book he published. The average number of books sold per title in the United States for an established higher grade mystery writer like Street was around 3,000 copies. Assuming Street indeed sold 3,000 copies per title published in both the United States and Great Britain, his average yearly income in the 1930s would have increased to about $80,000. If his sales reached 4,000 per title in both countries — this seems a reasonable assumption — Street might well have averaged $100,000 a year. Including sales in other countries as well as sales of paperback copies, Street's average yearly earnings from his profuse stream of mystery novels in the 1930s may well have surpassed $100,000 annually in modern-day dollars. The author, who also was drawing income from

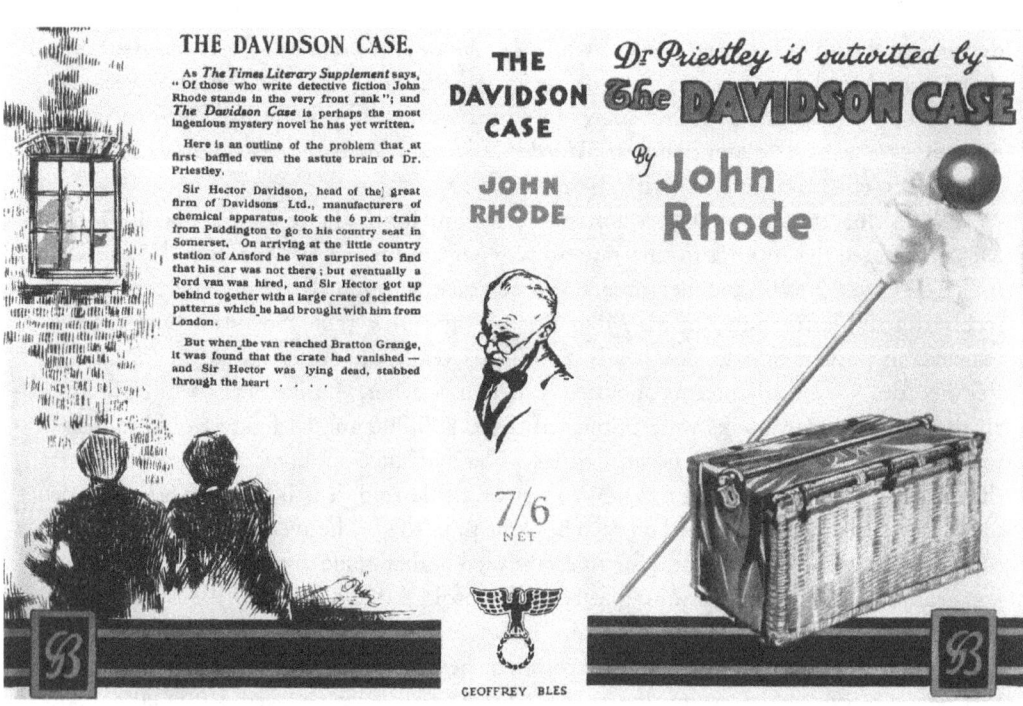

Top: John Rhode, *The House on Tollard Ridge* (1929); John Rhode, *The Davidson Case* (1929). A pivotal year for John Rhode, 1929 saw the appearance of the author's first great detective novels.

an army pension and evidently had inherited private means from his wealthy maternal grandfather, appears to have lived comfortably for the rest of his life. At his death he left an estate worth nearly $800,000 in current U.S. dollars.[37]

A 1929 review in the *Times Literary Supplement* of Street's *The House on Tollard Ridge* gives an idea of the status "John Rhode" had attained by this time. "Among the numerous company of those who write detective fiction there are comparatively few who care more for their plots than their thrills," wrote the reviewer, in a jab at the Edgar Wallace school of mystery authors. "In this select company Mr. John Rhode stands in the front rank with Mr. Wills Crofts and Mr. Connington." Moreover, the reviewer added, in words that *A Catalogue of Crime* would echo over forty years later, readers could "rely upon [Mr. Rhode's] name for tales which are good puzzles without ceasing to be good tales as well."[38] The Priestley novels, it seems, had both narrative logic and grip, at least in the eyes of John Rhode's appreciative between-the-wars readers.

Though it is not his best or best-remembered tale from the twenties, *The House on Tollard Ridge* is an impressive crime story. The novel details events following the discovery of the murdered Samuel Barton at his gloomy house on lonely Tollard Ridge. In the first part of the novel, the local official investigator, Superintendent King, methodically builds a case against Barton's black sheep son, Arthur, who is arrested and brought to trial. The second part of the novel concerns the affairs of Samuel Barton's attractive ward and heir, Kitty Hapgood. Living an isolated, dull existence with her guardian, Kitty had drifted into marriage with the prosperous local farmer James Hapgood; and now that she will be inheriting the money of her "Uncle Sam," she is contemplating drifting out of that marriage, as she indicates in a series of disillusioned reflections to young Dick Sinclair (who is desperately in love with her):

> "You cease to be a woman when you're married, and become a wife. In exchange for the privileges you're supposed to gain, you lose many others. Men listen to women, they don't listen to their wives.... [M]arriage isn't a sort of idyllic form of existence.... [I]t's a job, and just about the hardest possible job to make a success of.... [Y]ou mustn't expect any help from your employer.... People will say ... I am married still, whether I like it or not. I say that, my marriage never having meant anything to me, I see no harm in putting it aside, forgetting it, as one might forget any other job one held."

Such hard-bitten observations coming from the lips of the nominal heroine of a Golden Age detective novel are rather remarkable, especially when coming from the pen of a "Humdrum." Moreover, the independent-minded Kitty refuses the opportunity to divorce her husband and marry Dick Prescott, at least for the time being, expressly desiring to enjoy the freedom that her guardian's money has given her. "Women talk a lot of rot about their freedom," she declares, "but precious few of them ever have it."[39] Kitty, however, now has the liberty that comes with financial independence, and she does not mean to immediately relinquish it, even to the ardent and appealing Dick Prescott.

Before Kitty Hapgood can follow her resolution, another mysterious death occurs at the house on Tollard Ridge. In the final section of the novel, Dr. Priestley, Harold Merefield in tow, arrives on the scene, soon establishing that the second death was murder. As the Professor continues his investigations, he finds to his bliss a complex murder plot. "The ingenuity of the criminal upon whose track we find ourselves is really out of the ordinary," Priestley delightedly tells Harold. "I shall never regret the visit I have paid to

Lenhaven."⁴⁰ Eventually he is able to demonstrate how the dark deeds were accomplished, and a double murderer is apprehended. The novel ends with Priestley wickedly suggesting, much to Harold's mortification, that he might purchase the house on Tollard Ridge for use by himself and his secretary as a snug writing retreat.

With its tightly focused plot centering on a puzzle involving clever murder mechanics, *The House on Tollard Ridge* set the standard for the many successful John Rhode tales that would follow over the next three decades. Additionally, it also offered twenties readers some atmospheric passages concerning the sinister house of double death and a pleasingly adult and sensible female character in Kitty Hapgood. Interestingly, the germ of *Tollard Ridge's* plot came from Rudyard Kipling's 1902 short story, "Wireless," which Street mentions explicitly in his novel.⁴¹

Good as *Tollard Ridge* is, the best remembered of the twenties Priestleys is 1928's *The Murders in Praed Street*, which is the second of the two John Rhode titles designated mystery cornerstones by Ellery Queen. *Praed Street* made a strong impression in its day, **[SPOILER ALERT]** as it evidently is the first instance of the admittedly now well-worn plot in which a series of killings is motivated by a desire on the part of the murderer to revenge himself on the members of a jury who found him guilty of a crime decades earlier. The novel receives added piquancy from the fact that Dr. Priestley served as foreman of the jury and thus is the madly vindictive murderer's ultimate target. **[END SPOILER ALERT]** *Praed Street* also remains the sole filmed Street novel, having been adapted into the Sidney Gilliat scripted British movie *Twelve Good Men* in 1936 (with Priestley deleted).

Another strong point of the tale is the setting in Praed Street and its lower-middle class environs. "Praed Street," the author informs us, "is not at any time one of London's brighter thoroughfares." Lending the tale a sense of every day conventionality not found in the typical twenties country-house gentry mystery story, most of the victims of the murderer are modest shopkeepers, like James Tovey, the greengrocer hopefully styling himself a "fruit and vegetable merchant," and his tobacconist friend Sam Copperdock. The weakness of the tale occurs when Dr. Priestley, having astutely deduced the linking factor among all the murder victims, nevertheless fails to penetrate the murderer's guise, one likely to be clear enough to the modern reader. "Priestley does nothing but blunder around and get himself nearly gassed," grouses the normally admiring authors of *A Catalogue of Crime*.⁴² While this admitted lapse in the Professor's normally keen mental processes may disappoint the readers, *Praed Street* nevertheless is a most readable tale.

Street's best twenties puzzle is found not in *Praed Street* or *Tollard Ridge*, but in 1929's *The Davidson Case*, the simple title of which belies one of the Major's most deftly knotted conundrums. In the novel a series of events at Davidson's, Ltd., designers and manufacturers of chemical apparatus, culminate in the murder of the head of the firm, Sir Hector Davidson. A classic example of the mystery novel murderee, Sir Hector is a mendacious, selfish and dissolute baronet who has given several people ample motive to murder him. Having inherited both his father's title and controlling interest in Davidson's, Ltd., Sir Hector proceeds to drive his conscientious and brilliant cousin, Guy Davidson, out of active involvement in the firm, allowing Sir Hector to use Davidson's, Ltd. "merely as a sponge from which to squeeze the greatest possible profit for himself." In addition to ignoring the long-term interests of the business by maximizing share dividends and neglecting reserves ("In his eyes, Davidson's existed only to minister to his pleasures,"

Street informs us. "What happened to the firm after his death was a matter of complete indifference to him."), Sir Hector, an inveterate lecher, attempts amorous assault on his secretary, the beautiful Olga Watkins, and terminates from employment at Davidson's, Ltd. her boyfriend, machinery designer Philip Lowry, in part to give himself less obstructed access to Olga. Another black mark against Sir Hector is his treatment of the family country home, "a beautiful old house in Somersetshire" named Bratton Grange. Disliking the country and "preferring the distractions of the West End," Sir Hector retains Bratton Grange to serve as his weekend love nest, having discharged the old servants and replaced them with "a married couple less critical of his doings."[43]

One Saturday evening, Olga having strenuously repulsed Sir Hector's latest and hardest-pressed invitation to a weekend in the country and agilely escaped from the office, the baronet departs alone for Bratton Grange with a large, padlocked wickerwork box full of valuable machinery patterns. At the Somersetshire train station, Sir Hector hires a van to take him and his box to Bratton Grange, insisting, because of the cold weather, on riding with the box in the van itself. After completing the five mile drive to Bratton Grange, the driver opens the van doors to help Sir Hector with the box, but finds no box, only Sir Hector's dead body, stabbed to the heart with "a piece of stout steel wire, about seven or eight inches long." One end of the wire "had been ground to a fine and very sharp point, the other had been driven into a plain wooden ball, about a couple of inches in diameter. The weapon formed, in fact, a very efficient stiletto."[44] Some days later, the wickerwork box, with the machinery patterns still inside, is discovered in a nearby wood.

The problem having been brought to him by his friend Guy Davidson (now Sir Guy, Guy having succeeded to his cousin's title, as well as his shares in the business), Dr. Priestley investigates, quickly finding himself at odds with Scotland Yard's Inspector Hanslet. [**SPOILER ALERT**] Soon enough, Priestley has destroyed Hanslet's case against Olga Watkins, demonstrating that the murder weapon could not have been used by her. Yet despite his past proclaimed indifference to the fates of criminals in murder cases he has solved, the Professor proves reluctant to voice to Hanslet his opinion as to who the guilty party in the case actually is. He finally explains his quandary to the Scotland Yard inspector:

> "I find myself in a very difficult position, Inspector.... I have known since yesterday evening ... that Sir Guy Davidson killed his cousin. To you this fact makes him a criminal, to be pursued with the utmost rigor of the law. To me, on the other hand, to whom human retribution is not a scientific principle, he appears a benefactor of humanity. You cannot deny that, the more we learn of the two cousins, the more we learn what an excellent thing it is for everybody concerned that Sir Hector should have given place to Sir Guy. Apart altogether from the advantage to the firm of Davidson's and its employees, we know that Sir Hector led a vicious life, which, even from the narrow point of view of justice, was better terminated."[45]

Wrestling with the question of whether to place his evidence before Hanslet, the Professor finds the Inspector has discovered on his own evidence implicating Sir Guy, which thankfully settles the matter: "The withholding of my knowledge could only delay, it could not avert, the inevitable tragedy [of Sir Guy's arrest]." Sir Guy goes to trial, charged with the murder of his cousin, but the defense has a surprise for the prosecution. Calling the eminent toxicologist, Sir Alured Faversham, to the stand, the defense reveals that Sir Alured, upon being shown an exhumation order, examined Sir Hector's exhumed body and concluded that Sir Hector had died not from stabbing, but from "poisoning by one of the organic arsenical compounds, probably of the kakodyle series," the poison having been administered some twenty to thirty minutes before Sir Hector's death in the van.[46] Sir Guy, if he indeed stabbed Sir Hector, stabbed a man already dead. The defense suggests that Sir Hector poisoned himself in his railway carriage on the journey between London and Somersetshire. Impressed with this expert evidence, the jury finds Sir Guy not guilty.

Admitting to Sir Alured that he erred by not himself attending the inquest at Bratton Grange (instead sending Harold in the company of Sir Guy) and accepting the country doctor's testimony that Sir Hector had died from a stab wound, Priestley nevertheless affirms that he continues to believe in Sir Guy's guilt. But if Sir Guy poisoned his cousin, how did he do it? Why would a chemist use a poison that left detectable traces in the body long after death? Why stab Sir Hector after poisoning him? Priestley ruminates — then one evening Harold is awakened in the middle of the night by his employer:

> "Hullo, sir, what is the matter?" exclaimed Harold.
> "Nothing, nothing," replied the Professor, testily. "When Davidson traveled down to Bratton Grange to attend the adjourned inquest, did he take any luggage with him?"
> "Why, yes, sir," said Harold, slowly struggling to collect his thoughts. "I think so. Yes, of course! He had a suitcase with him, and a good-sized trunk in the van. I remember that he told me he did not know how long he might stay."
> A grim smile passed across Dr. Priestley's face. "Thank you, my boy," he said. "I am sorry I disturbed you. Good night."[47]

The classic moment of illumination has occurred and the Great Detective has solved the mystery. Dr. Priestley emerges from Westbourne Terrace with Harold for some personal investigation and verifies his solution, which he explains at a small dinner party at his house, with Harold and Sir Guy present. Sir Guy, realizing that Priestley has grasped the essential facts, fills in the missing pieces of the puzzle.

Cognizant of Sir Hector's office habits, Sir Guy was able to take advantage of the fact that his cousin invariably drank a whiskey and soda before leaving his office on Saturday afternoons. Sir Hector made his own soda water with a sparklet, a small steel reservoir filled with compressed carbon dioxide. On the previous Friday, Sir Guy replaced the box of sparklets with a box containing a single sparklet, one Sir Guy had specially prepared in his own private laboratory by filling it "with a particularly deadly gas of the kakodyle series." When Sir Hector attempted with the sparklet to aerate water for his drink, he painlessly but fatally gassed himself. After entering the deserted office, Sir Guy stabbed Sir Hector's corpse with the specially prepared wire, taking care "to bruise and lacerate the edges [of the wound], so that it would be impossible to detect that the blow had been inflicted after death." He then put his own blood on his cousin's shirt to give the appearance that blood had flowed from the wound. Having placed Sir Hector's body in the wickerwork box, Sir Guy, disguised as Sir Hector (the reader was previously informed that the cousins bore a close resemblance to one another, Sir Hector looking "very like a coarsened edition of his cousin"), made the journey via train and van to Bratton Grange.[48] Once in the van, he simply dumped out Sir Hector's corpse and departed with the empty box to the disused ice-house of Bratton Grange, where he left the box and used a previously hidden bicycle to depart the vicinity. Upon returning to Bratton Grange for the inquest,

Sir Guy carried with him in a "good-sized trunk" (the one Harold had recalled when queried by Priestley) containing the patterns that ostensibly had been in the wickerwork box when the false Sir Hector made his "fatal" journey. Once in the ice-house, Sir Guy placed the patterns in the box and then dumped the box in a nearby wood, so as to lead to the later discovery of the box with the patterns. Sir Guy deliberately left clues for Dr. Priestley to discover that would lead to him as the culprit of the so-called "false murder"— the stabbing of Sir Hector — because he knew that if he were arrested for the false murder, evidence of the "true murder"— the poisoning of Sir Hector — would lead to his acquittal. Once acquitted of Sir Hector's murder, he could not be tried for it again, even were his guilt in the true murder discovered.

Once these remarkable revelations have taken place, Sir Guy reveals that his motive for murder was selfless:

> "Hector was a man who had no thought beyond the pursuit of pleasure.... As head of the firm he had no interest beyond squeezing the last penny out of it for himself, regardless of the future of the firm.... Davidson's was to him nothing more than a convenient organization by which to make money.
>
> To me ... Davidson's was almost sacred. It had been the life work of two generations before me, a monument of skill and patient effort. I have never regarded it as belonging to any one man, but as a trust.... Nor was the guardian of the trust responsible for the firm alone. He was in charge of the welfare of his employees, many of whom had grown up in the firm, as well. My uncle felt this keenly, as had his father before him.
>
> Yet there was I, compelled to stand helplessly aside and watch the firm going steadily downhill, while my cousin squandered its resources upon drink and women.... [I]f his policy had been allowed to continue, the firm could not have lasted for many more years.... The edifice ... would have fallen, bringing disaster upon hundreds of innocent workers, who had given the best years of their lives to the firm.
>
> Only one thing could save the situation — my cousin's death."[49]

Sir Guy explains that he had to remain at liberty so the he could accomplish the vital reorganization of the business. Then he dramatically reveals to his dinner companions that he is "suffering from an incurable complaint," from which he is sure to die in no more than a few years. He is leaving all his shares in Davidson's to Olga Watkins and Philip Lowry, who can be trusted to carry on the firm "as the first two Davidsons would have wished." He has prepared another fatal sparklet for himself, and he will retire to Bratton Grange and use it when he feels his mortal disease "getting the upper hand." Sir Guy believes it fitting that he will mete out the same fate for himself as he did for the cousin he slew: "An eye for an eye, a tooth for a tooth — after all, isn't that justice, Professor?"[50]

With *The Davidson Case*, Street produced a quite sophisticated Golden Age mystery. Not only the puzzle but also the theme — when, if ever, is murder justified?— is of interest. Both Davidson and Priestley are allowed by the author to make cases in favor of the moral utility of murder. Against Priestley's objection that Sir Guy's arrest, conviction and execution "will merely have the effect of undoing all the good which Sir Guy's action [murdering Sir Hector] has effected," Inspector Hanslet, representative of the machinery of "justice," can merely respond with a rote invocation of occupational duty: "That's all very well, Professor ... But it's my job to collect evidence which will lead to the arrest and conviction of the criminal."[51] Of course, in time-honored mystery fashion, the murderer is required to expire, even if by his own hand several years after the end of the novel; but only after his crime has paid off—both for himself and many others.

The Davidson Case is of interest as well for its characterization. Puzzle predominates, but Street succeeds with Olga Watkins and Guy Davidson in creating characters that engage the reader. Half-Czech and half-English, Olga, in addition to the "dogged British persistence" of her father, has a strain of "quick, passionate impulsiveness" inherited from her mother. A charming, sociable young woman, Olga yet is also intensely proud of her accomplishments at work: "She, a friendless girl, had become a wheel of real importance at the eminent firm of Davidson's."[52] Olga refuses, even near the novel's end, when she has agreed to marry Lowry, to give up her position in the firm, so that, unlike such fluttery social butterflies of twenties mystery fiction as April Priestley, she stands for something more than the frivolous love interest.

Sir Guy is remarkable for his dedication to Davidson's, Ltd. In his concern for the firm and its workers (for whom he is willing to risk what remains of his life), Sir Guy stands in stark contrast to the debauched, selfish Sir Hector, representing instead the progressive, responsible capitalist, interested in technological advance and the welfare of his work force, like the celebrated real-life Sir Alfred Mond, who, three years before *The Davidson Case* was published, had been responsible for the consolidation of British chemical firms as Imperial Chemical Industries.[53] Only in the hands of such men as Sir Guy Davidson (with the help of such women as Olga Watkins) can industrial capitalism survive in a world beset by the Bolshevik menace, Street might well be suggesting [**END SPOILER ALERT**].

Two years after the publication of *The Davidson Case*, Street again considered the morality of murder and portrayed out-of-the-ordinary women characters in another finely plotted John Rhode detective novel, *The Hanging Woman* (1931). Two deaths quickly take place in the tale. First there is the demise of the pilot Andres Vilmaes in a supposedly accidental plane crash that occurred when Vilmaes attempted to make a landing on the private airstrip of his employer, the brilliant research scientist Charles Partington. Soon following is the supposed suicide by hanging at a deserted country house of a woman, Cynthia Bartlett, who was thought to have been romantically involved with Vilmaes. At the inquest on Bartlett, both local Superintendent Everley and Inspector Hanslet are taken aback to learn that the woman actually was murdered, but Hanslet's association of several years with a certain acidulous scientist provides a guiding star for the inspector. "I know very well what's the first thing I'm going to do," announces Hanslet, who very shortly is consulting Dr. Priestley.[54] Through a series of brilliant deductions, Priestley determines that not only Bartlett but also Vilmaes was murdered [**SPOILER ALERT**] and that the murderer is Charles Partington, who was running a drug smuggling operation to finance his legitimate scientific work and was being blackmailed by Vilmaes and Bartlett. Priestley allows Partington a chance to escape England and its hounds of justice, later telling Hanslet: "In my eyes his guilt ... is a very small matter compared with the scientific discoveries which he might have made through his experiments." After the failure of his escape attempt, Partington commits suicide, leaving Priestley to pronounce his epitaph:

> "A remarkable man!" he said softly. "A lover of science who allowed his passion to possess him to the exclusion of every other sentiment. Even the sanctity of human life was not worthy, in his estimation, to stand in the way of his research. And who dare say that he was not right?

Millions have been killed in wars waged for the furtherance of much less estimable ambitions.... His death is so great a loss to science that it seems to me too great a price to pay in retribution for the murders of Vilmaes and Miss Bartlett."[**END SPOILER ALERT**]

A bemused Hanslet can only regard Priestley "curiously" and counter that "it's lucky for ordinary folk that we don't look at things at the Yard in the same way you do, Professor."[55]

Another interesting aspect of *The Hanging Woman* is the portrayal of Cynthia Bartlett and her friend and flatmate Miss Carroll. Though we never see Cynthia among the living, a sense of her cheerfully amoral, grasping nature is convincingly conveyed by the author. Both she and her friend Miss Carroll are more then capable of dispensing with men and acting purposively for themselves. Miss Carroll, we learn, is secretary of the "Women's League of Amity," and she scoffs at Hanslet's notion that Cynthia might have killed herself out of despair over a man: "I suppose you think that because a woman has committed suicide, there must be a man concerned in that matter. Let me assure you, once and for all, that Cynthia's regard for men, collectively or individually, was not sufficiently great to induce her to commit suicide on their account." It is Miss Carroll who intervenes in the case and establishes that Cynthia Bartlett was murdered — though this fact does not stop Hanslet from suspecting the determined, independent Secretary of the Women's League of Amity of her friend's now-established murder! The inspector's deeply-ingrained male chauvinism allows him to waive aside all commonsensical objections to his new theory:

> "I don't think there's any great trouble there. Women don't as a rule read the newspapers very carefully."
>
> "I've thought of that, Professor.... You must remember that we're concerned with a woman, subject to all a woman's fancies and indecisions."[56]

Priestley, though himself not immune to sexual chauvinism, finds these facile explanations impossible to swallow, and discovers the true murderer.

Presaged by 1929's *The House on Tollard Ridge* and *The Davidson Case*, the next fifteen years saw the flowering — perhaps in keeping with the theme of murder I should say congealing — of Street's crime fiction talent, with the appearance of a score or so of masterful tales of detection under the John Rhode name. Of the 34 John Rhode titles published over this amazingly prolific period (1930–1944), I would select as notable on grounds of ingenuity, besides *The Hanging Woman*, the following works: 1930's *Pinehurst*, 1932's *Dead Men at the Folly*, 1933's *The Motor Rally Mystery*, *The Claverton Mystery* and *The Venner Crime*, 1934's *The Robthorne Mystery*, *Poison for One* and *Shot at Dawn*, 1935's *The Corpse in the Car*, *Hendon's First Case* and *Mystery at Olympia*, 1937's *Death on the Board* and *Proceed with Caution*, 1938's *Invisible Weapons* and *The Bloody Tower*, 1940's *Death on the Boat Train*, 1941's *Death at the Helm* and *They Watched by Night*, 1943's *Dead on the Track* and *Men Die at Cyprus Lodge* and 1944's *Vegetable Duck*. About half of the seventeen John Rhode titles that Street produced from 1945 to 1953 are worthy works, with 1950's *Family Affairs* in particular approaching the mastery of his best earlier Rhode books. With the fifteen Rhode tales that Street published between 1954 and 1961, there is a strong decline in quality; and it is hard to designate a fully successful book from this period, although the very late *Licensed for Murder* (1958) has some strong features.

Clever plotting and impressive technical mastery characterize the best John Rhode novels from the 1930s and 1940s. Readers of Golden Age detection greatly prized the authorial ingenuity found in the works of such genre masters as Agatha Christie, with her fiendishly misleading but fair clueing, and John Dickson Carr, with his seemingly miraculous but rationally explained "locked room" puzzles. John Street's major contribution to the great game of Golden Age detection is his carefully constructed and exceptionally ingenious murders. Milward Kennedy once insightfully observed that "John Rhode" must have been the type of boy who, driven by a passion to know how things work, "takes his uncle's watch to pieces and puts it together again in approved working order," for Rhode's murders consistently had this sort of clockwork precision. "Though [Rhode's] characters are always adequate," Kennedy noted in another review, "it is the mechanics that are outstanding. He must hold the record for the invention of ingenious ways of taking human life." Dorothy L. Sayers agreed with Kennedy about the commanding cleverness of Street's murder methods, affirming that she believed the method employed in *Poison for One* would work because "Mr. Rhode says so." Sayers felt certain John Rhode was "the kind of man who [first] tries everything out on the dog in his own back kitchen (under proper safeguards, of course, for the dog)."[57]

The John Rhode books from Street's peak period reveal the author as a master at deviously devised destructive designs, including not only the means for introducing poisons into bodies in such works as *The Claverton Mystery*, *Poison for One*, *The Corpse in the Car*, *Hendon's First Case*, *Death at the Helm*, *Men Die at Cyprus Lodge* and *Vegetable Duck*, but also, in various other novels, murder by ingeniously original means of shooting, freezing, bombing, and burning. At no location on earth is one safe in a Rhode novel — not in dwellings modern or ancient (even buildings can kill), nor in car, boat, train, or, for that matter, boat train. *Death on the Board* provides a cornucopia of killings, variously by means of an explosion, a fire, poison and two distinctive gassings. *Mystery at Olympia* offers a Rasputin-like corpse that has been poisoned both by arsenic and carbon dioxide as well as shot, yet in reality suffered a death induced by some other means. Given his genius in murder (to borrow the clever title of an E.R. Punshon detective novel), it is a fortunate thing indeed for England that Major Street contented himself with dealing out death in novels and never turned to a life of true crime.

Street excelled at dispatch by poison, rivaling Agatha Christie is his adept use of this particularly devious weapon. In *The Claverton Mystery* (*The Claverton Affair* in the United States), when Sir Alured Faversham pronounces that Dr. Priestley's recently deceased friend, Sir John Claverton, died from the perforation of his stomach wall, the reader, aware he is reading a murder mystery, naturally knows that this fatal perforation must have resulted from the action of a malign human agent; [**SPOILER ALERT**] but of course it takes Dr. Priestley to determine that the perforation resulted from Sir John's ingestion of metallic sodium laid for him by the murderer. The ailing Sir John had regularly been taking prescribed gelatin capsules, and into one of those capsules the murderer introduced metallic sodium, with deadly effect. A showman composed of one part Hercule Poirot and one part Mr. Wizard, Dr. Priestley one evening arranges for Faversham to give a demonstration in an experiment before his assembled guests:

> A brass tea kettle stood in the fireplace. Faversham picked this up, and from it poured some warm water into a saucer on Dr. Priestley's desk. Into this he dipped one of the capsules which he had prepared. It floated on the surface, but for a few moments nothing happened. Then,

Miles Burton, *Murder of a Chemist* (1936). Whether writing as John Rhode or Miles Burton, John Street rivaled Agatha Christie in his prolific and ingenious use of poison as a murder weapon. In *Murder of a Chemist*, someone places oxalic acid in Josiah Elvidge's fatal lemon crush.

when the gelatin coating had dissolved, there was a sudden pop. A yellow flame shot up from the capsule, which began to dart erratically about the surface of the water. After a few seconds the substance had entirely disappeared, and the flame went out.[58]

Metallic sodium, we learn, would "flame in exactly the same way if introduced into the contents of the stomach," which is what happened to poor Claverton.[59] Enclosed in a gelatin capsule, the sodium passed harmlessly though Claverton's body, without leaving a trace of caustic action, until it reached his stomach. Once the gelatin had dissolved, introducing the contents of the capsule into the stomach, the hydrogen derived from the water caught fire, causing instant perforation of the stomach wall. The sodium then combined with the chlorine of the gastric juices to form sodium chloride, or common salt, a substance which attracted no marked attention in the course of the medical autopsy. **[END SPOILER ALERT]**

Poisons continued to slay mercilessly throughout the thirties and forties in a series of clever Priestley tales. In *Poison for One* the lecherous Sir Gerald Uppingham is found dead at his desk in the study of his country home, Bucklersbury Park. On the desk is found a tray with a decanter of whiskey, two siphons, three tumblers, a decanter of port, two wine glasses and a bottle labeled "Chaffey's Cough Linctus." Hydrocyanic acid has been added to this medicine, and Inspector Hanslet concludes that Sir Gerald died from drinking some of the poisoned linctus from one of the wine glasses—though, oddly, no one recalls Sir Gerald having complained recently of suffering from a cough. In a consultation with Hanslet, Dr. Priestley cuts to the quick **[SPOILER ALERT]**:

> "If a person drinks any liquid, especially a viscous liquid such as linctus, from a glass, the mark of the lips is invariably found round the rim of the glass. Has any search been made for such a mark?"
>
> "I don't suppose it has ever occurred to anybody, Professor," Hanslet replied.
>
> "Then I suggest that a further examination should be made without delay," said Dr. Priestley. "Until that has been done, it is merely a waste of time to discuss the matter further."[60]

Of course Priestley's suspicion that the cough linctus was a blind laid by a wily murderer is correct, and there are no lip prints on the wine glass that contained the linctus. Priestley eventually deduces that the murderer gassed Sir Gerald with hydrocyanic acid, by spraying his victim with an uncorked hot water bottle containing the gas. To protect himself from the deadly effect of the gas, the murderer wore over his head a gas mask (a souvenir of the Great War) charged with caustic soda. In the fatal study at Bucklersbury Park, Priestley demonstrates how the murder was accomplished, with himself in the role of murderer and Harold as victim, fortunately for Harold using bottled ammonia instead of hydrocyanic acid. **[END SPOILER ALERT]** Dorothy L. Sayers complained that this clever tale was "rather spoilt" for her by the jacket illustration, which depicted the frightening, indeed nightmarish, image of the murderer in full killing regalia. "Get your bookseller to remove the jacket before you sit down to enjoy Mr. Rhode's latest mystery," she urged.[61]

In probably Street's greatest thirties poisoning mystery, *The Corpse in the Car*, Dr. Priestley confines his choice of demonstration subjects to cats and leaves his hapless secretary alone. In this novel, the corpse found in the locked car is that of the tyrannical and capricious Lady Misterton, another of Street's classic murderees. One of Lady Misterton's "many unpleasant habits," we learn in the book's prologue, is having her long-suffering chauffeur, Fitchley, drive her round the countryside most afternoons, "fondly believing that she was in some way benefiting her health by so doing." Frequently she would have Fitchley pull over and turn on a portable wireless set, so she could sit for an hour or more listening to the current program while working on her latest petit point needlework. The day she becomes the corpse in the car, Lady Misterton informs Fitchley — after he has driven them some three and a half miles from her home, Clandown Towers — that she has forgotten her bag and he must walk back to get it, leaving her in the car. Fitchley is not pleased: "*But this was the limit! To ask him to walk seven miles to fetch her blasted bag! The old....* He checked himself hurriedly. Lady Misterton had an uncanny knack of reading people's thoughts." Off Fitchley goes, after adjusting the wireless set for his mistress and leaving her listening — ominously, if not overly subtly — to the strains of Saint-Saens' *Danse Macabre.* Upon reaching Clandown Towers, he learns that Lady Misterton had taken the bag with her after all and thus deliberately sent him on a fool's errand. He heads back, deciding to stop on his way at the local public house, the Three Frogs, for a quick pint ("a *few minutes more or less could make no possible difference*"). Stepping outside the Three Frogs after having his drink, Fitchely is hit by a motor-cycle and side-car and sent tumbling into a ditch. Fitchley goes to the hospital, while his mistress goes to her Maker. That evening, Lady Misterton is found dead in her car, wrapped in her rug, her needlework in her hands, the radio still running. The cause of death cannot be determined, as the autopsy could discover only minute traces of arsenic, insufficient to cause death, that were presumably left by the neuralgia medicine Lady Misterton was taking. Hanslet — now a superintendent thanks to Priestley's deductive efforts — is frustrated by the report, but not Dr. Priestley:

> [T]he report had put Dr. Priestley in an excellent humor. He rubbed his hands together and beamed at the Superintendent through his spectacles. "We look at these things from entirely different standpoints," he said. "You are a policeman, concerned solely with the legal aspect of the matter. I am a scientist, faced with what I believe to be a fascinating problem. It is inconceivable that Lady Misterton should have died from what are commonly called natural causes. Therefore an external agency has been employed, exceedingly sudden and powerful in its action, and having the most valuable property of leaving no traces in the dead body. This is the occasion for which I have always hoped, since my first interest in criminology was awakened."[62]

Fired with this new enthusiasm, Dr. Priestley emerges from Westbourne Terrace to conduct a personal investigation at Clandown Towers. Soon Miss Letchworth, the late Lady Misterton's fluttery paid companion, is confronting an "elderly gentleman of rather forbidding aspect," who wants to know all about Lady Misterton's pet cats.[63] **[SPOILER ALERT]** Preferring cats to humans, Lady Misterton doted on the animals in her mansion, and upon their deaths had them preserved by her chauffeur Fitchley, who was also a trained taxidermist, and mounted in glass cases. Priestley learns that one unfortunate cat, Miggles, was found inexplicably dead in Fitchley's workshop. Priestley also is informed by the chatty Miss Letchworth that the talented Fitchley serves as Clandown Towers' general handyman, usually managing to mend any broken thing about the place. Priestley then investigates the objects found with the corpse of Lady Misterton in the locked car: a brown silk bag (the one Fitchley had been sent to Clandown Towers to find), a workbag, the needlework, two india-rubber hot water bottles (each in a crocheted woolen cover), a large fur rug, a bottle of aspirin and the portable wireless set.

Going through all these objects, Dr. Priestley eventually determines that one of the radio batteries in the portable wireless set was overfilled and unexpectedly contained aluminum in the acid. The Professor makes note of these anomalies, without being able to determine their significance. Then one day, Superintendent Hanslet, at Westbourne Terrace in consultation with Dr. Priestley about the increasingly odoriferous red herrings in the case, lights a cigarette, crushes the empty packet and throws it into the study's lighted fireplace. The paper wrapping on the packet immediately catches fire, leaving the aluminum foil interior, apparently unchanged, in the heart of the flames, until it suddenly shrivels and vanishes. While Hanslet talks on, Dr. Priestley regards with "rapt attention" the disappearance of the cigarette packet in the fire. After Hanslet makes his leave, Harold is called upon to assist Priestley in a series of experiments with aluminum foil, and the Professor discovers his solution. He later demonstrates to an audience — using as his test subject an unlucky cat — how the deaths of both Lady Misterton and her cat Miggles (a run-through for the murder of Lady Misterton) were accomplished. As in the 1815 case of the German chemist Adolph Gehlen — which Priestley had suddenly recalled after seeing the foil in the fire — Lady Misterton died from exposure to arseniuretted hydrogen, or arsine, a deadly colorless, odorless gas. "Now, as it happens," Dr. Priestley cheerily explains, "arsine is very easily produced. The action of sulphuric acid upon zinc arsenide evolves it in considerable volume. Zinc arsenide, though not an article of commerce, is in turn very simple to prepare. It is only necessary to heat together arsenic and zinc, and quite a moderate temperature is required."[64] Knowing that Lady Misterton was in the habit of sitting alone in a closed car with a portable wireless set, Fitchley created the gas by inserting an aluminum foil-wrapped pellet of zinc arsenide into the sulphuric acid of the battery. It was necessary to overfill the battery to make sure that the pellet would act upon the acid; and the overfilled battery was the anomaly Dr. Priestley had noticed, allowing him to detect through chemical analysis the strange presence of aluminum in the battery. Fitcheley knew that the presence of small amounts of arsenic in Lady Misterton's body would be attributed to her neuralgia medicine, but realized that the overfilled battery conceivably might lead to suspicion. The chauffeur had hoped as a precaution against detection to replace the radio battery, but he had been injured in the road accident outside the public house and laid up in hospital. This unforeseen accident made it possible for Dr. Priestley to examine the wireless set, thereby sealing yet another poisoner's fate. [END SPOILER ALERT]

Rhode's "grand new way of eliminating people" in *The Corpse in the Car* made Dorothy L. Sayers, in her review of the book in the *Sunday Times*, figuratively hug herself with delight, though she registered disapproval of the mayhem directed against cats in the novel. Sayers admitted that Lady Misterton richly deserved to figure as the book's titular corpse, and it is hard to disagree with her. The widow of Sir James Misterton, who bequeathed to her a fortune made from his "Foam-Flowers for the Feet," Lady Misterton is an objectionable, unpleasant person, showing affection only for her cats, which she had stuffed and mounted in glass cases upon their demises, before placing them in a bizarre museum in her house, which she had hoped to have maintained after her death as part of the Misterton Cat Sanctuary. Lady Misterton's snobbish brother, Theodore Ormskirk, cannot contain his scorn at the idea of wasting all that good money on a glorified cat's home: "[T]he Misterton Sanctuary for Cats! Why, that yahoo of a husband of hers would turn in his grave if he got wind of it! Whatever else he may have been, he was a good man of business."[65]

The tryingly eccentric Lady Misterton was also unfailingly tightfisted and unscrupulous; **[SPOILER ALERT]** and she once laid a trap for her employee Fitchley that led, with poetic irony, to her demise at his hands. Shortly after his employment by Lady Misterton in the rather unusual position of chauffeur-handyman-taxidermist, Fitchley had been sent by his mistress to repair the floor of the lumber room, which had given way from dry rot. Under the boards, between the joists, Fitchley later explains, he found a small canvas bag containing "a lot of old silver and copper coins, with Queen Victoria's head on them. I counted them, and they came to two pounds thirteen shillings and seventeen pence." Facing a summons for several pounds that he owed a man, Fitchley, believing that the bag must have been hidden and forgotten decades ago, told himself "findings keepings" and filched it, only to discover that Lady Misterton had deliberately left the bag there in order to entrap him into a supposedly criminal act. After informing Fitchley that she would turn him over to the police unless he contracted to remain in her employment at her pleasure for the weekly wage of thirty shillings, Lady Misterton obtained Fitchley's signature to a highly exploitive contract. "It struck Hanslet that this had been a pretty mean trick on Lady Misterton's part" is Street's commentary on the affair, which ended up costing Lady Misterton her life. Seven years later, wanting to marry a parlor maid at Clandown Towers and hoping to find employment at less penurious wages, Fitchley, believing himself entrapped by Lady Misterton's contract, finally resorts to murdering his employer. "We know that the agreement which Fitchley was induced to sign was not worth the paper it was written upon," explains Dr. Priestley, "but Fitchley had no such knowledge. Men of his class have the very vaguest ideas of the operation of the law. He believed, no doubt, that at the very first symptom of revolt the police would be summoned and he would find himself in jail. This would put an end to his plans for the future." The Professor continues to reflect on Fitchley's motivation to kill, declaring: "In my opinion the achievement of liberty, even though the existing servitude is merely fanciful, is one of the strongest motives by which a man can be inspired." The imperceptive Superintendent Hanslet, who earlier had felt sympathy for the unjustly exploited chauffeur, now refers to Fitchley as "a damned clever scoundrel," missing the gist of the Professor's reflections entirely.[66] While modern readers might scoff at the legal ignorance attributed by the author in 1935 to "men of [Fitchley's] class," Street's attitude toward the matter of social class is interesting. Lady Misterton, like another fictional member of Britain's wealthy elite, Sir Hector Davidson, failed to meet obligations of basic decency to the working class, choosing instead to live life as a selfish social parasite. In both cases, death resulted. **[END SPOILER ALERT]**

Hendon's First Case, also from 1935, introduces the well-born police inspector Jimmy Waghorn, Superintendent Hanslet's eventual replacement in the Priestley series. This novel concerns yet another cleverly contrived poison death, this one by means of ptomaine poisoning at a restaurant, evidently from a fatal dish of calf's head (the *plat du jour*). When young Inspector Jimmy Waghorn, a fresh Hendon Police College graduate and protégé of Superintendent Hanslet, gets too close to the truth, the resourceful and remorseless murderer attempts to dispatch the young man by getting him to lick envelopes with gum heavily impregnated with the deadly ptomaine. In her review of the novel in the

Sunday Times, Dorothy L. Sayers deemed its plot "an exceedingly good one," while Barzun and Taylor in *A Catalogue of Crime* pronounced thirty-six years later that it was "one of Rhode's best."[67]

John Street continued to put poisons to rather quite nasty use in the 1940s. In *Death at the Helm* (1941), an adulterous couple dies of poisoning aboard the yacht *Lonicera*, after consuming a luncheon that included a couple glasses of *Hampden's Gin Blimp, the Connoisseur's Cocktail*, a circumstance that allows Street, strictly a beer and whiskey-and-soda man himself one surmises, to have his bit of fun with the makers of bottled cocktails. After obtaining his own bottle of Gin Blimp from a wine merchant, young Inspector Jimmy Waghorn looks at the mixture skeptically, thinking: "Now Hampden's Gin Blimp might be, and probably was, a highly artificial drink. But it was unlikely that its toxic properties were so great as to cause the deaths of two people immediately upon drinking it." Returning with the bottle to his office at Scotland Yard, where he meets his soon-to-be-retired superior, Superintendent Hanslet, Jimmy announces: "I am about to sacrifice myself upon the altar of duty.... This sticky and somewhat viscous beverage is Hampden's Gin Blimp. Here's to crime!" Though Jimmy survives his nauseating taste of the "pungent, slightly sweet, and faintly alcoholic" cocktail, he asks Hanslet: "I wonder what kick folks get out of drinking concoctions like that?"[68] In the case of the poisoned couple on board the *Lonicera*, they got quite a kick indeed, as the Gin Blimp they imbibed turned out to have been poisoned with extremely deadly distilled water dropwort.

In *Men Die at Cyprus Lodge* (1943), a paranormal investigator, Sir Philip Briningham, is fatally dispatched in a reputedly haunted house, not by ghosts, but by a booby-trapped hidden compartment, designed by a human hand with lethal intent. Investigating the source of a series of nocturnal noises heard in the house, Sir Philip reaches his hand into the hidden compartment, cuts his wrist on a surgical knife and dies in less than twenty minutes. Inspector Waghorn reports: "[T]he blade [of the knife] had been dipped in a mixture of aconitine and gum, which, on drying, had formed a thick coating. There was enough aconitine deposited on the blade to kill dozens of people." Of this novel, American reviewer Anthony Boucher approvingly wrote: "At his best, nobody can touch Rhode for ingenious murder gadgets and few can top him for meticulous unraveling; he's very close to his best in this one."[69]

Though written before the end of World War II, *Vegetable Duck* (1944) has a post-war setting; and so, fittingly enough, the setting of the murder is not a baronet's country home, but a relatively modest London service flat. Her husband having been called away by a telephone call, Mrs. Fransham dines alone on a fine dinner, including vegetable duck, "a marrow, not too big, stuffed with minced meat and herbs, and baked whole." Analysis shows that the vegetable marrow is riddled with digitalis and extremely lethal, but there is one point that baffles the Yard pathologist, Sir Oswald Horsham: "Our experiments have shown that every part of the flesh, of the rind and of the seeds, is equally and powerfully toxic ... I can't quite understand how this came about." Sir Oswald cannot, but Dr. Priestley, of course, can. **[SPOILER ALERT]** The murderer, he finds, had fed the fatal marrow during its growth with a liquid mixture including digitalis, so that it became infused with the deadly poison. He then sent the marrow up to the Franshams' flat via a tradesman's lift connected to the scullery, where it was prepared by the cook, who assumed Mrs. Fransham had ordered it. Inspector Waghorn, believing that the poison had been administered within the flat, mistakenly suspects Mrs. Franhsam's innocent husband, whom the murderer had decoyed away from the fatal dinner with a fake telephone call. [**END SPOILER ALERT**] The erring Jimmy finds himself subjected to the scorn Hanslet had stoically endured from Priestly for so many years. Commenting at one of Priestley's postprandial crime conferences on Jimmy's eventual arrest of the real murderer, a friend, Dr. Oldland, asks: "What made you so absolutely certain that [X] was the man you were after? Inspiration?" To which query "from the depths of his chair" Dr. Priestley rhetorically strikes: "Somewhat belated inspiration, if so." Jimmy explains his inspiration, encouraged by the Professor: "Go on, Inspector. A review of your mental processes can hardly lack interest." Such an ironic utterance would have passed over Hanslet's head completely, but Jimmy has sufficient perspicacity "to doubt how far he could regard this as a compliment." Yet Jimmy need not have felt so abashed at his slowness in this case, considering Anthony Boucher's apt comment on the tale: "Poisoned vegetable marrow starts a trail of almost unbelievingly ingenious false clues." The central idea of *Vegetable Duck* seems clearly inspired by an R. Austin Freeman short story, but Street's novel is both an elaboration and improvement on Freeman's already clever tale.[70]

Although Street excelled with poisons, he was as well a dab hand with sundry other murder devices. A look at a few more John Rhode titles from his peak period may suggest his murderous fecundity at this time. Two of his most ingenious non-poisoning murders are found in *They Watched by Night* (1941) and *Shot at Dawn* (1934). The former book is a wartime novel in which both Hanslet — now retired from active police duty in Scotland Yard — and Waghorn, both under aliases, are sent to the village of Hoxdown to investigate the mysterious signaling to German planes, which threatens a secret military base in a nearby wood. When the charred remains of Chief Constable Lamberhurst are discovered in the ashes of his summerhouse, Hanslet and Waghorn find themselves involved in investigating murder, as well as fifth-column activity. Naturally it becomes necessary to summon Dr. Priestley, now alone in his fastness at Westbourne Terrace, Harold having entered war service and the Professor having steadfastly refused to abandon London in spite of the Blitz. Hanslet and Waghorn, as well as the local police, are unable to determine why Lamberhurst could not have escaped to safety from the summerhouse fire, yet the dauntless professor is able to deduce all from assorted clues, [**SPOILER ALERT**] including the beer bottles Lamberhurst had delivered to the summerhouse on the day of his death:

> There was nothing in any way extraordinary about the [beer bottle]. It held a quart, was made of thick and nearly opaque glass, stood a foot high and was three and a half inches in diameter. The neck was secured with a screw stopper, and this was covered with a paper cap, kept in place by a rubber band.
>
> Dr. Priestley contemplated the bottle for a moment or two. "The bottles standing in the crate outside the summer house were exactly similar to this?"
>
> "Exactly," [Hanslet] replied. "This bottle and those in the crate all came from the same place, the Antelope [the public house at Hoxdown]."
>
> "The disadvantage of this deeply colored bottle glass is that one cannot tell whether the beer is clear or not before pouring it out," Dr. Priestley remarked. "In the case of Mr. Lamberhurst, I think, this disadvantage proved fatal."
>
> "What on Earth do you mean, Professor?" [Hanslet] exclaimed. "You're not suggesting that he died of drinking thick beer, are you?"
>
> "I'm not suggesting that he died of drinking anything at all," Dr. Priestley replied.[71]

In a teatime confrontation between the three men and the murderer, all is revealed. The murderer had poured out a bottle of beer and replaced the beer in the bottle with a deadly concoction of his own: A pint of water, into which "a quantity of finely divided white phosphorus" had been mixed, followed by gasoline and a teaspoon of baking powder. He then hastily replaced the stopper, the paper cap and the rubber band, and substituted his doctored bottle for a bottle of beer in the crate left outside Lamberhurst's summerhouse. Baking soda rendered the contents of the bottle evanescent, so that, as soon as Lamberhurst removed the stopper, some of the mixture foamed over his hands and clothing and on to the floor. Since phosphorous heats instantly upon exposure to air, it set fire to the gasoline contained in the mixture, which in turn ignited the phosphorous itself. The phosphorous, explains the unrepentant murderer, "burned with an intense heat, throwing off clouds of a suffocating smoke of phosphorous pentoxide.... Lamberhurst must have been enveloped in a sheet of flame and a cloud of choking smoke, giving him not the slightest chance of escape."[72] As it had been revealed previously, again by Dr. Priestley, that Lamberhurst was the fifth-column signaler and as it turns out that the murderer had an amply justified personal motive for his violent act, Hanslet and Waghorn allow the murderer to remain at liberty; and this man, who had been prepared to commit suicide by drinking a cup of poisoned tea, instead picks up his walking stick and serenely takes his leave of the assembled company. [**END SPOILER ALERT**]

The *Spectator* reviewer of *They Watched by Night*, it will be recalled from Chapter One, dismissed the resolution of the book's puzzle as Dr. Priestley shying the *Encyclopaedia Britannica* at the reader's head. Here the reviewer betrays critics' increasing impatience with carefully explained applied science in mystery novels. Many reviewers were coming to much prefer the conspicuous literary quotation dropping of such arty detectives as Ngaio Marsh's Roderick Alleyn, Nicholas Blake's Nigel Strangeways and Michael Innes' John Appleby; yet some readers, at least, still enjoyed Street's methodical and scientifically sound murders. Science professor Wendell Hertig Taylor in *A Catalogue of Crime* lamented that "this otherwise ingenious tale [*They Watched by Night*] ... should be blemished by Priestley's failure to know enough about the effects of high temperature upon the mineral calcite"; but, as this "blemish" concerns only the method of plane-signaling employed by the Nazi spy and not the murder itself, we need not chastise Street too forcefully over the matter of the mineral calcite. For his part E.R. Punshon in the *Manchester Guardian* found that in the novel "Mr. Rhode's extraordinary fertility of invention is shown once more in a fine flower of ingenuity." [73]

Barzun and Taylor deemed *Shot at Dawn* "a fine example of an early Rhode." It is certainly that and more. In addition to a brilliant and scientifically sound sleight of hand concerning the murder, *Shot at Dawn* boasts one of the most original *denouements* of the Golden Age. [**SPOILER ALERT**] As Street modestly explained two years after publishing *Shot at Dawn*, "I ventured to end with an acquittal." Street's allowing a murderer to emerge unscathed from the grinding mills of justice titillated one jaded crime fiction reviewer, Ralph Partridge, who wrote in the *New Statesman and Nation*, "I actually got a thrill out of the verdict of the jury!" Moreover, in addition to allowing his murderer to escape scot free, Street engaged the reader's sympathy with the murderer by making his victim a thoroughly wicked blackmailer. Street admitted in 1936 that he had tired of the convention of having the murderer die at the end of the novel, either by his own hand

John Rhode, *Shot at Dawn* (1934). One of the most praised John Rhode novels, *Shot at Dawn* offered scientifically-inclined readers a heady mixture of natural science and ballistics, as well as a brilliant piece of sleight of hand. After reading the novel, a delighted Dorothy L. Sayers declared with mock indignation that the author had led her innocence up the garden (courtesy Mark Terry).

or that of the state. "Acquittal rather spoils the moral of the story," he reflected. "Therefore some more or less artificial element must be introduced. Some damning piece of evidence must be invented for the detective to secure, or a confession must be secured. Personally, I don't like it, but it can't be helped."[74] In *Shot at Dawn*, however, Street demonstrated that he could help it, and in bravura style. [**END SPOILER ALERT**]

Shot at Dawn concerns the murder of Arthur Crosland, who is found dead one morning aboard his yacht, the *Alondra*, which had spent the night at anchor near the mouth of the River Ridding. Crosland's head is shattered from the impact of a rifle bullet, fired sometime, as the title of the book indicates, around dawn. [**SPOILER ALERT**] Colonel Peniston, Chief Constable of the County, explains to Superintendent Hanslet that due to tidal movement the bows of the *Alondra* would have been facing east at the estimated time of the shooting, so that the shot which killed Crosland must have come from south of the vessel. Hanslet believes it likely that the shot came specifically from Sir Charles Bransbury's home property, Daneswell Park, where a rifle range had been set up, nearly two miles from where the Alondra had anchored; and he conducts his investigation accordingly. It takes Dr. Priestley to determine that the crucial factor concerns not tides but winds. At the time the murder had taken place, the Alondra was wind-rode, not tide-rode, meaning that it had turned in accordance with the direction of the prevailing winds, not the tides. Thus its bows were facing west, not east, and the shot which killed Crosland would have come from the north side of the vessel, not the south side. Dr. Priestley also deduces how a rifle bullet that appeared to have been shot at long range really was fired at short range. Thus reinterpreted, the evidence turns out to implicate Chief Constable Peniston himself, who, we find, had been one of Crosland's blackmail victims. Peniston is arrested, but, in the *denouement* that so pleased Ralph Partridge, he is acquitted by the jury. [**END SPOILER ALERT**] Like Partridge, Dorothy L. Sayers also gave high praise to the book, particularly admiring how with a simple yet sound trick its author had, in a "perfectly heartless manner," led her "innocence up the garden."[75]

With 1937's *Death on the Board*, Street combined the murderous technical genius of his best detective novels with the multiple slayings of *The Murders in Praed Street* for a book that delighted reviewers. "The murders are most ingeniously planned and executed," wrote Isaac Anderson in the *New York Times*, "and even Dr. Priestley is put to a severe test before the story is ended." Across the ocean, Milward Kennedy in the *Sunday Times* sounded similar words of praise: "John Rhode, always prodigal of plans for murder, has never been more prodigal or more ingenious than in *Death on the Board*."[76] In addition to coming up with a particularly clever plot, Street also returned to the reflections on the nature of capitalism in the twentieth century that graced *The Davidson Case* eight years earlier, making *Death on the Board* one of his most interesting works.

Death on the Board opens literally with a bang, as the patrolling police constable Frean hears a massive explosion that momentarily sends him mentally back to the trenches during the German bombardment of March, 1918:

> For an instant all power of reasoning left him. A shell had burst not many yards away, one of those high-velocity things that gives no warning of its coming. In a flash he was down on one knee to avoid the splinter which he could hear whizzing through the air towards him. It struck his helmet, knocking it off his head and sending it spinning into the roadway.
>
> The loss of his helmet brought Frean abruptly to his senses. He sprang into the road and recovered it, feeling as he did so that something was embedded in it. Then suddenly a red sword of light pierced the darkness and by this he saw the object was half a tile.[77]

The recovered Frean looks about and sees "that the red sword of light was a single tongue of flame rising vertically from one of the houses bordering Barming Road.... The Privetts, the respectable and probably desirable residence of Sir Andrew Wigginhall." The constable enters the house and finds an hysterical, fleeing housemaid, an unconscious, wounded cook, and, last and most disturbing of all, "a mangled human leg torn off at the thigh."[78] The explosion had been centered in the upstairs bathroom, where Sir Andrew Wigginhall, having returned that evening from a trip abroad, had been preparing to bathe before dining.

The obliteration of Sir Andrew Wigginhall turns out to be the opening salvo in a brutal, unrelenting campaign of elimination by an unknown murderer against the Board of Directors of Hardware, Ltd., a giant business with "branches in nearly every provincial town." [**SPOILER ALERT**] Over the course of the novel, four more directors are terminated: Andrew Wigginhall's brother; Percy; his brother-in-law, Colonel James Flotman; Samuel Grimshaw, the firm's chief buyer; and Bernard Tunstead, the manager of one of its larger branches. Several of these murders are diabolically ingenious, on par with John Rhode's cleverest killings. Bernard Tunstead, a habitual cigarette smoker, is found one night in his bedroom, "hairless, blinded, scorched out of recognition," burned to death in his bed. It is assumed he fell asleep with a lit cigarette in his hand, setting fire to the bedclothes and to himself. Oddly, however, Tunstead appears to have slept that night between two blankets, with no sheets; and the blankets had not been entirely consumed by the fire. As the perplexed doctor explains on the scene, "There's no trace of either a top or bottom sheet here. The blankets, upper and lower, are badly singed.... I can't understand how it is that all the bedclothes haven't been completely burned." The coroner waves aside such concerns on the part of the doctor, but the interest of the ever-inquisitive Dr. Priestley, who has read an account of the inquest in a newspaper, is piqued. Eventually he deduces the solution: "Mr. Tunstead's sheets, pillowcases and the pajamas he was wearing on the night of his death had been nitrated." By treating these linens with a mixture of concentrated nitric and sulphuric acid the murderer was able to ensure that when they came into contact with lighted cigarette ash, "an extremely fierce and rapid flame would ensue," completely consuming all the nitrated material and inflicting fatal burns on Tunstead.[79]

Looking back over the earlier strange death of Hardware, Ltd. board member Sir Andrew Wigginhall, Priestley is able to determine how the explosion that blew apart Sir Andrew in his bathroom was engineered. Having obtained access to the bathroom for a mere minute or two while Sir Andrew was away traveling, the murderer was able to insert a small "infernal machine" between Sir Andrew's bathtub and the wall next it. Because Sir Andrew always ran his hot water into the bath first, the metal tub heated rapidly, radiating with heat the tongue of metal in the explosive device. The tongue of metal bent in the form of a circle, with the tip of it making contact with a wire, completing the electrical circuit from the battery and igniting a tuft of nitrated cotton wool, causing the deadly explosion. Since the bath would not be used in Sir Andrew's absence, notes Dr. Priestley admiringly, the murderer had laid a perfect death trap for his chosen victim.

Before police discover the culprit of these brilliant crimes, he manages to dispose of three more board members, one by a rather conventional liquid poisoning, but two others by clever gassing methods. Samuel Grimshaw is dispatched in a manner similar to Sir Hector Davidson in *The Davidson Case* and Sir Gerald Uppingham in *Poison for One.* Whereas those two august murder victims were eliminated by means of poison gas contained in, respectively, a soda sparklet and hot water bottle, Grimshaw, a buyer for

Hardware, Ltd., meets his end when testing a new sample tin opener on a tin of peas. The tin, unfortunately for Grimshaw, contains not merely peas, but cacodyl cyanide, "one of the deadliest poisons known to science."[80] Colonel Flotman follows Grimshaw to his own nasty demise shortly later, extinguished by chlorine gas in the private plant providing electrical power for his house, the murderer having poured salt into the plant's battery and locked Flotman inside the building.

What had the Board of Directors of Hardware, Ltd. done to inspire such murderous rage? Hardware, Ltd., it seems, had reached its eminent position by drastically underselling provincial competitors, driving them to ruin when necessary. "The path of success for that enterprising firm had been paved with other men's failures," writes Street. "Its competitors had been ruthlessly shouldered aside, helpless victims on the altar of modern salesmanship." Listening to the fulsome eulogy given by Samuel Grimshaw at the Board meeting held after Sir Andrew's death, Bernard Tunstead finds himself wondering "how on earth the other two members of the audience could swallow it ... here was that tiresome gas bag Grimshaw, spilling endless words upon the subject of Sir Andrew's benevolence of heart and mind!... Everybody knew what Sir Andrew had been like. Hard as nails and not caring a damn what happened to anybody as long as he got his own way. That was the way to get on in business, of course." The murderer turns out to be the son of a small businessman, one Shillingstone, whose concern was economically destroyed by competition with Hardware, Ltd., driving him to kill himself in despair over the loss of his livelihood. One of Shillingstone's contemporaries, a Mr. Phipps, asks of the investigating Jimmy Waghorn: "What's a man to do when his property's mortgaged, and he's up to his ears in debt?" He adds:

> That was the question that Shillingstone found himself faced with. Well, he answered it his own way, though it broke his wife's heart.... He got up quietly in the middle of the night without waking her and went down into the shop. He had a rack of sporting guns there fixed up against the wall. Well, he took one of those guns, loaded it, and blew out his brains with it. And it wasn't many months before Hardware, Ltd. had taken over the premises from the mortgagees and moved into them. You've only got to walk down the High Street to see them for yourself.

Mr. Phipps declares peremptorily: "There ought to be a law to stop these big firms doing things like that." As there was neither a law to prevent nor to punish such actions, Shillingstone's son took matters into his own hands. Having insinuated himself into the management of Hardware, Ltd., he succeeds with his inside knowledge in destroying the men he holds responsible for his father's death (and, indeed, his mother's death as well, as she, grief-stricken, had quickly followed her husband to the grave) and then kills himself as Hanslet and Waghorn come to arrest him, dramatically declaring: "My job in life is finished with the execution of the last of my father's murderers!"[81]

As in *The Davidson Case*, Street highlights problems he perceived as resulting from the activities of a conscienceless capitalism, in this case the negative social consequences of unrestrained business concentration. The penalty extracted from the members of the Board of Directors of Hardware, Ltd., for their role in the death of the man Shillingstone is high indeed, but Street presents their executioner in a sympathetic light. And Dr. Priestley, as unbound by conventional morality as ever, effusively praises the murderer's technical genius: "We cannot deny that his brain, though perverted, was phenomenally acute. His crimes were executed with a skill which must command our admiration." Street indulges a moment of irony when he has Sir Andrew Wigginhall's brother and fellow Board member, Percival Wigginhall, self-righteously attempt to pin the murder of his brother on "criminally minded people who refuse to see the virtues of capitalism," perhaps communists seeking "to strike a blow at the foundations of British commerce."[82] Of course, to the contrary, the danger to Hardware, Ltd. comes not from communists, but from the son of a hardworking small businessman annihilated by a bigger company able to practice economy of scale.

Death on the Board holds out some hope that after the wholesale massacre of its Board of Directors, Hardware, Ltd. may come to be run on more humane lines. Anthony Wiggenhall, son of Sir Andrew, effectively runs Hardware, Ltd. by the novel's end. Reflecting the retrograde concerns of the company's older generation of capitalists, the soon-to-be murdered Samuel Grimshaw views the elevation of progressive young Anthony with some reservation:

> He'd have to be watched pretty carefully at first. Already, as head of one of the departments of Hardware House, he had shown an undue interest in things that didn't concern him. He was always talking about the welfare of the staff and putting ideas into the heads of the younger folks. Getting up cricket clubs and football clubs and things like that. These modern young men and women were flighty enough without encouraging them to think of games when they ought to be attending to business.[83]

Caroline Wigginhall Flotman, sister of Andrew and Percival Wigginhall and wife of Colonel James Flotman — themselves all wiped out by the vengeful son of Shillingstone — in a symbolic statement of continuity with the aggressive past is made chairman of Hardware, Ltd. at the novel's end, but real power resides with the company's Managing Director, Anthony Wigginhall. **[END SPOILER ALERT]**

A John Rhode novel from the next year, *Invisible Weapons* (1938), demonstrates yet again Street's murderous ingenuity. Here Street devised two slayings, seemingly by "invisible" means, the first a bludgeoning that takes place in the locked cloakroom of a suburban house. The cloakroom has only a small window, access to which was under observation at the time of the victim's death. "If only I could make out how the crime was committed, I might form some theory of who did it," declares Inspector Waghorn.[84] Dr. Priestley, Harold in tow, bestirs himself to do some on-site investigation near the end of the novel and is able, in his inimitable way, to provide for the stymied Waghorn and Hanslet a classic demonstration of exactly how the first crime was accomplished, as well as an explanation of the second.

While Street's employment of ingenious murder means became his signature plot device in the 1930s and 1940s, making him the most prominent exponent of scientific detection after his illustrious predecessor R. Austin Freeman (1862–1943), Street occasionally produced works more reminiscent of that other famed Freeman (with whom he has been yoked in iron for decades now as one-half of the great Humdrum ox team of mystery), Freeman Wills Crofts. A few of Street's novels, most particularly the John Rhode titles *Proceed with Caution* (1937) and *Death on the Boat Train* (1940) and the Miles Burton tales *Murder of a Chemist* (1936) and *Mr. Westerby Missing* (1940) turn on alibi-busting, the technical element most famously associated with Crofts' many detective stories. *Proceed with Caution* has an interesting plot structure in which the reader sees separate investigations by Hanslet and Waghorn come to crashing halts, only for Dr. Priestley to come to the rescue by showing how the two seemingly discrete crimes are connected. Included in the novel are a couple of lengthy timetables, a feature often seen in Crofts' works and associated with Humdrum authors, but in fact used but infrequently by Street. Perhaps the most arresting devices in this clever novel are the murderer's use of a rented hearse to carry his victim's corpse (this idea delighted Milward Kennedy, who found it "a brilliantly simple answer to the conundrum, how to transport a corpse inconspicuously across the face of England") and the dumping of that corpse into a roadside tar boiler, a grisly yet effective way of obliterating all its exterior physical features.[85] For its part, *Death on the Boat Train* turns on a brilliantly simple alibi trick, one that is apt to bamboozle the reader and compares with the best deceptions of Crofts.

With the onset of World War II, Street kept up his prolific pace of writing, though his personal life, like everyone else's in Britain, at first was sharply disrupted. Major Street was reported to be working at the War Office in September 1939 and going "around in battle dress" in November 1940, but by early 1941 he and Eileen Waller had left London and returned to their beloved countryside. From about this time through 1948 — a period when he was still producing some of his most interesting work — John and Eileen resided in the village of Swanton Novers. This remote East Anglian settlement was originally an

The Cottage, Swanton Novers. Located in the remote East Anglian village of Swanton Novers, The Cottage was the home of John and Eileen throughout most of the 1940s (courtesy Barry Tomlinson).

estate village for Melton Constable Hall, longtime home of the Astley family. In correspondence with Dorothy L. Sayers, Anthony Gilbert (the pseudonym of detective novelist Lucy Beatrice Malleson), painted a short but colorful print picture of Swanton Novers, based on information received from her friends John and Eileen: "I haven't seen the place but hear it is charming and entirely removed from civilization. There is a Vicar faintly discernible between the beetling boughs of trees and about six cottages of natives. No car, no bus, no road service of any kind and apparently no shops. What an opportunity for the *News of the World* to spread themselves. *CANNIBALISM IN NORFOLK!*" Though noting dryly that it sounded rather as though Street had "deliberately solved the traveling problem by returning out of the way of trains," Dorothy L. Sayers worried: "But how does he get anything to eat?" While this portrait of the rural isolation of Swanton Novers was exaggerated — and the Major evidently found plenty to eat there — as late as 2005 the village was described by Simon Knott as being still unshaken from "feudal" slumbers. "The hills and woodlands encroach; the only sound is the impatient calling of the sheep in the pastures," writes Knott. "The narrow lane from the village twists and dips, and, just before it turns into a sandy track, there is [the church of] St. Edmund. It really feels as if you might fall off the edge of Norfolk if you go any farther."[86]

John and Eileen lived in the high street of the village in a two-story, bow-windowed, Georgian-style house modestly known as "The Cottage." The house boasted a drawing room, dining room and sitting room, as well as three bedrooms and a bathroom, a kitchen and scullery, a conservatory, a boot room, a laundry and a study (the latter room, where John wrote the many books he produced while residing in Swanton Novers, was isolated from most of the rest of the house, being at the end of a wing located to one side of the rear courtyard). On the three acres of grounds was a glasshouse as well as an outbuilding housing a garage, stables and storehouse. While living at The Cottage the Major and Eileen became friends with their neighbors the Neales. Interestingly, given Street's later strongly-voiced criticism of the Labor party in his novels, Mrs. Lilian V. Neale was a Labor J.P. deeply committed to her party's cause. Mrs. Neale's young granddaughter, Paula, who went to live with her grandparents at this time, recalls that her grandmother expected her "to help address envelopes which contained a message from the Labor candidate and then deliver them to every house in the village." Major Street and Mrs. Neale did not allow any political differences they might have had to get in the way of their friendship, however, and Paula visited John and Eileen every Saturday morning, carrying with her fresh eggs from her grandfather's chickens. Eileen used the eggs in the little cakes she baked for Paula, a few years later teaching the child, to her delight, how to make cakes herself. During each of her Saturday visits, the Major would leave his study and take a walk to the local public house, The Bell, the time and length of his visits never varying. Paula recalled Street as a large man "but in my eyes so gentle and quiet." A longtime motoring enthusiast, the Major made a great impression on Paula when he showed the child his and Eileen's newly purchased Armstrong-Siddeley model. Eileen, a slim and elegant lady, had a great fondness for cats, treating them rather like the children she never had. The Major resultantly developed a great familiarity with the animals that he put to good use in two of his novels, *The Corpse in the Car* and *The Cat Jumps*. After the war, the Streets enjoyed again taking cruises, including one in 1950 to the Caribbean.[87]

With the exception of Anthony Gilbert, who managed to find her way to Swanton

John Street and Eric the Skull. A former electrical engineer, John Street wired the eye sockets of Eric the Skull, the Detection Club mascot, to glow blood red in the darkness during initiation ceremonies. Dorothy L. Sayers deemed the 1936 photograph, which was taken by John Dickson Carr, "superbly characteristic" of Street (courtesy Douglas G. Greene).

Novers during wartime for occasional visits, Street seems to have seen little or nothing of his Detection Club friends during much of the war. In addition to keeping up his steady pace of writing, Street may have been involved in Home Guard activities in Swanton Novers (his Home Guard mystery, *Night Exercise*— the only non-series John Rhode mystery novel after 1925 — is extremely detailed in its depiction of this organization). Although John Dickson Carr described Street as his "greatest friend" from the Club, he and his wife Clarice appear never to have visited with the Major and Eileen after the older couple left Kent ("John Carr ... is the world's worst correspondent," complained Anthony Gilbert in a letter to Dorothy L. Sayers in 1941. "Even the Rhodes never hear from him now."). Before the war, Street was quite involved in Detection Club activities, motoring up to London for Club dinners, where alcohol tended to flow abundantly. Certainly Street could drink his share, and more. The bibulous Carr admiringly recalled watching the Major "polish off ten pints of beer before lunch, and more than that after dinner." But apparently Street was a generous treater as well. In the Detection Club Suggestion Book, Anthony Gilbert humorously wrote: "Suggest that when we go out we should not allow John Rhode [as he was known within the Club] to buy *all* the drinks."[88]

John Street contributed more to the Detection Club in the thirties and forties than generous rounds of drinks. With what Douglas Greene has aptly termed his "technical wizardry," the former electrical engineer was able to wire the Club's mascot, Eric the Skull, so that Eric's eyes would glow a bright blood red during membership initiation ceremonies.[89] Street also participated in the Detection Club's profit-seeking publishing ventures: the novels *The Floating Admiral* and *Ask a Policeman*; the true crime study *The Anatomy of Murder;* and the anthology *Detection Medley*. With the latter volume, Street accepted the job of editor, which left him the onerous task of collecting contributions from the Club's far-flung and not easily herded membership.

Over the summer of 1939, Street corresponded with Dorothy L. Sayers about his triumphs and tribulations with *Detection Medley*. In his first letter in this exchange, Street, who had notoriously crabbed handwriting, requested Sayers with mock resignation to "observe that, in deference to loud and sustained protests, I have taken to one of these infernal machines [a typewriter]." A week later Street reported that he had had some success and "even roped in [Hugh] Walpole and [A.A.] Milne." He could not, however, locate "that mysterious individual Mrs. Victor Rickard," who was a founding member of the Club from 1930 but had been little seen or heard of since. Street sent Sayers an additional missive the next day, after receiving "another dead letter this morning [R.C.] Woodthorpe this time." He grumpily suggested "a rule that people who do not keep the Secretary informed of their addresses should cease to be members." Finally Street decided to set June 30 as the closing date for contributions, extending the deadline so that he might catch a few additional "valuable fish," like the Baroness Orczy, famous author of the Man in the Corner detective stories and *The Scarlet Pimpernel*. In July, he was ready to think about a title, and he asked Sayers to set her "brilliant brain to work" on the matter. "Remember," he added, "the contributions are not all stories. And we want something snappy." Whether or not Sayers had been forthcoming, six weeks later Street was not happy with the title suggestions he had received, which included the precious *Detective's Ditty-bag*, *Detection Pie*, and *Here's to Jack Ketch*, the clichéd *Murder Will Out*, and the banal *Murder: In Fact and Fancy* and *Tales and Essays in Murder and Detection*.

"I can't say that I am personally in love with any of them," reflected Street. Finally, he went with a different title, *Detection Medley*. Yet one more problem arose in the fall, when the publisher, Hutchinson's, failed to include the names of all the contributors on the book jacket. "The jacket!" exclaimed a horrified Street to Sayers, "My dear, if you only knew the commotion that I ... have kicked up about that jacket." Finally, however, *Detection Medley* made it to print. Street told Sayers that in the end he was "quite pleased with the book and particularly proud of having extracted that most excellent introduction from [A.A. Milne]."[90]

During the 1930s Street also provided technical assistance for detective novels by his friends John Dickson Carr and Dorothy L. Sayers. As John Rhode, Street actually received co-authorship credit for John Dickson Carr's *Drop to His Death/Fatal Descent* (1939), though Street's contribution to the book likely was limited to providing the clever murder method used to dispose of a man descending alone in a closed elevator. Though Street did not receive any share of authorial credit for Sayers' *Have His Carcase* (1932), Sayers did give "grateful acknowledgements" to "Mr. John Rhode" for the "generous help" he had given her "with all the hard bits." Among these "hard bits" in this superb novel certainly is the exceedingly thorny Playfair Cipher solved by Lord Peter (about which Sayers and Street corresponded at this time) and quite possibly as well additional elements of the murderer's plot — surely one of the most complex in all detective fiction.[91]

In addition to his 1930s book collaborations, Street figured as the inspiration for John Dickson Carr's fictional detective "Colonel March" in a series of clever stories Carr published between 1938 and 1941. According to Douglas Greene, both Colonel March's "personality and physical appearance" were based on Major Street. Carr describes March as a "large amiable man (weight seventeen stone) with a speckled face, an interested blue eye, and a very short pipe projecting from under a cropped moustache which might be sandy or grey," a description which matches the 1930 Howard Coster photo of Street. Professor Greene notes that Colonel March "is fond of working out all sorts of puzzles" and possesses a great "fund of useless information."[92] Colonel March puts these qualities to good use as the head of Scotland Yard's Department D-3, the Department of Queer Complaints; while Major Street wrote detective novels with devilishly queer killings.

After World War II, Street remained active in the Detection Club for a few more years, and during this time he continued to believe in offering creative assistance to a fellow author. Michael Gilbert, admitted to the Detection Club in 1949, never met Street, but Christianna Brand, who became a Club member a few years earlier in 1946, remembered Street well. Nearly forty years after the event, she particularly recalled Street's offer to her when he heard she was suffering from writer's block: "My dear, come down to my place — I've got rows and rows of my books, look though them and use one of my plots, you're most welcome." Brand, a new author and still a dewy innocent where mystery series publishing was concerned, "nearly fainted" at the idea of borrowing an old master's plot, generous as the offer was.[93]

By the late forties, when Street invited Christianna Brand to rummage for a plot through the "rows and rows" of his books, Street had published over four score of crime novels, unveiling before enthralled readers *Dead Men at the Folly*, *Tragedy on the Line*, *Peril at Cranbury Hall*, *Murders in Praed Street* and *Mystery at Olympia*. *Death*, seemingly omnipresent, was to be found lurking *at the Crossroads, at the Club, at Breakfast, at Low*

Tide and *at the Helm*, as well as *in the Tunnel, in the Hopfields, in Harley Street*, and *on the Boat Train*. It is no wonder that by this time much of the zest was departing from Street's books, with narrative performances becoming ever more rote. Indeed, by this time, according to Freeman Wills Crofts, Street was reeling off his customary four books year into a Dictaphone, doing little subsequent revision after his typist had typed them. Even in the Street-admiring *Catalogue of Crime*, we see this admission in the capsule review of 1947's *Nothing but the Truth*: "Rhode now goes at his plots like a contractor; the deliberate laying out of equipment on ground carefully surveyed generates a powerful tediousness."[94]

A nostalgic note entered Rhode's work in the early forties, perhaps suggesting a realization on Street's part that much of his best work lay behind him. In 1941's *Death at the Helm*, we learn that Hugh Quarrenden, the famous barrister whose wife is found dead aboard the yacht *Lonicera* at the beginning of the novel, defended not only the boat train murderer of the recent *Death on the Boat Train* (1940), but also the murderer in *The Corpse in the Car* (1935). Street makes another reference to *The Corpse in the Car* later that year in *They Watched by Night* when he has an amateur criminologist recall to Inspector Waghorn "the case of the old lady who was found dead in her car in Windsor Great Park."[95] And in *Dead on the Track* (1943), Superintendent Hanslet is able to discover the true cause of death of a murder victim by recollecting a deduction made by Dr. Priestley fully a dozen years earlier in *Tragedy on the Line* (1931).

While much of Street's wartime crime fiction bears comparison with his best thirties work, in general postwar John Rhode novels show an increasingly steep decline in quality. Postwar Rhodes are monotonously cut from an identical narrative pattern. Inspector (soon Superintendent) Jimmy Waghorn is put in charge of a murder investigation, most often in a rural or provincial town setting. Several times throughout the story, Jimmy attends Saturday dinners at Dr. Priestley's house, afterwards thrashing out his current case with a trio of old men, the retired ex-superintendent Hanslet, the virtually retired Dr. Mortimer Oldland (a character introduced in 1933's *The Claverton Mystery*) and of course Priestley himself. A nearly mute and mostly vestigial (as far as any relation to plot goes) Harold Merefield takes notes and attends Dr. Priestley. Eventually Jimmy solves the case, aided with a hint here and there from the increasingly perfunctorily-employed, somnolent and desk-bound Professor. All this can make for wearying narratives, even when the problem offered in a particular book is a clever one. For example, of *Death in Harley Street*— a book cited in some sources as Street's masterpiece among John Rhode novels — Anthony Boucher noted that its author had offered the public "one of the year's most ingenious criminal plots" (how an unnatural death could be neither accident nor suicide nor murder) but sadly buried it "in endless static talk." Even Barzun and Taylor are quite harsh in their comments on some of the Rhode books from this period, particularly of titles from the late 1950s and early 1960s: "Routine stuff" (*Three Cousins Die*, 1959); "The dullest conceivable Rhode.... Well-nigh unreadable" (*The Fatal Pool*, 1960); "dull in the extreme" (*The Vanishing Diary*, 1961). So it is no wonder that Julian Symons, reviewing the uninspired *Three Cousins Die* (1959) in the *Sunday Times*, proclaimed John Rhode England's reigning "master of the humdrum" (Freeman Wills Crofts having expired two years previously).[96]

Nevertheless, there are notable bright spots among the post–World War II John Rhode titles, particularly in the late forties into the early fifties. *The Telephone Call* (1948)

John Rhode

John Rhode's list of detective stories grows and grows, and so does the public's appetite for his particular blending of humdrum everyday life with the startling appearance of the most curious kind of crimes. It was the Sunday Times who said of John Rhode that "he must hold the record for the invention of ingenious forms of murder". And The Times Literary Supplement describes him as "standing in the front rank of those who write detective fiction". Many of his books have been chosen by The Star as Thrillers of the Month.

is a realistic, police procedural reconstruction of the Julia Wallace murder case of 1931, one of England's most notorious unsolved crimes. The Wallace case clearly fascinated Street, who made several references to it four years earlier in *Vegetable Duck*; and in *The Telephone Call* the author fashioned an intriguing and sober fictionalized study of this baffling and frustrating mystery, suggesting a motive for the crime rooted in sexual infidelity. Another Rhode novel from this period, *Death at the Dance* (1952), offers a clever plot with, unusual for Street, a hard-to-spot murderer and motive, as well as an appealing rural setting: a mysterious, Hardyesque landscape of abandoned nineteenth-century tin mines, known as the "Enchanted Land." Other Rhode tales from this period that are of interest include the psychologically bleak and scientifically astute *The Lake House* (1946), where Dr. Priestley leaves his house to visit the titular lake house and conclude the case with a flourish by giving the last of his bravura scientific expositions; *The Paper Bag* (1948), a tale of an insidious murders-for-hire conspiracy; *Blackthorn House* (1949), a complex case involving murder, arson and the activities of a stolen car ring in austerity England; *The Two Graphs* (1950), which sees Rhode successfully returning to the teasing twins theme he had previously mined in *The Robthorne Mystery* (1934); *The Secret Meeting* (1951), which invokes the Cold War and has an aged Priestley briefly emerging from his abode (with the aid of the strong arm of Harold Merefield) to personally investigate the scene of one of the crimes; and *Death at the Inn* (1953) (more imaginatively retitled *The Case of the Forty Thieves* in the United States), concerning a clever criminal pilfering operation.

Four novels from the late 1940s and early 1950s — *The Telephone Call, Blackthorn House, The Paper Bag* and *Death at the Inn* — reflect an original element in the Rhode novels of this period: the influence of the burgeoning postwar police procedural crime novel subgenre. In the first two of these novels, Street pays so much attention to professional investigative apparatus that Dr. Priestley, heretical as it may be to say, seems incidental to the main action. In *Blackthorn House*, for example, Priestley does little until the very end of the tale, when he rises from his chair at Westbourne Terrace to interview a couple of suspects and more or less intuit the solution. The investigative legwork, which proves quite interesting, belongs to Jimmy Waghorn and other policemen. Despite the lack of true ratiocination on Dr. Priestley's's part, the novel was praised for its up-to-datedness by Anthony Boucher, while an English reviewer raved that its plot was "amazingly ingenious and [its] denouement well-delayed and convincing."[97]

In addition to their intricate criminal schemes both *The Paper Bag* and *The Case of the Forty Thieves* boast interesting poisoning murders. [**SPOILER ALERT**] In *Death at the Inn*, the murderer contrives the death that takes place at the Ariadne Inn by dropping a cocktail cherry impregnated with the poison Deltagon into his victim's mixed vermouth ("Some people have unusual tastes," comments Dr. Priestley dryly on being informed the victim's preference in drinks).[98] In *The Paper Bag*, a nefarious "Murders, Incorporated" style criminal organization steals poisons for use in devising contract murders of various undesired individuals. One murderee, a chronic alcoholic, is disposed of with methanol-

Opposite: John Street in the 1950s. Street continued to produce four detective novels a year in the 1950s, even as his inspiration began waning, giving rise for the first time in his career to the "humdrum" appellation. Even the publisher of John Rhode novels at this time referred to the author's portrayal of "humdrum everyday life."

tainted whisky, so that his death is first taken to be merely the result of accidental alcohol poisoning. Another victim, a huntsman who died after eating "high game" (rather putrid partridge) is assumed to be a casualty of food poisoning, but in reality succumbed to the poison doryl, which the murderer had added to the gravy in the gravy boat. Reference is made in the book to wartime plans by the Nazis to poison members of the invading Allied armies with doryl injected into sausages and methanol added to alcoholic beverages, indicating that Street had remained alert to the newest poisoning methods of the most advanced modern murderers. [**END SPOILER ALERT**]

The plot gambit of *The Paper Bag*, which involves the investigation of two seemingly unrelated murders that turn out to connect, is one used again by Street in probably his best post-war Rhode novel, *Family Affairs* (1950). In this impressively-constructed tale, the first murder to confront Jimmy Waghorn is that of a brewer's traveler, Edward Drayton, who is found dead in a wrecked car, his face badly cut by the smashed windshield, with all the money he had collected from inns that day missing from his vehicle. The last man to have seen Drayton traveling in his car is Warbling Willie, the local wandering "diddy," (slang for diddikai, or gypsy), whose nickname comes from the tin whistle on which he plays. Naturally Willie attracts some police suspicion, of theft at least, but a search of his caravan and the nearby wood fails to yield the missing money. Attention focuses on the woman Willie saw in Edward Drayton's car immediately before it crashed. A woman's grey suede glove, soaked in drying blood, is discovered between the two front seats of the smashed car, but the woman herself seems to have vanished. The deceased Edward Drayton was a son of the wealthy brewer Aylmer Drayton, and it comes to appear that the motive for Edward's murder, if murder it is, may have arisen from, as Dr. Priestley suggests, a family affair, with the theft of the money from Drayton's car being merely a murderer's blind. Jimmy, however, is unable to bring the case to a conclusion.

Eight months later, Jimmy is sent to investigate another fatal "family affair," this time the death of Sir Leonard Tamar at Mingley House on the night of his birthday. Sir Leonard was found by his son dead in his study behind a locked door, "his face spotted with little clots of dried blood, which had oozed from a number of small punctures" made from a light bulb that had fallen from a ceiling pendant over the table at which Sir Leonard had been sitting.[99] Oddly, the French window to the study was closed, though Sir Leonard liked fresh air on a warm evening, such as was the evening of his birthday. Additionally, a bundle of bank notes is missing from the study. Is this a case of theft, or is it, as Jimmy and Priestley suspected with the death of Edward Drayton, a family affair, with the theft merely acting as a blind?

Whatever the motives might have been, Priestley is able to suggest how the deaths of Edward Drayton and Sir Leonard Tamar might both have been murder. [**SPOILER ALERT**] In both cases, notes the Professor, "there is a mention of broken glass." In both cases a murderer could have projected into the faces of his victims a poisoned glass splinter. In the case of Drayton, any facial wounds would have been explained by the smashed windshield of the wrecked car, while in the case of Tamar, the murderer might have resorted to breaking the light bulb from the ceiling pendant and driving the glass splinters from it into Tamar's face, so that the wound from the poisoned splinter would be effectively hidden. Priestley then proceeds to give a hint to Jimmy: "You may retain some dim memory of the arithmetical problems of your schooldays. You were set the task of discovering the Highest Common Factor between two numbers.... I would recommend you to apply your own brain to a search for a common factor between these two cases. It may prove to be higher than you expect."[100]

Jimmy eventually tumbles to the truth: the Highest Common Factor is the diddy Warbling Willy, who was present in both areas when the crimes occurred. The motive for the two murders indeed was theft — family affairs they precisely were not. Willy killed both Drayton and Tamar with a blow-pipe that he had picked up on a Brazilian sojourn (as Jimmy observes, Willy did not use all his breath on his tin whistle). The mystery woman seen with Drayton was Willie's fabrication, one that, impressively, took in not only Jimmy but Dr. Priestley as well. Forced to acknowledge "initial error," the Professor reflects: "The crime was obscured by its very simplicity."[101]

As far as readers are concerned, the crime also is obscured by Street's having cleverly played a typical reader's assumption against him, namely the assumption that a simple diddy in a classical British mystery would be incapable of devising ingenious murders. To the typical genre reader a diddy would be, to borrow a term from John Dickson Carr, below suspicion. In Golden Age British detective fiction, "passing tramps" often are accused of murders, but it is a rare book indeed when one such tramp actually does the dirty deed. Unfortunately, Street somewhat spoils the pleasant effect of seeing a social inferior contrive clever killings by revealing that Warbling Willie actually is one William Blackburn, whose father "had a flourishing business of some kind in the Midlands" and sent his son to "one of the minor public schools"— proving once again the murderous utility in British mystery of decent birth and a public school education.[102] **[END SPOILER ALERT]**

Humbler murder victims in a humbler setting are found in *Licensed for Murder* (1958), the best of Street's mostly tedious succession of late John Rhode books (another title worth mentioning is 1954's *The Dovebury Murders*, though it is marred by Superintendent Waghorn's extreme obtuseness in grasping a rather obvious point). Tellingly, Anthony Boucher, who often could be extremely dismissive of Street's work at this time, praised *Licensed for Murder* rather highly: "The detection is competent; the murders have ingenuity and novelty to recommend them; and the background details on the management of a village inn are fascinating. Slow and heavy, but kind of nice." Similarly, *A Catalogue of Crime* makes positive note of *Licensed for Murder*'s "ingenious plot."[103]

Anthony Boucher was acutely discerning in his observations on this novel. Its murder plot is one of Street's cleverest and the late-1950s declining rural inn setting is done with conviction and authenticity, reflecting in plain prose the author's over half-century familiarity with public houses and his old artillerist's fascination with geography and landscape. *Licensed for Murder* opens with the managing director of Hinkley's Brewery, Mr. Godstow, learning that the elderly tenants of the Knapper's Arms plan shortly to give up the tenancy of the inn, one they have held for twenty-nine years. Godstow fears that finding new tenants will prove a stiff challenge:

> The Knapper's Arms was certainly not an attractive proposition. A century ago Famford had been a flourishing center of the flint-knapping industry.... But the industry had long since ... come to an end. The population of the straggling village had decreased, and now consisted almost entirely of laborers on the surrounding farms.... How was a tenant to be found for such

a house as the Knapper's Arms? ... the property included six acres of land, enough for a small-holding. But it wasn't everybody who would be attracted by the prospect of serving in the bar during opening hours and working on the land for the rest of the day.... Electricity had been laid on during the past five years, but water still had to be pumped by hand from a well, and there was no bathroom. The only available public transport was the bus service along the main road between Maltchester and Whitby.[104]

Godstow drives to Famford to get a look for himself at the lie of the land, which he finds, as he expected, unpromising:

From Hall Farm the village of Famford was hidden by an intervening hill. But when Godstow had driven to the crest of this, the village lay spread out before him: the flint-built church, with its squat tower; the vicarage; a few scattered cottages; and in the centre of all the Knapper's Arms. It was large for a village inn and by no means attractive in appearance. A central block built of brick, with a roof of blue slate. To this additions had been made from time to time, built of flint or of the local stone. The whole effect was ugly and without symmetry. Godstow could imagine a prospective tenant shuddering at first sight of it.[105]

Despite his doubts about the prospects of leasing the Knapper's Arms, Godstow is able to find an interested couple, the Bilstons. Surprisingly, the Bilstons are Londoners who want to give up their city jobs and live in the country, confounding Godstow's prediction that "No Londoner would ever take the Knapper's Arms." After a couple weeks when the Knapper's Arms is left untenanted, the Bilstons take up occupancy. Not unexpectedly, the locals — such as Mr. Kensal and his wife, the owners of Hall Farm, and the agricultural laborers who work for them — feel the Bilstons don't quite fit in at Famford. As Kensal tells his wife after first meeting the Bilstons: "A more unlikely couple to settle down at the Knapper's Arms, I can't imagine.... I'm not very greatly taken with him. He's got a superior way I don't like.... As for the woman.... I can't believe that her true vocation is to become the landlady of a village pub.... If she makes the chaps feel that they are her inferiors, they'll take to going to the Blue Boar. They don't like people who put on airs." This concern, however, is soon forgotten in the excitement that ensues when Mr. Bilston, taking down sheets of corrugated iron that had been put up over the inn's great, disused stone fireplace, discovers "a charred and utterly unrecognizable human form."[106] Cause of death cannot be determined, but murder looks likely and Superintendent Waghorn is called in on the case. It is assumed that the body was placed in the fireplace and burned during the period between tenancies, but, since the identity of the corpse cannot be definitely established, Jimmy finds his going very rough, even after a consultation with Dr. Priestley.

[SPOILER ALERT] During this time, Mrs. Bilston's widowed uncle, Richard Snape, a retired builder's foreman, decides to come and live with the Bilstons and help them with improvements they want to make on the Knapper's Arms. Unlike his niece and nephew, Snape becomes a popular fixture among the inn *clientele*, but regrettably he dies only a few months after moving to the Knapper's Arms from a cold that rapidly worsens into pneumonia. To her expressed shock, Mrs. Bilston inherits some twenty-five to thirty thousand pounds from her uncle, who had won big in a football pool several years earlier. Snape had a son, Fred; but he, a scapegrace, had been disinherited by his father. However, as Snape's attorney tells Jimmy, the retired builder's attitude toward Fred had been "that of the father of the Prodigal Son."[107] Had a penitent Fred returned to his father, he would have been reinstated in the will.

Spurred onward by Dr. Priestley, Jimmy eventually discovers what turn out to be two key facts: that Fred Snape had been released from prison shortly before the Bilstons took the tenancy of the Knapper's Arms and that Richard Snape had taken cortisone for a rheumatic complaint. Once treated with cortisone, a patient, Jimmy learns, must be treated with it again after contracting even a minor ailment, such as a cold, or otherwise the normally minor ailment could prove fatal. Suddenly the sequence becomes clear. Having found that their relation had won a fortune in the pools, the Bilstons determined to get that money for themselves. With the Knapper's Arms carefully selected as the ideal site for their first crime, the Bilstons successfully lured a credulous Fred Snape to the empty inn upon his release from prison, murdered him and burned his body in the ample fireplace. Soon afterward, they took up their tenancy at the inn, and Mr. Bilston "discovered" the charred corpse. With Fred out of the way, his father could be invited to live with his loving niece and nephew-in-law, who could make sure that when Uncle inevitably caught a cold, he would not get his vital cortisone treatment.

Street presents us with a clever crime plot indeed in *Licensed for Murder*, but its very cleverness is the book's undoing. Unable to obtain evidence that could credibly lead to the Bilstons' convictions for their despicable acts, Street resorts to having Mr. Bilston implausibly betray himself and his wife during a browbeating (and surely illegal) interrogation from Jimmy. [**END SPOILER ALERT**]. This is a rather unsatisfactory turn of events, but Street at least gives Dr. Priestley the novel's final words, which are characteristically scolding of the mental lapses of a representative of the law:

"And what do you think about it all, Priestley?"
"I think that if Jimmy had not allowed himself to be misled by appearances, he would have solved his problem considerably earlier."[108]

Besides providing a good puzzle, *Licensed for Murder* offers readers a glimpse of the changed landscape of even traditional English mystery in the 1950s. In *Family Affairs*, published eight years earlier, Street had noted that, due to "crushing taxation" that had "reduced revenues almost to vanishing point," Sir Leonard Tamar had been forced to put his family estate, Craymore Park, on the market and retire to live on a smaller property, Mingley House. Late in the novel Jimmy views the unoccupied dwelling house at Craymore Park and sees in it the passing of an era: "It was large and imposing, of the early Georgian period. But it had a desolate and untended appearance, as though its former glories had departed. No smoke came from any of its countless chimneys, and the windows were closed and shuttered."[109] *Licensed for Murder* has no settings of baronets and country houses, only of smallholders and laborers. Even the owners of Hall Farm, the Kensals, are plain, practical people, who concern themselves not with planning house parties for weekending society ladies and men-about-town, but rather with workaday matters like scrubbing eggs and spraying sugar-beets. Moreover, the ex–London, pub-purchasing couple, the Bilstons, come from decidedly unglamorous background—he a male nurse in a mental home and she a manager of the drapery section of a department store—while Richard Snape began his working life as a greengrocer. With *Licensed for Murder*, we are far removed from the glamorous, sophisticated English country house murders of stereotype.

Part Three: Miles Burton

To return from 1958's *Licensed for Murder* to the inception of John Street's "Miles Burton" novels in 1930 is to plunge back into the stereotyped setting of pre–World War II British mystery (the Miles Burton pseudonym may combine a play on Street and Rhode in the word "Miles" with a borrowing from Street's daughter's birthplace, the tiny Lincolnshire village of Gate Burton — customarily shortened to Burton). The Dr. Priestley novels having established "John Rhode" as one of the foremost exponents of British detection, Street appears initially to have envisioned his Miles Burton line of tales as thrillers in the manner of the hugely popular English crime writer Edgar Wallace. Street soon seems to have tired of the thriller form in the Burton line (as he did with the early Rhode thrillers), however; yet he continued publishing Burtons as straight detective novels. So prolific of plot devices was the author that he found he regularly could write at least four true detective novels a year. Unfortunately, publishers did not wish to publish four mystery novels a year by any single author. In 1936, for example, Street's American publisher, Dodd, Mead, turned down the Rhode novel *In Face of the Verdict*, in part because they thought it "not quite up to the author's standard" but mostly because, as they complained, "Mr. Rhode is writing more books than we can possibly publish." Dodd, Mead allowed that they might annually "publish three but couldn't promise more than two"— and four simply was out of the question. By establishing a second line of mysteries under the Miles Burton name, Street helped make sure that publishers could accommodate his seemingly endless procession of detective novels.[110]

In contrast with most of the later Burtons, both *The Hardway Diamonds Mystery* and *The Secret of High Eldersham*, published in 1930, are pure thrillers, with criminal organizations boasting "master brains" and heroes and heroines put in peril of their lives. The first of these novels, *The Hardway Diamonds Mystery*, is an entertaining pastiche of the genre. Who is behind the rash of daring jewel thefts, most recently including the celebrated Hardway Diamonds? That ingenious criminal brain, the "Funny Toff," it seems, but the police are unable to get near him. In desperation Assistant Commissioner of Scotland Yard Sir Edric Conway turns to young Dick Penhampton, a family friend and the brother-in-law of Lord Hardway himself. "Very few people guessed that behind the blasé air of the man about town," Street informs us, "was a keen and tireless brain, and energy carefully conserved for anything worth doing." Sir Edric Conway, apparently having despaired of the ability of the vast array of professionals within his own Department, tells Dick that "it's brain-power we want, if we are to circumvent the Funny Toff." Ever compliant and with time to spare, Dick goes to work on the case. In this endeavor he naturally is aided by his ever-ready "man," Jerry Gould, who, we learn with no great surprise, had devotedly served Dick throughout the Great War, "and was almost more a trusted friend than a servant" (almost). Eventually Dick discovers what most readers likely suspected on page forty-six of the British edition: **[SPOILER ALERT]** that, in yet another coincidence (this one staggeringly unlikely), the master criminal brain is no less than Dr. Weathersleigh, "that distinguished antiquary" and father of Dick's fiancée, Alison. Love conquers all, of course, and eventually, after Dr. Weathersleigh meets his demise in a climactic confrontation with law enforcement, Alison and Dick marry, retiring to a "beautiful old house" where the loyal Jerry Gould "is constantly in attendance upon them."[111] **[END SPOILER ALERT]**

Miles Burton, *The Hardway Diamonds Mystery* (1930). As this dust jacket certainly suggests, the Miles Burton series of novels began as thrillers.

Later in 1930, Street took many of the same clichéd ingredients from *The Hardway Diamonds Mystery*— the amiable amateur of independent means and his loyal "man," the sinister conspiracy, the criminal brain, the lovely daughter of a distinguished father — and folded them into a much more original tale, *The Secret of High Eldersham*. This novel stands out amid the many forgettable formula thrillers of its time in its strongly-conveyed rural setting and in its colorful use of the witchcraft theme. *Eldersham* also is notable for its introduction of amateur investigator Desmond Merrion, who after 1932 would serve as Miles Burton's sole series detective and eventually appear in a total of fifty-nine Miles Burton novels — making him a near rival, at least in terms of number of appearances, with Street's other, more famous detective, Lancelot Priestley.

Desmond Merrion, we learn in *The Secret of High Eldersham*, is "a bachelor of independent and very considerable means." Like Street, he served in World War I, first in the armed services, then, after being wounded, in military intelligence. However, Merrion was in the Royal Naval Volunteer Reserve rather than the Royal Artillery and the intelligence branch of the Admiralty rather than the M17b. In the latter capacity Merrion met Inspector Young of the Yard, impressing the latter man as "a living encyclopedia upon all manner of obscure subjects." The two kept up their friendship after the War, with Young often visiting Merrion's "luxurious rooms in Mayfair" to solicit his friend's help in unraveling the more tangled criminal matters that happened to come his way.[112]

Tangled as a cat's cradle is the strange affair at High Eldersham, where the publican of the Rose and Crown, ex-policeman Samuel Whitehead, has been found brutally murdered. Summoned to the backwater East Anglian village to investigate the case, Inspector Young comes to suspect, to his bemusement, that locally-practiced witchcraft may have bearing on the matter, and he seeks investigative aid from his friend Merrion, the "living encyclopedia on all subjects." The two friends, along with Merrion's steadfast man, the old ex-sailor Newport ("You can trust Newport," explains Merrion at one point. "He was with me all though the war, and I've had him ever since") soon find themselves confronting a local coven that is very active indeed.[113] Eventually Merrion and Young discover a link between the witch coven at High Eldersham and a drug-smuggling operation, and they are able by novel's end to resolve criminal and heretical matters alike in a manner both thrilling and logically satisfying to the reader.

The amiable and appealing Inspector Young regrettably appears in only one more Miles Burton novel, *The Three Crimes*, but Desmond Merrion after *Eldersham* settles down to a three decades long career of amateur crime investigation. At the end of *Eldersham* the ex–Navy man marries Mavis Owerton, daughter of the local squire, Sir William Owerton of High Eldersham Hall. Sir William dies within a few months of the marriage, leaving Merrion as the master of the Hall, which he uses as his base when not towning it in Mayfair with Newport in tow. For nearly two decades Mavis herself remains contentedly in the background, typically off visiting friends when a case comes up for Desmond, leaving her husband a free hand for dabbling in detection. Beginning with *Heir to Lucifer* (1947), however, Mavis makes occasional appearances again in the novels, typically in some gentrified seaside resort at which she and Desmond are vacationing, where murder has the poor taste to put in an appearance.

For his Miles Burton series, Street clearly fashioned his presiding investigator from the Lord Peter Wimsey gentleman amateur detective mold. By the time Desmond Merrion debuted in 1930, Dorothy L. Sayers' Lord Peter had appeared in four highly successful detective novels and a short story collection, establishing the aristocratic sleuth as a popular and colorful creation. Befitting the more restrained writing style of Street, Merrion is a far less memorable (positively or negatively) character than Lord Peter. However, in addition to independent means, a loyal manservant and a keen brain, Merrion, like Sayers' master detective, is endowed by his creator with an ever-ready stock of flippancies, as can be seen in these excerpts of his repartee with Young's successor, Inspector Arnold, and with Assistant Commissioner of Scotland Yard Sir Edric Conway:

> "Don't you ever develop an inflamed imagination, Arnold. It will give you far more trouble than an enlarged heart or a floating kidney, or even an ingrown toenail."
>
> "By Jove, Arnold, it's lucky you didn't choose [to drink from] the [poisoned] rum decanter! There would have been the sound of revelry by night in the underworld if one of the leading lights of the Yard had been suddenly removed by the hand of Providence."
>
> "Oh, come off it!" Conway exclaimed. "You're not going to repeat all that Balder nonsense again, are you?"
>
> "Balderdash, you might have said."[114]

More facetious than forbidding, Desmond Merrion also differs from Street's other famous detective, Dr. Priestley, in that where the Professor frowns on conjecture, Merrion merrily gives free reign to his imagination, much to the friendly derision of Inspector Arnold (who nevertheless usually relies on the amateur detective to solve his cases for him). "Let your imagination work first to propound a likely theory," pronounces Merrion in *Murder in the Coalhole*, "then look for the facts to prove it."[115] One imagines that had Dr. Priestley ever encountered Desmond Merrion, he would not have approved of this brash gentleman of leisure.

Merrion berates Arnold freely throughout the long series of Miles Burton tales, but Arnold — unlike Hanslet and Waghorn in the Priestley series — gives back as good he gets, the two men seemingly enjoying their constant bickering, rather like an old married couple. Merrion frequently derides Arnold for what Merrion sees (usually rightly) as the inspector's lack of imagination. "Why don't you tell me what you're driving at, instead of asking me all these silly questions?" demands Arnold at one point in *Murder in the Coalhole*, to which Merrion responds: "Because it might put ideas into your head, and that would probably be fatal." For his part, Arnold frequently scoffs at what he sees (usually wrongly) as Merrion's overactive imagination. Later in *Murder in the Coalhole*, when Merrion crows about one of his conjectures proving to be correct, Arnold does not hesitate to rebuke the effusively imaginative amateur detective: "Oh shut up! You've had so many contradictory ideas in this business that one of them was bound to be right."[116]

A Catalogue of Crime contends that the Burton tales "tend to be wittier and less dependent on mechanical devices, as well as more concerned with scenery and character" than the Rhodes. Apart from the Burtons being less dependent on mechanical devices than the Rhodes, this contrast is overstated. In his own acerbic way, Dr. Priestley is as witty a figure as the facetious Merrion, and scenery and character can be more interesting in the Rhodes than in the Burtons (for example, *The Bloody Tower* and *Death at the Helm*, John Rhode titles discussed at greater length below, have stronger depictions of, respectively, scenery and character than most Burtons). Certainly Burton tales like *Death in the Tunnel* (1936), *Death at the Club* (1937) and *Death Takes a Flat* (1940) take place in settings that are, as the bland titles indicate, about as generic as one might find anywhere within the genre at this time. A *New York Times* book review of *Death in the Tunnel*, a novel *A Catalogue of Crime* finds "a most readable affair," highlights this quality of blandness: "The story holds little physical action, no adventurous excitement, no romance, very little atmosphere, and nothing that could be described as charm. What slight picturesqueness it offers us lies wholly in the fact that its background is English" (this latter aspect presumably offered little picturesque impact for English readers). In his review in the *Sunday Times*, Milward Kennedy similarly emphasized the novel's flatness, complaining of its characters that "one has to take it for granted that they may have done or do whatever Mr. Burton chooses — one can form no estimate of one's own."[117] However, several of the Miles Burton titles admittedly are among Street's most colorful and engaging, with one, *Murder M.D.* being probably Street's single best written novel under any pseudonym.

Novels by Miles Burton most typically have village and provincial town settings (*The Secret of High Eldersham*, *The Menace on the Downs*, *Fate at the Fair*, *Death at the Crossroads*, *The Charabanc Mystery*, *Murder of a Chemist*, *Where Is Barbara Prentice?*, *Murder in Crown Passage* and many more), yet these settings are not unknown in the John Rhode books as well (*Mystery at Greycombe Farm* and *Death in the Hopfields* are the two most significant examples). On the whole, however, it is fair to conclude that the Burton titles often offer cozier reads, with more emphasis on village and provincial ways and less emphasis on mechanically complex and scientifically rigorous puzzles. It may well be that Street was aiming with the Miles Burton books at a less stereotypically masculine audience, as the more coldly analytical Rhodes have been dismissed, along with Freeman Wills Crofts' tales, as "men's books really, concerned with timetables and tides and the numbers on tickets and all that." Those preferring scientific and mechanical complexity to cozy settings will find the John Rhode books generally superior to the Burtons. However, from the twenty-year period following the appearance of *The Secret of High Eldersham* certainly a score or so of Burton titles can lay claim to superior puzzles and/or storytelling. Another Burton novel, *Death Takes the Living* (1949), deserves mention, not for its sub-par puzzle ("a very poor tale in which the motive and identity of the criminal are obvious from the beginning," harrumphs *A Catalogue of Crime*), but for its unique position in the Street canon as first and foremost a deliberately-designed critical commentary on British politics.[118] After the 1940s, the Burton novels, like the Rhodes, began declining sharply in quality, becoming of interest primarily as the foci for expressions of the author's growing distaste with life modern Britain. Several late Burtons have merit, however, particularly *Ground for Suspicion* (1950), *Murder in Absence* (1954) and *Bones in the Brickfield* (1958), all of which will be discussed below.

The two 1931 Miles Burton novels immediately following *The Secret of High Eldersham* are in the thriller mold, though both are far poorer in thrills compared with Street's first two Burton efforts. By 1933, however, the Burton books had begun gelling into the form they would take for the rest of the series, with Merrion and Arnold (Arnold very occasionally solo) investigating formal detective problems. The last real thriller in the Burton series is *To Catch a Thief*, which entertainingly places Merrion and Arnold amidst the machinations of two rival jewel thieving crime bosses. In an opening scene similar to that in Dorothy L. Sayers' *The Nine Tailors* (which appeared the same year), car trouble in the wintertime forces Merrion and his man, Newport, to seek shelter in the closest village. Street provides some enjoyable banter between master and servant:

> "What's the date? January 13th, isn't it? Well, let this be a lesson to you to never start out on a long drive on the thirteenth, Newport, my lad."
> "I did pass a remark this morning that the weather looked none too promising, sir...."
> "And now I suppose you're glad this has happened, you damn Jonah! Oh, lord, just look at it, man! There isn't a house in sight, it's freezing like the devil, it's been snowing for the last hour, and it's nearly dark already. Anything else you can think of to cheer us up?"
> "The cover on the spare wheel we've just put on is nearly smooth, sir," replied Newport promptly. "We haven't got any chains with us, or we could put them on."
> "You'd be a jolly companion at a funeral, wouldn't you?" The nearest place of any size seems to be Farley Midsomer.... It's fifteen miles ahead, and it'll probably turn out to be Farley Midwinter when we get there."[119]

Newport plays a large role in the tale, as does Ada Rayburn, a crook's girl turned avenging fury when her man is murdered by one of the crime bosses. After witnessing Ada calmly unload an automatic at the car she believes her enemy is driving, the traditionalist Arnold is apoplectic: "Upon my word, I don't know what you young women are coming to these days!" The more worldly and sophisticated Merrion, who refers to the young woman ironically, in reference to her gun play, as "the ministering Ada," takes a more benign view.[120] Indeed, we learn at the end of *To Catch a Thief* that Merrion actually helped Ada evade Scotland Yard's clutches.

None of the Miles Burton true detective novels from 1932 to 1935 are comparable with the best John Rhodes from the same period, though both *Death of Mr. Gantley* (1932), the first pairing of Merrion and Arnold, and *The Devereux Court Mystery* (1935), an inventive London-based mystery, have definite merit. However, 1936 was the banner Burton year, seeing the publication of a trio of top-line Miles Burton novels, *Death in the Tunnel*, *Murder of a Chemist* and *Where Is Barbara Prentice?* The first of these, *Death in the Tunnel*, was only the third Miles Burton novel selected by Doubleday, Doran and Co. for publication in the United States, though it was the fourteenth novel Street had written under the Burton pseudonym. The tale has divided critics from its publication until more recently, when Barzun and Taylor in *A Catalogue of Crime* (1971) and H.R.F. Keating in *Murder Must Appetize* (1981) sharply differed over the matter of its merit. Some reviewers found it flatly written and colorless while others praised it for having an uncommonly ingenious puzzle. The conclusion of Barzun and Taylor is favorable indeed: "Among railway stories the present tale ranks very high, as it does also among Burton's large output ... a most readable affair." However, Keating, while conceding that the murder in *Death in the Tunnel* was "devilishly ingenious," deemed the tale "run-of-the-mill" and "a comparative dud." In a puckish mood, Keating took time to mock the novel's "thickety prose," its notably stodgy concluding sentence ("They were duly hanged"), and the absence of a spicily "unconventional sex life" on the part of the murder victim, "a bachelor of sixty" (Keating maintained the latter possibility would be something "which almost every crime writer of today would feel bound to pursue, often at length"). Keating's critique perhaps could be set aside as the naturally biased expression of a modern-day aesthetic against an outmoded one, but for the fact that contemporary reviewers made some similar criticisms (though I have found no review that echoed Keating's regret over the novel's failure to provide an "unconventional sex life" for the murderee). Milward Kennedy found *Death *in the Tunnel* characterless, while *New York Times* reviewer Kay Irvin, who actually liked the novel a great deal, believed it lacked atmosphere. What Irvin, as well as another American reviewer, the *New York Herald Tribune's* Will Cuppy, and the British reviewer "Torquemada," who called *Tunnel* Miles Burton's best work, admired about the novel was the mechanics of its meticulous puzzle, which rivals some of the cleverest found in the John Rhode tales. The publisher's blurb in the novel's American edition attempted to mend this critical rift. Emblazoning the dust jacket of *Dark is the Tunnel* (the more evocative American title of *Death in the Tunnel*) with the declaration that the novel was "The Season's Most Baffling Mystery," Doubleday, Doran went on to claim on the inside front flap that "Mr. Burton's plots are the ultimate in bafflement. Though lacking in physical action, his plots are tense with emotional conflict and suspense and move with a celerity which prohibits boredom."[121] Modern readers may miss, as I did, the tense emotional conflict and boredom-prohibiting celerity the writer of the book's plot description discerned, but they should be intrigued, as I was, by a baffling puzzle that does not, in my view, overstay its welcome.

Death in the Tunnel concerns the shooting death of businessman Sir Wilfred Ponsonby in a locked train compartment while the train was traveling through a railway tunnel. "It's a pretty clear case of suicide.... Sir Wilfred was in a locked compartment by himself all the time," announces one investigator; yet Inspector Arnold, first introduced to Miles Burton readers in 1931's *The Menace on the Downs* and investigating cases in tandem with Desmond Merrion since 1932's *Death of Mr. Gantley*, is more experienced with outré Golden Age crime and thus dubious about the suicide theory. "I'm never quite easy in my mind about locked doors," he sagely announces. After naturally turning for enlightenment to his friend Merrion, still "something of an amateur criminologist," the pair are able to discover how the death of Sir Wilfred in the railway tunnel was contrived; and eventually the *how* leads to *why* and *who*. Those responsible for the crime are arrested and, we learn, in the phrase that so amused H.R.F. Keating, "duly hanged."[122]

In its dependence on cardboard ciphers involved in a business conspiracy, *Death in the Tunnel* bears close resemblance to a novel by Freeman Wills Crofts, an author to whom Street is frequently, though somewhat inaccurately, compared. While Keating found the tale dated in its manner of telling, I am more in agreement with Barzun's and Taylor's assessment that the novel is a "most readable affair," with an interesting puzzle and an investigation that moves at a good pace. Moreover, contrary to contentions in some reviews, there is some notable atmosphere conveyed by Street, when, in one memorable chapter, Merrion and Arnold, guided by an intelligent and articulate railway ganger, investigate the tunnel of death itself:

> Up till now there had been a path beside the down line, which, though uncomfortably close to the trains as they roared past, still afforded a measure of safety. But at the entrance to the tunnel the path ended. Thence it was necessary to walk on the permanent way, keeping a sharp lookout for trains, taking to the down line if an up train was heard, and vice versa. Here and there within the tunnel were refuges, caves dug out of the wall in which the three of them could barely crouch. More than once they were forced to seek shelter in one of these, when both an up and a down train approached them simultaneously.
>
> The atmosphere was, in any case, positively suffocating, though the ganger assured them that conditions were extremely favorable. "Why, in some weather you can't see a flare a dozen yards away," he said. "It's tricky work then, I can tell you, gentlemen. You've got to keep your wits about

you, for you know the drivers can't see you any more than you can see them. And as to breathing, you've got to take a mouthful of air when you can and think yourself lucky to get that."

They had a mild taste of this when a heavy goods train came through, steaming hard against the gradient. A torrent of red sparks poured from the funnel of the engine.... As the engine passed, the whirl of disturbed air seemed to snatch at them in an endeavor to drag them under the wheels. Then immediately they were enveloped in a warm clinging murk of steam and sulphurous smoke. The hot cinders descended on the backs of their necks, the trucks roared and clanged past within a few inches of them. Not until the train passed and the air had cleared a little did they venture to leave the refuge in which they had taken shelter.[123]

After leaving the tunnel and drawing deep breaths to cleanse "his lungs of the fumes he had inhaled," Merrion expresses his intense relief to be out of there: "'My word!' he exclaimed. 'That confounded tunnel must be as near an approach to hell as human ingenuity can devise. My classics are getting a bit rusty, but wasn't it Hercules who went down into the infernal regions to rescue his pal's wife?... I never realized before what a plucky chap he must have been. A dozen distressed damsels wouldn't tempt me into that tunnel again.'" Arnold looks at his watch and finds that "it had taken them nearly two hours to traverse the two and a half miles of the tunnel." Admittedly this episode from the novel is a mere vignette, yet in it Street manages to convey his familiarity with — and respect for — the work done by manual laborers. A comparable passage is lacking in two celebrated train mysteries from the period, Agatha Christie's *Murder on the Orient Express* (1934) and Freeman Wills Crofts' *Sir John Magill's Last Journey* (1930).[124]

The other two Miles Burton titles from 1936 — *Murder of a Chemist* and *Where Is Barbara Prentice?* — are entertaining tales that poke fun at the murderous morals of English suburbia. Both novels delighted as keen a critic (and practitioner) of the genre as C. Day Lewis. In addition to some amusing satire, the two tales also offer solid puzzles. That of *Murder of a Chemist* turns on an alibi problem — just who during a coach tour had the opportunity to poison with oxalic acid an unlikable chemist's lemon crush — while the latter trickily deals with that perennially interesting situation, that of the location of a vanished person. Indeed, in *Where Is Barbara Prentice?*, the whereabouts of Barbara Prentice may well elude most readers until the end of the tale. "The secret of what became of Barbara Prentice is so startling and so ingenious that only by superb self-control does the reviewer prevent himself from blurting it out to all the world with the triumphant cry: 'There now, did you ever hear the likes o' that?'" delightedly gushed Street's fellow detective novelist E.R. Punshon, in his review of the novel in the *Manchester Guardian*.[125]

Street produced another well-received Burton title in 1937, with *Death at the Club*. This tale makes nods to both a previous Burton story, *The Secret of High Eldersham*, with the club of the title being the Witchcraft Club, and to Street's own life, with the Witchcraft Club having monthly dinners and speakers, suggesting the practice of the real-life Detection Club. In *Death at the Club*, a corpse with a cut throat is discovered on the premises of the Witchcraft Club, an event that proves embarrassing to one of its thirteen members, Sir Edric Conway, an Assistant Commissioner of Scotland Yard. Conway (who, it will be recalled, was originally introduced into the Miles Burton series in the first Burton novel, *The Hardway Diamonds Mystery*) is in the especially awkward position of having discovered the body himself. Soon enough he calls his friend Merrion into the affair, telling Merrion that he fears Inspector Arnold, who is in charge of the case, could well end up destroying "every clue that would even remotely suggest murder and fabricate others which would prove conclusively that Brockman [the murder victim] committed suicide," if the inspector comes to suspect (wrongly, Conway insists) that he, Conway, might somehow be involved in the death. "The sense of esprit de corps in the force is stronger than you might imagine," Conway avows. Once again Merrion and Arnold enjoyably investigate a murder case in tandem, with Merrion constantly advancing new theories with joyful abandon and Arnold retorting with acerbic comments about Merrion's overly active imagination. "Give my imagination leave to deal with the subsequent adventures of this X," pleads Merrion during a conjectural reconstruction of the activities of the murderer, to which Arnold retorts, "If he exists in your imagination, he'll have some pretty queer adventures."[126] After a police constable guarding the premises of the Witchcraft Club takes a nip from a rum decanter there and is poisoned by conine in the rum, the plot thickens, but Merrion, working out a slender clue, is able to force a decisive and dramatic confrontation with the killer.

Like *Death in the Tunnel*, *Death in the Club* has a series of essentially featureless characters and atmosphere is mostly lacking, despite the fact that the titular Club's interest is in witchcraft. Sir Edric and Merrion both allude to Merrion's earlier experiences in *The Secret of High Eldersham*, but those allusions only serve to remind readers of both novels how dry and academic this later tale is compared with the earlier one. Yet the investigation moves swiftly and interestingly to an exciting finish and there is as well some mildly humorous satire along the way aimed at the patent medicine business. Barzun and Taylor concluded of *Death at the Club* that its author's "management of people, events, clues and interrelations among Sir Edric Conway, Insp. Arnold, and Demond Merrion is masterly throughout," while the contemporary "Dr. Watson" of the *Manchester Evening Chronicle* pronounced the tale "an extremely good problem story, with a splendid trap at the end" before concluding that it belonged on "every fan's library list."[127]

Incorporating espionage elements but nevertheless very much remaining a true detective novel, *The Platinum Cat*, published in 1938, is one the best and most complex of the 1930s Miles Burton novels that followed in the wake of *The Secret of High Eldersham*. It boasts a neat, Rhodeian infernal device, an interesting investigation by an amusingly disputatious Merrion-Arnold team that probes the consequences of adultery and a pleasing twist at the end. Isaac Anderson in the *New York Times* considered *The Platinum Cat* "as neat a baffler as we have encountered in some time," while *A Catalogue of Crime* praises the novel's "fine passages of description and speculation" and adroit use of Norse legend. Merrion puts his knowledge of myth to good use, once again leaving Arnold foundering at sea (it is Merrion, of course, who realizes that "Nanna"— the name of the wife of the Norse god Balder — is a code appellation and not, as Arnold assumes, merely some woman's "pet name").[128]

The Platinum Cat opens with the discovery of a charred body in the smoldering ruins of a fired rural cottage on Lughorse Farm, near the village of Pascombe (locally pronounced Patchum). With the body are a pair of gold cuff-links bearing the initials "J.H.F." and "a lump of metal, very much discolored and at first apparently quite shapeless." This discolored lump of metal reveals itself "as the figure of a cat, about three-quarters of an inch long"— the platinum cat of the title. In the garden outside the ruined cottage is planted a stake, at the head of which is "a withered bunch of foliage"; but this object catches the attention of only the insomniac, Matthew Arnold quoting ("Balder Dead") Pascombe rector, who alerted authorities of the early morning fire. Through means of the initialed cuff-links, police identify the corpse as that of James Henry Fenchurch, a Ministry of Defense employee. Sir Edric Conway finds from the Defense Minister, Lord Hawkenbury, that Fenchurch was one of three people who shared a defense "secret of overwhelming importance ... the key to the co-ordination of the defense of London against aerial attack." Fenchurch's presumed death raises concern over the safety of the air defense secret that Fenchurch shared, particularly after it is learned that the man had the greatest difficulty living within his income, his parents having accustomed him to a high style of living. We also learn in passing that Fenchurch was an exceptionally attractive man, embodying "the popular conception of what the Vikings looked like." Inspector Arnold conducts the investigation but soon Desmond Merrion is called in at the behest of his old friend Sir Edric Conway, as the case turns infernally complicated.[129]

Notable as well are *Death Leaves No Card*, *Mr. Babbacombe Dies* and *Mr. Westerby Missing*, the first two tales published in 1939 and the latter in 1940. *Card* offers a rare (and rather shocking) instance of Inspector Arnold managing to solve a case unaided by a brilliant amateur, Merrion being unable to help him due to an attack of influenza (perhaps Street had come to wonder himself whether one of his police detectives could actually solve a complex crime when thrown on his own devices). In *Card*, Arnold is confronted with quite a sticky problem: how Basil Maplewood came to die of shock in a locked bathroom in a farmhouse with no source of electricity in or near the building. Despite his frequent disparagement of Merrion's imagination, Arnold, after enjoying a "nicely done steak and a tankard of beer" at the inn where he is staying, lights his pipe and asks himself, "now, how would Merrion have tackled the problem?" Unfortunately, Arnold's attempt to imitate the imaginative Merrion for a long time only leaves the dogged yet dull inspector at a loss when it comes to actually solving the mystery (though he does pull through eventually). "It would be nice," he groans in frustration at one point, "if just for once something happened in this case that wasn't absolutely impossible." The reader can sympathize, for the murder mechanics in the tale turn out to be some of Street's most ingenious, taking full advantage of the author's background as an electrical engineer. The *Daily Telegraph* found "first class ... ingenuity ... in the final twist which provides the solution to the murder of Basil Maplewood in his bath."[130]

Death Leaves No Card also boasts some amusing satirical writing, directed at the pretensions of the leisured investor class and the enthusiasms of technical experts. Street clearly enjoyed lampooning the murder victim's idle, mindlessly snobbish aunt, Monica Maplewood, who has only her patronage of the I.I.I. (Institute of Incurable Imbeciles) to occupy her time. During Arnold's interview with her, Miss Maplewood sniffs to Arnold that her niece is audaciously planning to marry someone beneath the Maplewoods socially:

> "Why, all our ancestors would turn in their graves if she walked out of Hithering Church on that man's arm. It isn't so much that he hasn't got any money. It's his impertinence in thinking himself fit to marry into the family. Just fancy! I remember him as a dirty little boy going to board school. And he didn't always touch his cap if one spoke to him either. Mind you, I haven't a word to say against his father, though he does talk the broadest Hampshire you ever heard."

The father of whom Miss Monica Maplewood speaks more favorably (despite his accent) is the estate manager for the Maplewood Hithering Court Estate. "He never presumed on his position in the least," recalls Miss Maplewood fondly of the good old days when every man knew and accepted his immutable station in life. "My father always used to have him to lunch on Saturdays, and he behaved beautifully. Of course, we were careful not to have any other visitors." After a small dose of Miss Maplewood's maunderings, Street's readers should be able to sympathize with another of the tale's characters, who declares of the lady and her Institute of Incurable Imbeciles, "if incurable imbecility is the only qualifier, she should be an inmate herself."[131]

[SPOILER ALERT] Mr. Welch, manager of the local electricity works, a figure rather resembling Street himself, comes in for more gentle ribbing. Called upon to demonstrate how the murderer accomplished his dark deed, Mr. Welch falls "into ecstasies" over the ingenuity of the killing apparatus. "In his enthusiasm," writes Street, "he would no doubt have repeated the experiment in its entirety could he have found a willing victim."[132] [END SPOILER ALERT] Here Street may have been amusedly recalling Dorothy L. Sayers' speculation that "John Rhode" for accuracy's sake probably tried all his murder methods on his hapless dog.

Like *Death Leaves No Card*, *Mr. Babbacombe Dies* offers amusing sardonic writing directed at useless members of the English gentry, in this case the various relations of the late magnate Mr. Babbcombe, who met his demise through arsenical poisoning. In structure (if not in tone) resembling the John Rhode title *The Claverton Mystery*, *Babbacombe* nevertheless interestingly diverges from John Rhode titles in relying almost entirely for the solution of its mystery on Merrion's intuitions. *Mr. Westerby Missing*, a novel which concerns the disappearance of an eccentric birdwatcher, appears to be something of an homage to Freeman Wills Crofts' famous novel *The Cask*, where a dead body is found in a cask and must be laboriously traced to its point of origin. In *Westerby*, Arnold and Merrion eventually discover poor Mr. Westerby dead from strangulation in a packing crate far from where he was last seen alive. As in many a Crofts novel, the solution is reached through the investigators' destruction of an ingenious alibi. Along the way, Street provides his readers a rare glimpse of life at a lorry pull-up (in American parlance a truck stop). Lorry drivers are presented in the usual respectful fashion the author employed when portraying the manual working class. Isaac Anderson of the *New York Times* highly praised this particular Miles Burton tale.

With World War II's arrival, Street began incorporating wartime elements into both his Rhode and Burton novels. Merrion, like Street himself, again joins up with Military Intelligence, but that doesn't prevent him from helping his friend Arnold solve murder cases that come his way. *Death Visits Downspring/Up the Garden Path* (1941)—where a butler did not do it but rather had it done to him—is an enjoyable wartime Burton tale; yet it is overshadowed by *Murder M.D.* (1943), which is not only probably Merrion's greatest case, but one of Street's finest detective novels. *Murder M.D.* is a rather different book for Street, in its strong focus on its well-conveyed setting, the seemingly near-feudal village of Exton Forcett, as well as in its sustained emphasis on misdirecting the reader concerning the identity of the murderer from a large group of suspects. Over his long writing career, Street excelled at murder methods, as has been shown above; but he was less successful at fooling readers over the matter of "whodunit," something which was the grand specialty of the long-reigning and best-selling Crime Queen, Agatha Christie. Typically in a Street novel, whether a "John Rhode" or a "Miles Burton," the reader can guess "whodunit" at some point before the last chapter of the book. For readers taking a great interest in the "how" question as well as the "who" question, this aspect of Street's mystery writing is not a damning one; but for those who elevate the "who" question high above all others, it can lead to disappointment. However, in *Murder M.D.*, the reader should be left in genuine suspense over the "who" question until Street reveals all near the end of the novel. In both its excellent village setting and its superlative misdirection, *Murder M.D.* comes closer to a Christie tale than anything else Street ever published. The novel has been rightly praised in *A Catalogue of Crime* as "one of B[urton]'s best-constructed tales — compact, well characterized, and full of legitimate surprises."[133]

In *Murder M.D.*, life in the placid village of Exton Forcett has been disrupted by the intrusion of a singularly undesired presence: Native-born Austrian and naturalized British subject Dr. Kurt Wiegler, who is serving as wartime *locum tenums* for village physician St. John Cecil, currently enrolled in the medical corps in Egypt. The obnoxious Wiegler, boarding at St. John's family home of two generations, Foursquare, brings distress not only to St. John's neurasthenic wife, Hermione, but to virtually every village denizen whom he encounters. As Wiegler arrogantly explains over coffee at Exton House to the local squire, Sir Mark Corringham, he is compelled to intervene in everyone's affairs because of the chronic stupidity endemic in a tradition-bound village:

> "Many years have I lived in London before I came here to look after this little parish for a time. I flattered myself that I was on the fringe of learning something about the mentality of the Londoners. Stupid some of them are, yes. But there is always some reason behind their stupidity. They haven't been taught, or they don't understand. The disease will respond to treatment, it can be cured. But here in this village the disease of stupidity is incurable. Shall I tell you why? Because the patient doesn't want to be cured! He'd rather remain stupid than risk the mental discomfort of intelligence."[134]

Wiegler faults the villagers for being resistant to new medical treatment, the absent St. John Cecil for general incompetence and the local builder Simon Plowman for defrauding the village in the construction of an air-raid shelter that did not meet safety specifications. The cost-cutting, short-shifting Plowman has already been responsible, notes Wiegler, for accidents to workers like Bert Hawthorne, who was tiling a roof when it collapsed, leaving him crippled. Sir Mark allows Wiegler's assertions, but insists that the doctor's obstreperous criticism does more harm than good: "You must realize that in these village communities there's got to be a certain amount of give and take.... You'll set the whole place by the ears, if you're not careful."[135]

Wiegler of course does not listen to Sir Mark's temperate words and is soon found dead, his head battered, presumably from a fall he took down a cliff after making an injudicious step while bird-watching. The villagers are happy to see him gone, many even having decided that in addition to being obnoxious and arrogant, the "foreign" Wiegler likely was a German spy — bird-watching obviously being a front for his espionage activities. Sir Mark comes to suspect that Wiegler may have been murdered, but he decides, out of loyalty to his village, to say nothing at the inquest to counter his original influential opinion of accidental death, a decision that weighs on his conscience, as he tells a visiting Desmond Merrion (Merrion serves with Sir Mark's son in the Admiralty): "All the folk here call me squire, and it's not by any means a formal title, I assure you. Rightly or wrongly, they look up to me as a person who has more experience of worldly affairs than they have, and most of them are prepared to accept what I say." Had he been right in keeping silent about his altered view, or should he now speak to the police? Merrion, who privately agrees with Sir Mark that the doctor likely was murdered, advises his friends to keep his own counsel: "Let's forget the conversation we've had this evening, and thankfully accept the jury's verdict. There's no sense in stirring up muddy water once it's been allowed to settle."[136]

Merrion for once gives bad advice, **[SPOILER ALERT]** for the death of St. John Cecil's first locum is followed by that of the second one, Dr. Alida Mountwell, in circumstances ruling out anything but murder. "I don't want to appear flippant," says a bemused Merrion, called to the scene by a distressed Sir Mark, "but are we to assume that there is someone here whose hobby is killing locums?" The presence of an attractive young lady doctor had scandalized some villagers, who found the very idea that a woman would take up such a profession unnatural and unsettling. At Foursquare, Hermione St. John was beside herself, for she assumed that Alida Mountwell and her husband, who himself had unexpectedly returned from Egypt, must have been lovers. Merrion, working with his friend Arnold in tow, is able to find a solution that, to Sir Mark's relief, exonerates the household at Foursquare. It seems that wheelchair-bound Bert Hawthorne had recovered the use of his legs, but kept that recovery a secret, preferring to enjoy the use of the pension that village subscriptions had provided him. Life for Bert, explains a caustic Merrion, had become "an idyllic round of having nothing to do and being paid for doing it," and Bert had no intention of giving up that life.[137] When first Kurt Wiegler and later Alida Mountwell penetrated the secret that had eluded the something less than competent St. John Cecil, they both had to be gotten out of the way.

Murder M.D. is one of Street's writing triumphs. Clues are cunningly placed, so that we can easily miss a motive that has been staring us in the face for virtually the entire novel. Moreover, setting and characterization are quite well done. For example, when Alida Mountwell turns out to be the second murder victim, the reader actually feels shock and distress at the striking down of this personable woman. And Alida's feminine nemesis, Hermione Cecil, surely is one of the most effectively exasperating characters in detective fiction. In America, however, critical opinion of *Murder M.D.* divided, with Isaac Anderson of the *New York Times* praising the "skillfully concealed" motive for the murders and Anthony Boucher of the *San Francisco Chronicle* simply sputtering outrage, in an unusually imperceptive review from him. Offended that Miles Burton had cast his murderer in the novel from the ranks of the "lower classes," an outraged Boucher tersely deemed *Murder M.D.* "ammunition for Anglophobes." In his next review of a Burton tale, Boucher had not relinquished his grudge against the author, complaining that Merrion's "specialty is clearing the aristocracy and proving that crime is a property of commoners." Clearly "Miles Burton" had offended Boucher's liberal democratic sensibilities, but in my view Boucher made a serious misreading of *Murder M.D.*[138] **[END SPOILER ALERT]**

Murder M.D. offers considerable criticism of life in Exton Forcett. Though Street unfailingly portrays Kurt Wiegler as an arrogant man, needlessly short with people's feelings, he nevertheless makes clear that Wiegler is objectively correct in much of his criticism of the village. The villagers *are* foolishly loyal to their clearly incompetent doctor, St. John Cecil, who, we learn in the course of the novel, is eased out of the medical corps in Egypt for botching two cases. Builder Simon Plowman *is* dishonest, and his shoddily built air-raid shelter would not have withstood bombing, had not the busybody Wiegler discovered the structural problem. Street's description of the entire grasping Plowman family leaving church is unfailingly harsh:

> Mr. Plowman, a heavily-built man with a walrus moustache, in his black Sunday suit and bowler hat. Mrs. Plowman, stout and florid, with a fur coat and a hat of the latest fashion, as interpreted in Marbeach, perched dizzily on the anterior portion of her head. Ethel Plowman, a younger version of her mother, but with a distressing squint. And Archie Plowman, also black-suited and bowler-hatted, with a cherubic expression upon his round and moonlike face.... It had always been a mystery why [Archie] was not called up. Helping his father on work of national importance was the pretence.... Archie was a slacker and, for all his church-going and sanctimonious expression, something of a bad character.[139]

To be sure, this negativity expressed toward the Plowmans can be dismissed as conservative, aristocratic disdain for the petit bourgeois; yet Street's etchings of St. John and Hermione Cecil, both indisputably of the village gentry, are just as acid. Sir Mark Corringham may fear that his friends the Cecils will be implicated in the murders, but he seems not to genuinely like them when it comes to it, as he constantly damns their many obvious shortcomings. St. John Cecil is lazy, selfish and demonstrably incompetent in his profession. He married his wife largely for her family money and looked on his service in Egypt as a wonderful opportunity for getting away from her for a time. As for Hermione Cecil, she is, to indulge in slang, something of a basket case. Persistently self-doubting and overwhelmed by an absent husband, the loss of servants and wartime rationing, Hermione can barely manage as it is, without the presence of first the exasperatingly carping Dr. Wiegler and later the aggravatingly appealing Dr. Alida Mountwell as boarders. It is easy to understand Hermione's dislike of Wiegler, who does not himself attempt to be agreeable, but her objection to Alida Mountwell is based simply on her neurotic jealousy of the younger woman and a blockheaded anti-feminism:

> The idea that St. John would send her a lady locum was one that Hermione in her wildest dreams had never contemplated.... She herself had done her duty as a woman. She had married St. John and made him a comfortable home. She had brought up a son to be a credit to her and to serve his country at the hour of need. All the friends of her youth had preserved their femininity. They had obeyed the age-old precept that a woman's place is the home. Not one of them had deviated into occupations properly reserved for men.... That a woman might prefer a professional career to becoming a wife and mother was entirely beyond her comprehension.... The only conclusion she could come to was that Alida had chosen this career so that she might meet men.... How much did she and St. John know of one another? Surely the fact that she never mentioned his name pointed to the existence of some secret intimacy between them. It was disgraceful that St. John should have admitted a woman of that sort to the chastity of his home.[140]

Even further demoralizing is when Dr. Mountwell upstages Hermione in her own domestic sphere at Foursquare, as the not so conquering hero St. John is due shortly to return home. When Hermione, compelled by the absence of her daily woman to clean curtains herself, cannot get the tiresome things back on their rods, she has *in extremis* to turn to Alida for help. The latter woman quickly takes care of the problem with her customary efficiency, provoking further resentment on Hermione's part: "She hated to be beholden to her for anything.... She imagined St. John and Dr. Mountwell laughing behind her back at her ineptitude. Beyond the baize door, where no doubt they would retire on the pretext of professional discussion."[141]

Hermione Cecil also is an utter snob who, when not worrying about running the house with just one live-in servant and one daily woman, spends considerable time fretting over social distinctions, like how to treat the other tenant of Foursquare, her husband's dispenser, Eileen Draper (to preserve social distance, Hermione insists on calling the young woman, who has lived at Foursquare for four years, Miss Draper, rather than Eileen): "Of course, the girl had to have meals with the family. Any other arrangement would involve too much work for the servants. But there her association must end.... Her men folk must be made to understand that the girl was on an entirely different plane from their own. It must be demonstrated that her place was in that uncertain sphere which had its orbit between the working classes and the people one called upon." One of the things about Dr. Mountwell that troubles Hermione is that Alida does not observe such carefully calibrated social distinctions, taking tea in the homes of the Plowmans and other tradespersons. "What could she find to talk about" with such people, wonders the continually perplexed Hermione.[142]

The people at the top of Exton Forcett's social pyramid, Lord and Lady Corringham, do not come in for direct criticism from the author, who likely agreed with their ethic of conservative-led, gradual change. Nevertheless, [**SPOILER ALERT**] it is Sir Mark's failure to speak out about Wiegler's death that leads to Bert Hawthorne committing a second successful murder, something of which Sir Mark is keenly and guiltily aware. As for Bert himself, it is true he is of the "working class" (even though he is not working), but I think it refreshing to find an occasional murderer in a British Golden Age mystery coming from that group. Boucher surely was too sensitive on this particular score. Too often Golden Age writers restricted the field of culpritude to what some critics of the time viewed as "worthwhile people" (i.e., the well-born), undermining both the puzzle element and the realism of detective novels of the era. [**END SPOILER ALERT**] Street should be applauded for his originality.

The following year Street produced another Miles Burton novel excelling at mystification, *The Three Corpse Trick* (1944). Barzun and Taylor praised this tale highly, noting that suspense, unusually for Street, is maintained "to the very end" and that the characters and setting are of uncommon interest. "Merrion is in top form, the remaining characters varied, and there is legitimate surprise," the critical duo enthusiastically concluded. Oddly, this novel was not accepted, in contrast with a majority of Burtons in this period, for American publication; and it is not well-remembered today, though in fact it is one of the most engaging and intricate Burton tales.[143] When Wendy Burge disappears in the hamlet of Goose Common while collecting funds for the county hospital fund, Merrion and Arnold find themselves enmeshed in a really baffling series of problems. Within this tiny community, Street masterfully weaves four different plot strands into a fascinating fabric of mystery. The often quite odd denizens of Goose Common add piquancy to the puzzle.

With *The Cat Jumps* (1946), we move from the reader misdirection and naturalistic portrayal of people in *Murder M.D.* and *The Three Corpse Trick* to a traditional "murder means" novel with strictly stock suspects and a guessable murderer. Yet the tale is notable for the novelty and ingenuity of its puzzle, which involves the late night stabbing murder of a wealthy widow in her locked house. The only apparent means of egress into the house that night was a small pane of window glass left open for the outdoor nocturnal perambulations of the pampered cat, Belisarius (named for a Byzantine general, the subject

Eileen Waller. John Street's companion Eileen is holding the likely inspiration for the pampered feline Belisarius in the Miles Burton novel *The Cat Jumps* (1946). She herself probably inspired the character of Eileen Draper in *Murder M.D.* (1943) (courtesy David Lane).

of both a Henry Wadsworth Longfellow poem and a 1938 Robert Graves novel). It takes Desmond Merrion — himself one of the legatees in the murder victim's will — to perceive that with Belisarius lies the key to the solution to the mystery. "I always prick up my ears when I hear the expression, 'it just isn't possible,'" Merrion confidently announces. "So many things seem impossible until one knows how they're done."[144] I will not divulge the solution of this "sealed house" mystery here, though I will note that it has the scientific ingenuity of a good John Rhode novel (there is resemblance as well to the solution of one of R. Austin Freeman's cleverest short stories). Additionally, Belisarius, portrayed by Street with insight and affection, makes an appealing — albeit non-human — character.

Situation Vacant, also published later that same year, is another interesting village tale. In "the straggling village of Nearbridge" the successive deaths of Mrs. Whyttington's two personal secretaries perplex investigators until Merrion appears on the scene, rather late in the story. Though the mystery here is not so complex as that in *Murder M.D.* or *The Three-Corpse Trick*, the tale offers some satirical humor and yet another original use of a unique poison. The humor comes at the expense of a picturesque married couple, the Whyttingtons, Mr. Whyttington being the author of a string of scientifically piffling yet extremely popular nature books and Mrs. Whyttington being a financial agent for the Ranch o' Rest, a dubious retirement home for horses in the Central American republic of El Matador. Mr. Clipsham, a gentleman of independent means who has retired in Nearbridge and is trusted by the local inhabitants as a disinterested, wise observer, speaks with amusing dismissiveness of Mr. Whyttington's literary efforts: "I've got Whyttington's last [book] here, for he presented me with an autographed copy. *Shrub-loving Birds*, or *Bird-loving Shrubs*, I forget which. It's the most infantile twaddle I've ever had the misfortune to read. He burbles on for page after page about the birds' nests he finds in his garden. There's not a hint of scientific observation from beginning to end." Nor does he think highly of Mrs. Whyttington's beloved Ranch o' Rest: "[Mr. Clipsham] remembered the photographs she had shown him.... Groups of happy-looking horses, being fed and watered by swarthy men in wide-brimmed hats. Children playing rather self-consciously under the camera, in shady wooden porches. Where exactly the children came in was not quite clear.... You had to drag children in somehow into any charitable appeal. The sentimental British public demanded them."[145] As for the poison in *Situation Vacant*, it is picrotoxin, found in fishberries; and it is quite cleverly utilized in the tale.

Another interesting Burton tale from this period is *Not a Leg to Stand On* (1945), a teasing work about the disappearance of a man with an artificial leg (the leg soon resurfaces, though not the man). By the late 1940s, however, it was evident that the Burton series was waning in quality. Yet Street nevertheless managed to produce one of his most interesting Burton novels in 1949 with *Death Takes the Living*. This pleasingly titled story is of significance not for its rudimentary puzzle, but for its sour take on postwar British politicians and morose view of British society. In this novel, the conscientious, young Reverend Jonathan Denby, veteran of the R.A.F., desires to take on the living at Clynde, an isolated fens village in East Anglia reminiscent of High Eldersham in 1930. As the Bishop of Fencaster semi-whimsically tells Jonathan, "I must warn you that any rector who accepts the living will not find his task an easy one. The parish has been without an incumbent for so long that the parishioners have had time for a complete lapse into paganism. It would not surprise me to learn that they offered sacrifices to Baal, or passed their children through the fire to Moloch." The Bishop approves of Jonathan for the position at Clynde, but tells the young man that he first must obtain the assent of the local bigwig, Alfred Victor Smith, the second Lord Mundesley, who has proven reluctant in the past to accept new candidates for the living. The Bishop informs Jonathan that Mundesley, the son of a hugely successful manufacturer of a patent medicine, Smith's Elixir, and a passionate member of the Liberal party, will be certain to oppose Jonathan's elevation to the living at Clynde if he thinks Jonathan's political views are the same as those of his cousin, Henry Denby, who is serving as Minister of Iron and Steel in the Labor government. Jonathan hastens to assure the Bishop that he has "no strong political views, either way. Party politics have always seemed to me rather like a nursery game."[146] After an interview with Jonathan, Lord Mundesley agrees to the appointment, but he informs the young cleric that he must wait to move to Clynde until Lord Mundesley has had a new dwelling built for him, as the old, rambling rectory has fallen into hopeless decay. Unfortunately for Jonathan, he decides one night to go ahead and establish himself in the old rectory. Hearing noises in the dwelling's abandoned wing (local legend of course has it that the rectory is haunted), Jonathan goes to investigate and is never seen alive again. Eventually his body is fished from the coastal waters. An autopsy determines that he died from a fractured skull.

Inspector Arnold, in charge of the investigation, naturally calls upon his old friend Desmond Merrion, whose village, High Eldersham, lies not far from Clynde. As usual, Merrion is quite familiar with the rural scene: "I've driven through Clynde more than once, and I've noticed that barrack of a rectory. I know Lord Mundesley, and once some years ago he invited me to a day's shooting at Bromhoe Castle." Arnold and Merrion go to interview Lord Mundesley, who attempts to put them off with aristocratic hauteur, much to Merrion's bemusement. "You'd think from his manner that he considered himself far too highly placed to concern himself with the death of a mere parson," the master of High Eldersham Hall tells Arnold. "Yet, as all the world knows, his father sold patent medicines."[147]

Merrion eventually determines — as the reader likely has done for some time — that [**SPOILER ALERT**] Lord Mundesley is the leader of a stolen goods black market ring, which uses the abandoned rectory as a warehouse. When Jonathan Denby unexpectedly appeared there the night of a delivery, one of the criminals coshed him, inadvertently killing him. As the investigation reaches its conclusion, another death occurs, this one of Jonathan Denby's father, Sir Ambrose Denby. It first is believed that Sir Ambrose died naturally, but later evidence indicates that he was poisoned by his nephew Henry Denby (the aforementioned Minister of Iron and Steel in the Labor government), whose motive was to secure Sir Ambrose's title and estate, now that his cousin Jonathan was dead. Sir Edric Conway insists on pursuing the case, even though Sir Henry is implicated: "Denby may be a Cabinet Minister, but he's subject to the law like all the rest of us. We are bound at least to ask him why he emptied that decanter of whiskey down the lavatory." Sir Henry commits suicide when he learns the police want to question him, while Lord Mundesley is arrested for his part in the stolen goods operation. The high-profile criminality of a Labor cabinet minister and a Liberal Baron shocks the public, and causes the Bishop of Fencaster to choose as the text for his next sermon words from the Psalms: "I myself have seen the ungodly in great power.... I went by, and lo, he was gone! I sought him, but his place could nowhere be found."[148]

Among the complaints lodged against *Death Takes the Living* in *A Catalogue of Crime* is that "the only likable character is killed off on p. 46 [p. 37 in the British edition]," yet killing off the likable Jonathan Denby was necessary to fulfill Street's artistic purpose of condemning the Labor and Liberal parties by having members of these parties behave utterly despicably. Prominent Liberal Lord Mundesley is a criminal who is morally, if not legally, responsible for Jonathan's death, while Jonathan's cousin, Henry Denby, Labor Minister of Iron and Steel (industries nationalized upon Labor's taking power in 1945), actually murders Jonathan's father, Sir Ambrose, by laying poison for Sir Ambrose with his own hand. Specific complaints lodged against the Labor government in *Death Takes the Living* are few, all stemming from Labor's unpopular postwar rationing and austerity measures. For example, when Jonathan Denby eats his lunch at the Clynde public house, the Anchor, the lunch consists of "a couple stale rolls, cut open and smeared with potted meat. The best austerity could provide." On the other hand, there is a great deal of generalized vituperation directed against politics and politicians. Jonathan Denby, as mentioned above, dismisses politics as "a nursery game." Street himself bitingly pronounces that the Laborite Henry Denby has "a natural gift for hoodwinking the simple electorate." When Sir Edric Conway learns of Sir Henry's perfidious murder of his Uncle Ambrose, he comments contemptuously, "The man always was an opportunist." Ambrose Denby himself sums up the point of Street's tale when he asks his son: "Has it ever struck you what a subtle jest it is that a successful politician should acquire the title of the Right Honorable? When any consideration of honorable behavior is the last thing to enter their calculations?"[149]

The clear moral center of the novel lies with the slaughtered Denbys, father and son. Jonathan Denby is a young, self-sacrificing former public school rugby player and Royal Air Force veteran who deliberately chooses to labor in a humble parish like that at Clynde, rather than at some prestigious clerical career stepping-stone like St. Withberga's, as his cousin Henry wants him to do. As for Sir Ambrose, he clearly is Street's ideal man: a baronet from a long, distinguished lineage (he is, we learn, the tenth baronet in his line), but one who as a second son largely had to make his own way, and in a mechanical field. Though left with but slender resources, Sir Ambrose purchased an interest in a small engineering firm (like Street had purchased an interest in a power company in Lyme Regis) and made a smashing success of it. "By dint of [Sir Ambrose's] hard work, aided by his mechanical genius, the firm had prospered and grown out of all recognition," Street informs us. "In 1946, he had retired, a rich man, from active participation in the business." Unlike the criminal Lord Mundesley, son of an ennobled slick purveyor of a quack nostrum ("I believe [Smith's Elixir] was responsible for the deaths of comparatively few people," comments the Bishop of Fencaster ironically), Sir Ambrose is a worthy man, who gave much of value to his country.[150] Surely in Street's mind, the extermination of such men's lives by representatives of the Labor and Liberal parties was meant to symbolize what he saw as the wrecking of the country by the taxation and nationalization programs that followed the defeat of the Tories in 1945. **[END SPOILER ALERT]** In his books from the twenties and thirties, Street had revealed himself as sympathetic to welfare capitalism, but that policy left capitalists in charge of the reform process. Upon coming to power in 1945, Labor had taken that power out of the hands of the capitalists and put it into the hands of the people — or, rather, as Street would have seen it, the hands of conniving politicians who had deluded a "simple electorate."

While none of Street's 1950s Miles Burton mysteries are outstanding, as a group they are worth noting because they served as the primary repository of the author's expressions of his alienation from modern Britain (this also may suggest a reason why the Burton books were permanently dropped by their American publisher in 1950). This sense of alienation Street shared with John Dickson Carr, Dorothy L. Sayers, Agatha Christie, Henry Wade, Freeman Wills Crofts and other Golden Age detective novelists who survived the war years. No doubt much of what people have found "cozy" about such books as the Burtons is their evocation, in a chaotic, rapidly changing world, of a secure social structure. After 1950, the Major—who had ceased visiting London, a symbol for the discontented of all that had gone wrong in Britain—increasingly set his Miles Burton tales in villages and provincial towns where a cohesive gentry still could claim a measure of social authority. For example, in *Ground for Suspicion* (1950)—one of the best tales from this group of conservative novels—the active and energetic upper-crust citizenry of the quiet seaside town of Shellmouth, where Desmond and Mavis Merrion are staying while long-needed repairs are made to High Eldersham Hall, are adamantly opposed to the purchase for development of a stretch of waste land known as the Marram Ground by a holiday camp concern, Harry's Happy Haunts, fearing an invasion of vulgar holiday trippers. Learning of the opposition movement from Mortimer Goole, an attorney and honorary secretary of the Shellmouth Society, Merrion wishes it "every success," noting that "unspoiled seaside towns are becoming scarcer day by day." **[SPOILER ALERT]** Ultimately Merrion discovers that Harry's Happy Haunts in reality had never contemplated buying the Marram Ground, Goole having devised an imaginary threat to the town as a way of getting the Shellmouth Society itself to buy the land, with the large sum of money ending up in his pocket. At the end of the novel, however, Nature herself intervenes to protect Shellmouth from any possibility of unsightly development, by means of a sudden, savage storm that renders the Marram Ground into "a salt lake, upon which seabirds floated."[151] **[END SPOILER ALERT]**

Another stronghold against the social upheaval wrought by the Labor government is found in a 1953 Miles Burton novel, *Heir to Murder*, at Dragonscourt, the near feudal domain of Lady Violet Vernham. Dragonscourt, the ancestral estate of the Vernham family, is hidden in the woods at the head of the Car Valley above the small fishing port of Carmouth. Here elderly Lady Violet, "in every respect a survival from the past," is "able to ignore the dearths and discomfort of the Welfare State, and to maintain at least the shadow of her former existence." Forced to part with her chauffeur and personal maid, Lady Violet thankfully is able to maintain a lady companion (who combines the above jobs), as well as a lodge-keeper, butler and parlor maid, the latter three individuals more "feudal retainers" than servants. When the Merrions call on Lady Violet (Mavis' mother was an old friend of Lady Violet's), they find a Georgian house that symbolizes the fineness and stability of an earlier age: "At first sight [the house] seemed unpromising, a vast square block without any ornament to relieve its primness, but at a second glance [the Merrions] appreciated the air of dignity and comfort expressed by its perfect Georgian proportions." At the excellent dinner, a gratified Desmond feels as if he has been "transported back to the early years of the century, when gracious living had not yet come to be regarded as a social crime."[152]

Little consideration is given in the later Burton novels to whether the lower classes might be benefiting under Labor's governance, though it is suggested that private charity is being eroded by a modern confiscatory tax regime. "My father had always the welfare of the County, and of those who lived in it, at heart," Lady Violet lectures Merrion in *Heir to Murder*. "In these days of restricted incomes I have not been able to follow his example." Still, she plans to leave what she has at her death to someone who will do good unto his or her less fortunate neighbors (this admirable determination is, sadly, the impetus to the series of murders and attempted murders in the tale). Less idealistically, these later Miles Burton novels suggest that, like many middle and upper class Britons, Street simply found life personally bleaker in post–World War II Britain. In addition to Street's unusually forthright authorial editorializing in *Heir to Murder*, he allows Merrion in *Ground for Suspicion* to take a potshot at Labor while discussing with Mortimer Goole life among the eighteenth-century Shellmouth gentry:

"They must have had enormous fun."
"I bet they did!" Merrion agreed. "Austerity and rationing were unknown to those circles."[153]

The servant problem comes in for discussion in *Beware Your Neighbor* (1951), which takes place in the city of Barncaster in a genteel residential backwater, Hallow's Green. This desirable neighborhood, Street informs us, is derided as "Prigs' Parade" by "those queer souls to whom any standard of living higher than their own was anathema." Though Hallow's Green may be an envied district, it too has servant troubles. For example, the Raynham household, composed of a mother, son and daughter-in-law, has to put up with the not-so-tender services of the maid Lotti, "a Displaced Person," the author informs us, "of uncertain age and rudimentary intelligence." Lotti, who bears a more than passing resemblance to the exasperating Mitzi in Agatha Christie's *A Murder Is Announced*, published the previous year, can always be counted on to serve potatoes "either as a watery paste or half raw" and to make "a sorry mess of the chicken casserole"; and she must be constantly supervised by the younger Mrs. Raynham if domestic disaster is to be averted.[154] To the genteel Hallow's Green residents, war-displaced Europeans like Lotti leave much to be desired, but as the elder Mrs. Raynham stoically concedes, even Lotti is better than nobody.

Not all the 1950s Burtons conform to this conservative pattern. *Murder in Absence* (1954), for example, draws on the peripatetic John and Eileen Street's practical knowledge of realtors and freighters to provide a convincing and original Miles Burton tale without political overtones. In *Absence*, Inspector Arnold investigates the murder of a wealthy, womanizing provincial realtor while Merrion is absent from England, having departed with his wife Mavis on a Mediterranean cruise while yet more repairs are being made to High Eldersham Hall. Even in absence, however, Merrion manages to discover the key facts that bring about the solution of Arnold's case.[155]

The best of the later Miles Burton novels, *Bones in the Brickfield* (1958), likewise eschews political criticism in favor of more mild social satire, here directed against the contingent of formerly urban middle-class and wealthy retirees who have settled in the sleepy farming village of Downfold. "New-comers," as they are known, are viewed with amused contempt by the locals, whose chief spokesman is the elderly but still energetic retired farmer, Mr. Eagles. After the murder of one of the new-comers brings Arnold and Merrion to the village, Merrion, knowing from long experience the value of the local inn to a murder investigation, is quick to make the acquaintance of Mr. Eagles at Downfold's establishment, The Falcon. Eagles explains to the ever-inquisitive amateur detective (in no way slowed down after nearly thirty years in the detecting game) how the new-comer invasion began with the retired Glue King, Sir Horace Honiton, a well-meaning individual, interested in local ways (unlike many new-comers), but yet a man of unquenchable energy who found it necessary to stick his finger in every village pie. Gradually he and the other new-comers took over the farmers' Downfold Society and — with the best of intentions, no doubt — transformed it from a simple, rustic agrarian social club into a posh historical and archaeological association, leaving the perplexed farmers to drift away from the organization they had founded long ago. Mr. Eagles insists that the murder is a new-comer affair, and, after a succession of two more deaths, he finally is proved right. The mystery plot itself is not an overly complex one, but it dovetails nicely with the new-comers theme discussed above and incorporates some well-reasoned deductions from Desmond Merrion. Further, the counterpoint between the bustling — if ultimately futile — efforts of the Downfold Society to wrest dinosaur fossils from the nearby abandoned brickfield and the determined activities of the crime investigators, who keep finding human bodies there, is amusing and well-maintained.[156]

The nostalgic Mr. Eagles complains how the new-comers have changed the very landscape, recalling to Merrion,

> "If, when you were a young man, you'd climbed up the hill and looked down, you'd have seen as pretty a little place as you could want. Just the Street with the stream running along it, and nothing but fields all round. Now it's quite different. The Street hasn't changed much in my time. But the fields are all blotched with patches of brick, like a bull with the mange."

The next day, Merrion sets off from The Falcon to explore the surrounding downs. From a commanding position on them he looks about him and sees a still splendid pastoral vista:

> On the downs, both about him and across the valley, were flocks of sheep, moving slowly like white clouds across the green surface. In the valley lay the village, thatched roofs dominated by the church tower and the trees about it. The puffs of steam from a locomotive leaving the station rather added to than detracted from the scene, which fully merited Mr. Eagles' eulogies.... As for the villas and bungalows scattered among the farms and the fields, Merrion felt that he could ignore them, while fully understanding that Mr. Eagles could not. Downfold was his village, the ancestral home of generations of Eagles, and he loved it. To him these new accretions must be a sacrilege.[157]

Part Four: The Keys to the Streets

Judging John Street's body of mystery fiction from the 1950s Miles Burton novels alone would tend to lead one to the conclusion that the Major was the more backward-looking, pastoralist British Golden Age detective novelist of stereotype, but consideration of his other works suggests considerably more varied economic and social attitudes behind the books. Street's prewar interest in technology, business and manufacturing, seen already in the discussions of *The Davidson Case* and *Death on the Board*, runs counter to the agrarian nostalgia of the later Burton novels. Numerous further examples can be mentioned. The various makes of refrigerators owned by the suspects in the case becomes an important

John Rhode, *Mystery at Olympia* (1935, left); John Rhode, *Murder at the Motor Show* (1936). The British Motor Show was held at the Olympia exhibition center every year from 1904 to 1936. Street, a fervent auto enthusiast, regularly attended the shows. Certainly the great neon lights emblazoning "Mystery at Olympia" are at odds with the country house stereotype of Golden Age English mystery (though there is a country house in the tale). The dust jacket of the American edition of the title eschews literalism in favor of a stylized Art Deco design that emphasizes that noisy symbol of modernity, the car.

matter in one novel. That noisy symbol of modernity, the automobile, features prominently in such Street works as *Dead Men at the Folly*, *The Motor Rally Mystery*, *Mystery at Olympia* and *Blackthorn House*. In *Folly*, Hanslet and his local colleague spend much of the novel to-ing and fro-ing over the countyside in search of a mysterious, seemingly vanishing car linked to a series of local robberies. A railway and an under construction electrical transmission line also play roles in the tale. In *Mystery at Olympia*, the murder takes place at the crowded Olympia Motor Show, which Street, a car aficionado (his Armstrong Siddeley made a great impression in Laddingford, Kent), portrays in knowing detail. The post–World War II *Blackthorn House*, praised for its up-to-datedness by Anthony Boucher in his review of the novel in the *New York Times*, involves the activities of a stolen car ring in austerity England. In *The Motor Rally Mystery*, Street plunges participants in the British Motor-Car Rally into a murder case. He amusingly satirizes a pompous, Luddite coroner who uses his position to launch into an anti-auto diatribe at an inquest upon the deaths of two men supposedly accidentally killed in a car crash during the Rally. "I feel it to be my duty to express my opinion very strongly upon this point," declares the coroner self-importantly. "These two young men have fallen victims to the craze for speed which has become such a distressing feature of modern life. It is devoutly to be hoped that their deaths will serve as a warning to others." After pausing to make sure the reporters in court "had got his words correctly," the coroner, who in fact has very little conception of the true nature of a Motor Rally, closes the proceedings and departs.

The investigating police inspector admits that "the coroner is an ass" who "hates cars like the plague."[158] Unsurprisingly, the coroner's verdict of accidental death is incorrect, the two deaths having resulted not from reckless driving but premeditated murder.

As has been indicated in the discussion of Street's handling of characters like Sir Guy Davidson and Sir Ambrose Denby, Street clearly possessed great admiration for the British businessman ideal (and he is critical of his fictional British businessmen who do not adhere to that ideal). Conversely, Street damningly portrays old landed families who have not kept pace with the times, as in *Poison for One,* where Lord and Lady Cossington are hoping to hold on to the Cossington family estate by callously marrying off their daughter to Sir Gerald Uppingham, Chairman of the British Albanium Company and a notorious sexual wolf who has already impregnated a woman out of wedlock. Street describes Lord Cossington as "a dull, heavy-looking man, with weak eyes and an undecided chin." We learn that while the "first Viscount Cossington had been a judge in George the Third's reign, famous for his intellectual prowess," his intellectual prowess "had, unfortunately, not been transmitted to his descendants." Lord Cossington's son, Rupert, "a rather weedy-looking young man wearing round tortoiseshell spectacles," is a stock character of Street's, the ineffectual would-be great poet, whose verses are occasionally caught sight of near the crossword puzzle in a daily newspaper. Lord Cossington himself "never could understand why men occupied themselves with work" and querulously grunts his disapproval when he hears that Sir Gerald is occupied with business in his study (actually, Sir Gerald has been murdered).[159] Lady Cossington is a pretentious snob who worries pompously about setting bad examples for the servants and tries to forget that her maiden name, inherited from a father who made his fortune as a manufacturer of woolens, is Muggs. In short, the Cossingtons do little to trumpet the virtues of ossified landed gentry.

In a later novel from the thirties, *The Bloody Tower,* we see a gentry family portrayed even less favorably than the Cossingtons. This novel seems Street's literary nod to the English "rural gloom" genre associated at this time with the novels of Mary Webb and memorably satirized by Stella Gibbons in her 1932 comic novel, *Cold Comfort Farm.* In *The Bloody Tower,* Simeon and Caleb Glapthorne, father and son, live in squalor at their decaying Georgian country home, Farningcote Priory, attended by two slatternly servants. Caleb Glapthorne, who at the beginning of the novel is found dead with half his face blown away by a rifle shot, was a debauched wastrel who spent "his evenings in his own kitchen drinking gin with the cook," when not pursuing a neighboring farmer's daughter. Years before, Simeon Glapthorne had insisted that his eldest son remain at home as a proper landed gentleman and help him maintain the family estate, even though for some time there had barely been an estate left to maintain. Simeon's sister had lost caste in her brother's eyes after marrying a man who owned a nearby pottery, Simeon judging it "an unforgivable crime for a Glapthorne to marry a man who made his money by manufacturing drainpipes." Simeon's other son, admiringly depicted by Street, as a boy had enjoyed playing with toy boats and a clockwork engine and later made his escape from rural desuetude at Farningcote Priory by becoming a marine engineer. Simeon disapproves of this too, regarding it as "beneath the dignity of a Glapthorne to wipe his hands on a piece of cotton waste." Another mark against Benjamin is that (like the author) he has been known to drink "in public houses with commercial travelers and people of that type," rather

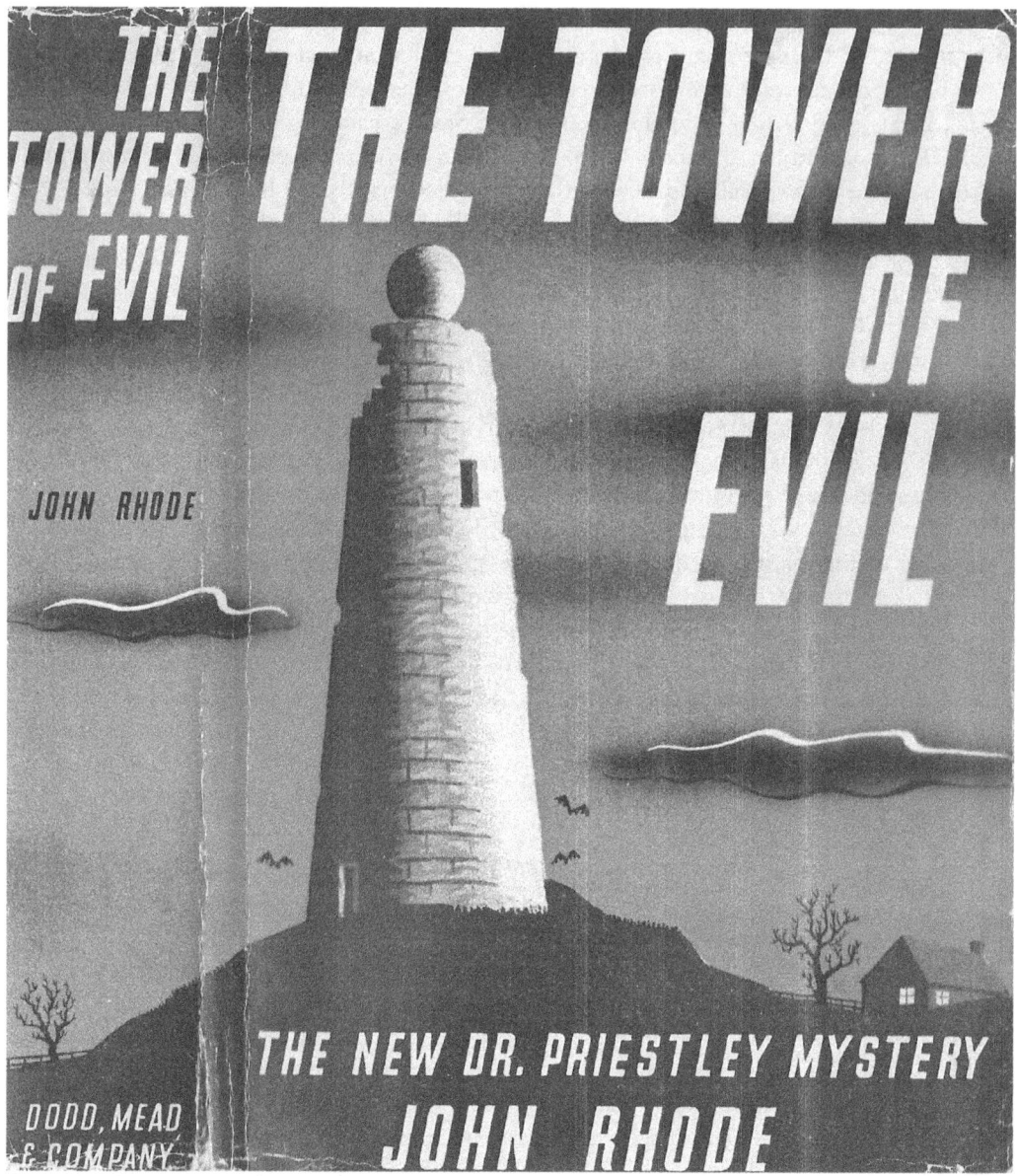

John Rhode, *The Tower of Evil* (*The Bloody Tower*) (1938). This gloomy 1938 Rhode novel demystifies the life of landed gentry, portraying a bleak world of rural squalor.

than getting hopelessly inebriated with a servant in the privacy of home like Simeon's favored son, the slain Caleb.[160]

A Catalogue of Crime dismissed *The Bloody Tower* as "pretty dreary stuff," but its dreariness is intentional and quite well-portrayed. In truth, it is one of Street's most atmospheric works. Moreover, it boasts as well a clever solution depending on carefully elucidated principles of structural engineering, no doubt familiar to Street from his perilous World War I days of forward observation on the Western Front. In likeness with

P.D. James' *The Black Tower,* the "Bloody Tower" of Street's novel is a bizarre architectural folly — "not unlike a truncated factory chimney with a ball balanced on top of it," explains the author. It was erected by Thaddeus Glapthorne, the eccentric eighteenth-century founder of the family's now-diminished fortune. Thaddeus' somewhat cracked descendant Simeon fervently believes in the claim of the tower's inscription that so long as the tower stands, "So long shall Glapthorne dwell in Farningcote." Street appealingly structures the tale's mystery around that prophecy.[161]

In addition to landed gentry, career army officers, another group important in Street's own family background, sometimes fall under the view of the author's cocked eye. In *The Corpse in the Car,* the unappealing murder victim's equally unappealing brother is the cantankerous retired army officer Theodore Ormskirsk, who never tires of reminding an exasperated Inspector Hanslet that his sister married socially beneath her when she wed Lord Misterton, the celebrated maker of "Foam-Flowers for the Feet." "But, good lord, for an Ormskirsk to marry Foam-Flowers for the Feet!" he fulminates at one point. "Why, man alive, don't you know that the Ormskirks came over with William the Conqueror?"[162] Hanslet replies that the Yard does not possess a copy of the passenger list, but his sarcasm fails to put a stop to the flow of Ormskirk's classist invective.

Less obnoxious but equally snobbish and fundamentally useless is Colonel James Flotman of *Death on the Board.* Flotman serves as one of the members of the Board of Directors of Hardware, Ltd., although he knows nothing about the business, functioning essentially as the puppet of his business-savvy wife, Caroline Wiggenhall Flotman. Colonel Flotman, formerly of the Army Service Corps, has "no ambition to achieve distinction in the world of commerce," having already achieved his utmost ambition by marrying a rich woman, though admittedly one mixed up in trade: "The fact that [Caroline Flotman] was the daughter of a small hardware merchant did not trouble him. That phase of her life had long been forgotten. When he first met her she was Miss Wiggenhall, the sister of Sir Andrew who had just been knighted. Surely a knight's sister might be counted a suitable match, even for a Flotman."[163] Sadly for Colonel Flotman, although he is the one Hardware, Ltd., Board member who contributes nothing whatsoever to Board decisions, he too is marked down for death by the novel's implacable murderer.

Street's scorn for gentlemanly slackers who look down their noses at those who condescend to work in business is so marked that one is forced to wonder whether it indicates any personal experience on his part. The Major's own ancestry reflects a landed gentry background in which military service was highly respected; yet perhaps business employment, which Street entered when he became not merely a stockholder in but as well the electrical engineer for the Lyme Regis Electric Light & Power Company, Ltd., may not have been so favorably regarded. Street's strongest statement against the aristocratic anti-business attitude can be found in the Miles Burton novel *Mr. Babbacombe Dies* (1939). This novel presents the stock situation of the wealthy uncle surrounded by nieces and nephews to whom he most inconveniently denies money; yet, rather than depict the uncle as a selfish monster, Street portrays him as an admirable self-made man and his relatives as greedy incompetents. As a young man, Adrian Babbacombe had left his decaying family seat to find work in the office of a string factory. "I know on that Saturday morning when I was given ten bob as my first week's wages, I felt that I was the only member of the family who had done anything useful since the old Crusading ancestor who lay in the

Parish Church with crossed legs and a broken nose," Babbacombe colorfully puts it to his friend Desmond Merrion. Eventually the hardworking and energetic Babbacombe made a fortune in the string business. As his fortunes rose and those of the rest of the family declined, however, the relations who had shunned him when he went into salaried employment decided it was worthwhile having social connections with Adrian Babbacombe after all. After his death (by arsenic poisoning), his various nieces and nephews express their dissatisfaction over receiving among themselves only half of the Babbacombe estate, the other half having been divided among people connected with Babbacombe's business. Though he himself is a member of the landed gentry as the master of High Eldersham Hall, Desmond Merrion has no sympathy for Babbacombe's relations. "You'll admit, I suppose," he says to Arnold, "that making string is a more useful occupation than sitting round in a big house twiddling one's thumbs? Babbacome thought so, anyway, and I agree with him." Of Babbacombe's nieces and nephews, Merrion concludes dismissively, "They haven't got the necessary push and resolution to succeed in life, and if they had got those gifts they would think it beneath their dignity to employ them." Similarly, concerning the testamentary disposition of Babbacombe's estate Merrion feelingly declares: "Half of his money he bequeathed to those who would know how to make use of it. The other half he scattered over the bog for his relatives to squander. They're damned lucky, though they don't realize it."[164]

Just as Street had great respect for honorable and accomplished businessmen, he wrote with sympathy and knowledge of the lives of hard-working and resourceful market farmers and rural entrepreneurs in *The Menace on the Downs* (1931), *Mystery at Greycombe Farm* (1932), *The Charabanc Mystery* (1934) *The Milk Churn Murder* (1935), *Death of Two Brothers* (1941), *Death Visits Downspring* (1941), *Murder Unrecognized* (1955), *Licensed for Murder* (1958) and numerous other tales. Moreover, he empathetically treated humbler village folk in numerous books that appeared from the 1930s through the 1950s. In the chapter he contributed to the Detection Club Round Robin novel *The Floating Admiral* (1931), for example, Street focuses most of his narrative attention on a roughhewn old sailor, Neddy Ware. In the John Rhode tale *Dead Men at the Folly*, with the exception of a local mill owner and his wife (who live in the ancestral mansion of a long departed gentry family), virtually all the characters are working class types, presented by the author naturally, without the condescension toward "rustics" and "yokels" associated with the mystery genre in the Golden Age. In answering a query from Dr. Priestley about his investigation of the two murders that have taken place during the course of the tale, Superintendent Hanslet replies offhandedly that "there's no accounting for what ignorant country people will do"— to which the professor sharply retorts: "In my experience, they display more commonsense than the townsmen." Similarly, when in *The Charabanc Mystery* Inspector Arnold concludes that the murder that took place in the charabanc (touring car) was the work of one of the drunken members of the Dribbleford Chequers Darts Club, which had been traveling round in the vehicle to various pubs when the murder occurred, Merrion chastises Arnold by contrasting the occasional innocent bender of the honest, hardworking countryman with the perpetual and prolonged debauches of the decadent urban sophisticate:

> Look here, Arnold, I know a lot more about life in an English village than you do. I ought to, since I live in one. I'm willing to bet that all these fellows, for three hundred and sixty-four

days in the year, are thoroughly good fellows. Honest, sober, industrious, and as good company as you'd find anywhere. On the remaining day, they are out to enjoy themselves thoroughly, and they all get happily and gloriously drunk. You must admit that it's a jolly sight more respectable than getting sozzled on cocktails every day of the week.[165]

Street not only defended humble village natives from the townsman's classist scorn, he also wrote favorably of maligned migrant workers in the villages. Following George Orwell by six years, the Major (who was living in the Kentish village of Laddingford at the time) produced in 1937 a highly-informed work on hops-picking in Kent, *Death in the Hopfields* (the title, apparently considered too esoteric for a U.S. audience, was changed by Street's American publisher to *The Harvest Murder*). While the criminous aspect of the novel does not compare with the complexity of Street's best work, there is indeed much interesting social detail about seasonal hop-pickers in *Hopfields*, and Street registers considerable sympathy and appreciation for these people. In chapter nine of the novel, hop farmer Mr. Velley takes Inspector Waghorn on a tour of the hopfields, giving his companion from London a virtual sociological lecture on the labor force. "You don't have much trouble with them?" asks Waghorn. "Wonderfully little," avows Velley:

> "Some people treat them like dirt, because they come from the poorer parts of London. I won't say their ways are everything you might wish.... But they're thoroughly decent, respectable people at heart, and, speaking for myself, I've little fault to find with them. The greater part of the money they earn they spend in the district, which means a lot in a place like this. It isn't only the shops and the pubs that benefit either. There isn't a cottage round about that doesn't sell them flowers, or fruit or vegetables or eggs, or maybe a chicken now and then. We may be glad to see the back of them, but we've got to admit we couldn't do without them."

The broadminded, perceptive Velley even endorses the employment of government Inspectors to see that farmers maintain proper accommodations for the hop pickers.[166]

Though some reviewers, having no desire to be edified about British working conditions when reading a mystery novel, dismissed *Death in the Hopfields* as a bore, others found the novel highly worthy of praise. For example, the *London Mercury* declared: "The setting of Mr. Rhode's detective story is so well done, with its festooned hops-gardens and orchards, its oast-houses and its weather-beaten but still unvanquished old timbered inns, that it would fill an evening agreeably even with a less generous and capably presented assortment of crime." Respected literary critic Edward Shanks wrote favorably in *John O'London's Weekly* of the novel's "vivid glimpses of the background of the hop-garden," while the Liberal newspaper the *News-Chronicle* went so far as to pronounce *Death in the Hopfields* "Mr. Rhode's best book." Whether or not one agrees with that assessment, it is true that *Hopfields* offered mystery readers of the period an unusual essay in "social realism" by a Golden Age British detective novelist; and it is perhaps closer to the real England of those days than is, for example, Dorothy L. Sayers' beloved and vastly better remembered crime novel *The Nine Tailors*. Certainly the English brewers Whitbread & Co., Ltd., strongly vouched for the novel in its quarterly journal, *House of Whitbread*, affirming that "those who have been privileged to read his manuscript have been struck with the accuracy of Mr. Rhode's description of hop-picking and the ways of the pickers, and with the vivid way in which he explains farm management and the whole process of gathering, drying and pressing the hops."[167]

Throughout his novels Street shows respect for good workmen who know their

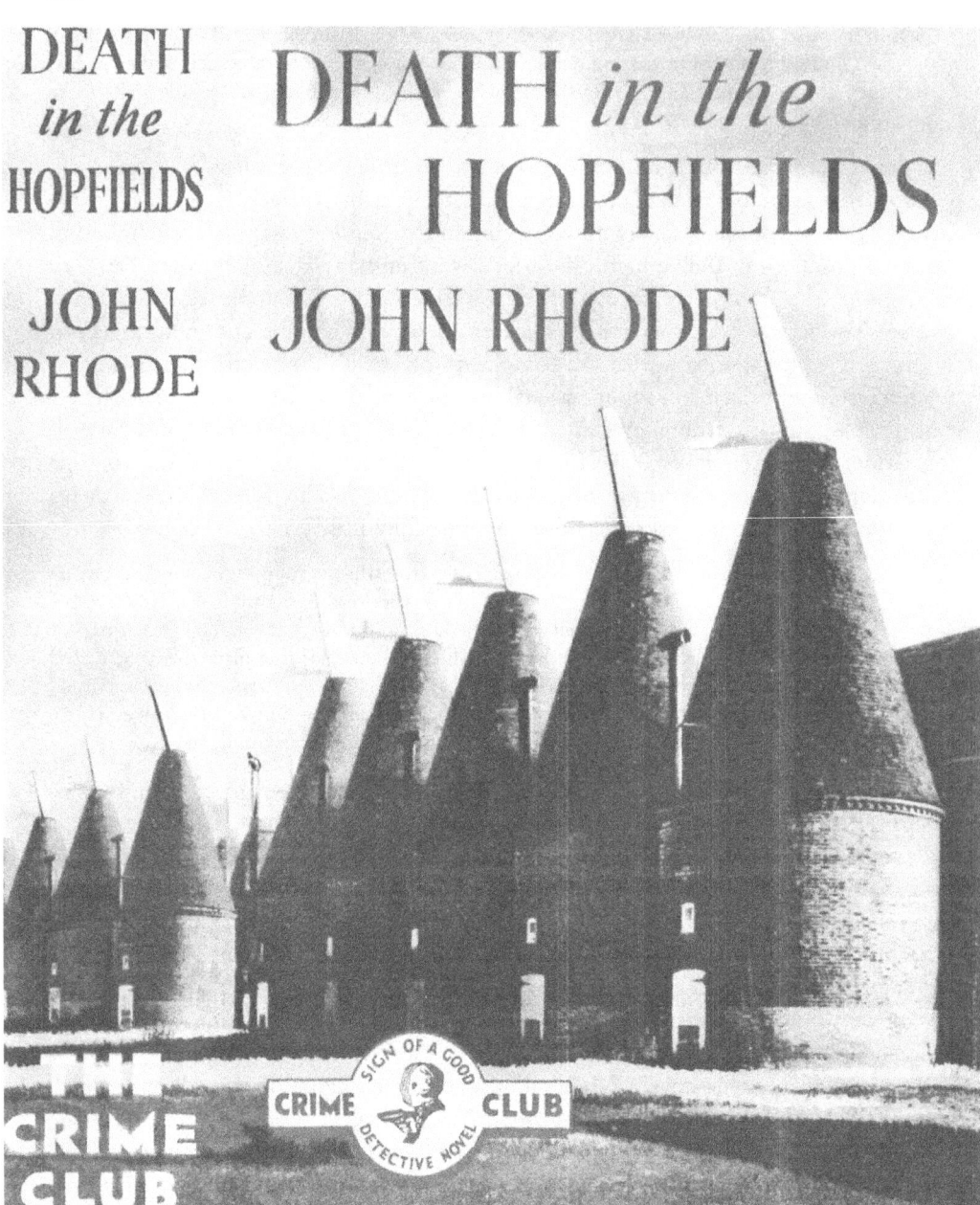

John Rhode, *Death in the Hopfields* (1937). In this 1937 novel, Rhode takes a great interest, as had George Orwell, in agricultural farm laborers.

trades. "A very decent, hardworking chap, and one of the most useful people in the town," comments Inspector Richings of Mr. Marle, craftsmen and keeper of a local second-hand furniture shop in *Dead Men at the Folly*. "Before the morning was out [Merrion] had acquired a deep respect for Pratt as a craftsman," similarly notes the author himself in *To Catch a Thief*. "He worked with a skill and expedition which would have made the village carpenter [in High Eldersham] open his eyes." Of the two Elvidge brothers in *Murder of a Chemist*— Josiah, the titular chemist, and Reuben, a furniture maker — it is not difficult to discern whom Street sees as the worthier man, after we follow the words of Reuben: "[Josiah] was always trying to make a big name for himself in the town.... He bought that house in Ottershaw Terrace simply to improve his social position. He didn't like it said his brother worked with his own hands in a tumbledown shop in a back street. And yet I dare say I'm worth as much as he is."[168]

Street extended this respect for good workmen to William Fitchley, the chauffeur-handyman in *The Corpse in the Car*. In that novel Lady Misterton, it will be recalled, left old coins under floorboards for Fitchely to discover in the course of performing work and then take, so that she could accuse him of theft and force him to sign an iniquitous contract. Street used similar material five years later in the Miles Burton title *Murder in the Coalhole*. In this book the obnoxious murderee, Vernon Polesworth, subjects Joe Masters, who is doing some work on Polesworth's bathroom, to his own honesty test by deliberately leaving a half-crown on the floor. Savvy and pugnacious, Masters drills a hole in the half-crown and nails it to the floor. When Polesworth angrily demands reimbursement of his half-crown, Masters spiritedly tells Polesworth that he will see him in hell first. Desmond Merrion's response to the episode —"a pretty low-down trick it is in my opinion"— echoes that of Inspector Hanslet to the Misterton-Fitchley affair in *The Corpse in the Car*: "A pretty mean trick on Lady Misterton's part." Street's use of this coin theft material in two different books leads one to suspect that the author may have heard of such an incident in actual life, perhaps in a public house from a workman himself, and docketed it for future writing use. An incident involving Street, a working-class man and a half-crown actually occurred in Swanton Novers in the 1940s, when Street, according to Paula Simpson, "gave the local milkman a half-crown on learning that he had just become a dad"— certainly a far cry from the fictional exchange between Vernon Polesworth and Joe Masters.[169]

Though Street manifests respect for the humble laborer in such works as *The Hanging Woman, Dead Men at the Folly, The Corpse in the Car, Death in the Tunnel, Murder of a Chemist, Death in the Hopfields, Murder in the Coalhole, Mr. Westerby Missing* and *Mr. Babbacombe Dies*, he evinces scorn for plutocrat financier Sir Hesper Bassenthewaite in *Death on the Boat Train*. Sir Hesper is an utter profligate, lustfully engorging himself on the pleasures of feminine flesh and material splendors. The author clearly disapproves of Sir Hesper's lifestyle, as can be seen in Superintendent Hanslet's bemused description of his official visit to the deceased titan's stately country mansion:

"Biggish place, isn't it?"

"Biggish!" Hanlet exclaimed. "It seemed to me that the house alone covered as much space as a small town, to say nothing of the park and the garden and the lawns and what-nots..."

"... The morning room, I may tell you, is about as big as the average police court and chock-full of furniture. The sort of stuff you see in antique shops, marked up with fancy prices. I felt as if I was in a museum and half expected a guide to turn up and show me round..."

"... So I asked [the butler] who else there was in the house. And it turns out there were thirty-two of them [servants].... Domestic staff, male and female, ranging from the butler to the fifth kitchen maid. And even then that number only included people actually living in the house.... And all for the purpose of looking after one solitary widower. I simply couldn't believe my ears."[170]

In Street's view the humble laborer who performs his work well is superior to such a profligate liver as Bassenthwaite. He is superior as well to the gentrified idlers who appear in many of Street's works, such as the occupants of the suburban "guest house" in *Death on Sunday*. Living incognito among them as part of a police investigation, Inspector Waghorn finds himself clinically contemplating his fellow guests and their foibles:

> It seemed to him extraordinary that they should be content to spend their lives doing absolutely nothing. They would eat more lunch than was good for them, and they would spend the next hour or two in digestive somnolence. They would then arouse themselves sufficiently to consume a hardy tea, after which they might indulge in a very little gentle exercise. Dinner time would find them capable of assimilating half a dozen courses. Later they would retire to bed, feeling, no doubt, that they had spent a most enjoyable day.[171]

Street's tone here is strikingly corrosive when one considers that he is writing of the class of people ostensibly beloved by Golden Age authors of this era.[172]

Street also directed scorn at men of property who declined to support the villages in which they resided, like Mr. Speight of Paddock Croft, Marling in *Death in the Hopfields*. "In [Police Sergeant] Wragge's opinion a man of Speight's position and means might do a little more for his poorer neighbors than he did," the author notes pointedly. "He was reputed to be a hard man and was not over-popular in the village." Street himself seems invariably to have taken a strong interest, in terms of both time and treasure, in local affairs. In Laddingford, Kent, for example, the author is recalled as a "true benefactor" of the village. Street served both as a local school governor, making many of the administrative decisions and paying out of his own pocket to send schoolchildren to concerts, and as the primary sponsor of the village cricket club, for which he acquired a sports field and pavilion, later donating both to the village when he and Eileen left Laddingford.[173]

Conversely, Street's work generally is restrained in its dealing with the servant class, avoiding the egregious condescending tendency in some Golden Age British detective fiction—derided by Colin Watson in *Snobbery with Violence*—to depict maids as rather dim, hysterical "Alices" ("Alices abounded in crime fiction," writes Watson, taking the name from a female domestic in Agatha Christie's *The Mystery of the Blue Train*. "They were undersized, had chronic sniffs, and were very easily moved to tears").[174] Sometimes in Street's novels female domestics are used for comic effect, as in *Vegetable Duck*, where the peppery cook, Ellen Runton, simply cannot stop talking, or in *The Dovebury Murders*, where the sour Mrs. Lines continuously grumbles about her near pathological skinflint employer (the splendidly-named Mr. Headcorn) and his continued refusal to buy a new cooker for the kitchen; but the humor is lightly done and genuinely amusing, without a sense of mean-spiritedness (indeed, it is clear that Mrs. Lines is quite right about that cooker).

Street offers the reader a more sustained look at household servants in the John Rhode title *Death Pays a Dividend* (1939), where, incidentally, the ingratiating young Inspector Waghorn becomes romantically attached to the cook of the London townhouse where murder has been done (however, the cook, Diana Morpeth, who Jimmy eventually marries, is not the rotund, imperious cook of mystery fiction stereotype, but a slim and sophisticated beauty of good birth who took up cooking due to her genteel family's unfortunately reduced circumstances). Besides Diana Morpeth, the servants in the household are the butler, John Taswell, the housemaid, Ivy Walker, and the parlor maid, Grace

John Street, Patron of the Laddingford Cricket Team. Street believed in supporting village institutions, such as, in this case, the grateful Laddingford cricket team. In his books Street condemned tightfisted wealthy village inhabitants, like *Death in the Hopfields*' Mr. Speight, who, in the opinion of Police Sergeant Wragge, "might do a little more for his poorer neighbors than he did" (courtesy Anthony Kremer).

Loveday (it can be seen that we even learn their full names). The first chapter is seen from Ivy's perspective, as she rises at half past seven in her "little room at the top of the house in Rufford Square" to get tea for the household and then go to work with her lantern, dustpan and brush. As she gets out of bed in "her clinging artificial silk nightie," we are told that Ivy is "young, slim and passably good-looking." Her thoughts as she gets to her early-morning tasks are not those of a nitwit Alice, but a perfectly competent and intelligent young woman:

> Ivy emptied the teapot into the sink. Then with the caddy spoon she put the tea into it: Six teaspoonfuls of old-fashioned, honest-to-goodness Indian tea. One for each person and one for the pot: That's what her mother had always taught her to do. She filled the pot with boiling water and sat down while she waited for the concoction to brew.... While she sat she hummed gaily a few bars of *Good King Wenceslas*. Christmas was already in the air. Ivy's thoughts wandered to her home where she would be on the following Saturday afternoon: The rambling, old pub kept by her father and mother, tucked away in the Kentish countryside. All her brothers and sisters would be home for Christmas — seven of them all told, including her. They'd have a topping time together. They always did.[175]

An immediate indicator of Ivy's virtue and good character to any practiced John Street reader is the young woman's lineal descent from pub-owning parents. When Ivy discovers a dead body on the front stairs, in her horror she does drop lantern, dustpan and brush, as anyone might do in the circumstances, but otherwise she keeps her head and sensibly reports the horrifying news to the butler.

Street's nuanced treatment of Superintendent Hanslet offers further evidence of the author's subtle approach to the matter of class. Unlike his protégé Jimmy Waghorn — a Cambridge man and Hendon Police College graduate born of a wealthy, professional father — Hanslet comes from a humble background and worked his way up within police ranks. In some 1930s novels, such as *Death at Breakfast* (1936), Hanslet can be maddeningly obtuse at times (as some contemporary reviewers on occasion complained, Hanslet never seems to understand that Dr. Priestley is Always Right) and he invariably fails to comprehend the literary allusions made by the more learned Dr. Priestley, Dr. Oldland and Inspector Waghorn. Justifiably, Dr. Priestley in *Hendon's First Case* concludes that Jimmy is the keener of the two men; yet both the professor and the author respect Hanslet's doggedness and determination. Indeed, in many ways Hanslet resembles the author, with his large size and weight, gruff humor and his love of beer, pipe and pub. In the late 1930s, the superintendent begins to feels his age and contemplates his impending retirement. Yet with the outbreak of war and the calling up of younger men, he finds himself kept on in service, increasingly grumbly and sleepy, like a bear kept from entering hibernation. Street portrays what I suspect may have been in many ways his fictive alter ego at this time with considerable wry self-awareness.

In *Dead on the Track* (1943), a case in which Hanslet functions as the sole lead investigator for the first time since 1935 (Jimmy, employed in Military Intelligence during the war, makes only a cameo appearance — albeit an important one — near the end of the tale), the local inspector delegated to meet Hanslet at the railway station is about to depart, "supposing that the man had missed his connection, when he is accosted by an elderly man, whose naturally imposing bulk was rendered vast by being swathed in a heavy overcoat and muffler." The vast muffler-swathed bulk announces that he is Superintendent Hanslet, much to the initial skepticism of the local man: "His first reaction was that this old museum piece was trying to pull his leg. Why should he be looking out for a wanderer from some institute for nonagenarians?" But "a deep chuckle" comes "from somewhere low down behind that preposterous muffler." "You weren't expecting to see an old dodderer like me, were you?" asks an amused Hanslet. "Can't we get somewhere out of this confounded draught, and I'll show my official card.... [N]ow all the younger chaps are busy hunting down folks who sell a turnip for a penny when the controlled price is three farthings, so we old fossils have to go out on less serious cases, such as murder."[176]

After lunch at 1:00 and a half-hour doze in a chair to digest his meal, Hanslet fills and lights "a large and evil-smelling pipe" ("There's no difficulty about getting the tobacco I like.... It's so rank no one else wants it") and proceeds to impart wisdom to the local man. In his twilight war years on the force, Hanslet finally cheerfully admits that his longtime friend Dr. Priestley is a man "who's very much cleverer than I am" and that "at least a dozen times I've backed the wrong horse." He now avows: "I've learnt by now to be a bit more cautious." Truth be told, the superintendent gives probably the most astute performance in this tale — though of course it is Priestley who ultimately puts every piece in the puzzle together.[177]

In another tale from that year, *Men Die at Cyprus Lodge*, Hanslet shows up late in the story, only to be less than graciously received by the local superintendent, who complains to Jimmy Waghorn, also in the neighborhood on an intelligence job, that the best Scotland Yard could find to help him with his murder case "was a superannuated buffer of the name of Hanslet." "I thought of offering him a bath-chair, with one of my chaps to pull it along," adds the superintendent contemptuously. Later Jimmy seeks Hanslet out in the older man's room in the local inn and finds him "washing his face in the basin with a prodigious spluttering." Jimmy, now on a more even level with his old mentor, ribs him with the story of the bath-chair gibe, to which Hanslet responds: "Bath-chair!... It's an electric chair he needs. Give him a shock to shake him up a bit. Never mind, I'll show him."[178]

Such moments as these make Hanslet one of the better realized police detectives of the Golden Age. This writer, at least, finds it easier to believe in Street's Hanslet than in both the exquisitely refined (and occasionally ever so twee) Roderick Alleyn and the uncompromisingly bland and virtuous Joseph French. By 1944's *Vegetable Duck*, which is preemptively set in the postwar period, Hanslet is finally permanently retired and insisting that he will soon remove himself from his London rooms out to a country cottage; yet somehow he never manages to do so (Hanslet is a somewhat misanthropic bachelor — he accepts assignment to a provincial case over Christmastime in order to get away from his relatives). Street might have employed a retired Hanslet as a way of introducing new cases in the Rhode series; but unfortunately the creatively flagging author henceforward allowed Hanslet only a role as part of the old man's chorus gathered at Dr. Priestley's weekly crime round table — a disappointing finale for a good character.

As with his attitude toward class, Street's attitude toward authority is not so easy to pigeonhole as the Symons-Watson school of criticism might suggest. Street definitely gave expression to anti-authority sentiment in his works. Aside from a dislike of Communism, which we see evidenced over the years in such works as *The Double Florin* (1924), *The Paddington Mystery* (1925), *The Platinum Cat* (1938), *The Secret Meeting* (1951), *Murder out of School* (1951) and *Licensed for Murder* (1958), Street's most persistent political stance over the decades, if it can be viewed as "political," was his opposition to compulsory closing hours for pubs (a passionate opposition that he shared with Golden Age detective novelist Rupert Croft Cooke, who wrote under the name Leo Bruce). A cantankerous Superintendent Hanslet can be seen speaking for the author when, in *Proceed with Caution* (1937), he denounces a host of trivial crimes on which he is forced to waste his professional time. Breaches of the licensing laws head his list of "things which are only crimes because some regulation or other makes them so," but he also takes time to denounce the Gambling and Shop Hours Acts. There are additional libertarian — some might say anarchic — sentiments in Street's novels. In *Murder in the Coalhole*, when Inspector Arnold learns that members of the local football club broke one of the windows in Vernon Polesworth's house after he kept a ball of theirs that was inadvertently kicked into his garden, Arnold admits, "I don't know that I altogether blame them." More seriously, as will have been seen already, murderers in Street's books frequently act with some measure of justification in the author's view. In *Death on Sunday*, when asked why the murderer slew the victim, Inspector Waghorn, knowing that the "victim" was blackmailing the murderer, replies quietly: "Because it was the only thing [X] could do."[179]

One of Street's most interesting denunciations of authority is found in *Night Exercise* (1942), his non-series World War II novel about murder among the Home Guard. At one point in the tale, Major Ledbury — who seems a clear Street surrogate (he even makes field observation from a church tower, as Street so often had done during World War I) — reflects bitterly on the incompetence of higher military authority:

> Ledbury glanced once more at the letters, and then laughed mirthlessly. They came to him through Battalion, but their reference numbers showed that they had originally emanated from Group, or possibly higher up still, from Zone or even from Area. His practical mind experienced a sudden revulsion at this long, rusty, and wholly unnecessary chain of command. Group, Zone, Area: each and all were controlled by incapable but possibly well-meaning senior officers. Soldiers with a fine reputation — gained, one would imagine, in the glorious fields of Victorian peace. They dwelt secure in a world of Olympian dreams, utterly remote from any contact with sordid reality. They had no idea of the difficulties of Volunteer Jones or his employer, or the loss of revenue suffered by Platoon-Commander Smith in devoting his time to the performance of his duties. And the maddening thing was that far from being of any use to the organization, they were a fifth wheel wobbling erratically in front of the coach.
>
> It was true ... that in this case the particular Group Commander concerned had been removed from the scene [though murder]. But that merciful event would benefit nobody. As Amurath to Amurath succeeds, so another officer of high rank, with a breast full of medals, a brain full of sawdust, and a mind incapable of appreciating the peculiar needs of the Home Guard, would appear from the limbo of obscurity to fill the vacant space.[180]

Such jaundiced reflections surely place Major Street at a far remove from Colonel Blimp.

Though he was not personally hostile to religion and indeed was, as his World War I writings make clear, a believer in a non-sectarian Higher Authority, Street in his fictional work often takes a skeptical view as well of those professing their religious/moral superiority. Like Rupert Croft-Cooke and his good friend John Dickson Carr, the Major greatly disliked religious Puritanism. In *Murder in the Coalhole,* Vernon Polesworth, surely one of Street's most deserving murderees, is revealed as a contemptible Puritan who prides himself on his great virtue but has no charity in his heart. "The only things that interested him were those blessed orchids of his," complains an acquaintance of Polesworth. "If any of the poorer folk of the village were in trouble he wouldn't stretch out a finger to help them.... He didn't drink and he didn't smoke, and it seemed to be a definite grievance to him that others did." Even the local Vicar comes in for a bit of tweaking, when he primly expresses his horror at a female schoolteacher spending an hour and a half alone in her room with a man ("I have no doubt that they were together guilty of the greatest impropriety"). Ministers, in fact, typically are portrayed in Street's novels as rather useless scatterbrains (if not brainless nincompoops), as in *To Catch a Thief* and *Death at the Club.* In the former novel, for example, the Reverend Alban Murrain of Poppleford Rectory is depicted as a sententious bore who persistently hogs the best seat at the fireplace in the lounge of a snowbound inn and talks the ears off anyone foolish enough to get too near him. "People with a voice like that were never happy unless they were inflicting it on someone else," reflects a disgusted Merrion.[181]

Colin Watson and H.R.F. Keating have accused Street of being prudishly shy about broaching the subject of sex in his books, but this accusation is far off the mark, as already indicated by the above quotation from *Murder in the Coalhole,* as well as by Street's having taken the time in *Death Pays a Dividend* to mention the passably attractive sight of housemaid Ivy in her clinging nightie and by his attribution of rather randy thoughts to Harold Merefield in *The Paddington Mystery.* Certainly the author's own life strongly suggests that the author took a broadminded view of human sexual relationships. A thorough reading of his fiction makes clear that adultery, out-of-wedlock sex and even implicit homosexuality are not subjects he feared addressing in his tales, as the following examples should more than suffice to show.

Adulterous wives are murder victims in both *Where Is Barbara Prentice?* and *The Telephone Call*. In *Death on the Boat Train,* a calculating and sexually amoral secretary becomes the mistress of a business tycoon, thereby providing a motive for the tycoon's murder to yet another man enamored with her. In *The Claverton Mystery*, we learn that one of Dr. Priestley's old friends has an illegitimate child, while another, Dr. Mortimer Oldland, had an adulterous affair and left his indifferent wife to live with his mistress (the author sympathetically treats both indiscretions). In *Death Invades the Meeting* (1944), a lawyer informs Superintendent Hanslet concerning the publican Mr. Tarrant and his wife that the woman living with him as Mrs. Tarrant "isn't really his wife. They aren't married, and he's got a wife alive who for reasons of her own won't divorce him." The lawyer adds regretfully: "There are women like that" (surely the situations in both *Claverton* and *Meeting* at least partially reflect Street's real-life personal circumstances). The actions of an unfaithful wife provide one of the motives for murder in *Death at Low Tide*, a novel that also sees a ship captain thinking longingly of his attractive wife's "delicious body." A gentleman believed to be using a country cottage for sexual weekend trysts comes under official scrutiny in a murder investigation in *Invisible Weapons*. In *Peril at Cranbury Hall*, a Belgian professor speculates of a missing man to a scandalized English attorney that "he may in Ostend have sought solace which Cranbury Hall, even your rigid England, could not have yielded him," before pronouncing: "Love is less fettered in Ostend than in Hyde Park, my friend." In *Shot at Dawn*, we learn that the murdered blackmailer possessed a collection of pornographic books ("he's got some books which I should be ashamed to let anyone see," comments a mortified Superintendent Hanslet). One of the blackmailer's victims is a middle-aged man, "rather florid-looking ... with sensual eyes and mouth," who admits that had his indiscretion been made public he would have been "utterly ruined, socially and professionally" and left with "no alternative but suicide." This dramatic admission is left vague by Street, but in its very vagueness it allows readers to imagine the possibility of something truly "awful," such as a homosexual encounter (implicitly homosexual males appear in three other Street novels: a Rhode, *Tragedy on the Line*, where reference is made to a male poet's "boyfriend"; and two Burtons, *Murder in the Coalhole* and *Heir to Murder*, in each of which an effeminate man falls under the influence of a stronger, more masculine one). In *Men Die at Cyprus Lodge*, a character explains that among previous tenants of the reputedly haunted house of the title were "three remarkably sprightly young women" who ran Cyprus Lodge as "what they called a guest-house, the guests being exclusively members of the opposite sex." He wryly adds that the young women "never complained about the house being haunted. One may venture the opinion that at night they were otherwise engaged than in listening for ghosts." Another prostitution reference is found in *Where is Barbra Prentice?*, where a young gentleman wastrel is jilted by his fiancée after she discovers that he spent a night with a prostitute in London. In *Invisible Weapons*, Dr. Oldland says of a jaded London society woman that "there was something about her that would have shocked a respectable prostitute." In *Death in the Hopfields*, Sergeant Wragge when visiting the local pub, The Chequers, ruminates as he surveys the posteriors of cavorting female hop pickers: "The girls were slim enough, good-looking too, most of them. But their mothers! You'd have a devil of a job to seat them five in a row in a railway carriage." After the murder of her nephew, Miss Maplewood of *Death Leaves No Card* tells Inspector Arnold, "I shall always be terrified of a man getting into my bedroom at night." Arnold glances at her figure and "feelingly" declares, "I don't think you need have any fears on that score, Miss Maplewood." Sexual banter is especially common in *Death Pays a Dividend*, as when housemaid Ivy tells Diana Morpeth in Diana's bedroom that their employer's private secretary had not been in his own room in the morning to have his tea. Diana naughtily replies, "Well, he's not in here, I can assure you. You can look under the bed and see if you like. Perhaps Grace [the angular parlor maid] knows something about it." Ivy giggles, finding Diana's banter "too funny for words." Brought up in a large family, Ivy knows "how to take a joke." Like Ivy, Street was no prude about sex.[182]

As indicated by his portrayals of Ivy Walker and Diana Morpeth, Street was capable of portraying women effectively when he chose. Street allows his male characters the occasional misanthropic comment, as has been seen already in *The Hanging Woman* and can be further glimpsed in an exchange in *The Davidson Case* between Inspector Hanslet and Dr. Priestley. Hanslet, believing that the murderer in the case is Olga Watkins, contends that she could have used a map to find her way around a countryside with which she was presumably unfamiliar, to which Priestley acerbically responds, "In my experience, the most certain means of ensuring that a woman will lose herself is to give her a map." Yet not all is from the male point of view. Street, who in Eileen Waller must have found an exceptionally independent-minded partner, shows considerable empathy for such unconventional, outspoken women characters in his books as Kitty Hapgood in *The House on Tollard Ridge*; Olga Watkins in *The Davidson Case*; Nancy Wickenden in *Tragedy on the Line*; Miss Carroll in *The Hanging Woman*; Ada Rayburn in *To Catch a Thief*; Caroline Flotman in *Death on the Board*; Miss Derwent in *Death on the Boat Train*; Stella Gargrave in *Dead on the Track*; Dr. Alida Mountwell in *Murder M.D.;* Lettice Baydon, the spirited yet kindly middle-aged spinster in *Death of Two Brothers*; and Jill Tattersett, the cynical girl's school teacher in *The Two Graphs* (1950), whose "profession of teaching had embittered her towards the human race, at all events as represented by her pupils." Moreover, Jimmy Waghorn's fiancée and later wife, Diana Morpeth, is an engaging creation who greatly humanizes Jimmy, but, regrettably, she appears in only *Death Pays a Dividend, Death on the Boat Train, The Fourth Bomb* (1942), *The Paper Bag* and *Up the Garden Path* (1949).[183]

Of all these women, probably the two most interestingly developed after Kitty Hapgood in *The House on Tollard Ridge* are Nancy Wickenden and Stella Gargrave. Perhaps not coincidentally, the two novels in which the women appear, *Tragedy on the Line* and *Dead on the Track*, are thematically linked (both have shooting murders disguised to look like accidents on train tracks and Hanslet in fact tumbles to this ploy in the latter novel by recalling Priestley's elucidation of the murder method in the former one). Nancy Wickenden and Stella Gargrave represent two different paths for women, that of independence and dependence. Wickenden, who earns her own living as a journalist, is a frank and free-living woman, who smokes, drinks, swears and speaks her mind on all subjects, including sexual ones, throughout the novel. Far from disapproving of her, the author allows her to function as the moral center of the tale and to win Dr. Priestley's approval. Indeed, Dr. Priestley is so taken with the woman that he engages in mildly flirtatious banter with her, somewhat surprising behavior for the formidable professor:

"Will you marry me, Dr. Priestley, and become the laird of Colingrove?"
"If I were thirty years younger, Miss Wickenden, I would close with your offer unhesitatingly."[184]

In her early thirties, Nancy is already divorced from one man and currently living with another, though she claims the relationship is platonic. Such behavior seems shocking to her smugly conformist, domestic sister-in-law, who complains about Nancy's wayward ways to Dr. Priestley:

"Nancy's outlook has always been abnormal, I suppose because she took up journalism when hardly more than a girl. I always think that women who call themselves independent and set out to earn their own living get distorted ideas.... She divorced her husband rather more than a year after she married him.... [S]he refused to give up her work and lead a normal domesticated life.... I sometimes think that Nancy has absolutely no moral sense."[185]

It is not difficult to discern which woman has the sympathies of both Dr. Priestley and the author.

Twelve years later, Street with the character Stella Gargrave sympathetically portrayed the pathos of a talented woman who gave up her independence for domestic security. Gargrave, we are told, had possessed great artistic promise, but was driven by her fear of poverty to relinquish her calling and meekly keep house for an imperious, self-centered brother she despised. When Hanslet interviews Miss Gargrave after the murder of her brother, he is surprised by her forcefully expressed ill will toward the deceased man. Hanslet cannot understand why she should have been unhappy. Street portrays the police superintendent ironically as obviously obtuse:

Hanslet felt the uncomfortable bewilderment he always experienced when confronted by a psychological problem.... To Hanslet's conventional mind this was very shocking. A sister should at least display a decent respect for her brother's memory, even if she didn't feel it.... [He] could not quite grasp what her grievance had been. She was living in the lap of luxury, and there were thousands of women who would have jumped at the chance of stepping into her shoes.[186]

Though Hanslet is perplexed by the complicated Miss Gargrave, it is her intelligence and powerful persuasive ability that drives him onward to solve — with Dr. Priestley's help of course — the murder of the brother she loathed, after the man she had once hoped to marry is implicated in the crime.

Street's perceptive eye caught the liberating effect of World War II on domestically confined British women. In contrast to the harassed traditionalist housewife Hermione Cecil in *Murder M.D.*, war wives in the village of Hoxdown in *They Watched by Night* (1941) find the global conflict a personally liberating event, as they paint their lips and fingernails, put on brightly-colored "trousers" and, so attired, invade the saloon bar of The Antelope, where they outrage at least one traditionalist male patron, who sourly complains to Jimmy Waghorn:

"I hate this place in the evening.... I don't like the company.... All talking at once."
"It's a bit of a Babel, certainly," Jimmy agreed.
"It's far worse. Babel was at least built in open air. This place is like the Black Hole of

Calcutta.... It's always full of women, chattering like so many magpies. Look at those two over there, tastefully dressed in trousers. Mrs. Quarrie and her friend Mrs. Otway. They live together at Cherry Garden Cottage on the Lower Road. Grass Widows. Both their husbands are serving somewhere in something.... I believe they are perfectly virtuous, though they do their best not to look like it."[187]

Women murderers in Street's books are a comparative rarity, even in the Burtons, which typically demand less mechanical expertise of murderers than do the Rhodes; yet they do exist. **[SPOILER ALERT]** Street's most interesting female culprit is the socially-ambitious Mrs. Wroughton in the Miles Burton novel *Murder of a Chemist*. Widow of the town's then Borough Sanitary Inspector, Mrs. Wroughton is dismayed when her son, Peter, another one of Street's heavily-caricatured moony-eyed, would-be poets, takes a job as a mere grocer's clerk. Her attempt to produce a monetarily advantageous marriage for Peter, so that she can restore her own social standing in her provincial town, leads eventually to her committing murder by putting oxalic acid in chemist Josiah Elvidge's lemon crush. In both *Chemist* and the immediately following Burton title, *Where Is Barbara Prentice?*, both from 1936, Street critiques furious (and occasionally fatal) feminine social competition in modern English provincial towns. "It's the ambition of every woman in Bridgeworthy to have a fur coat, even if she has to economize on her underclothes, I dare say," grumbles Superintendent Rowley in *Where Is Barbara Prentice?* "They seem to think it's a mark of social standing, like having a piano in the front room."[188]

Though she is a murderee, not a murderer, Barbara Prentice, the titular missing woman of the above novel, is one of Street's most interesting female characters: a malevolent, middle-aged gossip with a rapacious sexual appetite. Despised by and despising her physician husband, Mrs. Prentice puts the make on several younger men in town, finally succeeding in using her ill-gotten knowledge of dirty secrets to blackmail one of them into having a physical relationship with her. Barbara finally meets her quietus, but not before she has wrought considerable havoc on those unfortunate enough to have crossed her path. Though we never see Barbara Prentice alive, she makes a strong impression, rivaling Hermione Cecil of *Murder M.D.* as Street's most vividly unsympathetic female. **[END SPOILER ALERT]**

The most significant female murderer portrayed in Street's writings is the notorious, self-confessed killer Constance Kent, about whom Street wrote in *The Case of Constance Kent* (1928). The Constance Kent case is one of England's great true crime murders, one that has been the subject of numerous studies in articles and books, the most recent of which is Kate Summerscale's award-winning *The Suspicions of Mr. Whicher* (2008). Summerscale's book has been lauded as "eloquent" and "absolutely riveting."[189] Street's account is something less so, being told in a matter-of-fact and rather dry manner, reminiscent of Dr. Priestley himself. Yet his *Constance Kent* has significance as the first full-length study of the murder and, of further note, it served as the catalyst for an amazing development in the case, one no one could have anticipated at that late date. In 1928, the year that Street published his analysis of the infamous affair, sixty-eight years had passed since the murder had taken place. In 1860, Francis Saville Kent, the three-year-old son of Samuel Saville and Mary Pratt Kent, was found dead with his throat cut, in the household's outdoor privy. Jonathan Whicher, the celebrated Scotland Yard inspector eventually called in to help a floundering local police force, soon charged the dead boy's sixteen-year-old half-sister, Constance, with the horrible crime. This charge against her was dismissed by magistrates, leading to Whicher's public humiliation and premature retirement. Five years later, however, Whicher was vindicated when Constance, who had come under intense religious influence, confessed that she had indeed done the dark deed with her own hand. After serving twenty years in prison Constance was released and she left the country for parts unknown. At the time of the publication of *The Case of Constance Kent*, Constance had been absent from England for forty-three years and was assumed to be dead.[190]

Street's account of the murder demonstrates the same unsentimental, no-nonsense views of his contemporaneous political works. Street does not hesitate to find fault with the folly of various players in the drama, such as Constance's father, Samuel Kent, and the local police chief, Superintendent Foley. These two men particularly come in for much criticism from the author, Kent for his incompetence as the head of his family and Foley for his incompetence as the head of the murder investigation.

Samuel Kent married twice. His first wife, Mary Ann Windus, died in 1852. Fifteen months after her death, Samuel Kent married the family governess, Mary Pratt; and between 1854 and 1860, the couple had five children, including the future murder victim, Francis Saville. By his first wife Samuel Kent had produced ten children, five of whom died in infancy. In 1836, the first Mrs. Kent's state of health began breaking down, due, it was reported at the time and still accepted in Street's day, to the onset of insanity. Nevertheless, Samuel Kent continued to father, in rapid succession, six more children by his wife, four of whom died. Constance, a survivor, was born in 1844. A brother born the next year, William Saville, also lived to adulthood. Mary Ann Kent's health is said to have collapsed completely at this point, and she had no more children before her death in 1852. Himself a father of one child, Major Street was not enamored with Samuel Kent's conception of family planning. The author evinces no sympathy with Victorian concepts of patriarchy. Samuel Kent "seems to have been the typical mid–Victorian father, ruling his family and household by the light of stern puritanical principles," Street notes scornfully. "So long as his wife remained in good bodily health, he seems to have considered it right and fitting that she should continue to become the mother of defective children, irrespective of her mental condition. There can be very little doubt that this attitude on his part was responsible for the tragedy which subsequently occurred."[191]

Inspector Whicher quickly came to believe that Constance hated her new "mother"—her former governess—and spitefully murdered her own half-brother in order to exact vengeance upon the woman. Making a canny deduction in a matter involving Constance's three nightdresses (as a fictional mystery in the Golden Age the case could well have been titled *The Mystery of the Missing Nightdress*), Whicher charged Constance with the crime. Though his charge against Constance was dismissed by magistrates and Whicher was publicly disgraced for a time, he ultimately was vindicated when Constance confessed to the crime five years later. Street is unfailingly admiring of Whicher's mental capacity and professionalism, and he strongly contrasts the Scotland Yard man with blundering local police (the Scotland Yard man who shows up the natives is a staple of Golden Age works of detection). "Of Superintendent Foley ... it is difficult to speak without impatience," writes the author. In thusly dismissing the local Superintendent, Street specifically cited the undue deference Foley paid to Samuel Kent, a locally prominent man. "Foley ... was hardly the stuff of which great detectives are made," Street comments witheringly. "He was a partially educated man who had risen through the ranks through no particular merit of his own, and the occurrence of a crime in the house of a man whom he regarded as far above himself in station had entirely upset his faith in human nature and the essential fitness of things." Street argues that the local Superintendent became mentally paralyzed when he realized that his murder investigation threatened to implicate individuals within a higher class household, for "his chief idea was not to offend the gentry, as opposed to the common folk."[192] The result was that Foley had utterly bungled the case before Inspector Whicher's arrival.

Street himself thought that Constance Kent was "undoubtedly guilty," though he found aspects of her 1865 confession "frankly incredible." Like his fictional creation Dr. Priestley, Street looked beneath the surface of things and dispassionately proceeded to demonstrate point-by-point logical flaws in the document. Again like the Professor, Street even performed an experiment to test the plausibility of one point in the confession:

> The wound on the [child's] chest was inflicted through such remarkably unyielding substances as the blanket and the child's clothing. Now, I recommend anybody who is prepared to accept this statement that this wound was inflicted with a razor to try the following experiment. Wrap a stale loaf of bread in a blanket and endeavor to inflict such a wound as is described upon it with an ordinary razor. It is difficult enough to make a long cut on the loaf, but to stab it, as the child was undoubtedly stabbed, is utterly impossible. The end of the razor is not sharp enough, and the blade cannot be held sufficiently rigidly to allow the necessary force to be exerted.

"For some reason or other," Street finally concluded, "Constance Kent preferred not to tell the exact story of the happenings at Road Hill House on the night of June 29th, 1860." The author suggests a desire on Constance's part "to concentrate the guilt upon herself," but he does not elaborate this point.[193]

Less than six months after Street published *The Case of Constance Kent*, Geoffrey Bles, publishers of the book, received an astounding letter postmarked from Sydney, Australia. "Rhodes [sic] in his 'Case of Constance Kent' has made a great feature of insanity. Was Mrs. Kent insane?" began the missive. The writer then went on to explain that the first Mrs. Kent was not mad, as had been asserted in Street's book, that the governess and second Mrs. Kent had been sleeping with Samuel Kent while his first wife was alive and that the latter woman was cruel and vindictive toward Constance. Constance, determined to revenge herself upon this woman for the wrongs committed against her and her mother, committed "her most callous and brutal crime," the murder of her three-year-old half-brother.[194]

Naturally when his publisher showed Street this letter, the author was highly intrigued. Was an eighty-four year old Constance Kent alive and living in Australia and had she reached out, not from beyond the grave but from over the oceans, to correct Street's record of this terrible affair of nearly seventy years ago? After the Detection Club formed in 1930, the Major donated the letter to the Club library of crime fiction and history, where it was later lost or destroyed amidst the chaos in London during World War II (fortunately, Street typed a copy of the letter himself and this copy was later discovered in his papers after his death). When the Detection Club published a collection of true crime essays in 1936, *The Anatomy of Murder*, Street took the opportunity to revisit the Kent case with this new piece of evidence, which he dubbed the Sydney document.

Again Street took time to fault local law enforcement for class-related inhibitions that hobbled the pursuit of justice. "The proceedings at the inquest were farcical," declares Street peremptorily:

> The one aim of the coroner and of the foreman of the jury seems to have been to exonerate the members of the family. They could not believe that persons of their station in life could have committed such a crime. Much the same reluctance even to consider their guilt seems to have inspired the local police. They acted from the first upon this theory. No member of the family could possibly have committed the crime. Therefore the criminal must be sought among the servants, or some intruder from outside must be imagined.[195]

Street also continued to heap scorn on Samuel Kent. Noting that in determining to revenge herself on her stepmother by slaying her stepmother's and father's young son, "it did not seem to occur to Constance that the blow would be almost as acutely felt by her father, to whom she was apparently genuinely attached," the author hypothesizes:

> Perhaps she believed that her father would soon recover from his sorrow at the death of his youngest son. Mr. Kent had endured such bereavements before without showing any signs of being overwhelmed by them. At the date of the crime he had already had thirteen children, and was expecting the arrival of a fourteenth. Five of these had died in their infancy. Surely by this time such calamities must have lost their power to depress him unduly![196]

However, Street's main interest in this essay, "Constance Kent," was to explore "the curious personality of the criminal herself" through means of the Sydney document. Street seems impressed with the intelligence and determination of the girl, however perverse her act. Noting that Constance was contemporaneously described as wearing an expression in court more of "stupid dullness than intelligence," Street avers, "we can only suppose that her expression on this occasion belied her. Stupid dullness is certainly not a characteristic of her crime and of her subsequent conduct." Street suggests that Constance anticipated that "such a callous and brutal murder would not be attributed to a girl of sixteen." The author argues further that Constance felt a sense of "justification" in her bloody deed, finally confessing "under the influence of religious emotion," not in order "to save her own soul, but to remove the load of suspicion from others." Possibly, he speculates, that "original idea of justification never left her until very much later."[197]

Despite his speculations on Constance's character, Street admitted that he continued to find Constance "an elusive personality." One thing the author had very much wanted to determine for once and all in this vexing case was whether Constance herself had written the Sydney Document, as he for one believed. The writer of the Sydney document had declared that Constance Kent had "changed her name and gone overseas and, single-handed, fought her way to a good position, and made a home for herself, where she was well-liked and respected before she died."[198] Street suspected that this claim of death was subterfuge from the hand of the Road Hill House murderess. The next year, Street had the letter analyzed by a prominent handwriting expert, C. Ainsworth Mitchell, who unfortunately concluded that the letter had not been written by Constance Kent. Not until 1979, with the publication of Bernard Taylor's magnificently researched *Cruelly Murderered: Constance Kent and the Killing at Road Hill House*, was it established conclusively that Constance Kent had indeed migrated to Australia, become a highly respected nurse there, and, after reading Street's book, written the Sydney document. And only in 2008 did Kate Summerscale offer a theory, based on unpublished confidential reports made by Inspector Whicher in 1860, that Constance was aided by her fifteen-year-old brother,

William, who stabbed the young boy with a knife while Constance cut his throat with a razor. This theory explains the presence of the numerous discrepancies which Street had noted between the facts of the case and Constance's confession, such as Street's point about the impossibility of making stab wounds through a blanket with a razor. Once again, Street had proven adept at the mechanics of murder, even in a true crime context. He also demonstrated interest in that supposed *bete noire* of the Humdrum writer, criminal psychology, in this case that of a truly exceptional sixteen year old girl.

Accusations that Street held anti-Semitic attitudes have already been discussed and dismissed, outside the context of his detective novels. As far as Street's detective novels are concerned, they are almost entirely free of anything that might be perceived as anti-Jewish commentary. Indeed, to the contrary, Street's thriller *The Double Florin*, as already discussed, is arguably philo-Semitic. As for the detective tales, Jews rarely appear in them. When Street put his knowledge of the real-life Polna ritual murder case to use in *The Menace on the Downs*, for example, he changed the religion implicated in the murders from Judaism to a fictional pagan cult. Admittedly, the murder victim in *The Paddington Mystery* is an unattractive, unsympathetic Jew, but Street portrays him, Shylock-like, as a bigot infuriated when his daughter marries a Christian. The stance taken by Street in the novel is unlike that found, say, in the works of G.K. Chesterton, in that it is implicitly assimilationist in its view of the proper relationship between English Jews and Christians. This same assimilationist stance can be glimpsed again in a later 1951 John Rhode title, *The Secret Meeting*. London second-hand clothes dealer Steinie Gunberg is introduced as "a young, flashily-dressed man" with a smile "exhibiting an assortment of gold-filled teeth." Jimmy Waghorn initially is dubious about Steinie Gunberg, but by his second meeting with him, Jimmy has begun "to acquire a liking for Steinie. He was certainly bright, and there was nothing in any way furtive in his manner."[199] Jimmy to his gratification finds Steinie thoroughly Anglicized.

Unquestionably, Jews come off better in Street's books than do his old nemeses from his wartime intelligence years, the Catholic Irish, who are treated scornfully in both *The Bloody Tower* and *The Three-Corpse Trick*. "You aren't making allowances for his native Irish wrong-headedness," Desmond Merrion tells Inspector Arnold of the fifth-columnist Dermot O'Malley in the latter work. In the former title, the husband of the Irish-born servant Mrs. Horning defends his wife's drinking like a fish and wailing like a banshee thusly: "You must excuse her little ways, sir, but she's Irish and can't help it."[200]

A final word needs to be said about John Street's qualities as a writer, a subject not even considered worthy of mention by those, like Julian Symons, who have dismissed his books as mere puzzles. Certainly Street made no claims for himself as a serious novelist. "There is a very large class of reader," he once asserted matter-of-factly, "which likes a book in which something happens. This class is concerned with plot rather than characterization.... The average reader ... wants a good story rather than anything else."[201] It is clear that Street as a genre writer valued plot first and foremost. As I have endeavored to show, at his best he was a very good plotter indeed, in my opinion one of the finest in the genre. But Street's tales also have more color and humor than they have been credited with having. It seems to me that an author's personality inevitably comes forward in his work, and Street's genial, worldly and intelligent personality comes forth in his. His best works have strong plots and tell good stories as well.

Need more be said for them? Some will want to know whether they are good *novels*, as works by Sayers, Allingham, Marsh, Innes and Blake often are said to be. I hope I have demonstrated that there actually are interesting ideas to be found in Street's detective fiction, but I would not go so far as to compare them with the better serious mainstream novels. After his early, bathetic attempts at "love interest" in such twenties works as *A.S.F.* and *The Alarm*, Street for a time abandoned attempts to channel stronger emotional currents into his tales. However, something of a change can be detected in his writing over the course of the 1930s, as his books lose much of their remaining Victorian reserve from the twenties and become more "modern" and sexually frank. It would also appear that Street was influenced to some extent by the rise at this time of the detective novel of manners, as popularized by the famed trio of Sayers, Allingham and Marsh, with its sophisticated gentlemen detectives and their equally sophisticated love interests (Lord Peter Wimsey and Harriet Vane, Albert Campion and Amanda Fitton, Roderick Alleyn and Agatha Troy). Inspector Jimmy Waghorn, introduced by Street in 1935, comes of a good family, has been to public school and Cambridge and by 1939 has fallen in love with a lovely, witty and talented modern woman, Diana Morpeth. One does not have to be a Great Detective to see the influence of the Crime Queens here.

During this time Street also wrote a more atmospheric tale, *The Bloody Tower*, as well as a couple persuasive novels of character, the Burton title *Murder M.D.* (discussed above) and the Rhode title *Death at the Helm*. In its ironic narrative tone *Murder M.D.* approaches the brilliant village manners novels of Agatha Christie (see especially *The Murder of Roger Ackroyd* and *The Murder at the Vicarage*), while with *Death at the Helm* Street makes a greater attempt to locate murderous impulses in human passions and to portray the tragic human consequences of murder. In *Death at the Helm*, Hugh Quarrenden, the renowned King' Counsel, is a well-conveyed and ultimately moving character, as recognized in *A Catalogue of Crime*. Lending an air of more stylish sophistication to the book is its sympathetic presentation of a modern artist and his often scantily-clad model, Poppy, a somewhat bohemian couple who earlier in their relationship had cohabited without benefit of marriage.[202] The means by which the double poisoning is accomplished is interesting as well, but what one remembers most about the book is the heavy emotional toll that murder takes from a couple of the novel's characters.

Death at the Helm is presaged by two earlier sober Rhode titles from 1933, *The Claverton Mystery* and *The Venner Crime*. In the latter title, overpowering remorse by a murderer plays a key role in the unfolding of a highly complex plot, in which one can feel empathy for all those entangled in its meshes, and even Dr. Priestley, who normally "treated detection as he would have treated a game of chess," is not left unscathed.[203] In *The Claverton Mystery* (1933), Street sensitively treats the theme of adultery and its consequences for personal happiness. The more serious tone of the two 1933 Rhode novels perhaps may have been inspired in part by the 1932 death, at the quite untimely age of twenty-five, of Verena Street, the Major's daughter by his estranged wife. In *Claverton*, Priestley's old friends Dr. Mortimer Oldland and Sir John Claverton are revealed as, respectively, an adulterer and the father of an out-of-wedlock child. Street treats the pair of morally erring men sympathetically, at the end of the tale even affording Oldland's son from his broken marriage and Claverton's illegitimate daughter the promise of impending happiness in the form of wedded matrimony together. Perhaps with *Claverton* Street indulged in imagining a happier outcome for fathers and children than the one which in fact had materialized for him and Verena.

To be sure, Street's writing style is deliberately plain, without the stylistic flourishes desired by many from a novel. Unlike his friend John Dickson Carr, Street typically eschews romanticizing his works with Gothic-style backgrounds (*The House on Tollard Ridge* and *The Bloody Tower* are partial exceptions, though any romantic Gothicism one might find in the latter tale is undercut by its uncompromisingly squalid agrarian realism). For example, in the haunted house mystery tale *Men Die at Cyprus Lodge* Street makes the novel's reputed ghost not that of some medieval monk or Jacobean cavalier, but that of a prosaic Victorian-era tradesman. However, Street occasionally does share with Carr and other Golden Age detective novelists like Gladys Mitchell a sense of the colorfully odd, which we can see, for example, in his depictions of the bizarre room of stuffed cats in *The Corpse in the Car* and the poisoned plate of calf's head in *Hendon's First Case*, as well as in his Monty Pythonesque use of a green-hued hedgehog as an instrument of death in *The Ellerby Case*.

Street's writing occasionally can be rather arresting, as in this passage from *The Bloody Tower*, which conveys the dismal state of squalor into which Farningcote Priory and its denizens have fallen:

> She nodded toward a half open door, and at this invitation, Appleyard and Jimmy entered the room to which it led. It had a stone-flagged floor, damp-streaked walls and a ceiling from which most of the plaster had fallen, revealing the laths above. Bare of furniture but for a couple battered packing cases, and with a single iron-barred window set high up in the wall, the room was reminiscent of a prison cell. It had probably been intended by the architect of the house as the servants' hall.
>
> They had hardly entered the room when Mrs. Horning, who had repossessed herself of the saucepan, followed them. She went up to Jimmy whom, apparently, she mistrusted slightly less than Appleyard. She put her face so close to his ear that he could feel her hot nauseous breath at the back of his neck. "I was wondering if you had a drop of drink in your pocket by any chance," she whispered hoarsely.[204]

In the same novel, Street does not stint on portraying the gruesomeness of a shooting murder, in contravention of Colin Watson's claim in *Snobbery with Violence* that violence in Golden Age detective fiction is "conformist, limited, unreal." Asserts Watson: "A bullet-hole almost invariably is 'neat' (as a putt in golf, perhaps).... Blood is generally a 'spreading stain' or a 'pool,' both fastidious expressions that convey nothing of the terrible glistening mess that is made of human butchery." Yet in the aptly named *Bloody Tower* there are none of Watson's neat bullet holes: "The right side of his face was completely blown away, leaving nothing but naked and shattered bone. His dark hair was matted with blood and his left eye, apparently uninjured, stared glassily toward the cobweb hung rafters." Later the farmer's boy who discovered the corpse describes with the callous relish of adolescence what he saw: "When I got closer, I see that his head was all bashed in. Coo, wasn't there a muck of blood, too! I never see the like since Charlie—his dad's a butcher—took me into the yard to see a pig stuck."[205]

In addition to being able to depict a vivid scene, Street is capable of employing a pithy comment or turn of phrase. When Jimmy Waghorn skeptically asks the designing Miss Derwent of *Death on the Boat Train* whether she was happy as Sir Hesper Bassenthwaite's latest mistress, the lady is characteristically unsentimental and matter-of-fact about the value of true love versus that of material security: "Love in a cottage wouldn't appeal to me I'm afraid; I vastly prefer indifference in a mansion." Similarly amusingly blunt is the reply of the acerbic Dr. Prentice in *Where Is Barbara Prentice?*, when he is asked by the police whether he can assure them that his missing wife is not hiding in his house: "My dear, sir, I can assure you of nothing. For all I know or care, my wife may be hiding in the attic, living upon the cheese from the mousetraps." And in *Death on Sunday*, a hirsute minister's face is picturesquely described as follows: "Mr. Lextable's features were barely visible behind the veil of eyebrows, side whiskers, mustache and beard. Only when he raised his head did you become aware of mild blue eyes hiding like frightened dryads in an impenetrable forest."[206] Unquestionably, Street was a plain, straightforward writer, but that does not mean that his writing completely lacked all charm or piquancy.

What John Street's novels most typically offer is an engaging grounding in solidly English settings, especially the great institution of the British public house, which to Street, like to G.K. Chesterton and H.G. Wells, was a locus of all that was good in his native land. "If you take my tip, Mr. Richings, you'll never neglect the pub," Superintendent Hanslet fervently advises a local police inspector in *Dead Men at the Folly*. "If the landlord keeps his ears open, he can hear more of what's going on than the squire, the parson, the schoolmaster and the policeman put together. And I'll go so far as to say that if he's a decent, right-minded man, he can do more good in a little place than any of them." Even Dr. Priestley — certainly not a man given to pub crawling — in conversation with Harold Merefield pays tribute to the utility of pubs in murder investigations: "Really, my boy, the public-house is the finest possible place in which to obtain information." In *The Robthorne Mystery*, Street indicates that, like his characters, he saw the publican as having edged the patrician from his place of prominence in the English village, an occurrence all to the good: "Mr. Bolsom was an illustration of the old adage that the rulers of an English village are the squire, the parson, and the publican. The squire was dead, and the Manor house empty, so Mr. Appleby [the parson] and Mr. Bolsom [the publican] were left to divide their kingdom between them."[207]

Particularly in the Burton novels, but also in the Rhodes as well, detectives pay homage to publicans by spending a great deal of time in their places of business, extracting details from the locals and, not altogether incidentally, consuming copious amounts of food and drink. In *Murder in the Coalhole*, Desmond Merrion and Inspector Arnold are at the Red Lion dining on beer, roast lamb, potatoes and Brussels sprouts on page nine, devouring "an enormous homemade cake, two pots of jam and a huge pile of bread and butter" on page fifty-one (Merrion declines dried haddock) and gorging on boiled pork on page 207. By page 230 Merrion is ready for yet more sustenance, burbling happily: "Ah, here comes lunch. I can hear Mrs. Cadby's fairy footsteps on the staircase." No wonder the gentleman detective is moved to impart to Arnold the revelation that "the English race owes its virtue of sound common sense to substantial joints accompanied by beer." In another Miles Burton novel, *Fate at the Fair*, we learn that during his rural England murder investigations Merrion vastly prefers as lodging "the old-fashioned inn to the modern and usually dreary hotel." Newly arrived in the town of Middleford and looking for a place to spend the night, Merrion turns up his nose at gentry-patronized The Golden Fleece, choosing instead a humble abode favored by commercial travelers. "Trust the commercial to make himself comfortable," pronounces the amateur detective, as he settles comfortably in for the night. The coziness of Street's inns and pubs is such that when, in *Proceed with Caution*, an abandoned hearse, complete with a coffin in the back, is glimpsed by a publican early one morning outside his establishment, the image is particularly disquieting, like a crow on the cradle.[208]

One does find in Street's detective stories literary quotations and allusions, particularly to Biblical and classical sources and to Victorian-era writers like Charles Dickens, Alfred Lord Tennyson, Matthew Arnold and Algernon Charles Swinburne. For example, Lettice Baydon, a middle-aged clergyman's daughter in *Death of Two Brothers* (1941), at one point recalls a line from Swinburne's 1865 verse play, *Atalanta in Calydon*: "And lo, the feast turned funeral." Sometimes these references are quite apt. In *Murder in the Coalhole*, Miss Day, cleaner at the Middleden Elementary School, fearing an intruder, brandishes a poker "in an attitude of Ajax defying the lightning," a reference made ironically humorous by the dumpy Miss Day's incongruity with imposing figures from Greek myth.[209] Similarly, a doctor's suburban home in *Invisible Weapons* is named Epidarus (after a city state in Greece, thought to be the birthplace of Apollo's son Asclepius, the healer)—a source of much irritation to the local constabulary, which deems the name pretentious. Occasionally, Street will surprise the reader with a reference to an unusual work like Rudyard Kipling's science fiction story "Wireless" (*The House on Tollard Ridge*) or Robert W. Chambers' macabre collection of tales, *The King in Yellow* (*Invisible Weapons*). Admittedly Street does not parade in his work the "artsy" learning of a Sayers, Blake or Innes, but he displays a greater depth of literary knowledge than critics wedded to the Humdrum stereotype and unfamiliar with his books have been willing to grant him.

Though not a great literary quotation dropper, Street's Dr. Priestley is a true Great Detective, one of the most impressive in the genre in his implacable truth seeking. While Desmond Merrion retains charm and appeal, he remains a somewhat derivative figure, one less colorful then his gentlemanly brothers in detection, Wimsey, Campion and Alleyn. Priestley, however, is an awesome figure, one of talismanic power. "I am merely one of those people whose business it is to reach logical conclusions," he declares mildly in *Shot at Dawn*—and what amazing displays he makes of that business. Remorseless logic is a wondrous thing to behold. No wonder then that in his novels Street likens this oracle of detection to a graven image. "It was like offering supplications to a graven image," thinks a World War II military officer after bringing his problem to the great Dr. Priestley. In *The Two Graphs*, when Priestley abruptly snaps at a suspect, "When did you last see Harry Binfield, Mr. Downing," the man gasps and hesitates, utterly shaken. "It was as though a graven image had suddenly become animate with this startling question."[210] In Dr. Priestley's hands, truth inevitably will out, and all questions will be answered. No mere mortal, however clever, can resist him.

Whatever greater literary qualities might be claimed for the author's work, John Street himself likely would have asked for no more than to be recognized as a prolific spinner of frequently ingenious tales of fair play detection. In his introduction to 1933's joint Detection Club novel, *Ask a Policeman*, Street wrote, with humorous self-deprecation: "I have come to the conclusion that writing detective stories is just like any other vice. The deed is done without one's having any clear knowledge of the temptation which led up to it." Whatever temptation led John Street to take up the "vice" of writing detective stories, readers are fortunate that he did so, for he left many entertaining works well worth perusal, even in today's less patient times. "Mr. Rhode has devised more brilliant and unusual ways of getting rid of unwanted members of the human race than any other writer I know," author Sheila Kaye-Smith once admiringly observed of her favorite living detective novelist.[211] Indeed "John Rhode" had, with "Miles Burton" contributing his share too. John Street, the man behind those pseudonyms, should be remembered as a significant and accomplished figure within the detective fiction genre, one of its supreme artisans of murder.

CHAPTER THREE

Freeman Wills Crofts (1879–1957)

The Greatest Puritan of Them All

IN HIS 1972 SURVEY OF THE DETECTIVE FICTION GENRE, *The Puritan Pleasures of the Detective Story*, Congregationalist minister Erik Routley designated railway engineer turned celebrated mystery novelist Freeman Wills Crofts as "perhaps the greatest puritan of them all." To my mind there is no "perhaps" about it. Crofts' work characteristically has been noted for its carefully structured plots, seemingly impregnable alibis and exhaustively-detailed timetables, and for good reason. During the Golden Age of detective fiction, when readers placed a great premium on clever puzzles, Crofts was one of the genre's most popular writers, being generally considered, as a Collins Crime Club report stated of the author in 1931, England's "supreme technician" of mystery plot construction. Beyond question, an appreciation of Crofts' once much-lauded technical mastery (in contrast with his often less than felicitous prose style) is essential to understanding the great success that he enjoyed as a writer of detection. In addition to his still acknowledged mystery milestone, *The Cask* (1920), Crofts produced in his peak period (roughly 1927 to 1936) at least eight genre masterpieces: *Inspector French and the Starvel Tragedy* (1927), *The Sea Mystery* (1928), *Sir John Magill's Last Journey* (1930),

Freeman Wills Crofts. The master of the railway timetable detective novel was also one of the Golden Age British detective novelists most influenced by intense religious feeling (Bassano, 13 June 1939, © National Portrait Gallery, London).

Mystery in the Channel (1931), *The Hog's Back Mystery* (1933), *Mystery on Southampton Water* (1934), *Crime at Guildford* (1935) and *The Loss of the "Jane Vosper"* (1936). In terms of theme, however, Crofts' most important quality is, as Erik Routley asserted, his religious Puritanism. Of the famous mystery novelists who began writing in the Golden Age of detective fiction, Freeman Wills Crofts is the one most clearly and strongly influenced in his work by a rigorous moral sense grounded in evangelical, Low Church spirituality. His books often can be read as moral parables of murder, warning readers of the dangers offered to the human soul by worldly temptations, most notably avarice. It is important to comprehend of Crofts that not only was he once classed among the greatest writers working in the mystery genre ("an oracle of detective fiction"), but also that he remains — however one today may appraise his purely literary ability — one of the genre's most singular voices, unquestionably "the greatest puritan of them all."[1]

Religion played a central role in Freeman Wills Crofts' life from his early childhood, with Crofts having grown up in the home of his Anglican minister stepfather, the Venerable Jonathan Harding. Crofts' father, a surgeon-lieutenant in the British army and scion of a County Cork landed gentry family that included several Church of Ireland ministers, had died of fever in Honduras before Crofts was born; and his widowed mother married Reverend Harding when Crofts was but three years old. The small family lived in the little Ulster mill town of Gilford, where Harding was minister for thirty-five years (he later became Archdeacon of Dromore). Crofts attended grammar school at Methodist and Campbell Colleges in Belfast before apprenticing in 1897, at the age of eighteen, to his maternal uncle, Berkeley Deane Wise, chief engineer of the Belfast and Northern Counties Railway from 1888 to 1906. Engineer Wise was a celebrated figure in Northern Ireland at that time, as he additionally functioned as architect and landscaper for this important railway company, designing and building railway stations as well as "tea rooms, promenades, beaches, bandstands, paths and footbridges at beauty spots all along the [BNCR]." Crofts himself worked as a railway engineer in Northern Ireland until the success of his books in the 1920s allowed him to retire from the engineering profession in 1929 and fully devote himself professionally to his writing. In 1912 Crofts had married the daughter of a bank manager in Coleraine, and, after his retirement from railway work, he and his wife moved from Northern Ireland to the English village of Blackheath, in Surrey. There Crofts, who had already written nine mysteries between 1920 and 1929, would publish another two dozen novels, a book of short stories and a religious work in the period from 1930 to 1951. When not writing, tinkering in his workshop or traveling with his wife (Crofts especially enjoyed sea cruises, sharing with his Inspector French a wistful attachment to the sea), Crofts busied himself with village church activities, training choirs and playing the organ at services.[2] Terminal cancer slowed his great productivity and he was only able to publish a volume of radio plays, a collection of previously ungathered tales and a final novel before his death in 1957.

As the above suggests, there were two great influences on Freeman Wills Crofts, railways and religion. Both influences can be seen dominating Crofts' mystery writing as well, with his engineering background determining plot structure and his religious background determining thematic content. As the extreme technical complexity of Crofts' plots came to wane over time, the moral themes waxed ever greater, particularly in the openly and rather daringly evangelistic *Antidote to Venom* (1938), but also in other late works, such as *Man Overboard!* (1936), *The End of Andrew Harrison* (1937), *Fatal Venture* (1939), *Golden Ashes* (1940), *James Tarrant, Adventurer* (1941) and *Silence for the Murderer* (1948). One of the few literary references in Crofts' work is found in *The Box Office Murders* (1929), when Molly Moran, imprisoned in a house by a gang of criminals, looks through some dusty, old books piled in a room corner and finds among them *Pilgrim's Progress* and *The Fairchild Family*, the former of course John Bunyan's great Christian allegory and the latter a once-famous nineteenth-century moralizing children's novel that warned readers of their innate depravity and need for redemption. Did such works constitute Crofts' own reading material when he was young? One can imagine the influence that youthful exposure to *Pilgrim's Progress* and other works of Christian didacticism might have had on Crofts in the writing of his mysteries, for Crofts' fictional characters in their earthly journeys consistently confront the alluring paths of temptation to sin, crime and murder, sometimes avoiding them and reaching happy endings, sometimes following them, to their moral and material ruin.

Plot structure predominates over theme in Crofts' first detective novel, his landmark 1920 work, *The Cask*. Decades later, as Crofts' reputation declined, critics still continued to pay formal homage to this novel as a genre cornerstone. Written by Crofts in 1916 during convalescence from illness, it was stored away by the author for a time before he looked at it again in 1919 and decided that it merited submission to a publisher, namely Collins, the great British Golden Age detective fiction publishing house. After Crofts at Collins' request revised the third section of the novel (excising a trial sequence), *The Cask* appeared in print the next year, and its great critical and popular success — nearly 100,000 copies had sold by 1932 — established Crofts as a mystery author of first rank.[3] Together with Agatha Christie's *The Mysterious Affair at Styles*, likewise written in 1916 and published in 1920 (though it had much more trouble finding a publisher), *The Cask* today can be seen as having launched in full force the Golden Age of detective fiction.

When *The Cask* was reprinted by the House of Stratus in 2000, the publisher chose for the book a cover illustration of glamorous English society people playing shuffleboard on an ocean liner. Such an image may be the sort of thing people associate with Golden Age British mystery today, but it is at odds with the subject matter of the actual book that it purports to illustrate. Crofts and glamour are two things that emphatically do not go together. What *The Cask* does offer readers is a highly detailed and dogged investigation by Inspector Burnley to determine who murdered the woman whose body was found in a wine cask at St. Katherine's Docks, during unloading by the Insular and Continental Steam Navigation Company. The cask and its grisly contents get mislaid, with the result that the first section of the book, roughly a fourth of a long novel, deals with Burnley's effort to track it down again. When it is discovered, fully opened and the body removed, the result is highly satisfactory to all lovers of melodrama:

> On the throat [of the body] were two discolored bruises ... thumb-prints of the animal who had squeezed out that life with relentless and merciless hands.
> When the paper was removed from the dead face, the eyes of Felix seemed to start literally out of his head.
> "God!" he shrieked in a thin, shrill tone. "It's Annette!"
> He stood for a moment, waved his hands convulsively, and then, slowly turning, pitched forward insensible on the floor.[4]

In the second section of the novel, we learn that poor Felix is "entirely prostrated from the shock" of his discovery and that his very life is imperiled. Inspector Burnley is forced to travel to France to try to identify the unfortunate Annette. As Burnley travels on a train toward the coast, he thinks over how he will proceed, giving the reader a glimpse of the kind of attention to investigative detail for which Crofts became celebrated:

> There was first of all the letter to Felix. The signatory, M. Le Gautier, assuming such a man existed, should be able to give a clue. The waiters in the Toisson d'Or Cafe might know something. The typewriter with the defective letters was surely traceable.
>
> The clothes in which the corpse was dressed suggested another line of attack. Inquiry at the leading Paris shops could hardly fail to produce information. And if not there were the rings and the diamond comb. These would surely lead to something.
>
> Then there was the cask. It was a specially made one, and must surely have been used for a very special purpose. Inquiry from the firm whose label it had borne could hardly be fruitless.
>
> ... Burnley felt he was well-supplied with clues. Many and many a thorny problem he had solved with less to go on.
>
> He continued turning the matter over in his mind in his slow, painstaking way, until a sudden plunge into a tunnel and a grinding of brakes warned him they were coming into Dover.[5]

Slowly and painstakingly the investigation goes on, eventually becoming an effort, in the third section of the novel, to break down the suspected murderer's seemingly impregnable alibi involving his trip to Brussels and his visit to the Theater de la Monnaie to see Berlioz's opera *Les Troyens*. Much time is spent by investigators trying to determine where the suspected murderer was when, a matter that Crofts, a man with over two decades of working familiarity with railway timetables, handles with facility. Eventually the alibi is broken and the murderer confesses all, **[SPOILER ALERT]** revealing that the crime turned entirely on a sexual motive, the murderer being an adulterous husband desiring to rid himself of an unwanted wife. This, we will see, is unusual for Crofts, who over his long career preferred monetary gain as the motive for his murderers. Even when sexual desire is involved, that desire is usually coupled with — and subsidiary to — avarice. Perhaps *The Cask*'s primary setting in France, long viewed by British readers and writers as a land of unseemly and ungovernable carnal passions, accounts for this unusual emphasis. In any event, Crofts takes time to give the reader a moral on crime, however motivated, when he has the murderer reveal that his mistress died of natural causes soon after his violent killing of his wife: "The week after I destroyed my soul with the ghastly crime of which I will tell you, she [his mistress] got a chill. It turned to pneumonia, and in four days she was dead. I saw the judgment of Heaven beginning."[6] **[END SPOILER ALERT]**

Meticulously planned murders and didactic morals go together in Crofts' detective fiction throughout the next decade. In setting, Crofts' second work, *The Ponson Case*, is as paradigmatic as any English detective novel from the 1920s (though the intensive focus on Croft's plotting specialty, alibis and timetables, is exceptional). The opening paragraph of *The Ponson Case* introduces the reader to what became a celebrated Golden Age detective novel trope, that of the Georgian country home as a symbol of English social stability: "The dying sun of a July evening shone rosily on the old Georgian house of Luce Manor.... A fine old house, finely set on the summit of a low hill, and surrounded by wonderful old trees, it seemed to stand symbolical of the peace, security and solid comfort of upper-class rural England." Not content to imply symbolism, Crofts explicitly explains it to his readers, also emphasizing the oldness of the setting by using the word *old* three times in the short space of two sentences. Murder soon disrupts the idyllic, placid life at Luce Manor, when Sir William Ponson is found dead in the backwater of a river on his estate. Sir William's murder provides police with two prime suspects, his son, Austin — something of "a Socialist in politics"— and his nephew, Cosgrove, an idler who lives "the careless life of a man about town" and runs with "a rather fast set." Especially eyebrow-raising about Austin Ponson is the recent angry confrontation he had with Sir William over his engagement to a local bookseller's daughter, Lois Drew, a woman whom Sir William deemed unsuitable for marriage into the Ponson family on the grounds of her insufficient social standing. On the other hand, Sir William's wife Ethel and his daughter, Enid — the latter of whom is described by the author as "sweet-tempered and charming," "beloved by all" and "her father's heart and soul"— are quickly dismissed from suspicion by Inspector Tanner, who is, we learn, gifted as "a reader, so far as he was able, of hearts." During an interview with the bereaved pair of women, the reader of hearts is certain from their "bearing and manner" that they are "telling him the absolute truth" and are "ignorant of anything which might have been at the bottom of the affair."[7] Exit Ethel and Enid!

A true Crofts detective, Inspector Tanner is soon busy checking the minutiae of the alibis of Austin and Cosgrove Ponson. "To him time-tables were the breath of life," writes Crofts of a character in a later novel, but this trait manifestly is as well true of Inspector Tanner. An extract from Chapter Five of *The Ponson Case*, "Inspector Tanner Becomes Convinced," will provide a flavor of the Crofts detective at work:

> Before [Inspector Tanner] did anything else, every point of Austin's alibi must be gone into with the most meticulous care.
>
> Accordingly, having refilled his pipe, [Tanner] set himself to go over in detail the story Austin Ponson had told him of his movements on the night of the murder....
>
> Tanner took a sheet of paper, and, looking up his note of the times it had taken him to walk the various distances and estimating for the rowing, he made a statement something like a railway timetable.[8]

For the moment Austin Ponson's alibi holds, so Inspector Tanner begins probing that of Cosgrove Ponson. As an extract from Cosgrove's labored explanation of his alibi reveals, it is a nettlesome matter of times:

> "It appeared there was a comparatively slow train to Dundee at 8.30, but the next to Montrose was the express at 10.30.... I decided my best plan would be to take the 10.30....
>
> 'And what about my things that have gone on in the 7.15,' I asked.
>
> 'That will be all right,' the clerk answered. 'The first stop of both the 7.15 and the 10.30 is Grantham, and I shall wire the agent there to have your things collected from the 7.15, and handed in to you on the 10.30.'
>
> ... My little adventure had made me restless.... I would have liked to go to the Follies and see my friend Miss Betty Belcher, but I knew she was acting all the evening except during part of the second act, say from about 9.30 till 10.0. To pass the time till 9.30 I at last decided to go to the Empire.... I left my rooms almost at once, drove to the Empire, sat there for an hour or so, and then went to the Follies. From about 9.30 till 10.0 I sat with Miss Belcher in her room, then when it was nearly time for her to go on again I made my adieux and returned to King's Cross. I took care not to miss the 10.30, and at Grantham I got out and found a porter looking for me with my things. I duly reached Montrose about half past eight next morning."[9]

[SPOILER ALERT] Surprisingly, the cousins Ponson both turn out to be innocent,

Sir William's death having resulted from an accident during an altercation with Ethel Ponson's dissolute first husband, Tom Dale, long believed to have died when the ship on which he was traveling struck an iceberg off Newfoundland. Ethel Dale later married William Ponson, thereby unwittingly committing bigamy. After several decades passed, a down-on-his-luck Dale returned to England to attempt to blackmail Sir William, an action ultimately resulting in Sir William's accidental death. [**END SPOILER ALERT**]

The sad and unfortunate circumstances of Ethel Ponson's early marriage to Tom Dale give Crofts an opportunity to discourse to readers like a veteran temperance lecturer on the threat posed by alcohol to the happy home, in a passage that reads like it could have been drawn from a famous Currier and Ives lithograph, "The Drunkard's Progress." Young Ethel Osborne, we learn, had rashly accepted a proposal of marriage from Tom Dale, "outwardly a rather fascinating personality, good looking, always well dressed, and with attractive matters, though at heart ... a rotter." Sadly though not surprisingly, poor Ethel regretted marrying Tom Dale "from the first evening, when [Dale] returned drunk to the small seaside hotel at which they were spending their honeymoon." Crofts sententiously adds that "things went from bad to worse" in the unhappy marriage, with Dale continuing drinking, the couple getting into debt, and Ethel beginning "to fear her husband's dismissal and [their] consequent poverty."[10] [**SPOILER ALERT**] Though Ethel made a far wiser choice in her second marriage, her earlier wedding of a drunkard ultimately resulted in the violent (though accidental) death of her second husband, Sir William, over three decades later. [**END SPOILER ALERT**]

The Ponson Case is characteristic of much of Crofts' later work in the 1920s not merely in its intricate alibi mechanics and its at times heavy moralizing, but also in its neo–Victorian love story and its presentation of the tiresomely plucky heroine, Lois Drew. Lois Drew represents another staple of Golden Age mystery, the young woman of respectable middle class social position nobly withstanding the cruel rigors of a reduced income. When, in pursuance of his investigation of Austin Ponson's alibi, Inspector Tanner visits Elm Cottage, the Drew's "small detached villa," he finds in the drawing room that "everything bore traces of culture and taste, but also rather straightened means. The room wanted papering, the carpet was worn, the furniture shabby. But what there was of it was good, there was everywhere neatness and spotless cleanliness.... If the room bore the impress of Miss Drew's character, as Tanner suspected, it showed her a fine girl, bravely determined to make the best of things which she could not remedy."[11]

What precisely are the "traces of culture and taste" in the drawing-room of Elm Cottage beyond flowers in bowls and vases Crofts never makes clear, but the important thing is that the reader is to understand they are there. When Lois herself appears (Tanner had been shown in by an "elderly general servant," presumably the residuum of a once larger staff), she confirms the good impression that her interior decoration has already made on Tanner. Lois strikes Tanner as a young woman of character and determination, one who would only use her great inner strength to further a cause that "she believed just and right." She soon has a righteous cause for which to fight when Tanner arrests her fiancée for his father's murder. At first Lois is hit hard by the news, reflecting mournfully that "since the tragedy [of Sir William's murder] it had been as if some Dread Shade lurked ... ready at any minute to step forward and intrude its baleful presence into Austin's life and hers." However, a good lunch, consisting of a "hot stimulant and ... fresh rolls and butter," dispels dismal thoughts of the Dread Shade and soon Lois, aided by her lawyer cousin Jimmy Daunt, is making a strenuous effort to exonerate her beloved. To spare Lois public humiliation over his arrest, Austin had requested that Lois break their engagement, but of course the plucky girl refuses. Perhaps needless to add, the novel ends with the mystery explained to everyone's satisfaction and an announcement "in the fashionable papers" of the marriage of Austin and Lois.[12]

As the reference to Lois' fear of the Dread Shade indicates, there is a whiff of Victorian melodrama about Crofts' writing when it is called upon to depict the stormier human emotions, a whiff that lingers in *The Ponson Case* when Austin Ponson describes his fear of having his mother's bigamy exposed (actually Austin and presumably the author seem to think his father is guilty of bigamy as well, though he would seem to be "guilty" merely of cohabiting with a previously married woman). In recounting his ghastly shock and dismay over the whole affair, Austin helpfully recalls and reenacts (over fourteen pages!) for the police entire conversations held among different individuals:

> "I was appalled and horrified. Though upset on my own account, I ask you to believe that what distressed me most was its [the news of Tom Dale's return] possible effect on my mother and sister. Of my mother I just couldn't bear to think, and it also hurt me beyond words to believe that any such secret should have power to throw a shadow over Enid's life."
> "Did you speak to your father on this particular point?" Tanner interjected.
> "Speak? I should rather think so. I was beside myself with horror."
> "Can you recollect the exact words you used?"
> ... "I said as the thing began to dawn on me, 'And my mother — it can't be that she —?' I did not wish to speak the words and my father completed my sentence for me. 'Yes, there's no escape from it; she is the wife of that drunken ruffian.'"

Austin also believed that Lois Drew might reject him if she heard of his family's scandal, a rejection he would not risk: "I thought if the circumstances of my birth came out she might have nothing more to do with me.... I could not see that I was called upon to chance the wrecking of my happiness on what was after all a mere technical matter only. God forgive me, I did not intend to tell that angel. I feared the stigma would remain."[13]

To be sure, Crofts was not alone among Golden Age detective novelists in using fear of the exposure of unknowing bigamy as a mystery plot device, particularly in the earlier years of the period. As sardonically noted by Bill Pronzini in *Gun in Cheek*, his satirical survey of "alternative classics" of crime fiction (books so bad they become entertaining for their badness), in Gwen Bristow's and Bruce Manning's 1930 American mystery thriller, *The Invisible Host*, it is precisely mortification over the threatened exposure of her unintended bigamy that causes a "reputable cafe-society matron to die on the spot."[14] Yet Crofts' persistent devotion to such hackneyed, melodramatic devices, particularly in his 1920s novels, is rather singular. Such writing gives his work a backward-looking, nineteenth-century feel, more akin to that of inferior sensation novelists of the Victorian era than to the chroniclers of the bright young things associated with the Jazz Age.

Another recurring quality of Crofts' work that we first see in *The Ponson Case* is the author's tendency to divide people into good and evil camps. Though Cosgrove Ponson with his man-about-town ways perhaps can be seen as having one foot on both sides of the moral division, the characters otherwise cleave neatly, with only Tom Drew acting truly vilely in the course of the novel's events (the latter man's shameful actions are attributable to his having long ago succumbed to the malign influence of the Devil's brew). The women — Lois Drew and Ethel and Enid Ponson — are dismissed as possible culprits practically on sight by Inspector Tanner (a reader of hearts, it will be recalled), leaving only two obvious suspects for the reader, Austin and Cosgrove Ponson, both of whom have involved alibis to be investigated. Such plotting differs greatly from that in, say, Agatha Christie novels, where, as Robert Barnard has pointed out, it seems that anyone can be guilty of murder, from a nine-year-old child to a ninety-year-old dowager. Crofts' ingenuous narration may reduce reader suspense over the *who* question, but it is entirely in accord with the author's moral schematic, where humanity is cleft in twain, with the good who have resisted worldly temptation parted from the evil who have succumbed to it.

A final recurrent aspect of Crofts' work that we find in *The Ponson Case* is the running travelogue. In his own life, Crofts loved sea cruises and travel in Britain and the European continent, and this love manifests itself in his books in stretches of tedious guidebook-style commentary, as in *The Ponson Case*, when Inspector Tanner finds himself obliged to pursue a suspect to Portugal:

> When Tanner emerged into the brilliantly lighted streets and gazed down the splendid vista of the Avenida da Liberdade, he literally held his breath in amazement. The Portuguese he had always looked on as a lazy, good-for-nothing set, but this great new boulevard made him reconsider his opinion....
>
> At six o'clock Tanner was down on the Placa do Commercio, admiring in the brilliant sunlight the splendid river which flowed before him, and the charming setting of the town on its range of hills....
>
> ... Tanner stood leaning on the rail of the upper deck, watching the pleasantly situated town slip slowly astern. He could see the Cathedral of Belem standing, damaged, just as it was left by the earthquake of 1755. Then out of the mouth of the river and past the picturesque pleasure resort of Mont Estoril, with, just beyond it, the sleepy, old world village of Cascaes.[15]

Crofts' most famous detective, Inspector Joseph French, who appears in all Crofts' mystery novels published between 1924 and 1957, shares Inspector Tanner's (and Crofts') love of travel. He also proves, like Tanner, an accomplished reader of hearts and an indefatigable breaker of alibis. Before French debuted in the rather precipitately titled *Inspector French's Greatest Case*, however, Crofts published two other mysteries, a thriller, *The Pit-Prop Syndicate* (1922), and a detective novel, *The Groote Park Murder* (1923). Both works can be discussed relatively quickly.

Although Julian Symons in 1957 unexpectedly chose *The Pit-Prop Syndicate* as one of "the one hundred best crime stories," the book seems most remarkable to me for its introduction of another characteristic Crofts mystery novel element, his police detectives' frequently illegal and amateurish searches. Often 1920s critics praised the impressively methodical and deliberate Crofts as an expert on police procedure, but this in fact is an insupportable claim rightly dismissed in *Bloody Murder* by Symons, who declared peremptorily that "Crofts knew nothing about Scotland Yard." In *The Pit-Prop Syndicate* Crofts with unintended humor treats readers several times with instances of the intrepid Inspector Willis' highly advanced lock-picking skill, which depends on the simple medium of a single bent wire:

> [Willis] crept from his hiding place, and approaching the depot, tried the gate in the fence. It was locked, but few locks were proof against the inspector's prowess, and with the help of a bent wire he was soon within the enclosure.... Next he tackled the desk, picking the lock with his usual skill.... The other cupboard was locked.... Again the wire was brought into requisition, and in a moment the door swung open....
>
> Willis moved round behind the house, and once again producing his bent wire, in a few moments had the back door open.... The cupboard was locked, but with the help of the bent wire it soon stood open....
>
> Willis ... moved round to the office door.... His bent wire proved as efficacious with French locks as with English, and in a few moments they stood within, with the door shut behind them.

Only once does Willis let discretion get the better part of valor and refrain from resorting to his trusty bent wire, though not without a pang of speculative regret: "The front door was shut, and though [Willis] might have been able to open it with his bent wire, he felt that to adventure himself into the hall without any idea of the interior would be too dangerous."[16]

Let us leave Inspector Willis and his bent wire behind us and briefly note Crofts' continued indulgence in emotional melodrama between his lovers:

> "Madeleine! Madeleine!" he cried brokenly. "My own one! My beloved!" He almost sobbed as he attempted to strain her to his heart.
> But she wrenched herself from him.
> "No, no!" she gasped. You must not! I told you. It cannot be."

The unfortunate Madeleine's father, it seems, is implicated in a criminal conspiracy, having been brought into "financial embarrassment" from heavy losses incurred through gambling.[17]

The Groote Park Murder introduces two other plot elements in addition to Crofts' patented alibi-busting: misdirection over the identity of a corpse and impersonation. It is a well-conducted tale, but unfortunately soppy emotional melodrama again weighs down large sections of the book, as pressure is brought to bear on Crofts' heroine, Marion Hope, to break her engagement with her fiancée, who has been arrested (wrongly, of course) for murder. Marion, the author tells us, has "a sweetness of disposition which made her the absolute idol of her father, and endeared her to all those with whom she came in contact." However, the modern reader may find her something of a tiresomely passive daddy's girl:

> "Oh, daddy," she threw her arms once more about his neck, "I can't have him left there [in prison] without any sign of our sympathy, without even a letter.... If I may not see him, you go, daddy. They would let you, his employer, his future father-in-law." Mr. Hope winced. "Say you'll go now, right now before you do anything else."
> As Mr. Hope still demurred, Marion's expression suddenly changed.
> "It's not that you don't want to go," she cried anxiously. "Oh, daddy, say it's not that!"[18]

Part of *The Groote Park Murder* takes place, as the title might suggest, in South Africa, where Inspector Vandam proves slightly more sophisticated than Inspector Willis in carrying out his searches, using a bunch of skeleton keys rather than Willis' favored instrument: "[The dispatch case] was locked, but locks were but slight obstacles to Inspector Vandam, and with the aid of a skeleton key from a bunch he always carried, it soon stood open." Amusingly, Inspector Vandam during his investigation seems as concerned with regular feeding as with actually tracking down the murderer:

> Though it was considerably after his usual lunch hour when he left his Chief's office, [Vandam] contented himself with a five-minute pause for a sandwich and a cup of coffee in a restaurant before starting the next phase of his investigation.
>
> Puzzled and uncertain as to his next step, [Vandam] returned to the center of town and entered his favorite restaurant to partake of a long overdue lunch.
>
> [Vandam] looked at his watch. "Half past twelve. Soon time for a bit of lunch."

Perhaps not surprisingly, it is left to the less gastronomically-preoccupied Inspector Ross of Scotland to ultimately bring to book the true murderer, who pays at novel's end, we learn, "the supreme penalty for his crimes." "Such was the just ending," Crofts weightily intones, "of one of the most cold-blooded monsters of the century."[19]

While *The Cask* is considered Crofts' greatest mystery novel, his by far most famous detective, Inspector Joseph French, did not appear until four years later, in 1924, with the publication of *Inspector French's Greatest Case*. Although French essentially is no different in kind from his earlier incarnations, Burnley, Tanner, Willis, Vandam and Ross, as a consequence of his appearance in thirty mystery novels (including a cameo in a children's mystery, *Young Robin Brand, Detective*) and numerous short stories he necessarily boasts a bit more of a biography. In his first appearance, French is described by Crofts as "a stout man in tweeds, rather under middle height, with a clean-shaven, good-humored face and dark blue eyes, which, though keen, twinkled as if at some perennially fresh private joke." His nickname at the Yard, we find, is "Soapy Joe," because of the persuasiveness of his suavity of manners. At various times in the series of French mysteries, Crofts is careful to show us examples of how the Inspector is able to get what he wants from a witness by means of his "soapy" ways. For example, in *Inspector French's Greatest Case*, French charms an asthmatic witness by asking about his illness. "The Inspector had found from long experience," Crofts instructs his readers, "that the time spent in discussing his illness with an invalid was not wasted. The pleasure [French] gave had the effect of creating a sympathy and good feeling which assisted him when he came to the second part of the interview, the favor he wanted for himself."[20] The expenditure of a little human sympathy, we learn, can reap rich material rewards.

Inspector French also is endowed with some elements of a personal life, including a wife, Emily, or Em for short. Emily French is a firmly domesticated woman devoted to her "mysterious household employments"; yet, when listening to her husband's recitation of a case on which he is working, she nevertheless occasionally will "take a notion" and give French a valuable hint on how to proceed in the solution of his problem. We see Emily French take notions in *Inspector French's Greatest Case* and *The Box Office Murders*, but in the 1930s she recedes into inconsequentiality. Although Em accompanies her husband on a pleasure boat during his criminal investigation in *Fatal Venture* (1939), no further "notions" from her are recorded by the author.[21]

In addition to a wife, Inspector French claims a family. I have never seen a critic or reviewer mention it, but Joseph and Emily French evidently had two children, a son killed in World War I and a daughter named Eliza, who is living in her parents' home when the events described in *Inspector French's Greatest Case* take place. This critical oversight is understandable, as Crofts himself later failed to recall French's offspring ("I have been wondering whether [French] has children," the author confessed in 1935. "It's like a dream to me that in one book children were mentioned, and that in another their existence was denied. But as I can't find either reference, I can only note the point as one to be avoided."). Yet reference to a son, at least, is indisputably clear in *Inspector French's Greatest Case*:

> It was that damned war, responsible for this as well as most of the troubles of the times. It had probably made a difference to the Inspector also?
> "Lost my eldest," said French gruffly, and turned the conversation.[22]

Later in the novel a girl named Eliza appears in the French home and, although the context is somewhat ambiguous, she appears to be a daughter, not a housemaid (surely the Frenches were too quintessentially bourgeois at this time to employ a live-in housemaid).

Both Crofts as well as critics saw Inspector French as the outstanding example of the plain, "everyman" police detective in Golden Age British mystery fiction. French explained his innovation in a 1935 article, "Meet Chief-Inspector French." A would-be detective novelist, Crofts pronounced, had first to decide whether his detective would be "brilliant and a 'character,'" or merely an "ordinary humdrum personality." Crofts concluded for two reasons to take the humdrum route with his detective: first, because he felt that doing so would offer an innovation in detective stories, there being already in the genre a great many "'character' detectives," lineally descended, for the most part, from Sherlock Holmes; and second, as Crofts admitted with disarming frankness, because "striking characteristics, consistently depicted, are very hard to do." This question settled to his satisfaction, Crofts attempted with his Inspector French to create "a perfectly ordinary man, without peculiarities or mannerisms." Yet the author admitted, seemingly somewhat ruefully, that "of course [French] had to have *some* qualities." Clearly Emily French and the children were a mild step in that direction. But, as Crofts' consignment of the French offspring to literary oblivion and his drastic reduction of Em's role in the novels indicate, French failed to do much in the way of making Inspector French an interesting character. Julian Symons complained, correctly in my view, that in succeeding so well in making his series detective "commonplace," Crofts made him "uninteresting" (at least as an individual rather than an archetype).[23]

In a late French novel, *James Tarrant, Adventurer* (1941), Crofts narrates an appealing little domestic interlude that indicates what Inspector French might have been, had his creator been inclined to really develop the character. It is eleven o'clock on Sunday morning and French, "dressed in a disreputable pair of grey trousers and an old brown paint-spotted coat," has just "emerged from his kitchen door into the tiny strip of garden at the rear of his house." He crosses to a small shed in the yard, removes a spade and then stands "directing a predatory eye upon his microscopic plot of grass." There is "something furtive in his manner"; indeed, he looks as if he is about to do "what he knew he ought not, and taking a risk about it too."[24] Hesitating but a moment, he plunges his spade into the grass.

What is French up to here? In a suspense novel, he might be preparing to bury the brutally battered Emily French, who perhaps finally had one notion too many, in the back garden. But in actuality the inspector, indulging a mildly adventurous urge buried deep within him, merely is attempting to reset the path to the couple's "little summerhouse" so that it will curve instead of run straight. Mrs. French, who opposes the plan, is at church, giving her husband his great chance to effect the alteration and present Em "with a *fait accompli* on her return."[25]

More such incidents from home life as these might have improved French as a character, but Crofts does not offer them. Nor does Crofts actually make French a realistic police detective, as Julian Symons noted and Crofts himself candidly admitted:

> French I made an inspector of Scotland Yard rather than a private detective because I hoped in this way to gain realism. But at once a horrible difficulty loomed up: I knew nothing about Scotland Yard or the C.I.D. What was to be done? The answer was simple. I built on the great rock which sustains so many of my profession: If I knew nothing of my subject, well, few of my readers would know more.... I found this rock not quite so steadfast as I hoped. It has been pointed out to me that French has at times done things which would make a real inspector of the Yard shudder.[26]

Although Crofts never made a sustained effort to endow French with persuasive human or professional qualities, the author did invest his series detective with one of his own great passions, love of travel. Fortunately for French but perhaps unfortunately for the reader, the good Inspector is able to indulge his passion with some frequency over the course of his many investigations. In his *Greatest Case* alone, French gets to spend a considerable amount of time in Switzerland and France, allowing Crofts his chance to provide the reader with yet more tedious guided tours of Continental beauty spots, rather in the matter of a host who cannot bring himself to halt the slideshow of the family vacation:

> [French] had been to France and Germany on a previous occasion, but never to Switzerland, and he was looking forward to getting a glimpse of some of the wonderful mountain scenery of that country.
> He disembarked at Calais, passed through customs, and took his seat in the Lotschberg-Simplon express with true British disapproval of all that he saw. But later the excellent dinner served while the train ran through the pleasant country between Abbeville and Amiens brought him to a more acquiescent mood, and over a good cigar and a cup of coffee as he had seldom before tasted, he complacently watched day fade into night. About half-past six o'clock next morning he followed the example of his countless British predecessors, and climbed down on the long platform at Bale to drink his morning coffee. Then again on through scenery of growing interest, past Bern to Spiez, where he found the Lake of Thun really had the incredible coloring he had so often scoffed at, but secretly admired, in the Swiss posters he had seen at London....
> Next morning he took the southbound train, and having passed through the nine miles of the Loetschberg tunnel, he gazed with veritable awe into the dreary waste of the Loetschenthal and the great gulf of the Rhone Valley, marveling as the train raced along the side of the stupendous cliff. He changed at Brigue, passed down the Rhone Valley, and changing again at Martigny, spent another four hours on what a fellow traveler with a nasal drawl described as "the most elegant ride he'd struck," through Vallorcine and Argentiere to Chamonix. On crossing the divide, the panorama which suddenly burst on his view of the vast mass of the Mont Blanc massif hanging in the sky above the valley, literally took away his breath, and he swore that his next holidays would certainly be spent in the overwhelming scenery of these tremendous mountains.[27]

Like Inspectors Willis and Vandam, Inspector French is handy at searches, both legal and illegal. At times, one begins to wonder whether the mild French harbors subconscious burglarious urges. In *The Box Office Murders*, for example, French continually flouts the law in his determination to collect evidence without the tiresome inconvenience of first obtaining a search warrant. On pages 97 to 99 of my edition of this tale, the inspector is breaking into and searching the office of a suspect, on pages 116 to 120 breaking into a garage though a window in order to search this suspect's car and on pages 122 to 127 conniving at a colleague's entering this suspect's house under the false pretense of being a workman so that the man might snoop over the premises. "By hook or by crook, [French] would examine that car," writes Crofts at one point, "even if he had to commit a felony." As his implement of choice for facilitating invasions of private homes and businesses French prefers an ever-trusty bunch of skeleton keys to Willis' primitive (yet still amazingly efficacious) bent wire. However, the man is no slouch himself with the art of the bent wire, as we see, for example, in *Inspector French and the Starvel Tragedy*, where French, encountering a lock that is "too large" for his skeleton keys, needs "but a few moments' work with a bit of bent wire" to do the trick. Additionally, in another novel, *The Sea Mystery*, the wily French goes his investigative predecessors one better in having mastered the quite advanced detective technique of opening envelopes with razor blades to read documents contained within and then resealing them so that no one is the wiser:

> French carried an old razor blade in his pocket and in less than a minute the envelope was open. The note read:
> "Danger. Meet me tonight at old time and place."
> French swore softly in high delight. He had them now! Here was convincing proof of their guilt.
> But it was insufficient to bring into court. He must get something more definite. With skillful fingers he re-closed the envelope and put it back where he found it.[28]

Inspector French is best understood not in terms of realism, but as an archetypal Everyman figure bringing good out of dauntless industry. "It's like any other job," pronounces French of police work, "you get results by pegging away." Like any man when confronted with challenges, French at times loses heart, but he always regains his equanimity and in the end triumphs. After a hard day investigating *The Sea Mystery*, French, "tired and not a little out of sorts," reflects resignedly: "Evidently in this case, as in most others, there was no royal road to success. He must simply go on trying to amass information in the ordinary humdrum routine way, in the hope that sooner or later he might come on some fact which would throw the desired light on the affair." Happily, sleep alleviates French's momentary depression, giving cause for the author to declare reassuringly, if sententiously: "It is wonderful what an effect a good night's sleep and a bright morning will have on the mind of a healthy man." Continues the moral-minded author: "French had gone to bed tired and worried about his case. He woke cheery and optimistic, philosophic as to his reverses, and hopeful for the future.... As he looked out of his window French felt that life was good and that to squander it in sleep was little better than a sin." And, surely enough, the rejuvenated Inspector finds his way. At novel's end French has, despite a few missteps here and there, "taken the criminals and added to his reputation with his superiors," leaving him "on the whole ... satisfied."[29]

For many years, readers and critics alike were more than satisfied with Freeman Wills Crofts' Inspector French detective tales. Crofts' standing as one of the supreme practitioners of detection lasted well into the 1930s, declining somewhat only in the years immediately before World War II. In the 1940s and 1950s his reputation dropped considerably, yet even today his position as the supposed best representative of the Golden Age "Humdrum school of detective novelists," as Julian Symons designated him, still stands.

Comparatively few mystery readers today have patience for tales larded with thickly detailed alibis and timetables, but in Crofts' day many people found such problems fascinating. "Long and intricate timetables have always been a weakness even for the brightest people," pronounced an American reviewer in passing in 1931. Arnold Bennett may have fulminated in 1930 against the banality of the writing of the railway engineer turned writer, but at the time the esteemed author and critic was fulminating, many *litterateurs* and intellectuals in Britain treated Crofts as one of the greatest living detective fiction writers, if not the very greatest. Recalling her husband's *entree* into the ranks of detective fiction authors twelve years earlier, Margaret Cole, wife of prominent socialist thinker G.D.H. Cole, wrote in 1935 that "it was just about the time when Mr. Freeman Wills Crofts' first stories were coming out, and all the intelligentsia were very much excited by them." For his part, T.S. Eliot regularly praised Crofts highly in the pages of his journal, the *Criterion*. In June 1927, for example, Eliot coupled Freeman Wills Crofts with R. Austin Freeman, dubbing the authorial pair "our two most accomplished detective writers." Later that same year, in a review of S.S. Van Dine's *The Canary Murder Case*—a novel that had taken America by storm, rising into the bestseller lists—Eliot opined that "Mr. Van Dine has not written anything to equal the best work of either Mr. Freeman or Mr. Croft [sic]." Reviewing Van Dine's even more successful *The Greene Murder Case* over a year later, in September 1928, Eliot allowed that Van Dine now stood "in the front rank of detective writers," though still "a little lower than Mr. Freeman and Mr. Crofts."[30]

Additional esteemed individuals, such as E.C. Bentley, Charles Williams and Harold Nicolson, as well as lesser reviewers, continued to pay Crofts high tribute into the middle thirties. Bentley found *The Hog Back's Mystery* (1933)—along with Crofts' *Sir John Magill's Last Journey* and Dorothy L. Sayers' *The Five Red Herrings* surely the *ne plus ultra* in locational timetable mysteries—"as pretty a piece of work as Inspector French has done" and "on the level of Mr. Crofts' very best; which is saying something." Williams deemed the same novel "in the highest flight of detective aeroplanes." He resoundingly added: "The delight it will give in the crudest reader is miraculous; to the sensitive it is catastrophic. In fact, it is a very good book, one of Mr. Crofts' best, and that is to say one of our best." For his part, Harold Nicolson declared *Mystery on Southampton Water* (1934) "exactly what a detective novel should be—ingenious, lucid, reasonable, intricate and exciting." Similarly, *Crime at Guildford* (1935) provoked an outpouring of enthusiasm, with, for example, Torquemada of the *Observer* crying "Brilliant" and "Dr. Watson" of the *Manchester Evening Chronicle* proclaiming "here is greatness." Such was Crofts' reputation at this time that even hard-boiled American mystery writer Raymond Chandler, notoriously no keen admirer of the Golden Age British detective novel, wrote favorably of Crofts' books and their plot construction, dubbing Crofts "the soundest builder of them all."[31]

While Crofts never quite outgrew the fame of *The Cask* and it always remained tied to his name, like *The Murder of Roger Ackroyd* long did to that of Agatha Christie, it was Crofts' post–*Cask* Inspector French novels that sustained his high pre–World War II reputation with his readership. Notable French novels from his greatest period of investigative triumph, 1924 to 1936, include *Inspector French's Greatest Case* (1924), *Inspector French and the Starvel Tragedy* (1927) and *The Sea Mystery* (1928), all of which offer ingenious and what in their day were highly original plot twists; *Sir John Magill's Last Journey* (1930) and *The Hog Back's Mystery* (1933), Crofts' greatest timetable novels; *The 12.30 from Croydon* (1934) and *Mystery on Southampton Water* (1934), his most celebrated "inverted" tales;

Mystery in the Channel (1931) and *Crime at Guildford* (1935), complex tales of corporate corruption; and *The Loss of the "Jane Vosper"* (1936), the author's nearest attempt to a full-scale police procedural novel. After *"Jane Vosper,"* plotting in the French novels tends to become less complex, while, as mentioned above, moral themes become more overt in some works. Here I will look in greater depth at the eight French novels from this period that I think best illustrate the finer qualities in his detective fiction: *Inspector French and the Starvel Tragedy; The Sea Mystery; Sir John Magill's Last Journey; Mystery in the Channel, The Hog's Back Mystery; Mystery on Southampton Water; Crime at Guildford* and *The Loss of the "Jane Vosper."*

Inspector French's Greatest Case has certain clever plot elements but suffers from some of Crofts' negative stylistic qualities as a writer, qualities most pervasive in his 1920s output. In *Greatest Case* we find those tedious travel guide *longueurs* as well as the author's overuse of "picturesque" dialect, the latter most regrettably evident in his scene with the wealthy American matron Mrs. Chauncey S. Root (wife of the noted Pittsburgh steel manufacturer). In depicting Inspector French's conversation with Mrs. Root, Crofts never misses an opportunity to indicate that the good lady is 100 percent genuine, grade–A all–American:

"I guess you better tell me first."

"Say, now, what started you on that yarn?"

"You have interested me quite a lot. Start right in and tell me the story."

"Here are some pictures I took with my Kodak.... Next is Haidee Squance, daughter of Old Man Squance of Consolidated Oil. I've known her since I've known anything."[32]

Almost entirely set in Yorkshire (with, blessedly, not an American in sight), *Inspector French and the Starvel Tragedy*— which followed the lightweight thriller *Inspector French and the Cheyne Mystery* by one year — offers an ingenious plot revolving around the burning of an isolated manor house on the bleak moors. Three bodies are found in the smoldering ruins of the building and an inquest is soon held. The coroner's jury determines (1) that the bodies are those of the old miser who owned the manor house and his two servants, a married couple who had come into his employ within the last year and (2) that the fire was accidentally set. However, it is pointed out (if rather belatedly) that the safe in which the miser's hoard of paper money incinerated was fireproofed. How, then, did the paper money catch fire? Soon Inspector French is on his way to Yorkshire.

In *Starvel* there is a love story subplot involving the dead miser's bland and uninteresting niece/ward and her beau, a young gentleman rather alarmingly named Pierce Whymper; however it is an unobtrusive affair that recedes as French's investigation unfolds. The intricate puzzle plot is quite original for its day and suspicion is deftly manipulated by the author. With its narrative culminating in a railway station confrontation between Inspector French and a grimly determined murderer — one in which French (and Inspector Tanner from *The Ponson Case*, who, along with Inspector Willis from *The Pit-Prop Syndicate*, makes a cameo appearance in *Starvel*) is almost blown apart by a grenade —*Starvel* is one of the bravura Crofts mystery tales, deserving the praise meted it by T.S. Eliot.

Although in *The Sea Mystery* there is one paragraph devoted to the sightseeing pleasures of Plymouth and an excess of genre-stylized working class Cockney dialect, this 1928 tale is if anything superior to the excellent *Starvel*. Shorter than the earlier somewhat wordy Crofts novels and more credible in its depictions of character, *The Sea Mystery* was justly lauded in *A Catalogue of Crime* for having more persuasive "motives behind the deed" and "people more distinct than was to be the case in other tales." Essentially the story is a stripped-down version of Crofts' seminal novel, *The Cask*. Suggesting the similarity between the two tales is the fact that a more accurate title for *The Sea Mystery* would have been *The Crate*, a crate being the container in which a corpse is discovered in this later tale. After the crate with the corpse is fished from the sea by a leisure boating father and son and its grisly contents discovered, Inspector French is called into the case. With rare humor Crofts has French tell the local police doctor that the affair "reminds me of a case investigated several years ago by my old friend Inspector Burnley"—a certain case involving a cask. "Very interesting," comments the doctor. "I remember reading of that case you mention. The papers were absolutely full of it at the time. I thought it an extraordinary affair, almost like a novel."[33]

Like Inspector Burnley ("retired now," we learn), French finds himself tasked with tracking the origin of the corpse container. Doing so proves a cumbersome job, provoking French to reflect, no doubt to the delight of readers of the tale, that "this ... was going to be one of those troublesome cases in which an ingenious criminal had enveloped his evil deeds in a network of false clues and irrelevant circumstances to mislead the unfortunate detective officer."[34] Nevertheless, the dauntless French traces the crate to the Vida Works, a company which recently suffered a double blow in the deaths of its junior partner, Charles Berlyn, and its traveling representative, Stanley Pyke, both of whom disappeared together while traversing a moor. Both Stanley Pyke's cousin, Jefferson Pyke (in England on a visit from the Argentine), and Mr. Berlyn's widow, Phyllis, are able to identify the corpse, the face of which had been battered beyond recognition, from its distinctive birthmark. **[SPOILER ALERT]** French comes to believe that Berlyn is still really living and that he murdered Pyke, with the connivance of another man, Colonel Domlio, an investor in the Vida Works. The motive for the two men, French concludes, was jealously over Phyllis Berlyn's romantic relationship with Stanley Pyke (Domlio himself is infatuated with Mrs. Berlyn, but she has shown no reciprocation of interest in him). Eventually French learns the truth, which is that the true murderer is the presumed dead Stanley Pyke—who enjoyed the assistance of Phyllis Berlyn—and the true victim was Charles Berlyn. Jefferson Pyke had died suddenly while in France and Stanley Pyke had assumed his identity, as part of a plan to enable him to murder Charles Berlyn and thus be able to "live with Phyllis in good social standing." In his guise as Jefferson Pyke, Stanley Pyke, along with Phyllis, falsely identified the corpse of Charles Berlyn as that of himself! It is an admirably mind-bending scenario, the sort of thing that prefigured such later works as Agatha Christie's celebrated novel *The Body in the Library* (1942) and several amusingly outrageous identity-switching detective tales by Michael Innes, such as *A Night of Errors* (1947). Further pleasures may be found in the novel with French's exposure of some clever alibis and a faked car breakdown. **[END SPOILER ALERT]**

Sir John Magill's Last Journey, which followed *The Sea Mystery* after two years, was a book held in especial affection by Crofts, who declared it the best of his works. Authorial judgments on such matters are notoriously disputable, but here I might venture to agree with the author. Published in 1930, *Last Journey* was the first Crofts mystery to appear after the author and his wife left Northern Ireland and settled in retirement in England. Part of the novel, which concerns the disappearance and possible murder of retired Irish linen manufacturer Sir John Magill, is set in Northern Ireland and it is dedicated by Crofts "To MY MANY GOOD FRIENDS IN NORTHERN IRELAND." In writing the book, Crofts clearly drew inspiration from his Irish associations. The Northern Ireland village of Gilford, where Crofts as a boy had resided with his mother and his vicar stepfather, is a contraction of "Magill's ford," which was named after a seventeenth-century landowner, Captain John Magill. Moreover, the village had grown up around a successful linen mill.[35]

Once Crofts had completed writing his latest novel and submitted the manuscript to his publisher, Collins, he found himself having to go to battle with Collins over the proposed title. Crofts preferred *Sir John Magill's Last Journey*, Collins *The Magill Mystery*. "However for the first time I stuck to my guns" wrote the normally self-effacing Crofts proudly to Dorothy L. Sayers in 1930, and he got his (much superior) title. Once it appeared in print, *Last Journey* became a very successful novel, seeing eight impressions in Britain between 1930 and 1935 and three in the United States in 1930. In the latter country the tale was chosen by Pocket Books in 1941 as the first Inspector French mystery reprint in their popular paperback editions; and in Britain it was reprinted by Penguin as late as 1955. In the *Times Literary Supplement*, a British reviewer compared the novel favorably with Crofts' *The Starvel Tragedy*, which the reviewer regarded "as the high-water mark of detective fiction"; while in the United States, the *New York Times*, perhaps reflecting a characteristic difference in national temperament, happily discerned "plenty of action in this thriller." Crofts himself opened the tale with a flourish, declaring on the opening page that "the Sir John Magill Case proved perhaps the most terribly baffling of all the baffling cases French had tackled.... [M]any times before the case dragged on to its inevitable and dramatic close French found himself wishing nothing so much as that he had never heard of the unfortunate man who gave [the case] its name."[36]

There is some action near the end of *Sir John Magill's Last Journey*, when Inspector French cleverly lures the culprits of the crime into a police trap. Yet most of the novel is a mental exercise in pure detection, admittedly with French engaging in considerable to-ing and fro-ing around England, Scotland and Ireland in his investigations of an exceedingly cold-blooded and dastardly crime. The novel opens in Scotland Yard with the personable Detective-sergeant Adam M'Clung of Northern Ireland explaining to Inspector French the circumstances of retired linen manufacturer Sir John Magill's disappearance. Sir John had traveled by rail from his stately Knightsbridge home to Scotland before taking a boat to Ireland, where he thereupon vanished. The chief suspects seem to be Sir John's son, Malcolm, who runs the family mills in Ireland; his nephew, Victor, who is known to have a fondness for betting; and Breene, Sir John's private secretary (as John Dickson Carr once noted, in Golden Age detective novels private secretaries always are a good bet for murderer). Additionally, shadowy agents of industrial espionage also are a possibility. **[SPOILER ALERT]** Although the top suspect initially is Malcolm Magill, especially after an anonymous letter leads police to the discovery of Sir John's corpse buried on the grounds of Malcolm's home, it later turns out that Sir John never arrived alive in Ireland after all, but was murdered on the train in Scotland and impersonated in Ireland. No less than four men are involved in the crime, one of whom is Victor Magill, his motive for participation in the heinous plot having been the substantial legacy provided for him in his uncle's will. The conspiracy necessitated the creation of

Freeman Wills Crofts, *Sir John Magill's Last Journey* (1930, left); Freeman Wills Crofts, *Mystery in the Channel* (1931). Freeman Wills Crofts' most famous fictional creation, Inspector Joseph French, is one of the most mobile of Golden Age detectives, regularly traveling far-flung distances by rail and by boat in order to collar evildoers.

alibis for each of the men, and in order to smash these alibis, French undertakes a lengthy investigation of their movements by rail, by boat and by car. [**END SPOILER ALERT**] The logistical complexity of it all undeniably is quite impressive, all Crofts' skill as a railway man in knowing precisely how to get people where they want to go and when being brought to bear on the tale's problem. Additionally, Crofts here refrains from tediously indulging in long guidebook details and provides background settings that are functional, economical and convincing. A final appealing aspect of *Last Journey* is the entire absence of one of the author's bathetic love stories, what little "love interest" there is being tepidly supplied by the private secretary Breene and Magill's oldest daughter (both near middle age), who, we learn in the course of the novel, plan to marry. The reason for the presence of even this very minor love interest is not the author's desire to involve us emotionally in "love's young dream," as in other such Crofts' novels as *The Ponson Case*, *The Pit-Prop Syndicate*, *The Groote Park Murder*, *The Cheyne Mystery* and *The Starvel Tragedy*, but rather his practical need to provide Breene with a motive for murdering his employer. All in all, *Sir John Magill's Last Journey* is a satisfyingly complex, no-nonsense specimen of the unbreakable alibi detective novel; and it was rightly deemed by critic H. Douglas Thomson in *Masters of Mystery: A Study of the Detective Story* (1931) to be the best of Crofts' books up to that time, with "one of the best red herrings ever dangled before the reader."[37]

With *Mystery in the Channel* (1931), Crofts shifted his transportation emphasis from trains to boats, as Inspector French investigates the shooting murders of two businessmen found dead on a yacht floating in the English Channel. Crofts ably manages the opening discovery scene and throughout the novel keeps his writing terse and direct, barring an unneeded dose of "stage Cockney" working class dialect (with an abundance of misplaced "haitches"). The two dead men were the chairman and vice-chairman of Moxon's General Securities, a firm of investment bankers standing on the verge of financial collapse. Over the course of French's investigation, it becomes clear that someone in Moxon's not only is responsible for the two murders but also for the defalcation of a million and a half pounds. Yet discovering just who is responsible for these crimes proves quite a formidable task for French, who at one point late in the tale becomes so frustrated that he is moved to make what for him is a shocking statement: "Curse it ... I could do with a bottle of beer" (sadly, we are denied our view of the abstemious Inspector French quaffing beer in a pub with his chief underling, Sergeant Carter, because the Inspector has a sudden insight that leads to his solving the case). In addition to its marvelously well-constructed plot, *Channel*, the first novel Crofts conceived and wrote entirely after the Great Stock Market Crash of 1929, is of interest for the author's forcefully expressed moral outrage over criminality in high financial circles (for more on this point, see below). That astute critic Charles Williams praised *Channel* in strong terms, avowing that the novel "is one of the best mysteries that Inspector French has ever solved, and one of the best books that Mr. Crofts has ever written.... I always expect Mr. Crofts' books with reverence, but I await the next with excitement."[38]

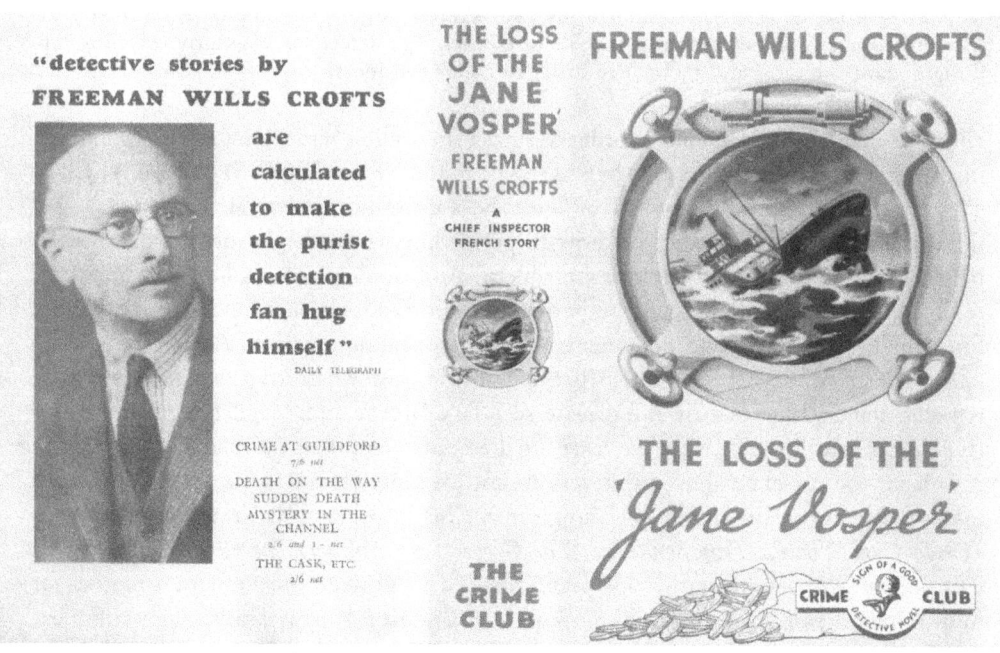

Freeman Wills Crofts, *Man Overboard!* (1936, opposite) and *The Loss of the 'Jane Vosper'* (1936, above). At the apex of Crofts' transatlantic appeal in 1936, his American publishers, Dodd, Mead and Company, contrasted the author's bourgeois series detective with insouciant gentleman amateurs like Dorothy L. Sayers' Lord Peter Wimsey: "Inspector French has been definitely built up as a foil to the theatrical and eccentric fictional sleuth, and is, therefore, a model of thoroughness, persistency and hard work." For its part, the Collins Crime Club guaranteed the author's appeal to the "purist detection fan."

FREEMAN WILLS CROFTS

FREEMAN WILLS CROFTS was born in Dublin, Ireland, and educated in Belfast. He early became assistant construction engineer on the Irish Railways and later chief assistant engineer in the London, Scotland and Midland system.

In 1929 he resigned his engineering work to devote his entire time to novels, although the railroad background still persists in his writing.

Like many detective-story writers, he has a number of hobbies—gardening, carpentering, motoring and music. His Inspector French has been definitely built up as a foil to the theatrical and eccentric fictional sleuth, and is, therefore, a model of thoroughness, persistency and hard work.

"Crofts tells a straight-forward story of crime and detection," writes Vincent Starrett, "filled with human, everyday characters and with careful attention to detail. It's the right sort of novel for the genuine detective-story addict, who likes to work on the case himself."

Of all fictional detectives, Chief-Inspector Joseph French is first and foremost in breaking down alibis. An interesting verbal picture of him is presented in a letter from Mr. Crofts to his publishers. "French is a rather stoutish man, slightly below middle height, blue-eyed, with a pleasant, comfortable, cheery expression. He does not wear a uniform. His manner is suave, pleasant, even kindly, partly because by nature he is a decent man and partly because if he sets those he is interrogating at their ease he gets more out of them. He would be dressed in an ordinary lounge suit with probably a soft hat and without stick or gloves."

The Inspector French stories have been translated into Swedish, Danish, Dutch, French, German, Italian, Czecho-Slovakian and Portuguese.

Other Titles by FREEMAN WILLS CROFTS

THE CASK · THE STRANGE CASE OF DR. EARLE
CRIME ON THE SOLENT · THE LOSS OF THE "JANE VOSPER"
MAN OVERBOARD! (Fall 1936)

DODD, MEAD AND COMPANY

Though fewer forms of transportation are involved in the commission of the investigated crimes in *The Hog's Back Mystery*, this 1933 Crofts novel is similarly intricate to *Journey* and *Channel* in its construction of alibis; indeed, the novel boasts perhaps the longest, most complex timetables in the literature of Golden Age detection (it is actually graphed by Crofts). Additionally, at the end of the novel every clue on which French based his deductions Crofts keys by page number, an impressive authorial feat. The tale concerns the disappearances of no less than three individuals around the Hog's Back, a ridge near Crofts' own home village of Blackheath. At times it appears as if the one man, a local doctor named Earle, and two women literally vanished off the face of the Earth, giving the tale a sinister edge unusual for Crofts. Discerning a motive for the murders proves especially difficult, though as usual Crofts is scrupulously fair to his readers (while praising the novel highly, Eric Gillett in the *Sunday Times* complained that Crofts gave his readers no "early indication of possible motives for the crime," a claim that in my view reflects more poorly on Gillett's deductive skills than on Crofts' clueing).[39] Eventually French solves one of his most complex cases, giving in the last chapter a deft and charmingly self-deprecating drawing room exposition before his outwardly rather deflating (though inwardly admiring) colleagues.

Mystery on Southampton Water, the second of two inverted crime novels published by Crofts in 1934, is in my view the superior of the two, though the other novel, *The 12.30 from Croydon*, is better remembered today. While *Croydon* follows the standard man-plots-death-of-rich-relative pattern (see more below), *Southampton Water* deals with a more unusual topic in the Golden Age crime novel, industrial espionage. A rivalry between cement manufacturing companies in the vicinity of Southampton eventually escalates into three murders, including a double homicide by means of an explosive device. While Crofts unfolds the story in his usual plain style, the narrative nevertheless grips the reader, as he follows the stratagems and counter-stratagems of the two ruthless companies, as well as those of French and the other official investigators. As usual, Crofts is prodigious with clever criminal devices, including the means of drugging one of the cement factory executives while he is traveling on a train and the devising of an explosion of a small boat carrying the managing directorate from the same firm. It is quite an entertaining tale; and if it is not necessarily, as Harold Nicolson stated, "exactly what a detective novel should be," it certainly is exactly what a Freeman Wills Crofts detective novel should be.[40]

Crofts followed *Southampton Water* in 1935 with another tale of business theft and murder, *Crime at Guildford*. Quite well-received at the time, *Guildford* is filled to abundance with ingenious elements, though it is rather imitative of *Southampton Water* in its basic design and one key joist in the plot span is shaky. *Guildford* involves the theft of a fortune in gems from Norne's jewelers and the murder of one of the company's executives. Much of the novel revolves around how keys to the company safe were obtained, a plot point repeated from *Southampton Water*, though admittedly with a different — and quite clever — mechanism. **[SPOILER ALERT]** However, the novel's murder plot requires impersonation of the victim by a look-alike actor involved in the conspiracy, and here Crofts stretches credulity to the breaking point by having one of the victim's longtime colleagues taken in by the trick, even though the colleague had talked for some time to the impersonator (albeit in a darkened room). Even if such a ploy really would have worked, it is quite arguable whether a group of murderers would have staked their own lives on such a chancy venture. [**END SPOILER ALERT**] In "The Simple Art of Murder," Raymond Chandler's famous essay criticizing the classical detective novel, Chandler, who actually enjoyed Crofts' books more than he did those of most English mystery writers, with justification criticized this ploy in *Guildford* as "too fancy." Additionally, there is some unfortunate travelogue near the end of the novel when Inspector French travels to the Netherlands. Still, *Crime at Guildford* stands as a fine example of the Golden Age detective novel.

Arguably the best Crofts' tale involving corporate conspiracy is *The Loss of the "Jane Vosper,"* one of Crofts' most popular books since its publication in 1936 (in England "Jane Vosper" went through five printings by 1937, was reprinted by Penguin in 1953 and 1965 and was selected by Julian Symons for the 1980 Crime Club Golden Jubilee Series). This story opens with a bang, or four of them to be precise, as multiple explosions sink the merchant vessel *Jane Vosper* in the southern Atlantic. After a bravura opening detailing the foundering of the ship, the next chapters follow the genesis of the investigation by an insurance company suspecting fraud. When the insurance investigator disappears, French is put on the case. What follows is the gradual uncovering by French and his team of a very clever yet credible crime. Here Crofts pays more attention to realistic police procedure and provides patient readers with a fascinating story, praised by both Nicolas Blake and Milward Kennedy. The latter reviewer reflected perceptively on the odd strength of the tale, and Crofts' style in general:

> His gift is to interest the reader in a pedestrian account of the search for a needle in a haystack. His latest book is perhaps his most astonishing performance; for when it is two-thirds over neither Inspector French nor the reader has discovered anything at all towards the elucidation of the mystery. Mr. Crofts can interest us in repeated scrutinies of wisps of hay and repeated discoveries that they are not needles.[41]

Contrarily, two other author-reviewers, Margaret Cole and Julian Symons, criticized Crofts for having populated his novels with essentially featureless characters. "Not characters at all," complained Cole in 1931, but rather "extremely simple structures provided only with name labels and impregnable alibis." Echoing this sentiment nearly a half-century later, Symons asserted that "Crofts' characters are no more than names, and have so little individuality that they might just as well carry labels saying Managing Director, Works Foreman, Ship's Engineer." Yet in Crofts' novels flat characters are a virtue rather than a vice, for they allow readers to focus on what they should realize is his strength as an entertainer, plotting. Crofts' most problematic novels in my view are those taking the form of pietistic narratives where the author attempts to emotionally engage readers in the moral plights of his characters, rather than offer them a complexly plotted mystery. Indeed, with the possible exceptions of *Enemy Unseen* (1945), a return to Crofts' older style, and an unusual wartime espionage tale, *Death of a Train* (1946), Crofts in my opinion never produced a top-flight detective novel again from 1937 onwards, a period when the author regrettably began relying less on plotting and more on characterization, as will be seen below. Reflecting a common view, critic Eric Partridge once mentioned of Crofts in passing that his writing style debarred "purple-passaged dramas."[42] This in fact is manifestly untrue of much of Crofts' work, as my discussion above of the bathetic neo–Victorian style infecting a number of his twenties novels should have demonstrated. Purple passages occasionally would appear even in the best French period, 1927 to 1936, and all too frequently afterwards in the mostly unchecked decline of the French franchise that followed.

Signs of eventual collapse can be seen in 1932's *Sudden Death* and *Death on the Way*, efforts by Crofts to offer readers more psychologically developed characters, something his peculiar writing talent was not equipped to carry off successfully. *Sudden Death* is a country house mystery, with events seen through the perceptions of housekeeper Anne Day. Left on the death of her clergyman father "homeless and with an income of barely thirty pounds a year," Anne was about "to take a position as scullery maid in a large house," when the housekeeping job with the Grinsteads at Frayle came her way. Unfortunately, Anne as a person is not remotely interesting; and the second of the novel's two murders fizzles miserably. Indeed, this murder might well be the most prosaically explained locked room killing in a British Golden Age detective novel: [**SPOILER ALERT**]

> As Grinsmead turned back towards his desk Edith shot him. She locked the door ... wiped the pistol, pressed his fingers on it, laid it in his hand, and placed herself behind the door. She knew she would be hidden between the door and the cabinet.... When the door was burst open and the others were staring spellbound at Grinsmead, she simply ran forward from behind the door. As she had foreseen, none of them noticed that she had not come through it. [**END SPOILER ALERT**]

As a solution to a locked room problem this is underwhelming, to say the least, and it suggests why French normally was better off sticking to his timetables.[43]

Attempting in *Sudden Death* to provide greater character interest for his readers, Crofts unfortunately falls back on the same dreadfully overwritten melodrama that mars some of his twenties books: [**SPOILER ALERT**]

> And then she looked across at Edith and suddenly, in a ghastly flash of enlightenment, she knew. More than that, she saw that Edith realized that she knew.
> Anne could have screamed from sheer horror as she gazed, as if hypnotized, at Edith's expression. There sat, not the quiet, rather hard, and more than rather self-centered Edith Cheame, but a fiend, a devil in human form. For moments which seemed like an eternity they sat facing each other, while Anne felt that she was looking down into a suddenly uncovered abyss of human evil, more appalling that she could have imagined.[44]

In this storm of melodramatic writing the heavy clichés come down upon the reader like hailstones: "sheer horror," "gazed as if hypnotized," "a devil in human form," "moments which seemed like an eternity," "abyss of human evil." After being pelted by such weighty phrases, it is hard for the dazed reader to share the author's concern over the fates of saintly Anne and fiendish Edith. [**END SPOILER ALERT**]

Death on the Way is a definite improvement over *Sudden Death*, both in its solidly grounded and well-conveyed railway setting and in the construction of its two murder problems involving a group of railway engineers, but over-prominent characterization again is a weakness. Here the problem centers on the characterization of the murderer. [**SPOILER ALERT**] Seemingly borrowing from Agatha Christie, Crofts makes the murderer the sympathetic central character of the book, Clifford Parry. However, Crofts does not demonstrate the narrative mastery needed to carry off the celebrated "Roger Ackroyd trick." We are allowed into Parry's mind, but so selectively as to open the author to the charge that he here violated the Golden Age canon of fair play. The most interesting thing about *Death on the Way*, besides the appealing railway setting, is the author's attempt, through French, to make the novel's double murderer sympathetic to the reader:

> "I don't know if you are familiar with Clifford Parry's history. In a sense I suppose it would be fair to say that all this trouble is due to the War. Parry served and left the army a wreck. During his service his father died, and his mother was left hard up. Fortunately about that time they came in for a legacy of some L500. It was decided that this money should be spent in Parry's finishing the course in engineering which had been interrupted when he joined up. His health having somewhat improved, he qualified. Immediately afterwards his mother died. Her little income died with her and Parry was left alone and penniless. Worse almost than that, debts that he contracted had not been paid off."[45]

In debt, Parry lets himself get inveigled into a scheme to commit fraud upon the railway company for which he works, which in turns leads to the greater crime of murder. People falling into the path of crime because of large debts they have incurred (often, though not in this case, through gambling) is an extremely common circumstance in Crofts' novels and short stories, but far less typical is an attempt by the author to provide a psychological explanation in partial mitigation of a crime. In *Death on the Way* French is led by his study of Parry's case history to declare: "I think there might be a defense of unsound mind arising from shell shock. I feel sure he's not normal."[46] **[END SPOILER ALERT]**

In 1934 was the publication of Crofts' first inverted crime novel, *The 12.30 from Croydon*, a tale that presaged Crofts' increasing concern in the late 1930s and 1940s with moral issues. In this novel we watch as the protagonist, Charles Swinburn, needing money for his failing business and to marry a demanding woman ("I may as well tell you at once that under no circumstances would I marry a poor man," this ostensibly fatally charming woman, Una Mellor, charmlessly announces), succumbs to the temptation to murder his wealthy uncle, Andrew Crowther. Half-senile and pigheadedly adhering to an outdated, absolutist Victorian conception of laissez-faire, the old man refuses to give his desperate heir any financial aid, telling Charles that he will have to be satisfied with inheriting his estate upon his death. Debating whether to go forward with a plan thusly to precipitate that death, Swinburn argues to himself that "all this morality business," as he dismissively terms it, is "only an old wives' tale.... What was politic was right. What was the greatest good of the greatest number?"[47] **[SPOILER ALERT]** Like Guy Davidson in John Street's *The Davidson Case*, **[END SPOILER ALERT]** Swinburn tells himself that he is taking a relative's life to save the employees in his business, though Crofts makes clear to the reader that Swinburn is deceiving himself and that purely personal considerations are paramount with him. Once resolved on his murderous course, Swinburn carries out his plan with considerable ingenuity, but of course unforeseen contingencies crop up, as well as a bland yet implacable nemesis in the form of Inspector French.

Although Crofts' first essay in inverted murder was one of the author's most praised crime novels, his characterization ability is too slight to sustain a plausible narrative in *Croydon*. Swinburn's supposedly overwhelming passion for the utterly unsympathetic, grasping Una Mellor is never made remotely credible. "*A marriage with Una! Heaven! Heaven on earth, irrespective of anything else!*" moonily thinks an enraptured Charles at one point, though this reader strongly suspects marriage with Una might well have made the earth resemble a rather more fiery region. However, it must be conceded that *Croydon* traditionally has been considered one of Crofts' best works. Indeed, Charles Williams wrote of a woman reduced to tears when reading *Croydon*, because "she couldn't bear the nice murderer to be hanged." Williams joked that the weeping woman should have known better, as the "nice murderer" had deliberately killed two people (both his tightfisted uncle and a blackmailing butler) and an upright man like Crofts could never have allowed him to go unpunished. Indeed, as Swinburn, on trial for his life, awaits the jury's verdict, Crofts takes the opportunity to moralize about the man's current dire position: "His thoughts went back to certain incidents in his life. Now he would give everything he had if he could have lived them differently. How thankful now would he not be if he could have a clear conscience, his freedom, and poverty. And Una! He had sacrificed himself for Una, and at the first breath of trouble she had let him down!"[48] Crime, one can but conclude from this interior monologue, does not pay. Existing as a character in a Freeman Wills Crofts novel, Swindon really should have seen it coming.

Crofts' moralism becomes more and more pronounced over the thirties, as he focused less on complex plotting and more on the portrayal of his characters' confrontations with temptation and sin. Greed is the besetting vice that leads to the downfall of many a man in these novels, particularly greed in business. Of the sixteen novels Crofts published between 1930 and 1941, fully eleven (nearly 75 percent) cast businessmen in some negative light: *Sir John Magill's Last Journey* (1930); *Mystery in the Channel* (1931); *Death on the Way* (1932); *The 12.30 from Croydon* (1933); *Mystery on Southampton Water* (1934); *Crime at Guildford* (1935); *The Loss of the "Jane Vosper"* (1936); *Man Overboard!* (1936*); The End of Andrew Harrison* (1938); *Fatal Venture* (1939); and *James Tarrant, Adventurer* (1941). Before 1930, out of nine published mystery novels in only one is corruption in a legitimate business made the operative factor in the murder puzzle. That this chronological cleavage in Crofts' work coincides with the onset of the Great Depression scarcely seems coincidental.

Before 1930, Crofts' comments tend to be more dismissive of labor than of capital. In *The Sea Mystery*, for example, Crofts asserts rather huffily that "consideration on the part of the employer ... was vastly more common than the unions would have the public believe," chidingly adding that "gratitude on the part of the employee was not so frequent." In *Inspector French's Greatest Case*, Crofts, perhaps thinking of himself, laments how many a time French's dream of enjoying "a long, lazy, delightful evening with a pipe and book" is dashed by work demands. "Not for him was the eight-hour day, overtime at high rates, 'on call' or country allowances, expenses," writes Crofts, in a shot across the bow of an obstreperous working class. "[French's] portion was to get his work done, or take the consequence in lack of promotion or even loss of such position he held."[49] After Crofts' retirement from railway engineering, which occurred the same year as Black Tuesday in the United States, the now fulltime author became much more critical of business. One is forced to wonder whether Crofts took hits in his investments that were sufficiently hard to cause him, like others in the middle class, to wonder for the first time about the equity of modern capitalism and high finance.

Whatever happened in Crofts' own life, in his books from the 1930s onward rapacious businessmen wreak havoc on the lives of the innocent, variously through physical theft (*Mystery on Southampton Water*), financial fraud (*Death on the Way, The Loss of the "Jane Vosper," Man Overboard!, James Tarrant, Adventurer*), promotion of vice (*Fatal Venture*) and irresponsible speculations (*Mystery in the Channel, The End of Andrew Harrison*), all of which end up leading to murder. *Mystery in the Channel*, written in the immediate wake of the world financial crash, decisively sounded this note in Crofts' work. In this novel, multiple murders are precipitated by the collapse of Moxon's General Securities, "one of the biggest financial houses in the country." **[SPOILER ALERT]** Having realized that a crash was inevitable, four partners decided to convert the firm's capital into easily portable diamonds and abscond with them, a plan which turned deadly when one of the men murdered his three criminal colleagues and seized the diamonds for himself. **[END SPOILER ALERT]** Early on in the affair, Inspector French's chief at Scotland Yard, Sir Mortimer Ellison, is moved, in regard to the failure of Moxon's, to damn the venality of criminal financiers:

> "When I think of all the innocent people who are going to suffer through these dirty scoundrels, I'd give a big part of my salary to know they were safe in Dartmoor. Two old maiden ladies living close to us, friends of my wife ... invested their whole worldly goods through Moxon's General Securities. What is there for them now? The poorhouse? And their case will only be one of thousands.... Think of all the people who will now have to give up sending their sons to a decent school. And all that will have to do without their holiday and little pleasures they had been counting on for years. I tell you, French, it'll not be the fault of this department if those fellows have any more happiness in the world."

To this sentiment, French agrees "whole-heartedly."[50]

French later reflects on how Ellison's harsh attitude toward crooked financiers markedly contrasts with his more sympathetic views of other criminals:

> [Sir Mortimer] always deplored the punishment of the out-of-work or the poorly paid who, seeing his family in want, had stolen to relieve their immediate needs. Even on occasion he had surprised French by expressing regret as to the fate of murderers. Murderers, he held, were by no means necessarily hardened criminals. In their ranks they numbered some of the most decent and inoffensive of men. But for the wealthy thief who stole by the manipulation of stocks and shares and other creditable methods known to high finance, whether actually within or without the limits of the law, he had only the most profound enmity and contempt.[51]

In a later case, recounted as *The End of Andrew Harrison*, French investigates the sealed room murder of a widely-despised financier. Andrew Harrison "had an unpleasant reputation," Crofts informs his readers condemningly. "His brilliancy in business was admitted on all sides. Even his obvious enemies admired, if ruefully, his financial dexterity.... But of his humanity and honesty ... not one word. 'Crooked as they make them,' was perhaps the most flattering description." At one point, French, who admits having himself lost money on the stock market, reflects perplexedly on the oddly quasi-religious nature of modern finance:

> Amazing how important people's beliefs were! He had once heard a man arguing that the whole structure of finance was built on faith, or credit, as it was technically called. This man said it didn't matter whether or not money really existed so long as people believed it did. French could not accept that view. He remembered that faith had not put money in the Humbert safe. Yet without faith he could not see that modern commerce and finance could function. It was an interesting question and sometime he must think it out.[52]

Certainly Crofts in these works is not ignoring the Depression, as Julian Symons in *Bloody Murder* has contended was done "in almost all the detective stories of the Golden

Age." On the other hand, Crofts' preoccupation remains with the small investor class of which he formed a part: aged gentlewomen on fixed incomes threatened with outright poverty; white-collar fathers not able to send sons (a thought for the educations of daughters apparently never arises) to "decent" schools; and nice middle class families having to forego special holidays. Crofts does refer occasionally to the problem of the manual unemployed, but he never imaginatively treads in the worn boots of the laboring class, members of which had to give up more "little pleasures" in their lives than the hope of a holiday. In his novels Crofts is much more interested in the plights of downtrodden members of the genteel class, like Anne Day in *Sudden Death* and Betty Stanton in *Golden Ashes*, who must find salaried employment as housekeepers, or *The End of Andrew Harrison's* Markham Crewe (he of the "dark handsome face, with its aquiline nose, sensitive mouth and innate stamp of breeding"), who is forced to seek the position of social secretary under that awful parvenu millionaire financier Andrew Harrison. Fortunately, such occupations seem to involve little in the way of actual duties (though murder always seems to be lurking round the corner). Betty Stanton even finds time to write a novel "about the successful struggle of a girl against poverty" (with, even more surprisingly, "a striking and original plot"). By the end of *Golden Ashes*, Betty, that nasty murder behind her, is herself on her way to financial security, with her book published and now "a very good seller" and a contract for three more novels in her pocket.[53]

On one occasion Crofts allows the oh-so-bourgeois French to be brought up short by his less financially secure assistant, Sergeant Carter, in the course of their investigation of the murder of Andrew Harrison. Comparing the effect on stocks of the death of millionaire financier Andrew Harrison to that which occurred when Ivar Kruger, the so-called Swedish Match King, who committed suicide in 1932, French comments: "That affair may be responsible for some of the present trouble. People remember Kruger and it makes them nervous. And quite reasonably. I was stung myself over Swedish matches, and if I had money in Harrison's, I'd see about getting it out before I did anything else." Carter grins and responds, "I believe you, sir. And so should I if I was lucky enough to have to decide." This remark, reports Crofts, "set French to thinking. He had lost £500 in that crash.... Was he so lucky? He hadn't thought so at the time. And yet was it not better to save and lose £500 that never to be able to save at all? Yes, he supposed Carter was right."[54]

A favored narrative pattern of Crofts in the thirties and forties, used in *Man Overboard!*, *Fatal Venture*, *James Tarrant, Adventurer* and *Silence for the Murderer* (1948), is to tell the tale of some inherently decent and honest person ("straight" is the now apt to be misleading adjective often used by Crofts to describe such people) who lands in trouble through his or her naive association with some shady business promoter/s enticing get rich quick scheme, but ultimately is redeemed through the relentless detection of the good Inspector (actually now Chief Inspector) French. In *Man Overboard!*, the narrative focus is diffused between the investigators (French and his old North Irish friend and colleague from *Sir John Magill's Last Journey*, Sergeant M'Clung) and the nice young woman, Pamela Grey, whose fiancée is wrongly arrested for the novel's murder. Pam is the classic Crofts' heroine, one we see over and over in his books. She is physically appealing, but not so much so as to compel unseemly carnal thoughts: "Pam was not exactly pretty, and she was not beautiful at all. All the same she was a sight to gladden tired eyes." Most importantly, Pam simply is *good*: "The overwhelming impression she gave was of what used to be called wholesomeness.... In her face there was character." When French meets Pam, he, a true reader of hearts, is immediately struck by her goodness: "A nice girl, he thought. Decent and straight and dependable, he felt sure. Good looking too in a mild sort of way. But not remarkable. Would make a good wife for someone."[55]

Unfortunately, Pam and her fiancée have been inveigled by a couple of fraudsters into involvement in a business scheme to market inflammable inert petrol, a scheme which of course leads to murder. The real murderers' plot itself is uninteresting, reusing some tricks from *Sir John Magill's Last Journey*, and perfunctorily investigated by French; but Crofts' main interest in the novel is narrating the narrow escape of Pam and her fiancée from the mortal snare set by avarice. Love of money is the root of all the evil in *Man Overboard!* "Suddenly and unexpectedly there had come a promise of money," writes Crofts. "Not a little money — not even a competence. What was dazzling their bewildered gaze was the prospect of a vast fortune; wealth almost infinite; utterly beyond ordinary limits; staggering in its magnitude."[56]

Crofts is at his least subtle as a writer in drawing a moral from Pam's brief lapse into sinful greed:

> Pam was intoxicated with the amazing prospect of wealth. But Pam could not foresee the future. She didn't realize that very often Fate offers her benefactions with her tongue in her cheek. They come as promised, but not alone. Some ingredient is added which robs them of their value. Pam didn't know that a day was coming ... when she would have given everything she had if only she had never heard of the fortune or of any person or thing connected with it. She didn't know that instead of bringing joy and freedom to herself and Jack, the whole affair would grow into a ghastly horror whose memories threatened to stay with them during every remaining moment of their lives.[57]

Jack's threatened incarceration, which becomes a reality over the course of the novel, leads for Pam to some quite vexing emotional moments ("awful ghastly terror," Crofts now calls it, this presumably being even worse than the aforementioned "ghastly horror"). Crofts must have drawn on all his vast melodramatic resources (as well as his typewriter's exclamation point key) to convey Pam's agitated mental state to the reader:

> How she wished that Jack was back! How she wished to see him and hear him and to be comforted by what he would have to tell her!
> Because that this would comfort her, she never for a moment doubted. Never for a moment! And yet.... Oh, how she wished he would come!...
> An icy hand seemed to close round Pam's heart.... So it had come.... Jack arrested! *Jack!* And for murder!....
> ... Oh, how crookedly things had happened! If only Platt had not lost his head in the cottage on that Saturday morning! If only Jack had appeared a few seconds earlier or later than he did! If only he had not crossed that night and by the same boat!... It was as if Fate was against them.[58]

Fortunately for Pam, Chief Inspector French arrives on the scene to drive from her life the looming menace of all this ghastliness. Like it shall be, we are told, on the Day of Judgment, the good stand revealed when Pamela Grey and Joseph French confront one another. Just as French senses righteousness radiating from Pam, she perceives the great well of goodness in him: "Chief Inspector French was not only polite and appeared to be straight, but she thought he looked kindly and decent." French finds the true murderers and Jack is released by the police. Pam at first is "intensely disappointed" when it is revealed that the formula for inert petrol was a fiction all along, but she grows "reconciled to the loss, particularly as in her heart of hearts she believed real happiness was more likely to be achieved in comparatively humble circumstances."[59]

The troubles of Harry Morrison in *Fatal Venture* and Merle Weir in *James Tarrant, Adventurer* stem from their participation in what Crofts and many others perceived as unethical businesses, casino gambling in the former novel and patent medicines in the latter one. Both Harry Morrison and Merle Weir are favored characters of Crofts, plucky orphans of good family thrown upon their own resources by the deaths of their parents. Merle Weir, we learn, is "in character ... one in a thousand, straight and kindly and decent and unselfish." After the death of her father, a country doctor, she is cast into the world to wend her own way, so she goes into the nursing profession. A prudent young woman, Merle divides the capital inherited from her father, "setting aside half for the necessary [nursing] training, and retaining the rest against the proverbial rainy day." All goes well until she meets the unscrupulous James Tarrant, the *Adventurer* of the book's title. Merle falls hard for this bounder, her love blinding her to the telltale signs of dishonesty in his physical appearance, notably a "long face ... strengthened almost to brutality by the ... firm jaw" and eyes "too shrewd for complete confidence" (throughout Crofts' work "shrewdness" in businessmen is seen by the author not as a virtue, but a vice, connoting not admirable horse sense, but potentially ruthless determination to get ahead unfairly at the expense of others). With promises of marriage, the smoothly scheming Tarrant persuades Merle to lend her capital to his patent medicine scheme, despite Merle's concern that the scheme is not quite "straight." Tarrant is rightly convinced that he holds Merle's heart in the palm of his hand: "He could get what he liked out of her. And as to her conscientious scruples, a few amorous looks and kisses would put them right."[60] Eventually the lying and cheating Tarrant meets his Maker as the result of violence, and Merle is arrested and tried for murder; though of course French saves the poor wronged woman when he belatedly discovers the truth.

Crofts' strongest attack on business is found in *Fatal Venture*, where unethical businessmen start a floating luxury gambling casino just outside British territorial waters, dragging the intrinsically honest and decent Harry Morrison along into their shady affair. Like Merle Weir, Harry is an orphan, who found himself forced to become self-supporting after the deaths of his parents and the unhappy revelation that debts resulting from his father's "secret speculation" had nearly wiped out his entire legacy. Morrison has a crisis of conscience about participating in a gambling concern, yet he succumbs for a time to temptation: "He didn't like the idea that he would be helping to carry on a gambling hell. What would he feel like ... if he learnt that his livelihood had brought someone else to suicide? Then he told himself that such ideas were morbid.... He mustn't be a sentimental fool."[61]

Harry meets another inherently good person like himself when he encounters Margot Stott, the niece of the gambling ship's unscrupulous backer. Margot is yet another classic, virtuous-but-not-exactly-pretty Crofts heroine. "Her coloring was dark, and though not in any sense beautiful, her features were regular and well-formed," Crofts writes of Margot.

Opposite: Freeman Wills Crofts, *James Tarrant Adventurer* (1940). Businessman James Tarrant's moral corruption manifests itself physically in his "long face ... strengthened almost to brutality by the ... firm jaw." With such novels as *Tarrant*, Crofts questioned business ethics in Depression-era Britain.

FREEMAN WILLS CROFTS

A NEW INSPECTOR FRENCH NOVEL
JAMES TARRANT, ADVENTURER

However, "it was not the details of the appearance," the author adds significantly, "but the general impression he received from her, that affected Morrison. She seemed to radiate goodness in all its forms.... On her kindliness as well as complete straightness he would have banked his future." Margot agrees with Harry that the ship would far better have been devoted to providing holiday cruises for nice middle class patrons, rather than serving as a gambling den for the dissolute, sensation-seeking rich (each cabin even has a private bathroom!), and she effectively becomes his guiding angel of good conscience:

> Morrison was startled.... "You don't approve of gambling?"
> She shook her head decidedly. "No, nor the luxury. I feel it's all wrong. Don't you think so yourself, Mr. Morrison?"
> Morrison hesitated. "Well, I confess I was brought up to consider gambling an evil...."
> She turned in her chair and looked at him.... "Tell me more of Mr. Bristow's original idea. That would have been really good. It would have given health and pleasure to a lot of people who couldn't afford all this."[62]

Naturally French and his wife, who improbably accompanies him on his shipboard investigation, are favorably impressed with the moral paragon that is Margot: "The more French saw of Margot, the more he admired her. He had liked her when they first met.... Mrs. French had quite fallen in love with her, proclaiming her delight in meeting any young person so good and kind and unspoilt." Of Harry, French shares a similar high opinion and doubts that a man of his "apparent character" could be guilty of murdering Margot's uncle. One of the murderer's qualifications, as French sees it, is that "he must have the necessary selfish, cruel and determined character." After arresting someone who does have this necessarily bad character, French goes through the casino's papers and discovers the unpleasant truth about this "gambling hell": "In the seventeen months during which the ship had been running, there had been nine cases of more or less complete ruin. Three men and one woman had committed suicide, three had gone abroad and disappeared, and two had been reduced to beggary at home; besides which there were many letters telling of serious loss."[63] At Margot's urging, her father, who inherits the casino, decides to sell the ship for scrap. Margot and Harry marry two months later, making sure to send a wedding invitation to Joseph and Emily French.

Crofts' pronounced faith-based moralism in such works should be sufficiently clear. However, his most explicitly religious work, one in which he directly tries to evangelize readers, is the inverted crime novel *Antidote to Venom* (1938). Crofts' works are notably lacking in that Golden Age detective fiction staple, the absent-minded, head-in-the-clouds village vicar, perhaps at least partly because Crofts likely felt that religion was not a subject for levity in fiction (humor is rare in any case in Crofts' books). But religious feeling, as I have endeavored to show, suffuses Crofts' writing more completely than that of any other Golden Age detective fiction writer, with the exceptions of G.K. Chesterton and H.C. Bailey. In 1949, Crofts would make his profound devotion to the Christian faith patently clear with his publication of what the author viewed as his magnum opus, *The Four Gospels in One Story*, a time-consuming effort to streamline the Gospels and tell them in the language of the plain man. "Contact with Christ changes people's nature," avowed Crofts in his preface to the book, "giving them the qualities of integrity, courage and unselfishness so universally needed." Occasionally in his fictional works, Crofts will make a direct religious reference, as when, in *James Tarrant, Adventurer*, he pointedly notes that the "church choir practice, which seemed the chief excitement of a Friday evening [in the village of Lydcott], evoked in [Tarrant] no answering thrill" (this statement carries added force when we recall that Crofts himself directed church choirs in Blackheath).[64] Only with *Antidote to Venom*, however, did Crofts consciously adopt in his mystery fiction an overtly pietistic narrative, examining the effect on humans of communion with the Holy Spirit.

In December 1937, not long before he published *Venom*, Crofts wrote Dorothy L. Sayers — now known for her religious play *The Zeal of Thy House* as well as her detective fiction — trying to interest her in the activities of the Christian evangelical organization known as the Oxford Group. Crofts reminded Sayers that he had sent her a copy of the Group's journal, *Rising Tide*, which was dedicated to "illustrating what was being done in an attempt to solve some of our present day problems"; and he informed her that an effort now was afoot to send a copy to every member of the Society of Authors, so as to win support for the Group's visionary aim of "world re-building." Here the author is clearly referencing the Oxford Group's philosophy of "Moral Re-Armament," grandiloquently explicated in a 1938 London speech by its founder, the American Christian missionary Dr. Frank Buchman. "The [world] crisis is fundamentally a moral one," pronounced Buchman. "The nations must re-arm morally. Moral recovery is essentially the forerunner of economic recovery. Imagine a rising tide of absolute honesty and absolute unselfishness sweeping across every country!... A wave of absolute unselfishness throughout the nations would be the end of war." A true believer in this "Buchmanism," Crofts avowed to Sayers that the Oxford Group was "really making for better living" around the world.[65]

Sayers' reply to Crofts' letter was sufficiently squelching ("I must admit frankly that there are aspects of the Group Movement which to me, as an English Catholic, are distasteful. I am sorry, but there it is!"), but that Crofts wrote the formidable and High Church Sayers such a letter in the first place suggests that the mild author indeed had become something of an evangel by this time. Certainly two novels Crofts published shortly prior to *Antidote to Venom*, *Man Overboard!* and *The End of Andrew Harrison*, reflect Moral Re-Armament philosophy, with their emphasis on "straightness." Indeed, the closing paragraph of *Andrew Harrison* would have been right at home as a homily in *Rising Tide*. "Poor people," French reflects as he thinks of the miserable family of the despised, deceased Andrew Harrison, "they played so much for their own hand that they missed their own happiness."[66] Moral Re-Armament, one can imagine Crofts thinking, would have brought true happiness to Harrison's family by vanquishing their base, selfish urges, and it would have made the great financier himself deal straighter in business.

In *Antidote to Venom*, Crofts for the first time directly writes about the saving, transformative effect of religious faith. As in other novels, the protagonist of *Antidote to Venom*— George Surridge, Director of the Birmingham Corporation Zoo — allows himself to be drawn into nefarious activity, this time murder. Surridge made the mistake of wedding a woman of a higher social station, one made unhappy by household economies. ("When ... she found they were traveling second class on their honeymoon to Switzerland, she had frowned, though without remark. And when at Pontresina they had gone to a comparatively primitive hotel with small rooms and without private baths, she had been a little short.") Worse yet, he "had been idiotic enough ... to get into a gambling set at his club," with the result that he was losing "more than he could afford, and yet he didn't want to stop playing." When he falls for another woman and needs yet more money, his fatal course toward the commission of murder is determined. Vivid memories of his "religious upbringing" are insufficient to sway him, as "he had long ceased to believe in that sort of thing." However, after murder is done and Surridge has reaped his worldly reward, he finds that religion is not so easily cast aside:

> He was conscious of a fundamental unrest and disquietude of spirit. He was obtaining the material advantage he had sought, but he had got with it an intangible load which seemed to bear him down like an actual weight.... [H]e had done what he had done ... because he had wanted to amuse himself with a mistress.... It was for this ... that he had become a murderer. It was for this that he had lost his peace of mind and taken on his shoulders a load from which he could never be rid.... [H]e saw that he had exchanged financial worry for a moral burden.[67]

George tells himself that his "thoughts of conscience" are only "nonsense retained in the mind from the false teaching of childhood. In this world, if you wanted anything you had to take it." Yet he is not able to banish such thoughts from his mind. As he comes to fear imminent arrest and falls to "his very lowest" point emotionally, his thoughts return to the religious teaching of his childhood: "Some old words that he had then learnt had recurred to him, about going to Someone and being given rest.... [H]e knew beyond doubt or question that he had been deceiving himself: that there was a God, that good and evil in his life did matter, and that if there were hope for him at all, it was through the Divine Man who had spoken these words." The penitent George is brought to prayer and ultimately to the confession of his crime to police authorities (naturally the unstoppable French was on the verge of arresting him anyway). Blessedly, these actions constitute "the first steps to a vital contact with the Divine ... he now knew himself to be forgiven, cleaned from his load of guilt, and with a power and confidence to face the future to which he was moving, such as he had never experienced." For good measure George's wife Clarissa also finds "a contact with the Divine" and the reformed couple is able to glimpse "what life on such a basis of honesty and love might have been, if only they had found it earlier."[68]

In an author's note at the beginning of the novel, Crofts describes *Antidote to Venom* as "a two-fold experiment: first, it is an attempt to combine the direct and inverted types of detective story, and second, an effort to tell a story of crime positively." Crofts expressed desire "to tell a story of crime positively" confused the usually perceptive *Sunday Times* crime fiction reviewer Milward Kennedy, but Crofts' goal here seems clear to me: he wanted to publish a crime novel in which a criminal genuinely repents and is saved literally by the grace of God.[69] The motif of the story, venom, of course recalls the original sin instigated by the serpent in Eden. Venom figures literally in the tale, both through the lethal Russel's Viper used as an instrument of murder and figuratively in the evil that poisons George's heart and leads him into sin. The novels' final chapter, in which George finds his way to God, is titled "Venom: the Antidote."

During this time in the late thirties and beyond when Crofts' moral concerns came to find their most explicit expression in his books, his grip on plotting — his most praised quality as a writer — began to slacken. Some of his plots from these years have been criticized on technical points, like those in *Man Overboard!*, where a post-mortem fails to find physical evidence that a man found floating dead in the sea had previously been chloroformed and drowned on land; *Golden Ashes*, where the inheritor of an entailed estate tries to sell it; and *The Losing Game*, where a professional blackmailer signs his true name and address on an explicit blackmailing letter to one of his victims. Furthermore, Crofts' insistence on so clearly demarcating fallen characters from sanctified ones can have a suspense-killing effect in the context of a detective novel (when it is not inverted). Not for Crofts is Agatha Christie's unveiling of shocking reversals of character in the final pages of her novels, revealing lambs as wolves.

Crofts' best novel from this later period, 1937–1957, 1945's *Enemy Unseen*, is an intricate village mystery that abandons the overtly pietistic narrative form of most of the author's later works (*Death of a Train*, a tale from the following year about German sabotage in Britain that makes good use of workaday railway atmosphere, also is worth noting). In *Enemy Unseen*, Chief Inspector French is called to a village in Cornwall to investigate the death of a local man killed by the explosion of a rigged grenade during his daily walk along the shore. Crofts mostly focuses on French and his investigation, without digressions for emotional outpourings by the various goodhearted if dull female characters (who include, besides several village matrons, an ingénue with love interest in tow). Hinging more on matters of geography and mechanical engineering than timetables, the solution shares an affinity with John Rhode tales and the shifting of suspicion is deftly handled by the author, despite his overly generous instant exoneration of the "nice" characters ("her ... expression showed kindliness and goodwill"; "he was highly educated, had excellent manners and was truly upright and good-hearted"; "a man of the highest type, with his open face, shrewd but honest eyes, and kindly expression"; "she was obviously kind and good-hearted"). Furthermore, one of the characters for whom Crofts does not personally vouch is a writer of mystery thrillers ("poor stuff, designed like most films for the less intelligent sections of the community") and another is a composer of crossword puzzles, allowing Crofts an opportunity to indulge in a few pages of rare wit. Crofts' catalogue of over-ingenious crossword clues is amusing and the thriller author's thoughts on genre writing (conveyed to French) pertinent:

> "I write thrillers.... The detective story is the story of the elucidation of a problem. The solution is reached by inference and deduction from the given facts. In any story worthy of the name all the facts are given to enable the reader to find out the truth for himself. If he fails ... he can watch the detective succeed by the reasoning he should have employed."
> "He always does succeed! Unhappily that's where one departs from real life."
> "Oh, yes, he must succeed or else the story has no ending."
> "I wish we could say the same of our cases."[70]

Crofts makes the wealthy owner of the local manor — a pushing, parvenu public man named Charles Savory — genuinely unlikable. Indeed, Savory is one of the most persuasively unsympathetic (one is tempted to say unsavory) characters in Crofts' fiction, giving most of the other characters plenteous motives to kill him and Chief Inspector French good reason to wonder whether he, Savory, might have been the intended victim of the murderer all along. Yet despite the considerable unpleasantness raised by the grenade murder (and another that succeeds it), by the end of the tale the intrepid Chief Inspector French has restored the *status quo ante homicidium*, in the classic fashion memorably apotheosized by W.H. Auden in his essay "The Guilty Vicarage." "With the cloud of unsolved murders removed," declares Crofts pacifically, "the little town settled down once more to its accustomed quiet" (albeit minus a goodly number of its citizens).[71] Anthony

Boucher praised *Enemy Unseen* for having "an even more intricate puzzle than usual" with Crofts. "For the patient only," he concluded of the tale, "but for them a rewarding treasure." Similarly, Jacques Barzun and Wendell Hertig Taylor in *A Catalogue of Crime* lauded the novel's "ingenious plot" and its solution, the secret of which is "so ably maintained to the end."[72]

Enemy Unseen and, to a lesser extent, the intensively detailed *Death of a Train* reflect the Indian summer of Crofts' mystery fiction writing. The four detective novels (including one for children) that the author published in the last ten years of his life, 1947 to 1957, unfortunately are the negligible creations of an increasingly tired writer. Even the generally

Freeman Wills Crofts, *Murderers Make Mistakes* (1947). As the titles hints, Crofts's first short story collection is a gathering of moral parables on the folly of murder (courtesy Mark Terry).

sympathetic Barzun and Taylor damningly conclude of *French Strikes Oil* (1951), for example, that "it reads like an office report."[73]

Of greater interest than the last novels are the 1940s radio plays of Crofts, published in revised form as two volumes of short stories, *Murderers Make Mistakes* (1947) and *Many a Slip* (1955). The plots of the stories, all turning on some minor technical point that exposes the murderer, are of no great moment, but from a thematic standpoint they are strikingly reminiscent of moral parables, revealing as they do the dreadful consequences of man's succumbing to the temptation to kill. Once a man murders, he dooms himself, for murder inevitably will out (the theme is emphasized in the splendid Bip Pares jacket illustration of *Murderers Make Mistakes*, which depicts a great hand, like the Hand of God, pointing at a murderer in the act of committing his crime). "But as many another evil-doer has found," pronounces Crofts warningly in *Many a Slip*'s "The Flowing Tide," "things did not work out exactly as ... intended."[74]

The moral failing of Crofts' murderers in these two story collections is one that should have been extremely familiar to the author's readers by this time: improvident spending. In *Many a Slip*'s "The Medicine Bottle," for example, Joe Gresley's "trouble was money. He was extravagant. He liked his little luxuries, particularly he liked running around with girls. Unhappily his income would not stretch to it. When his own cash was gone he had borrowed. Now repayment was due and he could not meet the call." Similarly, in "Boomerang," from the same collection, the trouble of murderer-to-be George Broad is "money, money, money! His income ... was adequate enough, yet the money just melted through his fingers.... Broad had been received into a circle of people richer than himself, and he could not live up to their standards. He knew he should leave it and retrench, but he stayed on because he liked the society and the feeling of superiority it gave him."[75] Over and over in Crofts' works living beyond ones means and getting into debt yields fatal consequences.

Even when in these stories a murderer's motive hinges on a man's desire for a woman, desire for money is implicated as a motive as well, either because attainment of the woman is not possible without the man's first achieving a greater income or because the man desires the woman's income as well as the woman herself. Of future murderer Charles Howard in "The Case of the Enthusiastic Rabbit-Breeder" (from *Murderers Make Mistakes*), we learn that he had fallen in love with John Gray's wife and she with him. Yet Crofts assures us that "for mere love Howard would never risk murder. His real motive was more compelling. Muriel Gray was rich."[76]

By now, the reader will have some notion of Crofts' social and political views, based on my discussion of his attitude toward religion and business. Still, a few more words should be added to clarify matters. Leftist mystery writer and genre critic Julian Symons contends in *Bloody Murder* that "it is safe to say that almost all of the British writers in the twenties and thirties ... were unquestionably right-wing" and "overwhelmingly conservative in feeling." How true of Freeman Wills Crofts is Symons' contention? Crofts' strong religious sense of the wickedness of avarice, coupled with his distress over the Depression, actually led him to become at times quite critical of aspects of capitalism. "Golden Age writers would not have held it against Sigsbee Manderson [the financier of *Trent's Last Case*] that he had become rich by speculation," writes Julian Symons in *Bloody Murder*, "although they might have regretted his brashness and vulgarity."[77] But the cautious Crofts' long time distrust of speculative money schemes and his dismay over the crisis of world capitalism in the 1930s clearly caused him, like many other individuals of the time, to cast a critical eye at the Sigsbee Mandersons of the world. Indeed, Crofts' Andrew Harrison is Sigsbee Manderson by another name and he is portrayed by the author in a correspondingly negative light.

In his books Crofts repeatedly indicates that shrewdness in business is evidence of bad character. In *Crime at Guilford*, for example, the Chairman of the Board of Nornes, Limited, an important jewelry firm, is described by the author as "a man of great ability and force of character." One might see this as a compliment, but then the author adds: "In the City his keenness and efficiency were universally admired, through faith in his absolute straightness under all circumstances was not so strongly marked." Of men involved in the casino gambling business in *Fatal Venture*, Crofts disapprovingly writes, "There was that altogether too wide-awake expression about their eyes which made it hard to bank too heavily on their good faith." Again, the term "wide-awake" is one traditionally regarded in business culture as indicative of a positive attribute, but Crofts clearly does not see it as such. **[SPOILER ALERT]** In *The Loss of the "Jane Vosper,"* French concludes from the appearance and manner of one of his businessmen suspects that he has "force of character, determination, and ability." Regrettably, French also decides that the man shows "no corresponding suggestion of high moral traits." Ultimately French arrests the man for the commission of fraud and murder. Interestingly, the government of the Soviet Union, which had been a contracting party to the businessman's fraudulent sale of stolen goods, is portrayed by Crofts in a markedly laudatory fashion. The Soviet Government representatives, the author notes, "were horrified to learn that the sets which they had bought were stolen" and "now behaved handsomely," offering to make full financial restitution to the firm that was the victim of the murderer's fraud.[78] **[END SPOILER ALERT]**

Crofts' most insistent condemnation of business in his detective novels appears in *The Affair at Little Wokeham*, a 1943 tale. Arriving in Little Wokeham in the wake of yet another murder and soon hard at work interviewing suspects, French immediately dismisses from suspicion Christina Winnington, another in Crofts' line of sympathetic distressed gentlewomen (Christina keeps house for a brother and sister, her deceased "country gentleman" father, Marmaduke Winnington, having lived off his capital and left at his death merely "a pittance ... to be divided among his children"), because French is "impressed by her transparent honesty and kindliness." With businessman Guy Plant, however, the Chief Inspector's sensitive moral antennae are immediately raised:

> Very different was the impression he received when Guy Plant came into the room. Here was a tight-lipped, shrewd-eyed man with a hard, unpleasant expression and a streak of furtiveness in his manner; a watchful man who obviously considered carefully the implications of his answers before making them. He would be, French imagined, what is often called a "good" businessman, i.e. one who has a heart like a flint and would allow no considerations of decency or honor to stand between him and whatever money he could legally filch from his competitors. In short, he would be just the type of man to commit a murder, provided the profit was big enough and his safety could be assured.

Perhaps Crofts' moral philosophy at this time is best summed up with this Pippa-esque observation from his children's mystery, *Young Robin Brand, Detective*: "What a difference to everything people made! When they were decent it was a different world!"[79]

The Oxford Group's concept of "Moral Re-Armament" clearly exercised a great influence on Crofts' writing and thinking at this time. The financial collapse of the Depression caused many hitherto complacent people to look suspiciously on the activities of once revered Captains of Capitalism and to regard more favorably calls for direct state intervention in the economy. Crofts' sympathetic portrayal of organs of the Soviet Government, including the Commissariat of Agriculture (this shortly after the state-induced Great Famine), suggests he looked sympathetically on Soviet efforts to reshape Russian society; though obviously the author, as a Christian, would have preferred Moral Re-Armament to Communism as the ideal Utopian solution to the world's manifold ills.[80] In regard to his economic views, then, Crofts is an exception in some respects to Symons' sweeping and unnuanced characterization of the conservatism of Golden Age mystery novelists.

To be sure, Crofts never rejected capitalism wholesale, but rather merely desired that it be practiced in a more ethical, or "straight," way by men who had morally re-armed themselves. And Crofts did not give labor a critical pass by any means. Crofts' specific criticism from the twenties of labor politics has been quoted already. It must be added as well that the author at times could be quite dismissive and contemptuous of individual members of the working class portrayed in his books. In 1922's *The Pit-Prop Syndicate*, for example, Crofts at one point introduces us to "a middle-aged man of the laboring classes, slow, heavy, and obese." Not content with that description, Crofts adds for good measure that "in his rather bovine countenance hardly any spark of intelligence shown." In 1940's *Golden Ashes*, an American inherits an entailed British landed estate, Forde Manor, and returns to his ancestral homeland to live the life of a country gentleman. Unfortunately, Crofts makes sufficiently clear, the man simply is *not* a gentleman; and he is received coldly by the local gentry. Forde Manor's newly hired housekeeper, distressed gentlewoman Betty Stanton, reflects that, given her employer's "undistinguished features" and "squeaky high-pitched voice with its suggestion of working-class America," it is only natural for such shunning to have taken place. "It's no use his trying," bluntly agrees one of Betty's genteel friends. "He seems a decent sort of fellow, but he's not their type.... There are plenty of people — nice people — whom he could entertain." As late as 1945, when "The Case of the Fireside Mountaineer" first appeared (it was performed that year as a radio play and later was included in the short story collection *Murderers Makes Mistakes*), Crofts writes of "typical specimens of the better-class British workmen, decent-looking, well-mannered, and obviously honest, if not over-intelligent," a patronizing description illustrative of the social gulf that Crofts still perceived as existing between himself and the "laboring classes."[81]

Despite his long association with railroads — his hallmark as a detective novelist — Crofts displayed a marked affection for the English countryside and a pronounced distaste for London both in his own life (he retired to the village of Blackheath, located on the scenic "hog's back" ridge, and his preferred vacation locales were rural areas, cruise ships and Continental pensions) and in his novels, through the character of Inspector French. Whenever a case takes French, who cares dearly for his tiny domestic patch of garden, out of the city and into the fields, so to speak, it is cause for rejoicing on the part of the detective. In *Fatal Venture*, for example, French reflects how "for some time now he had been working on unpleasant cases: tedious, wearisome, sordid.... They had taken him either to slums, or to areas which were rapidly becoming slums: a world of grimy bricks and mortar, of smells and insects and unwashed humanity. He was sick of the work and of his less fortunate fellow citizens, and longed for a breath of clean, fresh air and the green of the country." It is not difficult to discern in such a passage a certain antipathy for the British urban working class, however much Crofts may have loved all humanity in a philosophical, Christian sense. In *Anything to Declare?*, a final, lackluster novel that Crofts, terminally ill with colorectal cancer, struggled for some half-dozen years to complete (it finally appeared in 1957, but weeks before his death), the author makes clear where his ultimate class allegiance lay when he has his heroine, Nancy, describe her genteel domestic employers to herself "by a word which has almost disappeared from the language ... *gentlefolk*, with all the straightness and kindness and regard for feelings of others which that [word] meant." Yet ironically the doubtlessly gentle Crofts' references to members of the working class are not always so kind.[82]

Unlike John Street, Crofts — who had, as we have seen, an unfortunate fondness for "colorful" dialect as well as travelogue — continuously has his working class men (whether in London or the distant countryside) speak in what Colin Watson in *Snobbery with Violence* disgustedly termed as the "outrageous pseudo-Cockney" of mystery genre convention. Here, being questioned by French in 1930's *Sir John Magill's Last Journey*, is a railway attendant, the tellingly named Henry Pugg:

"That's the gent wot afterwards disappeared, isn't it?" he asked...

... "Yes, sir, I remember 'im well. I saw about the disappearance in the paper and I remembered 'im well. A small old gentleman with white 'air...."

... "I mightn't be able to tell you if it 'adn't been for that there account in the noospaper."[83]

Contrast this highly stylized patter with the more naturalistic speech of railway workers Ben Porter, a laborer, and Joe Sparling, a foreman porter, in John Rhode's *Tragedy on the Line*, published a year later:

Hullo, Ben, what's up?" he exclaimed. "Why, you look as white a sheet!"

"Like enough, too," panted Ben. "So would you be, if you'd had a turn same as I have. There's a dead man up the line, Joe. Lying there, just clear of the road by Colingrove Crossing he is, with his face bashed in something horrible."

"One of they suicides, I expect. You didn't by any chance recognize him did you, Ben?"

Ben shuddered. "Recognize him? There's no one this side of the grave as could do that. Why, he ain't got no face left, I tell you."[84]

Whereas in Street's works members of the working class who stand up to their employers (even resorting to murder) can be treated with sympathy, in Crofts' books ill-mannered servants are portrayed negatively, the author casting them either as accomplices of gangs or as uncooperative witnesses who must be bullied for information with threats of arrest and incarceration. In both *Inspector French and the Cheyne Mystery* (1926) and the children's detective novel *Young Robin Brand, Detective* (1947), for example, sullen maids treacherously align themselves with crooks menacing their masters. Crofts makes the discontent of both women manifest on their faces. Susan, a parlor maid to the Cheyne family who deliberately admits burglars to their home, is "tall with rather heavy features, and good looking after a somewhat coarse type." Similarly, in *Young Robin Brand, Detective*, the maid Ada, who is involved in a kidnapping plot directed against the family for whom she works, is "a tall, dark young woman, not at all bad-looking, though with a sinister expression." Both women grudge the household chores they are expected to perform. Ada, we are told, has a "short" manner about her and does unwillingly all she is asked to do by her mistress; while Susan, when away from the Cheyne home, profusely spews venom on her employers: "I was fed up, I can tell you! Susan this and Susan that! 'Susan, we'll have tea now,' 'Susan, you might bring up a tray and take up the mistress' breakfast,' 'Susan, you might light the fire in the study, Mr. Chenye wants to work.' Yah! I guess I've about done my share."[85]

The treacheries of the ungrateful Susan and Ada are eventually exposed, but members of the lower classes cause difficulties in other ways as well. In *Inspector French's Greatest Case*, when French has to question the former parlor maid of a crime suspect, he finds that she is a "tall, coarsely good-looking blonde" who regards him "with something approaching insolence out of her rather bold eyes." Sizing her up as a fresh type, French quickly is threatening her with prison if she does not answer his questions satisfactorily. Soon he has "banished the girl's look of insolence and reduced her to a suitable frame of mind." Similarly, in *The Sea Mystery*, when French in the course of his investigations encounters Alf Beer, a former packer who left his job out of anger at being reproved by a superior, the Inspector finds him a man "with a sullen face and heavy, discontented expression." When Alf proves recalcitrant under questioning, French tells the young man: "That's obstruction and you'll get six months for it. Come along to the station. And unless you want a couple of years you'll come quietly." The craven Alf of course completely collapses at the Inspector's "bluff" (Crofts' habitual euphemism for this practice — others might have said "lie") and French gets the information he wants. French is secretly relieved by Alf's quick capitulation, Crofts admits, because "statements obtained by threats are not admitted as evidence and he felt he had been sailing rather near the wind."[86] Indeed.

French worries considerably less about the warrantless searches and seizures he commits in a number of books by means of his ever-handy skeleton keys. Indeed, in a later novel, *The Affair at Little Wokeham* (1943), French is openly mirthful at the notion that a subordinate might be expected to obtain a search warrant before conducting a search: "'[You searched] without a search warrant!' French's voice sounded outraged. 'I'm ashamed of you, Carter, and deeply pained. I've always been ashamed of myself and deeply pained when I've done the same thing. I hope you had luck?'"[87] Similarly, in the previous year's *Fear Comes to Chalfont*, French and his new police college educated subordinate, Sergeant Rollo, cavalierly forge an anonymous letter and show it to a suspect, hoping to obtain a damaging admission from him.

Generally Crofts seems convinced that law, as embodied by the kindly and decent Inspector French, is on the side of the angels and should be extended considerable leeway in bringing criminals to justice. In *French Strikes Oil* (1951), Crofts gives French (now a Superintendant) the voice of millions of British citizens disgruntled with post-war social conditions when he has him disgustedly throw down a file of papers in his office and reflect how he is "sick to death of these hooligan youngsters with their guns and coshes and their attacks on defenseless old women. They made his work duller and more sordid than ever." Yet the author was not a vindictive man, and he makes haste to add that "the thought of all these young people going wrong [distressed] French intensely."[88]

Occasionally Crofts allowed such a reformist impulse to appear in his pages. In 1947's

Young Robin Brand, Detective, for example, Chief Inspector French tells a querying youngster that life in prison is "not very pleasant, of course." Yet French assures the boy that "it's nothing like it was even a few years ago. Formerly the idea was to make prisoners suffer.... Now the idea is to give them a chance to reform." In addition to endorsing the goal of prisoner reform rather than punishment, Crofts also writes, through the voice of Pamela Grey in *Man Overboard!*, of the need for quality state-appointed defense attorneys. As her fiancée goes on trial for his life, Pam in her mind damns the State for not living up to its moral obligation to provide judicial proceedings that would assure equal justice for all, regardless of wealth:

> And, why, Pam thought, should the defense be left to the friends of the accused? The State is acting against the accused, why shouldn't the State arrange for the trial to be fair? Why should private individuals have to pay huge sums to get justice? Suppose they hadn't the money? Pam thought of the agony of having to put up with perfunctory or second-rate help because one couldn't afford to give one's loved one the best chance for his life.... It was all wrong![89]

Crofts' work from the early 1920s reveals less sympathy for an oft-derided group in Golden Age mystery fiction, English Jewry. Unseemly encounters between law enforcement and repellently portrayed Jewish citizens occur in two of the author's early novels — *The Ponson Case* and *The Pit-Prop Syndicate*— but do not recur in later works, suggesting that at some early point in his writing career realization dawned on Crofts that such material was unworthy of him (though surprisingly in the 1944 radio play "The Case of the Avaricious Moneylender," he provided a Jewish name for the predictably loathsome moneylender of the title, a name that was retained when the play was recast as a story and published three years later in *Murderers Make Mistakes*). In *The Ponson Case*, Inspector Tanner goes to moneylender Moses Erckstein — "stout and dark with a short black beard and Semitic features"— to obtain some needed information. Tanner has to threaten Erckstein "with a summons to Court, where his books and his methods would be probed mercilessly in public," before the moneylender will comply with his demand. In a gratuitous sneer, Crofts adds that though Erckstein had been a German before the war he has since opportunistically made his nationality Polish. A Jew also proves an aggravating if minor obstacle in Inspector Willis' investigation in *The Pit-Prop Syndicate*. When Willis confronts a restaurant manager for answers to some queries, he finds the man "a sly, evil-looking person of Semitic blood." Not surprisingly this unpleasing person tries to hedge his answers, causing Willis to "cut him short with scant ceremony": "Now look here, my friend.... I haven't time to waste with you. That man you were talking to is wanted for murder, and what you have to decide to do is whether you're going to act with the police or against them. If you give us any trouble you may find yourself in the dock as an accomplice after the fact." Later, when the man proves dubious over Willis' demand that he make his premises available for a police eavesdropping operation, Willis tells him he has no choice, but will be reimbursed "reasonably well." He then looks the man "aggressively" in the face and adds: "You'll not lose if you act on the square, but if not ... if the slightest hint of my plan reaches any of the men — well, it will be ten years [for you] at least." His threat achieves the desired result:

> "It shall be done! All shall happen as you say."
> "It had better," Willis rejoined, and with a menacing look strode out of the restaurant.

Immediately after terrorizing the hapless restaurant manager, Willis questions a hotel "manageress," presumably an English-born Gentile, and the difference in treatment is striking. Crofts rather smugly informs readers that the Inspector's gentle manner with this lady "was very different from that displayed to the German Jew."[90]

A Jew is questioned in one other early Crofts' novel, *The Groote Park Murder*, though this time he is treated politely by the investigating police officer, South Africa's lunch-loving Inspector Vandam. Nevertheless, Crofts did not restrain himself from offering the reader one more nasty description of a Jewish character: "Moses Goldstein was dark and oily of countenance, with Semitic features and a pair of furtive, shifty eyes."[91] Six years later, in another novel, *The Box Office Murders*, Crofts mentions the presumably Jewish Esther Isaacs — a box office cashier girl — in passing, without negative reference; yet it is the Irish cashier Molly Moran who French ends up befriending and rescuing from the clutches of a ruthless criminal gang.

Crofts' portrayal of women often is much more positive than his portrayals of businessmen, Jews or members of the lower classes, though it is not all that much more nuanced. Middle- and upper-class women tend to fall in three categories in Crofts' works: "good girls," who usually provide love interest; "bad girls" (a much smaller group), who are murderers or accomplices of murderers, and stout, "motherly," nurturing older women (this regiment is led by Emily French), who play only peripheral roles in the tales. In the six books Crofts published between 1921 and 1927, "good girls" figure prominently; and they recur as well in the author's later books in the thirties and forties, sometimes, as with Pamela Grey in *Man Overboard!*, as narrative focal points. In a few novels Crofts varies the pattern by making the "good girl" somewhat older, as in *Sudden Death*, *Found Floating*, *Golden Ashes* and *James Tarrant, Adventurer*; yet, whatever their age, they are uniformly uninteresting characters representing bland and naive goodness. The only ones with any real sparks of animation are the thriller heroines Joan Merrill, of *Inspector French and the Cheyne Mystery*, and Molly Moran, the plucky if dim theater cashier of *The Box Office Murders*. Molly Moran is the lone genuine "working class" good girl (her "stubborn little chin showed she had no lack of character"), while Joan even more surprisingly is by occupation an artist (we are assured, however, that her doctor father on his death "left her enough to live on fairly comfortably"). Like other Crofts heroines, Joan is, in the thoughts of the novel's idiot hero, "not perhaps exactly pretty, but jolly looking, the kind of girl it is a pleasure just to sit down and watch."[92] Joan is vastly more intelligent than her partner in adventuredom, Maxwell Cheyne; but, disappointingly, not long after she arrives on the scene she gets kidnapped and we see nothing of her again until the end of the novel. More commonly Crofts' heroines are passive, if virtuous, nonentities, like Ruth Averill, of *Inspector French and the Starvel Tragedy*. Like so many of her ingenuous sisters in Crofts novels, Ruth exists to fret.

Crofts adopted what he evidently conceived to be a feminine tone of voice when portraying his good girls, which means readers get a great parade of emotional agonizing and hand-wringing that quickly palls. Occasionally Crofts even goes so far as to adopt the much-derided "Had I but Known" style of narration associated with the Mary Roberts Rinehart school of American mystery fiction, as in this example from the opening of *The Starvel Tragedy*, where Crofts clearly hoped to curdle the blood in his readers' veins: "She [Ruth Averill] did not know then, though she realized it afterwards, that the message he was bringing her was to be the herald of a series of terrible and tragic happenings, so dark and sinister and awful that had she foreseen them she might well have cried out in horror and dismay." As this passage indicates, when Crofts as narrator attempts to portray heavy emotional situations, he frequently employs the sort of loaded words associated with lesser Victorian sensation novelists. In *Sudden Death*—to cite another example—we are repetitively told after a murder in the household that "the rest of the day passed as a nightmare" and that "life at Frayle had indeed become a nightmare." A day of police interrogations behind her, Anne Day, the "good girl" of the novel, "had seldom felt so weighed down by foreboding.... The very air seemed to be charged with horror.... It was if she was waiting ... for something dreadful to happen.... Dinner was a nightmare."[93]

The melodrama-conveying word to which Crofts most commonly resorted, however, was not "nightmare," but *ghastly*. In *The Affair at Little Wokeham* alone, his copy editor evidently having nodded, the dread word is found no less than fourteen times: "this ghastly retribution"; "ghastly enough"; "this ghastly project"; "'It's been ghastly!'"; "what a ghastly affair!"; "'this ghastly business'"; "caught in a ghastly trap"; "'this ghastly affair'"; "God, how ghastly!"; "this ghastly mischance"; "this ghastly Monday morning"; "absolutely ghastly"; "such a ghastly connection"; "that ghastly room."[94] Crofts' rare hard-nosed bad girls are preferable to his good girls, if only because they do not encourage the author to indulge in this banal—I hesitate to say ghastly—writing.

As one might surmise from Crofts' persistent refusal to make his heroines beautiful or even exactly pretty, sex occupies little place in the author's books. Indeed, when a woman tells Inspector French in *The Box Office Murders* that a man gave her assurance the job he was offering her involved "nothing immoral or connected with sex," it comes as a surprise that such a thing even could be raised as a possibility in a Crofts novel. Surely unintentionally on the author's part, the most sexually suggestive passage in Crofts' works actually occurs between two (heterosexual) women:

> "Dear Sybil! You may count on me to the utmost!..."
> ... "Oh, Anne, no matter how this finishes up, I'm thankful you're here!" And sitting up in bed, Sybil threw her arms round Ann's neck and kissed her hungrily.

The only time it is indicated in Crofts' works that a good girl actually has had sex, to my recollection, is in *James Tarrant, Adventurer*, when Merle Weir, on trial for the murder of James Tarrant, is forced on the stand to admit, with a "warm flush" of embarrassment on her cheeks, having "lived with the deceased" in an unmarried state.[95]

Not surprisingly, given Crofts' difficulty portraying credible female characters, some of the author's best novels are those in which women play peripheral roles, such as *Sir John Magill's Last Journey*, *Mystery in the Channel*, *Mystery at Southampton Water*, *Crime at Guildford* and *The Loss of the "Jane Vosper."* Indeed in the second of these books, which takes place primarily at two cement works and at various police stations, there literally are no female characters at all, with women being only very occasionally even referred to by the men. Since Crofts mostly was unable to portray sexual passion as a credible motive for murder [**SPOILER ALERT**] (he skates by in *The Sea Mystery* by studiously avoiding entering the criminal couple's minds and emphasizing their calculated desire to maintain acceptable "social standing," thus avoiding his usual bathos), [**END SPOILER ALERT**] this laser-like focus on workplace economic conflicts to the entire exclusion of domestic concerns is not to be regretted.

When Crofts does attempt to portray sexual passion he creates a problem of belief for the reader. For instance, in *Found Floating*, a novel with admittedly clever plot mechanics, we are asked to believe that Mant Carrington's lustful desire for Eva Dugdale gave Eva and her husband a motive to murder him (Mant employs Eva's husband), though this ostensibly murder-provoking lust is dealt with only tentatively, at secondhand. "Mant Carrington was pestering her with unwanted attentions," is how the local Inspector primly puts it to French. When French concludes that "it was obvious that the simplest way out of difficulty for both the Dugdales would be that Mant should die," the reader should be left dubious. [SPOILER ALERT] At the end of the novel the rather unlikely murderer writes in a confession: "Then the climax came. I happened to discover Mant was making himself objectionable to my niece, Eva Dugdale. This was the last straw. A wave of fierce hatred swelled up in me. From that moment I began to plot Mant's death."[96] [END SPOILER ALERT] This confession is as unbelievable as French's speculations over the possible guilt of the Dugdales, because nowhere in *l'affaire Dugdale* has Crofts portrayed an emotional conflict intense enough to have driven real people (as opposed to fictive puppets) to commit murder. It is worth noting in this context that although Croft's late mystery novel *Young Robin Brand, Detective* was written by the author expressly for juveniles, its overall emotional tone varies but slightly from that of the books he wrote for adults.

Crofts demonstrated this lack of perception of the emotional bases of darker human behavior in his 1938 account of an infamous true life murder in the anthology *Great Unsolved Crimes*. Crofts' contribution to this anthology was titled "The Gorse Hall Mystery." In six pages he detailed the facts of this unsolved murder and suggested an entirely unsatisfactory solution. To recount the case briefly, wealthy businessman George Henry Storrs was stabbed to death by an intruder in his home, Gorse Hall, in November 1909. Two months earlier, police had been called to Gorse Hall after a man supposedly had shot through a window of the house. The police could find no evidence that this shooting incident actually had taken place, but Storrs being an important man, they consented to keep a special watch on the house. Additionally a large bell was installed on the roof, so that the police could be given an alarm if the intruder returned. Late in October, the bell was sounded and the police appeared as bidden, only to find that Mr. Storrs was just testing them. Not altogether surprisingly, the police watch was withdrawn. Only two days later, the tragedy occurred. When police found Storrs at his home, badly knifed and in fact dying, they asked him who his assailant was, but Storrs professed not to know. Two men successively were tried and found not guilty, which left the mystery unsolved nearly thirty years later, when Crofts wrote his account of the affair.

Impressed by one of the reported exclamations of the mysterious murderer as he attacked Storrs ("I've got you at last"), Crofts concludes, quite sensibly, that the man was known to Storrs and nursed some grievance against him. Yet Crofts also argues that "owing to Mr. Storrs' upright character and kindly disposition," Storrs' secret, whatever it was, "was nothing with which he could reproach himself." In Crofts' view the grievance that the murderer held against Storrs must have been a delusional one. Why then would Storrs have held his tongue about the identity of this man, even in his dying moments? Struck by witness claims that the murderer was a young man, Crofts lamely suggests that Storrs did so out of a sense of "pity for the misguided youth."[97]

If Crofts' conclusion strikes readers as implausible (which is how it struck me), they should be pleased to learn that in 1983 the great true crime expert Jonathan Goodman published an alternative theory in his book *The Stabbing of George Henry Storrs*. Finding that Storrs' behavior was inexplicable were Storrs not hiding *something*, Goodman suggested that the murdered man's character had not been quite so upright as Crofts had assumed and that he had in fact done something with which he could — and did — reproach himself. Goodman found that a German governess in the household of one of Storrs' few close friends had drowned herself in 1907, under circumstances strongly suggesting that the unmarried woman was pregnant. Since it appeared to Goodman that Storrs was "the only man with whom she was ever alone," Goodman concluded that Storrs had "ruined" the woman and that a brother of hers killed Storrs in revenge. Goodman's theory, which has recently received corroboration on the British television program *Julian Fellowes Investigates*, seems a more realistic assessment of the facts of the case and the complexities of human nature than does the charitable construction provided by Crofts, who perhaps in this instance over-imbibed the milk of human kindness. But then, as Crofts himself reflected in another discussion of true crime that he wrote, "A New Zealand Tragedy" (published in 1937 in the Detection Club's *The Anatomy of Murder*), "Real life stories have an atmosphere of sordidness and evil which is happily absent from almost all detective novels."[98] Certainly this is true of the novels of Freeman Wills Crofts.

As discussed in Chapter One, Arnold Bennett several times in reviews forcefully denounced Crofts for banal writing, in which credible human emotions are indiscernible; and, some half-century later, Julian Symons wrote dismissively of Crofts' inability to create rounded characters. More recently, in 2001, sociology professor Ian Carter echoed Bennett and Symons, noting that "Crofts displays the engineer's marked distaste for human quiddities; his characters scarcely manage to rub together two dimensions, let alone three." Crofts himself downplayed characterization in his commentaries on mystery writing, placing primary importance on plotting. The retired railway engineer not surprisingly found that his former employment aided him immeasurably in devising plots. In a humorous reference to himself in *Young Robin Brand, Detective*, Crofts has one character, railway engineer Mr. Carr, reveal to the titular young Robin Brand, a detection enthusiast, that "one of our engineers left us and took up the writing of mystery stories, and he told me that in essentials there was little to choose between the jobs." Robin expresses his surprise at this statement, so Mr. Carr explains:

> "My friend put it like this: 'If I want to plan the layout of a station yard ... I begin by working out what movements are required.... Then I plan a layout that will enable these things to be done. Similarly ... in starting a book I begin with the important adventures or happenings, and then I plan the necessary characters and situations and locations to enable these adventures to take place.' He said it really was the same kind of thing."[99]

By all accounts Crofts was a nice, mild, devoutly religious man, without any of the writer's eccentricities or personality quirks that might have enlivened his crime fiction. Crofts found embarassing the Detection Club's elaborate initiation rituals involving murder weapons and a skull, in contrast with John Street, who not only participated with great gusto, but also had wired the skull's eyes to glow red in the darkness. Fellow Detection Club member Gladys Mitchell recalled Crofts during dinners sitting at table "bolt upright and very neat" and at an initiation ceremony holding a revolver and reciting a short piece in too quiet a voice, obviously viewing the whole affair as rather silly. So it is not surprising in Crofts' works when the atmosphere lacks color and the human element exists simply as track upon which the plot's engine can run smoothly to its intended destination. When Crofts does attempt "atmosphere," he typically gives us merely guidebook detail, and his attempts at deeper characterization merely plunge us into bathos. Indeed, it can fairly be said of Crofts' characters that, with the exception of the Everyman figure of Inspector French, they are entirely forgettable, a charge that cannot be laid so sweepingly against Crofts' fellow Humdrum authors John Street and Alfred Walter Stewart.[100]

Similarly, Crofts' works are nearly bereft of the sorts of cultured milieus employed by the two groups of the British Golden Age detective novelists still widely read today, the Crime Queens and Detection Dons. Over and over Crofts portrays the same business men found so indistinguishable by Margaret Cole and Julian Symons, eschewing the artists, actors, writers and intellectuals who populate novels by such writers as Marsh, Allingham and Innes. What few references Crofts makes to the arts professions tend not to be complimentary. "It's my brother, Roland Brand," wails a shamefaced Betty Stanton to Chief Inspector French in the novel *Golden Ashes*, in the tone of someone confessing to the secret shame of a loathsome venereal disease. "He has artistic temperament and he couldn't stick regular business."[101]

Though like Arnold Bennett and Ian Carter I hold no great admiration for Crofts' writing style, which truly achieves the quintessence of humdrum, I believe nevertheless that the best books by Freeman Wills Crofts retain value for their simultaneous plotting complexity and clarity, hallmarks of a highly capable literary engineer. Additionally, I think Crofts has interest as an intensely religious writer, a point that surprisingly seems to have occurred previously only to Eric Routley, a veteran mystery reader and Congregationalist minister. "He had indeed something of the Puritan in his composition," Crofts writes pointedly of the murder victim in *Fear Come to Chalfont*, "though without the strength and the genuine goodness of the Puritans' religion." Crofts' himself had much of the Puritan in him as well, *with*, I think one can fairly conclude, a strength and genuine goodness drawn from his religion. While Crofts' piety fostered his simplistic characterization and hindered him from writing more realistically about human relations, it gave him as well genuine sympathy for repentant sinners and an openness to progressive solutions to social and economic ills not typically associated with British mystery fiction authors of the Golden Age. Additionally, Crofts' writing occasionally rises to a higher level when it achieves a dignified Biblical cadence, as in these passages:

> Knowledge is not always power. Sometimes it is weakness and death. It was so with Sutton. He knew too much; therefore he died. (*The Loss of the "Jane Vosper"*)
>
> Harrison had gone to his account. No longer would he dominate his home and the money market. No longer would his deals leave a trail of ruined homes and make his rivals sweat with fear. Never again would he quarrel with his wife and make his daughter curse him. His day was over. (*The End of Andrew Harrison*)
>
> But the heavens remained as brass above him. (*Mystery in the Channel*)
>
> So to an end came the dreams and schemes of two miserable men. (*The Hog's Back Mystery*)[102]

In the mystery fiction of Freeman Wills Crofts we see a world where the mortal sin of avarice threatens to overwhelm all of us, both through direct temptations to ourselves and through the menace posed to us from others who have succumbed to it. Those who weakly give in to base urges and kill are themselves destroyed, for the wages of sin is death. The simple and unassuming yet utterly relentless and determined Inspector French functions as Providence's instrument of justice, saving the innocent and smiting the guilty. "As for French," writes Crofts after Molly Moran's dramatic rescue from the clutches of a vicious gang of cutthroats at the conclusion of *The Box Office Murders,* "the consciousness of work well (if slowly) done was its own reward.... [H]e had not only...saved Molly Moran's life and the lives of other girls who might have fallen into the hands of the gang, but had cleared out a nest of evildoers whose removal was essential to the welfare of the entire country."[103] In the fictive world of Freeman Wills Crofts, murderers always make mistakes and evildoers, no matter how crafty, invariably meet their match in the phlegmatic Joseph French.

CHAPTER FOUR

Alfred Walter Stewart (*J.J. Connington*) (1880–1947)
Survival of the Fittest

THE THIRD MEMBER OF THE HUMDRUM TRIUMVIRATE, Alfred Walter Stewart, who wrote as J.J. Connington, is the Crassus of the authorial trio, overshadowed by his fellow triumvirs today. Yet in the 1920s and 1930s "J.J. Connington" stood with John Street and Freeman Wills Crofts as the foremost British practitioner of the science of pure detection. I use the word "science" advisedly, for the man behind J.J. Connington, Alfred Walter Stewart, was an esteemed scientist who held the Chair of Chemistry at Queens University, Belfast, for twenty-five years, from 1919 until his retirement in 1944. A small, unassuming, mustached polymath," Stewart was "a strikingly effective lecturer with an excellent sense of humor, fertile imagination, and fantastically retentive memory," qualities that also served him well in his detective fiction. During roughly this period, the busy Professor Stewart found time to author a remarkable apocalyptic science fiction tale, *Nordenholt's Million* (1923), a mainstream novel, *Almighty Gold* (1924), and, between 1926 and 1947, twenty-four mysteries (all but one true tales of detection), among them at least eight classic examples of the Golden Age detective novel at its considerable best. The *Times Literary Supplement* doubtlessly reflected the views of many Golden Age devotees of true detective fiction when it proclaimed in 1930 that "Mr. Connington is one of the clearest and cleverest of masters of detective fiction now writing," as did the *London Daily*

Alfred Walter Stewart. The brilliant and acerbic Professor Stewart left a fine body of detective fiction as a literary legacy, as well as a disturbing apocalyptic science fiction thriller, *Nordenholt's Million* (1923) (courtesy Geoff Bradley and Irene Stewart).

193

Mail when the same year it emphatically declared: "For those who ask first of all in a detective story for exact and mathematical accuracy in the construction of the plot, there is no author to equal the distinguished scientist who writes under the name of J.J. Connington."[1]

Just as the occupational backgrounds of Street and Crofts are reflected in their crime stories, so is Stewart's background as a man of science, not only narrowly in terms of his much-praised plots but also more broadly in terms of characterization and theme. The most famous character in the J.J. Connington mystery tales, Chief Constable Clinton Driffield (the detective in seventeen of the twenty-four Connington crime novels), can be a strikingly highhanded and ruthless investigator, occasionally taking into his hands the functions of judge and jury as well as chief of police. Absent from the literature of Connington is the hail-fellow-well-met quality found in Street's works or the religious ethos suffusing those of Crofts. In their place we see instead a certain cynicism about the human animal and a marked admiration for detached supermen with superior intellects. For this reason, reading Connington sometimes can be a challenging experience for modern readers inculcated in today's gentler social beliefs. However, in my view there is no question but that the author produced some fine detective novels, with well-wrought puzzles, bracing characterization and an occasional leavening of dry humor. Not long after his death in 1947, Connington's work undeservedly fell entirely out of print. A number of Connington titles are well worth reviving, particularly *Murder in the Maze* (1927), *Tragedy at Ravensthorpe* (1927), *The Case with Nine Solutions* (1928), *The Sweepstake Murders* (1931), *The Castleford Conundrum* (1932), *The Ha-Ha Case* (1934), *In Whose Dim Shadow* (1935) and *A Minor Operation* (1937). In this chapter the plotting of these masterfully-devised detective novels is examined in detail, along with aspects of other tales that shed light on Connington's fascinating if not always comforting social and political views. Additionally, I analyze the recently uncovered correspondence between Alfred Walter Stewart and the famous horologist Rupert Thomas Gould, which is supportive of my interpretation of the Connington works. The Stewart-Gould correspondence reveals a man with knowledge of an impressively wide array of subjects — encompassing literature as well as science — and a mordant yet often appealing wit. Like his detective Sir Clinton Driffield, Stewart did not suffer gladly the legion he considered fools, but he was a formidably intelligent man whose detective fiction is eminently deserving of revival.

Alfred Walter Stewart had significant religious influences in his life, his father having been a longtime Professor of Divinity at Glasgow University and his father-in-law a Baptist minister and member of an extremely prominent Scottish manufacturing and Christian philanthropic family, yet religious sensibility seems absent from the Connington corpus. The pseudonym "J.J. Connington" itself was derived from a nineteenth-century Oxford Professor of Latin and translator of Horace, indicating that Stewart's own literary interest lay not in religion but rather in the pre-Christian classics ("I prefer the *Odyssey* to *Paradise Lost*," the author once avowed). In his tales Connington tends to address sexual subjects more explicitly than other British Golden Age detective novels, albeit from a rather clinical, scientific viewpoint. Most striking about theme in Connington's work is the streak of philosophical Social Darwinist authoritarianism running through it, with his investigative superman, Sir Clinton Driffield, behaving at times in an extraordinarily highhanded fashion. Julian Symons once wrote that "it would have been impossible" for British Golden Age detective novelists "to have created a policeman who beat up suspects," yet with Sir Clinton Driffield J.J. Connington gave readers a policeman who remorselessly contrives the suicide of a murder suspect in one case and in another actually slays the murder suspect by his own hand.[2] Admittedly, this aspect of Connington's work receded in significance in the 1930s, yet Driffield in my view remains until his final appearance in 1947 one of the least empathetic of the Golden Age's Great Detectives.

The authoritarian strain in the J.J. Connington novels is apparent from the first, in the author's striking and frightening apocalyptic science fiction tale, *Nordenholt's Million*. This novel has been analyzed as an essentially fascistic futurist fantasy in W. Warren Wagar's *Terminal Visions: The Literature of Last Things* (1982) and Nicholas Ruddick's *Ultimate Island: On the Nature of British Science Fiction* (1993), an interpretation with which I am in agreement. To give context to *Nordenholt's Million*, I should point out that the novel was published at a time of fearsome economic and social discord in much of Europe, including Great Britain, and that the desire for a redeeming strongman to sweep away all the ills plaguing his country hardly was limited to the author. It should be recalled that 1923, the year *Nordenholt's Million* was published, saw the rise in Italy of Mussolini and his National Fascist Party. Two years earlier, Connington's own revered model as a detective novelist, R. Austin Freeman, had published his long cherished eugenicist study, *Social Decay and Regeneration*, which posited unchecked migration to Britain of southern Europeans as a dire threat to the kingdom. Connington had read Freeman's book and expressed a favorable opinion of it fifteen years later (though he had forgotten its title), suggesting the work influenced *Nordenholt's Million*. Moreover, Connington admitted at this later date that he had at the time of the composition of *Nordenholt's Million* felt much pessimism about Britain's position in the world; and this pessimism clearly is reflected in the book's dark and violent vision of the country's future.[3]

Nordenholt's Million chronicles the rise in Britain of the dynamic and ruthless capitalist Stanley Nordenholt ("the Platinum King, the multi-millionaire, the wrecker of two governments") amidst an apocalyptic global calamity, the blighting of the world's plant life by a strain of rapidly reproducing denitrifying bacteria. Facing an imminent collapse of the food supply and the resulting starvation of the entire British population, Parliament proves incapable of meaningful action and bends to the superior will of the masterful Nordenholt, who demands and receives ostensibly temporary dictatorial powers to implement his own uncompromising solution: the creation of a "Nitrogen Area" in the Clyde Valley of Scotland, to be populated by the five million individuals (drawn from a population of fifty million) Nordenholt regards "as most fitted to survive." The remaining population is informed, in a deliberate lie, that the "Nitrogen Area" eventually will produce food for the entire population; yet once preparations are completed, communications and transportation networks outside the Nitrogen Area are destroyed, effectively "quarantining" the unfortunates in the rest of the country and consign them to cruel deaths from starvation (leaflets are dropped from planes falsely informing the desperate people that the population of the Nitrogen Area has succumbed to plague, so no salvation can be found from that quarter). Of Ireland, we learn that the country has been secretly raided for all its remaining livestock, resulting in fighting with and numerous casualties among the native population. "Not that it mattered much," dispassionately notes Connington's narrator, Nordenholt's right-hand man, Flint, "since all were to die in any case before very long."[4]

Once the rest of Britain has been successfully segregated from the Nitrogen Area, Nordenholt announces the dissolution of Parliament, which had transferred to Glasgow. His potential political opponents, including the Prime Minister, are arrested and hauled off by Nordenholt's "Labour Defense Force," to be deposited with their families to face certain demise outside the Nitrogen Area. In addition, members of the House of Commons judged "of no personal value in this enterprise" by Nordenholt are similarly exiled to their doom. One surmises that Nordenholt was saved the unfortunate necessity of eliminating the King and the Prince of Wales by their earlier convenient determination to die with the overwhelming majority of their people (in this connection it should be noted that Connington never makes clear the fate of the House of Lords).[5]

Nordenholt does not rest with the extermination of recalcitrant politicians. "Before long," notes Flint, "both the Committees and Nordenholt had an extensive black list of 'inefficient' workers; and the stage was being set for another drastic lesson." As the admiring Flint tells it, Nordenholt acts to liquidate an undesired group of people with a dispatch and efficiency that Hitler and Stalin no doubt would have admired:

> The morning papers contained a full report of [Nordenholt's] speech; but before they were in the hands of the populace, Nordenholt had acted. All the ca'canny workmen had been arrested during the night, along with their families, and removed to the southern boundary, where they were placed on trains and motors ready for transport to the Border.... Nordenholt knew the advantage of mystery; and he proposed to make these disappearances strike home on the public mind. The inefficients vanished without leaving a clue behind.... Ten thousand men had been condemned.[6]

With slackers purged and labor cowed, work proceeds admirably, like something out of a Nazi or Soviet propaganda poster, as visualized by Flint:

> I leave to the imagination of my readers the task of picturing that gigantic concentration of human effort: the eternal smoke-cloud from a thousand chimney-stalks lying between us and the sun; the murky twilight of the streets at noon; the unintermittent thunder of trains pouring coal into the city; and, above all, the half-naked figures in the factories, toiling, toiling, shift after shift in one incessant strain through the four-and-twenty hours.[7]

Nordenholt is no man of faith, declaring that religious creeds are "empty things; life left them long ago." Recognizing, however, that religion has its uses in motivating the populace to work, he includes "ministers of the various denominations" among his elect. When one minister gets out of hand and preaches "end-of-days" fanaticism to his followers, Nordenholt has no compunction about having them all mown down with machine guns. There is, one suspects, room for only One True God in Nordenholt's domain, and that is Nordenholt himself. Certainly Flint on meeting the great magnate describes him in theistic terms. "Under that slow and minute inspection, eye to eye," he humbly avows, "I felt all my human littleness, all my petty weaknesses exposed and weighed."[8]

This short survey of Nordenholt's "Nitrogen Area" reveals that in many respects it could have served as a blueprint for between-the-wars Fascists and Communists, a fact that can hardly endear liberal-minded people to the novel today. Professor Ruddick puts the point well in *Ultimate Island*: "The features of [Nordenholt's] regime, offered approvingly to the reader, are familiar to us from the various totalitarian regimes that have sullied the history of this century: the band of brothers forming the power elite; the secret police; the neighborhood informants; the disappearances of political opponents; the disinformation campaigns; the sacrifice of everything to the efficiency of the state."⁹ A later section of *Nordenholt's Million*, in which Flint surveys the awful fate that has befallen London since its isolation from the Nitrogen Area, is even more repellant to modern sensibilities.

Safe in the Nitrogen Area's confines, Flint has been designing dream cities of a hopeful future with Nordenholt's winsome niece, Elsa Huntingtower; and Nordenholt, cognizant of their visionary schemes, tells Flint that he needs to be made aware of what humanity really is like by seeing what has become of London. "London is thronged with people just the same as those down there in the [Nitrogen Area] factories," he notes ominously. "I want you to see what it amounts to when you take off the leash.... [G]o down to London and see it with your own eyes." Accordingly, Flint flies to London, landing at Hendon aerodrome ("Nordenholt had spared the Hendon aerodrome in the general destruction of the exodus," Flint informs us, "though he had burned all the aeroplanes which were there at the time"). Accompanied by an armed escort, Flint sallies forth to see what the blight has wrought on the population that remained in Britain's once great capital. He finds to his disgust that London has evolved into a city of savages and undesirables, revealed by the author in a series of disturbingly vivid vignettes: an "indescribably filthy" Jew offering gold and gems for a rat to eat ("It enraged me to hear this filthy object profaning all the material splendors of the world," declares an unsympathetic Flint, "and I thrust him aside roughly"); vicious "foreign scum" (presumably German Jews) seizing sections of London and crucifying interlopers; a degenerate female English aristocrat, Lady Angela, consorting with a "huge negro," Herne the Hunter, who leads a pack of human animals in hunting down human prey. It becomes horrifically evident to Flint that London has devolved into a sewer collecting all the ostensible vermin in the Kingdom, from racial and ethnic minorities to the dissolute rich, and that its demise actually is a fortunate event. When Lady Angela attempts to seduce Flint's guide, Geoffrey Glendyne — a former friend of hers — Glendyne warns her off brutally, in words that mingle racism with a fear of assertive female sexuality: "It's no good, Angela. You're corrupt to the core, and you can't conceal it. I've no use for you. You couldn't be straight if you tried. Do you think I want the associate of a nigger? And what a nigger at that!"¹⁰

After Flint returns to the Nitrogen Area disgusted and disillusioned with what he has seen in London, Nordenholt shockingly makes clear to his acolyte that the blight actually is a fortunate occurrence, for it has given them a chance to cleanse and correct a soiled and broken world:

> With decent luck, you ought to have a clean slate to start with. Most of our old troubles have solved themselves, or will solve themselves in the course of the next few months. There's no idle class in the Nitrogen Area; money's only a convenient fiction.... [T]here's no Parliament, no gabble about Democracy, no laws that a man can't understand. I've made a clean sweep of the old system; and the rest will go down before we're done.¹¹

Against this advocacy of pitiless social engineering of the scale soon to be put into effect with incalculable human tragedy in Hitler's Germany and Stalin's Russia, only Elsa Huntingtower is allowed to speak, but her liberal humanitarianism is but a weak reed. Rather improbably to say the least, Elsa had been left in ignorance that everyone outside the Nitrogen Area is dying from starvation and other calamities; but when she finally discovers the truth she turns against her uncle as well as Flint, excoriating them for their appalling inhumanity. Yet Elsa's arguments are dismissed as simply the predictable triumph of emotion over reason in the softer female mind. "The great barrier of sex divides us," reflects Flint of men and women, "and our outlook upon the world can never be the same." As with other women, concludes Flint, Elsa's problem was that "emotion, and not intellect, was the guiding star. The picture of starving millions which had broken upon her without warning had overpowered her normally clear brain."[12]

Like John Street's Professor Sanderson in his thriller *The Double Florin*, published a year after *Nordenholt's Million*, Flint and his master Nordenholt believe in the despotism of pure reason; yet whereas Street emphatically rejects this idea and has Sanderson vanquished by the forces of a resilient and resourceful western liberalism, Connington endorses it and hands his authoritarian despot and his lackeys the laurels of victory. Nordenholt dies before the realization of his Promised Land, the dream city of Asgard (appropriately named, given the novel's Nordic associations), but his deputy Flint lives to write about it. Utopia in Connington's world is an exclusive place indeed, with most of the denizens of the Nitrogen Area deemed unworthy to enter its precincts. The "mass of manual laborers whose intelligence unfitted them for anything beyond bodily toil"—the people whose labor actually built Asgard—are excluded from the city, Flint informs his readers, because Asgard "is only for those who can enjoy its beauties."[13]

Noted genre editor and bibliographer Everett F. Bleiler justly praised *Nordenholt's Million* for having "good characterizations, excellent detail, and an imaginative sweep." J.J. Connington's daughter, Irene Stewart, recalled to me the case of a landscape gardener of her acquaintance who had been caught up in the book's undeniable "imaginative sweep." Having spotted her copy of *Nordenholt's Million*, the man proceeded to quote to her "word for word the last two paragraphs." He was, according to Miss Stewart, much "interested in Daddy's theories." Yet Bleiler also deemed *Nordenholt's Million* "a nasty book"; and most modern readers likely would feel hard pressed to deny this assessment.[14] With the benefit of modern hindsight, Connington's fantasy of an improved society in *Nordenholt's Million* seems scarily in accord with that of the cruelly ambitious schemes of Nazi and Communist planners in the 1930s, wherein people were treated only as mechanical parts of the great social machine, to be worked until broken and then discarded (parts judged for whatever reason "defective" of course were dispensed with at the outset). Never again would J.J. Connington produce anything approaching the relentless ruthlessness of *Nordenholt's Million*; yet the tale holds significance for analysis of the author's later tales, in that it lays out memes seen again in his work, most importantly admiration for elite authority, disdain for the lower classes and non–Anglo-Saxon ethnicities, and unease over aggressive female sexuality.

J.J. Connington's second novel, *Almighty Gold* (1924), actually marks a retreat from the authoritarianism of *Nordenholt's Million*, indicating, perhaps, that the inhuman calculus of the earlier novel had caused even its tough-minded author to blanch. *Almighty Gold* suggests that the elites themselves may well be as unworthy as the masses. Like *Nordenholt's Million*, the 1924 novel details the career of a business tycoon, through the narration of the great man's chief assistant. However, the titan of *Almighty Gold* is in truth a mere financial swindler with feet of baser material, clay; and he is brought to his deserved ruin by the end of the tale.

In *Almighty Gold*, Connington continues to accept as an article of faith the public's susceptibility to strongmen, noting through his narrator that "the crowd will follow a man and forsake an idea any day, if only the man be big enough or persuasive enough to grip them." Yet in this novel authoritarian heroes are hard to find. Connington's narrator disdains not merely the modern corporate capitalist, but England's traditional landed aristocracy as well. Of the ancient family of the novel's venal aristocrat, Cyril Le Venner, the narrator damningly declares that "honor, pride, money, blood, women and friendship" had been "sacrificed each in turn to broaden the lands of Dene Royal [the Le Venner family estate]. To gratify this sinister avarice they had sunk to the level of werewolves."[15] In *Almighty Gold*, both England's traditional and modern elites lack a grand design for the world, instead pursuing self-aggrandizement as its own end. In detective fiction, however, Connington would again find a capable strongman worthy of admiration, in the form of one of Golden Age detective fiction's most noteworthy Great Detectives, Sir Clinton Driffield.

In Connington's first detective novel, *Death at Swaythling Court* (1926), the author deliberately devised a highly traditional setting in the village of Fernhurst Parva, complete with its local squire, the arch-conservative agrarian Colonel Sanderstead, its unctuous, pompous, compulsively Latin-quoting minister, Reverend Flitterwick, and even its very own village idiot, 'Sappy' Morton. A dark cloud has floated over this placidly feudal community in the form of the low-born, nouveaux riche Hubbard, who affrontingly takes up residence at a fine local estate of great antiquity, the imposing Swaythling Court. Hubbard evidently is not a Jew (unless the name is an alias), but he is described in terms of loathing often reserved for Jews in British mystery fiction of this period: "Hubbard was not an attractive character. He was a big clumsy man with an expression of slyness which sat ill upon a person of his bulk. Somehow, with his little close-set eyes, his red face, his ugly hands with their vulgar display of rings, his large and slightly flat feet, he looked out of place between Jimmy and the Colonel." To top off this list of physical imperfections that make Hubbard deserving of elimination, Connington gives the poor man a highly affected lisp, as in this instance when he responds to the Vicar's quoting Ovid: "'I never read him, parthon. They didn't teach Greek in my school. I gather he'th amusing, from what you thay. Got the goodth, eh? Hot thtuff? You fellowth know where to nothe it out.'" "'Greasy fellow,'" pronounces the visiting man-about-town, Jimmy Leigh. "'Not our sort,'" huffs the Colonel.[16]

Hubbard meets his quietus soon enough. The ensuing investigation is of little interest ("pathetically bad," sniffs the *Catalogue of Crime* of the novel's plotting), but the solution is quite striking in its endorsement of casual murders of inconvenient persons. [**SPOILER ALERT**] It seems that Hubbard was a professional blackmailer who was attempting to ensnare Jimmy Leigh's sister, Stella. Stella had been waiting the granting of her divorce decree so she that could marry Colonel Sanderstead's nephew, Cyril Norton. Before the decree had been granted, however, a maid at a house in which Stella and Cyril happened to be staying overnight witnessed Cyril blundering out of a passage leading to several bedrooms, one of which was Stella's. No sex was involved, mind you, Cyril informs his Uncle, merely some missteps in the dark:

> "The old place was a rambling one; and when I got to the bottom of my flight of stairs, I took the wrong turn and wandered along a passage. It came to a blank end at last, with nothing but bedroom doors all along it. So I turned back to try my luck in the other direction.... One of the servants was coming along in the corridor in the opposite direction. I explained that I wanted to get my motor coat. The maid looked at me rather queerly, I thought."[17]

The maid proceeded to inform Hubbard of this "impropriety" and Hubbard commenced his blackmail attempt. "Hubbard had only to drop a note to the King's Proctor," declares an outraged Cyril, "and Stella's divorce was in the soup.... Would anyone have believed the true story in the face of the obvious interpretation of the facts?"[18] The only thing to do was to murder Hubbard, which Cyril promptly did, with the help of the always amiable Jimmy Leigh. Cyril and Jimmy slay the offensively vulgar blackmailer by first drugging him and then force feeding him cyanide drip solution through his nose. After hearing Cyril's and Jimmy's confession, Colonel Sanderstead concludes that, since Hubbard only got what was coming to him, he will ignore his legal obligation as a county official and keep silent about everything.

To my mind, the resolution of *Death at Swaythling Court* is problematical in several ways, all stemming from the extermination of the admittedly verminous Hubbard. First, the primary motive for the murder is a weak one, which makes the ostensibly sympathetic murderers seem merely bloodthirsty. Would Stella's divorce really have been blocked on those shaky grounds? Cyril and Stella were not caught in bed together, or even in the same room together. It seems that the more natural reaction would have been to have cried "publish and be damned" and turned the matter over to the police. Second, whatever we might think of the morality of the actions of Cyril and Jimmy as private individuals, Colonel Sanderstead as a county official violated his trust in shielding his nephew and his friend from the consequences of a coldly deliberated crime. It would seem that in the vicinity of Fenhurst Parva there is one law for squires and their family and friends and another for everyone else. Finally, the sadistic manner of the murder — the cyanide solution force feeding — is told with unseemly pride and gusto by the murderous pair, leaving the reader with a queasy feeling of distaste about the whole thing. [**END SPOILER ALERT**] Vastly more appealing as a novel and skillfully constructed as a puzzle is Miles Burton's *Murder M.D.*, which has a similar setting.[19]

Readers were soon to see similar questionable actions taken in the Sir Clinton Driffield series of detective novels, which Connington launched the next year with *Murder in the Maze* (1927). In his first recorded case, Sir Clinton Driffield, who served in "a big post" in the South African police, returns to England to claim ownership of a landed country estate and the post of Chief Constable of the county. Driffield is given his fullest description in *Murder in the Maze*, where we find that he, like the plutocrat Stanley Nordenholt, is a masterful man indeed:

> Sir Clinton was a slight man who looked about thirty-five. His sun-tanned face, the firm mouth under the close-clipped moustache, the beautifully-kept teeth and hands, might have attracted a second glance in a crowd; but to counter this there was a deliberate ordinariness about his appearance.... Only his eyes failed to fit in with the rest of his conventional appearance; and even them he had disciplined as far as possible. Normally, they had a bored expression; but at times the mask slipped aside and betrayed the activity of the brain behind them. When fixed on a man they gave a curious impression as though they saw, not the physical exterior of the subject, but instead the real personality concealed below the facial lineaments.[20]

As described above, Sir Clinton Driffield's incisively penetrating gaze rather resembles that of the God-like Stanley Nordenholt ("under that slow and minute inspection, eye to eye, I felt all my human littleness, all my petty weaknesses exposed and weighed"). Although Sir Clinton never aspires to commit murder on a mass scale like the great

Nordenholt, he nevertheless reveals similar authoritarian tendencies in the course of his investigations. In *Murder in the Maze*, twin brothers Neville and Roger Shandon are slain by poisoned darts in the maze garden of Neville's country estate, Whistlefield. [**SPOILER ALERT**] The surprise culprit is the remaining brother, Ernest, a physically defective weakling reminiscent in his all-around unsuitability to the murder victim Hubbard in *Death at Swaythling Court*:

> The third brother, Ernest, seemed hardly to belong to the same family as the twins. Though five years younger, he had none of the vitality and energy which were so manifest in his elders; and the contrast was accentuated by the weakness of his eyes.... [W]hen his brothers had made their fortunes, he had slipped into the role of parasite without a thought, had transferred himself to Whistlefield, and had continued to live there ever since.[21]

Realizing he has been unmasked as the murderer by Sir Clinton, Ernest Shandon, armed with a gun, retreats into the Maze, thereby precipitating a remarkable dénouement. Sir Clinton, who had planned for this eventuality, has his men set fire to beds of sulfur, so that the fumes drifting over the Maze will convert Shandon's redoubt into a horrid death-trap. Nearly overcome by the deadly choking gas, the desperate Shandon commits suicide, as Sir Clinton had hoped and expected. As Sir Clinton indifferently explains some time later to his friend and frequent investigative Watson, the great local landowner Squire Wendover, Shandon was "dull, selfish, callow and stupid"— an unworthy specimen, essentially unfitted for life. "I could have arrested the brute," Sir Clinton admits. "Then we'd have had a trial. And the Hawkhursts [Ernest Shandon's niece and nephew] would have been branded as relatives of a murderer. I thought things could be done just as efficiently by making Ernest Shandon his own executioner." Sir Clinton admits regretfully that "we had to hold an inquest, of course." Fortunately, he was able to get away with providing the jury "the bare legal minimum of evidence; just enough to prove suicide.... [W]e've stifled [talk] as far as we possibly could; and the reporters got so little [information] that the thing was hardly talked about in the newspapers." Sir Clinton's last words in *Murder in the Maze* express his extreme self-satisfaction in having subverted the letter of the law to have reached the end he personally deemed just: "I wonder what [the newspapers] would have made of it if they'd known all about our methods! Perhaps I wasn't quite orthodox. Perhaps I ought to have got him nicely hanged — and incidentally run the public in for a big bill for the prosecution. I can only say that my conscience is quite clear; it doesn't give me a twinge."[22]

In *Murder in the Maze*, Clinton Driffield imperiously acts not only in his duly authorized role of investigator but also as Ernest Shandon's judge and jury. He does not technically become Shandon's executioner as well, though his coldly calculated actions virtually make him such. It takes until the fifth Clinton Driffield detective novel, *Nemesis at Raynham Parva*, for Sir Clinton to act as a *literal* executioner, killing by his own hand the man he judges the culprit in the murders he has been investigating. [**END SPOILER ALERT**]

Nemesis at Raynham Parva sees Driffield, having retired from the chief constableship to devote himself to his landed estate, visiting his widowed sister and her two children at their country home, Fern Lodge. There he learns from his concerned sister, Anne Thornaby, that his niece, Elsie, has married an Argentinean. This dramatic revelation launches the brother and sister into a fascinating discussion of the advisability of English girls marrying South Americans. "He's foreign — not our sort," complains Mrs. Thornaby of Elsie's new husband. "His manners are all right — only too much so, if you know what I mean." However, Sir Clinton reminds her that "Spaniards aren't necessarily dagoes, you know, Anne. Some of them are sound stuff.... Though I admit I'd have been better pleased if Elsie had kept to her own people and left foreigners alone. Rex Brandon was the man I was betting on ... he's a likeable young cub. Pity!" Despite Driffield's "reassuring" words to his sister, when he meets Elsie's husband, an exceedingly smooth-talking Argentinean named Francia, he is careful to closely scrutinize him with his penetrating gaze; and he too is displeased. Why, he wonders, could Elsie not have married Rex Brandon, "a youngster one could take to and trust with Elsie, because he was one's own sort." In conversation with Elsie's friend Estelle, Sir Clinton is further troubled to find that his and his sister's distaste for the Argentinean is shared by this young woman, one of Elsie's own more open generation:

"Oh, he's all right. A bit swalmy, you know."
"Swalmy?"
"Oh, you know what I mean. Rather..."
A vague gesture completed her description.
"Thanks. My own thought put neatly into words," Sir Clinton interjected.[23]

Sir Clinton's sister concludes that her great mistake was having allowed Elsie to travel unchaperoned to London, where she "got among a rather weird lot" and picked up "a lot of futile ideas" about "freedom, and living your own life." Most troubling to Elsie's mother are the ideas of this "rather weird lot" that concern sex: "A man and a girl go about together for a while; and then, one day, they decide to get married — if they take the trouble — and they drop into the registry office and fix it up without telling anyone.... I don't think much of it." Sir Clinton commiserates in his sister's concern about Elsie, recalling that his niece "was always such a pretty, trustful kiddie.... Never been hurt, and thought everybody was as straight as herself."[24]

[**SPOILER ALERT**] The concerns of Sir Clinton and his sister are revealed as amply justified when we learn that Francia is no less than the head of a white slavery ring and that the scoundrel plans to ship Elsie and several of her friends off to Argentina, where they will be forced into lives of sexual servitude (over the course of the novel Francia murders two people as well). Upon discovering the truth himself, Sir Clinton, like Cyril Norton and Jimmy Leigh in *Death at Swaythling Court*, resolves to take justice into his owns hands by committing murder. Weighing the matter over in his mind, he reflects: "If Francia fell into the hands of the law and [he] supplied the evidence in his possession, then Francia would undoubtedly be convicted.... But this meant that Elsie would be stamped as the wife of a murderer and a trader in women.... That was an ugly possibility ... to publish the very evidence which would put a stain upon his niece."[25] Rather than "put a stain upon his niece" by resorting to a public trial, Sir Clinton executes a private killing. As a bonus, Sir Clinton speculates, Elsie, her husband out of the way, will be left free to marry the of-the-right-sort and very English Rex. Once again, as in *Murder in the Maze*, Sir Clinton spares the reputation of gentlefolk (this time his own), by highhandedly and ruthlessly arranging events so that the truth about family murder scandals remain discretely within the family's purview.

Even Connington evidently was aware that to have his series detective, a chief constable, himself commit murder was problematical, since the author makes clear at the outset of *Raynham Parva* that Driffield had retired from his post. Moreover, Driffield did not appear in another Connington detective novel until 1931's *The Boat-House Riddle*, two novels with a new series detective, Superintendent Ross, having intervened between the two Driffield mysteries. Had Connington consciously planned *Raynham Parva* as Clinton Driffield's swan song and then relented and had Sir Clinton return, perhaps because his newer series detective, a rather dull dog, was not so popular with readers as Sir Clinton? Whatever the reasons for his revival, Sir Clinton came back to stay as Chief Constable, appearing over the next sixteen years in twelve of Connington's remaining fifteen mystery novels and arresting people for the very crime of premeditated murder that he himself had committed in *Raynham Parva,* a serious moral dichotomy that Connington leaves unexamined. Indeed, in *The Castleford Conundrum* (1932), Connington with no evident sense of irony has Sir Clinton lecture Squire Wendover, in response to the Squire's plea that Driffield do something to help a nice man and his daughter entangled as suspects in a county murder case: "What do you expect me to do, Squire? Call off the police, or what? There are limits, you know." Moreover, in a 1942 novel, rather ironically titled *No Past Is Dead,* Connington has Sir Clinton declare, either with deep disingenuousness or amazing absentmindedness, "When I take to crime, I hope I'll have enough wits left to scatter no clues of that sort about."[26] **[END SPOILER ALERT]**

After his return as J.J. Connington's series detective, Driffield never acts as highhandedly as he did in *Nemesis at Raynham Parva* and *Murder in the Maze*, but he continues to give an impression of barely containing within himself an extreme disdain for much of humanity. Asked in *Raynham Parva* by his sister how he enjoyed a holiday in Europe, he responds tersely: "I just wandered about and met a lot of interesting human specimens, here and there." Sir Clinton often speaks of the people he confronts in his cases as "specimens," as in *The Castleford Conundrum*, for example, where he contemptuously dismisses the murder victim's husband (the sympathetic narrative focal point of the first two chapters) as "a little shrimp of a man, the sort that apologizes to you profusely if you tread on his toes" and "a miserable little worm with a few redeeming points." The murder victim herself comes off little better, getting bluntly catalogued by Sir Clinton as "a brainless creature with some pretensions to good looks of a sort and a perfect genius for vapid chatter." Only the murder victim's stepdaughter is spared the scorn of Sir Clinton, who, like other middle-aged male characters in Connington novels, has a sympathetic eye for attractive "girls" under the age of thirty. "She was good-looking," Driffield recalls, "and she'd a nice, firm jaw."[27]

In another tale, *The Ha-Ha Case* (1934), **[SPOILER ALERT]** Driffield responds with philosophical detachment to Squire Wendover's regretful pronouncement that the resolution of the case "is a bad business for the Brandons.... One brother murdered and the other brother hanged." "Oh, let's look at the bright side," counters the Chief Constable. "Burling Thorn will fall into the hands of the only one of them who had any grit to work with a will for his living."[28] **[END SPOILER ALERT]** As in *Nordenholt's Million,* the weak have been winnowed out and the strong put in control, a socially desirable outcome.

Frequently Driffield's clinical observations come off as rather harsh, yet occasionally he can be amusing, as in one of his comments in *The Case With Nine Solutions* on an egocentric young man's journal, which is filled with callow observations on the young man's love affairs. "Now [he and his girlfriend] seem to have got the length of a distinct tiff, and he rushes at once to jot down a few bright thoughts on jealousy from H.G. Wells in support of his thesis," the Chief Constable observes wryly to a colleague. "It appears that this 'entanglement,' as he calls it, is cramping his individuality and preventing the full self-expression of his complex nature. I can't imagine how we got along without that word 'self-expression' when we were young. It's a godsend. I trust the inventor got a medal."[29] Even here, however, when one considers that at this point Driffield is investigating what may be a double murder, human sympathy on the Chief Constable's part over the essential tragedy of violent death seems lacking.

What empathy Driffield does exhibit in the Connington novels is mostly reserved for lovely young women (usually "girls" under thirty) of acceptable birth. Sylvia Hawkhurst in *Murder in the Maze* is a typical example of such a girl. After being orphaned, Sylvia was taken in by her wealthy uncles (her trustees) at their estate of Whistlefield. Sylvia serves as their housekeeper, and we are told that she runs the establishment better than any mere paid employee could. However, we learn as well that Sylvia is no domestic drudge, for housekeeping actually occupies "very little of her time," most of which is devoted to the proper pursuits of a between-the-wars, country gentlewoman in her twenties: hunting in season, motoring (Sylvia owns her own car), playing tennis ("well") and golf ("better still"), and dancing (Sylvia is "reckoned one of the best dancers in the neighborhood"). Unusually in a Connington novel, where women often are portrayed as consumed with jealously of other women's sexual appeal to men, the winsome Sylvia is "popular with girls as well as men," though this popularity with other girls is, Connington notes, "in spite of her looks."[30]

[**SPOILER ALERT**] It is his desire to save the lovely, charming and wealthy Sylvia from public embarrassment that prompts Sir Clinton to contrive her murderer uncle's suicide. In *Raynham Parva*, Sir Clinton resorts to committing murder by his own hand to save another winning girl from humiliation, this time his own niece, Elsie Thornaby. While suggesting that Sir Clinton feels an incestuous desire for Elsie would be to dip too far into the well of speculative sexual pathology, nevertheless it is clear that Driffield resents being supplanted in his niece's affections by another man (and an Argentinean, no less). His murderous determination to prevent Francia from putting "a stain upon his niece" does carry a sexual connotation, though it is one likely not intended by the author. In any event, Driffield does make sure that, by slaying Francia, Elsie ultimately will end up with someone more like himself, the of-his-sort Englishman Rex Brandon. [**END SPOILER ALERT**]

The other girls in *Raynham Parva* targeted as victims for the white slave trade are, like Elsie, attractive and genteel young ladies; and Driffield accordingly has a high opinion of the lot. Sir Clinton had some time ago been made an "honorary uncle" of Elsie's old friend Estelle Scotswood, a relationship that "had its perquisites later when Estelle grew up into a tall, graceful girl who was never bored when taken out to dinner or to the theatre." The final two newly blossoming English roses threatened with plucking by the white slaver, the somewhat down-on-their-luck Anstruther sisters, are judged by the retired Chief Constable "a nice, straight pair." Though Sir Clinton immediately notices that the sisters evidently have "not much cash to spend on their clothes," he generously decides "they've got good taste and they've done the best with what they have. No cheap shoes and stockings to ruin the effect."[31]

The plights of other good-looking, genteel girls suffering "reduced circumstances" receive attention from the author in a number of his novels. The twenty-three-year-old Una Menteith, sensitive about being employed as a governess when she meets Jim Brandon in *The Ha-Ha Case*, defensively reels off the dismal alternatives for a girl "left stranded in the world with two hundred or two hundred and fifty a year." Her list is a remarkable compendium of the horrors of life on limited income that preoccupied much between-the-wars middlebrow English fiction:

> You might live in a women's club or in some boarding-house, of course — very cheap ones. Can you guess what that means? I can remember the animals: the girl who fancies herself on the piano ... the old lady who always has trouble with her false teeth at meals ... the woman with the harsh voice that can be heard all over the room ... the maiden lady who's seen better days when she didn't have to mix with dreadful people like yourself.... No privacy unless you shut yourself up in a cheerless bedroom with a slot radiator and a penny-a-night book from a lending library. And most likely the whole establishment will be bathed in an inescapable smell of boiled cabbage or fried onions.[32]

London flats, Una informs Jim Brandon, are no better. "Half your income goes for rent," she complains, leaving you pinching every last one of the few remaining pennies: "[You] spend your mornings trailing from one local greengrocer to another, in the hope of getting potatoes a halfpenny a stone cheaper than last time. [You] shop at Woolworth's.... You can't afford a decent dressmaker. You wear somebody else's cast-offs — 'only been worn three times, moddom' — from the second-hand dealers in Bayswater. The theater, when you can afford a splash, means standing at the pit-door."[33]

Eileen Cressage, a character in Connington's slight but appealing second detective novel, *The Dangerfield Talisman*, could have greatly sympathized with Una Menteith's plight, though fortunately Eileen has never been driven to the desperate measure of actually taking salaried employment. Rather, she attempts to tide herself over from quarterly allotment to quarterly allotment with her bridge winnings at country house parties. As Eileen sits playing bridge for stakes at the splendid residence of the ancient Dangerfield family, she reflects worriedly on the "problems of a girl trying to keep up decent appearances on a tiny income."[34] The cash-strapped girl wins twenty-seven pounds that evening, but she later loses two hundred, a devastating sum. One of the guests, a caddish fellow aware of Eileen's financial difficulties, offers her a check for the amount, but with the proviso that she must come to his room later that night to collect it. This offer with nasty strings attached the sexually virtuous Eileen refuses; and, not surprisingly, her virtue is rewarded by the novel's end.

Women's sexuality is a prominent concern in the Connington novels, with men acting to protect pure women's reputations from "stain" in *Death at Swaythling Court* and *Nemesis at Raynham Parva* and with unchaste women coming to bad ends, like the debauched Lady Angela in *Nordenholt's Million*. When a witness avows of a murder victim in *The Case with Nine Solutions*, "He told me he was going out to dinner with that hussy next door," Sir Clinton interrupts the man with a mordant observation: "I'm afraid you'll have to be more definite. There are so many hussies nowadays." And indeed there are some notable "hussies" in the world of Connington's novels, beginning with Yvonne Silverdale, in *The Case with Nine Solutions*. Yvonne, one of several apparent murder victims in the novel, is native French and therefore, of course, of an unusually (by British standards) passionate and flirtatious nature. "Not altogether a nice school-girl," comments Sir Clinton of Yvonne after reading part of the diary she kept at her convent academy.[35] **[SPOILER ALERT]** Although a married woman, Yvonne had launched into a Platonic affair with a somewhat younger man, Edward Hassendean, like her husband a chemist at the city research institute. This "harmless" public liaison with Hassendean actually was being cynically manipulated by Yvonne to cover the real sexual affair she was having with yet another man. Unfortunately for Yvonne, Hassendean, who was frustrated by his Platonic paramour's continued refusal to sexually consummate their relationship, dosed the woman with hyoscine, one of the drugs known today as a "date rape drug." A careless worker, Hassendean inadvertently gave Yvonne too much of the drug, causing her death. The panicked Hassendean then shot Yvonne in the head, hoping to make her death appear the result of suicide [**END SPOILER ALERT**]

Another sexually rapacious woman in Connington novels who meets her death is the notorious adventuress in *The Boat-House Riddle* quaintly named "Cincinnati Jean." Clinton Driffield memorably describes Cincinnati Jean as "a nasty little specimen of our baser social vermin." In her heyday, Jean's game was to get men photographed in compromising positions with her, making them susceptible to blackmail. During what Driffield calls "the weird mix-up in our social classes just after the Armistice," Jean found a particularly rich crop of victims, including wealthy landowner Colin Keith-Westerton, who she maneuvered into marrying her.[36] Some years later, Keith-Westerton, believing Jean dead, remarried. Naturally Jean slithers on to the scene at the newly-wedded Keith-Westerton's pastoral country home, Silver Grove, demanding money for her silence, and the wicked Jean is permanently silenced.

Not only are bad women victims of violence in Conningtons' tales, they also are perpetrators of it. **[SPOILER ALERT]** In *The Castleford Conundrum* and *The Twenty-One Clues* (1941), women of loose morals connive at the murder of those standing in the way of their love affairs. In the former novel, Constance Lindfield shoots her half-sister Winifred Castleford as part of a plot to get her half-sister's money and to eliminate her as a rival for the hand of the attractive ne'erdowell Dick Stevenage. In the latter tale, Helen Barratt—having made, like Colin Keith-Westerton in *The Boat-House Riddle*, the grave error of marrying beneath her own social class—finds herself trapped in an unhappy marriage. Reflecting on her mistake in having wed an earnest but impecunious evangelical minister (of the Church of Awakened Israel), she reflects to her uncle:

> "I was so young, and I'd no real idea about things. It seemed grand, marrying on next to nothing with a career of good works and so on in front of one. But it bores me stiff nowadays.... They're all so frightfully narrow-minded, not like an ordinary church, somehow. And they're not my sort. I can't make friends amongst them. They're not my class, and they think differently from me."

Later Helen angrily confronts her husband with her discontents:

> Because I married you with your poor salary I've had to go without a good many things which a girl of my class looks on as necessities. We've no maid, and I have to act as one. You can't afford a car, and there isn't a girl I know who hasn't got one. And now you want me to give up the few amusements that I've got left [smoking, dancing and playing bridge for stakes]. I don't feel inclined to."[37]

What Helen does feel inclined to do is murder her unsatisfactory husband, which she proceeds to do, with the help of her younger lover. [**END SPOILER ALERT**]

J.J. Connington, *Murder Will Speak* (*For Murder Will Speak*) (1938). Far from the stolid country house tale of stereotype, this late Connington novel chronicles illicit sexual relationships in a modern English urban setting.

The most intensive exploration by Connington of women and sexuality is found in a 1938 Clinton Driffield novel, *For Murder Will Speak*. Though its puzzle, while acceptable, is not the author's most distinguished, the tale itself retains considerable interest for its handling of its five main female characters: the attractive, amoral secretary Olive Lyndoch; the thirty-something society wife Linda Hyson; the twenty-something, more recently married Nancy Telford; the frustrated spinster Ruth Jessop; and the servant Cissie Worgate.

Olive is having an affair with her businessman boss, Ossie Hyson, and is furiously facing the prospect of losing him to another of his secretaries, the less intelligent but younger Kitty Nevern. Linda, Hyson's wife, is understandably unhappy in her childless marriage with the philandering Ossie, but refuses to consummate a Platonic friendship she has with the gentlemanly Norris Barsett. ("I can't.... I wish I could. I do wish I could, dear. But it's the way I'm made, and I'd be no good to anyone if I broke through that.") Nancy Telford, once happily married, seems on edge about something. Spinster Ruth Jessop— "a plump little woman of about thirty-six, who had just missed prettiness by a very little"— is unbecomingly desperate to land a man. Ruth's problem is shared by the Hyson's maidservant Cissie Worgate, "a shy, unattractive little thing" whom "no man had ever given ... more than a passing glance."[38]

Women's lives in *For Murder Will Speak* revolve entirely around actual or desired sexual/emotional relationships with men (this is true even of the bubble-headed Kitty Nevern, who is mad about matinee idols). Ruth Jessop and Cissie Worgate suffer from their inability to attract males. The former woman is a reflection of the author's belief that females in their mid-thirties have passed their physical shelf date. Unable to snag a husband, Ruth takes out her frustrations by indulging in spiteful gossip. Possessed of "no looks, no sex appeal, no private income, and no social standing"— Cissie Worgate is even worse situated than Ruth Jessop. To escape from the drab reality of her manless life, Cissie spends all her spare time at the cinema watching romance films, which to her mean "hot kisses, passionate embraces, and the world well lost, if need be."[39]

[SPOILER ALERT] In contrast to Ruth Jessop and Cissie Worgate, Nancy Telford sees too much of "hot kisses" and "passionate embraces." A chronic nymphomaniac as a result of an unfortunate glandular disorder, Nancy is compulsively driven to seek sexual encounters with men, despite being happily married to an adoring husband. When the spiteful Ruth Jessop, who has witnessed a clandestine assignation between Nancy Telford and Ossie Hyson, mails Nancy a poison pen letter telling her all about what she saw, a distraught, despairing Nancy commits suicide. "There's where tragedy comes in," Sir Clinton (his discriminating sympathy aroused) tells Squire Wendover. "She was in love with Jim Telford, ardently in love with him.... And she was a perfectly straight girl, too. But that gland had gone wrong and the result threw her into Hyson's hands.... She did her level best to hold it in check, but the disease was too much for her. Imagine the thoughts and feelings of a straight girl landed in that position, Squire."[40] Clearly Nancy Telford is seen as an object of sympathy, unlike the similarly promiscuous Lady Angela in *Nordenholt's Million*, but this is because Nancy's glands made her do it (and do it), rendering her a fitting object for male chivalric sympathy.[41] **[END SPOILER ALERT]**

Connington made a commendable effort with *For Murder Will Speak* to advance beyond the landed gentry, country house milieu and to write realistically about sex in a modern English urban setting; yet the discussion about glands comes off as rather clumsy and heavy-handed today, making the novel seem a sometimes unintentionally amusing oddity of its time. At one point, the novel's specialist in treating glandular disorders, Dr. Malwood, explains lesbianism as simply another malady of the glands:

> "I don't discuss my own patients ... but there's no harm in telling you about a case that fell into the hands of a fellow specialist in my line. The patient was a girl, round about twenty, very attractive, quite feminine, and engaged to a decent young man. Then, in a very short time, she

changed completely. She broke off her engagement — couldn't stand male endearments. Instead, she took to frequenting young girls, putting her arm round them, kissing them eagerly and so on. Finally she showed signs of an incipient moustache."

Fortunately, removal of "a tumor pressing on the suprarenal glands" caused all the girl's "pseudo-masculine characteristics" to vanish and she soon, *sans* moustache, became engaged again, "as keen on her old fiancé as anyone could wish."[42]

In *For Murder Will Speak*, most modern readers likely will find Connington's treatment of female psychology, like his treatment of lesbianism, over-simplified. The author sees women's lives as revolving around the great sexual competition for men. Independent intellectual interests on the part of females are absent. In considering Cissie Worgate's personal dilemma, Connington notes the qualities lacking in her that a woman needs in order to have allure for a man: looks, sex appeal, private means and/or social standing. Intellect and/or personal accomplishments seem not to enter into consideration as possibly appealing female attributes. Even in the case of the sympathetic and apparently intelligent Linda Hyson, who is sadly neglected by her philandering husband, Connington omits reading books (even detective stories!) from his list of her leisure activities. Like the stupid Kitty Nevern and Cissie Worgate, Linda loves the cinema. She also plays golf (like Sylvia Hawkhurst in *Murder in the Maze*) and enjoys evenings of bridge (like Eileen Cressage in *The Dangerfield Talisman* and Helen Barratt in *The Twenty-One Clues*), when not sitting chastely on the sofa having those heart-to-heart talks with her gentleman caller, Norris Barsett. Admittedly, Linda Hyson, Ruth Jessop and Nancy Telford are upper middle-class ladies of comparative leisure (though Linda complains of having to manage with only Cissie Worgate as a servant). In contrast with these women, Olive Lyndoch, the hard-nosed secretary having an affair with Nancy's husband, has a job (and she is good at it), but she is portrayed as far more preoccupied in her amorous relationship with her boss than with any actual work she does for him.[43] Yet the novel retains considerable historical interest today, as a tale out of the Golden Age rut.

[**SPOILER ALERT**] In penning a poison pen letter that drives someone to suicide, Ruth Jessop serves as an example of the havoc and discord that female sexual anxiety can wreak in Connington's novels. The author discusses this supposed central feature of female psychology at greatest length in *The Twenty-One Clues*. In deducing that Helen Barratt had taken a lover younger than herself and with him plotted to kill her husband, Clinton Driffield draws on two literary sources: Karin Michaelis' *The Dangerous Age* and Benjamin Franklin's "Advice to a Young Man Concerning the Choice of a Mistress." Michaelis' once notorious novel, originally published in 1910, when Alfred Walter Stewart had just entered his thirties, deals with an unhappily married forty-three-year-old woman who has an affair with a man eight years her junior. Franklin's famous letter of advice recommended the worth of older women (past childbearing years) as lovers, famously in part because "they are so grateful." Evidently unable, in contrast with Karin Michaelis and Benjamin Franklin, to contemplate that a woman past the age of forty could possess any sexual attractiveness to a man, Connington in *The Twenty-One Clues* made Helen Barratt's dangerous age "round about thirty-six" and her lover about twenty-seven. Thirty-six, notes Sir Clinton sympathetically, is "just the age when age may begin to tell on a woman. See her in the street and you might take Mrs. Barratt for twenty-seven or twenty-eight. See her close at hand, and you'd perhaps notice those tiny betraying wrinkles about the mouth which destroy the illusion of fresh youth. She must have seen them herself in the mirror and understood that they were the forerunners of further ravages to come. That's an awkward discovery for a woman."[44] [END SPOILER ALERT]

Similar awkward discoveries are made by "older" women in *The Castleford Conundrum* and *The Eye in the Museum*. In the former novel both Winfred Castleford, thirty-five, and her half-sister, Constance Lindfield, thirty-three, despise Winifred's twenty-year-old stepdaughter, Hillary Castleford, because they believe men find the young woman more alluring than they. Poor Winifred, we learn, looks "her full thirty-five years," while Constance Lindfield, like Helen Barratt in *The Twenty-One Clues*, has "lost the freshness of youth." In *The Eye in the Museum* (1929), young Joyce Hazlemere complains bitterly of her life with her forty-something aunt and guardian Evelyn Fenton, rhetorically asking her fiancée: "How would you like to be under the thumb of a woman of over forty who was jealous of your looks and hates you because she knows that at her age she can't compete with a girl amongst men?" Like *The Castleford Conundrum's* Winifred Castleford, for whom she seems to be the prototype, Evelyn Fenton looks "every day of her age" in spite of the desperate efforts she makes "to compete with the younger generation."[45]

The proper thing for such women to do is retire from the game and fade as gracefully as they can into respectable — if not desirable — matronhood. Yet Ruth Jessop, Helen Barratt, Winifred Castleford, Constance Lindfield and Evelyn Fenton stubbornly refuse to do this (significantly, all the women are childless), resulting in unfortunate outcomes indeed: [SPOILER ALERT] Ruth Jessop is arrested for writing poison pen letters and Helen Barratt for the murder of her husband; Constance Lindfield is exposed as the murderer of her half-sister and commits suicide; and Winifred Castleford and Evelyn Fenton are murdered. [END SPOILER ALERT] On the other hand, chaste, alluring girls still enjoying "the freshness of youth" (such as the females menaced by white slavers in *Raynham Parva*) are proper objects of active masculine sympathy and protection, from which they benefit accordingly.

Just as Connington's views of gender and age seem rather rigidly defined, so do his views of social class. We have already seen how marriage outside one's class produces misfortune in *The Boat-House Riddle* and *The Twenty-One Clues*. In the latter novel, Clinton Driffield fully sympathizes with the mortification Helen Barratt soon suffered from having rashly married a man socially beneath her. "She has a very natural leaning toward her own class and its ways," he tells Squire Wendover. Her murdered husband "was no doubt a decent enough man, but he came from a lower class." How could he compare in her eyes with her lover Callis, a "good-looking young fellow" with "nice manners" and a "social position about the £800 or £900 a year mark," who "speaks well with a good accent"? In a slightly earlier novel, *For Murder Will Speak*, it is Driffield's "Watson," Squire Wendover, with his finely sensitive nose for class distinctions, who first scents a couple's problem: "Now there's a case of trouble," the Squire tells Sir Clinton. "She married a fellow called Hyson. Not quite our sort, Hyson. I haven't seen much of him and I don't want to see more. He's a shade below her socially, just a shade, but it makes all the difference."[46]

Jean Trent, the newlywed wife honeymooning with her husband, Colin, on the Scottish islet of "Ruffa" in Connington's entertaining mystery thriller *Tom Tiddler's Island*, would have agreed with Squire Wendover's conclusion. She and the evidently rather idle

Colin are enjoying a long honeymoon indeed, with three weeks already spent in luxury hotels and now "a month or so" on Ruffa. Learning that her new acquaintance on the islet, a nice girl named Hazel, is unenthusiastic about Ruffa, Jean speculates to herself that boredom is the cause: "Evidently Mr. Arrow was so wrapped up in his scientific work that he spared no time to his niece. The other three men [who lived with them] were not of the same class. It must have been a deadly monotonous existence for a girl." Though Jean is, the author informs us, an imaginative girl, she — clearly no Lady Chatterley — simply cannot imagine any way in which a man from a lower class could conceivably be interesting. Indeed, Jean's own friendly interest in her and Colin's neighbor Mr. Northfleet lessens when Colin informs her that the man is a "consulting chemist":

> "Do you mean he keeps a shop and makes prescriptions?"
> Jean's enthusiasm was slightly damped.

Happily, Jean's suddenly-raised "doubts" about Northfleet's worth as an individual are quickly dispelled when Colin explains that consulting chemists are important men, advisors to large factories on chemical processes.[47]

Like Squire Wendover and Jean Trent, Driffield believes "class-mixing" an ill-advised activity, particularly for members of the upper, or as Sir Clinton would put it, "better" class. It will be recalled that in *The Boat-House Riddle*, Driffield refers unfavorably to the intermingling of classes that occurred in the aftermath of the Great War. During his murder investigations, the Chief Constable when making deductions very much adheres to his belief in the importance of class distinctions. In *Mystery at Lynden Sands* (1928), for example, Driffield reasons that one of the men who overpowered and murdered Peter Hay must have been a "better-class fellow," else Peter naturally would have remained in shirt-sleeves when he went to meet them, rather than have put on a jacket. Sixteen years later, in the midst of a great society-altering conflagration, Driffield and implicitly the author are still drawing the same class-based inferences. In *Jack-in-the-Box*, the Chief Constable agrees with Wendover's speculation that the murderer of one Pirbright was "a better-class person than his host" because he brought a good brand of whiskey with him to share with his victim.[48]

Members of both the middle and the lower classes come in for condescending treatment in Connington's works. In *The Boat-House Riddle* and *The Ha-Ha Case*, Driffield finds the middle-class backgrounds of his detective inspectors quite limiting. Of Inspector Severn in the former novel, the Chief Constable reflects to Squire Wendover: "He may be all right in his judgment of people like Horncastle [one of the Keith-Westerton gamekeepers]. But he's a middle-class Protestant. What chance has he of fathoming the motives of a Roman Catholic like Mrs. Keith-Westerton, let alone those of my friend the Abbé Goron? He and Mrs. Keith-Westerton come from different social strata." Similarly, Inspector Hinton in *The Ha-Ha Case* is hobbled by class limitations when making his investigations. Smarting over his inferior economic background and classical education, Hinton is foolishly reluctant to defer to the superior knowledge of Sir Clinton, even in little matters:

> "Now about this case of yours," Sir Clinton went on briskly. "There's a little bit of doggerel I've found useful sometimes. There's a Latin original, but I'll give you an English version...."
> "I can construe Latin," Hinton interrupted.

He hated those university fellows with their assumptions that they were the only educated people in the country. They thought nobody knew Latin unless he'd been birched at their old school. He'd been at secondary school himself and was as well educated as they were.

"Oh, very well, if you'd rather have the original," Sir Clinton concurred blandly, "here it is: 'Quis, quid, ubi, quibis auxiliis, cur, quomodo, quando?'"

"Who, what, where..." the inspector translated. It doesn't make sense, sir. There isn't a verb in it."

"Oh, it's sensible enough," Sir Clinton assured him, tactfully ignoring Hinton's obvious discomfiture. "Here's an English version. It's easy to remember, because it rhymes: 'What was the crime? Who did it? When was it done and where? How done, and with what motive? Who in the deed did share?'"

At the end of the novel, Sir Clinton in conversation with Wendover concedes of Hinton that the man is "a bit uncouth, I admit."[49]

In other Connington works middle class characters are faulted for additional flaws besides an insufficient knowledge of Latin. These failings typically involve dress and/or accent. Connington's final detective novel, *Commonsense is All You Need* (1947) has several passages in which "that dilettante bibliophile Collingbourne" and his niece Diana Herne, who reside at the stately country home Friar's Pardon, ridicule Diana's co-worker, the librarian Mr. Oakley, for his myriad inadequacies, mostly centering around his appearance and speech. "If he had £10,000 a year," Diana (who to her amusement has been romantically linked to Oakley) tells Squire Wendover, "one might put up with things like these; but love in a slum on £225 per annum is not my cup of tea." After the inadequate Oakley's murder, Diana reflects: "He was a common little man, quite unattractive ... with a dreadful accent and no ... well, no poise ... he was either boasting or else cringing and over-polite in an underbred sort of way. That side of him set my teeth on edge." Diana's uncle concurs with his niece's assessment: "Shabby little fellow with a dreadful accent and no *savoir-faire*. Not a scrap. Not out of the top drawer, by any means.... I wasn't going to allow this underbred fellow to lay down the law in my house."[50]

Similarly underbred and distressingly undistinguished in social background (though wealthier) is *The Ha-Ha Case*'s shady businessman Mr. Hay, rather a spiritual descendant of the abominable Mr. Hubbard from *Death at Swaythling Court*. Like Diana Herne in *Commonsense Is All You Need*, Una Menteith in *The Ha-Ha Case* finds the presence of this ill-mannered man in her company at a fine country house difficult to tolerate:

"He doesn't seem to fit in here somehow," Jim volunteered....

"Of course he doesn't," [Una] agreed contemptuously. "Look at him. His clothes are all right; he goes to a first-class tailor. And yet he manages to look over-dressed in a short coat and black tie. You'd know there was something wrong, even before he opened his mouth...."

... "His manners are imitative and not natural.... He knows what to do when he can't help sneezing, for he's seen well-bred people in that fix, and he copies what he saw them do. The same with shaking hands and not shaking hands.... But he swills drink like ... like a cow, because that's natural to him and he probably doesn't notice that he's different from his models in that."[51]

In *Tragedy at Ravensthorpe* (1927), a classic English country house mystery from the 1920s, lovely Joyce Chacewater of Ravensthorpe Castle merrily mocks the idea of being reduced to dreary lower middle-class status after her impending marriage:

"I can see it all coming. I can see the fat ankles"—she glanced down at her own slim ones—"and the artificial silk stockings at three-and-eleven the pair.... Michael's business will always be mismanaged, with him at the head of it.... I'll have that red nose that comes from indigestion; because ... we won't be able to keep a maid, and I never could cook anything whatever."[52]

Needless to say, charming Joyce evades such a dire fate for herself and Michael, Sir Clinton Driffield restoring a satisfactory order at Ravensthorpe by novel's end.

Members of the lower class — particularly the servants tasked with maintaining the many country homes that, like Ravensthorpe, one finds in the pages of Connington's novels — come in for similar dismissive treatment, being depicted by the author either as comical, nitwitted incompetents or shiftless, malicious scoundrels. In the family home in Belfast, recalls Irene Stewart, the family employed a live-in "cook-general" and a series of Irish maids, allowing her mother "infinite leisure to keep up with her friends in their golf and bridge." Of the family's "series of Irish maids" Irene Stewart writes in detail and with fond affection: "Lily, who came from a farm near the mountains of Morne ... Rachel, the only person who could control our Scottie dog.... Sophie, who was with us when my father died, and with whom I kept in touch for many years, after she moved back to Donegal. All these were really my friends."[53]

Irene Stewart's undoubted empathetic regard for the family maids is not made evident by her father in his Connington fiction, however. For example, the author fully embraces the Golden Age British mystery novel convention that maids will immediately become hysterical upon the discovery of a murder. This phenomenon can be observed in greatest detail in a classic servant scene from *Murder in the Maze*, when Vera Forrest, a guest at Whistlefield who has just escaped from the garden maze in which her two hosts have been slain with curare-tipped darts, stumbles into the house, "disheveled, breathless, and without shoes on her feet," to encounter the doubtful providence of Shelton the maid.

> "Are there any men in the house, Shelton? Quick, don't waste time."
> The maid stared at the haggard girl before her as though in this strange figure she could hardly recognize the cool and graceful Miss Forrest of normal life.
> "What's come to you, Miss?" she asked, without replying to the question.
> "Mr. Shandon's been murdered. Is Mr. Stenness here, or Mr. Hawkhurst? Or anyone else? Go and find them immediately, if they're anywhere about."
> Then, as the girl seem dazed by the news:
> "Can't you do as I tell you? Hurry! There's no time to lose."
> ... The maid's slowness irritated her overwrought nerves.
> "*Will* you go?"
> But by this time the idea of murder had penetrated the dull mind of Shelton and produced a reaction which Vera had not foreseen.
> "Mr. Shelton murdered, and the man creeping about the place! I'd never dare go out of this room, Miss. He might be there in the hall now, waiting for me. Oh, oh!"
> Her voice rose in hysteria. Vera looked at her wearily.[54]

Deciding to make use of Shelton's rising fear, Vera leads her to the front door, where the maid lets loose with a series of lusty screams, attracting the attention of two more "panic-stricken maids," as well as Stenness, the private secretary ("Thank goodness, a man at last!" cries the grateful Vera). Stenness first deals with the company of dimwitted maids, who are uselessly "clinging to each other for company":

> "Go up and get fresh shoes and stockings for Miss Forrest. Can't you see she needs them?"
> When the girls had gone he turned to Vera.

"Nothing like making them do something, otherwise we'd have the whole lot down with their nerves."[55]

Poor Cissie Worgate, in addition to the other demerits remorselessly ticked off by the author in *For Murder Will Speak*, shares the nervous temperament of the maids at Whistlefield, as is seen when she discovers the body of her master, Ossie Hyson, in the kitchen:

With staring eyes, she shrieked in panic...
Asprawl on the floor lay the body of a man, with head and shoulders inside the gas-oven from which the fumes were escaping. Cissie recognized the clothes; it was Mr. Hyson. She shrieked again ... then she rushed to the back door and screamed at the pitch of her voice. Then, with terror pursuing her, she fled the corner of the house and down to the gate, screaming as she went.
For a while she lost track of events.[56]

Finally, the strain of having seen the body of an apparent suicide, an employer for whom she had no shred of affection, proves too much for Cissie and she collapses, naturally, "in hysterics."[57] It is difficult to understand the logic here, as Cissie, in contrast with Shelton in *Murder in the Maze*, could not have believed, however improbably, that she was in danger herself of being murdered by a ruthless killer still lurking on the premises. Her behavior only makes sense if one appreciates the attitude found in a considerable body of Golden Age detective fiction that servants, evidently falling lower on the scale of human evolution, are far less intelligent than their social betters and thus inevitably behave like absolute ninnies in a crisis.

Mrs. Butterswick, housekeeper for Hazel Deerhurst in *A Minor Operation*, appreciates the problem of lower class nerves. After she discovers that her beloved mistress has unaccountably disappeared overnight and that there is blood on the parquet floor, "the first problem" presenting itself to her after she rings the police concerns the matter of the housemaid, Evie. "Evie ... was a bit high-strung and nervous. Like enough, she might fly off the handle, get hysterical and silly, if she found herself in a 'murder house' with only Mrs. Butterswick for company and support. Better let her learn of the tragedy after the police had arrived, with their reassuring masculinity."[58]

Mrs. Butterswick adores her mistress, as a good domestic employee should. The thought that a policeman might see her Hazel's precious articles of underclothing, let alone touch them, fills her with horror. When a searching officer glances at Hazel's "unslept-in bed with the filmy nightdress stretched on it," the housekeeper hastily intervenes between him and the bed, "feeling that it was next door to profanation that this man from the police station should be feasting his eyes on Hazel's night attire." It is with a great sense of relief when she learns the investigator will allow her to personally conduct the search though the bedroom wardrobes and drawers: "Alien hands were not to profane her mistress' 'pretties.'"[59]

Not all servants can be expected to possess the admirable loyalty of a Mrs. Butterswick, who devotes herself like some sort of vestal matron to the worshipful care of the temple that is Hazel Deerhurst's bedroom. In *The Eye in the Museum*, Inspector Ross encounters a particularly nasty specimen of the disloyal servant, the "second gardener" Nathan Sturry, who wants to sell him information for money. Ross is unimpressed with the human specimen confronting him: "Greed and slyness were written large on the dull face; and his manner, as he entered the room, was a combination of self-importance and suspicion." Ross meets Sturry's attempts to wheedle cash for information by the same means employed by Inspector French in the tales of Freeman Wills Crofts: implicitly threatening the second-gardener with prison. ("Ever hear of being an accessory ex post facto or of committing misprision of felony? Pretty serious offenses, both of them.") Sturry having "no knowledge of the law, and ... a very considerable fear of consequences" collapses immediately and tells Ross what he wants to know *gratis*.[60]

Unlike the surly, grasping Sturry, the lady's maid Tobin in *Truth Comes Limping* (1938) is more than anxious to "spill" on her mistress, but she does so not out of a sense of public duty but rather from a feeling of private, petty malice against the lady. We learn Tobin is a bad character from Wendover's appraisal on encountering her: "Good-looking ... in a hard sort of way, but he didn't like the set of her mouth. She hadn't exactly a vinegary expression, but she might develop into a shrew in time.... [S]he was just the sort to give her mistress the courtesy she was paid for while taking a real delight in sneering at her behind her back." For her pains, Tobin is warned by Clinton Driffield that telling tales out of school could land her in serious trouble: "What you've said to me is official; but if you go talking in that strain outside, as you've been doing, you'll get yourself into trouble.... [I]f there's any fresh talk in the village, we'll know where it comes from, you understand? You can go now. Send Maverton [the valet] to me at once." After Tobin has departed, Sir Clinton, always ready to discuss feminine psychology, speculates to Wendover that "jealousy of some sort is at the back of [Tobin's spite].... Probably Miss Carfax [Tobin's mistress] is better looking or something like that."[61]

Excepting *Nordenholt's Million*—written, as explained above, at a time when Connington was extremely pessimistic about his country's future—there is little discernible racism in Connington's mystery novels, outside the late work *Jack-in-the-Box*, surprisingly praised by Anthony Boucher as a "flawless specimen of [the] detailed British school." **[SPOILER ALERT]** One of the key villains in the novel is a fiendish mulatto religious charlatan, Jehudi Ashmun, who is shot at the tale's climax by Sir Clinton himself. ("'It does hurt, when you get it amongst the metacarpals,' said Sir Clinton unsympathetically, 'Well, my man, you've earned it.'") Before he ends up shooting Ashmun amongst the metacarpals, the Chief Constable had seemed to defend the mulatto mystic against an outraged Squire Wendover.[62] Nevertheless, Ashmun is proven unfit for decent English society, just like the bestial Herne the Hunter in *Nordenholt's Million*. **[END SPOILER ALERT]**

Connington's seeming lack of sympathy for his fellow creatures (always excepting attractive, well-born and "straight" girls) extends from the socially "inferior" to the economically destitute as well. In *The Ha-Ha Case*, a family crisis emerges when the heir to the Brandon estates becomes determined to distribute much of the family landholdings to the urban poor. Johnnie Brandon, who with the author's evident sympathy is characterized by one character as an "inexperienced dullard," naively lectures his brother Jim on the virtue of boundless charity:

> "It's like this.... Things aren't properly distributed. Some of us have far more money than we need. Other people haven't got enough to live decently.... Think of the slums, Jim. Think of all those poor devils cooped up in those dens. Some of them never see a green field in their lives. They ought to be given a chance. They ought to be taken clean out of those beastly rookeries and planted down in the country with allotments and smallholdings."

"It was the crude socialism of adolescence," reflects the author of *Nordenholt's Million*, "a froth of generous feeling untempered by the slightest experience of the world."[63] The ruthless and experienced Stanley Nordenholt, it will be recalled, solved the problem of need in Britain by facilitating the deaths of forty-five million people, those dispassionately deemed by him to be merely burdens on a society fighting for its very survival. A "modest proposal" for the physical disposal of the superfluous poor, rather than one for helping to alleviate their poverty, seems to draw considerably more enthusiasm from Connington, or at least to provide greater inspiration for his imagination.

To be fair, Connington does maintain through Clinton Driffield an affectionate indulgence for the man who functions as Sir Clinton's "Watson" figure in most of his tales, the conscientious, agrarian traditionalist landowner, Squire Wendover. A humane paternalist, Wendover recognizes that the landowner has reciprocal obligations in his relationships with his rural dependents. In *Truth Comes Limping*, the Squire, though ever-reluctant to criticize fellow members of his gentry class, cannot refrain from making caustic comments to Sir Clinton about his great landowning neighbors, the ancient Carfax family, who selfishly neglect their quasi-feudal obligations. "They're damned bad landlords," he tells the Chief Constable:

> "From father to son, it goes on just the same.... They're inconsiderate with their tenants, even with men who've been on their land generation after generation. If rents aren't paid on the nail — out you go! And they pinch on repairs to a scandalous extent by my standards. It's not a mere matter of money.... It's simply that they haven't got a spark of sympathy with the people who live on their land."[64]

Squire Wendover is viewed tolerantly by Sir Clinton as an anachronism, but an entirely admirable one. In this context it must be recalled that, though Connington in *Nordenholt's Million* told of Stanley Nordenholt's smashing of the House of Commons with great relish, he left the fate of the House of Lords vague. While he viewed incompetent members of the gentry like the simpleminded socialist Johnnie Brandon and the shortsightedly selfish Carfaxes as best dispensed with, Connington clearly admired the Squire Wendovers of Britain, who through good (and traditional) management could keep the rural masses in line.

In terms of his treatment of the modern political and social touchstones of class, gender and race, J.J. Connington stands as one of the more conservative of British writers of Golden Age detective fiction. While the sociopolitical attitudes reflected in his novels can make much in them off-putting to the reader of today, it is only fair to evaluate Connington as well on his own aesthetic terms, as a maker of interesting and entertaining puzzles. Although he generally does not match the ingenuity of either Street or Crofts in their respective specialties, murder means and alibi construction, Connington nevertheless devised during his best years some excellent tales of detection, qualifying him, in my view, as one of the major mystery genre writers of the period. Already in the late 1920s he was seen by critics as belonging in "the front rank of detective-story writers" (*Times Literary Supplement*) and "the front row of detective story writers" (*Criterion*); and he fittingly became one of the charter members of the Detection Club in 1930. I will look in greater depth at eight Connington novels from his best period (1927 to 1937, all with Sir Clinton Driffield): *Murder in the Maze* (1927), *Tragedy at Ravensthorpe* (1927), *The Case with Nine Solutions* (1928), *The Sweepstake Murders* (1931), *The Castleford Conundrum*

(1932), *The Ha-Ha Case* (1934), *In Whose Dim Shadow* (1935), and *A Minor Operation* (1937). Not only do Connington's best mystery tales provide readers with well-wrought puzzles, they also offer a bracing contrast with many other mysteries of the period in their generally cynical view of human nature.[65]

Connington made his break to the front of the murdermongers' pack with his third detective novel, *Murder in the Maze*, in which Sir Clinton Driffield debuted as the author's great series detective. No less a fan of the genre than T.S. Eliot praised *Murder in the Maze* for its construction ("we are provided early in the story with all the clues which guide the detective") and its liveliness ("The very idea of murder in a box hedge labyrinth does the author great credit, and he makes full use of its possibilities"), deeming it "a really first-rate detective story." For his part, H.C. Harwood declared in *The Outlook* that with the publication of *Murder in the Maze* Connington "demands and deserves comparison with the masters ... buy, borrow, or — anyhow get hold of it." Two decades later, in his 1946 critical essay, "The Grandest Game in the World," the great locked room detective novelist John Dickson Carr echoed Eliot's assessment of the novel's virtuoso setting, writing: "These 1920s ... thronged with sheer brains. What would be one of the best possible settings for violent death? J.J. Connington found the answer, with *Murder in the Maze*."[66]

Murder in the Maze, like *Tragedy at Ravensthorpe*, which appeared later that year, is centered, as are many 1920s Golden Age detective novels, on criminous events at a country house. In both novels, Connington's no-nonsense detective, Chief Constable Sir Clinton Driffield (lately returned from South Africa), oversees the restoration of order at a fractious rural estate. Attending a weekend house party at *Murder in the Maze*'s Whistlefield, the estate of Roger Shandon, are the following individuals: Roger Shandon himself; Shandon's fraternal twin brother, Neville, and his other brother, Ernest; his niece and nephew, Sylvia and Arthur Hawkhurst; his private secretary, Ivor Stenness; and his charming young houseguests, Vera Forrest and Howard Torrance. Ne'er-do-well Ernest's continual presence at Whistlefield is a constant source of mild irritation to Roger Shandon, but of more concern to him of late is his nephew Arthur Hawkstone, who has exhibited a disturbing lack of mental balance after coming down with "sleepy sickness" (encephalitis lethargica).[67] Further, both of the elder Shandon brothers are involved in contentious business matters: Neville, an attorney, is King's Counsel in the controversial Hackleton case; while Roger, who made his fortune from mysterious doings in South Africa and South America, has been vaguely threatened by a former colleague, who accuses Roger of having cheated him. Finally, the private secretary, Ivor Stenness, clearly is up to something untoward.

A day of gentle lazing at Whistlefield is soon disrupted by double murder. The elder Shandon brothers are found dead in Whistlefield's celebrated hedge maze, both felled by curare-tipped darts. The awful discoveries are made by Whistlefield's two houseguests, Vera Forrest and Howard Torrance, who had entered the Maze to have a race to reach its double centers. The dire events that follow unfold from Vera's perspective as she wanders alone through the Maze, able to hear but not see Howard. She comes to realize she is trapped in the Maze with a murderer:

"Howard! I'm frightened. What's happened?"

"One of the Shandons has been killed. I blundered into the center trying to get to you. There's blood on his coat..."

... "There's somebody moving about in the Maze, Howard. I hear footsteps."

> ... It came over her how safe and peaceful the world was — and now, in pursuit of an aimless piece of amusement, she had come into the slaughterhouse. The Minotaur was afoot in the labyrinth.[68]

As T.S. Eliot and John Dickson Carr both noted, this section of *Murder in the Maze* is grippingly-narrated and well-deserving of praise. Indeed, the novel as a whole is something of a triumph, boasting well-managed suspense and true detection (though perhaps some red herrings are not as forcefully presented as they could be). As mentioned earlier, the climax of the novel is disturbingly ruthless but also dramatically apposite, with readers again being taken back to the site of the menacing Maze, where we find that Clinton Driffield has held all the threads in his hand for some time and has arranged for all those concerned in the mystery a most fitting exit, in accordance with his own private conception of justice (among other things he essentially exterminates Whistlefield's very wicked murderer). At the tale's end even a wedding is in the offing, with Driffield offering a good job to a certain worthy affianced young man: "I've some small influence in South Africa, and it so happens that a man out there asked me to look round for someone to fill a post. The pay's good enough to marry on."[69]

Debuting with Sir Clinton Driffield in *Murder in the Maze* is Driffield's best friend, Squire Wendover. The Squire appears in fourteen of the seventeen Driffield novels (he is entirely absent from three of the first five Driffields, but appears in every one from 1931's *The Boathouse Riddle* through 1947's *Commonsense Is All You Need*), serving as Driffield's Watson figure as the Chief Constable marches from one investigative triumph to another. As in *Murder in the Maze*, Driffield often is staying over at his fellow bachelor's ancestral country estate, Talgarth Grange, when he is called into a local murder investigation. Driffield seems to have a dry affection for his friend, but that does not prevent him from frequently twitting the Squire, whose enthusiasm for the art of amateur detection somewhat exceeds his skill at practicing it:

> "You've made out quite a fair case against both Hackleton and young Hawkhurst *as suspects*, Squire; but there isn't a tittle of evidence there that a jury would look at, you know."
> "Oh, I see that well enough," Wendover admitted. "But the case against other people isn't half as strong. Ardsley's a possible suspect [Ardsley is a local toxicologist whom Wendover dislikes, in part because the man experiments on animals]. He has possession of curare; he knows the Maze intimately..."
> "And he's had a squabble with Roger Shandon over fishing rights. I'm afraid even Izaak Walton would hardly have thought that matter was a sufficient ground for murder, Squire."[70]

Although the resemblance of Driffield and Wendover to Holmes and Watson is specifically referenced by the pair themselves in *Murder in the Maze* ("I see," announces Wendover at one point. "I'm to be Watson, and then you'll prove what an ass I am. I'm not over keen"), in this novel Connington takes pains to make clear that Wendover is no mere "idiot friend," as the Watson figure in the detective novel was often called:

> [Wendover] was one of those red-faced, hearty country gentlemen who, on first acquaintance, give an entirely erroneous impression of themselves. Met casually, he might quite easily have appeared to be a slightly fussy person of very limited intellect and even more restricted interests; but behind that façade lived a fairly acute brain which took a sly delight in exaggerating the misleading mannerisms. Wendover was anything but a fool, though he liked to pose as one.[71]

Squire Wendover indeed is a more interesting character than Agatha Christie's Colonel Arthur Hastings and many of the other "fairly acute" to outright dim individuals who filled the stolid ranks of the Watson phalanx in Golden Age detective fiction, though he was never as fully limned by his creator as he might have been. We learn, for example, that Wendover has an instinctive and indulgent sympathy for "pretty girls," but Connington never really lets us glimpse any deeper emotional life that the Squire might have (even Watson had a wife, however briefly). Yet Wendover's warmer, more humane presence admittedly provides relief from the brilliant but formidable and sometimes forbidding Sir Clinton Driffield.

Squire Wendover is regrettably absent from *Tragedy at Ravensthorpe*, which, like *Murder in the Maze*, was published in 1927. In this tale Sir Clinton with the help of one of his men, Inspector Armadale (obviously the inspector's name is a nod to the Wilkie Collins novel), cleanses yet another country house, this time Ravensthorpe, the home of old family friends, the Chacewaters. As at *Maze*'s Whistlefield, there are three siblings in the family. Like Sylvia Hawkhurst in *Maze*, Joan Chacewater is charming, beloved by all and clearly above suspicion of anything unseemly; however, brothers Maurice and Cecil Chacewater are at odds, both over a lovely woman, Una Rainhill, and over the plan of the tightfisted elder son, Maurice, to sell the Medusa Medallions — attributed to Leonardo Da Vinci and the prize acquisitions in the private museum at Ravensthorpe — to Mr. Foss, the representative of a "Yank millionaire" (the brothers' deceased father, a firm believer in primogeniture, left his entire estate to Maurice).

Great complications soon ensue, however. There is a burglary — or two — during a masked ball at Ravensthorpe, but it becomes unclear just what was stolen and one of the burglars seems to have vanished into thin air. Then Mr. Foss winds up stabbed to death in the museum and Maurice Chacewater is found shot — but was the unlikable Maurice the murderer of Mr. Foss or a murder victim himself? Soon Clinton Driffield has untangled this quite tangled affair, exhibiting some impressive feats of ratiocination. Arguably the tale skirts with violating one or even two of the "rules" of detective fiction (T.S. Eliot thought so and thus ranked the tale below *Murder in the Maze*), but to my mind these infractions are but slight and the tale is first-rate. Particularly appealing are Connington's explanation of the miracle problem of the burglar's vanishing and his use of fairy folklore (possibly inspired by the recent hubbub over the Cottingley Fairies photographs that took place in England in the early 1920s).[72]

The crime fiction reviewer for the *Spectator* hailed *Tragedy at Ravensthorpe* in the strongest terms, declaring of the novel: "This is more than a good detective tale. Alike in plot, characterization, and literary style, it is a work of art." Both Connington's 1928 detective novels, *Mystery at Lynden Sands* and *The Case with Nine Solutions* received much praise as well. Although to my mind the former novel is marred by melodramatic thriller elements, *The Case with Nine Solutions* is one of Connington's very finest works and one of the best English mysteries from the 1920s. The *Times Literary Supplement* lauded the novel as "a very well-constructed story ... with a criminal worthy of Mr. Connington," while in the United States Frederic F. Van de Water declared: "This book is a thoroughbred of a distinguished lineage that runs back to 'The Gold Bug' of Poe. It represents the highest type of detective fiction." Even Dashiell Hammett, not traditionally considered a great friend of the classical British puzzle novel, conceded, in his review of *Nine Solutions*

J.J. Connington, *The Case with Nine Solutions* (1929). Alfred Walter Stewart later reflected of his highly-praised *The Case with Nine Solutions*, which explores potentially lethal sexual tensions and jealousies at the Croft-Thornton Research Institute, that the novel "made rather a neat problem in elimination."

in the *Saturday Review of Literature*, that it was "a very conventional, not altogether exciting, but quite readable detective story," with the solution reached "quite satisfactorily." When in 1929 Arnold Bennett — definitely no friend of the classical British puzzle novel — asked "an independent and erudite student of detective fiction" to recommend to him a "supreme modern masterpiece" of the genre, that unnamed friend named *The Case with Nine Solutions*.[73] Though reading the novel did nothing to convince the obstinate Bennett that the modern detective novel had any artistic merit whatsoever (as discussed in Chapter One), in fact *The Case with Nine Solutions* indeed is a fine example of the classical form, offering an intellectually engaging puzzle as well as characters that seem surprisingly modern in some ways; and it merits reading today, just as it did over eighty years ago.

The novel opens effectively with a fearsome welter of murder. Dr. Ringwood, a *locum tenens* newly arrived in the provincial city of Westerhaven, is rung up on a foggy night and urgently requested by a nervous housemaid to visit the residence where she is employed so that he can treat the other maid at the house, who has become violently sick (the two maids have been left alone in the house for the evening). A friend of Ringwood's familiar with the city, Dr. Trevor Markfield (a chemist at the local Croft-Thornton Research Institute), has just made a personal call on Dr. Ringwood; and he volunteers to guide his friend through the treacherous fog to the house, which happens to be that of Dr. Silverdale, the head of the Research Institute's chemical department, and his wife Yvonne. Markfield leaves Ringwood at the end of the avenue of private homes in which Heatherfield, the house he is seeking, is located; but Ringwood, confused by the fog, mistakenly enters the wrong house, the next-door Ivy Lodge, home of Edward Hassendean, another chemist at the Research Institute.

At Ivy Lodge, Ringwood finds not the expected sick maid, but a young man bleeding copiously on the smoking room chesterfield. The man, who turns out to be Edward Hassendean, has been shot twice through the lungs and is clearly dying. He manages to gasp out the words "caught me ... thought it was ... all right ... never guessed..." to Dr. Ringwood before expiring from his wounds.[74] Realizing he is in the wrong house and now in urgent need of a telephone, Ringwood crosses over to Heatherfield and briefly interviews the maid who had earlier rung him. Before seeing the sick woman in her bedroom, Ringwood excuses himself, rings up Clinton Driffield (Ringwood knows Driffield from having treated the Chief Constable's butler during the short time he has been practicing at Westerhaven) and informs him of the presence of a dead, bullet-pierced body at Ivy Lodge. After visiting with the ill maid (whom he diagnoses as having come down with scarlatina), Ringwood crosses back over to Ivy Lodge, where he encounters Driffield and police inspector Flamborough, who have come to investigate the violent death of Edward Hassendean.

At Ivy Lodge Driffield and Flamborough commence investigations, which include an interview with Edward Hassendean's returning uncle and aunt, who inform the investigators that young Hassendean had planned to go to a dance that night with his neighbor Yvonne Silverdale. Crossing over to Heatherfield to further investigate this aspect of matter, Driffield and Flamborough find the sick maid still in bed and now delirious, as well as the other maid on the landing of the stairway, stone dead. "She's been strangled pretty efficiently," announces Sir Clinton coolly.[75]

The next day, the Chief Constable receives an anonymous letter which reads, "Try hassendean bungalow lizard bridge road justice." Following the tip from "Justice" ("a member of the Order of the Helpful Hand, perhaps," suggests the cynical Driffield), the Chief Constable, Flamborough and Dr. Ringwood journey out to the sea view bungalow owned by the Hassendeans and discover the corpse of Yvonne Silverdale sitting upright in an arm-chair, a bullet wound to the side of her head, an automatic pistol at her feet. "She was dead before the shot was fired, of course," declares Sir Clinton. "There wasn't half enough blood scattered about the place." On-the-spot examination from Dr.

Ringwood leads the doctor to conclude that the true cause of Yvonne Hassendean's death was a fatal dose of a mydriatic drug.[76]

So, in the course of an evening and the following day, Driffield and his police force have been presented with three violent deaths, yet only one—that of the strangled Silverdale maid—is certain murder. The "nine solutions" of the title refer to the various possible combinations of causes of death for Edward Hassendean and Yvonne Silverdale: accident/accident; suicide/suicide; murder/murder; accident/suicide; suicide/accident; accident/murder; murder/accident; suicide/murder; murder/suicide.[77] It all adds up to a very tricky set of problems for Sir Clinton. Clearly there must be some vital link connecting all this mortal carnage in a provincial town, but what? And why is "Justice" being so helpful to the police with those anonymous letters?

Writing much more would spoil enjoyment of a teasing puzzle-novel that climaxes with quite a bang, followed by an interesting postscript of excerpts from Sir Clinton's notebook, explaining step-by-step how the Chief Constable arrived at his solution. However, I feel I would be remiss in not noting a few more aspects of the tale. Arnold Bennett criticized the novel for being dry and detached and for lacking atmosphere, contrasting it unfavorably with the melodramatic, nineteenth-century mysteries of Emile Gaboriau; but what might favorably strike a reader today about *The Case with Nine Solutions* is its bleak modernity. The Croft-Thornton Research Institute turns out to be a workplace hotbed of sexual tensions and jealousies on the parts of a generally unlikable and emotionally unsatisfied group of men and women, rather reminiscent of the sort of novel P.D. James has been writing since 1963's splendid *A Mind to Murder* (set at the Steen Psychiatric clinic). **[SPOILER ALERT]** Especially striking is the revelation that Yvonne Silverdale died from being accidentally overdosed with the "date rape" drug hyoscine by the contemptible, narcissistic and sexually frustrated Edward Hassendean. Mrs. Silverdale was calculatedly using her Platonic relationship with young Hassendean to shield from her husband (whose own romantic attention is elsewhere engaged as well) her true sexual affair with another man, but that hardly makes Hassendean's action any less grotesque. **[END SPOILER ALERT]** All in all, *The Case with Nine Solutions* is the sort of mystery novel one finishes with a thorough dislike for most everyone in it. One also might well feel some appreciation for Dr. Markfield's biting declaration: "Still got the notion that human life's valuable? The war knocked that on the head.... Human life's the cheapest thing there is."[78] No wonder Arnold Bennett thought the book inhuman. But the "read' is none the worse, in my opinion, for being a sour one.

By the end of the decade of the 1920s, J.J. Connington had achieved a high reputation indeed among detective fiction connoisseurs. Connington's new English publisher, Victor Gollancz, did not stint on praise for the author in the publisher's blurb on the dust jacket of his latest tale, *The Eye in the Museum* (1929), informing readers that "J.J. Connington is now established as, in the opinion of many, the greatest living master of the story of pure detection. He is one of those who, discarding all the superfluities, has made of deductive fiction a genuine minor art, with its own laws and its own conventions." *The Sweepstake Murders*, an excellent 1931 Connington mystery, offers proof that the author continued to excel at his art in the new decade.[79]

While *The Sweepstake Murders* is not as astringent a novel as *The Case with Nine Solutions*, none of its characters are particularly likeable. The series of slayings in the tale may well strike most readers as it does Inspector Severn, to whom "the whole affair presented itself as a mere puzzle to be solved, like a chess-problem."[80] Fortunately, the "mere puzzle" in *The Sweepstake Murders* is quite an interesting one, involving the perennially popular multiple murder plot, specifically in this case a succession of deaths among the members of a sweepstake syndicate that has just won nearly 250,000 pounds. After the accidental death of one of the syndicate members, the surviving group of men (which includes Squire Wendover) contracts that only living members of the syndicate should share in the winnings. When litigation delays the distribution of the award and in the interim members of the syndicate start dying suspiciously, Clinton Driffield and Inspector Severn come to the conclusion that one member of the syndicate is seeking to increase his share of winnings by eliminating his fellow stakeholders.

With *Sweepstake Murders*, Connington provides the reader both an extremely clever alibi mechanism and a plausible, ingeniously simple murder contraption. Like John Street, Connington centered his mystery plots far less on "unbreakable" alibis than did Freeman Wills Crofts, but in this novel he devised one of the best in the literature for the first of the tale's killings.[81] Additionally, one of the murder means that Connington employs in *Sweepstake Murders* has some of the design ingenuity often found in Street's works, and it is, moreover, clued with pleasing subtlety. Despite his background in chemistry, Connington tended less to build his plots around a technically brilliant murder method than to use his scientific expertise to fashion subsidiary mystery elements, but with the novel's second murder the author firmly focuses the ratiocinative interest on an unusual means of inducing death.

Obnoxious elements obtrude on the reader's enjoyment less in *Sweepstake Murders* than they do in a number of other Connington tales. Being himself one of the members of the sweepstake syndicate, Squire Wendover necessarily plays an integral role in the events, and does not seem tacked on by the author as he sometimes does. Clinton Driffield actually takes a role in the novel secondary to Inspector Severn (who here is allowed to function rather efficiently, with no cutting remarks from his superior about his middle class limitations). Indeed, Sir Clinton is absent from much of the tale's investigative proceedings, reappearing only near the end to provide, with his usual bland competence, the final stunning revelations.

The additional members of the syndicate besides Wendover are, as Barzun and Taylor put it in *A Catalogue of Crime*, "an unprepossessing lot whom it is a pleasure to see gradually eliminated." All the men come, interestingly, not from Connington's favored country house milieu, but from the rising commercial class, an entity of which the author, through the thoughts of Squire Wendover, seems to disapprove. At one point in the novel, the squire, who on a whim agreed to participate in the syndicate in order to be a sport (and certainly not because he needed the money his share of the winnings would provide him), reflects unfavorably on his fellow stakeholders:

> These people belonged to a circle different from his own. They cared nothing for the countryside or the country people. They represented new trades and factories which were springing up like mushrooms south of the old industrial block of the midlands. They cast their eyes about for districts where the rates were low; and where one came, another followed.... These invading things weren't like the old staple trades: coal, iron, shipbuilding, and so forth. They were all based on flimsy articles, or next door to that.... Blackburn with some office gadget or other....

Redhill with his under-capitalized place in Stanningleigh turning out fancy brands of enamel.... Falgate over in Ambledown with his acetate silk factory (which might not last much longer).... Mackworth with his ZZZ Sauce.... Coniston with his motorbuses ... old Thursford with his cinemas (not forgetting young Thursford's ten per cent. partnership).... Checkey's venture in toffee. These people quite obviously didn't think along the same lines as himself. One might accept them as neighbors, but one stuck to one's own group when it came to choosing friends.[82]

The only female character of significance in the novel is Viola Langdale, a fiancée of one of the syndicate members. Viola is of some interest as another example of the pathos of the girl of good social station made cynical and hardened by her reduced circumstances:

[Viola] had a tiny income, just sufficient to scrape along on by living in the house her parents had left her. Within limits, of course, she could live as she liked; there was no one to interfere with her. And in some ways, if all tales were true, she had made the limits wide enough.... Wendover disliked thinking about that sort of thing where a girl was concerned. Instead, he turned to another mental picture: Viola, with her worn suede golf-jacket and her dingy little car, keeping a footing with her richer friends as best she could, and covering all her difficulties with that bright, hard smile.[83]

Always attempting to err on charity's side where a pretty girl is concerned, Wendover reflects that Viola is "outwardly ... feminine enough" despite that certain hardness. She looks "her twenty-seven years," admittedly, "but not a day older." Regrettably, Viola at her relatively advanced age is no dewy-eyed innocent, having "been engaged to three men before, without mentioning other affairs"—a lapse in character that troubles the fastidious Squire. Ultimately the perforce materialistic Viola becomes implicated in the novel's slayings, but I will leave future readers to discover for themselves the full truth about the mystery. E.C. Bentley in the *Daily Telegraph* particularly praised *Sweepstake* at the time for "an alibi that is a triumph of ingenuity" (after stating "Mr. Connington writes admirably always") while Barzun and Taylor in *A Catalogue of Crime* label the tale "one of Connington's best conceptions."[84]

Strikingly unlikable women, as well as men for that matter, are found in *The Castleford Conundrum*, one of Connington's finest detective novels. In this tale, the author does an extremely effective job of portraying an odious, stupid second wife, Winifred Castleford, and her detestable, sponging in-laws. Even her seemingly sympathetic second husband, Philip, an impecunious miniaturist who married the wealthy, masterful Winifred (widow of a war profiteer who made a quick pile before conveniently expiring in the 1919 flu epidemic) only after she accidentally maimed his painting hand and effectively destroyed his career, is offhandedly dismissed with contempt by Clinton Driffield as a cringing weakling. Only Philip's daughter (and Winifred's stepdaughter), Hillary, is portrayed by the author with real sympathy, she being the typical beautiful, chaste young girl specially favored by Connington. If one desires to read a novel with a houseful of scheming, contemptible relations and a cleverly arranged murder of the one person with all the money — a favored situation in classical mystery tales — one could not do better than *The Castleford Conundrum*.

The novel opens at Winifred Castleford's country house, Carron Hill, with the author detailing the multiple after dinner animosities (all centering on the very wealthy Winifred) simmering among the various people there that night. In the one camp we find

Philip Castleford and his daughter Hillary, in the other Winifred's designing relations: Constance Lindfield, Winifred's half-sister and companion; Laurence and Kenneth Glencaple, her brothers-in-law from her first marriage (a country doctor and a struggling businessman respectively); and Francis Glencaple, Kenneth's brutish, seemingly near semi-moronic fourteen-year-old son. Not part of the menagerie at Carron Hill, but of great concern to the three women who live there, is Dick Stevenage, an utter waster nevertheless found intensely interesting by the local female population.

In *The Castleford Conundrum*, Connington casts his scorn for humanity about in heaps. Winifred is an utterly worthless being — pushy, selfish and common — eminently deserving of murdering. Thirty-five and with "calves like a sturdy dairy-maid's," "Winnie," as she likes to be called (one of her irritating qualities is her insistence that everyone, even adults, be called by diminutives: hence Winifred/Winnie; Constance/Connie; Hillary/Hillie; Laurence/Laurie; Kenneth/Kennie; Francis/Frankie), despises her younger, prettier stepdaughter and makes her life miserable in every petty way that she and her half-sister Connie can devise. Constance is resentful of the presence of Phillip and Hillary at Carron Hill and does all she can to undermine them. Thirty-three years of age and, like Winnie and Hillary, powerfully attracted to the handsome Dick Stevenage, she also is intensely jealous of Hillary Castleford. The main concern of the calculating Laurence and the piggish Kenneth is to get their hands on Winnie's fortune, inherited from their deceased brother, by getting Phillip and Hillary essentially written out of Winnie's will. Kenneth's son is possibly the worst of the worthless lot, a horrid young brute whose favorite pastimes are torturing animals and playing with the rook rifle his doting Aunt Winnie has given him. "I could shoot you, Aunt Winnie. Look!" he yells proudly on receiving the weapon, foreshadowing his aunt's imminent demise.[85]

Soon enough the egregious Winnie Castleford is discovered shot dead in a chair on the porch of her summer chalet by the chalet caretaker, Mrs. Haddon. Connington portrays Mrs. Haddon with more care than he typically lavishes on underlings, though he gives her the customary servant's avidity for the notoriety that accompanies the role of corpse-finder in a village murder mystery ("at the back of Mrs. Haddon's mind was a vision of herself, a really important person for once, breaking the tragic news in Thunderbridge village") and saddles her as well with a contemptible, Bolshevist husband. Mr. Haddon, "a disgruntled devil with his knife in the police and the upper classes," turns out to be the author of a recent rash of nasty anonymous letters, telling tales out of school about the various amours of members of the local moneyed class. In an episode reminiscent of Inspector Ross' exchange with the surly and greedy second gardener in *The Eye in the Museum*, Clinton Driffield finds himself confronted with the need to extract information possibly related to the murder from the conniving, shiftless Haddon. Driffield consents to pay Haddon for his information, but he does so in a manner calculated to strongly convey both his disgust for the man and his stout determination that members of the lower classes must not be allowed to trifle with their superiors:

> Sir Clinton opened the note-case, leafed over the contents, extracted the dingiest ten-shilling note he could find, and passed it over to Haddon.
> "Rather dirty money, I'm afraid, Mr. Haddon. But you're not the sort to object to that, I'm sure."
> Haddon seized the note and stowed it away in his pocket. Then he seemed to catch the second meaning in the Chief Constable's remark.

"If people didn't do things, there'd be nothing to write about," he declared impudently.

"If you ever put pen to paper in that way again," Sir Clinton said decisively, "I'll see you goaled for the full two years. You can count on that. In the meantime, if you breathe a word on this affair, we'll have to take up the case against you. So you're warned."

Haddon shrugged his shoulders as though making light of the threat; but his pretence was a feeble one. The Chief Constable's tone had carried conviction.[86]

Another lower-class character subjected — though more gently — to Connington's scorn in *The Castleford Conundrum* is Police Constable Ebenezer Gumley, who dreams of great conquests in the field of criminal investigation, but is inevitably dashed in his hopes by his poor choice of reading material. "Literature is an elastic form," notes the author, "but in the case of P.C. Gumley it meant two things and two only: a manual of *Police Law* and the cheaper type of detective stories." Expanding on the subject of the latter literary form, Connington explains: "His day's duty done, [Gumley] retired to his bedroom at his lodgings. After thumbing over the long row of tattered, paper-bound volumes on the shelf, he plunged with zest into a re-perusal of the rounding-up of Thick-Eared Mike or the tracking-down of Slim Harry, the International Crook."[87] Evidently feasting on a steady diet of crude Edgar Wallace potboilers and American pulps, poor P.C. Gumley has not a prayer of reaching the solution in an intellectually sophisticated Connington detective novel.

To be sure, Connington holds the well-born idler Dick Stevenage and his mother in every bit as much contempt as he does Mr. Haddon and P.C. Gumley. While working on an exceedingly long-gestating novel, we learn, Stevenage lives with — and off — a so-eager-to-be-modern mother, who indulges her charming boy's every whim to the extent her fixed income will allow. "Caught up in the swirl of new ideas which followed the war," Connington witheringly notes, "she had assimilated everything without digesting anything."[88] For Dick's part, when not working on his novel (which is most of the time), he contemptibly strings along Constance Lindfield and Hillary Castleford, all the while carrying on a covert flirtation with the wealthy Winnie Castleford.

Clinton Driffield and his friend Squire Wendover do not appear on the scene until the final third of the book, but they then find their hands full with a highly complex crime. Before the relentless Sir Clinton reveals all in a classic drawing-room lecture to the suspects gathered at Carron Hill, he sportingly provides Wendover a list of the nine key points in the case, for the Squire to work his way through, if he can. These include such intriguing details as the following (all making use of the author's chemistry knowledge): ash found in the grate of the Chalet having "a much greater quantity of aluminum than should normally be present"; fibers in Winifred Castleford's head wound containing pine wood pores and "some ribbony structure"; and the fact that the weather was very warm when someone from Carron Hill checked out law books from the village library.[89] Cryptic clue tabulations like this one were eagerly devoured by the puzzle gluttons of the Golden Age, and Connington certainly does not stint his readership its meat and drink in *The Castleford Conundrum*, a novel full of good things.

[SPOILER ALERT] In his drawing room lecture, Sir Clinton methodically lays out the case against Philip Castleford, before proceeding to up-end it completely, revealing instead that the true killer is Constance Lindfield. The two then engage in a battle of wits, with Constance attempting to demolish Driffield's case against her, but she is inevitably overmastered by the great sleuth. In a return to his old ways, Sir Clinton allows Constance, a bad girl if ever there were one, to escape trial by committing suicide upstairs. He explains to the shocked people in the drawing room that this decision was no chivalric caprice, but a practical concession to the difficulty in Britain of securing a murder conviction against a woman:

> Sir Clinton glanced at Westerhaven, who nodded reassuringly.
> "It's quite all right, sir. I gave the orders. She can't get out of the house."
> Sir Clinton made no reply. He leaned back in his chair, outwardly indifferent, but alert for a sound. Suddenly it came, the sharp crack of a small-bore pistol in an upper room. The Chief Constable was the only one of the group who did not start.
> "Sometimes a jury of one is more effective than twelve men in a box," he said in a level tone. "And British juries have a rooted distaste for sending a woman to the drop if they can wriggle out of it with any decency. Will you go up with the Inspector, Dr. Glencaple? I have an idea we might need a medical man here."

Sir Clinton then recommends to Philip Castleford that he get his daughter, Hillary (the one straight girl in the tale) "off the premises.... This isn't a nice business, and she's better out of it."[90] **[END SPOILER ALERT]**

The Castleford Conundrum presented crime fiction critics with no puzzle as to its quality. "In *The Castleford Conundrum* Mr. Connington goes to work like an accomplished chess-player. The moves in the games his detectives are called on to play are a delight to watch," raved the reviewer for the *Sunday Times*. He added that "the clues would have rejoiced Mr. Holmes' heart." For its part, the *Spectator* concurred in the *Sunday Times*' assessment of the novel's masterfully-constructed plot: "Few detective stories show such sound reasoning as that by which the Chief Constable brings the crime home to the culprit." Additionally, E.C. Bentley, much admired himself as the author of *Trent's Last Case*, took time to praise Connington's purely literary virtues, noting: "Mr. Connington has never written better, or drawn characters more full of life."[91]

J.J. Connington again combined interesting if unlikeable characters with a strong plot in the next Sir Clinton Driffield mystery, *The Ha-Ha Case*. At a country house weekend at Edgehill, ancestral estate of the Brandon family, various people gather, including the three at-odds Brandon brothers, a discrete governess seemingly with some agenda of her own, a scheming tutor and his kittenish wife, and a coarse businessman of some sort. When Johnnie, the youngest of the Brandon brothers, is shot dead at the ha-ha while rabbit hunting (a ha-ha is a sunken wall designed to delineate boundaries while not obstructing views), everyone is quick to proclaim the "tragedy" an accident, but the ambitious middle-class, secondary school educated Inspector Hinton soon scents other possibilities, namely suicide or even murder. His investigation eventually brings in Clinton Driffield (along with Squire Wendover), who in short order solves the case, which revolves around fine points of rifle ballistics and English law.[92]

The Ha-Ha Case is yet another Connington novel characterized by a hard-as-nails cast of characters. Here, for example, is the blunt assessment of Johnnie Brandon's next elder brother, Jim, on Johnnie: "Johnnie was always a bonehead. A rabbit would be hard put to it to earn a living if he changed brains with my young brother." Admittedly, one couple does emerge during the course of the novel's events, but the couple's relationship is not treated romantically by the author. As unlikable as any of the suspects is Inspector

Hinton himself, a middle class cop with a chip on his shoulder and an uncanny knack for alienating everyone he interrogates. Sir Clinton gets much mildly sadistic amusement out of baiting his hapless subordinate. "Hinton writes a first-class report" is Driffield's refrain to Wendover throughout the novel, always uttered at the end of a catalogue of Hinton's deficiencies. "I have a suspicion you think [Hinton's] a bonehead," says Driffield to Wendover at one point, in a masterpiece of a backhanded compliment. "He's not that. I should say he has the knack of seeing the obvious just a shade quicker than most people."[93]

Connington also devises some humorous exchanges among Inspector Hinton, the village tobacconist and grocer, Mr. Copdock, and Copdock's relation Jane Anne Tugby, a maidservant at Edgehill. Miss Tugby's nose for gossip at the Big House inspires Connington to make an amusing comparison between the maid's amateur sociological researches and the experiments of men of science (like Alfred Walter Stewart):

> Miss Tugby, in fact, like many a distinguished scientist, "wanted to know about things." The pursuit of knowledge for its own sake, without ulterior design, was her object. And since the field of her researches was human nature, it would ill become the most eminent student of mere atoms and molecules to disclaim spiritual kinship with so zealous an investigator.
>
> In most scientists the thirst of knowledge is accompanied by the desire to publish to the world the results which they have acquired.... Here the orthodox scientist had a decided advantage over Miss Tugby, who had no *Journal* or *Transactions* in which to record her discoveries. But Nature ever finds a way.[94]

Praised at the time by both Dorothy L. Sayers and "Francis Iles" (the name under which crime novelist Anthony Berkeley Cox did book reviews), *The Ha-Ha Case* continued the impressive run of sardonic mystery novels by the "Clever Mr. Connington" (as he was now dubbed on book jackets by his English publisher, Hodder and Stoughton). In her review of the tale, Sayers rightly took time out to note its effective characterization, something rarely associated today with Humdrum authors:

> There is no need to say that Mr. Connington has given us a sound and interesting plot, very carefully and ingeniously worked out. In addition, there are the three portraits of the three brothers, cleverly and rather subtly characterized, of the [governess], and of Inspector Hinton, whose admirable qualities are counteracted by that besetting sin of the man who has made his own way: a jealousy of delegating responsibility.[95]

The reviewer for the *Times Literary Supplement* suggested hopefully that perhaps Clinton Driffield had actually mellowed in *The Ha-Ha Case*: "Those who have never really liked Sir Clinton's perhaps excessively soldierly manner will be surprised to find that he makes his discovery not only by the pure light of intelligence, but partly as a reward for amiability and tact, qualities in which the Inspector [Hinton] was strikingly deficient."[96] This is true enough, but the reader still sees much of the classic Sir Clinton is his subtly sarcastic treatment of Hinton, as well as in the unsentimental Social Darwinist sentiments he utters at the end of the novel.

The next year saw Clinton Driffield return in yet another excellent tale, *In Whose Dim Shadow*, refreshingly set not in a country house but rather a modern suburban neighborhood and dealing with matters of adultery, bigamy and blackmail. The mystery plot is well-clued and compelling, the kicker of a closing paragraph is a classic of its kind, and, additionally, the author paints some excellent character portraits, particularly those of a pushy freelance journalist, a callow Christian evangelist, a careworn Frenchwoman in a marriage of convenience to a bigamist and an introverted, elderly clerk who dreams of traveling to Japan. Surprisingly in a Connington tale, the clerk, Mr. Mitford, is a figure presented with some poignancy. Mitford's one great goal in life is to visit the storybook Japan of his dreams before it is vanquished entirely by the forces of modernization, but, alas, he is not destined to achieve his goal. I fully agree with the *Sunday Times* assessment of the tale: "Quiet domestic murder, full of the neatest detective points.... [T]hese are not the detective's stock figures, but fully realized human beings."[97]

Nearly twenty months elapsed between the publication of *In Whose Dim Shadow* (1935) and the author's next book, *A Minor Operation* (1937)—an unusually long time for Connington, who published one book (and sometimes two books) every year between 1926 and 1940, with the exception of 1936. The reason for the author's delay in production was the onset in 1935–36 of the afflictions of cataracts and heart disease (he ultimately would succumb to the latter in 1947). When nearing the end of his composition of *In Whose Dim Shadow* in the spring of 1935, Connington found his own eyesight was going dim. "I was really surprised on looking over the book," Connington later recalled to his friend Rupert Gould, "to find how I managed to keep up the lightheartedness of dialogue toward the end, for the latter part of the book was written when I was so blind I couldn't read a word I was typing." The author was blinded by cataracts in both eyes and had to have operations later that year to restore his eyesight. In February 1936, nearly a year after he had completed *In Whose Dim Shadow*, Connington was "still putting off from week to week the start of a new book, with a conscience worrying me daily over it. Since these two operations on my eyes, I don't seem to have got back into proper trim, for some reason or other." However, soon the author was reporting to Gould that "in connection with a new tec yarn, I have been thinking over the problem of sending a message which could not be traced to the sender." Connington had devised a gimmick for making it more difficult to identify the type used in a telegram message, and this gimmick found its way into a new detective novel manuscript. Additional eye operations in April (three in ten days) interrupted the author's work; but by the fourteenth he had had his final daily dose of atropine and was able to get back to writing. "When I saw my specialist this time," Connington informed Gould, "he wanted to know how I was going to meet his challenge to write a tale dealing with a nursing home; but I think I took him aback by saying he'd find a cataract operation in my next book!" The title of the new Connington mystery opus would be *A Minor Operation*.[98]

Yet fate had not tired of hazarding with Connington's health. On May 29, 1936, the author had his first heart attack, an event he detailed, with the mordant humor of his creation Clinton Driffield, eight days later in another letter to Gould, "written in bed, recumbent, with a drawing board looming over me": "[On May 29] woke up at 3 A.M. feeling Browning was mistaken when he said 'All's right with the world.' An hour later, felt quite sure he was wrong + clamored for morphia to dull the pain. If I'd had only myself to consider, I'd have given in + passed in my cheques, I imagine." Not until August 21, nearly three months later, would doctors allow Connington to "descend and ascend a stair once per diem, and resort to my study four hours a day." On August 31, however, the author informed Gould that his agent having "booked me to turn out a short story in less than a week," he had been "able to get an idea, work it out, write it up and deliver the M.S.

Alfred Walter Stewart's house in Belfast (built in 1923 or 1924). According to Stewart's daughter, Irene, "the bottom left hand window was that of the Study — it deserves a capital 'S' — where his books were written, and the family also lived" (Irene Stewart to the author, 14 August 2011, courtesy Irene Stewart).

in London last Saturday (less than four days occupied in all)." This feat convinced him that he was "slowly recovering normal brain power." Connington spent much of September with his wife and daughter motor touring his beloved Scottish highlands (his wife doing the driving); but after this trip he was again hard at work on *A Minor Operation*. He reported having completed the tale ("with a sigh of relief") in a letter to Gould dated October 26. "I find that I have written about 30,000 words in less than a month," wrote the author, "which is at least proof that I haven't lost fluency completely."[99]

Of his latest work, Connington reflected, "I'm not much enamored with it; but then one never feels satisfied with anything one has just finished." Critics were much more admiring than the author, finding the new novel a strong addition to the Connington corpus. Milward Kennedy opened his *Sunday Times* review by noting that "it is a long time since I had the good fortune to read a book by J.J. Connington." With *A Minor Operation*, Kennedy declared, his fellow author had proven "again that the murder-plot is capable of as many variations as the love-story, and that he has very few superiors in its construction." For its part, the *Times Literary Supplement* asserted that *A Minor Operation* treated the reader "to exactly the right mixture of mystification and clue." In addition to its impressive construction, the *TLS* added, the novel had "character-drawing above the average," particularly in the case of the ex-convict Nicholas Adeney. More recently, *A Catalogue of Crime* deemed the tale "in many ways a classic," with "Sir Clinton ... in his very best form."[100]

A Minor Operation is indeed a strong Connington, although it is more streamlined than his other best tales, possibly reflecting the author's medical problems at the time of its composition. The novel involves the intertwined mysteries of the disappearance of a classic Connington "pretty girl" ("To judge from Mrs. Butterswick's description," reflects Inspector Dornfell, "Hazel Deerhurst must have been the kind of girl that men would look twice at, and railway officials and bus conductors are human, like the rest of us") and the murder of her despicable businessman husband, only just released from jail.[101] The mystery of Hazel Deerhurst's disappearance is extremely well-clued and cleverly deduced by Driffield, who indeed is in top form. Two-thirds of the way through the novel, Driffield tabulates for Inspector Dornfell and Squire Wendover (and the reader) a dozen clues to the whereabouts of Hazel Deerhurst, but chances are the reader, like Dornfell and Wendover, will still not see the truth. The murder problem is marginally less successful, because the case against the murderer seems to come together too easily in a rather summary last chapter. Additionally, the characterization, which starts out quite strongly, fades somewhat later in the tale (and the lower-class characters are the usual caricatures). Still there are as well clever dodges concerning chemistry and typewriters and altogether *A Minor Operation* is an outstanding example of a Golden Age detective novel.

As it turned out, *A Minor Operation* also became Connington's last fully successful Clinton Driffield tale. The drop in quality between this novel and his next, *Truth Comes Limping*, which appeared the next year, 1938, is startlingly steep, with the latter tale offering only a lackluster mystery plot with dull characters and turgid writing. Better is *For Murder Will Speak*, also from 1938, but this novel remains of interest today primarily for reasons of social history discussed above. Of Connington's later mystery works, those that come closest to his previous level are the two Mark Brand tales, *The Counsellor* (1939) and *The Four Defences* (1940), and a single Driffield, *No Past Is Dead* (1942). The Mark Brand mysteries concern a short-lived series detective Connington introduced in 1939, Mark Brand, a radio advice-giver known as "The Counsellor." Brand's introduction suggests that the author had tired of his sardonic Great Detective, but Brand, though he is a good conception, never becomes a rival to Sir Clinton. Connington gives Brand a few specific character traits, such as a penchant for loud clothing, a brash manner and a love of quotations from the classics (usually misattributed by him), as well as a feisty professional sidekick, Sandra Raynham, a nice variation on the usual bland and genteel pretty girls who populate so many Connington tales. Had Connington carried through this conception with energetically paced narratives in sustained milieus, the author might have been successful in giving the world another notable detective. Unfortunately, by the time of his composition of the Counsellor tales, Connington's zest for writing novels seems to have departed (additionally, Irene Stewart has noted that "'The Counsellor' wasn't a popular move as a detective, I feel that my father wasn't really at home with him"). The first Counsellor tale — titled, reasonably enough, *The Counsellor*—is especially disappointing, though it opens promisingly, with Mark Brand determined to use his massive resources as a hugely popular radio personality to solve a mystery himself. "Seriously, Mark," asks a dubious Sandra, "do you really mean to go down there as the complete detective?" "Absolutely," responds The Counsellor, invoking the Great Detectives as his spiritual guides:

I shall take with me all the necessities. A hypodermic syringe, cocaine, a violin, a pound of shag, a Thorndyke research case, Sir Clinton Driffield's copy of Osborn's *Questioned Documents*, some of Mr. Fortune's intuitive capacity in my vest-pocket, Lord Peter Wimsey's collection of jade — I can get that into a sack over my shoulder ... and some of Poirots's little grey cells.[102]

To be sure, the puzzle in *The Four Defences*, the second Counsellor tale, is one of the author's most inspired constructions, indeed one of the most fiendishly complex of the era, Connington taking an infamous real life murder case, the Rouse blazing car affair, as his theme and composing from it a stunning set of criminal variations. The reviewer for the *Times Literary Supplement* acutely noted of the novel:

> This is in the cold-blooded category which ... excites a crossword puzzle kind of interest. Nothing in the Rouse case would prepare you for these complications upon complications.... What they prove is that Mr. Connington has the power of penetrating into the puzzle-corner of the brain. He leaves it dazedly wondering whether in the records of actual crime there can be any dark deed to equal this in its planned convolutions.[103]

With practically non-existent atmosphere and the thinnest of cardboard characters, the tale depends entirely for its interest on its brilliant murder plot, making it one of the most notable examples — for good or ill — of the Golden Age detective novel as pure puzzle.

Connington's last four novels — *The Twenty-One Clues* (1941), *No Past Is Dead* (1942), *Jack-in-the-Box* (1944) and *Commonsense Is All You Need* (1947) — are Driffield tales clearly not comparable in quality to his best earlier ones (though *No Past is Dead*, partly based on a real-life murder case, boasts an intricate plot with an ingenious alibi gambit) that were published as the heart disease that eventually killed the author worsened. Ill health forced Connington's retirement from Queen's University in 1944, the same year *Jack-in-the-Box* appeared. "I am afraid," Connington wrote a friend, the chemist and forensic scientist F. Gerald Tryhorn, in August 1946, eleven months before his death, "that I shall never be much use again. Very stupidly, I tried for a session to combine a full course of lecturing with angina pectoris; and ended up by establishing that the two are immiscible." He added that since retiring in 1944, he had been physically "limited to my house, since even a fifty-yard crawl brings on the usual cramps." After what he characterized as "my complete crack-up," Connington admitted that he "didn't feel inclined to write a tec yarn." Instead he relaxed for a time from the technical requirements of mystery plotting and composed a dozen essays on a diverse array of subjects, among them a fascinating French true crime case (which he also used as the basis for his novel *No Past is Dead*), drug use, atomic power, and Scottish legends (including that of the Loch Ness Monster), indicating a wide range of imaginative scope on his part. In these elegant short works, Irene Stewart avows, "was something of himself." The author collected his essays into a volume, *Alias J.J. Connington*, which was published, along with his final detective novel, the pithily titled but evidently over-hastily written *Commonsense Is All You Need*, in 1947, the year of the death, at the age of 66, of Alfred Walter Stewart, Emeritus Professor of Chemistry at Queen's University, Belfast. Three of Connington's works of fiction were reprinted in paperback editions after his passing: *Nordenholt's Million* (in 1948) and his mysteries *The Case with Nine Solutions* and *Death at Swaythling Court* (in 1949 and 1954 respectively), but afterward his body of work fell into decay. Strong praise in *The Catalogue of Crime* in 1972 revived a certain level of interest in Connington, however. Even Julian Symons admitted in the final edition of *Bloody Murder* (1992) that for his seminal work of criticism he had reread novels by Connington, an author he recalled favorably from "adolescent memories."[104] Yet Symons found Connington did not live up to those memories.

In my view *A Catalogue of Crime* more accurately measures Connington's worth as a writer of detective fiction. The author's best work has lasting value, both for the ingenuity of the puzzles and soundness of the detection as well as for the bracing, sometimes acerbic, narration, so at odds with the cozy stereotype of the period. Connington had a distinct and memorable voice in Golden Age detective fiction, setting him apart from not only his fellow so-called Humdrums but also from other writers in the genre. This voice can be heard as well in a cache of recently discovered correspondence between Connington and Rupert Thomas Gould, the brilliant author, radio lecturer and horologist (scientist of time measurement) best known today for having restored eighteenth-century inventor John Harrison's marine chronometers, devices which helped to measure the east-west position, or longitude, of ships at sea (the story of Gould's restoration of the marine chronometers was portrayed in a well-received 2000 film, *Longitude*). The correspondence between the two men began in September 1935, shortly after Connington wrote Gould, who the previous year had published *The Loch Ness Monster and Others*, to tell the horologist of his having viewed on Loch Ness something resembling the infamous Monster while he and his family were on a motor tour of Scotland. Initially addressing each other as "Commander Gould" and "Professor Stewart," the two men soon were going informally by just Gould and Stewart. Although the pair never actually met in person, the two men developed a warm friendship by mail, writing each other lengthy letters every month through December 1936 (sometimes nearly twenty pages in length), addressing a host of matters, including literature (the pair often lent each other books), politics, science, religion, popular culture, family, work and sex. The Alfred Walter Stewart of the correspondence often reflects the J.J. Connington of the novels: dryly humorous, frequently ironic and acerbic in his commentary on human folly and blunt and unflappable in his discussion of sexual matters. "The Titanic was the most striking of all the [sea] catastrophes," he reflected to Gould at one point, in a classic instance of a Sir Clintonesque observation. "I was here [in Belfast] when she was built, and the amount of brag about the 'unsinkable' was fairly God-provoking."[105]

Literature was the subject addressed most often by the two men in their letters to each other. In his correspondence with Gould, Connington is revealed as a voracious reader of fiction, someone whose interests spanned far beyond his professional area of expertise, chemistry. Connington, who like John Street could read French, was a great admirer of French as well as classical literature. He also enjoyed the imaginative literature of escape, including children's tales as well as science fiction and the supernatural (with the latter genre he showed great familiarity, referencing works by M.R. James, H.R. Wakefield, William Hope Hodgson, Edgar Allen Poe, Algernon Blackwood, M.P. Shiel, Arthur Machen, Marjorie Lawrence, Oliver Onions, May Sinclair, L.P. Hartley and C.H.B. Kitchin). J.J. Connington surely was one of the best read of Golden Age detective novelists, an accomplishment for which he has until now gone entirely uncredited.

Though he never established himself as a literary critic like Dorothy L. Sayers did, Connington was quite at ease in his Gould letters discussing authors and their works. Here he is, for example, on the careers of Edgar Allen Poe and Mark Twain:

[Poe and Twain] seem built for contrast. Twain got everything Poe didn't get: cash, public admiration, and a wife who kept him in leading-strings. Twain was always the great crusader boldly showing up things that didn't matter a rap, such as the Feudal system of England (!), but carefully avoiding giving any offense by tackling things that he knew needed exposure in the American system. In fact, he played for safety all along the line.... Whereas Poe fought like a tiger for his own ideals and cared nothing for unpopularity.... And there is a curious similarity between Poe and Mark Twain in the fact that their best stuff in each case is obviously "escape literature" for the author. Poe made his escape into an "unreal" world, whereas Mark Twain escaped into the Peter Pan world of Huck Finn, Tom Sawyer and the Life on the Mississippi.[106]

In explaining his disappointment with the tales of M.R. James, the Dean of the Golden Age British ghost story, Connington explained:

He never makes me speculate beyond the story, whereas to my mind the high-water mark in these affairs is to make the reader muse further over the possibility that the "normal order" is not perhaps the whole story in the Universe. Machen at his best produces this.... It's difficult to define what I mean, but it comes to this: that [Machen's] "The Great God Pan" suggests a whole possible Universe juxtaposed to ours, whereas James's ghosts seem to be mainly ex-humans who have left some little job undone and have come back to clear up this purely personal affair.[107]

Connington also reflected on the rarity of good children's literature:

Born writers for children are very rare birds indeed. In the last century or so, we have had Lear (1812–88), Kingsley (1819–75), Carroll (1832–1898) and then E. Nesbit who flourished in the nineties, and A.A. Milne in the nineteen-twenties. In fact, just about one per generation. And the surprising thing is that no "second-classers" have survived at all. Of course I exclude all such horrors as "Sandford & Merton," "The Fairchild Family," and "Little Lord Fauntleroy" from consideration. It is a surprisingly difficult genre, since apparently all the successful ones have succeeded in writing books which will amuse both children and adults.[108]

Connington's one great aversion was to post-1910 ("modern") literature, which he rather facilely declared "to be based on one abiding principle — doing things by the 'awfully easy' method, which needs no skill, talent, or pains." James Joyce's *Ulysses*, which he had read from a smuggled edition (the book was banned as obscene in Britain until 1936), he deemed "one of the dullest books I'd ever struck." The author was also dismissive of psychological fiction, noting trenchantly that while Guy de Maupassant had been sane he had been a materialist, but "as his own brain disease deepened, he turned more and more to the psychological novel." He dryly added: "From which you will have little difficulty in surmising that I don't rate the psychological novel very highly."[109]

It should be noted that Connington objected to Joyce's *Ulysses* not on grounds of obscenity, but on grounds of "dullness." Connington's Gould letters indicate that he was not easily offended by the subject of sex. Indeed, he adopted a rather detached and cynically amused attitude about humanity's sexual foibles. On sexual matters, wrote the author to Gould, again sounding reminiscent of his fictional detective Sir Clinton Driffield, "I have got, like Nietzsche, 'Beyond Good and Evil' and I am not of the shockable breed. Quite case-hardened, in fact." Illustrative of Connington's assertion is his observation in one letter concerning "a large tome on the witch cult, by a lady graduate of London University, a Miss Somebody or other." She "speculates at large on the sexual endurance in the Sabbath and avows that it seems more than human," noted Connington humorously. "How does *she* know?" Still, he matter-of-factly agreed with the good lady in her conjecture that "an artificial member was employed by the man personating Satan."[110]

Connington was equally amused (and very much interested) by a book on the infamous Pemberton-Billing trial sent him by Gould. In 1918, the right-wing newspaper of Noel Pemberton-Billing, a member of parliament, published an article, "The Cult of Clitoris," alleging that performers and attendees at the premiere stage performance of Oscar Wilde's long-banned play *Salome* numbered among an alleged list of 47,000 prominent "perverts" being blackmailed by the Germans into betraying the war effort. Maud Allen, the lead performer in *Salome*, sued Pemberton-Billing for libel, alleging that the M.P. was accusing her of lesbianism. The trial degenerated into mayhem, with Pemberton-Billing putting Oscar Wilde on trial yet again — Wilde's former lover, Lord Alfred Douglas, now a devout Catholic, even appeared to testify to Wilde's malign intentions with *Salome*. In the end, Pemberton-Billing was found not guilty.[111]

After reading the book of the trial in bed while convalescing from his heart attack, Connington wrote Gould delightedly: "The Pemberton-Billing Affair kept me amused for a day.... What an affair! I've seldom seen so much ignorance displayed in any trial by presumably competent legal lights. Fancy a judge who had never heard the word "orgasm," and a barrister who confuses sadism with necrophilia. Surely they might keep a dictionary at hand when they take on cases of this kind."[112]

Sympathizing with Lord Alfred Douglas, who he thought had "tried to live down his disgrace," Connington expressed disgust with the attempt by the plaintiff's attorney to rake up Douglas' past. Yet of Oscar Wilde himself, Connington wrote in a later letter, "I think he got what he deserved. I have pity for the natural invert, whose position seems a dreadful one; but Oscar was a pure pervert, with whose case I haven't a spark of sympathy."[113] Here the author was expressing sentiments that would find their way a couple years later into his 1938 detective novel *For Murder Will Speak*, which shows sympathy for "inverts" driven by physical causes to engage in abnormal sexual behavior. No doubt Connington saw Oscar Wilde as a willful homosexual profligate, hence a "pure pervert."

Connington evidently saw no suggestion of perversion in his correspondent Gould's rather ingenuous confession in one letter of a fascination with female bondage. Indeed, Connington was able to recommend to the horologist several works that might fit his peculiar taste for what Connington termed "abductiana," including a couple French novels, *Peril Bleu* and *Caresco, Surhomme*, as well as S. Fowler Wright's *The Island of Captain Sparrow*, in the latter of which, Connington blithely informed Gould, "the heroine is taken prisoner by a genuine half-breed satyr with horns complete."[114] To be sure, Gould assured Connington that he loathed actual cruelty and violence and had no interest in "acting out" his own peculiar sexual fantasies, which admittedly marks a difference between Gould and Wilde, who in contrast with Gould gloried in physically actualizing his desires.

Connington assured Gould that he too hated physical cruelty: "There seems to be enough of it in the world without my going out of the way to add to the sum total." Yet, indicative of the sometimes harsh strain in the Connington works, the author, on hearing of the IRA assassination of Vice-Admiral Somerville (he had recruited for the Royal Navy in County Cork) speculated to Gould on "whether capital punishment should not be reinforced by a good sound course of scientific torture — e.g. coupling up with a big induction coil for five minutes at a time throughout the day before the actual execution." Calculated "poisoners and gunmen really need something more than mere painless hanging as a deterrent," he concluded wrathfully.[115]

A certain elitism and cultural conservatism emerges in Connington's letters. Sometimes this is amusingly expressed, as when the author commented on one of his favorite essays in Edmund Lester Pearson's *Books in Black and Red* (1923), another book Gould lent him:

> The tale of the 'literary man' on page 88 reminded me that once I leased a furnished flat from a young married couple. I found that their library consisted of six volumes of the pocket edition of Kipling. "Well, after all, they do read something," I mused charitably. Then I took down the books and found the pages still stuck together by the gilt edges! They'd never been opened since some misguided friend had given them as a wedding present apparently. So at least that bride was spared the horror of finding out she'd married a literary man.

About another book he enjoyed Connington concluded bluntly that it "would never be popular with the man on the street. Its allusions demand some sort of education in the reader to get the full pleasure of it, and that must cut down the possible public very considerably."[116]

In his letters to Gould, Connington expressed deep distaste for aspects of modern popular culture. Coming across ads for practical joke devices, including a whoopee cushion ("WHEN ANYONE SITS DOWN IT GIVES THE MOST INDESCRIBABLE NOISES") and surprise soap ("WHEN YOU TRY TO WASH, YOUR FACE TURNS BLACK"), Connington deemed that they give "a more depressing picture of humanity than even Swift." Similarly, after seeing an obnoxiously conspicuous billboard on a Scottish motor tour the author concluded that "modern advertising is the limit":

> Going down Glencoe [cite of the infamous 1692 massacre of the MacDonald clan], we passed a huge board about 20 feet square, with the lettering:
> FORK RIGHT FOR THE BLANK HOTEL
> *ON THE SITE OF THE MASSACRE*
> LUNCHEONS, TEAS, ETC.

"I suppose after the next war," Connington concluded mordantly, "Macaulay's New Zealander will be faced with a hoarding: SITE OF LONDON/TEA, BED AND BREAKFAST/TERMS MODERATE/PARKING PERMITTED."[117]

Concerning political matters, Connington emerges in his letters as a typical enough specimen of the British conservative of the period, committed to the idea of the Empire and hopefully espying imperial resurgence just around the corner. Despite the authoritarian tone and Nordic symbolism of *Nordenholt's Million* and his own pre–World War I education in Germany, Connington held a poor opinion of the country under the Nazi regime, writing, for example, "German diplomacy is running true to type again [i.e., clumsily bellicose]. That race has never been civilized, probably owing to the fact that it never had any share in the Roman civilization." He placed the blame for German savagery on the Prussian influence in the country, reflecting that during his years in Germany he had "found the South German a decent enough creature." It was the Prussian whom he found he could not "abide at any price." Nor did Connington hold the French in much higher political esteem than he did the Germans (despite his love of French literature), complaining of them at one point: "These beggars seem to think that we are some sort of vassals of theirs in European questions." His solution to the problem of renewed German aggression in Europe was to let Germany and France battle it out, while England stood aside and rearmed. "If they want to fight," declared Connington, "my inclination is to let them mutually exhaust themselves and then we could step in with real effect and dictate a peace rather better then Versailles." If only Britain would keep out of European entanglements until she had completed rearmament, Connington avowed with misplaced confidence, the country "very soon will be once again the biggest factor in international affairs."[118]

Not altogether surprisingly, the author based his condemnations of Germany — as well as Italy and Japan — not on any abstract humanitarian concerns, but rather on matters of pure power politics. The public moral outrage over the Italian invasion of Ethiopia, for example, Connington dismissed as misplaced sentimentalism. What concerned him was not the fate of "this Selassie fellow" and his followers, but "the possibility of the Gippies [Egyptians] beginning to intrigue against us with their new Italian neighbors."[119] The League of Nations he dismissed as utterly inept and useless as a means of preventing war, although he conceded the organization had done some good in suppressing drug trafficking and white slavery.

Also not unexpectedly, Connington tends to write dismissively of religion and religious figures. "I never did like St. Paul," he admits at one point, "I'm sure I'd never have asked him in to tea, had he been a contemporary. What a tortuous mind the fellow had!" Of American evangelicalism, a subject raised by Gould, Connington tells his friend that "one of my young fellows [a student of his at Queen's College] was over in America with a Rockefeller Fellowship last year and he penetrated into the Fundamentalist Belt at one time and got a severe shock when he found it wasn't all newspaper chat! He had never really believed there were people like that!" Another time he related a more personal experience when he tells Gould how the young woman he had got engaged to in his mid-twenties "died suddenly after the wedding-presents had come in.... I heard that a parson had the good taste to use my case as an illustration in his sermon on the following Sunday! All was grist that came to his mill, evidently; but I'm afraid I never spoke to him again." Similarly, Connington wrote of his distaste of having to visit his parson brother-in-law (one of his wife's elder brothers, Reverend Holms Coats, then Principal of the Scottish Baptist College) while motor touring in Scotland. "Did you ever meet your mental and spiritual antithesis (or perhaps antipole would be a better word)," he sardonically asked Gould. "I had to drop in and see my brother-in-law while across the water and, as usual, we hadn't a single subject where we weren't at cross-purposes. It's a long-standing business.... Now he is a parson and 'gooder' than ever and still we seem unable to see eye to eye on any subjects whatever. It's quite an education to see what one would look like if one were turned into one's mirror-image."[120]

In many of the sentiments expressed in his books and letters, Connington comes off as rather clinical, even scornful at times; yet he maintained numerous friendships with colleagues and students, enjoying a wide list of correspondents like Rupert Gould, and he seems to have gotten along well with his wife, Lily, and daughter, Irene (born 1921), which suggests a more personable side to the private man. To be sure, he occasionally wrote with exasperation of the follies of the students at Queen's College, like the young woman who nearly blew up a room with a bottle of ether or the third-year medicals who came close to combusting his entire department. "But you've no notion what a nerve-wracking business it is, dealing with the modern student," he informed Gould. "Not so long ago, a third-year girl was discovered hugging an eighty-ounce bottle of ether, with which she was soaking her over-all in order to remove stains (that's hardly what we supply ether for). Anyhow, there she was, dripping with ether, and with a lighted Bunsen burner within a few feet of her. Luckily someone made a dash for it and turned it off." Disaster was averted in this instance, but there was another close shave Connington recalled having had. "Most people think the academic life delightfully free from petty worries. Just judge for yourself," he wrote Gould. Connington, it seems, had lent a colleague his lecture theater, for use with a class of boisterous third year medicals; and things degenerated rapidly from there:

> Yesterday, these bright young things, full of Guy Fawkes spirit, brought a load of squibs into the place and amused themselves by setting them off while waiting for my colleague to arrive and start his lecture. Result, one squib got through a crack in the floor and fell into the space below, which is our only store for empty packing-cases, wood-shaving packing, and other tinder. Luckily someone happened to be in the store and put his foot on the squib instanter. Had he not been there, my Department would have gone up in flames.... Between this sort of thing and the cases of damsels cleaning grease from their over-alls with ether a foot or two from a Bunsen flame, you can imagine that the Staff leads an anxious life. I sometimes wish I had gone in for an English lecture chair instead of a chemistry one![121]

Despite his complaints, however, Connington always was pleased to see a student of his make good. Discussing the case of one of his students, who had made a great success of studying river pollution in the Tees Valley, Connington proudly admitted, "it's very nice to see one of one's cubs tackling a complex affair of that sort and coming out successfully ("cub" is a term of rough affection the author often uses for younger males in his mystery novels). Connington also maintained a warm correspondence with a number of his professional colleagues and intellectual acquaintances, like Gerald Tryhorn and Rupert Gould. While he did not suffer gladly those whom he deemed fools, he happily engaged and supported those whom he could intellectually respect. One professor whom Connington recalled fondly not altogether surprisingly "feared neither God nor man and had a tongue like a file." Connington amusingly retailed to Gould an anecdote of how the professor, nicknamed Cocky, had put a pretentious young prig of a student back in his proper place:

> One day at the start of a session — not in my time — he began to call the roll and got down to the S's. 'Mr. Smith?' No answer. 'Mr. J. Smith?' Whereupon arose a dandiacal gentlemen and said: 'Excuse me. Professor Young, but my name is Smythe.' Cocky glared at him for a moment, then snorted, and said: 'H'm! Some people call it shit, others call it shite! Same thing!'[122]

To be sure, Connington was as unsparing of erring colleagues as he was of blundering students, mirthfully discussing, for example, the case of a pedantic editor of the *Chemical Society Journal*

> who got the idea that he knew all about English and how it should be writ. Among his notions was one to the effect that "But" was a conjunction and could not be used at the beginning of a sentence. BUT (!) in this he had the misfortune to differ from another pedant and the second pedant proceeded to read through the complete works of Shakespeare, Milton, Dickens, Thackeray, and several others, with the sole object of reckoning up the number of cases in which they started sentences with "But." The ensuing correspondence reached 29 letters on either side — all of which I unfortunately had to suffer, since one of the combatants took me as his confidant.... [I]t is amusing to find people squabbling over such niceties when Shakespeare didn't even bother to make his verb agree with his subject.[123]

Alfred Walter Stewart with Lily (left) and with daughter Irene, c. 1932. Stewart loved motoring over his native Scotland with his wife, Lily, and his daughter, Irene. On one such trip, the family even made a "Nessie" sighting (which led to the establishment of Stewart's close epistolary friendship with Rupert Thomas Gould) (courtesy Irene Stewart).

During his discussion with Gould of the sexually explicit Aristophanes play *Lysistrata*, Connington could not refrain from mocking a colleague who recently had "assured me, almost with tears in his eyes, that Greek literature was absolutely pure as the driven snow.... I am left wondering whether he was an outrageous liar, or, alternatively, so childish that he didn't know what the Greeks were talking about at times." And with another man who tried to cadge copies of Connington novels from the author he was openly contemptuous. "A colleague ... discovered rather late in the day that I wrote tec yarns," Connington recalled. "One had just appeared and he remarked effusively to me: 'You must lend us a copy, so we can read it!' I'm afraid he was referred to the nearest circulating library." Once again sounding like his fictional creation, Sir Clinton Driffield, the author scornfully concluded: "Really, the human animal makes a curious specimen for study, if one had the time to bother about it."[124]

Connington referred with great affection to his only child, his daughter Irene, who was a teenager at the time he was writing the Gould letters. He kept Gould, who had two children himself, updated throughout the correspondence as to what books Irene was reading and what films she was seeing (Gould, though not Connington, was a film buff). During one of his *Children's Hour* lectures, Gould mentioned Irene by name, an event that Irene much to her consternation missed, she having gone with friends to see *Werewolf of London*. Gould later sent her a novelization of the film *King Kong*, complete with stills (Connington and Gould themselves were interested in how the effect of the giant ape clutching Fay Wray in his hand was managed).[125] Connington mentioned his wife, Lily, much less, though I should note that in my possession is a copy of *Nordenholt's Million* inscribed "from Lily Stewart in memory of her husband A.W. Stewart, J.J. Connington my intimate friend died July 30 1947."

An uncharacteristically sentimental note sounds in Connington's explanation for his turning down Gould's offer to send him the licentious *Lysistrata* illustrations by Aubrey Beardsley. Connington declined to see them not because of his wife, but out of respect for Beardsley, who begged on his deathbed that all copies of the illustrations be destroyed. "I expect [Beardsley] was really scared stiff by some priest or other on his death-bed, poor chap," reflected the author. "Some of those people are really merciless."[126] Still, out of respect to Beardsley, Connington felt bound to honor the last request of a man for whom as an artist he had so much admiration.

Certainly from the perspective of someone writing (or reading) about a detective novelist, the thoughts of that person on crime literature are of interest; and in his correspondence with Gould, Connington recorded some notable statements on mystery genre aesthetics. These statements, previously unknown, are especially significant coming as they do from one of the more important writers of detection in the period. Additionally, in several letters Connington also gave fascinating nitty-gritty detail, again previously unknown, about how he personally went about writing detective fiction. Taken cumulatively, this material offers an important addition to our knowledge of the theory and practice of the art of the Golden Age detective novel.

As his frequent term for his detective novels, "tec yarns," suggests, the author was modest about his work in the mystery genre. Connington rejected the view — at the time he was corresponding with Gould expressed, for example, by Dorothy L. Sayers in her bestselling novel, *Gaudy Night,* and by Milward Kennedy in the *Sunday Times* crime novel review column — that the detective novelist should aspire to raise the form to higher art. "You can't mix a detective story with a novel of character and manners, no matter what people say," Connington insisted. "If you are going to have a mystery, then you can't give the psychology of the murderer, or there is no mystery. And if you give the psychology of all the other characters, then the omitted actor is bound to be the murderer, and again there is no mystery. But people don't seem to see this."[127] Considering that *Gaudy Night* at this time was drawing much attention to Dorothy L. Sayers' detective novel as novel of manners advocacy, it is hard not to see Connington's words as a rebuke of Sayers specifically.

For his part, Gould informed Connington that he preferred the two earliest Connington novels, *Nordenholt's Million* and *Almighty Gold*, to the later tales of detection, because he found them the more serious works. "Your detective tales of murder and mystery are marvels of ingenuity, but they tell your readers little or nothing of what you think with regard to the big problems of modern life," Gould avowed. "I would rather have another *Nordenholt's Million* or *Almighty Gold* than a dozen thrillers." In response, Connington, though he wrote rather dismissively of *Almighty Gold* as an unsuccessful work, disclaimed on his part any serious intent whatsoever in the writing of detective novels, thus essentially conceding Gould's point. "Heaven forfend that you should imagine I take myself for anything out of the common in the tec yarn stuff," he self-deprecatingly declared. "I write these things because they amuse me in parts when I am putting them together and because they are the only writings of mine that the public will look at. Also, in a minor degree, because I like to think some people get pleasure out of them. But I should be surprised if anyone found a philosophy of life hinted at in them, for certainly I had no intention of putting it there, not even a 'little.'"[128]

In Connington's view, the greatest living detective novelist, who stood in a class by himself, was R. Austin Freeman, creator of the great scientific detective, Dr. John Thorndyke. Freeman was at this time the Dean of British detective novelists, Arthur Conan Doyle having died a half-dozen years earlier. Over the thirty odd years that Freeman had been writing detective fiction, Connington had derived great "intellectual amusement" from the elder man's works. Austin Freeman "is the best of our crew of detective story writers and the only one of us who has given a fresh twist to the detective story since it left Poe's hands," wrote Connington emphatically. "The pity is that he has not received anything like enough recognition for this originality." However, while Connington praised the authoritatively-presented science in Freeman's Thorndyke tales (clearly the "fresh twist to the detective story" to which he was referring), he deprecated what he saw as the excessive love interest in them, a critical take that should not come as a surprise to anyone familiar with Connington's own novels, which emphasize technical ingenuity and downplay romance. "Thorndyke's assistants have a distressing aptitude for falling in love with wronged heroines," conceded Connington of his hero's tales, to which Gould, also an admirer of Freeman's, concurred: "[T]he lovemaking is distressing."[129]

This minor criticism notwithstanding, Connington found the last Freeman novel he had read (probably *Dr. Thorndyke Intervenes*, 1933) "quite up to his standard, and that means much better than 90 percent of the rest of us." Indeed, Connington admitted that Freeman "is about the only tec writer I read nowadays. I avoid the others for fear of absorbing an idea from them, forgetting where it came from, and innocently producing it as my own later on." Fortunately, one could read Freeman "without any qualms of that sort, since his ideas are always stamped plainly with his individual seal and couldn't be mistaken for anyone else's."[130]

It was to the redoubtable Freeman that Connington turned when, after his heart attack, he needed to read aloud to get back into fettle for delivering his class lectures. Pulling off the shelf Freeman's first published Thorndyke novel, *The Red Thumbmark*, Connington began reading it for an hour or two daily to Irene Stewart. "I have been reading [Irene] 'The Red Thumbmark,'" explained Connington, "and Austin Freeman would be much flattered if he heard her comments on its interest.... [S]he spotted the criminal before a third of the book was read, and was able to give perfectly sound reasons for her selection." Connington added that the next book on their agenda was Freeman's *The Eye of Osiris*, which he hoped for Freeman's sake would defeat his daughter's "detective capacity."[131]

Himself a personal friend of Austin Freeman's, Rupert Gould urged Connington to write the great detective novelist (Connington and Freeman had never met, despite the fact that both men were charter Detection Club members). Finally Connington did so, and in December 1936 he was honored to receive a letter from the older author. "Some time ago, I pulled myself together and wrote to Austin Freeman," Connington informed

Gould, "and this morning I got a reply from him, though I had specifically asked him not to bother." Connington deemed the letter from Freeman "very nice indeed." The earliest works of Freeman went back to Connington's college days in London, not long after the turn of the century; and Connington clearly must have mentioned something of the romance of hansom cabs in these old tales, for he delightedly reported to Gould that Freeman "mentioned there is still at least one hansom cab in London."[132]

Connington also enjoyed the works of Arthur Conan Doyle, though he was dismissive of Doyle's interest in spiritualism ("when the spirits came in, the common-sense oozed out"). In one letter to Gould, Connington noted derisively that a critic once had accused the creator of Sherlock Holmes "of having 'no style'." What this really meant, Connington countered, in another statement of his aesthetic orthodoxy, was that Doyle "wrote so clearly that one's attention was never distracted by 'stylistic' displays." In other words, Doyle knew how to tell a straightforward, entertaining tale without adding a lot of unnecessary, "literary" folderol. "My own explanation of the present vogue of the tec yarn," Connington expounded, "is simply that current novels are such poor stuff that any tec yarn gives better entertainment than they do."[133]

Despite Gould's expressed preference for Connington's earlier, "serious" works and Connington's own modesty about his "tec yarns," as the two men's correspondence lengthened Connington was pleased to find that Gould was reading some of his detective novels as well. The exchanges between these two distinguished men on the subject of Connington's mystery fiction offer an interesting glimpse on how Golden Age readers of classical tales of detection regarded this particular writing craft. Both Gould and Connington emphasized technical ingenuity and fair play, though Gould occasionally praised some of the tales on grounds of literary style as well.

In April 1936 Gould bought and read a copy of Connington's *The Ha-Ha Case* and was soon mentioning in a letter to his friend how much he had enjoyed it. Part of his pleasure he derived from having deduced the murder method: [**SPOILER ALERT**] "I am proud to say that I spotted the trick with the cut cartridge and the smooth-bore. Previously, I thought the murderer might have used what the Boers call Loopers—slugs loosely wired together." He did, however, make a tentative criticism of the tale on fair play grounds, explaining to Connington that "you had so effectively enlisted my sympathies on [X]'s side in the earlier chapters that I felt vaguely that I had been sold a pup when [X] turned out to be the murderer."[134] Interestingly, Gould effectively was suggesting to Connington—who had disclaimed any intention of trying to make his tec yarns novels of character—that the detective novelist had made his murderer in *The Ha-Ha Case* too rounded and sympathetic.

In his response Connington countered that he had not sold his killer as a pup, but, to the contrary, had fairly clued the negative side of that person's personality: "I don't know why your sympathy was enlisted on [X]'s side, because I took special pains to show that [X] could hardly open [his/her] mouth without making some remark about money. [X's] peculiar fascination escaped me!" On the matter of the cut cartridge and the smooth bore, Connington congratulated his friend on his pertinacity: "If you got the length of spotting the cartridge you were laps ahead of the field." Connington wryly mentioned receiving shortly after the novel's publication two letters by "almost the same post": in the first the writer had complained that the murder method portrayed in *The Ha-Ha Case* (which involved the use of cut cartridges) was an impossibility, while in the second the writer had assured the author that he himself "used cut cartridges regularly for some shots and had even fired them from a choke-bore."[135] **[END SPOILER ALERT]**

Pleased that Gould had enjoyed *The Ha-Ha Case*, Connington sent his friend copies he had come across of several other of his tec yarns: *The Eye in the Museum*, *The Sweepstake Murders*, *The Case with Nine Solutions* and *Nemesis at Raynham Parva*. Of these titles he was dismissive of two, *The Eye in the Museum* ("I don't reckon it as one of my best") and *Nemesis at Raynham Parva* ("personally, I think the White Slavery book is rather a poor one"), while he was rather more proud of the remaining pair. *The Case with Nine Solutions* "made rather a neat problem in elimination" he still believed; while he assured Gould of *The Sweepstake Murders*, "you can take it that the photographic stuff in that book is quite accurate, as I tried the whole thing out myself to make sure it 'worked'."[136]

In one of his letters Gould mentions having read both *Sweepstake* and *Nemesis* before passing them on to a solicitor friend of his who was a great fan of detective fiction. **[SPOILER ALERT]** Of the former he boasted of spotting how the second murder was committed, which "rather gave the show away." Further, he asserted that another of the novel's key gimmicks (involving photography) had appeared in similar form in the L.T. Meade and Robert Eustace story "East of North" (he even cited the exact issue of *The Strand* in which the story had appeared, October 1899). Gould also candidly admitted, "I hae ma doots bout the forged typewritten letters," in that the novel's villain took enormous and arguably foolish risks typing and planting them. **[END SPOILER ALERT]** However, he added a note of praise for one of the characters — "a most natural old beast" — and declared himself "lost in admiration at the way in which your opening chapter manages to introduce most of the characters, and give one a good idea of their personalities, by natural dialogue, without any forcing."[137]

Of *Nemesis*, Gould first declared himself "entirely at one with Sir Clinton in my opinion of what ought to be done to such people [as white slavers]." **[SPOILER ALERT]** Yet he added that he thought Sir Clinton "took enormous risks" in murdering Francia, the villainous white slaver of the tale. "Suppose Francia had chucked the papers down, and got up out of the chair, as soon as Driffield had left the room: or had even shifted his position slightly. The shot might have missed him altogether, or only wounded him — and then the fat *would* have been in the fire."[138] **[END SPOILER ALERT]**

To the brilliant polymath Gould — who is occasionally termed "pedantic" by his biographer, Jonathan Betts — this picking of logical nits must have been irresistible, and Connington took the critique in good stride, standing his ground on some points, but giving way on others. **[SPOILER ALERT]** Of *Sweepstake*, he countered:

> I think you do me some injustice over the typing of the incriminating letters. Suppose the villain had been spotted at the typewriter by a visitor or the maid; all he had to do was to drop that part of his plan and not use the letters. He was not endangering himself until he actually used them. And I took care to point out that the maid, in the garden, was out of earshot. However, I believe in confessing my errors, and you are undoubtedly on the nail when you say the letters should have been signed by an initial and not in full.[139]

Concerning the photography gimmick, Connington insisted, "I am quite innocent of any plagiarism of intent." However, he admitted that he had read the Meade and Eustace stories in *The Strand* over thirty years previously "and it is possible that the idea may have floated up out of the subconscious when I needed something of the sort." He reiterated that "it is just the fear of this happening which keeps me from reading my competitors nowadays." However, he added, "I really think that in this case I was independent of previous suggestions."[140] **[END SPOILER ALERT]**

After running Gould's critical *Sweepstakes* gauntlet, the detective novelist thanked him "for the compliment on the character drawing," admitting he found it "very pleasant" to read that he "had managed to pull it off." Of Gould's points against *Nemesis*, Connington said much less, conceding, as mentioned above, that he now thought the tale "rather a poor one"; yet he did remind Gould that "every murder implies risks to the criminal and luck must play an enormous part in a successful murder."[141]

At one point, Gould and Connington debated not merely plot detail in Connington's own books, but as well the broader matter of crime novel aesthetic standards. Here, Connington again revealed himself as holding a more traditional view of the matter, disdaining literary innovation on fair play grounds. When Gould suggested the idea of a Jekyll-Hyde type murderer — a "Jekyll" who had no notion the murderer was himself in his "Hyde" persona — Connington dashed cold water on the idea, arguing that it would be seen by reviewers as a cheat on the reader. In his next letter, an undaunted Gould responded. "I note what you say about the dual personality murderer, and about reviewers damning such a plot as not legitimate," wrote Gould. "But surely the laws of detective fiction are themselves fictitious.... I regard 'The Murders in the Rue Morgue' as a masterpiece. Is it a fair criticism to say that making an ape the murderer is 'illegitimate'?"[142]

Before receiving this response from Gould, Connington had already written his friend another letter, in which he mentioned reading a review in the *Times Literary Supplement* damning a novel for having employed precisely the dual-personality murderer device that Gould had coincidentally suggested! A week later, now having received Gould's response, Connington conceded that Gould was "quite right about the idea of the 'laws' of detective fiction, which have mainly been erected by folk who do not write it themselves." Connington himself believed there was "only one reasonable convention" in detective fiction, that of fair play: "The reader should always know exactly as much as the detective is supposed to know, and certainly not less than this."[143]

Connington's correspondence with Gould concerning the art of writing detective fiction suggests that the detective novelist constructed his "tec yarns" around some sort of clever technical gimmick or dodge, with characters and settings being developed later on in the writing process. *The Case with Nine Solutions*, for example, saw its inception as a mathematical question of elimination: given two deaths that could be accident, suicide or murder, how many possible combinations of outcomes are there and how can the false combinations be eliminated to reach the one true one? With *The Sweepstake Murders*, Connington emphasized most in his exchanges with Gould his bit of ingenuity with photography, while *A Minor Operation* started, as we have seen above, with a notion for sending an untraceable typed message (and as he began to plot the actual events of the latter novel, the author added his own recent real life experience of cataract operations). The novel that immediately followed *A Minor Operation* the next year (1938), *Truth Comes Limping*, began when Connington decided that he wanted his new tale to include archery. "Do you know anything about archery?" he asked Gould in November 1936, shortly after he had sent *A Minor Operation* to his publishers. "I have a glimmering notion of using it in a forthcoming book.... If you have any practical experience, I'd be glad to draw on that later on when I get the idea more or less developed."[144] He already had ordered a copy of Longman's and Waldron's 1894 book, *Archery*, he noted. Material and technical detail, not psychology or social manners, is what fascinated J.J. Connington as an author of detective fiction.

The critical tide has long turned against the Golden Age's great materialist technicians of detection — indeed, the waters already were shifting in the 1930s — but this fact does not efface J.J. Connington's standing as one of the major mystery authors of his time. For over twenty years, Alfred Walter Stewart diligently and creatively applied himself to the writing of his fair play tec yarns, and during his best years (roughly 1927 to 1937) he produced at least eight fine examples of the Golden Age art. The author's aesthetic conservatism, something to which he steadfastly adhered throughout his career as a detective novelist, led to his being damned as a "Humdrum" by those impatient with exterior, material detail; yet, while Connington has the technical expertise and plotting soundness implied by that appellation, he also can be a forceful and memorable writer, with an often strikingly blunt and cynical narration. Admittedly, in many ways Connington in his aesthetic and political conservatism conforms to the accepted and expected Golden Age mystery paradigm; yet his authorial voice nevertheless is interesting and original, not only in his fascinating if philosophically troubling apocalyptic thriller *Nordenholt's Million*, but additionally in his bracingly intelligent works of detection. J.J. Connington put not merely his scientific and technical facility into his detective fiction, but his own distinct personality as well (even if he did disclaim any conscious intention of putting into it a "philosophy of life"); and his best works emphatically merit survival.

Appendix I

Notable Criminous Works by Cecil John Charles Street

Works by "John Rhode"

Fiction

1. *The Paddington Mystery* (1925) (not a great detective novel, but it introduces a future Great Detective, Dr. Lancelot Priestley)
2. *Dr. Priestley's Quest* (1926) (Dr. Priestley emerges as a genuine Great Detective)
3. *The Ellerby Case* (1927) (a lively — and deadly — Priestley thriller in which a green hedgehog becomes an instrument of death)
4. *The Murders in Praed Street* (1928) (a mass murderer is at work, with Priestley as an intended victim)
5. *The House on Tollard Ridge* (1929) (mechanically ingenious murder, with an unconventional heroine)
6. *The Davidson Case* (1929) (Priestley's greatest case from the 1920s asks whether murder can ever be philosophically justified)
7. *Pinehurst* (1930) (Hanslet rides a bicycle; Priestley digs into a meaty mystery)
8. *The Hanging Woman* (1931) (something of a thematic sequel to *The Davidson Case*)
9. *Dead Men at the Folly* (1932) (murder on the go)
10. *The Motor Rally Mystery* (1933) (the great automotive murder case)
11. *The Claverton Mystery* (1933) (early poisoning masterpiece, darker than most of this author's tales)
12. *The Venner Crime* (1933) (something of a sequel to *The Claverton Mystery*)
13. *The Robthorne Mystery* (1934) (a clever and legitimate reworking of the identical twins device)
14. *Poison for One* (1934) (one of Street's comparatively few country house mysteries and another classic poisoning tale)
15. *Shot at Dawn* (1934) (one of the bravura performances of the Golden Age)
16. *The Corpse in the Car* (1935) (perhaps Priestley's greatest poisoning case)
17. *Hendon's First Case* (1935) (introduces Jimmy Waghorn and more poison)
18. *Mystery at Olympia* (1935) (a man is shot and poisoned — twice — but dies from another cause)
19. *Death in the Hopfields* (1937) (social realism detective novel)
20. *Death on the Board* (1937) (unscrupulous Board of Directors liquidated with a remorseless efficiency that Stalin would have envied)

21. *Proceed with Caution* (1937) (Crofts-like tale of timetables, oiled by a good pub setting and some piquant bits involving hearses and tar boilers)
22. *Invisible Weapons* (1938) (Dr. Priestley makes the murder weapons "visible")
23. *The Bloody Tower* (1938) (atmospheric, anti-romantic tale of country house squalor)
24. *Death Pays a Dividend* (1939) (Jimmy Waghorn meets Diana Morpeth)
25. *Death on Sunday* (1939) (a good deal of satire in this tale of murder at a genteel guest house)
26. *Death on the Boat Train* (1940) (good alibi and an entertaining look at a mega-millionaire's milieu)
27. *Death at the Helm* (1941) (murder matters in this tale)
28. *They Watched by Night* (1941) (ingenious spying and even more ingenious murdering)
29. *Dead on the Track* (1943) (Superintendent Hanslet's Greatest Case)
30. *Men Die at Cyprus Lodge* (1943) (a house lethally haunted by an inoffensive Victorian tradesman)
31. *Vegetable Duck* (1944) (amazingly ingenious poisoning case)
32. *The Lake House* (1946) (a bleak and mechanically complex tale)
33. *Death in Harley Street* (1946) (much praised by Barzun & Taylor; ingenious yet extremely static)
34. *The Paper Bag* (1948) (unusual poisonings in this interesting murder-for-hire tale)
35. *The Telephone Call* (1948) (sober recreation of the infamous Julia Wallace case)
36. *Blackthorn House* (1949) (interesting police procedural involving a stolen car ring in austerity England)
37. *The Two Graphs* (1950) (profitably revisits territory explored in *The Robthorne Mystery*)
38. *Family Affairs* (1950) (probably Dr. Priestley's best-knit postwar murder affair)
39. *The Secret Meeting* (1951) (complex case involving Cold War elements)
40. *Death at the Dance* (1952) (unusually for Street, here the "How?" question is less interesting than the "Who?" and the "Why?")
41. *Death at the Inn/The Case of the Forty Thieves* (1953) (entertaining exploration of ingenious pilfering scheme in postwar England)
42. *The Dovebury Murders* (1954) (some clever plot elements in this provincial poisoning tale, as well as the scrappy charwoman Mrs. Lines and her near-pathological, miserly employer, Mr. Headcorn — though the tale is marred by Jimmy Waghorn's staggering slowness to perceive a certain possibility)
43. *Licensed for Murder* (1958) (non-glamorous English murder, fifties-style, at John Street's great good place, the pub)

Non-Fiction

1. *The Case of Constance Kent* (1928)
2. "Constance Kent," in *The Anatomy of Murder* (1936)

Works by "Miles Burton"

1. *The Secret of High Eldersham* (1930) (this classic village witchcraft tale introduces gentleman amateur detective Desmond Merrion, less celebrated today than Peter Wimsey and Albert Campion, but withal no less clever)
2. *Death of Mr. Gantley* (1932) (first pairing of Desmond Merrion with Inspector Arnold)

3. *To Catch a Thief* (1934) (lively saga of "the ministering Ada")
4. *The Devereux Court Mystery* (1935) (a rare London Burton)
5. *Death in the Tunnel* (1936) (an ingenious murder in a railway tunnel)
6. *Murder of a Chemist* (1936) (middle class murder in the provinces)
7. *Where Is Barbara Prentice?* (1936) (more provincial middle class murder)
8. *Death at the Club* (1937) (murder implicating the highest level of Scotland Yard)
9. *The Platinum Cat* (1938) (a teasing tale of espionage and murder)
10. *Death Leaves No Card* (1939) (left to his own devices, Arnold somehow manages to solve an ingenious locked bathroom murder)
11. *Mr. Babbacombe Dies* (1939) (Street's greatest excoriation of the idle gentry)
12. *Mr. Westerby Missing* (1940) (a sort of homage to Freeman Wills Crofts' *The Cask*)
13. *Death Visits Downspring/Up the Garden Path* (1941) (pleasing wartime mystery)
14. *Murder, M.D.* (1943) (one of the classic village mysteries of English detective fiction)
15. *The Three-Corpse Trick* (1944) (complex and clever village murder)
16. *Not a Leg to Stand On* (1945) (teasing tale of the missing man and his missing leg)
17. *The Cat Jumps* (1946) (murder in a locked house — what does Belisarius know?)
18. *Situation Vacant* (1946) (village murder with dotty authors, daft charities and deadly fishberries)
19. *Death Takes the Living* (1949) (a Golden Age detective novelist takes on the Labour Government)
20. *Ground for Suspicion* (1950) (opposition to commercial development proves lethal)
21. *Murder in Absence* (1954) (Desmond and Mavis Merrion take an interesting cruise)
22. *Bones in the Brickfield* (1958) (the best of Burton's later village tales)

Works by "Cecil Waye"

This was a very short-lived Street pseudonym. There are four in number and very hard to find. I have read two and I found neither work memorable.

Appendix II

Notable Criminous Works by Freeman Wills Crofts

Novels

1. *The Cask* (1920) (massive cornerstone work of mystery fiction)
2. *The Ponson Case* (1921) (overlooked country house mystery text from the twenties)
3. *Inspector French's Greatest Case* (1924) (introduces one of the great detectives, in a good — though not in fact his greatest — case)
4. *Inspector French and the Starvel Tragedy* (1927) (burnt bodies in Yorkshire, done to a turn)
5. *The Sea Mystery* (1928) (a pleasingly stripped down version of *The Cask*, without most of Crofts' twenties period flaws)
6. *The Box Office Murders* (1929) (quaintly entertaining thriller about murders of theater cashiers)
7. *Sir John Magill's Last Journey* (1930) (Crofts' alibi tour de force, a complex affair of times and distances, not for the faint of mind)
8. *Mystery in the Channel* (1931) (early post–Depression instance of a Golden Age corporate malfeasance detective novel; economically written and extremely well-plotted)
9. *Sudden Death* (1932) (an attempt by Crofts at a domestic, "feminine anxiety" tale, but rather beyond his skill level and with a disappointing locked room)
10. *Death on the Way* (1932) (good railway setting; poorer treatment of murderer)
11. *The Hog's Back Mystery* (1933) (another amazingly complex alibi timetable novel)
12. *The 12.30 from Croydon* (1934) (an early inverted mystery tale, traditionally well-regarded)
13. *Mystery on Southampton Water* (1934) (inverted mystery tale of corporate malfeasance; Crofts' best inverted in my opinion)
14. *Crime at Guildford* (1935) (another meaty corporate corruption tale, though it carries one of Crofts' favorite gambits rather too far for complete plausibility, as Raymond Chandler noted)
15. *The Loss of the "Jane Vosper"* (1936) (Crofts' closest attempt to a true "police procedural" novel; masterfully detailed)
16. *Man Overboard!* (1936) (morality tale in which Crofts' tediously ingenuous heroine Pam learns that great riches may create more problems than they solve)
17. *Found Floating* (1937) (possibly the Crofts novel most resembling an Agatha Christie tale, plus the love song of Runciman Jellicoe)
18. *The End of Andrew Harrison* (1938) (an attack on high finance dressed up as a detective novel)

19. *Antidote to Venom* (1938) (an inverted mystery novel that is also an earnest expression of the author's religious faith)
20. *Fatal Venture* (1939) (an attack on casino gambling dressed up as a detective novel)
21. *James Tarrant, Adventurer* (1941) (an attack on patent medicines dressed up as a detective novel)
22. *The Affair at Little Wokeham* (1943) (yet another inverted novel that functions as a morality tale)
23. *Enemy Unseen* (1945) (well-designed village mystery that breaks with Crofts' later pattern of mystery as overt pietistic narrative)
24. *Death of a Train* (1946) (wartime sabotage thriller with notable railway atmosphere, of technical rather than romantic nature, as befits the personality of the author)

Short Story Collections

1. *Murderers Make Mistakes* (1947) (parables of murder and its comeuppance)
2. *Many a Slip* (1955) (the slighter sequel)
3. *The Mystery of the Sleeping Car Express* (1956) (ragbag collection including the 1921 title story, a mechanically clever train murder that was Crofts' first published short story, and 1956's "The Raincoat," the last short story he wrote)

Appendix III

Round Robin Writer
Freeman Wills Crofts' Contributions to The Floating Admiral *(1931) and* Double Death *(1939)*

In the 1930s Freeman Wills Crofts made significant contributions to two round robin detective novels, *The Floating Admiral* (1931) and *Double Death* (1939). As the term *round robin* indicates, both were collaborative efforts, with chapters written successively by different individuals. Though neither novel is an unqualified success, the contributions Crofts made to them are worth noting.

A publishing product of the newly formed Detection Club, *The Floating Admiral* had twelve chapters by thirteen Club members (the second chapter is jointly credited to G.D.H. and Margaret Cole, though it likely was written by Margaret), plus a prologue by Club president G.K. Chesterton. On the whole, the round robin form seems to me not an accommodating one for the detective story, which probably more than any other literary form calls for scrupulous plotting; and in my view *The Floating Admiral*, over-loaded with complications from too many eager hands, begins to take on water and sink well before reaching its destination. Nevertheless, the individual contributions (which include not only the chapters themselves but notes on the chapters) often are quite interesting.

In a January 9, 1932, essay in the *Illustrated London News*, G.K. Chesterton singled out the contribution of Freeman Wills Crofts (along with that of Ronald Knox) for special mention. Dismissing his own prologue to the tale, written last, as "merely ornamental," Chesterton went on to amusedly note that his fellow contributors' "discord is even more entertaining than their harmony." He particularly liked how the methodical Crofts, who was responsible for a later chapter (nine), politely but remorselessly seized the opportunity to correct obvious points of procedure missed or botched by his more careless predecessors:

> Mr. Freeman Wills Crofts ... concentrates (as I hope we all know) on really practical and businesslike crime, with reliable dates and details.... Mr. Freeman Wills Crofts is himself a patient plotter, and was content, like the villain of melodrama, to bide his time. He also was prepared; he was waiting round a dark corner with a sandbag ... waiting for his revenge on the earlier collaborators and contributors. And when his turn comes to take up the story, he manifestly takes a savage delight in seizing on all the practical steps that have been left out, or all the practical difficulties that have been left unconsidered, by less precise or perhaps less prosaic detectives. But he preserves the ironical politeness to his colleagues, and preserves it beautifully. He says, in an airy way, something like: "Inspector Rudge had now a moment to attend to what he

should have arranged before," or "Inspector Rudge made up for the delay in the performance of," etc. And then we learn, by these elegant insinuations, that the earlier writers had forgotten to have the body properly identified; had forgotten a variety of things which Mr. Freeman Wills Crofts, wandering through the world, Bradshaw in hand, invariably remembers.[1]

My favorite of these Crofts mid-course investigative corrections noted by Chesterton is, "[Inspector Rudge] was a good deal worried that he had not yet been able to arrange for an adequate identification of the remains."[2] But Chesterton was mistaken in assuming that Crofts' genuine politeness was "ironical" and that the author took "savage delight" in correcting his colleagues' lapses. Though both men were profoundly religious, they nevertheless had very different temperaments. Such stances as Chesterton describes would have been antithetical to Crofts' very nature. Without self-regarding fanfare, Crofts simply would have been modestly determined to set the facts right, as courteously as possible.

Often though erroneously labeled a product of the Detection Club, *Double Death* was produced by six collaborators, only two of whom, Dorothy L. Sayers and Freeman Wills Crofts, were in fact members of the Detection Club. Evidently originally published in serial form in the *Sunday Chronicle* in 1936 and appearing in book form (with some editorial revision) under the auspices of Victor Gollancz in 1939, *Double Death* is a more successful novel than the meandering *Floating Admiral*, although as a tale of detection it ultimately leaves something to be desired. For this lapse, however, the fault rests not with Sayers and Crofts, who provided ample and excellent clues and detection, nor with Valentine Williams, who follows them pretty ably, but rather with F. Tennyson Jesse, Anthony Armstrong and David Hume, who tend to skimp on material elements. In his notes to his contribution (the final chapter), David Hume freely admits his disinterest in detailed detection:

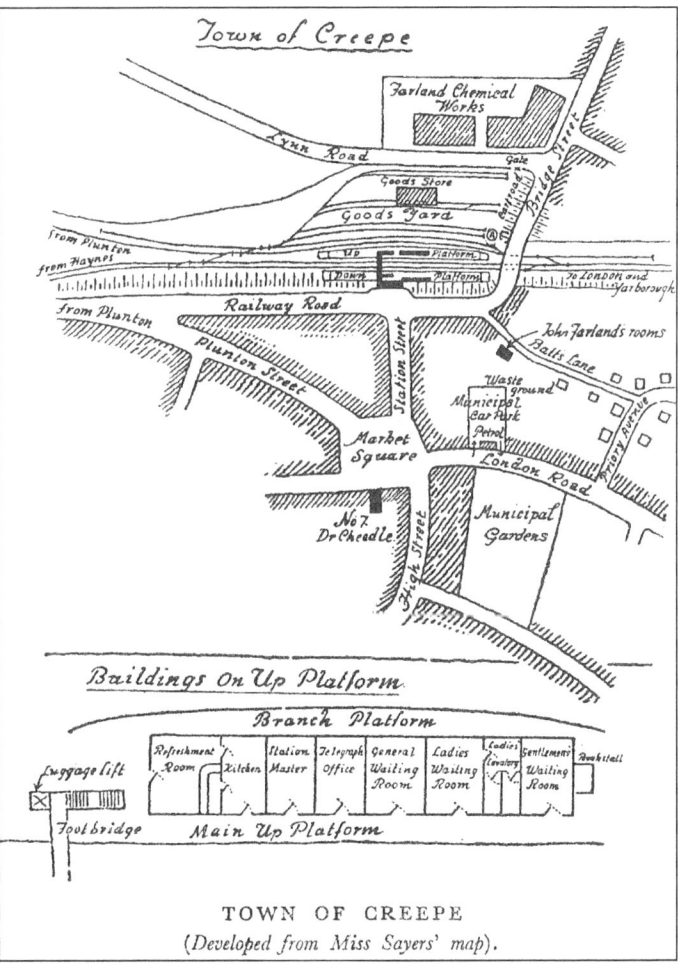

TOWN OF CREEPE
(*Developed from Miss Sayers' map*).

Map of the town of Creepe and the buildings on up platform in *Double Death* (1939). Freeman Wills Crofts' stunning map of the town of Creepe and Creepe Railway Station makes crystal clear the action is his entertaining chapter of this round robin detective novel.

"In common with [F. Tennyson Jesse] I have abandoned the ingeniously effective tables and plans of Sayers and Crofts. I imagine the reader is faced with a shoal of massive red herrings without being led through the maze of a Bradshaw, and the intricacies of Crofts' topographical adventure." Unfortunately Hume, Jesse and Armstrong clearly disrupt Sayers' and Crofts' original scheme, transforming the tale from one of detection to one of mere mystery (albeit a well-written one).[3]

As the authors of the first and second chapters, respectively, Sayers and Crofts corresponded about the story in the spring of 1936, while Crofts and his wife were touring Mediterranean ports via the steamship Letitia (this experience found its way into Crofts' 1937 detective novel, *Found Floating*). Sayers' memorable opening chapter introduces the classic situation of a household over which an imperious and capricious wealthy older woman tyrannizes. This woman, Mrs. Farland, thinks she is being poisoned, yet it is the new nurse, just arrived at the local railway station in the evocatively named town of Creepe, who dies, from an overdose of a powerful sleeping draught. Creepe station plays a major role in Sayers' chapter; and in her correspondence with Crofts, Sayers urged, "If I have made any of the [railway] people be in the wrong place or do the wrong jobs, please tell me and I will alter them."[4]

Sayers clearly had devised a scenario specially designed to appeal to her Detection Club colleague Crofts, and he responded with his own excellent chapter. In addition to having Inspector Billingham carefully track the movements and scrutinize the alibis of the various suspects (after first taking ten minutes, at his wife's insistence, to eat his supper), Crofts adds a tantalizing detail to the narrative mix: that Nurse Ponting had been the chief witness for the prosecution in a domestic poisoning case. Another contributor to *Double Death*, the journalist, author and criminologist F. Tennyson Jesse, pronounced Crofts' idea that the nurse had been previously involved in a murder trial "grand."[5] Crofts also drew a stunning map of the town of Creepe (with an inset of the buildings on the up platform of the railway station). Throughout the chapter, Crofts' writing is economical and direct, never lapsing into pointless detail or emotional bathos, even in its depiction of Mrs. Farland, now petrified that after the death of the nurse that she will be next to unnaturally expire. The last image of the blundering young blackbird suddenly appearing at Mrs. Farland's windowpane, like the Angel of Death, is a potent and arresting one — surprisingly so, coming as it does from the hand of Freeman Wills Crofts, a man not normally given to flights of metaphorical fancy.

APPENDIX IV

Notable Genre Works by Alfred Walter Stewart

Novels

1. *Nordenholt's Million* (1923) (not a detective novel, but a notable work of dark apocalyptic science fiction, important in understanding Alfred Walter Stewart as the writer J.J. Connington)
2. *The Dangerfield Talisman* (1926) (a murderless country house tale; slight but pleasant)
3. *Murder in the Maze* (1927) (introduces Chief Constable Sir Clinton Driffield and his Watson, Squire Wendover, as well as the brilliant idea of murder in a hedge maze)
4. *Tragedy at Ravensthorpe* (1927) (Clinton Driffield's second case, another intricate country house affair)
5. *The Case with Nine Solutions* (1928) (an excellent puzzle in a grimly bleak tale about human nature)
6. *Nemesis at Raynham Parva* (1929) (Sir Clinton temporarily exits, ruthlessly)
7. *The Sweepstake Murders* (1931) (Clinton Driffield confronts a series of related murders, all well-contrived)
8. *The Castleford Conundrum* (1932) (another country house murder affair, astringently told and complexly plotted)
9. *The Ha-Ha Case* (1934) (ballistics and inheritance law expertly treated in a sober country house setting; based on the notorious real life Ardlamont shooting case of 1893)
10. *In Whose Dim Shadow* (1935) (an interesting suburban murder investigation, with some surprisingly sympathetic characters, along with some utter stinkers)
11. *A Minor Operation* (1937) (makes creative use of recent events from the author's own life)
12. *For Murder Will Speak* (1938) (sex in the suburb)
13. *The Four Defences* (1940) (the second and last Mark Brand "Counsellor" mystery has a murder plot of extraordinary complexity, though it reads like a fictionalized crossword puzzle)
14. *No Past Is Dead* (1942) (of interest for an excellently constructed alibi and the fact that it is based on the Achet-Lepine murder case discussed by the author in "The Mystery of Chantelle" in his essay collection, *Alias J.J. Connington*)

Novella

1. *After Death the Doctor* (1934) (a non-series tale turning, Austin Freeman-like, on an interesting scientific gimmick).

Chapter Notes

Introduction

1. *London Daily Telegraph*, 2 September 2007, 22 August, 4 September 2009; *London Observer*, 9 September 2007; *London Times Literary Supplement*, 3 October 2007.

2. Josephine Tey sometimes is named as the fifth Crime Queen, but most of her genre work (as well as her most esteemed genre work) appeared after 1945.

3. Julian Symons, *Bloody Murder: From the Detective Story to the Crime Novel*, rev. ed. (1972; repr., New York: Mysterious Press, 1993), 14, 118.

4. *London Sunday Times*, 19 August 1959, 23; H.R.F. Keating, "A Double-Strung Crossbow," in *Julian Symons at 80: A Tribute*, ed. Patricia Craig (Helsinki: Eurographica, 1992), 114; Julian Symons, *The Detective Story in Britain*, rev. ed. (1962; repr., Harlow, UK: Longmans, Green, 1969), 23. Rules for writing detective fiction that emphasized the primacy of puzzle construction were promulgated by numerous figures in the 1920s and into the 1930s, most famously by American detective novelist S.S. Van Dine (the pseudonym of critic Willard Huntingdon Wright) and Ronald Knox, the prominent Catholic priest and British writer (among his other accomplishments, Knox penned six detective novels).

5. Symons, "Detective Story," 23. Symons' addition of Henry Wade to a later edition of *Bloody Murder* seems to have been a response to the high praise meted to Wade in Jacques Barzun's and Wendell Hertig Taylor's *A Catalogue of Crime*, an encyclopedic tome Symons earlier had admitted to finding "extremely eccentric" in its appraisal of mystery writers. Julian Symons, *Mortal Consequences: A History—From the Detective Story to the Crime Novel* (American edition of *Bloody Murder*) (New York: Harper & Row, 1972), 247. Symons gives no indication that he had actually read any Henry Wade novels in the interim, however. Since Henry Wade was one of the more consciously literary of British Golden Age crime writers, Symons' conscription of him into Humdrum ranks seems senseless. Possibly Symons was motivated more by pique with Barzun than anything else. "What Barzun finds entrancing I think dull," Symons dogmatically declares, ignoring the fact that the two men actually appreciated many of the same authors. Symons, *Bloody Murder*, 283.

6. Though I disagree with Symons' pejorative use of the word *Humdrum* in reference to these writers, the term has entered, seemingly permanently, into the lexicon of mystery genre criticism and I therefore adopt it for use in this study.

7. On the feminization of the Golden Age British detective novel, see note 9. Key texts positing the High Tory, backward-looking conservatism of Golden Age British detective fiction include, besides Julian Symons' *Bloody Murder*, the following works: W.H. Auden, "The Guilty Vicarage," *Harper's* 196 (May 1948): 406–412, reprinted in W.H. Auden, *The Dyer's Hand* (New York: Random House, 1962) and *Detective Fiction: A Collection of Critical Essays*, ed. Robin W. Winks, ed. (Woodstock, VT: Foul Play Press, 1988); George Grella, "Murder and Manners: The Formal Detective Novel," *Novel: A Forum on Fiction* 4 (fall 1970): 30–49, reprinted in Winks, *Detective Fiction* (as "The Formal Detective Novel"); Colin Watson, *Snobbery with Violence: English Crime Stories and Their Audience* (New York: St. Martin's Press, 1972); Stephen Knight, *Form and Ideology in Crime Fiction* (Bloomington, Indiana: University Press, 1980); Dennis Porter, *The Pursuit of Crime: Art and Ideology in Detective Fiction* (New Haven, CT: Yale University Press, 1981); Martin Priestman, *Detective Fiction and Literature: The Figure on the Carpet* (London: Palgrave Macmillan, 1991); Martin Priestman, *Crime Fiction: From Poe to the Present* (Writers and Their Work) (Plymouth, UK: Northcote House, 1998); Charles J. Rzepka, *Detective Fiction* (Cambridge, UK: Polity, 2005); John Scaggs, *Crime Fiction* (London: Routledge, 2005); P.D. James, *Talking about Detective Fiction* (Oxford: Bodleian Library, 2009).

8. Symons, *Bloody Murder*, 137; Leroy Lad Panek, *Watteau's Shepherds: The Detective Novel in Britain 1914–1940* (Bowling Green, OH: Popular Press, 1979), 12. For another significant example of this truncated coverage of Humdrum writers, see Stephen Knight's recent ambitious attempt at a broad genre survey, *Crime Fiction, 1800–2000: Detection, Death, Diversity* (Basingstoke, UK: Palgrave Macmillan, 2004). Professor Knight devotes three sentences to Crofts, one sentence to Street (for his pseudonym John Rhode) and none to Stewart. Despite this general neglect of Humdrum writers, a few recent studies have given some overdue attention to the scientific detective novelist R. Austin Freeman (1862–1943), a contemporary of Arthur Conan Doyle who might be styled the Father of the Humdrums. See Knight, *Crime Fiction*, 69–70; Lee Horsley, *Twentieth-Century Crime Fiction* (Oxford: Oxford University Press, 2005), 35–36. In addition to the Crime Queens, the British Golden Age novelists who have received the most critical attention in surveys are Anthony Berkeley Cox, who wrote crime fiction under the pen names Anthony Berkeley and Francis Iles,

and a pair of male authors who might be termed the Detection Dons: Nicholas Blake (pseudonym of poet and professor Cecil Day Lewis) and Michael Innes (pseudonym of literature professor John Innes Mackintosh Stewart). Other detective novelists one sometimes sees mentioned in surveys are the American-born (but, for much of his adult life, England-dwelling) author John Dickson Carr, master of the locked room, or impossible crime, mystery, and Gladys Mitchell, creator of the bizarre psychiatrist detective Mrs. Bradley. Little substantive analysis comparable to that performed on the Crime Queens has been done with these authors, however, though a fine biography of Carr and worthy short literary studies of the genre fiction of Innes and Cox have appeared in the last twenty-five years. See Douglas G. Greene, *John Dickson Carr: The Man Who Explained Miracles* (New York: Otto Penzler, 1995); George L. Scheper, *Michael Innes* (New York: Ungar, 1986); Malcolm J. Turnbull, *Elusion Aforethought: The Life and Writing of Anthony Berkeley Cox* (Bowling Green, OH: Popular Press, 1996).

9. Laura Thompson, *Agatha Christie: An English Mystery* (London: Headline Review, 2007), 374–376; Erin A. Smith, *Hard-Boiled: Working-Class Readers and Pulp Magazines* (Philadelphia, PA: Temple University Press, 2000), 39; Susan Rowland, "The 'Classical' Model of the Golden Age," in *A Companion to Crime Fiction*, ed. Lee Horsley and Charles A. Rzepka (Malden, MA: Wiley-Blackwell, 2010), 122. On the rise of feminist crime fiction studies since the 1970s see Heta Pyrhonen, *Murder from an Academic Angle: An Introduction to the Study of the Detective Narrative* (Columbia, SC: Camden House, 1994), 108–113, and Merja Makinen, *Agatha Christie: Investigating Femininity* (Basingstoke, UK: Palgrave Macmillan, 2006), Chapter One. Examples abound of this insistently gendered academic approach to Golden Age British detective fiction. For example, in her *Crime Fiction* survey, Lee Horsley notes that the British Golden Age of detective fiction is "generally thought of as a period during which detective fiction became feminized" (p. 38). John Scaggs declares that the "Golden Age in Britain was defined by" the Crime Queens Christie, Sayers, Allingham and Marsh (Scaggs, *Crime Fiction*, 26). Charles J. Rzepka asserts that Agatha Christie's audience was "largely female" (p. 157) and that during the Golden Age period "detective fiction shifted ... away from adventure elements that had traditionally appealed to male readers and toward plots of ratiocination ... which most women at the time were more inclined to admire" (p. 157–158). In *Murder by the Book? Feminism and the Crime Novel* (London: Routledge, 1994), Sally Munt insists that the Golden Age of British detection is "commonly conceived" as having run from "the first novel of Agatha Christie (1920) to the last novel by Dorothy L. Sayers (1937)" (p. 7) and she speculates that male critics who disparage the Golden Age are motivated by "a hidden agenda to repudiate women authors' work as relevant to a purely historic moment, an arcane form now superseded by the masculine hard-boiled thriller" (p. 209, n.28). The overly sweeping distinction between universally tough, "masculine" American mystery fiction on the one hand and universally genteel, "feminine" British mystery fiction on the other has been endorsed most recently in P.D. James' recent short genre survey, *Talking about Detective Fiction*. "A reader coming from Dashiell Hammett or Raymond Chandler to Agatha Christie or Dorothy L. Sayers could reasonably feel that these writers were living not only on different continents but in different centuries," declares James. In James' view, the differences between female-dominated British Golden Age detective fiction and the works of the American male hard-boiled writers "are so profound that it seems stretching a definition to describe both groups under the same category." James, *Detective Fiction*, 70, 72. Contradicting all this, sources contemporary with the Golden Age often expressed the view that both authors and readers of British detective fiction, particularly in the period from 1920 to 1935 or thereabouts, were predominantly male. For example, in a 1929 essay, "The Professor and the Detective," Marjorie Hope Nicolson, then Dean of Smith College (she later became the first female graduate school professor at Columbia University), asserted that "the detective story is primarily a man's novel" and that "the great bulk of our detective stories today are being written by men"— phenomena she attributed to mainstream fiction having become "too largely feminized." Marjorie Nicolson, "The Professor and the Detective," in *The Art of the Mystery Story*, ed. Howard Haycraft (1946; repr., New York: Carroll & Graf, 1992), 123. Additionally, George Orwell recalled in his "Bookshop Memories," originally published in 1936, that while "women of all kinds and ages" read novels by such mainstream bestsellers as Ethel M. Dell, Warwick Deeping and Jeffrey Farnol, men "read either the novels it is possible to respect, or detective stories.... [T]heir consumption of detective stories is terrific." George Orwell, "Bookshop Memories," *Fortnightly* (November 1936), reprinted in *George Orwell: An Age like This 1920–1940* (Collected Essays, Journalism and Letters, vol. I) ed. Sonia Orwell and Ian Angus (Boston, MA: David R. Godine, 2000), 244. For further consideration of this matter, see Chapter One, note 23.

10. For biographies of individual Crime Queens, see: for Agatha Christie, Janet Morgan, *Agatha Christie: A Biography* (New York, Alfred A. Knopf, 1985) and Thompson, *Agatha Christie*; for Dorothy L. Sayers, Barbara Reynolds, *Dorothy L. Sayers: Her Life and Soul* (New York: St. Martins, 1993); for Margery Allingham, Julia Thorogood [Jones], *Margery Allingham: A Biography* (London: Heinemann, 1991) (rev. ed., published as *The Adventures of Margery Allingham*, Chelmsford, UK: Golden Duck, 2009); for Ngaio Marsh, Margaret Lewis, *Ngaio Marsh: A Life* (London: Chatto & Windus, 1991) (reprinted by Scottsdale, AZ: Poisoned Pen Press, 1998) and Joanne Drayton: *Ngaio Marsh: Her Life in Crime* (Auckland: HarperCollins, 2008). For collective studies of the four Crime Queens (as well as, in the first book, Josephine Tey and, in the second book, P.D. James and Ruth Rendell), see Jessica Mann, *Deadlier Than the Male: Why Are Respectable English Women So Good at Murder?* (New York: Macmillan, 1981) and Susan Rowland, *From Agatha Christie to Ruth Rendell: British Women Writers in Detective and Crime Fiction* (Basingstoke, UK: Palgrave, 2001).

11. Smith, *Hard-Boiled*, 39. *Mystery in Southampton Water* is discussed in Chapter Two. For another Humdrum novel where female characters are practically nonexistent, see *Night Exercise* (1942) by John Rhode (Cecil John Charles Street). Among the women who briefly appear in the novel, which is about a murder that takes place during a Home Guard practice operation, only a pub keeper's wife and a Civil Defense secretary have even a few lines (though the secretary, Miss Purser, is admiringly described "as the sort of person who would carry out details of routine undisturbed with a Panzer division on her doorstep." John Rhode, *Dead of the Night* (English title: *Night Exercise*) (New York: Dodd, Mead, 1942), 241.

12. P.D. James, *Time to Be in Earnest: A Fragment of Au-*

tobiography (London: Faber and Faber, 1999), 33. In her detective novel *Have His Carcase* (1932), Dorothy L. Sayers acknowledged the help she received on certain technical points from John Street, while she gave co-authorship credit for her epistolary mystery *The Documents in the Case* (1930) to Dr. Eustace Robert Barton, who aided her with the book's medical and scientific details. Similarly, Ngaio Marsh gave co-authorship credit of her third detective novel, *The Nursing Home Murder* (1935), to a prominent New Zealand gynecologist and obstetrician, Dr. Henry Jellett.

13. Agatha Christie, *The Secret of Chimneys* (London: Collins, 1925), 228. Christie's other most famous series detective, Miss Marple, the elderly, genteel spinster living in the quaint English village of St. Mary Mead, is often treated as a major Golden Age figure, though in fact, as noted by Alison Light, she appeared only in one novel and one volume of short stories before 1940. Disdain for aristocratic English detectives and their social milieus clearly colored early influential criticism of British Golden Age detective novels made in the 1940s by the American man of letters Edmund Wilson and the great hard-boiled detective novelist Raymond Chandler (see Curtis Evans, "'The Amateur Detective Just Won't Do': Raymond Chandler and British Detective Fiction," *The American Culture*, http://stkarnick.com); and this disdain is often echoed today by genre critics writing about the hard-boiled tradition. "Christie's armchair supersleuth, Hercule Poirot ... can find the solution to any mystery with his ingenious faculties of deduction. After he solves the case, everyone breathes a sigh of relief while the butler pours a round of sherry," sarcastically writes Gene D. Phillips in *Creatures of Darkness: Raymond Chandler, Detective Fiction, and Film Noir* (Lexington: University Press of Kentucky, 2000), 1, in a statement representative of numerous others that can be found within the body of hard-boiled genre criticism.

14. James, *Detective Fiction*, 72; Auden, "The Guilty Vicarage," reprinted in Winks, *Detective Fiction*, 15, 21.

15. James, *Detective Fiction*, 70–71.

16. Symons, *Bloody Murder*, 108; Watson, *Snobbery with Violence*, 140, 171; Knight, *Form and Ideology*, 117–118; Porter, *Pursuit of Crime*, 194–195. For a concise statement of Watson's views, see Colin Watson, "Mayhem Parva and Wicked Belgravia," in *Crime Writers*, ed. H.R.F. Keating (London: British Broadcasting Corporation, 1978), 47–63. These views are echoed in such works as Martin Priestman's *Crime Fiction* ("The social vision of Christie's novels is, famously, very conservative. Country houses and/or upper-middle-class village communities ... purvey a typifying vision of British society as a whole strikingly at odds with many insistent realities of the inter-war years, from the devastation of the Great War to the mass unemployment and depression of the 1920s and 1930s.... [The detectives of Sayers, Allingham, Marsh and Innes] are very complete fantasy-projections of a readership anxious to believe that an establishment led by such well-bred, well-educated men could still be trusted to protect a threatened and divided British society from itself"— p. 21, 24); Charles J. Rzepka's *Detective Fiction* ("Here [in Golden Age British detective fiction] was a world embodying the values of the vanishing gentry class"— p. 153); and John Scagg's *Crime Fiction* ("Golden Age fiction, at least in its British version, often features a rural or semi-rural setting.... The characteristic desire of Golden Age fiction to restore or return to a lost order that, in all respects, is superior to the present world, reinforces this pastoral reading"— p. 50).

17. The characterization of Agatha Christie's novels as High Tory, backward-looking and pastoralist has been forcefully challenged by a chapter in Alison Light's *Forever England: Femininity, Literature and Conservatism between the Wars* (London: Routledge, 1992), in my view the most important work of literary criticism from the last twenty years touching on British Golden Age mystery. Light has influenced this study with her idea of "conservative modernity." Among authors of recent genre surveys, Lee Horsley recognizes that the "standard view of the uniformly insular and snobbish character of inter-war detective fiction is effectively challenged by ... Alison Light." Horsley, *Crime Fiction*, 39. See also: Gill Plain, *Twentieth-Century Crime Fiction: Gender, Sexuality and the Body* (London: Routledge, 2001), which challenges the liberal-conservative binary in comparing the works of the hard-boiled American crime novelist Raymond Chandler with those of Agatha Christie; and Susan Rowland, *Agatha Christie to Ruth Rendell*, which carefully notes nuances in the conservatism of the Crime Queens ("Despite the reputation gained by Christie, Sayers, Allingham and Marsh for providing unproblematically conservative country house mysteries, these rural economies prove surprisingly non-coherent and fragile"— p. 43).

18. For an especially illuminating academic study of the treatment of gender issues by a Golden Age detective novelist, see Makinen, *Investigating Femininity*.

19. James, *Detective Fiction*, 81. An exception to my generalization about genre studies of the last forty years, Ian Carter's *Railways and Culture in Britain: The Epitome of Modernity* (Manchester: Manchester University Press, 2001), offers an example of how an informed inclusion of Humdrum authors can enhance a literary study. In a chapter of eighteen pages (excluding notes) on Golden Age crime fiction and British railways, Professor Carter devotes three persuasive pages to the works of railway engineer turned mystery novelist Freeman Wills Crofts. Mention also is made of books by the other subjects of this study. For additional broader literary studies that include analyses of detective fiction, see Alison's Light's *Forever England*, Gill Plain's *Women's Fiction of the Second World War: Gender, Power, Resistance* (Edinburgh: Edinburgh University Press, 1996) and Nicola Humble's *The Feminine Middlebrow Novel, 1920s to 1950s: Class, Domesticity and Bohemianism* (Oxford: Oxford University Press, 2001) — all of which draw in part on works by the Crime Queens — and Chris Baldick's impressive comprehensive literary survey, *The Modern Movement* (The Oxford English Literary History, Volume 10. 1910–1940) (Oxford: Oxford University Press, 2004).

Chapter One

1. *London Sunday Times*, 19 August 1959, 23; Julian Symons, *Bloody Murder: From the Detective Story to the Crime Novel*, rev. ed. (1972; repr., New York: Mysterious Press, 1993), 118; H.R.F. Keating, "A Double-Strung Crossbow," in *Julian Symons at 80: A Tribute*, ed. Patricia Craig (Helsinki: Eurographica, 1992), 114.

2. Symons, *Bloody Murder*, 118, 124. For the most informed discussion of Gladys Mitchell and her work, see Nicholas Fuller's introduction to Gladys Mitchell, *Sleuth's Alchemy: Cases of Mrs. Bradley and Others* (Norfolk, VA: Crippen & Landru, 2005), 6–21.

3. Cecilia Tichi, *Shifting Gears: Technology, Literature, Culture in Modern America* (Chapel Hill: University of North Carolina Press, 1987), 98, 105.

4. Dennis Porter, *The Pursuit of Crime: Art and Ideology in Detective Fiction* (New Haven, CT: Yale University Press, 1981), 163; Leroy Lad Panek, *An Introduction to the Detective Story* (Bowling Green, OH: Popular Press, 1987), 123; H. Douglas Thomson, *Masters of Mystery: A Study of the Detective Story* (1931; repr., New York: Dover, 1978), 33; E.M. Wrong, Introduction to *Crime and Detection* (London: Oxford University Press, 1926), reprinted in *The Art of the Mystery Story*, ed. Howard Haycraft (1946; repr., New York: Carroll and Graf, 1992), 24; Dorothy L. Sayers, Introduction to *Great Stories of Detection, Mystery and Horror*, ed. Dorothy L. Sayers (London: Victor Gollancz, 1928), 44, reprinted in slightly truncated form as Introduction to *The Omnibus of Crime* in Haycraft, *Mystery Story*. Panek disparages "third rate writers" who placed "a high value on what they perceived to be the intellectual puzzle," rather than humor, psychology or the study of social manners; yet whether or not one agrees with it, Panek's personal preference as a matter of historical fact was by no means shared by all detective fiction readers of the Golden Age. See Panek, *Introduction*, 126.

5. The extracts from critical reviews are drawn from *Hobart Mercury*, 1 August 1930, 3; *Perth West Australian*, 30 August 1930, 4; *London Sunday Times*, 7 January 1934, 9; as well as the back flap of the dust jacket of *Mystery at Olympia* (London: Collins, 1936) and *Death at the Hopfields* (London: Collins, 1937) and the back matter in the following: Rhode, *Hopfields*; Miles Burton, *Death at Low Tide* (London: Collins, 1938); John Rhode, *Shot at Dawn* (London: Collins, 1934). The publisher's descriptions are drawn from the front matter of the American edition of *Death on the Boat Train* (New York: Dodd, Mead, 1940) and from the front dust jacket of *Death in the Hopfields*. Maps and plans still occasionally appear in modern day detective novels. See, for example, the front matter of Robert Barnard's retro-titled *The Corpse at the Haworth Tandoori* (New York: Scribner's, 1998) and the three books in Alan Bradley's award-winning Flavia de Luce series (set in the 1950s), *The Sweetness at the Bottom of the Pie* (New York: Delacorte, 2009), *The Weed That Strings the Hangman's Bag* (New York: Delacorte, 2010) and *A Red Herring Without Mustard* (New York: Delacorte, 2011). In a 2008 interview, Bradley noted his admiration of Golden Age detective novels: "I was brought up on Dorothy L. Sayers and Sherlock Holmes and a bit later worked my way through Agatha Christie, G.K. Chesterton and a host of others.... I'm still hoping to come across the works of Freeman Wills Crofts and Austin Freeman, which I've never managed to locate." See *Material Witness: Fiction for the Criminally Inclined*, 7 February 2009, http://materialwitness.typepad.com.

6. *Monthly Criterion* 8 (September 1928), 175; Charles Williams, *Westminster Chronicle & News-Gazette*, 7 April 1933, reprinted in *The Detective Fiction Reviews of Charles Williams, 1930–1935*, ed. Jared C. Lobdell (Jefferson, NC: McFarland, 2003), 94; *New York Times Book Review*, 16 September 1928, 67. The other quoted extracts from critical reviews are drawn from the back matter of Freeman Wills Crofts, *Crime at Guildford* (London: Collins, 1935). T.S. Eliot ranked Crofts above both the American detective novelist S.S. Van Dine, who at the time had taken the United States by storm with the first three titles in his Philo Vance "Murder Case" series of tales, *The Benson Murder Case* (1926), *The Canary Murder Case* (1927) and *The Greene Murder Case* (1928); and Agatha Christie, who had published four Hercule Poirot detective novels, *The Mysterious Affair at Styles* (1920), *Murder on the Links* (1923), *The Murder of Roger Ackroyd* (1926) and *The Mystery of the Blue Train* (1928), as well as four inferior thrillers, *The Secret Adversary* (1922), *The Man in the Brown Suit* (1924), *The Secret of Chimneys* (1925) and *The Big Four* (1927). The last listed of these thrillers, *The Big Four*, though it features Hercule Poirot, is a farrago of the most risible Edgar Wallace-Sax Rohmer devices that was compiled by Christie after the failure of her marriage and her subsequent mental breakdown; and it has been commonly considered one of her poorest efforts, including by the author herself, who referred to it as "that rotten book." Janet Morgan, *Agatha Christie: An Autobiography* (New York: Knopf, 1985), 163. On T.S. Eliot's mystery criticism, a subject that, oddly, has received little attention from genre critics, see David E. Chinitz, *T.S. Eliot and the Cultural Divide* (Chicago: University of Chicago Press, 2003), 155. Chinitz suggests that Eliot "helped create the intellectual vogue for detective fiction." Certainly he helped lend puzzle-oriented detective fiction considerable cachet, at least as far as intellectuals were concerned.

7. Williams, *Westminster Chronicle & News-Gazette*, 27 May 1930, reprinted in *Charles Williams*, 28. Little, Brown continued to emphasize Connington's merit as an author of fair play detection throughout the decade of the 1930s. "On both sides of the Atlantic, reviewers agree that J.J. Connington is a master of the story of pure detection," the publisher announced on the jacket of *The Boathouse Riddle* in 1931. "Mr. Connington has few peers in the writing of real detective stories," Little, Brown further asserted seven years later on the jacket for *Truth Comes Limping* (1938). Even as late as 1942, Little, Brown on the dust jacket for *No Past Is Dead* assured potential readers that "Mr. Connington's quick-witted sleuth arrives at his solution with only the use of evidence that is fairly presented to the reader."

8. *Saturday Review of Literature* 6 (9 February 1929): 670; *Monthly Criterion* 6 (July 1927): 90; *Monthly Criterion* 6 (November 1927): 568. The other quoted extracts from critical reviews are drawn from the front matter of J.J. Connington, *The Eye in the Museum* (London: Gollancz, 1929).

9. *London Daily Herald*, 7 January 1932, 13; 10 December 1931, 13; 4 June 1931, 13; 15 November 1934, 14; 6 June 1935, 15.

10. Will Cuppy, *The Decline and Fall of Practically Everybody* (1950; repr., Boston: David R. Godine, 1984), 2; *New York Herald Tribune Book Review*, 21 July 1935, 4; 7 July 1935, 8. In 1931, P.G. Wodehouse deemed Cuppy "America's leading reviewer of detective stories." P.G. Wodehouse, Introduction to Will Cuppy, *How to Tell Your Friends from the Apes* (1931; repr., Jaffrey, NH: David R. Godine, 2005), ix.

11. *New York Herald Tribune Book Review*, 20 November 1936, 36; 5 July 1936, 8; 27 October 1935, 12; 16 June 1935, 10; 8 November 1936, 16.

12. H.R.F. Keating, *The Bedside Companion to Crime* (New York: Mysterious Press, 1989), 36; P.D. James, *Talking about Detective Fiction* (Oxford: Bodleian Library, 2009), 52, 91, 92, 94.

13. Julian Symons, *Mortal Consequences: A History— From the Detective Story to the Crime Novel)* (English title: *Bloody Murder*) (New York: Harper & Row, 1972), 248.

14. Sheila Kaye-Smith, *All the Books of My Life: A Bibliobiography* (London: Cassell, 1956), 188; Josephine Pullein-Thompson to the author, 28 March 2006. A writer character in Cannan's *Death at the Dog* recalls: "I

tried to make my detective a brilliant kind of person—like Dr. Priestley, only young and attractive." Joanna Cannan, *Death at the Dog* (1941; repr., Boulder, CO: Rue Morgue Press, 1999), 151. Seventeen years later, in Cannan's *And Be a Villain*, a grandmother suspecting that murder has been done is urged by her grandsons to do armchair detecting, in the manner of Dr. Priestley (and Nero Wolfe). See Joanna Cannan, *And Be a Villain* (London: Victor Gollancz, 1958), 112.

15. Peter Ibbotson, "Sayers and Ciphers," *Cryptologia* 25 (April 2001): 81. *Time*, 6 May 1929, www.time.com/time/magazine/article/0,9171,732300,00.html. On the misconception of puzzle-oriented detective fiction as something that appealed to less intelligent readers, see Robert Kuhn McGregor with Ethan Lewis, *Conundrums for the Long Week-End: England, Dorothy L. Sayers and Lord Peter Wimsey* (Kent, OH: Kent State University Press, 2000), 33. "[A] detective story had to appeal to 'middlebrow' taste to at least be successful. This fact severely circumscribed the occasions for literary experimentation," declare the authors. To the contrary, the fair play Golden Age detective novel was itself a literary experiment, one that drew the interest of modernists and intellectuals, particularly in the 1920s. See Chris Baldick, *The Modern Movement* (The Oxford English Literary History, Vol. 10, 1910–1940) (Oxford: Oxford University Press, 2004), 273 ("[T]he detective story ... offered a sort of intellectual challenge that made it acceptable to the highly educated, and indeed sometimes addictive"). For genre critics noting T.S. Eliot's praise for Wilkie Collins' *The Moonstone* (but not his praise for the novels of Freeman Wills Crofts), see Symons, *Bloody Murder*, 50, and James, *Detective Fiction*, 23.

16. Herbert Read, "Answer to Lord Peter's Prayer," *Night and Day*, 8 July 1937, reprinted in Herbert Read, *Pursuits and Verdicts* (Edinburgh: Tragara Press, 1983), 5. On Alfred Lucas, see Mark Gilberg, "Alfred Lucas: Egypt's Sherlock Holmes," *Journal of the American Institute for Conservation* 36 (1997): 31–48.

17. This dedicatory note is found in Charles J. Dutton, *The Shadow on the Glass* (New York: Dodd, Mead, 1923). On Dutton, see his autobiography, *Saints and Sinners: The Story of a Clergyman* (New York: Dodd, Mead, 1940).

18. A membership list of Princeton's University League Book Club, Detective Group was discovered by me in an American first edition of David Frome, *The Black Envelope* (New York: Farrar & Rinehart, 1937). "David Frome" was a pseudonym of American novelist Zenith Jones Brown, also known for her "Leslie Ford" mysteries. Unfortunately, I am unaware of the existence of any reader's reports on these books, so have no way of knowing whether these eminent representatives of the sciences and the humanities reached differing conclusions concerning the merits of the respective books.

19. Kaye-Smith, *Books*, 187; *Canadian Forum* 36 (15 March 1936), 30. Dorothy L. Sayers published her last detective novel, *Busman's Honeymoon*, in 1937, afterwards turning to writing religious plays and essays as well as a translation of Dante's *Divine Comedy*, the latter of which she was working on at her death in 1957.

20. *Saturday Review of Literature* 16 (14 August 1937): 20; 16 (18 September 1937): 20; *New Yorker* 13 (30 January 1942):60; 15 (24 April 1943): 84; 16 (21 August 1943): 68; 19 (21 April 1945): 84; 22 (13 July 1948): 64. Innes' first two detective novels, published in 1936 and 1937, sold slightly over 2,000 copies in the United States, according to his American publisher, Dodd, Mead. Though Dodd, Mead expressed hope of considerably expanding Innes' sales beyond that level, the British detective novelist never became a big hardback seller in the United States. Innes' *One-Man Show* (*A Private View*), published in 1952, sold only 5,180 hardback copies and his final detective novel, *Appleby and the Ospreys*, which appeared many years later in 1986, reached 9,500. See Dodd, Mead & Co. to A.P. Watt & Son, 10 May 1938, Memo 19, March 1958, *Appleby and the Ospreys* Royalty Report, Box 11, Dodd, Mead Mss, Lilly Library Manuscript Collection, University of Indiana.

21. Kaye-Smith, *Books*, 186. On the life and writings of R. Austin Freeman, see Norman Donaldson, *In Search of Dr. Thorndyke: The Story of R. Austin's Freeman's Great Scientific Investigator and his Creator*, rev. ed. (1971; repr., Shelburne, ON: The Battered Silicon Dispatch Box, 1998) and Oliver Mayo, *R. Austin Freeman: The Anthropologist at Large* (Hawthorndene, SA: Investigator Press, 1980).

22. James, *Detective Fiction*, 118.

23. It should not come altogether as a surprise that in her survey P.D. James omits any mention of R. Austin Freeman, though he is one of the mystery genre's most important British authors. Born in 1920, James recalls eagerly reading *Gaudy Night* in 1936, a year after it was first published, as well as devotedly saving "pocket money to buy the new books by Dorothy L. Sayers or Margery Allingham"; yet she gives no indication of ever in her long life having perused a detective novel by a Humdrum author. P.D. James, *Time to be in Earnest: A Fragment of Autobiography* (London: Faber and Faber, 1999), 95, 144. James' preferences would have struck many Golden Age commentators as perfectly natural, though for a reason that perhaps would come as a surprise to many today. H. Douglas Thomson argued in *Masters of Mystery* in 1931 that true, puzzle-oriented detective novels appealed more strongly to men than women, men preferring to confront a puzzle in a mystery and women delighting more in an exhibition of "emotional values" on the part of the mystery's characters. "The average male reader reads the detective story for the problem," declared Thomson, "the female reader for the excitement of the setting. The man in the street loves a problem.... Not so with women.... To every woman who prefers the problem there are at least four who prefer the shocker [i.e., thriller]." Thomson, *Mystery*, 41. Similarly, "Judge Lynch" avowed that "women don't like puzzle mysteries *per se*," but rather put priority on the people in the mystery being "the kind you care about.... The bull-dog British brand of deliberate deduction, as exemplified by [Crofts'] Inspector French and [Rhode's] Dr. Priestley, positively infuriates them.... Stories with a scientific background or that depend on chemical formulae or the like for their elucidation are frequently used [by women] as doorstops." Judge Lynch, "Battle of the Sexes: The Judge and His Wife look at Mysteries," in Haycraft, *Mystery Story*, 369. Thus many at the time would have deemed as exceptional indeed a puzzle-loving, Humdrum-admiring female mystery reader such as Sheila Kaye-Smith. Interestingly, critic Stuart P. Mais praised Kaye-Smith's novels in explicitly phallocentric terms: "We read Sheila Kaye-Smith because she alone among the women writers of to-day writes with the sure touch of a man.... Miss Sheila Kaye-Smith has masculine strengths." Stuart P. Mais, *Why We Should Read* (London: Grant Richards, 1921), 157.

24. Herbert Read, "Answer to Lord Peter's Prayer," 5–8. The journal in which Read's article originally appeared,

Night and Day, was a short lived affair started by Graham Greene, who chose Evelyn Waugh to review mainstream novels and Read to review mystery novels. In his later introduction to the slim volume in which Read's *Night and Day* mystery reviews were reprinted, Greene noted that in these reviews Read "found an outlet for his hitherto repressed sense of fun" and added: "How glad I was to see him exercise it on the portentous and pretentious Dorothy Sayers." Ibid., 4. Even as late as 1949, a traditionalist reviewer praised a John Rhode novel, *Blackthorn House*, for avoiding "love interest": "There is no heroine, but John Rhode's readers need no such sop. They have enough to do trying to unravel this extraordinarily well-contrived puzzle." See the front flap of the dust jacket for John Rhode, *The Two Graphs* (London: Geoffrey Bles, 1950).

25. Arnold Bennett "Idleness and Dawdling," *London Evening Standard*, 24 January 1929, reprinted in *Arnold Bennett: The Evening Standard Years "Books and Persons" 1926–1931*, ed. Andrew Mylett (Hamden, CT: Archon Books 1974), 234.

26. Arnold Bennett, "'Crime' Novels Fail to Thrill," *London Evening Standard*, 25 September 1930, reprinted in Mylett, *Bennett*, 413. The title of Bennett's article illustrates that deriders of puzzle-oriented detective fiction often simply operated on different aesthetic assumptions from its admirers, who did not desire to be provided in their light reading with "thrills," but, rather, mental stimulation. Illustrating this point, one then current detective novel that Bennett did praise, Francis Everton's *The Dalehouse Murder*, has what must have struck more puzzle-oriented readers as a tiresomely melodramatic ending, in which the seemingly sweet young Margaret, abruptly revealed as a murderous fiend, chloroforms, binds and gags Janet, the heroine of the tale, and then threatens, before Janet's horrified fiancée, to disfigure her helpless victim's face with vitriol. "You she-devil, take it away!" cries the fiancée, who nevertheless, being the rather stiff narrator of the tale, immediately rationalizes his unmanly outburst, noting that, after all, he had been by this point "tortured beyond discretion" by wicked Margaret. After Margaret is foiled and properly institutionalized, another character helpfully (if belatedly) explains her murderous actions by noting: "There was insanity on both sides of the family." Francis Everton, *The Dalehouse Murder* (New York: Bobbs-Merrill, 1927), 274, 306. This is the tale Bennett deemed "at least as good as any modern detective-story I have read since Conan Doyle." Of it he also pronounced, "The character drawing is excellent." Arnold Bennett, "Mistakes Detective-Novel Writers Make," *London Evening Standard*, 27 March 1930, reprinted in Myles, *Bennett*, 361. Bennett pointed out in his book review column that he much preferred the "lowbrow" thrillers of Edgar Wallace to modern detective novels. His own attempts at writing mystery genre fiction were not notably successful. See John Lucas, *Arnold Bennett: A Study of His Fiction* (London: Methuen, 1974), 55–57.

27. The Detection Club oath is found in Haycraft, *Mystery Story*, 197–99. On Edgar Wallace, see Margaret Lane, *Edgar Wallace: The Biography of a Phenomenon* (New York: Double, Doran, 1939). On Sax Rohmer, see Cay Van Ash and Elizabeth Sax Rohmer, *Master of Villainy: A Biography of Sax Rohmer* (Bowling Green, OH: Popular Press, 1972). On Sapper, see Richard Usborne, *Clubland Heroes: A Nostalgic Study of Some Recurrent Characters in the Romantic Fiction of Dornford Yates, John Bucahn and Sapper*, rev. ed. (1953; repr., London: Barrie and Jenkins, 1974). On the effort to aesthetically segregate the detective novel from the thriller, see Leroy Lad Panek, *Watteau's Shepherds: The Detective Novel in Britain 1914–1940* (Bowling Green, OH: Popular Press, 1979), 11–14.

28. Douglas G. Greene: *John Dickson Carr: The Man Who Explained Miracles* (New York: Otto Penzler, 1995), 103; Thomson, *Masters*, 57. The most famous detective fiction rules were lain down in the 1920's by the American critic and mystery author Willard Huntingdon Wright, whose Philo Vance detective novels, written under the pseudonym S.S. Van Dine, included the bestselling *The Canary Murder Case* (1927), *The Greene Murder Case* (1928) and *The Bishop Murder Case* (1929), and by the British Catholic priest and writer Ronald Knox, who published a half-dozen detective novels himself and was a founding member of the Detection Club. These rules are found in Haycraft, *Mystery Story*, 189–196. That many of the rules of Wright and Knox and certainly the provisions of the Detection Club oath itself were designed to distinguish the relatively highbrow detective novel from the lowbrow thriller, thus elevating the detective novel as a literary art form, is a point that seems to have been missed by Julian Symons and P.D. James. For example, both Symons and James have trouble comprehending the point of the Chinaman prohibition, which clearly was a squib directed at the silliness of "Yellow Peril" thrillers. Symons deems the Chinaman prohibition "unintelligible," while for her part James finds it "difficult to understand." James allows the possibility that the prohibition was "obliquely referring to Dr. Fu Manchu," yet she does not credibly explain why it would have done so. See Symons, *Bloody Murder*, 107; James, *Detective Fiction*, 53.

29. *Hobart Mercury*, 1 August 1930, 3.

30. On the crime fiction of Anthony Berkeley Cox, see Malcolm J. Turnbull, *Elusion Aforethought: The Life and Writing of Anthony Berkeley Cox* (Bowling Green, OH: Popular Press, 1996).

31. Anthony Berkeley, *The Wychford Poisoning Case: An Essay in Criminology* (London: Collins, 1926), 143.

32. Anthony Berkeley, *Roger Sheringham and the Vane Mystery* (1927; repr., London: House of Stratus, 2003).

33. Symons, *Bloody Murder*, 111. Oddly, P.D. James, who generally shares Julian Symons aesthetic outlook on the historical development of the mystery genre, overlooks Cox in *Talking about Detective Fiction*.

34. Preface to Anthony Berkeley, *The Second Shot* (London: Hodder & Stoughton, 1930). Julian Symons reflects the usual critical view when he praises "the masterly way in which [the Francis Iles novels] broke away from the conventions of the detective story." Symons, *Bloody Murder*, 140. *Before the Fact* was famously filmed by Alfred Hitchcock, under the title *Suspicion* (1941).

35. Preface to Anthony Berkeley, *Panic Party* (London: Hodder & Stoughton, 1934).

36. Preface to Milward Kennedy, *Sic Transit Gloria* (London: Gollancz, 1936).

37. Symons, *Bloody Murder*, 135; James, *Detective Fiction*, 90. In Symons' view, the later Sayers novels, "with the exception of the lively *Murder Must Advertise* [1933], show an increasing pretentiousness, a dismal sentimentality, and a slackening of the close plotting that had been [Sayers'] chief virtue." Symons, *Bloody Murder*, 135. Today, however, it is apparent that among the scholars of British mystery, admirers of the "manners" trend in Sayers' later fiction outnumber detractors. See, for example, Barbara Reynolds, *Dorothy L. Sayers: Her Life and Soul* (New York: St. Martin's, 1993); Catherine Kenney, *The Remarkable*

Case of Dorothy L. Sayers (Kent, OH: Kent State University Press, 1990); and McGregor with Lewis, *Conundrums for the Long Week-End*. Kenney, for instance, with unbounded enthusiasm applauds the movement in Sayers' fiction "away from the artificial plot and into real human problems.... Few novelists of any stripe present a world as richly varied as hers; one must go back to Dickens to see as many levels and types reflected in the fictional mirror. In the novels of Dorothy L. Sayers, one may come to know England as it was between the two great wars." Of a Sayers work like *The Documents in the Case* (1930), written after the author's shift in aesthetic values had commenced, Kenney declares that "a reader who already knows the solution to the books' detective problem can return to it again and again, to savor its remarkable characterizations, its cogent comments on modern life, and its insights into human relationships and motivations." Kenney, *Remarkable Case*, 46, 49. This effusion of praise could not be more at odds with Julian Symons' categorical dismissal in *Bloody Murder* of the view that Sayers can be seen as a serious novelist. Symons' friend, fellow crime writer and successor as President of the Detection Club, H.R.F. Keating, explains concerning Symons' distaste for Sayers' work that "Miss [sic] Sayers' open admiration for the absurdly aristocratic Lord Peter Wimsey, the anti–Semitic remarks she allows him to make, the liberties she granted herself in the way of long-windedness had over the years irritated a writer [Symons] with a very different approach." Despite this concession, Keating asserts that Symons' "appraisal of [Sayers'] merits ... is ungrudging, and scarcely to be faulted." Sayers advocates, however, doubtlessly would find much to fault in Symons's overall assessment. Keating, "Crossbow," 113.

38. Sayers, Introduction to *Great Short Stories*, 37. The triolet is a poetic form originating in thirteenth-century France.

39. Ibid., 37, 38, 40.

40. Ibid., 33, 40, 44.

41. Dorothy L. Sayers, Introduction to *Great Short Stories of Detection, Mystery and Horror*, 2nd Ser., ed. Dorothy L. Sayers (London: Gollancz, 1931), 12, 17.

42. In the Golden Age a detective novel sold on average in the United States only about 2,000 copies (mostly to rental libraries), with even the most successful typically topping out at some 10,000 to 15,000 copies sold. The print runs of British first editions of Dorothy L. Sayers' mysteries published between 1930 and 1935 averaged 5,200 copies, but her final novels, *Gaudy Night* and *Busman's Honeymoon*, enjoyed initial print runs of 17,000 and 20,000 copies respectively. Janet Laurence, "Publishing in the Golden Age of Crime Fiction," in *AZ Murder Goes ... Classic: Current Crimewriters Revisit Past Masters*, ed. Susan Malling and Barbara Peters (Scottsdale, AZ: Poisoned Pen Press, 1997), 256. Sayers' *Gaudy Night* supposedly sold over 36,000 copies within a few weeks of its publication. *London Daily Herald*, 2 January 1936, 8. On detective novel sales in the Golden Age, see Marie F. Rodell, *Mystery Fiction: Theory and Technique* (New York: Duell, Sloan and Pearce, 1943), 213–220.

43. Dorothy L. Sayers, Introduction to *Tales of Detection*, ed. Dorothy L. Sayers (1936; repr., London: J.M. Dent & Sons, 1947), xII, xIII.

44. Symons, *Bloody Murder*, 118; *The Spectator* 146 (9 May 1931): 146–147; 155 (1 November 1935): 710; 156 (28 February 1936): 364.

45. See Curtis Evans, "Was Corinne's Murder Fairly Clued? The Detection Club and Fair Play, 1930–1953" *CADS Supplement* 14 (2011).

46. *London Sunday Times*, 25 February 1934, 9; 30 September 1934, 9. Evidence of Sayers' continued interest in the puzzle element of the detective novel is readily apparent from her correspondence with fellow Detection Club members in the late 1940s and early 1950s. In her letters concerning the suitability of various prospective new members, such as Elizabeth Ferrars, Douglas Browne, Andrew Garve, Michael Gilbert and even Julian Symons himself, it is clear that the self-deposed Crime Queen still believed in the primacy of detection in a detective novel. See Evans, "Corinne." Of Sayers' mystery fiction reviews in the *Sunday Times*, Sayers scholar Catherine Kenney has noted the irony of the fact that "Sayers herself could enjoy many more crime writers than do most of her [present day] admirers." Kenney, *Remarkable Case*, 33. The reading in McGregor's and Lewis' *Conundrums for the Long Week-End* of Sayers' critical works and detective novels as consistently anti-puzzle (see their Chapter Four) is passing strained.

47. *London Sunday Times*, 10 June 1934, 9; 11 November 1935, 9; 17 February 1935, 9.

48. Ibid., 2 February 1936, 9; 21 February 1937, 10; 19 July 1936, 10; 13 October 1935, 7; 6 June 1937, 11.

49. *The Spectator* 156 (1 April 1936): 764; 157 (30 October 1936): 770. Interestingly, Nicholas Blake's "crime, the whole crime, and nothing but the crime" comment was paraded by Collins as a badge of honor on Miles Burton dust jackets. See, for example, those for 1940's *Murder in the Coalhole* and *Mr. Westerby Missing*.

50. John Strachey, "The Golden Age of English Detection," *Saturday Review of Literature* 19 (7 January 1939): 12–13. A first cousin, once removed, of noted writer and Bloomsbury Group member Lytton Strachey, John Strachey later joined the Labour party and entered politics, serving in the Clement Attlee government.

51. Strachey, "Golden Age," 13.

52. Robert D. Denham, ed., *The Diaries of Northrop Frye, 1942–1955* (Toronto: University of Toronto Press, 2001), 14.

53. *The Spectator* 159 (30 July 1937): 214; 163 (20 October 1939): 555.

54. *The Spectator* 158 (5 February 1937): 232; 166 (5 December 1941): 538; 169 (1 January 1943): 16. E.B.C. Jones married a Cambridge literature professor, F.L. (Peter) Lucas, and was known among friends, who included members of the Bloomsbury Group, as Topsy Lucas. See Noel Annan, *The Dons: Mentors, Eccentrics and Geniuses* (Chicago: University of Chicago Press, 2000), 171, 180.

55. *New Statesman and Nation* 11 (29 February 1936): 316; 12 (20 June 1936): 913; 25 (27 March 1942): 293; 13 (6 March 1937): 374; 15 (26 February 1938): 343. Toward the end of his mortal stay at the *New Statesman*, Ralph Partridge frequently found, to his intense dismay, that even Agatha Christie was not proving worthy of Agatha Christie.

56. Symons, *Bloody Murder*, 167; *Adelaide Mail*, 10 October 1953, 14; 5 June 1954, 5. Indicative of his contempt for his subject, McElwain misidentifies the murderer in the John Rhode novel *Blackthorn House* (1949). He also inconsiderately reveals a major part of the solution of the Rhode tale *Family Affairs* (1950) in order to chastise the author for using what he deems too implausible a murder method. See *Adelaide Mail*, 19 March 1949, 9; 12 August 1950, 17. In a similarly scathing vein, Ralph Partridge wrote of John Rhode's *The Domestic Agency* (1955) that "Mr. Rhode's greatest virtue is that his

plots run true to real life, which ... is often dull, stodgy and repetitive." *New Statesman and Nation* 51 (9 April 1955): 512. During this decade Street's books actually received some good notices in provincial papers, however. The mid–1950s Miles Burton titles *A Crime in Time* and *Found Drowned* both were praised as "ingenious," for example, the former by the *Oxford Mail* and the latter by the *Wolverhampton Express and Star*. See the back dust jacket flap of Miles Burton, *The Chinese Puzzle* (London: Collins, 1957). Julian Symons himself displayed a personal aversion to the Great Detective in his own crime fiction. In his first published detective novel, *The Immaterial Murder Case* (1946), he introduces a rather heavy-handed caricature of the Great Detective named Teak Woode. It should not come as a surprise to learn that the Great Man does not solve the case.

57. Evidently there remained still a reliable if reduced Humdrum readership into the 1960s. As late as 1966, a publisher recalled of Christopher Bush, a Humdrum-affiliated detective novelist who published his last mystery in 1968, that "he has a considerable public, a 'steady Bush public,' a public that has endured through many years. He never presents any problem to his publisher who knows exactly how many copies of a title may be safely printed for the loyal Bush fans; the number is a healthy one too." Laurence, "Publishing in the Golden Age," 257. No doubt this point held true as well for John Street's steady stream of novels, particularly the John Rhodes, every title of which was published in both Great Britain and the United States from 1927 through 1961.

58. Jacques Barzun and Wendell Hertig Taylor, *A Catalogue of Crime* (New York: Harper & Row, 1971), 20–21, 357.

59. See H.R.F. Keating's Introduction to John Rhode, *The Claverton Mystery* (1933; repr., London: Collins, 1985), 6, 7.

60. Stephen Knight, *Crime Fiction 1800–2000: Detection, Death, Diversity* (Basingstoke, UK: Palgrave McMillan, 2004), 98, 105.

Chapter Two

1. J.K. Van Dover, *You Know My Method: The Science of the Detective* (Bowling Green, OH: Popular Press, 1994), 157. For the "Public Brain Tester No. 1" comment, see the back matter of *Death in the Hopfields* (London: Collins, 1937). Since R. Austin Freeman was a generation older than John Street and other true Humdrum mystery writers and published his first detective novel in 1907, thirteen years before the Golden Age is commonly considered to have started, he is not considered a Golden Age Humdrum novelist, even though he was active during the entire span of the period (roughly 1920 to 1940). As discussed in Chapter One, however, Freeman was the major progenitor of the Humdrum detection writers of the Golden Age.

2. *London Times*, 2 January 1965; Howard Haycraft, ed., *The Boy's Second Book of Detective Stories* (New York: Harpers, 1940), 255. Street was recently the subject of a short article in the July 2011 edition of *Gibraltar Magazine*. See Dave Wood, "Gibraltar-born MI7 Agent is famous Detective Novelist" (pp.40–41). Reflecting the current (and mistaken) wisdom derived from Julian Symons, Wood concludes in passing that the "critics were less kind" to Street's detective novels than the public (p. 41).

3. Patrick Mileham to the author, 18, 19 August 2008; "Cecil John Charles Street," *Oxford Dictionary of National Biography* (*ODNB*), vol. 53 (London: Oxford University Press, 2004), 61–62; Martin Roundell Greene to Curtis J. Evans, 18 April 2007; Martin Roundell Greene, *Electric Lyme* (Crewkerne, UK: Martin Roundell Greene, 2006), 19, 24, 27, 29; www.1911census.co.uk; Tony Medawar, "'Rhode' Closed," *CADS: Crime and Detective Stories* 43 (June 2003): 33–34; Brendan Clifford, *The Administration of Ireland, 1920 by Major C.J.C. Street with a Review of His Other Writings* (Belfast: Athol Books, 2001), 5–12. Some information on Street's military service (along with a photograph of Street) is found on the back of an American paperback edition of the John Rhode title *Death Sits on the Board*, published by Popular Library in 1943. The Kirwans were a prominent, ancient landowning family in Galway, Ireland. See Ronan Lynch, *The Kirwans of Castlehacket, Co. Galway* (Dublin: Four Courts Press, 2006). Eileen Waller, of Irish Cromwellian ancestry, was a daughter of a civil engineer and granddaughter of John Francis Waller, a poet famous for "The Spinning Wheel," a popular Irish song. Henry Boylan, ed., *A Dictionary of Irish Biography*, 3rd ed. (Dublin: Gill and MacMillan, 1998), 438. Eileen likely was named after the young woman in the poem.

4. See the quotations from critical reviews in the front matter of F.O.O., *The Making of a Gunner* (London: Everleigh Nash, 1916) and Robert Dunlop, review of *With the Guns* on Great War Forum, http://1914–1918.invisionzone.com/forums/index.php?showtopic=17364. In her conversations with historian Douglas Greene, Clarice Carr, the widow of mystery writer John Dickson Carr, recalled John Street as, to quote Professor Greene, "a great storyteller with entertaining accounts of his army experiences." Douglas G. Greene, *John Dickson Carr: The Man Who Explained Miracles* (New York: Otto Penzler, 1995), 202. Many of these accounts likely originally appeared in Street's war memoirs.

5. F.O.O., *Gunner*, 78–79.

6. Ibid., 79.

7. Ibid., 34.

8. Ibid., 42–43.

9. F.O.O., *With the Guns* (London: Everleigh Nash, 1916), 47–48.

10. F.O.O., *Gunner*, 104; F.O.O., *Guns*, 29, 50–51.

11. 1891 England Census, RG12, 555, 10, 14; Edward T. Law, "Huddersfield and District History: Storthes Hall, Thurstonland," http://homepage.eircom.net/~lawedd/STORTHESHALL.htm. On General John Alfred Street, see Sir Bernard Burke, *A Genealogical and Heraldic History of the Colonial Gentry*, vol. 1 (London: Harrison and Sons, 1891), 29, and *The Annual Register: A Review of Public Events at Home and Abroad for the Year 1889* (London: Rivingtons, 1890), 176. General Street was a veteran of the First Opium and Crimean Wars and also served in Gibraltar and India. Caroline Bill was General Street's second wife. By his first wife, who died in Ceylon from dysentery in 1874, he had three children, Alfred Edmund Campbell (1861), Sophia Catherine (1862–1947) and Louisa May (1864–1944). In 1882, two years before her half-brother Cecil John Charles Street was born, Sophia Catherine Street married Edric Frederick Gifford, 3rd Baron Gifford (1849–1911). Sophia, Baroness Gifford, sounds an interesting person. She converted to Catholicism and later served as a nurse in the Boer War, receiving the Queen's SA [South Africa] Medal. After her husband's death, she purchased Old Park, Bosham, Sussex, where she kept a pack of harrier hounds, serving as Master and

Huntsman until 1931. Neither John Street nor his much older half-sisters had issue, meaning General Street's line died with his children. See "Lady Gifford's Harriers Point-to-Point Steeplechases," www.nationalarchives.gov.uk/a2a/records.aspx?cat=182-amsl1846&cid=-1#-1.

12. 1891 England Census, 14; John Rhode, *Men Die at Cyprus Lodge* (London: Collins Crime Club, 1943), 65. "Firlands" earlier appeared as the home of the murder victim in the John Rhode novel *Mystery at Olympia*, where Street unsentimentally described the house as "an outstanding example of the worst type of Victorian domestic architecture. One felt that the designer's aim had been to achieve the maximum of pretentiousness without, and discomfort within." Nevertheless, the author allows that "the house was solidly built and in excellent repair." John Rhode, *Mystery at Olympia* (1937; repr., London: Collins Crime Club, 1935), 23. Street may have modeled Freddie Norton-Sandway, the exuberant fifteen-year-old in *Death on Sunday* (London: Collins, 1939), after himself: "He likes tinkering about with wireless sets and gadgets like that. His doting mother says he's got the scientific temperament and that it ought to be encouraged" (p. 8).

13. F.O.O., *Gunner*, 111–113.
14. Ibid., 121–123.
15. Clifford, *Ireland*, 178, 188.
16. F.O.O., *Gunner*, 89, 95, 160, 210. Indicative of Street's "realistic" view of warfare is a passage in *Gunner* concerning the deliberate shelling of churches. Street deems such actions regrettable but necessary: "If an observer can see from a church tower, he will most certainly use it; and it is an axiom of modern warfare that all possible observation posts must as far as possible be destroyed." F.O.O., *Gunner*, 62. Street himself frequently was a potential target of German fire as he observed enemy positions from British-held church towers.
17. Clifford, *Ireland*, 185, 187. For evidence of widespread English concern over the French use of African troops in the occupation, see the London *Daily Herald* article "Black Scourge in Europe: Sexual Horror Let Loose by France on the Rhine" and the pamphlet *The Horror on the Rhine*, both by English journalist, author and politician Edmund Dene Morel. It is worth noting that Morel was a pacifist and socialist, which places him at considerable political distance from Street. On Morel's writings, see Tina Marie Campt, *Other Germans: Black Germans and the Politics of Race, Gender and Memory in the Third Reich* (Lansing: University of Michigan Press, 2003), 36.
18. Clifford, *Ireland*, 187.
19. C.J.C. Street, *Thomas Masaryk of Czechoslovakia* (New York: Dodd, Mead, 1930), 127–136.
20. On the Marconi Scandal, see C.J.C. Street, *Lord Reading* (New York: Frederick A. Stokes, 1928), 94–140; Frances Donaldson, *The Marconi Scandal* (New York: Harcourt, Brace, 1962); H. Montgomery Hyde, *Lord Reading: The Life of Rufus Isaacs, First Marquess of Reading* (New York: Farrar, Straus and Giroux, 1967), 121–64; Denis Judd, *Lord Reading: Rufus Isaacs, First Marquess of Reading, Lord Chief Justice and Viceroy of India, 1869–1933* (London: Weidenfeld and Nicholson, 1982), 90–107. On the reactions of G.K. Chesterton and Rudyard Kipling, see Bryan Cheyette, *Constructions of "the Jew" in English Literature and Society: Racial Representations, 1875–1945* (Cambridge: Cambridge University Press, 1993), 86–87, 179–80.
21. Street, *Lord Reading*, 59, 76, 101, 114. Street took a dim view of Lloyd George's political rhetoric, terming it at various places in the book "vituperative abuse," "vulgar invective," "Socialistic oratory" and "clamorous invective against the upper and middle classes." Ibid., 67, 67, 75, 76.
22. John Cooper and B.A. Pike, *Detective Fiction: The Collector's Guide*, rev. ed. (1988; repr., Aldershot, England: Scolar Press, 1994), 258; Freeman Wills Crofts to Peter Ibbotson, 23 November 1949, letter in possession of the author. That Cecil Waye is yet another John Street pseudonym was a discovery made by Tony Medawar.
23. Jacques Barzun and Wendell Hertig Taylor, *A Catalogue of Crime*, rev. ed. (1971; repr., New York: Harper & Row, 1989), 455; John Rhode, *A.S.F.: The Story of a Great Conspiracy* (London: Geoffrey Bles, 1924), 6, 98.
24. Rhode, *A.S.F.*, 293, 299.
25. Ibid., 262, 311.
26. John Rhode, *The Double Florin* (London: Geoffrey Bles, 1924), 24, 26, 208, 235.
27. Ibid., 241, 243, 298.
28. Leroy L. Panek, *The Special Branch: The British Spy Novel, 1890–1980* (Bowling Green, OH: Popular Press, 1981), 80. On negative images of Jewish capitalists in British detective fiction, see Malcolm J. Turnbull, *Victims or Villains: Jewish Images in Classic English Detective Fiction* (Bowling Green, OH: Popular Press, 1998).
29. *The Alarm* is egregiously overwritten, as can be glimpsed from this extract from a speech by Aline, the feminine (and rather feminist) point of the novel's romantic triangle: "Do you imagine that I, being what God made me, should be content with what you had to offer me, not materially, but mentally? ... Slaves all men are, I know, slaves to influences over which they have no control. But your bondage is the hardest of all ... for it is your brain and not your limbs that wear the fetters. Could I consent to share a bondage such as that? ... I should beat my wings unceasingly in the cage you wrought for me, however spacious, however ornamented with the gilding you call fame.... Perhaps I am an outcast among women, a rebel born, feeling no reverence for the laws and ordinances of my sex.... Absolute freedom I did not demand, for absolute freedom pre-supposes the severing of all ties, the complete escape from the social system we call civilisation, and that no one can achieve. But for my husband I sought one upon whom the fetters lay as lightly as possible, an outlaw like myself who earned his life not as a wage-slave, but took from it what he needed and scorned the rest." John Rhode, *The Alarm* (London: Geoffrey Bles, 1925), 73–75. Incredibly, this formal philosophical discourse on freedom is presented as off-the-cuff conversation on Aline's part. Fortunately for the Major and his readers, in the coming Priestley novels he learned to make his characters talk more like actual human beings. Incidentally, both Aline's name and her free-thinking sentiments, if not necessarily the floridness of the writing, suggest the influence of Street's companion, Eileen Waller.
30. John Rhode, *The Paddington Mystery* (London: Geoffrey Bles, 1925), 17–18. Soon in the series, Priestley is being referred to the author as a scientist, not a mathematician, making Priestley more a direct descendant of R. Austin Freeman's great scientific detective, the medical jurist Doctor Thorndyke.
31. Ibid., 137, 193, 194, 201, 230.
32. John Rhode, *The Ellerby Case* (London: Geoffrey Bles, 1927), 40; John Rhode, *The Davidson Case* (London: Geoffrey Bles, 1929), 100; John Rhode, *The Corpse in the Car* (London: Collins Crime Club, 1935), 64.
33. Rhode, *Davidson*, 294; Rhode, *Ellerby*, 93.

34. John Rhode, *Dr. Priestley's Quest* (1926; repr., London: Geoffrey Bles, 1935).
35. See the critical excerpts on the front flap of the dust jacket of John Rhode, *Peril at Cranbury Hall* (London: Geoffrey Bles, 1930).
36. Correspondence, Box 19, Dodd, Mead Mss., Lilly Library Manuscript Collection, University of Indiana.
37. *ODNB*, vol. 53, 62. On the economics of mystery sales at this time, see Marie F. Rodell, *Mystery Fiction: Theory and Technique* (New York: Duell, Sloan and Pearce, 1943), 213–218. According to Rodell, "The vast majority of the mystery fans — about 99% of them" thriftily chose to borrow mystery books from rental libraries rather than purchase them, severely curtailing the potential profit mystery authors could earn from their books. Thus 60,000 people, say, might actually read a given mystery title that sold only 3,000 copies. By the 1940s a handful of what Rodell called the "most successful mystery writers, at the very top of the heap" — such as Agatha Christie — sold from fifteen to twenty thousand copies of each book they published. Rodell, *Mystery Fiction*, 214. John Street would not have risen to this level, but he may have surpassed the 4,000 copies figure I have attributed to him, particularly in the United States, which of course had a larger population than Great Britain. In that case his income in modern dollars would have surpassed an average of $100,000 a year, though it is unlikely that it would have reached $200,000.
38. *Times Literary Supplement*, 17 January 1929, 46. In her diary entry for May 20, 1936, the mystery-fancying Kansas farm wife, Stella Wilkinson, records finishing reading *The House on Tollard Ridge*, but sadly she makes no comment on the content: "Earle and I planted a good deal of the garden but the wind blew so hard we found working difficult. The dust is blowing, too. I finished reading 'The House on Tollard Ridge,' by John Rhode." See Stella Wilkinson Diary, www.wilkinson.ws/claude/stella/diary/may_1936.htm.
39. John Rhode, *The House on Tollard Ridge* (London: Geoffrey Bles, 1929), 154–60. Note the similarity of Kitty Hapgood's sentiments on marriage to those of Aline in *The Alarm*. Quite broadminded by Golden Age standards, Street's views on the marital relationship no doubt reflect experience from his own life.
40. Ibid., 288.
41. *The House on Tollard Ridge* also resembles an Agatha Christie short story bearing the same title as the Kipling tale and published in the *Sunday Chronicle Annual* in December 1926.
42. John Rhode, *The Murders in Praed Street* (London: Geoffrey Bles, 1928), 1; Barzun and Taylor, *Catalogue of Crime* (1989), 452.
43. Rhode, *Davidson*, 32, 34.
44. Ibid., 76.
45. Ibid., 202.
46. Ibid., 203, 253.
47. Ibid., 277.
48. Ibid., 11, 311, 315. [**SPOILER ALERT**] Guy's impersonation of Hector raised the critical hackles of no less than Dashiell Hammett, who, reviewing *The Davidson Case* in the *Saturday Review of Literature*, damned the novel as one "designed to earn the scorn of all true lovers of detective stories." Hammett concluded that the author had cheated "most abominably" by declaring, in his own voice, that the (disguised) man traveling to Bratton Grange was Hector Davidson, when it in fact was his cousin, Guy Davidson. *Saturday Review of Literature* 6 (21 September 1929): 164. A quarter-century later Agatha Christie used the same device as Street had, in the novel *After the Funeral* (1953). [**END SPOILER ALERT**]
49. Rhode, *Davidson*, 304–305.
50. Ibid., 317–318.
51. Ibid., 202.
52. Ibid., 31–32.
53. Sir Alfred Mond (1869–1930) "was one of the great industrialists and financiers of the early twentieth century.... He believed that the old laissez-faire was no longer the way to produce general prosperity, and he was an opponent of confrontational approaches to industrial relations.... He opposed lockouts and strikes as methods of resolving disputes, and thought that there should be profit-sharing, employee shareholding, and what today would be called a stakeholder economy." A.N. Wilson, *After the Victorians: The Decline of Britain in the World* (New York: Farrar, Straus and Giroux, 2005), 281.
54. John Rhode, *The Hanging Woman* (London: Collins, 1931), 106.
55. Ibid., 275, 306–307.
56. Ibid., 83, 113, 193.
57. *London Sunday Times*, 3 January 1937, 10; 13 October 1935, 7; 10 June 1934, 7.
58. John Rhode, *The Claverton Mystery* (London: Collins Crime Club, 1933), 247.
59. Ibid., 248.
60. John Rhode, *Poison for One* (London: Collins Crime Club, 1934), 92.
61. *London Sunday Times*, 10 June 1934, 7.
62. John Rhode, *Corpse in the Car*, 10, 11, 14, 60.
63. Ibid., 68.
64. Ibid., 206, 232–33
65. *London Sunday Times* 17 February 1935, 9; Rhode, *Corpse*, 74.
66. Rhode, *Corpse*, 114, 116, 239–40, 242.
67. *London Sunday Times*, 9 June 1935, 7; Barzun and Taylor, *Catalogue*, 451.
68. John Rhode, *Death at the Helm* (New York: Dodd, Mead, 1941), 187.
69. John Rhode, *Men Die at Cyprus Lodge* (London: Collins Crime Club, 1943), 88; Anthony Boucher, *San Francisco Chronicle*, 11 June 1944, reprinted in *The Anthony Boucher Chronicles: Reviews and Commentary, 1942–1947*, vol. II, *The Week in Murder*, ed. Francis M. Nevins (Vancleave, MS: Ramble House, 2002), 83.
70. John Rhode, *Vegetable Duck* (London: Collins Crime Club, 1944), 15, 56–57,182–183; Boucher, *San Francisco Chronicle*, 20 May 1945, reprinted in Nevins, *Chronicles*, 134. Surely *Vegetable Duck* is one of the oddest titles for a detective novel in the genre, but I think the title reflects Major Street's underappreciated, quirky sense of humor. For those bemused by the title, I append the following recipe, extracted from page 238 of *May Byron's Vegetable Book* (London: Hodder and Stoughton, 1916): 540. "Vegetable Duck: Take a young and tender vegetable marrow, slit it right down, remove the seeds, fill the two cavities with breadcrumbs, chopped onions, chopped sage, and about a tablespoonful of butter, mixed with one beaten egg. Season with pepper and salt. Bind the halves together again, and put in a slow oven till baked a good brown. Baste with a little melted butter." Granted, Ms. Barton's recipe does not include minced meat, but perhaps the determined reader can improvise. In *Dead on the Track* (1943; repr., Toronto: Collins, 1945), Street describes, with some horror, a wartime austerity version of vegetable duck, called vegetable goose. "[I]t's made of parsnips and

lentils with apple sauce," declares its confident creator. "Nice and tasty." The author, however, terms the dish "a livid and amorphous mess" (pp. 121–122).

71. John Rhode, *Signal for Death* (English title: *They Watched by Night*) (New York: Dodd, Mead, 1941) 261–62.

72. Ibid., 273–274.

73. Barzun and Taylor, *Crime* (1989), 454. For E.R. Punshon's assessment, see the dust jacket back flap for *The Fourth Bomb* (London: Collins, 1942).

74. Barzun and Taylor, *Crime* (1989), 454; Basil Hogarth, *Writing Thrillers for Profit: A Practical Guide* (London: A. & C. Black, 1936), 115; *New Statesman and Nation* 8 (10 November 1934): 678.

75. *London Sunday Times*, 11 November 1934, 9.

76. *New York Times Book Review*, 27 June 1937, 88; *London Sunday Times*, 6 June 1937, 11.

77. John Rhode, *Death Sits on the Board* (English title: *Death on the Board*) (New York: Dodd, Mead, 1937), 2.

78. Ibid., 2–3, 8.

79. Ibid., 10, 79, 80, 157.

80. Ibid., 211.

81. Ibid., 32, 29, 52–53, 181, 305.

82. Ibid., 44, 307.

83. Ibid., 50. Street himself was the most important supporter of the cricket team in Laddingford, Kent, where he resided in the 1930s.

84. John Rhode, *Invisible Weapons* (New York: Dodd, Mead, 1938), 76.

85. *London Sunday Times*, 14 November 1937, 11. On the Burton novels, see below.

86. Anthony Gilbert to Dorothy L. Sayers, 12 September 1939, 4 November 1940, 29 April 1941, 6 July 1941, Dorothy L. Sayers to Anthony Gilbert, 8 July 1942, Dorothy L. Sayers Papers [DLS Papers], Marion E. Wade Center, Wheaton College; Simon Knott, "St. Edmund, Swanton Novers," *The Norfolk Churches Site*, www.norfolkchurches.co.uk/swantonnovers/swantonnovers.htm. In her April 1942 letter, Anthony Gilbert wrote, "John Rhode is never coming to London again." Gilbert's novel *He Came by Night* (1944) is affectionately dedicated to Eileen Waller "in memory of the haunted village."

87. Juanita Hadwin, "Swanton Novers, Norfolk, England: The Village, its Inhabitants and its History," www3.telus.net/swanton_novers; Paula Simpson to Curtis J. Evans, 14 January 2004, 30 September 2008; Anthony Gilbert to Dorothy L. Sayers, 26 February 1950, DLS Papers. Paula Simpson reports that her grandmother approved of and often quoted the Labour party slogan, "Think of Tomorrow Vote Labour Today." Both her grandmother and Major Street "were in agreement that they should help the less well off in any way they could," she notes; and Street "always supported [the Village] financially." Paula Simpson to the author, 14 January 2004, 30 September 2008.

88. Greene, *Carr*, 202; Anthony Gilbert to Dorothy L. Sayers, 1941, DLS Papers; Michael Gilbert, Foreword to John Rhode, *Mystery at Greycombe Farm* (1932; repr., Bath, UK: John Curley, 1991).

89. Greene, *Carr*, 196.

90. "John Rhode" to Dorothy L. Sayers, 25 May, 2 June, 3 June, 4 July, 18 August, 22 November 1939, DLS Papers.

91. Peter Ibbotson, "Sayers and Ciphers," *Cryptologia* 25 (April 2001): 81. Street had previously used the Playfair Cipher in a 1930 John Rhode novel, *Peril at Cranbury Hall*.

92. Greene, *Carr*, 225.

93. Christianna Brand, "Detection Club Memories," *CADS: Crime and Detective Stories* 52 (August 2007), 7.

94. Freeman Wills Crofts to Peter Ibbotson, 23 November 1949, letter in possession of author; Barzun and Taylor, *Catalogue of Crime* (1989), 452.

95. Rhode, *Night*, 183. Quarrenden later resurfaces as an assizes judge in *The Lake House* (1946).

96. Anthony Boucher, *San Francisco Chronicle*, 27 October 1946, reprinted in Nevins, *Chronicles*, 219; Barzun and Taylor, *Catalogue of Crime* (1989), 447, 448, 451, 455; *London Sunday Times*, 19 August 1959, 23.

97. For critical praise of *Blackthorn House*, see the front flap of the dust jacket of *Family Affairs* (London: Geoffrey Bles, 1950). The inception of the police procedural mystery subgenre often is associated with the publication of American Hillary Waugh's *Last Seen Wearing* in 1952, yet Englishman Maurice Procter began writing well-received police novels in 1947. Notable thirties predecessors to Maurice Procter include Henry Wade and Basil Thomson. All too frequently in the later Waghorn tales, Street in order to make Priestley more relevant to the plot makes the once fairly keen Jimmy implausibly dim, spoiling a number of potentially excellent novels, such as *Death in Wellington Road* (1952) and *The Dovebury Murders* (1954).

98. John Rhode, *The Case of the Forty Thieves* (English title: *Death at the Inn*) (1953; New York: Dodd, Mead, 1954), 57.

99. John Rhode, *Family Affairs* (London: Geoffrey Bles, 1950), 145.

100. Ibid., 195, 198.

101. Ibid., 254.

102. Ibid., 251.

103. *New York Times Book Review*, 5 July 1959, 12; Barzun and Taylor, *Catalogue of Crime* (1989), 451.

104. John Rhode, *Licensed for Murder* (London: Geoffrey Bles, 1958), 9–10. On Street's fascination as an artillerist with the science of mapmaking, see his comments in F.O.O., *Gunner*, 178. Detailed topography is a common feature of the Rhode and Burton books, but unfortunately few have maps. There are, however, fine endpaper maps in the John Rhode titles *Dead Men at the Folly* (1932) and *Shot at Dawn* (1934) and excellent maps on the fronts of the dust jackets of the 1970s reprint editions of the Miles Burton titles *Murder, M.D.* and *The Three Corpse Trick*. Presumably all these maps were drawn by Street.

105. Ibid., 14.

106. Ibid., 16, 34–35, 39.

107. Ibid., 190.

108. Ibid., 256.

109. Ibid., 164, 225. "The end of [World War II] left most surviving landowners in circumstances more reduced and distressed than they had ever known," writes historian David Cannadine. "And in the austere and egalitarian world of Welfare State socialism that followed, there was a distinct feeling that their remaining economic privileges, political influence, and social status were no longer acceptable." David Cannadine, *The Decline and Fall of the British Aristocracy* (1992; repr., New York: Vintage Books, 1999), 638. *Licensed for Murder* is so up-to-date that one character even mentions "rock and roll"—unfavorably.

110. Dodd, Mead to Harold Ober, 18 September 1936, 23 September 1936, Dodd, Mead Mss, The Lilly Library, University of Indiana. Dodd, Mead in 1936 published two Rhodes, *Mystery at Olympia/Murder at the Motor Show* and *Death at Breakfast*. In 1937, Dodd, Mead again refused to

publish *Verdict*, instead publishing two other Rhode titles, *Death in the Hopfields/The Harvest Murder* and *Death Sits on the Board/Death on the Board*, both of which they reported liking much better than *Verdict*. Dodd, Mead to Constance Smith, 16 December 1936, Dodd, Mead Mss. *In Face of the Verdict* was not finally published in the United States by Dodd, Mead until 1940 (with two other Rhodes). Long and leisurely by 1930s standards and with several anachronisms, *Verdict* may have been written by Rhode in the 1920s and updated by him in 1936. Demonstrating how fertile Street's brain was in the 1930s, every year in that decade saw the author produce not only two or three Rhodes but at least two Miles Burton novels as well (1933 and 1936 saw him produce three). "Cecil Waye" was another, very short-lived, Street pseudonym.

111. Miles Burton, *The Hardway Diamonds Mystery* (London: Collins, 1930), 45, 46, 53, 106.

112. Miles Burton, *The Secret of High Eldersham* (1930; repr., New York: Garland, 1976), 47–48.

113. Ibid., 129–130.

114. Miles Burton, *The Clue of the Fourteen Keys* (English title: *Death at the Club*) (New York: Doubleday, Doran, 1937), 97, 185; Miles Burton, *The Platinum Cat* (London: Collins Crime Club, 1938), 143. Also like Lord Peter, Merrion boasts knowledge of a wide array of subjects, in his case including witchcraft and nautical lore (*The Secret of High Eldersham*), chemistry (*The Cat Jumps*), Norse mythology (*The Platinum Cat*) and anthropology (*The Chinese Puzzle*).

115. Miles Burton, *Written in Dust* (English title: *Murder in the Coalhole*) (New York: Doubleday, Doran, 1940), 209. Inspector Arnold does in fact manage to solve three cases on his own. See *Death Leaves No Card* (1939), *Death of Two Brothers* (1941) and *This Undesirable Residence* (1942). In the first of these tales he amusingly is forced to rely on his own devices when, in answer to his telegram requesting aid on a case, Merrion responds with the dire tidings that he is confined to bed with flu.

116. Ibid., 72, 267.

117. Jacques Barzun and Wendell Hertig Taylor, *A Catalogue of Crime* (New York: Harper & Row, 1971), 90; *New York Times Book Review*, 8 November 1936, 26; *London Sunday Times*, 5 January 1936, 9.

118. Brand, "Memories," 7; Barzun and Taylor, *Catalogue of Crime* (1989), 90.

119. Miles Burton, *To Catch a Thief* (London: Collins, 1934), 6.

120. Ibid., 213, 217.

121. Barzun and Taylor, *Catalogue of Crime* (1989), 88; H.R.F. Keating, *Murder Must Appetize*, (1975; repr., New York: Mysterious Press, 1981), 14–17; dust jacket of Miles Burton, *Dark is the Tunnel* (English title: *Death in the Tunnel*) (London: Doubleday, Doran, 1936). Keating refers to *Death in the Tunnel* as a "railway timetable mystery," although in fact the novel does not really involve railway timetables, which were far more a specialty of Freeman Wills Crofts. Keating, *Appetize*, 14.

122. Burton, *Tunnel*, 16, 49, 280.

123. Ibid., 69–70.

124. Ibid., 74. The dust jacket of *Murder on the Orient Express* evocatively portrays a worker heaping coal into the train's firebox, but such events remain confined behind the scenes in the novel's narrative, which concentrates on famed detective Hercule Poirot interviewing mostly genteel suspects and their servants in a first-class passenger car.

125. See the critical reviews section in the back matter of Miles Burton, *Death at Low Tide* (London: Collins Crime Club, 1938).

126. Burton, *Fourteen Keys*, 51, 66.

127. See the critical reviews section in the back of *Death at Low Tide*.

128. *New York Times Book Review*, 25 September 1938, 106; Barzun and Taylor, *Catalogue of Crime* (1989), 92. Inspector Arnold is fairly sophisticated in his first two appearances, in *The Menace on the Downs* (1931) and *Death of Mr. Gantley* (1932) — in the former novel he can read German and in the latter he has a doomed love affair with the pretty heroine of the tale — but he soon becomes comically bumptious. For example, in *The Charbanc Mystery* Arnold fails to recognize the name of Leonardo da Vinci. "By Jove!" exclaims Merrion at one point in that novel, "You ought to have a fresco painted on the walls of your room at the Yard. *The Triumph of the Obvious!* Pity Leonardo da Vinci's dead. He'd have loved it." An uncomprehending Arnold replies: "Sounds like one of those dagoes round Soho way, but I don't remember him, and we don't let fellows like that loose in the Yard, as you ought to know by this time." Miles Burton, *The Charabanc Mystery* (London: Collins Crime Club, 1934), 86.

129. Miles Burton, *The Platinum Cat* (London: Collins, 1938), 25, 38, 58.

130. Miles Burton, *Death Leaves No Card* (1939; repr., Toronto: Collins, 1942), 81, 147. The *Daily Telegraph* review excerpt is found on the front cover of the paperback edition.

131. Ibid., 69, 88. Other farcical charities in Street's works are the Ranch o' Rest for superannuated horses in *Situation Vacant* (see below), the Errand Boys' Aid Society in *Death Pays a Dividend* and the Lap-dog Protection Society in *Peril at Cranbury Hall*.

132. Ibid., 188, 190.

133. Barzun and Taylor, *Catalogue of Crime* (1989), 93.

134. Miles Burton, *Murder, M.D.* (1943; repr., Hornchurch, UK: Ian Henry, 1975), 6.

135. Ibid., 9.

136. Ibid., 45, 50.

137. Ibid., 186.

138. *New York Times Book Review*, 21 November 1943, 44; Boucher, *San Francisco Chronicle*, 21 November 1943, 21 May 1944, in Nevins, *Chronicles*, 52, 79. On Anthony Boucher's politics, see Jeffrey Marks, *Anthony Boucher: A Biobibliography* (Jefferson, NC: McFarland, 2008).

139. Burton, *Murder, M.D.*, 40.

140. Ibid., 66, 70–71. "Exton Forcett had remained immune from the corrupting influence of feminism," notes Street sardonically. "Even the Women's Institute under the able guidance of Mrs. Laverock had confined itself to domestic matters and remained aloof from local politics. It knitted comforts, it baked meat pies for farmworkers, it made jams of curious and hitherto unknown consistency. None of its members had ever aspired to a seat on the parish council." Ibid., 69.

141. Ibid., 96.

142. Ibid., 19, 71. Eileen Draper's name resembles that of Street's companion and later wife, Eileen Waller. That the name St. John Cecil appears to be a play on the author's own name, Cecil John Charles Street, seems another example of the author's subtle humor. Was Hermione a portrait of his first wife?

143. Barzun and Taylor, *Catalogue of Crime* (1989), 92–93. Between 1935 and 1949, Street published thirty-one novels under the Miles Burton name; nineteen of were published in the United States.

144. Miles Burton, *The Cat Jumps* (London: Collins, 1946), 163.

145. Miles Burton, *Situation Vacant* (London: Collins, 1946), 30, 47. Mr. Clipsham bears a suspicious resemblance to the author, being a pipe smoker and a large man, "over six foot tall and weighing some seventeen stone." Like Street, Clipsham at noon emerges from his study and walks to the local inn (here, The Speckled Trout) for a pint of bitter and chat with the locals. Having traveled widely, he possesses "a vast fund of miscellaneous knowledge, and a quick understanding of human nature and its failings." He takes "a genuine pleasure in helping people out in their difficulties, and if a pound or two could smooth them out, the necessary sum was forthcoming." Ibid., 9. At the time of the events detailed in *Situation Vacant*, he has even started writing a book — though not a detective novel!

146. Miles Burton, *Death Takes the Living* (London: Collins, 1949), 8, 10.

147. Ibid., 82, 122.

148. Ibid., 183, 192.

149. Barzun and Taylor, *Catalogue of Crime* (1989), 90; Burton, *Living*, 16, 21, 25–26, 177.

150. Ibid., 9, 21.

151. Miles Burton, *Ground for Suspicion* (London: Collins, 1950), 8, 256. Shellmouth is more fortunate than the village in *Devil's Reckoning*, a Miles Burton title published the previous year. The village in the latter tale is taken over by the military so that it may serve as a missile range and its luckless inhabitants are evicted (interestingly, this event, which takes place near the end of the novel and is portrayed caustically, was deleted from the American edition of the novel). Street's dissatisfaction with London is suggested by a line in his 1953 novel *The Case of the Forty Thieves*, wherein the author writes of a character (a surrogate for himself who is looking for a locale in which to retire) that "he had come to the conclusion that London was an abominable place" after spending merely a week there. John Rhode, *The Case of the Forty Thieves* (New York: Dodd, Mead, 1954) (published in England in 1953 as *Death at the Inn*).

152. The copy of *Heir to Murder* I have consulted is a digitalized one, found at *The Maywrite Library: E-Texts of Classical Golden Age Mystery Novels and Short Stories*, http://www.munseys.com/diskfour/heirmudex.htm.

153. Ibid; Burton, *Ground*, 10.

154. Miles Burton, *Beware Your Neighbour* (Collins: London, 1951), 5, 23, 25, 99. As early as 1946, Street gave hint of where his thoughts were trending on the social theme of Labour practicing the politics of envy when he gratuitously noted of the cantankerous village chemist of *Situation Vacant* that, his "political theories being of the advanced Left, he had a standing grievance against society in general and his neighbours in particular." Burton, *Situation*, 5.

155. Street still manages to get in a complaint about food rationing in *Absence*. Other above average fifties Burtons are *The Moth Watch Murder* (1957) and *Return from the Dead* (1959), the latter of which rather nicely bookends *The Secret of High Eldersham*.

156. Like *Licensed for Murder*, a Rhode title likewise from 1958, *Bones in the Brickfield* combines a strong setting with a solid plot. However, *Bones* is decidedly the more humorous of the two tales. When Sir Horace's widow, Lady Honiton, learns that the Downfold Society's prized fossilized dinosaur leg was lost in the conflagration of the organization's premises, she optimistically pronounces, "The dinosaur had four legs. There must be three more lying about somewhere." Miles Burton, *Bones in the Brickfield* (London: Collins, 1958), 255.

157. Ibid., 41, 51.

158. Tony Kremer, "A History of Yalding, Kent, England, http://yaldinghistory.webplus.net/page179.html; John Rhode, *Dr. Priestley Lays a Trap* (English title: *The Motor Rally Mystery*) (New York: Dodd, Mead, 1933), 62–63, 65. The novel is dedicated to "NUMBER 187 AND HER DRIVERS March 1st–3rd, 1932." Two of *Motor Rally*'s characters, both young manufacturers, previously appeared in *Tragedy at the Unicorn* (1928), which Street dedicated to "THE MERRY COMPANY." These characters were modeled on cronies of Street's who shared his fondness for pubs, cars and boats. The John Rhode title *Peril at Cranbury Hall* is dedicated to "THE SKIPPER," the nickname for one of these recurring characters from *Tragedy at the Unicorn* and *The Motor Rally Mystery*. For the Anthony Boucher review of *Blackthorn House*, see *New York Times Book Review*, 10 July 1949, 14. For the thesis that ideological opposition in Britain to technology, business and manufacturing has been exaggerated, see W.D. Rubinstein, *Capitalism, Culture, and Decline in Britain, 1750–1990* (London: Routledge, 1993). Certainly John Street represents a more pro-business ethos than has been customarily associated with the Golden Age of detective fiction, or, indeed, between-the-wars English fiction more generally. On the antipathy for industrialization, urbanization, suburbanization and technology in modern English literature, see Chris Baldick, *The Modern Movement: 1910–1940*, vol. 10 (The Oxford English Literary History) (Oxford: Oxford University Press, 2004), 304–310.

159. Rhode, *Poison*, 12, 13. Other examples of Street's feckless, futile would-be Great Poets can be found in *The Murders in Praed Street*, *Tragedy on the Line*, *Murder of a Chemist* and *Death in Wellington Road*.

160. John Rhode, *The Tower of Evil* (English title: *The Bloody Tower*) (New York: Dodd, Mead, 1938), 25, 81, 96, 149; Chris Baldick, *Modern Movement*, 295. To the criticism of Benjamin Glapthorne's public drinking, the local inspector tartly counters, "I can't see that it's any worse drinking with commercial travelers, who are usually very good fellows, than it is to drink with one's old nurse who ... is a holy terror." Rhode, *Tower*, 96.

161. Barzun and Taylor, *Crime* (1989), 447; Rhode, *Tower*, 4, 45. The English dust jacket for *The Bloody Tower* inaccurately portrays the tower as an attractive medieval structure, while the modernistic American dust jacket for *The Tower of Evil* (the American title) captures the tower's starkness. In a Miles Burton title, *Death of Two Brothers* (1941), Street damningly portrays the tale's pair of slain brothers, the callous gentry sons of Sir Spencer Mereworth, markedly contrasting them with the yeoman farmer Mr. Challock.

162. Rhode, *Corpse*, 76.

163. Rhode, *Board*, 47.

164. Burton, *Mr. Babbacombe Dies* (London: Collins, 1939), 16, 81, 83, 85.

165. John Rhode, *Dead Men at the Folly* (London: Collins, 1932), 192; Burton, *Charabanc*, 81. Street seems to have been intrigued by the evolution in English life of the rural carrier from horse-drawn carts to motorized vehicles, a process he traces in *The Menace on the Downs* and *The Charabanc Mystery*. The rural transport entrepreneurs described in these novels bear some similarity to Dick Dewy of Thomas Hardy's *Under the Greenwood Tree* (1872).

166. John Rhode, *Death in the Hopfields* (London: Collins, 1937), 137. George Orwell's account of hop picking is found in his article "Hop-picking," which originally appeared in the *New Statesman and Nation*, 17 October 1931. It can be found in Peter Davison, ed., *Orwell's England* (London: Penguin Books, 2001), 9–12. In a jab at low salaries paid hop pickers, Orwell concluded sardonically of hop picking that "it would be almost ideal if one could only earn a living by it." Noting that "a whole tribe of Government officials" now supervised the living accommodation afforded hop pickers, Orwell conceded that "presumably it is better than it used to be," before adding, "But what it can have been like in the old days is hard to imagine, for even now the ordinary hop-picker's hut is worse than a stable." Ibid., 10, 11.

167. See the critical review extracts in the back matter of John Rhode, *Mystery at Olympia* (1935; repr., London: Collins, 1937) and the publishers blurb on the dust jacket of *Death in the Hopfields*.

168. Rhode, *Folly*, 68; Burton, *Thief*, 132; Miles Burton, *Murder of a Chemist* (London: Collins, 1936), 104–105. Street even sympathetically portrays a beleaguered traveling salesman in *Death Takes a Detour* (London: Collins, 1958).

169. Burton, *Dust*, 161; Paula Simpson to the author, 14 January 2004.

170. John Rhode, *Death on the Boat Train* (New York: Dodd, Mead, 1940), 105–107.

171. John Rhode, *Death on Sunday* (London: Collins, 1939), 71–72.

172. Street's scathing portrayal of guest house society in *Death on Sunday* is reminiscent of Anthony Horowitz's depiction of a similar group in "The Funk Hole," a 2003 episode from the British World War II mystery series *Foyle's War*.

173. Rhode, *Hopfields*, 9; Kremer, "History of Yalding."

174. Colin Watson, *Snobbery with Violence: English Crime stories and Their Audience*, rev. ed. (1971; repr., London: Eyre Methuen, 1979), 141.

175. John Rhode, *Death Pays a Dividend* (New York: Dodd, Mead, 1939), 1, 3–4. Diana Morpeth curiously resembles the real life Monica Dickens, a great-granddaughter of Charles Dickens who published a celebrated account of her experience as a cook-general for the upper classes in *One Pair of Hands*, a book published the same year as *Death Pays a Dividend*.

176. John Rhode, *Dead on the Track* (1943; repr., Toronto: Collins, 1945), 41.

177. Ibid., 47–48, 51, 55.

178. Rhode, *Cyprus*, 159, 163, 164. So much emphasis in the later books is laid on Hanslet's stoutness and immobility that it comes as a surprise to read of him riding a bicycle down a country road in the early tale *Pinehurst*. But then Major Street had once been a comparative stripling himself.

179. John Rhode, *Body Unidentified* (English title: *Proceed with Caution*) (New York: Dodd, Mead, 1938) 1; Burton, *Dust*, 9; Rhode, *Sunday*, 252.

180. John Rhode, *Dead of the Night* (English title: *Night Exercise*) (New York: Dodd, Mead, 1942), 223–224.

181. Rhode, *Dust*, 101; Burton, *Thief*, 11. The most notable exception to this rule is that ill-fated, manly, young, practical Christian, the Reverend Jonathan Denbigh, in *Death Takes the Living*. Additionally, the Reverend Colin Carew in *Heir to Murder* is, like Denbigh, a veteran of the Royal Air Force and is treated with similar favor by Street. "And a man, I say, not a tea-party parson," approvingly says one character of Carew. "Kind-hearted as they make 'em, and doesn't shove his nose in where he isn't wanted." Burton, *Heir*. Here Street appears to have been drawing on William Makepeace Thackeray's witty portrayal of "A TEA-PARTY PARSON": "The Rev. Lemuel Whey is a tea-party man, with a curl on his forehead and a scented pocket-handkerchief. He ties his white neckcloth to a wonder, and I believe sleeps in it. He brings his flute with him; and prefers Handel, of course; but has one or two pet profane songs of the sentimental kind, and will occasionally lift up his little pipe in a glee. He does not dance, but the honest fellow would give the world to do it; and he leaves his clogs in the passage, though it is a wonder he wears them, for in the muddiest weather he never has a speck on his foot. He was at St. John's College, Cambridge, and was rather gay for a term or two, he says. He is, in a word, full of the milk-and-water of human kindness, and his family lives near Hackney." William Makepeace Thackeray, *Extracts from the Writings of W.M. Thackeray: Chiefly Philosophical and Reflective* (London: Smith, Elder, 1886), 381–382. This extract originally appeared in Thackeray's 1852 novel, *Men's Wives*.

182. John Rhode, *Death Invades the Meeting* (New York: Dodd, Mead, 1944), 78. Miles Burton, *Death at Low Tide* (London: Collins, 1938), 11; John Rhode, *Shot at Dawn* (New York: Dodd, Mead, 1934), 113, 211, 253, 254; John Rhode, *Tragedy on the Line* (1931; repr., London: Collins, 1973), 79; Rhode, *Cyprus*, 79; John Rhode, *Peril at Cranbury Hall* (1949; repr., London: Geoffrey Bles, 1930), 188; Rhode, *Weapons*, 165; Rhode, *Hopfields*, 60; Burton, *Card*, 41; Rhode, *Dividend*, 6. Perhaps harking back to events following the arrest and trial of Oscar Wilde for "gross indecency" some forty years earlier, Street informs readers of *Shot at Dawn* that the tale's blackmail victim with the dark sexual secret, in fear of being served with a subpoena, "prudently fled the country immediately after the arrest" of the murderer of the blackmailer. Rhode, *Dawn*, 274. In *Snobbery with Violence*, Colin Watson, accusing Street of sharing the "almost Victorian reticence" of other writers in the mystery fiction genre, claims that "in his *Tragedy at the Unicorn* (1928), a girl is included on the list of suspects simply because the murder victim had, on one occasion, caught her in his arms and tried to kiss her"; but this is a misleading assertion. Let the "girl," Joan, give her full explanation of the unseemly events at the Unicorn: "He caught me in his arms and tried to kiss me. When I ordered him to let me go, he said that he agreed that the passage was too public, but that I knew the number of his room. I was to tap on the door when the others had gone to bed. If I didn't come, he said that he would see to it that the Unicorn got such a reputation that no decent people would ever come and stay here again." *Tragedy at the Unicorn* (New York: Dodd, Mead, 1926), 76. A melodramatic situation, to be sure, but one need not be an extreme sophisticate to comprehend that clearly a bit more is involved here than an unsought kiss.

183. Rhode, *Davidson*, 149–150; John Rhode, *The Two Graphs* (London: Geoffrey Bles, 1950), 42. Interestingly, in *Death Pays a Dividend*, Diana, the charming wife-to-be of Jimmy, notes disparagingly of the murder victim's pious, drippy sister, "Rupert Bayle's sister is called Maud. She would be, you know." Rhode, *Dividend*, 64. Maud was the middle name of Street's first wife, surely something the author had not forgotten by the time he wrote *Death Pays a Dividend*. Jimmy writes Diana in

Death on Sunday (1939) and mentions her in *The Secret Meeting* (1951), but she does not make an appearance in either novel.

184. Rhode, *Line*, 252.
185. Ibid., 84.
186. Rhode, *Track*, 63–65.
187. Rhode, *Signal*, 92.
188. Miles Burton, *The Clue of the Silver Cellar* (English title: *Where Is Barbara Prentice?*) (New York: Doubleday, Doran, 1936), 12.
189. See the critical "blurbs" on the back of the dust jacket of the American edition of Kate Summerscale, *The Suspicions of Mr. Whicher: A Shocking Murder and the Undoing of a Great Victorian Detective* (New York: Walker, 2008).
190. This account is drawn from John Rhode, *The Case of Constance Kent* (London: Geoffrey Bles, 1928). The most significant book-length studies of the case that followed the Rhode are Yseult Bridges' *Saint-with Red Hands? The Chronicle of a Great Crime* (London: Jarrolds, 1954); Bernard Taylor, *Cruelly Murdered: Constance Kent and the Killing at Road Hill House* (1979; repr., London: Grafton Books, 1989) and Kate Summerscale's *Suspicions of Mr. Whicher*. Other notable figures who have written at shorter length of the Constance Kent case are George A. Birmingham, F. Tennyson Jesse and William Roughead.
191. Rhode, *Constance Kent*, 2, 5.
192. Ibid., 14–15, 16. In Sergeant Britcher of *Death of Two Brothers*, Street portrays a policeman very much like Superintendent Foley. Britcher firmly believes that "no member of the real gentry could be guilty of crime." Miles Burton, *Death of Two Brothers* (London: Collins, 1941), 151.
193. Ibid., 272, 274, 275, 277.
194. See the second edition of Bernard Taylor's *Cruelly Murdered* (London: Grafton Books, 1989), which reprints the Sydney letter in full in Appendix II (pp. 372–378). Taylor recounts Street's receipt and handling of the Sydney letter at pages 360–361. The writer of the Sydney letter hinted that the first Mrs. Kent's illness was due to syphilis contracted from her husband, a point not addressed by Street but convincingly handled by Kate Summerscale. See *Suspicions*, 296–298. Given Street's low estimation of Samuel Kent, he likely did not find the syphilis allegation unlikely, assuming he read "between the lines" of the Sydney letter and apprehended the allegation.
195. John Rhode, "Constance Kent," in *The Anatomy of Murder: Famous Crimes Critically Considered by Members of the Detection Club* (New York: Macmillan, 1937), 79.
196. Ibid., 72.
197. Ibid., 82, 83.
198. Ibid., 85.
199. John Rhode, *The Secret Meeting* (London: Geoffrey Bles, 1951), 10, 13, 22.
200. John Rhode, *The Three Corpse Trick* (London: Collins, 1944), 60; Rhode, *Tower*, 64. Interestingly, both of Street's wives came of noteworthy Irish descent. However, Eileen Waller very likely was Protestant and Harriet Maud Kirwan may have been as well (though the Kirwans originally were Catholic). In 1911, the Kirwan family home at Bawnmore was fired upon and stoned during troubles with Irish tenants. Street's then brother-in-law Dennis Agar Richard Kirwan was the owner of Bawnmore at this time. See Annaghdown GAA Club, *Bawnmore and the Land League*, http://www.annaghdowngaa.com/Annagh doiwnGAAfiles/Gallery/BawnmoreBool/Landleague.htm.
201. Hogarth, *Thrillers*, 30–31.
202. Street evidently liked Hugh Quarrenden enough to have him resurface five years later, now a judge, in *The Lake House*. Street also sympathetically portrays artists in *Blackthorn House*, contrasting them with a rather brutish, philistine provincial police inspector.
203. Rhode, *Claverton*, 52.
204. Rhode, *Tower*, 56–57.
205. Watson, *Snobbery*, 102; Rhode, *Tower*, 6, 48.
206. Rhode, *Boat Train*, 225; Burton, *Silver Cellar*, 88–89; Rhode, *Sunday*, 28.
207. Rhode, *Davidson*, 124; Rhode, *Folly*, 48; John Rhode, *The Robthorne Mystery* (New York: Dodd, Mead, 6).
208. Miles Burton, *Brothers*, 16; Burton, *Dust*, 51, 207, 230, Miles Burton, *Fate at the Fair* (London: Collins, 1933), 6. "Wonderful how the smell of beer seems to pervade this case," comments Merrion in *The Charabanc Mystery* (p. 122). On "country pubs" portrayed as "quintessentially English places" and "sanctuaries of immemorial English liberty" in English literature of this period, see Baldick, *Modern Movement*, 306.
209. Burton, *Dust*, 9.
210. Rhode, *Dawn*, 252; Rhode, *Cyprus*, 146; Rhode, *Graphs*, 246.
211. The Detection Club, *Ask a Policeman* (1933, repr., London: Macmillan, 1983), 1; Sheila Kaye-Smith, *All the Books of My Life: A Bibliography* (London: Cassell, 1956), 188.

Chapter Three

1. Erik Routley, *The Puritan Pleasures of the Detective Story* (London: Gollancz, 1972), 124. For the critical notices on Crofts' writing, see the jacket of Freeman Wills Crofts, *Mystery in the English Channel* (English title: *Mystery in the Channel*) (New York: Dodd, Mead, 1931). The best recent analysis of Crofts' as a writer is found in Ian Carter, *Railways and Culture in Britain: The Epitome of Modernity* (Manchester, UK: Manchester University Press, 2001), 179–182. As is obvious from the title, Professor Carter's book stresses Crofts background as a railroad engineer.
2. For biographical information on Freeman Wills Crofts, see his entry in the *Oxford Dictionary of National Biography*, vol. 14 (London: Oxford University Press, 2004), 257–258; James M. Crafts and William F. Crafts, *The Crafts Family: A Genealogical and Biographical History of the Descendants of Griffin and Alice Crafts of Roxbury, Mass. 1630–1890* (Northampton, MA: Gazette Printing Company, 1893), 7–8; Jim McCarthy, "Churchtown's History: Burton Park, Churchtown House and Ballydam," http://www.churchtown.net/Webpages/history/H-bur ton%20house.htm; "Hot on the Trail of Crime Writer Freeman Wills Crofts," 11 June 2004, http://www.getsur rey.co.uk/community/yesteryear/s/93312_hot_on_the_trai l_crimewriter_freeman_wills_crofts; "About the Author," in Freeman Wills Crofts, *The Loss of the "Jane Vosper"* (London: Collins, 1936); H. Douglas Thomson, *Masters of Mystery: A Study of the Detective Story* (1930; repr., New York: Dover, 1978), 176; Rosalind Davies, "Tullylish Parish," *Ros Davies' Co. Down, Ireland Genealogy Research Site*, http://freepages.genealogy.rootsweb.ancestry.com/~ rosdavies/PHOTOSwaordsTullylishAll.htm; Slater's Directory-Gilford (1881), *Sinton Family Trees*, http://www. bob-sinton.com/history/gilford/gilford_slater.php. On Berkeley Deane Wise, see William Alan McCutcheon, *The*

Industrial Archaeology of Northern Ireland (Belfast: Her Majesty's Stationer's Office, 1980), 130, 166, 167, 171, 172, 173, 185, 213; "Welcome to Whitehead Excursion Station," *The Railway Preservation Society of Ireland*, http://www.steamtrainsireland.com/whitehead/. Crofts was a great admirer of the sea adventure stories of Maurice Drake (1875–1923) and borrowed the surname of Maxwell Cheyne, the young protagonist of *Inspector French and the Cheyne Mystery* from a character in a 1913 Drake novel, *WO2*. Appropriately, the climax of *The Cheyne Mystery* takes place on the high seas.

3. For discussions of *The Cask*, see Thomson, *Masters of Mystery*, 187–189; Howard Haycraft, *Murder for Pleasure: The Life and Times of the Detective Story*, rev. ed. (1941; repr., New York: Biblo and Tannen, 1974), 123–124; Freeman Wills Crofts, introduction to *The Cask* (1920; repr., London and Glasgow: Collins, 1946) (Library of Classics), 7–10; "About the Author," in Crofts, *"Jane Vosper."* There is a divergence in the sources as to whether *The Cask* was written in 1916 or 1919. Haycraft and Symons give the year as 1919, but the "About the Author" page in *"Jane Vosper"* gives 1916. Given that Crofts in his introduction to the 1946 reprint edition of *The Cask* avers (1) that he wrote the manuscript of *The Cask* during a "period of convalescence" from illness, (2) that "the manuscript was put away and almost forgotten," (3) that upon coming across the manuscript again he read it aloud to a neighbor, Dr. Adam A.C. Mathers, who gave him "immense help" in revising it, (4) that after this revision Crofts sent the manuscript to Collins and Collins who returned it, provisionally accepting it but requesting a rewrite of Part III (originally an account of a murder trial), and (5) that *The Cask* appeared in print in 1920, I believe that the time element favors the earlier year, 1916. See Crofts, introduction to *The Cask*, 7–8.

4. Freeman Wills Crofts, *The Cask* (1920; repr., London: House of Stratus, 2000), 101–102.

5. Ibid., 110.

6. Ibid., 382.

7. Freeman Wills Crofts, *The Ponson Case* (1921; repr., London, House of Stratus, 2000), 1, 9, 19, 42, 63, 69. It is fortunate for Tanner that he is able to exclude the women from suspicion in this case, for we learn that, "though hardened by a life of contact with crime, he was a good fellow at heart, and he disliked intensely giving pain, especially to women." Ibid., 82.

8. Freeman Wills Crofts, *Death of a Train* (London: Hodder & Stoughton, 1946), 35; Crofts, *Ponson*, 77–78.

9. Crofts, *Ponson*, 102–104.

10. Ibid., 11–12.

11. Ibid., 80–81.

12. Ibid., 81, 145, 149, 291. As H.R.F. Keating has noted, regular meals are very important matters in Crofts' novels (see more on this below). Before that late lunch, poor Lois had been "almost fainting for food," while earlier in the novel, Dr. Ames, called to examine Sir William's dead body, had sadly to forgo having breakfast. Dr. Ames is a resourceful fellow, however. When the police sergeant on scene later asks the doctor to assist him in going through the pockets of the dead man's clothes, he finds Ames "just finishing a somewhat substantial snack in the dining-room" of Luce Manor. Ibid., 22, 149.

13. Ibid., 268–269, 275.

14. Bill Pronzini, *Gun in Cheek: A Study of Alternative Crime Fiction* (1982; repr., New York: Mysterious Press, 1987), 192.

15. Crofts, *Ponson*, 218, 220.

16. Julian Symons, *Bloody Murder: From the Detective Story to the Crime Novel*, 3rd rev. ed. (1972; repr., New York: Mysterious Press, 1993), 118; Freeman Wills Crofts, *The Pit-Prop Syndicate* (London: Collins, 1922), 202–203, 211–212, 260, 279. In many of Crofts' earlier books especially, his police detectives often seem to conduct investigations in an odd vacuum, even though they theoretically have one of the world's great police forces to support them in their investigative work. For example, in *The Box Office Murders* (1929), when Crofts' Inspector French decides to question householders on Southampton Water — one of whom, so he has hypothesized, might have had a boat stolen by the criminals — he does so entirely by himself, even though it takes a great deal of time and he is already under pressure from his superior to make quicker progress on the case. Later, when searching the velvet pocket lining of a car compartment that he knows once contained some vital evidence, French "in vain" longs "for the skill of [R. Austin Freeman's fictional detective] Dr. Thorndyke, who might have been able with his vacuum extractor to secure microscopic dust from [the lining's] fibres." Crofts, *The Box Office Murders* (1929; repr., London: House of Stratus, 2000), 119. One would have thought that Scotland Yard might have employed someone capable of performing such an operation (by 1946's *Death of a Train*, Crofts himself had realized this — see pages 230–31 of the Hodder and Stoughton edition, where Crofts again refers to Dr. Thorndyke's extractor).

17. Crofts, *Pit-Prop*, 149, 189, 194. We believe the author when he assures us that his hero's "whole future life and happiness lay between the dainty hands of Madeleine Coburn." Ibid., 58. In *The Hundred Best Crime Stories* Julian Symons deems *The Pit-Prop Syndicate* "one of [Crofts] livelier stories." Julian Symons, *The Hundred Best Crime Stories* (London: *Sunday Times*, 1958), 7. I disagree. Though there is a criminal gang behind the felonious shenanigans, the whole thing strikes me as slow-going. Even a chase at the end involves railway timetables (complete with a map): "[Willis] bought a time-table and began to study the possibilities.... The first northwards [train] was the 4 p.m. dining-car express from King's Cross to Newcastle. It left Doncaster at 7.56 and reached Selby at 8.21. Would Archer travel by it? And if he did, what would be his next move?" Crofts, *Pit-Prop*, 292.

18. Freeman Wills Crofts, *The Groote Park Murder* (1923; repr., London: House of Stratus, 2000), 129, 134.

19. Ibid., 33, 39, 78, 112

20. Freeman Wills Crofts, *Inspector French's Greatest Case* (1924; Amer. ed., New York: Thomas Seltzer, 1925), 9, 193.

21. Ibid., 96. Attempting to use Freeman Wills Crofts as evidence for her contention that "all in all, the golden age form is a feminized one," Susan Rowland in her essay "The 'Classical' Model of the Golden Age" (in *A Companion to Crime Fiction*, Malden, MA: Wiley-Blackwell, 2010), rather overgenerously credits Emily French's notion in *Inspector French's Greatest Case* with solving the case. "ABfortunately, [Inspector] French has a wife," writes Rowland. "With her help … French can escape from circular wandering into nabbing his man" (p. 121). Yet in the overwhelming majority of Inspector (later Superintendent) French cases, Emily French contributes nothing whatsoever to the elucidation of the problem (she often does not even appear). The "notion" that Crofts' mystery novels are "domestic" and "feminized" will not wash, in my view. To be sure, their masculine sensibility is of an evangelized sort markedly different from that of the American hard-

boiled tradition — though see Leonard W. Cassuto, *Hardboiled Sentimentality: The Secret History of American Crime Stories* (New York: Columbia University Press, 2009) — but I would not characterize them as "feminine."

22. Freeman Wills Crofts, "Meet Chief Inspector French," in *Meet the Detective* (Harrisburg, PA: The Telegraph Press, 1935), 83; Crofts, *Greatest Case*, 207.

23. Crofts, "Meet Chief Inspector French," 81; Symons, *Bloody Murder*, 118.

24. Freeman Wills Crofts, *James Tarrant, Adventurer* (London: Hodder & Stoughton, 1941), 149–150.

25. Ibid., 150.

26. Crofts, "Meet Chief Inspector French," 82.

27. Crofts, *Greatest Case*, 69–71. We also learn that Inspector French, like Georges Simenon's Inspector Maigret, smokes a pipe.

28. Crofts, *Box Office Murders*, 114; Freeman Wills Crofts, *Inspector French and the Starvel Tragedy* (1927; repr., London: House of Stratus, 2000), 197; Freeman Wills Crofts, *The Sea Mystery* 1928; repr., London: House of Stratus, 2000), 215. Contrast Crofts' blasé attitude with that the scrupulous one of Henry Wade, a Golden Age British detective novelist possessing a far stronger grasp than Crofts of true police procedure: "For a moment [Inspector Poole] was tempted to take advantage of her absence to search the house, but ... breaking in without a warrant was an illegal action and would get him into serious trouble if he were found out." Henry Wade, *Constable Guard Thyself!* (1934; repr., London: Hutchinson Library Services, 1971) 252.

29. Crofts, *Sea*, 23, 93, 262.

30. G.D.H. and Margaret Cole, "Meet Superintendent Wilson," in *Meet the Detective*, 118; *Monthly Criterion* 5 (June 1927): 360; 6 (September 1927): 377; 8 (September 1928): 175. The "long and intricate timetables" comment was found in a folder of newspaper review clippings in the Dorothy L. Sayers papers, located at the Marion E. Wade Center at Wheaton College, Wheaton, Illinois. Although attributed to both Coles, "Meet Superintendent Wilson" likely was written exclusively by Margaret Cole.

31. For Bentley and Nicolson, see the critical notices reprinted in Freeman Wills Crofts, *Mystery on Southampton Water* (1934; repr., London: Hodder and Stoughton, 1936). For Charles Williams, see Jared C. Lobdell, ed., *The Detective Fiction Reviews of Charles Williams, 1930–1935* (Jefferson, NC: McFarland, 2003), 40–41, 58, 77, 94, 109. For "Torquemada" and "Dr. Watson," see the critical notices reprinted in Freeman Wills Crofts, *The Loss of the "Jane Vosper"* (1936; repr., London: Collins, 1937). Raymond Chandler's comment on Crofts features prominently on the recent House of Stratus reprints of his novels. For more on Chandler's attitude toward Crofts' detective fiction, see my essay "'The Amateur Detective Just Won't Do': Raymond Chandler and British Detective Fiction," The *American Culture*, http://stkarnick.com.

32. Crofts, *Greatest Case*, 160, 161, 163. To be fair to Freeman Wills Crofts, in the 1920s even the American characters of Agatha Christie, who had an American father, tend to talk in this over-insistingly slangy manner as well.

33. Jacques Barzun and Wendell Hertig Taylor, *A Catalogue of Crime*, rev. ed. (1971; repr., New York: Harper & Row, 1989), 155; Crofts, *Sea*, 22–23.

34. Ibid., 22, 56.

35. On "Magill's Ford," see www.culturenorthernireland.org/YourArea.aspx?location=506.

36. Freeman Wills Crofts to Dorothy L. Sayers, 11 August 1930, Dorothy L. Sayers Papers, Marion E. Wade Center, Wheaton College. Freeman Wills Crofts, *Sir John Magill's Last Journey* (London: Collins, 1930), 9. For the quoted critical notices on the novel, see the 1941 Pocket Books paperback edition of *Sir John Magill's Last Journey*. In the latter, incidentally, Crofts' appealing original opening section is significantly truncated.

37. Thomson, *Masters*, 192.

38. Freeman Wills Crofts, *Mystery in the Channel* (1931; repr., London: House of Stratus, 2000), 241; Lobdell, *Charles Williams*, 58.

39. *London Sunday Times*, 9 April 1933, 11. A similar clue key that appears in *Obelists Fly High* (1935), by American mystery writer C. Daly King, is much celebrated, though in fact Crofts' use of the devise in *The Hog's Back Mystery* preceded King's by two years.

40. With such bits as the boat explosion and a scene where one of the conspirators has to drive a car with a murdered man propped up on the passenger seat beside him, *Mystery at Southampton Water* should film quite well, even without "love interest."

41. *London Sunday Times*, 2 February 1936, 9.

42. Margaret Cole, *Spectator* 146 (May 1931): 746; Julian Symons, Introduction to Freeman Wills Crofts, *The Loss of the "Jane Vosper"* (1936, repr., London: Collins, 1980); Eric Partridge, *Journey to the Edge of Morning: Thoughts upon Books: Love: Life* (London: Frederick Muller, 1946), 35.

43. Freeman Wills Crofts, *Sudden Death* (1932; repr., London: House of Stratus, 2000), 3, 4, 309. As a novel, *Sudden Death* feels stage bound and over emotionalized (*A Catalogue of Crime* refers to its "oddly feminine tone"– p. 156), so it is not surprising to learn that Crofts in 1937 adapted it into a play. The play was performed in Guildford, the county town of Surrey (located near Crofts' home village of Blackheath), but apparently it got no farther. Freeman Wills Crofts to Dorothy L. Sayers, 13 October 1937, DLS Papers. Crofts' *The End of Andrew Harrison* (1938) offers a better locked room problem than *Sudden Death*, but it is only a minor part of the mystery.

44. Crofts, *Sudden Death*, 301–302.

45. Freeman Wills Crofts, *Death on the Way* (London: Collins, 1932), 273–274.

46. Ibid., 270.

47. Freeman Wills Crofts, *The 12.30 from Croydon* (1934; repr., London: House of Stratus, 2000), 55, 91.

48. Ibid., 50, 327–28; Lobdell, *Charles Williams*, 109.

49. Crofts, *Sea Mystery*, 133; Crofts, *Greatest Case*, 209.

50. Crofts, *Channel*, 78–79.

51. Ibid., 79–80.

52. Freeman Wills Crofts, *The End of Andrew Harrison* (1938; repr., London: Hodder and Stoughton, 1940), 17, 130. Crofts' apt reference to the Humbert safe recalls the amazing case of the French fraudster Therese Humbert, who, incredibly, secured a fortune in loans over a twenty-year period based on a bogus claim that she had a fortune in a sealed safe. When the safe was finally opened on court order in 1902 (when Crofts was 23), it was found to contain only a brick and an English halfpenny. Thousands of smaller creditors and investors were swept up in the ensuing financial maelstrom and ruined. See Hilary Spurling, *La Grande Therese: The Greatest Scandal of the Century* (New York: Harper Collins, 2000).

53. Symons, *Bloody Murder*, 108; Crofts, *Andrew Harrison*, 9; Freeman Wills Crofts, *Golden Ashes* (1940; repr., London: House of Stratus, 2000), 38, 289.

54. Crofts, *Andrew Harrison*, 129–130.

55. Crofts, *Man Overboard!* (New York: Dodd, Mead, 1936), 1, 116.
56. Ibid., 2. The novel, indeed, recycles most of the Crofts bag of tropes. When French arrives in Northern Ireland, he expresses a desire to see "this Gorge of the Avon and suspension bridge that you hear so much about," and Crofts obliges with a paragraph-long guidebook description of the site. When investigating the murdered man's lodgings, French finds a locked desk; but, as ever, "stout locks could not prevail against skeleton keys ... wielded with French's skill." And from papers found in the desk French discovers that the man foolishly "had been gambling and ... was in the hands of the moneylenders." Ibid., 95, 98–99. In short, *Man Overboard!* is like a Crofts old home week.
57. Ibid., 3–4.
58. Ibid., 127, 222, 223.
59. Ibid., 124–125, 344.
60. Crofts, *Tarrant*, 20, 21, 22, 43. The patent medicine business is a frequent satirical target of Golden Age detective fiction.
61. Freeman Wills Crofts, *Fatal Venture* (1939; repr., Hornchurch, Essex: Ian Henry, 1984), 7, 53.
62. Ibid., 71, 72, 78.
63. Ibid., 171, 185, 186, 223.
64. Freeman Wills Crofts, *The Four Gospels in One Story, Written as a Modern Biography, with Difficult Passages Clarified and Explanatory Notes* (London: Longman's, Green, 1949), x; Crofts, *Tarrant*, 16. Crofts was a great supporter of Dorothy L. Sayers' controversial wartime religious radio play cycle *The Man Born to be King* (1941–1942), which also sought to give the Bible a modern voice, and he likely was inspired by its example. See Freeman Wills Crofts to Dorothy L. Sayers, 24 February 1942, DLS Papers.
65. Freeman Wills Crofts to Dorothy L. Sayers, 16 December 1937, DLS Papers. For the text of Buchman's speech, see Arthur H. Baker and J.P. Thornton, eds., *Remaking the World: Selections from the Speeches of Frank N.D. Buchman* (London: Heinemann, 1942), 85–87.
66. Barbara Reynolds, ed., *The Letters of Dorothy L. Sayers*, vol. II: 1937 to 1943 (New York: St. Martin's Press, 1997), 64; Crofts, *Andrew Harrison*, 319.
67. Freeman Wills Crofts, *Antidote to Venom* (1938; repr., London: House of Stratus, 2000), 8–9, 11, 102, 178–80.
68. Ibid., 180, 287–288, 290.
69. Ibid., Author's Note.
70. Freeman Wills Crofts, *Enemy Unseen* (1952; repr., London: Hodder and Stoughton, 1945), 20, 23, 62, 100, 124–124, 144.
71. Ibid., 256.
72. Anthony Boucher, *San Francisco Chronicle*, 29 April 1945, reprinted in Francis M. Nevins, *The Anthony Boucher Chronicles: Reviews and Commentary, 1942–1947* (Vancleave, MS: Ramble House, 2002), 130; Barzun and Taylor, *Catalogue of Crime* (1989), 153.
73. Barzun and Taylor, *Catalogue of Crime*, 153.
74. Freeman Wills Crofts, *Many a Slip* (London: Hodder & Stoughton, 1955), 22.
75. Ibid., 51, 146.
76. Crofts, *Murderers Make Mistakes* (London: Hodder & Stoughton, 1947), 127–128.
77. Symons, *Bloody Murder*, 108–109. Symons generously allows that "this is not to say that they were *openly* [emphasis added] anti–Semitic or anti–Radical." Ibid., 108.
78. Freeman Wills Crofts, *Crime at Guildford* (1935; repr., London: House of Stratus, 2000), 3; Crofts, *Venture*, 94; Crofts, *Vosper*, 131–132, 284, 315.
79. Freeman Wills Crofts, *The Affair at Little Wokeham* (1943; repr., London: House of Stratus, 2000), 15, 150–51; Freeman Wills Crofts, *Young Robin Brand, Detective* (1947; Amer. ed., New York: Dodd, Mead, 1948), 110.
80. Crofts' view of the Soviet Union (and Communism) had changed dramatically by New Years' Day, 1952, when he informed an admiring American correspondent that Britons "can never be grateful enough to your President [Truman] for striking in Korea: to my mind the outstanding act of the century. By doing it he turned international hopelessness into hope." Additionally, like other British Golden Age detective novelists, such as John Dickson Carr (a longtime American expatriate), Dorothy L. Sayers, Henry Lancelot Aubrey-Fletcher and John Street, Crofts welcomed the return of the Tories to political prominence: "Vast numbers of us feel more hopeful about the situation now that Churchill is again in power. Most of the Labour men were good honest men doing their best, but their training and background made them think too much of social services — splendid if one can afford them — and not enough of fundamental solvency and foreign relations." He discontentedly added, "I reckon that three-fourths of my income goes in taxes of one kind or another." Freeman Wills Crofts to Mrs. Martin, 1 January 1952, typescript in possession of author.
81. Crofts, *Pit-Prop*, 64; Crofts, *Ashes*, 31–32, 34; Crofts, *Mistakes*, 265.
82. Crofts, *Venture*, 132; Freeman Wills Crofts, *Anything to Declare?* (1957; repr., London: House of Stratus, 2000), 56.
83. Colin Watson, *Snobbery with Violence: English Crime Stories and Their Audience*, rev. ed. (1971; repr., London: Eyre Methuen, 1979), 140; Crofts, *Last Journey*, 111–112.
84. John Rhode, *Tragedy on the Line* (London: Collins, 1931), 17–18.
85. Freeman Wills Crofts, *Inspector French and the Cheyne Mystery* (1926; repr., London: House of Stratus, 2000), 28, 78; Crofts, *Robin Brand*, 62–63. Personally, I felt like cheering the refreshingly saucy Susan at this point in the novel, though I suspect this was not the reaction Crofts was aiming to provoke in his readers.
86. Crofts, *Greatest Case*, 229, 230; Crofts, *Sea*, 148.
87. Crofts, *Wokeham*, 181.
88. Freeman Wills Crofts, *French Strikes Oil* (1951; repr., London: House of Stratus, 2000), 46.
89. Crofts, *Brand*, 143; Crofts, *Overboard*, 227–228.
90. Crofts, *Ponson*, 95; Crofts, *Pit-Prop*, 284–286.
91. Crofts, *Groote*, 72.
92. Crofts, *Box Office Murders*, 102; Crofts, *Cheyne*, 93, 97.
93. Crofts, *Starvel*, 4; Crofts, *Sudden Death*, 90, 199, 205.
94. Crofts, *Wokeham*, 1, 61, 61, 81, 104, 110, 184, 185, 198, 253, 256, 288, 292, 301.
95. Crofts, *Sudden Death*, 54; Crofts, *Tarrant*, 277.
96. Freeman Wills Crofts, *Found Floating* (1937; repr., London: Hodder and Stoughton, 1941), 206, 277, 278, 308.
97. Freeman Wills Crofts, "The Gorse Hall Mystery," in *Great Unsolved Crimes* (London: Hutchinson, 1938), 178, 180.
98. Jonathan Goodman, *The Stabbing of George Harry Storrs* (London: Allison and Busby, 1983), 208–212; Free-

man Wills Crofts, "A New Zealand Tragedy," in *The Anatomy of Murder* (New York, Macmillan, 1937), 336.

99. Carter, *Railways and Culture*, 181; Crofts, *Robin Brand*, 61–62.

100. Gladys Mitchell's description of Crofts at the Detection Club meeting is found in Julian Symons' introduction to the 1980 edition of *The Loss of the "Jane Vosper."* J.J. Connington himself concurred with Mitchell's description of Crofts, writing to a friend in 1946, "I knew [Crofts] slightly when he was over here [in Belfast] as Assistant-Engineer on the N.C. Railway. He was a very decent man, not a bit puffed up by his success, and, in fact, rather diffident about it, and very modest about his books." A.W. Stewart to F. Gerald Tryhorn, 30 August 1946. Letter in possession of author. Similarly, Crofts struck Clarice Carr, who attended Detection Club dinners as the wife of John Dickson Carr, as a "polite" yet "undemonstrative" older gentleman (he actually was only fifty-seven when she met him), who always gave her "the impression that his thoughts were elsewhere." Douglas G. Greene, *John Dickson Carr: The Man Who Explained Miracles* (New York: Otto Penzler Books, 1995), 201.

101. Croft, *Ashes*, 228.

102. Freeman Wills Crofts, *Fear Comes to Chalfont* (1942; repr., London: House of Stratus, 2000), 7; Crofts, *"Jane Vosper,"* 280; Crofts, *Andrew Harrison*, 95; Crofts, *Channel*, 234; Freeman Wills Crofts, *The Hog's Back Mystery* (1933; repr., London: House of Stratus, 2000), 299.

103. Crofts, *Box Office*, 237. Crofts' rhetoric here is reminiscent of more recent utterances by a prominent world leader of evangelical Christian faith.

Chapter Four

1. On the academic career of Alfred Walter Stewart, see his entry in *Oxford Dictionary of National Biography*, vol. 52 (London: Oxford University Press, 2004), 627–628. For the critical praise from the *Times Literary Supplement* and the *London Daily Mail*, see the front jacket flap to *The Two Tickets Puzzle* (Boston: Little, Brown, 1930).

2. A.W. Stewart, *Alias J.J. Connington* (London: Hollis & Carter, 1947), 215; Julian Symons, *Bloody Murder: From the Detective Story to the Crime Novel*, 3rd rev. ed. (1972; repr., New York: Mysterious Press, 1993), 108. On the personal life of Alfred Walter Stewart, see *ODNB*, vol. 52, 627–628. Connington wrote affectionately of his father at several points in *Alias J.J. Connington*.

3. A.W. Stewart to R.T. Gould, 27 November 1935; 15 February 1936. Photocopies in possession of Jonathan Betts. For more on Connington and R. Austin Freeman, see below.

4. J.J. Connington, *Nordenholt's Million* (1923; repr., London: Ernest Benn, 1926), 48, 58, 101. Connington's distaste for Irish Catholics (whom he derisively termed "our local fauna") is made clear at several points in his letters to Rupert Gould, where the author caustically notes local support for violent actions by the Irish Republican Army. See, for example, A.W. Stewart to R.T. Gould, 10 April 1936. Though Nordenholt's plan calls for the selection of five million individuals, the tycoon gives the public the figure of one million, thinking it catchier; hence the book's title.

5. Connington, *Million*, 106, 107. Connington later wrote that the resignation of Edward VII (the Prince of Wales in 1923) was "most depressing" and a "sad affair." The only solace to draw from the whole episode, he concluded, was that "the monarchy has a very strong hold on the people, or they would not be in this state over a constitutional crisis." A.W. Stewart to R.T. Gould, 12 December 1936.

6. Connington, *Million*, 111, 113.

7. Ibid., 114.

8. Ibid., 66, 122.

9. Nicholas Ruddick, *Ultimate Island: On the Nature of British Science Fiction* (Westport, CT: Greenwood, 1993), 116–117. Connington's brief comments on the construction of similar "Nitrogen Areas" in Japan and the United States further illustrate the novel's partiality for authoritarian forms of government. When the food crisis struck, "Japanese statesmen" (with their "practical minds") confronted "a simpler problem" than did English politicians, Connington explains, since the former of course "could ignore public opinion entirely." As a result, the creation of a Nitrogen Area run on Nordenholt's lines proceeded smoothly in Japan. Ibid., 211. Conversely, in the United States, a country beset by a weak central government and an unassimilated, ethnically diverse population, much chaos ensued before a Nitrogen Area could be successfully fashioned.

10. Connington, *Million*, 154, 156, 162–163, 168, 178, 179, 185.

11. Ibid., 190.

12. Ibid., 231, 241. As Professor Ruddick has pointed out, Elsa's surname (Huntingtower) suggests that she is looking for a hard, strong man to yield to; and Flint's surname suggests that he is that man. Ruddick, *Ultimate Island*, 118.

13. Connington, *Million*, 299, 302.

14. Everett F. Bleiler, *Science Fiction: The Early Years* (Kent, OH: Kent State University Press, 1990), 152; Irene Stewart to the author, 22 June 2011.

15. J.J. Connington, *Almighty Gold* (London: Constable, 1924), 155, 243–44.

16. J.J. Connington, *Death at Swaythling Court* (1926; repr., London: Ernest Benn, 1930), 18, 25–26, 27–28.

17. Jacques Barzun and Wendell Hertig Taylor, *A Catalogue of Crime*, rev. ed. (1971; repr., New York: Harper & Row, 1989), 139; Connington, *Swaythling*, 271.

18. Ibid., 272.

19. Certainly *Death at Swaythling Court* is an exception to W.H. Auden's influential formulation of the classical detective story in "The Guilty Vicarage" as one where, in order for "innocence" to be restored to the "Edenic" community where the murder took place, the murderer, guilty of "demonic pride," must meet his end either through execution, suicide, or madness. See W.H. Auden, "The Guilty Vicarage," reprinted in *Robin W. Winks, Detective Fiction: A Collection of Critical Essays* (Woodstock, VT: Foul Play Press, 1988). For the murderers in *Swaythling Court*, murder offers them not an end, but a beginning. The community is cleansed not by the punishment of the murderers, but the commission of the murder.

20. J.J. Connington, *Murder in the Maze* (Boston: Little, Brown, 1927), 55–56, 58.

21. Ibid., 5.

22. Ibid., 273, 288–289, 289–290.

23. J.J. Connington, *Nemesis at Raynham Parva* (London: Gollancz, 1928), 25–26, 41, 126.

24. Ibid., 23, 27.

25. Ibid., 191.

26. J.J. Connington, *The Castleford Conundrum* (Boston: Little, Brown, 1932), 228; J.J. Connington, *No Past Is Dead* (Boston: Little, Brown, 1942), 181.

27. Connington, *Nemesis*, 21; Connington, *Castleford*, 227, 228. A second-tier series detective of Connington's, Superintendent Ross, has similarly dour views as those of Sir Clinton, thinking in *The Two Tickets Puzzle* (1930): "He [the murder victim] can't have been a very likeable creature.... But if unlikableness justified murder, I suppose a fair proportion of the human race would be wiped out of existence to-morrow." J.J. Connington, *The Two Tickets Puzzle* (London: Gollancz, 1930), 108.
28. J.J. Connington, *The Ha-Ha Case* (1934; repr., London: Hodder and Stoughton, 1936), 310. Left unclear is whether the Brandons of *The Ha-Ha Case* are relations of Rex Brandon of *Nemesis at Raynham Parva*. One assumes not.
29. J.J. Connington, *The Case with Nine Solutions* (Boston: Little, Brown, 1928), 127.
30. Connington, *Maze*, 13.
31. Connington, *Nemesis*, 44, 77.
32. Connington, *Ha-Ha*, 17, 18.
33. Ibid., 18.
34. J.J. Connington, *The Dangerfield Talisman* (Boston: Little, Brown, 1926), 5.
35. Connington, *Solutions*, 44.
36. J.J. Connington, *The Boat-House Riddle* (London: Gollancz, 1931), 192, 193.
37. J.J. Connington, *The Twenty-One Clues* (Boston: Little, Brown, 1941), 10, 13.
38. J.J. Connington, *For Murder Will Speak* (Boston: Little, Brown, 1938), 15, 34, 52, 148.
39. Ibid., 148, 150.
40. Ibid., 299.
41. No one in the tale seems to consider whether lecherous murder victim Ossie Hyson might not be a victim of *his* glands.
42. Connington, *Speak*, 70.
43. Connington's daughter, Irene Stewart, recalls her mother as "a much more simple character than my father ... who had infinite leisure to keep up with her friends in their golf and bridge," suggesting that, from Connington's standpoint, there may have been considerable verisimilitude in his portrayal of Linda Hyson and her social set in *For Murder Will Speak*. Irene Stewart to the author, 22 July 2009.
44. Connington, *Clues*, 310.
45. Connington, *Castleford*, 7, 11; J.J. Connington, *The Eye in the Museum* (London: Gollancz, 1931), 19, 25–26. In *Tom Tiddler's Island*, the lovely young newlywed Jean reflects to her husband on "the way strangers at the next table look at you covertly when they think you don't see them.... [T]he middle-aged women looking you up and down, half envious and half superior. And the middle-aged men staring at me and envying you — oh, yes, I know they did." J.J. Connington, *Gold Brick Island* (English title: *Tom Tiddler's Island*) (Boston: Little, Brown, 1933), 14.
46. Connington, *Clues*, 289, 291, 309; Connington, *Speak*, 63.
47. Connington, *Gold Brick*, 13, 67, 70.
48. J.J. Connington, *Mystery at Lynden Sands* (London: Gollancz, 1928), 59; J.J. Connington, *Jack-in-the-Box* (Boston: Little, Brown, 1944), 81, 84. The similarity of these deductions as well as the existence in both tales of forced marriage plots suggest that Connington had the earlier *Lynden Sands* in mind when he wrote *Jack-in-the-Box*.
49. Connington, *Boat-House*, 143; Connington, *Ha-Ha*, 245–246, 303–304.

50. J.J. Connington, *Commonsense Is All You Need* (London: Hodder and Stoughton, 1947), 20, 191, 196–197. One presumes that Diana Herne is no relation to Herne the Hunter of *Nordenholt's Million*.
51. Connington, *Ha-Ha*, 58–59.
52. J.J. Connington, *Tragedy at Ravensthorpe* (Boston: Little, Brown, 1927), 29.
53. Irene Stewart to the author, 22 July 2009.
54. Connington, *Maze*, 44.
55. Ibid., 45, 46.
56. Connington, *Speak*, 151.
57. Ibid.
58. J.J. Connington, *A Minor Operation* (Boston: Little, Brown, 1937), 42, 43.
59. Connington, *Operation*, 64, 65.
60. Connington, *Eye*, 134, 138.
61. J.J. Connington, *Truth Comes Limping* (Boston: Little, Brown, 1938), 184, 187, 188. **[SPOILER ALERT]** In the same novel the valet Malverton is beaten by his master (who turns out to be the murderer) after he provides Driffield with damning information about his master. **[END SPOILER ALERT]** Though he of course wanted the information, Sir Clinton nevertheless approvingly comments on the chastisement administered to the disloyal valet.
62. Anthony Boucher, "The Week in Murder," *San Francisco Chronicle*, 23 January 1944, in *The Anthony Boucher Chronicles: Reviews and Commentary 1942–1947*, ed. Francis M. Nevins (Vancleave, MS: Ramble House, 2002), 57; J.J. Connington, *Jack-in-the-Box* (Boston: Little, Brown, 1944), 155, 231. When Wendover declares that "nobody wants a mulatto cousin dumped on his doorstep out of the blue," Driffield implicitly rebukes the insular Squire: "I don't suppose I'd care to have a wastrel relation landing on me, whatever his colour was." Ibid., 173. **[SPOILER ALERT]** Yet Driffield's point is undermined by the fact that this particular mulatto turns out to be an exceptionally bad hat. **[END SPOILER ALERT]**
63. Connington, *Ha-Ha*, 48–49.
64. Connington, *Limping*, 28–29.
65. The *London Times Literary Supplement* review is quoted in the front matter of the third edition of J.J. Connington, *The Eye in the Museum* (1929; repr., London: Gollancz, 1933). For the *Criterion* review, which was written by T.S. Eliot, see *Monthly Criterion* 6 (November 1927): 568.
66. *Monthly Criterion* 6 (July 1927): 90. John Dickson Carr, "The Grandest Game in the World," reprinted in Douglas G. Greene, ed., *The Door to Doom and Other Detections*, rev. ed. (1980; repr., New York: IPL, 1991), 316. For the H.C. Harwood comment, see the front flap of the dust jacket of *Tragedy at Ravensthorpe* (Boston: Little, Brown, 1927).
67. Encephalitis lethargica is an unusual form of encephalitis that spread in a worldwide epidemic between 1915 and 1926, shortly before *Murder in the Maze* was published. Three years after the appearance of *Murder in the Maze*, Agatha Christie inflicted the disease on one of the characters in her novel *The Murder at the Vicarage* (1930).
68. Connington, *Maze*, 34–37.
69. Ibid., 265.
70. Ibid., 120–121. Izaak Walton (1593–1683) authored *The Compleat Angler*.
71. Ibid., 86, 160. For the supreme example of the true idiot friend in Golden Age detective fiction, see Agatha Christie's Captain Arthur Hastings in her Hercule Poirot tales.

72. Purportedly of actual faeries, The Cottingley Fairies photographs were taken by two adolescent cousins in 1917 and highly publicized in England by Arthur Conan Doyle (a fervent spiritualist after the death of one of his sons in World War I), who used them as the basis for his 1922 book *The Coming of the Fairies*.

73. *Spectator* 139 (1927): 359; Connington, *Museum*, front matter; *Saturday Review of Literature* 6 (9 February 1929): 670; Arnold Bennett, "I Take Up the Challenge of Detective Fiction Lovers," *Evening Standard*, 17 January 1929, reprinted in *Arnold Bennett: The Evening Standard Years "Books and Persons" 1926–1931*, ed. Andrew Mylett (Hampden, CT: Archon Books, 1974), 232. The Van de Water comment comes from the front flap of the dust jacket of *Grim Vengeance* (English title: *Nemesis at Raynham Parva*) (Boston: Little Brown, 1929).

74. Connington, *Nine Solutions*, 15.

75. Ibid., 52.

76. Ibid., 63, 72, 73.

77. Tellingly, the maid's death is treated by all involved in the investigation as a mere adjunct to the murders of the "significant" people. This of course turns out to be the correct approach.

78. Ibid., 6.

79. See book description on the front flap of *The Eye in the Museum* dust jacket, Gollancz edition.

80. J.J. Connington, *The Sweepstake Murders* (Boston: Little, Brown, 1931), 259.

81. It should be noted here, however, that Rupert Gould claimed that a similar alibi method had been used in an 1899 short story in *The Strand* (see below).

82. Barzun and Taylor, *Catalogue of Crime* (1989), 141; Connington, *Sweepstake* 49–50.

83. Connington, *Sweepstake*, 41.

84. Ibid., 40; Barzun and Taylor, *Catalogue of Crime* (1989), 141. For the E.C. Bentley praise see the back flap of the dust jacket of J.J. Connington, *The Ha-Ha Case* (London: Hodder & Stoughton, 1934).

85. Connington, *Castleford*, 35, 36.

86. Ibid., 79, 246–47. Even Haddon's wife regrets her husband's leftist inclinations: "Jack had been a changed man when he came back from the West Front.... He'd got among a bad set in the Army and picked up all sorts of notions about Bolshevism and the class-war.... Nowadays he spent most of his time in grousing against anyone better off than himself.... He was getting himself disliked by everybody." Ibid., 70.

87. Ibid., 82–83.

88. Ibid., 152.

89. Ibid., 308.

90. Ibid., 339–340.

91. For this critical praise, see the dust jacket of J.J. Connington, *The Ha-Ha Case* (London: Hodder & Stoughton, 1934).

92. Connington based *The Ha-Ha Case* on the real life Ardlamont Case, a sensation in Scotland and the rest of Great Britain in 1893. At Ardlamont, a large country estate in Argyll, Cecil Hambrough died from a gunshot wound while hunting. Cecil's tutor, Alfred John Monson, and another man, both of whom were out hunting with Cecil, claimed that Cecil had accidentally shot himself; but Monson was arrested and tried for Cecil's murder. The verdict delivered was "not proven," but Monson was then — and is today — considered almost certainly to have been guilty of the murder. Several key characters in *The Ha-Ha Case* are drawn directly from the Ardlamont case, as is the murder (shooting "accident" while hunting) itself; though Connington added numerous complications that take the tale in a new direction. On the Ardlamont case, see William Roughead, *Classic Crimes* (1951; repr., New York: New York Review Books Classics, 2000), 378–464.

93. Connington, *Ha-Ha Case*, 21, 252, 258. That two different characters contemptuously refer to two other characters as "boneheads" during the course of the tale seems not altogether unfitting in a Connington novel. Irene Stewart notes that her father had two brothers, an elder, Fred, a physician, and a younger, Charlie, a solicitor. "In good old Scottish tradition," she continues, "there was some quarrel [between Fred and] my father, and he never came to Belfast, and we never met. His name was never mentioned, and though I knew that I had a cousin, named Rhoda, it wasn't until her death, that the solicitor contacted me, and gave me news of her.... I could have had a cousin, but the old family quarrel came between." Irene Stewart to the author 22 July 2009. Brotherly conflicts feature significantly in *Murder in the Maze*, *Tragedy at Ravensthorpe* and *The Ha-Ha Case*.

94. Connington, *Ha-Ha Case*, 172–173. Mr. Copdock's name strongly resembles that of the tobacconist Copperdock in John Rhode's *The Murders on Praed Street*.

95. *Sunday Times*, 30 September 1934, 9. Another interesting character in *The Ha-Ha Case* is an escaped lunatic at the murder scene who is a fervent believer in the seventeenth-century prophecies of Coinneach Odhar Fiosaiche, or Dun Kenneth, the Seer, a figure discussed in one of the essays Connington collected in *Alias J.J. Connington*. See "Things in the North," in Stewart, *Connington*, 255–259.

96. *London Times Literary Supplement*, 18 October 1934, 718.

97. *London Sunday Times*, 14 July 1935, 8. In his collection of essays, *Alias J.J. Connington*, Stewart when discussing his friendship with a former professor of his, the renowned chemist and mountaineer, John Norman Collie, recalled that Collie's "collection of specimens of Chinese and Japanese art made his rooms a museum; and I remember hours spent there after dinner." Stewart, *Connington*, 271. No doubt Connington transferred his interest in Japan to the pathetic Mr. Mitford. Connington dedicated his first novel, *Nordenholt's Million*, to Collie.

98. A.W. Stewart to R.T. Gould, 14, 23 February 1936; A.W. Stewart to R.T. Gould, 10, 14 April 1936. Of the telegram gimmick, Connington in *A Minor Operation* has Sir Clinton declare, "It's clever, isn't it? ... I thought of it myself a long while ago. But that almost sounds like self-praise, doesn't it?" Later in the tale, confirming that Sir Clinton is something of an ego projection of the author, we read this: "'I'm not sorry I took chemistry at school,' Sir Clinton said with satisfaction as he tossed the burning envelope into the fireplace. 'It turns up usefully now and again.'" Connington, *Operation*, 236, 289.

99. A.W. Stewart to R.T. Gould, 7 June, 21, 31 August, 9 September, 26 October 1936. The "quickie" short story to which Connington refers likely was "Before Insulin," which appeared in the *London Evening Standard* on September 1, 1936. Connington appears to have written *A Minor Operation* in about four months, roughly in March, April, May and October 1936. His "record in quick writing," Connington had earlier explained to Gould, "was in my early stages when I planned and wrote a 70,000 word tec yarn in rather less than six weeks." A.W. Stewart to R.T. Gould, 27 November 1935. This speedily-produced "tec yarn" probably was the second Connington mystery tale, *The Dangerfield Talisman* (1926).

100. *London Sunday Times*, 20 February 1937, 10; *London Times Literary Supplement*, 27 February 1937, 150; Barzun and Taylor, *Catalogue of Crime* (1989), 140.

101. Hazel Deerhurst's physical allure is commented on throughout the tale, with a fair amount of focus on her intimate apparel. Her housekeeper, Mrs. Butterswick, as we have seen, is terrified lest the rough hands of any policeman fondle her mistress' "pretties," as she quaintly puts it to herself; while Squire Wendover shows interest in this subject as well. "Was she a pretty girl," the Squire asks immediately upon hearing of Hazel's disappearance. Later on he speculates that "a girl doesn't get into her dressing-gown and lingerie when she's going to interview a man she hates." For his part, Sir Clinton raises the possibility that Hazel Deerhurst might have been sexually assaulted by her just-released ex-convict husband: "Now what about Deerhurst? Here's a man who for over four years has been shut off completely from any association with women. His appetites must be all on edge, and from what we've heard of him he's apt to play the bully when he wants a thing. Hazel Deerhurst, one gathers, was a pretty girl." Connington, *Operation*, 97, 131–32.

102. Irene Stewart to the author, 22 June 2011; J.J. Connington, *The Counsellor* (London: Hodder and Stoughton, 1939), 22.

103. *London Times Literary Supplement*, 6 July 1940, 329.

104. A.W. Stewart to F.G. Tryhorn, 30 August 1946 (letter in possession of the author); Irene Stewart to the author, 22 July 2009; Symons, *Bloody Murder*, 323. Irene Stewart recalls that *Alias J.J. Connington*, not being detective fiction, "took some selling to a publisher." Irene Stewart to the author, 22 July 2009. Julian Symons was born in 1912, so presumably he was writing of twenties Connington, or else he remembered himself as younger than he was. The Connington novels *A Catalogue of Crime* ranks most highly are *The Boathouse Riddle*, *The Case with Nine Solutions*, *The Castleford Conundrum*, *The Dangerfield Talisman*, *The Four Defences*, *The Ha-Ha Case*, *A Minor Operation*, *Murder in the Maze* and *The Sweepstake Murders*. Only *The Counsellor* is not listed.

105. A.W. Stewart to R.T. Gould, 26 February 1936. On Rupert Thomas Gould, see Jonathan Betts, *Time Restored: The Harrison Timekeepers and R.T. Gould, the Man Who Knew (Almost) Everything* (London: Oxford University Press, 2006). Photocopies of the Gould-Stewart correspondence are in the possession of Jonathan Betts, who was kind enough to allow me to see them and quote from them. Why, or even whether, the correspondence halted in 1937 is not clear. Irene Stewart confirms the family Loch Ness Monster sighting in 1935, when she was fourteen: "Our sighting ... was real enough — there were three humps in line astern, each with its wake, but no head or tail. So I said, 'Och, they're only porpoises,' only to be told that porpoises don't live in fresh water, a proper putdown." Irene Stewart to the author, 22 June 2011.

106. A.W. Stewart to R.T. Gould, 3 November 1935.

107. A.W. Stewart to R.T. Gould, 28 February 1936.

108. A.W. Stewart to R.T. Gould, 10 May 1936.

109. A.W. Stewart to R.T. Gould, 25 April, 17 December 1936.

110. A.W. Stewart to R.T. Gould, 3 November 1935, 29 April, 17 December 1936. Connington is referring to Margaret Murray (1863–1963), at that time recently retired from an Assistant Professorship in Egyptology at the University College of London. The "tome" to which Connington refers is Professor Murray's *The Witch-cult in Western Europe* (1921), which hugely influenced popular understanding of witchcraft and such famous horror writers as H.P. Lovecraft and Dennis Wheatley (and also John Street's novel *The Secret of High Eldersham*, published under his Miles Burton pseudonym). Today, scholars tend to cast doubt on Murray's theories and her scholarship. Connington's own references to Murray seem rather tinged with condescension.

111. On the amazing Pemberton-Billing affair, see Philip Hoare, *Oscar Wilde's Last Stand* (New York: Arcade, 1998).

112. A.W. Stewart to R.T. Gould. 22 July 1936.

113. A.W. Stewart to R.T. Gould, 28 September 1936.

114. A.W. Stewart to R.T. Gould, 14 December 1935. "I have always been interested, and taken pleasure in, accounts of girls being kidnapped, gagged, blindfolded, bound hand and foot, handcuffed, fettered and otherwise reduced to a condition of complete helplessness." wrote the strikingly candid Gould. "Also in illustrations and/or photographs of the same." Betts, *Time Restored*, 275. Connington's own novels evince a consistent interest in pretty "girls" under the age of thirty. Occasionally these pretty "girls" are imperiled, as in *Nemesis at Raynham Parva*, with its ruthless white slavery ring, and in two other detective novels, *Mystery at Lynden Sands* (1928) and *Jack-in-the-Box* (1944), in both of which a pretty "girl" melodramatically is abducted and pressed to consent to marriage with the villain of the tale. Two pretty girls are abducted as well in the thriller *Tom Tiddler's Island* and rape and kidnapping is one of the possible fates of a vanished pretty girl in *A Minor Operation*.

115. A.W. Stewart to R.T. Gould, 14 December 1935, 14 April 1936. Connington classed "blood sports" under his definition of physical cruelty. "I can't reckon pheasant-shooting, hare-coursing, or otter-hunting as sports at all. As to the 'blooding' of kids at a fox-hunt, it merely sickens me," he wrote Gould emphatically. "I used to shoot a little, but only for the pot; which has some justification: but I haven't had a shot gun in my hands for thirty years now, and shall never pick one up again." A.W. Stewart to R.T. Gould, 14 February 1936. In *The Castleford Conundrum*, it will be recalled, a particularly odious teenage boy is revealed as an animal torturer.

116. A.W. Stewart to R.T. Gould, 25 January 1936.

117. A.W. Stewart to R.T. Gould, 27 September, 5 November 1936. The "Macaulay's New Zealander" reference is to historian and essayist Thomas Macaulay's verbal image of a New Zealander of the future contemplating the ruins of London. This image was later graphically portrayed in 1872 by Gustave Doré in a famous illustration.

118. A.W. Stewart to R.T. Gould, February 14, March 9, 12, 19, April 25 1936. It will be recalled that in *The Treachery of France* (1924) John Street had expressed similarly hostile views of positions taken by French governments. Connington's opinion of American political figures was rather low as well, the author having placed the blame for Europe's post–Great War difficulties on the direct intervention of United States President Woodrow Wilson and his close adviser Edward M. House into the Versailles Treaty negotiations. "It was deplorable that the destinies of the world should have been committed to two insufferably conceited creatures like Wilson and House," Connington wrote Gould scathingly. "When I read the House documents, I was surprised, and Wilson, to judge by the official life, must have been even worse. University men are useless in positions of that sort; and Wilson wasn't even a good specimen of a University man." A.W. Stewart to R.T. Gould, 19 March 1936.

119. A.W. Stewart to R.T. Gould, 1 May 1936.
120. A.W. Stewart to R.T. Gould, 14 December 1935, 25 April, 8 May, 27 September 1936. On the Reverend Holms Coats, see Kenneth B.E. Roxburgh, "The Fundamentalist Controversy Concerning the Baptist Theological College of Scotland," in *Baptist History and Heritage* 36 (Winter/Spring 2001), 251–272. "My father and Uncle Holms were rather oil and water," admits Irene Stewart. Irene Stewart to the author, 22 July 2009.
121. A.W. Stewart to R.T. Gould, 1 May, 11 May 1936.
122. A.W. Stewart to R.T. Gould, 11 November 1935, 22 November 1936.
123. A.W. Stewart to R.T. Gould, 26 October 1936.
124. A.W. Stewart to R.T. Gould, 23 March 1936.
125. Irene Stewart to the author, 22 June 2011. With his wife and daughter Connington did see *Things to Come*, an adaptation of the H.G. Wells novel *The Shape of Things to Come* (1933).
126. A.W. Stewart to R.T. Gould, 27 November 1935.
127. A.W. Stewart to R.T. Gould, 25 January 1936.
128. R.T. Gould to A.W. Stewart, 7 March 1936; A.W. Stewart to R.T. Gould, 9 March 1936.
129. A.W. Stewart to R.T. Gould, 3, 27 November 1935, 27 April 1936; R.T. Gould to A.W. Stewart, 25 November 1935.
130. A.W. Stewart to R.T. Gould, 14 April 1936. Despite his declaration that he never read "tec yarns" by authors other than Freeman, however, Stewart during his convalescence from his heart attack accepted a loan of books from Gould that included three mystery novels not authored by Freeman, Georgette Heyer's *Behold, Here's Poison*, George Goodchild's *The Monster of Gramont* and Patricia Wentworth's *Fear by Night*. The latter two novels are more accurately characterized as thrillers, but the former unquestionably is a work of detection.
131. A.W. Stewart to R.T. Gould, 21 August 1936.
132. A.W. Stewart to R.T. Gould, 12 December 1936.
133. A.W. Stewart to R.T. Gould, 14 February, 14 April 1936.
134. R.T. Gould to A.W. Stewart, 13 April 1936.
135. A.W. Stewart to R.T. Gould, 14 April 1936.
136. A.W. Stewart to R.T. Gould, 14 April, 8 May, 11, 26 October 1936.
137. R.T. Gould to A.W. Stewart, 29 October 1936.
138. Ibid.
139. A.W. Stewart to R.T. Gould, 26 October 1936.
140. Ibid.
141. Ibid.
142. R.T. Gould to A.W. Stewart, 25 April 1936.
143. A.W. Stewart to R.T. Gould, 25 April 1936.
144. A.W. Stewart to R.T. Gould, 5 November 1936. Somewhat surprisingly, given his reputation as the man who knew everything, Gould informed Stewart that his knowledge of archery was slight. Another tale clearly based on Connington's experience with failing eyesight was "After Death the Doctor," [**SPOILER ALERT**] an enjoyable novella with a central gimmick turning on the use of contact lenses. See *The First Class Omnibus* (London: Hodder and Stoughton, 1934). [**END SPOILER ALERT**]

Appendix III

1. G.K. Chesterton, "A Detective Story with Twelve Authors," *The Illustrated London News*, 9 January 1932, reprinted in Lawrence J. Clipper, *The Collected Works of G.K. Chesterton*, Vol. 36 (*The Illustrated London News, 1932–1934*) (San Francisco: Ignatius Press, 2011), 22–23.
2. The Detection Club, *The Floating Admiral* (1931; repr., Boston: Gregg Press, 1979), 165.
3. Various authors, *Double Death: A Murder Story* (London: Gollancz, 1939), 284. The editor of the novel—who grandiosely dubbed himself the "All-Seeing Eye"—was a seventh writer, John Chancellor. He took it upon himself to add a prologue that gives away David Hume's solution, evidently in an attempt to fairly clue it. Granted, Hume's solution is not fair play, but removing the mystery element entirely, as Chancellor does, seems merely foolish.
4. Dorothy L. Sayers to Freeman Wills Crofts, 13 March 1936; Freeman Wills Crofts to Dorothy L. Sayers, 11 April 1936; Dorothy L. Sayers papers, Marion E. Wade Center, Wheaton College, Wheaton, Illinois.
5. Various authors, *Double Death*, 190. Sayers' 1931 railway timetable detective novel, *The Five Red Herrings*, was an homage to Crofts.

Bibliography

Primary Sources

Diaries, E-mails and Letters

Alfred Walter Stewart to Frederick Gerald Tryhorn, 30 August 1946 (letter in possession of author)
Freeman Wills Crofts to Mrs. Martin, 1 January 1952 (letter in possession of author)
Freeman Wills Crofts to Peter Ibbotson, 23 November 1949 (letter in possession of author)
Irene Stewart to the author, 22 July 2009, 22 June 2011
Josephine Pullein-Thompson to the author, 28 March 2006
Martin Roundell Greene to the author, 18 April 2007
Patrick Mileham to the author, 18, 19 August 2008
Paula Simpson to the author, 14 January 2004, 30 September 2008
Stella Wilkinson Diary, www.wilkinson.ws/claude/stella/diary/may-1936.htm

Government Documents

1891 England Census
1901 English Census
1911 English Census

Magazines and Newspapers

Canadian Forum, 1936
The Criterion/The Monthly Criterion, 1927, 1928
(London) *Daily Herald*, 1931, 1932, 1934, 1935, 1936
(London) *Daily Telegraph*, 2007, 2009
(London) *Observer*, 2007
(London) *Sunday Times*, 1933, 1934, 1935, 1936, 1937, 1959
(London) *Times*, 1965
(London) *Times Literary Supplement*, 1929, 1934, 1937, 1940, 2007
New Statesman and Nation, 1934, 1936, 1937, 1938, 1943, 1955
New York Herald Tribune Book Review, 1935, 1936
New York Times Book Review, 1928, 1936, 1937, 1943, 1949, 1959
New Yorker, 1942, 1943, 1945, 1948
Saturday Review of Literature, 1929, 1937, 1939
The Spectator, 1931, 1935, 1936, 1937, 1939, 1941, 1943
Time, 1929

Manuscript Collections

Alfred Walter Stewart–Rupert Thomas Gould Correspondence, 1935–1936. Copies in possession of Jonathan Betts.

Dodd, Mead Mss. The Lilly Library Manuscript Collection. University of Indiana, Bloomington.
Dorothy L. Sayers Papers. Marion E. Wade Center. Wheaton College, Illinois.

Works by Freeman Wills Crofts, Alfred Walter Stewart, Cecil John Charles Street and Other Crime Writers

Berkeley, Anthony, *The Layton Court Mystery*. London: Herbert Jenkins, 1925.
_____. *Panic Party*. London: Hodder & Stoughton, 1934.
_____. *Roger Sheringham and the Vane Mystery*. 1927. Reprint, London: House of Stratus, 2003.
_____. *The Second Shot*. London: Hodder & Stoughton, 1930.
_____. *The Silk Stocking Murders*. London: Collins, 1928.
_____. *Top Storey Murder*. London: Hodder & Stoughton, 1931.
_____. *The Wychford Poisoning Case: An Essay in Criminology*. London: Collins, 1926.
Burton, Miles. *Beware Your Neighbour*. London: Collins, 1951.
_____. *Bones in the Brickfield*. London: Collins, 1958.
_____. *The Cat Jumps*. London: Collins, 1946.
_____. *The Charabanc Mystery*. London: Collins, 1934.
_____. *The Chinese Puzzle*. London: Collins, 1957.
_____. *The Clue of the Fourteen Keys* (English title: *Death at the Club*). New York: Doubleday, Doran, 1936.
_____. *The Clue of the Silver Brush* (English Title: *The Milk Churn Murder*). New York: Doubleday, Doran, 1935.
_____. *The Clue of the Silver Cellar* (English Title: *Where Is Barbara Prentice?*). New York: Doubleday, Doran, 1936.
_____. *Dark Is the Tunnel* (English Title: *Death in the Tunnel*). New York: Doubleday, Doran, 1936.
_____. *Death at the Crossroads*. London: Collins, 1932.
_____. *Death at Low Tide*. London: Collins, 1938.
_____. *Death Leaves No Card*. 1939. Reprint, Toronto: Collins, 1942.
_____. *Death of Mr. Gantley*. London: Collins, 1932.
_____. *Death of Two Brothers*. London: Collins, 1941.
_____. *Death Takes a Detour*. London: Collins, 1958.
_____. *Death Takes the Living*. London: Collins, 1949.
_____. *Death Visits Downspring* (English title: *Up the Garden Path*). New York: Doubleday, Doran, 1941.
_____. *The Devereux Court Mystery*. London: Collins, 1935.
_____. *Devil's Reckoning*. London: Collins, 1949.
_____. *Fate at the Fair*. London: Collins, 1933.
_____. *Ground for Suspicion*. London: Collins, 1950.
_____. *The Hardway Diamonds Mystery*. London: Collins, 1930.
_____. *Heir to Lucifer*. London: Collins, 1947.
_____. *Heir to Murder*. London: Collins, 1953.
_____. *The Menace on the Downs*. London: Collins, 1931.
_____. *Mr. Babbacombe Dies*. London: Collins, 1939.
_____. *Mr. Westerby Missing*. New York: Doubleday, Doran, 1940.
_____. *Murder in Crown Passage*. London: Collins, 1937.
_____. *Murder of a Chemist*. London: Collins, 1936.
_____. *Murder Out of School*. London: Collins, 1951.
_____. *Murder Unrecognized*. London: Collins, 1955.
_____. *Murder, M.D.* 1943. Reprint, Hornchurch, UK: Ian Henry, 1975.
_____. *Not a Leg to Stand On*. London: Collins, 1945.
_____. *The Platinum Cat*. London: Collins, 1938.
_____. *The Secret of High Eldersham*. 1930. Reprint, New York: Garland, 1976.
_____. *Situation Vacant*. London: Collins, 1946.
_____. *The Three-Corpse Trick*. London: Collins, 1944.
_____. *To Catch a Thief*. London: Collins, 1934.
_____. *Vacancy with Corpse* (English Title: *Death Takes a Flat*). New York: Doubleday, Doran, 1940.
_____. *Written in Dust* (English Title: *Murder in the Coalhole*). New York: Doubleday, Doran, 1940.
Cannan, Joanna. *And Be a Villain*. London: Gollancz, 1958.
_____. *Death at the Dog*. 1941. Reprint, Boulder, CO: Rue Morgue Press, 1999.
Christie, Agatha. *After the Funeral*. London: Collins, 1953.
_____. *The Big Four*. London: Collins, 1927.

_____. *The Body in the Library.* London: Collins, 1942.
_____. *The Man in the Brown Suit.* London: Collins, 1924.
_____. *The Murder at the Vicarage.* London: Collins, 1930.
_____. *The Murder of Roger Ackroyd.* London: Collins, 1926.
_____. *Murder on the Links.* London: Collins, 1923.
_____. *Murder on the Orient Express.* London: Collins, 1934.
_____. *The Mysterious Affair at Styles.* London: Collins, 1920.
_____. *The Mystery of the Blue Train.* London: Collins, 1928.
_____. *The Secret Adversary.* London: Collins, 1922.
_____. *The Secret of Chimneys.* London: Collins, 1925.
Connington, J.J. "After Death the Doctor." In *The First Class Omnibus.* London: Hodder & Stoughton, 1934.
_____. *Almighty Gold.* London: Constable, 1924.
_____. *The Boat-House Riddle.* London: Gollancz, 1931.
_____. *The Case with Nine Solutions.* Boston: Little, Brown, 1928.
_____. *The Castleford Conundrum.* Boston: Little, Brown, 1932.
_____. *Commonsense Is All You Need.* London: Hodder & Stoughton, 1947.
_____. *The Counsellor.* London: Hodder & Stoughton, 1939.
_____. *The Dangerfield Talisman.* Boston: Little, Brown, 1926.
_____. *Death at Swaythling Court.* 1926. Reprint, London: Ernest Benn, 1930.
_____. *The Eye in the Museum.* London: Gollancz, 1929.
_____. *For Murder Will Speak.* Boston: Little, Brown, 1938.
_____. *The Four Defences.* London: Hodder & Stroughton, 1940.
_____. *Gold Brick Island* (English Title: *Tom Tiddler's Island*). Boston: Little, Brown, 1933.
_____. *The Ha-Ha Case.* 1934. Reprint, London: Hodder & Stoughton, 1936.
_____. *Jack-in-the-Box.* Boston: Little Brown, 1944.
_____. *A Minor Operation.* Boston: Little Brown, 1937.
_____. *Murder in the Maze.* Boston: Little, Brown, 1927.
_____. *Mystery at Lynden Sands.* London: Gollancz, 1928.
_____. *Nemesis at Raynham Parva.* London: Gollancz, 1928.
_____. *No Past Is Dead.* Boston: Little, Brown, 1942.
_____. *Nordenholt's Million.* 1923. Reprint, London: Ernest Benn, 1926.
_____. *The Sweepstake Murders.* Boston: Little, Brown, 1931.
_____. *The Tau Cross Mystery* (English Title: *In Whose Dim Shadow*). Boston: Little, Brown, 1935.
_____. *Tragedy at Ravensthorpe.* Boston: Little Brown, 1927.
_____. *Truth Comes Limping.* Boston: Little, Brown, 1938.
_____. *The Twenty-One Clues.* Boston: Little, Brown, 1941.
_____. *The Two Tickets Puzzle.* Boston: Little, Brown, 1930.
Crofts, Freeman Wills. *The Affair at Little Wokeham.* 1943. Reprint, London: House of Stratus, 2000.
_____. *Antidote to Venom.* 1938. Reprint, London: House of Stratus, 2000.
_____. *Anything to Declare?* 1957. Reprint, London: House of Stratus, 2000.
_____. *The Box Office Murders.* 1929. Reprint, London: House of Stratus, 2000.
_____. *The Cask.* 1920. Reprint, London: House of Stratus, 2000.
_____. *Crime at Guildford.* 1935. Reprint, London: House of Stratus, 2000.
_____. *Death of a Train.* London: Hodder & Stoughton, 1946.
_____. *Death on the Way.* London: Collins, 1932.
_____. *The End of Andrew Harrison.* 1938. Reprint, London: Hodder & Stoughton, 1940.
_____. *Enemy Unseen.* 1945. Reprint, London: Hodder & Stoughton, 1952.
_____. *Fatal Venture.* 1939. Reprint, Hornchurch, UK: Ian Henry, 1984.
_____. *Fear Comes to Chalfont.* 1942. Reprint, London: House of Stratus, 2000.
_____. *Found Floating.* 1937. Reprint, London: Hodder & Stoughton, 1941.
_____. *The Four Gospels in One Story, Written as a Modern Biography, with Difficult Passages Clarified and Explanatory Notes.* London: Longman's, Green, 1949.
_____. *French Strikes Oil.* 1951. Reprint, London: House of Stratus, 2000.
_____. *Golden Ashes.* 1940. Reprint, London: House of Stratus, 2000.
_____. "The Gorse Hall Mystery." In *Great Unsolved Crimes.* London: Hutchinson, 1938.
_____. *The Groote Park Murder.* 1923. Reprint, London: House of Stratus, 2000.
_____. *The Hog's Back Mystery.* 1933. Reprint, London: House of Stratus, 2000.
_____. *Inspector French and the Cheyne Mystery.* 1926. Reprint, London: House of Stratus, 2000.
_____. *Inspector French and the Starvel Tragedy.* 1927. Reprint, London: House of Stratus, 2000.
_____. *Inspector French's Greatest Case.* 1924. New York: Thomas Seltzer, 1925.
_____. *James Tarrant, Adventurer.* London: Hodder & Stoughton, 1941.

_____. *The Losing Game*. 1941. Reprint, London: House of Stratus, 2000.
_____. *The Loss of the "Jane Vosper."* London: Collins, 1936.
_____. *Man Overboard!* New York: Dodd, Mead, 1936.
_____. *Many a Slip*. London: Hodder & Stoughton, 1955.
_____. *Murderers Make Mistakes*. 1947. Reprint, London: House of Stratus, 2000.
_____. *Mystery at Southampton Water*. 1934. Reprint, London: Hodder & Stoughton, 1936.
_____. *Mystery in the Channel*. 1931. Reprint, London: House of Stratus, 2000.
_____. "A New Zealand Tragedy." In *The Anatomy of Murder*. New York: 1937.
_____. *The Pit-Prop Syndicate*. London: Collins, 1922.
_____. *The Ponson Case*. 1921. Reprint, London: House of Stratus, 2000.
_____. *The Sea Mystery*. 1928. Reprint, London: House of Stratus, 2000.
_____. *Silence for the Murderer*. 1949. Reprint, London: House of Stratus, 2000.
_____. *Sir John Magill's Last Journey*. London: Collins, 1930.
_____. *Sudden Death*. 1932. Reprint, London: House of Stratus, 2000.
_____. *The 12.30 from Croydon*. 1934. Reprint, London: House of Stratus, 2000.
_____. *Young Robin Brand, Detective*. 1947. New York: Dodd, Mead, 1948.
The Detection Club. *Ask a Policeman*. 1933. Reprint, London: Macmillan, 1983.
Drake, Maurice. *WO2*. New York: Dutton, 1913.
Dutton, Charles J. *The Shadow on the Glass*. New York: Dodd, Mead, 1923.
Everton, Francis. *The Dalehouse Murder*. New York: Bobbs-Merrill, 1927.
F.O.O. *The Making of a Gunner*. London: Everleigh Nash, 1916.
_____. *With the Guns*. London: Everleigh Nash, 1916.
Freeman, R. Austin. "Rex v. Burnaby." In *The Famous Cases of Dr. Thorndyke: Thirty-Seven of His Criminal Investigations as Set down by R. Austin Freeman*. 1929. Reprint, London: Hodder and Stoughton, 1952.
_____. *Social Decay and Regeneration*. London: Constable, 1921.
Gilbert, Anthony. *He Came by Night*. London: Collins, 1944.
Iles, Francis. *Before the Fact*. London: Gollancz, 1932.
_____. *Malice Aforethought*. London: Gollancz, 1931.
Innes, Michael. *A Night of Errors*. New York: Dodd, Mead, 1947.
James, P.D. *A Mind to Murder*. 1963. Reprint, London: Faber and Faber, 2006.
_____. *Shroud for a Nightingale*. 1972. Reprint, London: Faber and Faber, 2006.
Kennedy, Milward. *Bull's Eye*. London: Gollancz, 1933
_____. *Corpse in Cold Storage*. London: Gollancz, 1934.
_____. *I'll be Judge, I'll be Jury*. London: Gollancz, 1937.
_____. *Poison in the Parish*. London: Gollancz, 1935.
_____. *Sic Transit Gloria*. London: Gollancz, 1936.
King, C. Daly. *Obelists Fly High*. 1935. New York: Dover, 1986.
Mitchell, Gladys. *Come Away, Death*. London: Michael Joseph, 1937.
_____. *The Rising of the Moon*. London: Michael Joseph, 1945.
_____. *St. Peter's Finger*. London: Michael Joseph, 1937.
_____. *Speedy Death*. London: Gollancz, 1929.
Rhode, John. *A.S.F.: The Story of a Great Conspiracy*. London: Geoffrey Bles, 1924.
_____. *The Alarm*. London: Geoffrey Bles, 1925.
_____. *Blackthorn House*. New York: Dodd, Mead, 1949.
_____. *Body Unidentified* (English Title: *Proceed With Caution*). New York: Dodd, Mead, 1938.
_____. *By Registered Post*. London: Geoffrey Bles, 1953.
_____. *The Case of Constance Kent*. London: Geoffrey Bles, 1928.
_____. *The Case of the Forty Thieves* (English Title: *Death at the Inn*). New York: Dodd, Mead, 1954. English Edition, 1953.
_____. *The Claverton Mystery*. London: Collins, 1933.
_____. "Constance Kent." In *The Anatomy of Murder: Famous Crime Critically Considered by Members of the Detection Club*. New York: Macmillan, 1937.
_____. *The Corpse in the Car*. London: Collins, 1935.
_____. *The Davidson Case*. London: Geoffrey Bles, 1929.
_____. *Dead Men at the Folly*. London: Collins, 1932.
_____. *Dead of the Night* (English Title: *Night Exercise*). New York: Dodd, Mead, 1942.
_____. *Dead on the Track*. 1943. Reprint, Toronto: Collins, 1945.
_____. *Death at Breakfast*. London: Collins, 1936.
_____. *Death at the Dance*. New York: Dodd, Mead, 1952.
_____. *Death at the Helm*. New York: Dodd, Mead, 1941.
_____. *Death in Harley Street. Death in Harley Street*. 1946. Reprint, New York: Harper & Row, 1986.

_____. *Death in the Hopfields*. London: Collins, 1937.
_____. *Death in Wellington Road*. New York: Dodd, Mead, 1952.
_____. *Death Invades the Meeting*. London: Collins, 1944.
_____. *Death on the Boat-Train*. London: Collins, 1940.
_____. *Death on Sunday*. London: Collins, 1939.
_____. *Death Pays a Dividend*. New York: Dodd, Mead, 1939.
_____. *Death Sits on the Board* (English Title: *Death on the Board*). New York: Dodd, Mead, 1937.
_____. *The Double Florin*. London: Geoffrey Bles, 1924.
_____. *The Dovebury Murders*. New York: Dodd, Mead, 1954.
_____. *Dr. Priestley Lays a Trap* (English Title: *The Motor Rally Mystery*). New York: Dodd, Mead, 1933.
_____. *Dr. Priestley's Quest*. London: Geoffrey Bles, 1926.
_____. *The Ellerby Case*. London: Geoffrey Bles, 1927.
_____. *Family Affairs*. London: Collins, 1950.
_____. *The Fourth Bomb*. New York: Dodd, Mead, 1942.
_____. *The Hanging Woman*. London: Collins, 1931.
_____. *Hendon's First Case*. New York: Dodd, Mead, 1935.
_____. *The House on Tollard Ridge*. London: Geoffrey Bles, 1929.
_____. *Invisible Weapons*. New York: Dodd, Mead, 1938.
_____. *The Lake House*. New York: Dodd, Mead, 1946.
_____. *Licensed for Murder*. London: Collins, 1958.
_____. *Men Die at Cyprus Lodge*. London: Collins, 1943.
_____. *The Murders in Praed Street*. London: Geoffrey Bles, 1928.
_____. *Mystery at Greycombe Farm*. London: Collins, 1932.
_____. *Mystery at Olympia*. London: Collins, 1935.
_____. *The Paddington Mystery*. London: Geoffrey Bles, 1925.
_____. *The Paper Bag*. London: Geoffrey Bles, 1948.
_____. *Peril at Cranbury Hall*. London: Geoffrey Bles, 1930.
_____. *Pinehurst*. London: Geoffrey Bles, 1930.
_____. *Poison for One*. London: Collins, 1934.
_____. *The Robthorne Mystery*. New York: Dodd, Mead, 1934.
_____. *The Secret Meeting*. London: Collins, 1951.
_____. *Signal for Death* (English Title: *They Watched by Night*). London: Dodd, Mead, 1941.
_____. *The Telephone Call*. London: Geoffrey Bles, 1948.
_____. *The Tower of Evil* (English title: *The Bloody Tower*). New York: Dodd, Mead, 1938.
_____. *Tragedy at the Unicorn*. London: Geoffrey Bles, 1928.
_____. *Tragedy on the Line*. London: Collins, 1931.
_____. *The Two Graphs*. London: Geoffrey Bles, 1950.
_____. *Up the Garden Path*. London: Geoffrey Bles, 1949.
_____. *Vegetable Duck*. London: Collins, 1945.
_____. *The Venner Crime*. London: Oldhams, 1933.
Sayers, Dorothy L. *Busman's Honeymoon*. London: Gollancz, 1937.
_____. *The Documents in the Case*. London: Ernest Benn, 1930.
_____. *The Five Red Herrings*. London: Gollancz, 1932.
_____. *Gaudy Night*. London: Gollancz, 1935.
_____. *The Nine Tailors*. London: Gollancz, 1934.
_____. *Strong Poison*. London: Gollancz, 1930.
Stewart, A.W. *Alias J.J. Connington*. London: Hollis & Carter, 1947.
Street, C.J.C. *Lord Reading*. New York: Frederick A. Stokes, 1928.
_____. *Rhineland and Ruhr*. London: A. Couldrey, 1923.
_____. *Thomas Masaryk of Czechoslovakia*. New York: Dodd, Mead, 1930.
Van Dine, S.S. *The Benson Murder Case*. New York: Scribner, 1926.
_____. *The Bishop Murder Case*. New York: Scribner, 1929.
_____. *The Canary Murder Case*. New York: Scribner, 1927.
_____. *The Greene Murder Case*. New York: Scribner, 1928.
Various Authors. *Double Death: A Murder Story*. London: Gollancz, 1939.
Wade, Henry. *Bury Him Darkly*. London: Constable, 1936.
_____. *Constable, Guard Thyself!* London: Constable, 1934.
_____. *Heir Presumptive*. London: Constable, 1935.
_____. *The High Sheriff*. London: Constable, 1937.
_____. *Lonely Magdalen*. 1940. Rev. ed., London: Constable, 1946.
_____. *Mist on the Saltings*. London: Constable, 1933.
_____. *Released for Death*. London: Constable, 1938.

Secondary Sources

Books

Annan, Noel. *The Dons: Mentors, Eccentrics and Geniuses.* Chicago: University of Chicago Press, 2000.
The Annual Register: A Review of Public Events at Home and Abroad for the Year 1889. London: Rivingtons, 1890.
Ash, Cay Van, and Elizabeth Sax Rohmer. *Master of Villainy: A Biography of Sax Rohmer, Master of Villainy: A Biography of Sax Rohmer.* Bowling Green, OH: Popular Press, 1972.
Baker, Arthur H., and J.D. Thornton., eds. *Remaking the World: Selections from the Speeches of Frank N.D. Buchman.* London: Heinemann, 1942.
Baldick, Chris. *The Modern Movement: 1910–1940.* Vol. 10. The Oxford English Literary History. Oxford: Oxford University Press, 2004.
Barzun, Jacques, and Wendell Hertig Taylor. *A Catalogue of Crime.* 1971. Rev. ed., New York: Harper & Row, 1989.
Betts, Jonathan. *Time Restored: The Harrison Timekeepers and R.T. Gould, the Man Who Knew (Almost) Everything.* London: Oxford University Press, 2006.
Bleiler, Everett F. *Science Fiction: The Early Years.* Kent, OH: Kent State University Press, 1990.
Bridges, Yseult. *Saint-with Red Hands? The Chronicle of a Great Crime.* London: Jarrolds, 1954.
Burke, Sir Bernard. *A Genealogical and Heraldic History of the Colonial Gentry.* Vol. I. London: Harrison & Sons, 1891.
Campt, Tina Marie. *Other Germans: Black Germans and the Politics of Race, Gender, and Memory in the Third Reich.* Lansing: University of Michigan Press.
Cannadine, David. *The Decline and Fall of the British Aristocracy.* 1992. Reprint, New York: Vintage Books, 1999.
Carter, Ian. *Railways and Culture in Britain: The Epitome of Modernity.* Manchester, UK: Manchester University Press, 2001.
Cassuto, Leonard W. *Hard-Boiled Sentimentality: The Secret History of American Crime Stories.* New York: Columbia University Press, 2008.
Cheyette, Bryan. *The Construction of "The Jew" in English Literature and Society: Racial Representations, 1875–1945.* Cambridge, UK: Oxford University Press, 1993.
Chinitz, David E. *T.S. Eliot and the Cultural Divide.* Chicago: University of Chicago Press, 2003.
Clifford, Brendan. *The Administration of Ireland, 1920, by Major C.J.C. Street with a Review of His Other Writings.* Belfast: Athol Books, 2001.
Cooper, John, and B.A. Pike. *Detective Fiction: The Collector's Guide.* 1988. Rev. ed., Aldershot, England: Scolar Press, 1994.
Crafts, James M., and William F. *The Crafts Family: A Genealogical Biographical History of the Descendants of Griffin and Alice Crafts of Roxbury Mass. 1630–1890.* Northampton, MA: Gazette Printing Company, 1893.
Denham, Robert D., ed. *The Diaries of Northrop Frye, 1942–1955.* Toronto: University of Toronto Press, 2001.
Dickens, Monica. *One Pair of Hands.* London: Michael Joseph, 1939.
Donaldson, Frances. *The Marconi Scandal.* New York: Harcourt & Brace, 1962.
Donaldson, Norman. *In Search of Dr. Thorndyke: The Story of R. Austin Freeman's Great Scientific Investigator and His Creator.* 1971. Rev. ed., Shelburne, ON: The Battered Silicon Dispatch Box, 1998.
Dover, J.K. Van. *You Know My Method: The Science of the Detective.* Bowling Green, OH: Popular Press, 1994.
Doyle, Arthur Conan. *The Coming of the Fairies.* New York: Doran, 1922.
Drayton, Joanne. *Ngaio Marsh: Her Life in Crime.* Auckland: HarperCollins, 2008.
Dutton, Charles. *Saints and Sinners: The Story of a Clergyman.* New York: Dodd, Mead, 1940.
Gibbons, Stella. *Cold Comfort Farm.* London: Longmans, 1932.
Goodman, Jonathan. *The Stabbing of George Harry Storrs.* London: Allison and Busby, 1983.
Gould, R.T. *The Loch Ness Monster and Others.* London: Geoffrey Bles, 1934.
Greene, Douglas G. *John Dickson Carr: The Man Who Explained Miracles.* New York: Otto Penzler, 1995.
Greene, Martin Roundell. *Electric Lyme.* Crewkerne, UK: Martin Roundell Greene, 2006.
Hardy, Thomas. *Under the Greenwood Tree.* London: Tinsley Brothers, 1872.
Haycraft, Howard. *Murder for Pleasure: The Life and Times of the Detective Story.* 1941. Rev. ed., New York: Biblo and Tannen, 1974.
Hoare, Philip. *Oscar Wilde's Last Stand.* New York: Arcade, 1998.
Hogarth, Basil. *Writing Thrillers for Profit: A Practical Guide.* London: A & C. Black, 1936.
Horsley, Lee. *Twentieth-Century Crime Fiction.* Oxford: Oxford University Press, 2005.
Humble, Nicola. *The Feminine Middlebrow Novel, 1920s to 1950s: Class, Domesticity and Bohemianism.* Oxford: Oxford University Press, 2001.

Hyde, H. Montgomery. *Lord Reading: The Life of Rufus Isaacs, First Marquess of Reading.* New York: Farrar, Straus and Giroux, 1967.
James, P.D., *Talking about Detective Fiction.* Oxford: Bodleian Library, 2009.
_____. *Time to be in Earnest: A Fragment of Autobiography.* London: Faber and Faber, 1999.
[Jones], Julia Thorogood. *Margery Allingham: A Biography.* London: Heinemann, 1991. Revised Edition published as *The Adventures of Margery Allingham*, Chelmsford, UK: Golden Duck, 2009.
Judd, Denis. *Lord Reading: The Life of Rufus Isaacs, First Marquess of Reading, Lord Chief Justice and Viceroy of India, 1869–1933.* London: Weidenfeld and Nicholson, 1982.
Kaye-Smith, Sheila. *All the Books of My Life: A Bibliobiography.* London: Cassell, 1956.
Keating, H.R.F. *The Bedside Companion to Crime.* London: The Mysterious Press, 1989.
_____. *Murder Must Appetize.* 1975. Rev. ed., New York: The Mysterious Press, and London: The Lemon Tree Press, 1981.
Kenney, Catherine. *The Remarkable Life of Dorothy L. Sayers.* Kent, OH: Kent State University Press, 1990.
Knight, Stephen. *Crime Fiction, 1800–2000: Detection, Death, Diversity.* Blasingstoke, UK: Palgrave Macmillan, 2004.
_____. *Form and Ideology in Crime Fiction.* Bloomington: Indiana University Press, 1980.
Lane, Margaret. *Edgar Wallace: The Biography of a Phenomenon.* New York: Doubleday, Doran, 1939.
Lewis, Margaret. *Ngaio Marsh: A Life.* London: Chatto & Windus, 1991. Reprint, Scottsdale, AZ: Poisoned Pen Press, 1998.
Light, Alison. *Forever England: Femininity, Literature and Conservatism between the Wars.* London: Routledge, 1992.
Lobdell, Jared C. *The Detective Fiction Reviews of Charles Williams, 1930–1935.* Jefferson, NC: McFarland, 2003.
Lucas, John. *Arnold Bennett: A Study of His Fiction.* London: Methuen, 1974.
Lynch, Rowan. *The Kirwans of Castlehacket, Co. Galway.* Dublin: Four Courts Press, 2001.
Mais, Stuart P. *Why We Should Read.* London: Grant Richards, 1921.
Makinen, Merja. *Agatha Christie: Investigating Femininity.* Basingstoke, UK: Palgrave Macmillan, 2006.
Mann, Jessica. *Deadlier Than the Male: Why Are Respectable English Women So Good At Murder?* New York: Macmillan, 1981.
Marks, Jeffrey. *Anthony Boucher: A Bibliobiography.* Jefferson, NC: McFarland, 2008.
Mayo, Oliver. *R. Austin Freeman: The Anthropologist at Large.* Hawthorndene, SA: Investigator Press, 1980.
McCutcheon, William Alan. *The Industrial Archaeology of Northern Ireland.* Belfast: Her Majesty's Stationer's Office, 1980.
McGregor, Robert Kuhn, with Ethan Lewis. *Conundrum for the Long Week-end: England, Dorothy L. Sayers and Lord Peter Wimsey.* Kent, OH: Kent State University Press, 2000.
Michaelis, Karin. *The Dangerous Age.* New York: John Lane, 1911.
Morgan, Janet. *Agatha Christie: A Biography.* New York: Alfred A. Knopf, 1985.
Mylett, Andrew. *Arnold Bennett: The Evening Standard Years "Books and Persons" 1926–1931.* Hamden, CT: Archon Books, 1974.
Munt, Sally. *Murder by the Book? Feminism and the Crime Novel.* London: Routledge, 1994.
Murray, Margaret. *The Witch-Cult in Western Europe: A Study in Anthropology.* Oxford: Clarendon Press, 1921.
Nevins, Francis, ed. *The Anthony Boucher Chronicles: Reviews and Commentary, 1942–1947.* Vol. II, *The Week in Murder.* Vancleave, MS: Ramble House, 2002.
Panek, Leroy. *An Introduction to the Detective Story.* Bowling Green, OH: Popular Press, 1987.
_____. *The Special Branch: The British Spy novel, 1890–1980.* Bowling Green, OH: Popular Press, 1981.
_____. *Watteau's Shepherds: The Detective Novel in Britain 1914–1940.* Bowling Green, OH: Popular Press, 1979.
Partridge, Eric. *Journey to the Edge of Morning: Thoughts upon Books: Love: Life.* London: Frederick Muller, 1946.
Phillips, Gene D. *Creatures of Darkness: Raymond Chandler, Detective Fiction, and Film Noir.* Lexington: University Press of Kentucky, 2000.
Plain, Gill. *Twentieth-Century Crime Fiction: Gender, Sexuality and the Body.* London: Routledge, 2001.
_____. *Women Fiction of the Second World War: Gender, Power, Resistance.* Edinburgh: Edinburgh University Press, 1996.
Porter, Denis. *The Pursuit of Crime: Art and Ideology in Detective Fiction.* New Haven, CT: Yale University Press, 1981.
Priestman, Martin. *Crime fiction: From Poe to the Present.* Plymouth, UK: Northcote House, 1998.
Pronzini, Bill. *Gun in Cheek: A Study of Alternative Crime Fiction.* 1982. Reprint, New York: Mysterious Press, 1987.
Pyrhonen, Heta. *Murder from an Academic Angle: an Introduction to the Study of the Detective Narrative.* Columbia, SC: Camden House, 1994.
Reynolds, Barbara. *Dorothy L. Sayers: Her Life and Soul.* New York: St. Martin's, 1993.

_____, ed. *The Letters of Dorothy L. Sayers.* Vol. 2, 1937 to 1943. New York: St. Martin's Press, 1997.
Rodell, Marie F. *Mystery Fiction: Theory and Technique.* New York: Duell, Sloan and Pearce, 1943.
Roughead, William. *Classic Crimes.* 1951. Reprint, New York: New York Review of Books Classics, 2000.
Routley, Erik. *The Puritan Pleasures of the Detective Story.* London: Gollancz, 1972.
Rowland, Susan. *From Agatha Christie to Ruth Rendell: British Women Writers in Detective and Crime Fiction.* Basingstoke, UK: Palgrave, 2001.
Rubinstein, W.D. *Capitalism, Culture and Decline in Britain, 1750–1990.* London: Routledge, 1993.
Ruddick, Nicholas. *Ultimate Island: On the Nature of British Science Fiction.* Westport, CT: Greenwood, 1993.
Rzepka, Charles J. *Detective Fiction.* Cambridge, UK: Polity, 2005.
Scaggs, John. *Crime Fiction.* London: Routledge, 2005.
Scheper, George L. *Michael Innes.* New York: Ungar, 1986.
Smith, Erin A. *Hard-Boiled: Working Class Readers and Pulp Magazines.* Philadelphia: Temple University Press, 2000.
Snow, C.P. *The Two Cultures and the Scientific Revolution.* The Rede Lecture 1959. Cambridge: Cambridge University Press, 1960.
Spurling, Hilary. *La Grande Therese: The Greatest Scandal of the Century.* New York: HarperCollins, 2000.
Summerscale, Kate. *The Suspicions of Mr. Whicher: A Shocking Murder and the Undoing of a Great Victorian Detective.* New York: Walker, 2008.
Symons, Julian. *Bloody Murder: From the Detective Story to the Crime Novel.* 1972. 3rd rev. ed., New York: The Mysterious Press, 1993.
_____. *The Detective Story in Britain.* 1962. Reprint, Harlow, UK: Longmans, Green, 1969.
_____. *The Hundred Best Crime Stories.* London: Sunday Times, 1958.
_____. *Mortal Consequences: A History—From the Detective Story to the Crime Novel.* New York: Harper & Row, 1972.
Taylor, Bernard. *Cruelly Murdered: Constance Kent and the Killing at Road Hill House.* 1979. Rev. ed., London: Grafton Books, 1989.
Thackeray, William Makepeace. *Extracts from the Writings of W.M. Thackeray: Chiefly Philosophical and Reflective.* London: Smith, Elder, 1886.
Thompson, Laura. *Agatha Christie: An English Mystery.* London: Headline Review, 2007.
Thomson, H. Douglas. *Masters of Mystery: A Study of the Detective Story.* 1931. Reprint, New York: Dover, 1978.
Tichi, Cecilia. *Shifting Gears: Technology, Literature, Culture in Modernist America.* Chapel Hill: University of North Carolina Press, 1987.
Turnbull, Malcolm J. *Elusion Aforethought: The Life and Writing of Anthony Berkeley Cox.* Bowling Green, OH: Popular Press, 1996.
_____. *Victims or Villains: Jewish Images in Classic English Detective Fiction.* Bowling Green, OH: Popular Press, 1998.
Usborne, Richard. *Clubland Heroes: a Nostalgic Study of Some Recurrent Characters in the Romantic Fiction of Dornford Yates, John Buchan and Sapper.* 1953. Rev. ed., London: Barrie and Jenkins, 1974.
Wagar, W. Warren. *Terminal Visions: The Literature of Last Things.* Bloomington: University of Indiana Press, 1982.
Watson, Colin. *Snobbery with Violence: English Crime Stories and Their Audience.* 1971. Rev. ed., London: Eyre Methuen, 1979.
Wilson, A.N. *After the Victorians: The Decline of Britain in the World.* New York: Farrar, Straus and Giroux, 2005.

Articles and Essays

"Alfred Walter Stewart." In *Oxford Dictionary of National Biography.* Vol. 52. London: Oxford University Press, 2004.
Auden, W.H. "The Guilty Vicarage." *Harpers* 196 (May 1948): 406–412. Reprinted in W.H. Auden, *The Dyer's Hand.* New York: Random House, 1962; and *Detective Fiction: A Collection of Critical Essays*, edited by Robin W. Winks. Woodstock, VT: Foul Play Press, 1988.
Brand, Christianna. "Detection Club Memories." *CADS: Crime and Detective Stories* 52 (August 2007): 3–7.
_____. Introduction to The Detection Club, *The Floating Admiral.* Boston: Gregg Press, 1979. Novel originally published 1931.
Carr, John Dickson. "The Grandest Game in the World." 1946. Reprinted in *The Door to Doom and Other Detections*, edited by Douglas G. Greene. New York: IPL, 1991.
"Cecil John Charles Street." In *Oxford Dictionary of National Biography.* Vol. 53. London: Oxford University Press, 2004.
Chesterton, G.K. "A Detective Story with Twelve Authors." *The Illustrated London News*, 9 January 1932.

Reprinted in *The Collected Works of G.K. Chesterton*. Vol. 36. *The Illustrated London News, 1932–1934*, edited by Lawrence J. Clipper. San Francisco: Ignatius Press, 2011.

Cole, G.D.H., and Margaret Cole. "Meet Superintendent Wilson." In *Meet the Detectives*. Harrisburg, PA: The Telegraph Press, 1936.

Crofts, Freeman Wills. Introduction to *The Cask*. London: Collins, 1946. Library of Classics.

_____. "Meet Inspector French." In *Meet the Detectives*. Harrisburg, PA: The Telegraph Press, 1936.

"The Detection Club Oath." In *The Art of the Mystery Story*, edited by Howard Haycraft. 1946. Reprint, New York: Carroll & Graf, 1992.

Evans, Curtis. "'The Amateur Detective Just Won't Do': Raymond Chandler and British Detective Fiction." *The American Culture* (http://stkarnick.com).

_____. "Was Corinne's Murder Fairly Clued: The Detection Club and Fair Play, 1930–1953." In *CADS: Crime and Detective Stories*, Supplement 14 (2011).

"Freeman Wills Crofts." In *Oxford Dictionary of National Biography*. Vol. 14. London: Oxford University Press, 2004.

Fuller, Nicholas. "Gladys Mitchell: The Body of Her Work." Introduction to Gladys Mitchell, *Sleuth's Alchemy: Cases of Mrs. Bradley and Others*. Norfolk, VA: Crippen & Landru, 2005.

Gilberg, Mark. "Alfred Lucas: Egypt's Sherlock Holmes." *Journal of the American Institute for Conservation* 36 (1997): 31–48.

Gilbert, Michael. Forward to John Rhode, *Mystery at Greycombe Farm*. 1932. Bath, UK: John Curley, 1991.

Grella, George. "Murder and Manners: The Formal Detective Novel." *Novel: A Forum on Fiction* 4 (Fall 1970): 30–49. Reprinted as "The Formal Detective Novel" in *Detective Fiction: A Collection of Critical Essays*, edited by Robin W. Winks. Woodstock, VT: Foul Play Press, 1988.

Haycraft, Howard. "John Rhode." In *The Boy's Second Book of Detective Stories*, edited by Howard Haycraft. New York: Harper's, 1940.

Ibbotson, Peter. "Sayers and Ciphers." In *Cryptologia* 25 (April 2001): 81–87.

"John Francis Waller." In *A Dictionary of Irish Biography*, 3rd ed., edited by Henry Boylan. Dublin: Gill and Macmillan, 1998.

Keating, H.R.F. "A Double-Hung Crossbow." In *Julian Symons at 80: A Tribute*, edited by Patricia Craig. Helsinki: Eurographica, 1992.

_____. Introduction to John Rhode, *The Claverton Mystery*. The Disappearing Detectives. London: Collins 1983.

Knox, Ronald. "A Detective Story Decalogue." Introduction to *The Best Detective Stories of 1928*. 1929. Reprinted in *The Art of the Mystery Story*, edited by Howard Haycraft. 1946. Reprint, New York: Carroll & Graf, 1992.

Laurence, Janet. "Publishing in the Golden Age of Crime Fiction." In *AZ Murder Goes Classic: Current Crime Writers Revisit Past Masters*, edited by Susan Malling and Barbara Peters. Scottsdale, AZ: Poisoned Pen Press, 1997.

Maeder, Thomas. Afterword to Will Cuppy, *The Decline and Fall of Practically Everybody*. 1950. Reprint, Boston: David R. Godine, 1988.

Medawar, Tony. "'Rhode' Closed." *CADS: Crime and Detective Stories* 43 (June 2003): 31–34.

Nicholson, Marjorie. "The Professor and the Detective." In *The Art of the Mystery Story*, edited by Howard Haycraft. 1946. Reprint, New York: Carroll & Graf, 1992.

Orwell, George. "Bookshop Memories." *Forthnightly* (November 1936). Reprinted in *George Orwell: An Age Like This 1920–1940*, vol. I, *The Collected Essays, Journalism and Letters*, edited by Sonia Orwell and Ian Angus. Boston: David R. Godine, 2000.

_____. "Hop-picking." *New Statesman and Nation* (17 October 1931). Reprinted in *Orwell's England*, edited by Peter Davison. London: Penguin Books, 2001.

Read, Herbert. "Answer to Lord Peter's Prayer." *Night and Day*, 8 July 1932. Reprinted in Herbert Read, *Pursuits and Verdicts*. Edinburgh: Tragara Press, 1983.

Rowland, Susan. "The 'Classical' Model of the Golden Age." In *A Companion to Crime Fiction*, edited by Lee Horsley and Charles A Rzepka. Malden, MA: Wiley-Blackwell, 2010.

Roxburgh, Kenneth B.E. "The Fundamentalist Controversy Concerning the Baptist Theological College of Scotland." *Baptist History and Heritage* 36 (Winter/Spring 2001).

Sayers, Dorothy L. Introduction to Dorothy L. Sayers, ed., *Great Short Stories of Detection, Mystery and Horror*. 1928. Reprinted in slightly abbreviated form in *The Art of the Mystery Story*, edited by Howard Haycraft. 1946. Reprint, New York: Carroll and Graf, 1992.

_____. Introduction to Dorothy L. Sayers, ed., *Great Short Stories of Detection, Mystery and Horror*, 2nd Series. London: Gollancz, 1931.

_____. Introduction to Dorothy L. Sayers, ed., *Tales of Detection*. 1936. Reprint, London: J.M. Dent, 1947.

Strachey, John. "The Golden Age of English Detection." *Saturday Review of Literature* 19 (7 January 1939).

Symons, Julian. Introduction to Freeman Wills Crofts, *The Loss of the "Jane Vosper."* London: Collins, 1980.

Van Dine, S.S. "Twenty Rules for Writing Detective Stories." In *American Magazine* (September 1928).

Reprinted in *The Art of the Mystery Story*, edited by Howard Haycraft. 1946. Reprint, New York: Carroll and Graf, 1992.

Wodehouse, P.G. Introduction to Will Cuppy, *How to Tell Your Friend from the Apes*. 1931. Reprint, Jaffrey, NH: David R. Godine, 2005.

Watson, Colin. "Mayhem Parva and Wicked Belgravia." In *Crime Writers*, edited by H.R.F. Keating. London: British Broadcasting Corporation, 1978.

Weber, William C. ("Judge Lynch"). "Battle of the Sexes: The Judge and His Wife Look at Mystery." In *The Art of the Mystery Story*, edited by Howard Haycraft. Reprint, New York: Carroll & Graf, 1992.

Wrong, E.M. Introduction to *Crime and Detection*. London: Oxford University Press, 1926. Reprinted in *The Art of the Mystery Story*, edited by Howard Haycraft. 1946. Reprint, New York: Carroll and Graf, 1992.

Wood, Dave. "Gibraltar-born MI7 Agent is Famous Detective novelist." *Gibraltar Magazine* (July 2011): 40–41.

Webpages and Websites

Annaghdown GAA Club. "Bawnmore and the Land League." http://www.annaghdowngaa.com/Annagh.doiwn/GAAfiles/Gallery/BawmoreBool/Landleague.htm.

Davies, Rosalind. "Tullylish Parish." Ros Davies Co. Down. *Ireland Genealogy Research Site*. http://freepages.genealogy.rootsweb.ancestry.co/~rosdavies/PHOTOSwaordsTullylishAll.htm.

Facsimile Dust Jackets L.L.C., http://www.facsimiledustjackets.com.

Hadwin, Juanita. "Swanton Novers, Norfolk, England: The Village Its Inhabitants and Its History." http://www3.telus.net/Swanton-Novers.

"Hot on the Trail of Crime Writer Freeman Wills Crofts." 11 June 2004. http://www/getsurrey.co.uk/community/yesteryear/93312_hot_on_the_trail_crimewriter_freeman_wills_crofts.

"Interview: Alan Bradley." *Material Witness: Fiction for the Criminally Inclined*. 7 February 2009. http://materialwitness.tyepad.com.

Knott, Simon. "St. Edmund's, Swanton novers." *The Norfolk Churches Site*. http://www.norfolkchurches.co.uk/swantonnovers.swantonnovers.wtm.

Kremer, Tony. A History of Yalding, Kent." *http://yaldinghistory.webplus.net/page179.html*.

"Lady Gifford's Harriers Point-to-Point Steeplechases." http://www.nationalarchives.gov.uk/a2a/records.aspx?cat=182-amsl1846&cid=-1#-1.

Law, Edward T. "Huddersfield and District History: Storthes Hall, Thurstonland." homepage.eircom.net/~lawedd/STROTHESHALL.htm.

McCarthy, Jim. "Churchtown's History: Burton Park, Churchtown House and Ballydam." http://churchtown.net/webpages/history/H-burton%20house.htm.

The Railway Preservation Society of Ireland. http://www.steamtrainsireland.com/whitehead/"Slater's Directory-Gilford (1881)."

Sinton Family Trees. http://www.bobsinton.com/history/gilford/gilford_slater.php.

"Welcome to WhiteheadExcursionStation." www.cultureofnorthernireland.org/yourArea.aspx?location=506.

Index

Adelaide Mail (newspaper) 42, 263
"Advice to a Young Man Concerning the Choice of a Mistress" (letter) 209
The Affair at Little Wokeham (novel) 182, 185, 188
"After Death the Doctor" (short story) 279
Agatha Christie: Investigating Femininity (critical study) 3
Agatha Christie's Secret Notebooks (critical study) 5
Ajax 144
The Alarm (novel) 60, 141, 265
Alias J.J. Connington (essay collection) 232, 277–278
All the Books of My Life (bibliographical memoir) 25
Alleyn, Roderick (character) 80, 131, 141
Allingham, Margery 1–2, 6, 8, 9–10, 24–27, 33, 38, 40, 43, 47, 141, 191, 258, 259, 267; *see also* Crime Queens
Almighty Gold (novel) 193, 198–199, 240
"'The Amateur Detective Just Won't Do'" (critical essay) 273
American Journal of Archaeology 26
The Anatomy of Murder (essay collection) 89, 138, 190
And Be a Villain (novel) 261
Anderson, Isaac 83, 106, 108, 110
Antidote to Venom (novel) 147, 176–178
Anti-Semitism 47, 55–57, 59, 140, 186–187, 197, 199
Anything to Declare? (novel) 42, 184
Apollo 144
Appleby, Inspector John (character) 80
Appleby's End (novel) 27

Ardlamont Murder Case 277
Aristophanes 239
Armstrong, Anthony 253–254
Armstrong Siddeley 120
Arnold, Inspector Henry (character) 101–108, 110, 115, 118, 124, 131, 134, 140, 143, 268
Arnold, Matthew 106, 144
Asclepius 144
A.S.F. (novel) 49, 57–58, 141
Ask a Policeman (novel) 57, 89, 144
Atlee, Clement 263
Auden, W.H. 11, 179, 275

Bailey, H.C. 2, 43, 176
"Balder Dead" (poem) 106
Baldick, Chirs 259, 261, 269
Baldwin, Stanley 25
Barnard, Robert 153, 260
Barzun, Jacques 1, 3, 8, 13, 25, 43, 47, 78, 80, 91, 103, 106, 110, 180–181, 223–224, 257; *see also A Catalogue of Crime*; Taylor, Wendell Hertig
Beardsley, Aubrey 240
The Beast Must Die (novel) 38, 40
The Bedside Companion to Crime (book) 24
"Before Insulin" (short story) 277
Before the Fact (novel) 33
Behold, Here's Poison (novel) 279
Belfast 10, 16, 147, 193
Belfast and Northern Counties Railway 147
Belisarius (character) 4, 113–114
Bell, Josephine 29
Belloc, Hillaire 56
Bender, Harold H. 26
Bennett, Arnold 29–31, 35, 159, 190–191, 220, 222, 262
The Benson Murder Case (novel) 260

Bentley, E.C. 35–36, 159, 224, 227
Berlioz, Hector 149
Betts, Jonathan 243, 278
Beware Your Neighbour (novel) 118
Beyond Good and Evil (book) 234
The Big Four (novel) 210
Bill, Charles Horsfall 53
Birmingham, George A. 271
The Bishop Murder Case (novel) 262
The Black Tower (novel) 123
Blackheath (Surrey) 147, 166, 177, 183, 273
Blackthorn House (novel) 93, 120, 263, 271
Blackwood, Algernon 233
Blake, Nicholas (Cecil Day Lewis) 2, 24, 27, 33, 37–38, 40, 43, 80, 167, 257, 263
Blazing Car Murder 232
Bleiler, Everett F. 198
blood sports 278
Bloody Murder (critical study) 2, 6–8, 11, 13, 15–16, 153, 180, 232; *see also* Symons, Julian
The Bloody Tower (novel) 71, 101, 121–123, 140–142, 269
Bloomsbury Group 41, 263
The Boat-House Riddle (novel) 203, 206, 210–211, 218, 278
The Body of Library (novel) 161
Bones in the Brickfield (novel) 102, 118–119, 269
Books in Black and Red (essay collection) 236
"Bookshop Memories" (essay) 258
"Boomerang" (short story) 181
Boucher, Anthony 78–79, 93, 95, 110, 120, 180, 216, 268
The Box Office Murders (novel) 148, 155, 158, 187–188, 192, 272

291

Bradley, Alan 260
Bradley, Mrs. Beatrice Adela Lestrange (character) 258
Bradley, Geoff 4
Bradshaw (Monthly Railway Guide) 38
Brand, Christianna 90
Brand, Mark ("The Couseller") 231–232; *see also* Stewart, Alfred Walter
Bridges, Yseult 721
Bristow, Gwen 152
Brown, Ivor 20
Brown, Zenith Jones (Leslie Ford/David Frome) 261
Browne, Douglas 263
Bryn Mawr 26
Buchman, Dr. Frank 177
Bull's Eye 34
Bunyan, John 148
Burnley, Inspector (character) 148–149, 155, 161
Burton, Miles (pseudonym of Cecil John Charles Street) 98–119 passim; Burton and Rhode novels distinguished 100–102; origin of pseudonym 98; *see also* Street, Cecil John Charles
Bury Him Darkly (novel) 34
Bush, Christopher 33, 264
Busman's Honeymoon (novel) 27–29, 36, 263
By Registered Post (novel) 60

CADS: Crime and Detective Stories (journal) 4
Cairo 25
Campbell College Belfast 147
Campion, Albert (character) 141
The Canary Murder Case (novel) 159, 260, 262
Cannadine, David 267
Cannan, Joanna 25, 33
Caresco, Surhomme (novel) 235
Carr, Clarice 264, 275
Carr, John Dickson 1–2, 38, 43, 45, 47, 50, 72, 88–90, 95, 117, 132, 142, 162, 217–218, 257, 264, 274–275; *see also* Street, Cecil John Charles
Carrington (film) 41
Carrington, Dora 41
Carroll, Lewis 234
cars 87, 120–121, 269
Carter, Ian 190–191, 259, 271
Carter, Sergeant (character) 164, 172, 185
"The Case of the Avaricious Moneylender" (short story) 186
"The Case of the Enthusiastic Rabbit Breeder" (short story) 181
"The Case of the Fireside Mountaineer" (short story) 183
The Case of the Forty Thieves (*Death at the Inn*) (novel) 93, 269
The Case with Nine Solutions (novel) 21, 29, 194, 203–206, 216, 219–222, 232, 243–244, 278
casino gambling 174, 176
The Cask (novel) 22, 42–43, 108, 146, 148–149, 155, 159, 161
Cassuto, Leonard W. 272
The Castleford Conundrum (novel) 194, 203, 206, 210, 216, 224–227, 278
The Cat Jumps (novel) 4, 87, 112–114
A Catalogue of Crime (encyclopedia) 1, 3, 8, 13, 43, 47, 78, 80, 91, 95, 101–103, 109, 116, 122, 141, 180, 199, 223–224, 230, 232–233, 257; *see also* Barzun, Jacques; Taylor, Wendell Hertig
Chambers, Robert W. 144
Chancellor, John 279
Chandler, Raymond 1, 159, 167, 259, 273; *see also* hard-boiled
The Charabanc Mystery (novel) 102, 124–125, 268–269, 271
Chesterton, Cecil 56
Chesterton, G.K. 56, 143, 176, 252–253, 260
The Children's Hour (radio lecture series) 239
Chinitz, David E. 260
Chitterwick, Ambrose (character) 32
Christie, Agatha 1–3, 7–12, 15, 24–26, 30, 38, 41, 43, 47, 58, 60, 72, 73, 105, 108, 117–118, 128, 141, 148, 153, 159, 161, 168, 179, 219, 258, 259–260, 263, 266, 276; criticism of novels as "mere puzzles" 5–6; *see also* Crime Queens
Churchill, Winston 274
"The 'Classical' Model of the Golden Age (essay) 9, 272
The Claverton Mystery (novel) 43, 71–72, 74, 91, 133, 141
Clifford, Brendan 54–55
Coats, Reverend Holms 237, 279
Cold Comfort Farm (novel) 121
Cold War 93, 274
Cole, G.D.H. 2, 7, 37, 159, 252
Cole, Margaret 2, 7, 37, 159, 167, 191, 252, 273
Collie, John Norman 277
Collins, Wilkie 3, 25, 29, 35, 263
Collins Crime Club 18, 43, 146, 148, 162, 164, 167, 263, 272
Commonsense Is All You Need (novel) 212, 218, 232
Conan Doyle, Arthur 20, 27, 62, 241–242, 257, 277
Conington, John 194
Connington, J.J. (pseudonym) *see* Stewart, Alfred Walter
Conundrums for the Long Week-End (critical study) 261, 263
Conway, Sir Edric (character) 98, 101, 105–107, 116
Cooke, Rachel 5
The Corpse at the Haworth Tandoori (novel) 260
Corpse in Cold Storage (novel) 34
The Corpse in the Car (novel) 22, 38, 71–72, 74–77, 87, 91, 123, 127, 142
Coster, Howard 90
Cottingley Faeries photographs 219, 277
The Counsellor (novel) 231–232, 278
Cox, Anthony Berkeley 2, 18, 33–34, 36, 43, 228, 257; role in transformation of detective novel 31–33, 262
Creatures of Darkness (critical study) 259
cricket 128–129
Crime at Guildford (novel) 23, 147, 159–160, 166–167, 170, 182, 188
Crime Fiction 1800–2000 (critical study) 43, 257
A Crime in Time (novel) 264
Crime Queens 1–3, 6, 8–13, 17, 24, 40, 43, 47, 191, 257–258; *see also* Allingham, Margery; Christie, Agatha; Marsh, Ngaio; Sayers, Dorothy L.; Tey, Josephine
Crispin, Edmund (Bruce Montgomery) 27, 48
The Criterion (*The Monthly Criterion/The New Criterion*) 21, 159, 216
Croft-Cooke, Rupert (Leo Bruce) 131–132
Crofts, Freeman Wills: alibis and timetables in novels of 146, 149–150, 153–154, 158–159, 163, 166–167, 223, 268, 272, 279; ancestry and family of 147; artistic temperament and Bohemianism 191; avarice 149–152, 170, 171, 173–174, 181–182; Biblical cadence in

writing of 191; business and capitalism 170–172, 174, 181–183; charity and kindliness 155, 173, 176, 182, 189; church activities of 147, 177; city and country 183–184; class 170, 172, 177, 183–185; debt 169, 174, 178, 181, 274; and creation and development of Inspector French 155–158; criticized by John Strachey 40; decline in health of and death of 147; decline in plotting complexity in novels of 147, 167–168, 170, 178–181; and Detection Club 190–191, 252–253; dialect speech in novels of 160, 164, 184; and Dorothy L. Sayers 27, 162, 177, 254; drinking 151; education of 147; gambling 174, 176–178, 274; Great Depression 164, 170–171; Harry S Truman 274; ingenuity and technical facility of plots in detective novels of 146–147, 149, 154, 159–164, 166, 179–180; and the inverted crime novel 160, 166, 169–170; the Irish 162, 187; Jews 186–187; juvenile delinquency 185; Korean War 274; and locked room plot device 168, 171; marriage of 147; meals 151–152, 155, 272; mild and self-effacing personality of 162, 190–191, 275; and Moral Re-armament/Oxford Group 177, 183; morally simple frameworks of novels and stories 150, 152–153, 170, 172–174, 176, 179; naiveté about human motivations and difficulty portraying credible characters 160–161, 167–169, 188–191; novels and short stories as moral parables 147–148, 158, 167, 181, 191–192; novels as "feminized" 272–273; patent medicine 174; as playwright 273; police 185; police procedure in novels of 153–154, 157–158, 185, 189–190, 272–273; popularity of and praise for novels of 20–23, 38–39, 146–148, 159, 162, 166, 164, 167, 180, 260; postwar Labour government 274; prisons and penal reform 186; purple prose and banal writing in novels of 149–152, 154–155, 158, 163, 167–168, 187–188, 191; questioning suspects and wit-

nesses (judges' rules) 185; railway detail in novels of 162–163, 169, 179; as railway engineer 147, 149, 165, 173–174, 190; rejection of "character" detectives 156, 164–165; religious Puritanism 191; religious sensibility of 146–148, 176–178, 181, 190–192, 274; the right to a fair trial 186; round robin mystery writing of 252–254; servants 274; sex 149, 181, 188–189; short stories and radio plays of 181; the Soviet Union 182–183, 274; thrillers 179; travel by and travel guide commentary in novels of 147, 153, 157, 160, 163, 167, 183, 191, 254, 274; true crime writing of 189–190; warrantless searches 153–154, 157–158, 185, 274; women 150, 154–155, 172–174, 176, 181, 184–185, 187–188, 272; on writing *The Cask* 272; *see also* detective novels; individual books and story titles
Cruelly Murdered (true crime study) 139, 271
"The Cult of Clitoris" (article) 235
Cuppy, Will 22–23, 104
Curran, John 5
Currier and Ives 151
Cushman, Joseph A. 26
Czechoslovakia 49, 55–56, 70

Daily Herald (newspaper) 22
Daily Telegraph (newspaper) 18, 224
The Dalehouse Murder (novel) 262
Dancers in Mourning (novel) 27
The Dangerfield Talisman (novel) 205, 209, 277–278
The Dangerous Age (novel) 209
Danse Macabre (tone poem) 75
Dante 261
The Davidson Case (novel) 62–64, 66–71, 82–83, 119, 134, 266
Dead Men at the Folly (novel) 18–19, 71, 90, 120, 124, 126–127, 143, 267
Dead on the Track (novel) 71, 91, 130, 134–135, 266–267
Death at Breakfast (novel) 22, 90, 130, 267
Death at Low Tide (novel) 90, 133
Death at Swaythling Court (novel) 199–202, 205, 212, 232, 275

Death at the Club (*The Clue of the Fourteen Keys*) (novel) 27, 90, 101, 105–106, 132
Death at the Crossroads (novel) 90, 102
Death at the Dance (novel) 93
Death at the Dog (novel) 260
Death at the Helm (novel) 71–72, 78, 91, 101, 141
Death in Harley Street (novel) 91
Death in the Hopfields (novel) 42, 91, 102, 125–129, 133–134, 268
Death in the Tunnel (novel) 22–23, 91, 101–105, 127, 268
Death in Wellington Road (novel) 267
Death Invades the Meeting (novel) 133
Death Leaves No Card (novel) 107–108, 134, 268
Death of a Train (novel) 167, 179–180
Death of Mr. Gantley (novel) 103, 268
Death of Two Brothers (novel) 4, 43, 124, 134, 144, 268–269, 271
Death on Sunday (novel) 128, 131, 143, 270
Death on the Board (*Death Sits on the Board*) (novel) 26, 39, 71, 82–85, 119, 123, 134, 268
Death on the Boat Train (novel) 18, 71, 85–86, 91, 127–128, 133–134, 142–143
Death on the Way (novel) 18–19, 168–169, 170
Death Pays a Dividend (novel) 128–130, 132, 134, 268, 270
Death Takes a Flat (novel) 101
Death Takes the Living (novel) 102, 114–116, 270
Death Visits Downspring (*Up the Garden Path*) (novel) 108, 124
The Decline and Fall of Practically Everybody (humour essays) 23
Delafield, E.M. 31
De Luce, Flavia (character) 268
de Maupassant, Guy 234
Detection Club 30–33, 38, 50, 57, 63, 88–90, 138, 190, 216, 252–254, 262–263, 275
Detection Club Oath 30–31, 33
Detection Dons 17; *see also* Blake, Nicholas; Innes, Michael
Detection Medley (collection of short pieces) 89–90
detective fiction: alibis and timetables in 37, 85–86, 158–159, 223, 268, 272, 279;

closed and country house settings in 18, 47, 149–150, 217–219, 224–228; collector interest in 43; conservatism of 8, 10–13, 47, 259, 269; cozy appeal of 28, 102; cozy stereotype of 122, 233; decayed gentlepeople in 121–123, 151, 204–205; distinguished from crime novels and sensation novels 6; distinguished from thrillers 30–31, 65, 179, 226, 260, 262; engineering values in 16–17, 121–122; ethnocentrism and racism of 10; fair play in 6, 16, 30, 168, 244, 260, 266; feminization of 8–10, 257–259, 261, 272–273; France in 150; gendered appeal of 102, 258, 261; intellectual appeal of 17–18, 20–29, 159, 260–261; literary modernism of 261; maps and floor plans in 18–19, 267; police procedure in 267, 273; pseudo-cockney dialect speech in 184; as puzzles 5–8, 15, 17–18, 20–31, 37–39, 65, 72, 102, 108–109, 158–159, 258, 260, 262–263; rules for 7, 257, 262; sales of 261–263, 266; scientific accuracy and scientific appeal of 10, 24–28, 80; sex in 270; sophistication in 26–28, 40, 80; transformation of 31–37, 39–42, 240, 245, 262–263; violence in 142; *see also* Crofts, Freeman Wills; "Humdrums"; Stewart, Alfred Walter; Street, Cecil John Charles

The Detective Story in Britain (pamphlet) 7
The Devereux Court Mystery (novel) 103
Devil's Reckoning (novel) 269
Dickens, Charles 144, 263
Dickens, Monica 263
The Divine Comedy (epic poem) 261
Dr. Priestley's Quest (novel) 60–63
Dr. Thorndyke Intervenes (novel) 241, 270
"Dr. Watson" (crime fiction reviewer) 106, 159
The Documents in the Case (novel) 259, 263
Dodd, Mead and Company 18, 63, 98, 164–165, 261, 267–268
The Domestic Agnecy (novel) 263

Double Death (novel) 252–245
The Double Florin (novel) 49, 57–60, 131, 140
Doubleday, Doran and Company 103–104
Douglas, Lord Alfred 235
The Dovebury Murders (novel) 95, 128, 267
Drake, Maurice 271
Driffield, Chief Constable Clinton (character) 194–195, 199–213, 215–219, 221–229, 231, 233–234, 243, 276–277
Drop to His Death (*Fatal Descent*) (novel) 90
Drummond, Bulldog (character) 30
"The Drunkard's Progress" (lithograph) 151
Duguid, Lindsay 6
Dun Kenneth, the Seer 277
Dutton, Charles J. 26, 261

"East of North" (short story) 243
East of Prague (book) 49
eBay 43
Edward VII 275
Egypt 237
Elgin, Joseph C. 26
Eliot, George 5
Eliot, T.S. 20–21, 25, 159, 160, 217–218, 260–261, 276
The Ellerby Case (novel) 61, 63, 142
Ellison, Sir Mortimer 171
"The Elusive Bullet" (short story) 26
Encephalitis lethargica 276
Encyclopedia Britannica 41, 80
The End of Andrew Harrison (novel) 148, 170–172, 177, 191, 273
Enemy Unseen (novel) 167, 179–180
Epidaurus 144
Eric the Skull (Detection Club mascot) 88–89
Ethiopia 237
Eustace, Robert 243
Everton, Francis 262
The Eye in the Museum (novel) 210, 214–215, 222, 243
The Eye of Osiris (novel) 241
The Eye-Witness (journal) 56

Fairchild, John 41
Family Affairs (novel) 71, 94–95, 97, 263
Farceurs 7
The Fashion in Shrouds (novel) 40
The Fatal Pool (novel) 91
Fatal Venture (novel) 41, 148, 155, 170, 172, 174, 176, 182–183
Fate at the Fair (novel) 102, 143–144
Faversham, Sir Alured (character) 67–68, 72
Fear by Night (novel) 279
Fear Comes to Chalfont (novel) 42, 185, 191
Fellowes, Julian 190
Ferrars, Elizabeth 263
Fitton, Amanda (character) 141
The Five Red Herrings (novel) 159, 279
Fleming, Ian 42
Fletcher, J.S. 7
The Floating Admiral (novel) 89, 124, 252–253
"The Flowing Tide" (short story) 181
For Murder Will Speak (novel) 208–210, 214, 231, 276
Forever England (critical study) 3, 259
Form and Ideology in Detective Fiction (critical study) 12
Fortune, Dr. Reggie (character) 232
Found Drowned (novel) 264
Found Floating (novel) 26, 41, 187, 189, 254
The Four Defences (novel) 231–232, 278
The Four Gospels in One Story (book) 176
The Fourth Bomb (novel) 134
Foyle's War (television series) 270
France 49, 55, 149, 157, 236–237, 265, 273, 278
Franklin, Benjamin 209
Freeman, R. Austin 2–3, 20, 26–28, 31, 45, 79, 85, 114, 195, 241–242, 257, 260–261, 264–265, 272, 279
French, Eliza (character) 155–156
French, Emily (character) 155–156, 176, 187, 272
French, Inspector Joseph (character) 12, 131, 153, 155–158, 160–173, 176, 178–179, 182–183, 185–186, 188–189, 191–192;
French Strikes Oil (novel) 181, 185
Frye, Northrop 40–41
Fuller, Nicholas 259
"The Funk Hole" (television series episode) 270

Gaboriau, Emile 29
Galsworthy, John 27
Garve, Andrew 263

Gate Burton (village) 98
Gaudy Night (novel) 24, 27, 36, 240, 261–263
"Gehazi" (poem) 56
Gehlen, Adolph 76
Gehman, Henry Snyder 26
Geoffrey Bles 138
Germany 49, 55, 79–80, 109, 157, 179, 186–187, 197, 236–237
Gibbons, Stella 121
Gibraltar 48, 264
Gifford, Edric Frederick (3rd Baron Gifford) 264
Gilbert, Anthony (Lucy Beatrice Malleson) 2, 50, 87, 89, 267
Gilbert, Michael 90, 263
Gilford (Northern Ireland) 147, 162
Gillett, Eric 166
Gilliat, Sidney 66
Glencoe Massacre 236
"The Gold Bug" (short story) 219
"The Golden Age of English Detection" (essay) 40, 263
Golden Ashes (novel) 148, 172, 178, 183, 187, 191
Goodchild, George 279
Goodman, Jonathan 190
"The Gorse Hall Mystery" (essay) 189
Gould, Rupert Thomas 194, 229, 233, 235–244, 275, 277–279
"The Grandest Game in the World" (essay) 217
Graves, Robert 114
"The Great God Pan" (short story) 234
Great Short Stories of Detection, Mystery and Horror (1st and 2nd series) (short story collections) 34–36
Great Unsolved Crimes (essay collection) 189
Green, Anna Katherine 3
Greene, Douglas G. 1, 3, 30, 88, 90
Greene, Graham 262
Greene, Martin Roundell 4, 48
The Greene Murder Case (novel) 159, 260, 262
The Groote Park Murder (novel) 153–155, 163, 187
Ground for Suspicion (novel) 102, 117
Guedalla, Philip 17
"The Guilty Vicarage" (essay) 11, 179, 275

The Ha-Ha Case (novel) 38, 194, 203, 205, 211–212, 215–217, 227–228, 242–243, 276–278
"Had I but Known" school 187
Hamlet, Revenge! (novel) 40
Hammett, Dashiell 1, 219–220, 258, 266; *see* hard-boiled
The Hanging Woman (novel) 70–71, 127, 134
Hanslet, Inspector/Superintendent (character) 61–62, 67, 69–71, 74–80, 82, 84–85, 91, 101, 120, 122, 124, 127–128, 130–131, 133–135, 270
hard-boiled 1, 8–9; *see also* Chandler, Raymond; Hammett, Dashiell
Harding, Rev. Jonathan 147
The Hardway Diamonds Mystery (novel) 98–100, 105
Hardy, Thomas 269
Hare, Cyril 43
Harper & Row 1, 43
Harrison, John 233
Hart-Davies, Rupert 41
Hartley, L.P. 233
Harwood, H.C. 21, 217
Hastings, Captain Arthur (character) 219, 276
Have His Carcase (novel) 90, 259
Haycraft, Howard 48, 272
He Came by Night (novel) 267
Heir Presumptive (novel) 34
Heir to Lucifer (novel) 100
Heir to Murder (novel) 118, 133, 270
Hendon Police College 77
Hendon's First Case 61, 71–72, 77–78, 130
Heyer, Georgette 279
The High Sheriff (novel) 34
High Tory 2, 12
Highsmith, Patricia 42
Hilsner, Leopold 55–56
The History and Present State of Electricity (book) 60
The History of Sandford and Merton (children's book series) 234
The History of the Fairchild Family (children's book series) 148, 234
Hitchcock, Alfred 262
Hitler, Adolf 196–197
Hodder and Stoughton 228
Hodgson, William Hope 233
Hog's Back 166
The Hog's Back Mystery (novel) 20, 147, 159–160, 166, 273
Holmes, Sherlock (character) 242, 260
Honduras 147
Hop-picking 270
Horsley, Lee 257, 259

House, Edwin M. 278
The House of the Arrow (novel) 35
House of Whitbread (journal) 125
The House on Tollard Ridge (novel) 63–66, 71, 134, 142, 144, 266
Howe, Charles Merrill 26
Humbert, Therese 273
Humble, Nicola 259
"Humdrums": decline in popularity and reputation of 39–44; defined 2–3, 6–8, 15–17, 257; disdain for 17, 24–25, 37, 39–42, 260, 263–264; distinguished from Crime Queens 2, 9–13; distinguished from Edgar Wallace school 31; engineering/scientific backgrounds of 7, 9–10, 16–17; influence of R. Austin Freeman on 3, 27–28, 45, 79, 85, 114, 195, 241, 264–265; loyalty of segment of the reading public to 264; neglect of 1–2, 6–8, 13, 43–44; popularity and praise for 17–18, 20–29, 31, 38–39, 43, 260, 264; social history interest of books 2; treatment of class, gender and race by 12–13; *see also* Crofts, Freeman Wills; detective fiction; Stewart, Alfred Walter; Street, Cecil John Charles
Hume, David (crime writer) 253–254, 279
Hun, John Gale 26
Hutchinson's 90
Huxley, Aldous 29
Hyde Park Mansions (London) 48

Ibbotson, Peter 25
Iles, Francis *see* Anthony Berkeley Cox
I'll Be Judge, I'll Be Jury (novel) 34
The Immaterial Murder Case (novel) 264
Imperial Chemical Industries 70
In Face of the Verdict (novel) 98, 268
In Whose Dim Shadow (*The Tau Cross Mystery*) (novel) 20, 23, 194, 217, 228–229
Innes, Michael (J.I.M. Stewart) 2, 24, 27, 38, 40, 43, 80, 161, 191, 257, 259, 261
Inspector French and the Cheyne Mystery (novel) 160, 163, 184–185, 187
Inspector French and the Starvel

Tragedy (novel) 146, 158–160, 163, 187
Inspector French's Greatest Case (novel) 153, 155–157, 159, 170, 185
An Introduction to the Detective Story (critical study) 17
The Invisible Host (novel) 152
Invisible Weapons (novel) 71, 85, 133, 144
Ireland 48, 140, 147, 161–162, 195, 213, 235, 271, 275
Irish Republican Army (IRA) 235, 275
Irvin, Kay 104
Isaacs, Rufus 55–56
The Island of Captain Sparrow (novel) 235
Italy 195, 237

Jack-in-the-Box (novel) 211, 215, 232, 276, 278
James, M.R. 233–234
James, P.D. 8, 10–13, 24–25, 28, 123, 222, 258, 261–262; see also Talking about Detective Fiction; Time to Be in Earnest
James Tarrant, Adventurer (novel) 148, 156, 170, 172, 174–175, 187–188
Japan 229, 275, 277
Jellett, Dr. Henry 259 n. 12
Jesse, F. Tennyson 253–254, 271
Jones, Emil Beatrick Coursolles 41, 263
Joyce, James 234
"Judge Lynch" (William C. Weber) 27, 261
Julian Fellowes Investigates (television series) 190
Jumping Jenny (novel) 33

Kaye-Smith, Sheila 24, 27–29, 145, 261
Keating, H.R.F. 24–25, 43, 103–104, 132, 263, 268, 272
Kennedy, Milward 2, 33, 37–38, 72, 83, 86, 102–103, 167, 178, 230, 240; role in transformation of detective novel 34
Kenney, Catherine 263
Kent, Constance (murder case) 47, 136–140, 271
King, C. Daly 273
The King in Yellow (novel) 144
King Kong (film) 240
Kingsley, Charles 234
Kipling, Rudyard 55–56, 66, 144, 236, 266
Kirwan, Dennis Agar Richard 271
Kirwan, Major John Denis 48

Kitchin, C.H.B. 233
Knight, Stephen 12, 43, 257
Knott, Simon 87
Knox, Ronald 7, 257, 262
Korean War 274
Kruger, Ivar (Swedish Match King) 172

Laddingford (Kent) 49–50, 128
Lady Chatterley (character) 211
The Lake House (novel) 93, 271
Last Seen Wearing (novel) 267
Lawrence, Marjorie 233
The Layton Court Mystery (novel) 31
League of Nations 237
Lear, Edmund 234
The Leavenworth Case (novel) 3
Lechard, Xavier 4
Leonardo Da Vinci 268
LeQueux, William 59
Lewis, Ethan 261
Lewis, Steve 4
Licensed for Murder (novel) 71, 95–98, 124, 131, 267
Light, Alison 3, 259
Little, Brown and Company 21, 260
Little Lord Fauntleroy (novel) 234
Lloyd George, David 57, 265
Loch Ness Monster 232–233, 278
The Loch Ness Monster and Others (essay collection) 233
Lonely Magdalen (novel) 34
Longfellow, Henry Wadsworth 114
Longitude (film) 233
Lorac, E.C.R. 2
The Losing Game (novel) 179
The Loss of the "Jane Vosper" (novel) 37–38, 147, 160, 164, 167, 170, 182, 188, 191
Lovecraft, H.P. 278
Lovesey, Peter 4
Lucas, Alfred 25
Lyme Regis (Dorset) 48
Lyme Regis Electric Light and Power Company 48
Lysistrata (play) 239–240

M17b 16
Macaulay, Thomas 278
Machen, Arthur 233–234
Magie, William Francis 26
Mais, Styart P. 261
Makinen, Merja 3, 12, 259
Malice Aforethought (novel) 33, 37
"The Man Born to Be King" (radio play) 274
The Man in the Brown Suit (novel) 260

Man Overboard! (novel) 148, 164, 170, 172–174, 177–178, 186–187
Manchester Evening Chronicle (newspaper) 106, 159
Manchester Guardian (newspaper) 80
Manchu, Dr. Fu (character) 30
Mann, Jessica 5–6
Manning, Bruce 152
Many a Slip (short story collection) 181
March, Colonel (character) 90
Marconi Scandal of 1912 56
Marks, Jeffrey 4
Marple, Miss Jane (character) 259
Marsh, Ngaio 1–2, 6–9, 10, 24–25, 27, 38, 40, 43, 47, 80, 141, 191, 258–259; see also Crime Queens
Masaryk, Thomas 52, 55, 56
Mason, A.E.W. 35–36
Masters of Mystery (critical study) 3, 163, 261
Mathers, Dr. Adam A.C. 272
May Byron's Vegetable Book (cookbook) 266
McElwain, A.R. 42, 263
McGregor, Robert Kuhn 261
M'Clung, Sergeant Adam (character) 162, 172
Meade, L.T. 243
Medawar, Tony 4, 48, 265
"The Medicine Bottle" (short story) 181
Men Die at Cyprus Lodge (novel) 71–72, 78, 130–131, 133, 142
The Menace on the Downs (novel) 102, 124, 140, 268–269
Merefield, Harold (character) 60–63, 65–66, 68–69, 74, 85, 91, 93–94, 132, 143
Merrion, Desmond (character) 42, 100–110, 112, 114, 117–119, 124–127, 132, 140, 143–144, 268
Merrion, Mavis Owerton (character) 100, 117–118
Messalina of the Suburbs (novel) 31
Methodist College Belfast 147
Michaelis, Karin 209
The Milk Churn Murder (novel) 124
Milne, A.A. 89–90
A Mind to Murder (novel) 222
A Minor Operation (novel) 26, 38, 194, 214, 217, 229, 230–231, 244, 277–278
Mist on the Saltings (novel) 34
Mr. Babbacombe Dies (novel) 107–108, 123–124, 127

Mr. Westerby Missing (novel) 85, 107–108, 127
Mr. Wizard 72
Mitchell, C. Ainsworth 139
Mitchell, Gladys 2, 16, 33, 43, 142, 190, 257, 275
Mond, Sir Alfred 70, 266
The Monster of Grammont (novel) 279
Monty Python 142
The Moonstone (novel) 3, 25, 35, 261
Moral Re-Armament 177, 183
Morel, Edmund Dene 265
The Motor Rally Mystery (novel) 71, 120–121, 269
The Moving Toyshop (novel) 27
Muller, Marcia 1, 3
Munt, Sally 258
The Murder at the Vicarage (novel) 141, 276
Murder by the Book? (critical study) 258
Murder in Absence (novel) 102, 118
Murder in Crown Passage (novel) 102
Murder in Hospital (novel) 29
Murder in the Coalhole (novel) 101, 127, 131–133, 143–144
Murder in the Maze (novel) 21, 194, 200–204, 209, 213–214, 216–219, 276, 278
A Murder Is Announced (novel) 118
Murder M.D. (novel) 102, 108–112, 114, 134–135, 141, 267
Murder Must Advertise (novel) 262
Murder Must Appetize (critical study) 103
Murder of a Chemist (novel) 39, 73, 85, 102–103, 105, 127, 136
The Murder of Roger Ackroyd (novel) 141, 168, 260
Murder on the Links (novel) 260
Murder on the Orient Express (novel) 105, 268
Murder Out of School (novel) 131
Murder Unrecognized (novel) 124
Murderers Makes Mistakes (short story collection) 181, 183, 186
"The Murders in the Rue Morgue" (short story) 244
The Murders on Praed Street (novel) 63, 66, 90
Murray, Margaret 278
Mussolini, Benito 195
The Mysterious Affair at Styles (novel) 260
Mystery at Greycombe Farm (novel) 102, 124

Mystery at Lynden Sands (novel) 21, 211, 219, 276, 278
Mystery at Olympia (novel) 37, 71, 90, 120, 265, 267
*Mystery*File* (website) 4
Mystery in the Channel (novel) 22, 147, 160, 163–164, 170–171, 188, 191
The Mystery of the Blue Train 128, 260
Mystery on Southampton Water (novel) 147, 159–160, 166, 179, 188, 273

National Fascist Party 195
Nazism 54–55
Neale, Lilian V. 87
Nemesis at Raynham Parva (novel) 201–205, 243–244, 276
Nesbit, E. 234
New Statesman and Nation (journal) 41, 80
New York Times (newspaper) 104, 106, 110, 120, 162
New York Times Book Review (newspaper magazine supplement) 20
New Yorker (journal) 27
"A New Zealand Tragedy" (essay) 190
Newport (character) 100, 103
Nicolson, Harold 159, 166
Nicolson, Marjorie Hope 258
Nietzsche, Friedrich 234
Night and Day (journal) 262
Night Exercise (novel) 41, 89, 131–132, 258
A Night of Errors (novel) 161
The Nine Tailors (novel) 27, 36, 102, 125
No Past Is Dead (novel) 203, 232
No Walls of Jasper (novel) 33
Nordenholt's Million (novel) 193, 195–198, 203, 205, 215–216, 232, 236, 240, 245, 275
Norris, John 4
Norwood, Gilbert 27
Not a Leg to Stand On (novel) 114
Nothing but the Truth (novel) 91
The Nursing Home Murder (novel) 249

The Odyssey (epic poem) 194
Ohl, Patrick 4
Oldland, Dr. Mortimer (character) 79, 91, 133, 141
One Pair of Hands (memoir) 270
1001 Midnights (critical study) 1, 3
Onions, Oliver 233

Orczy, Baroness 89
Orwell, George 48, 125–126, 258, 270
Ovid, 199
Oxford 9, 24
Oxford Group 177, 183

The Paddington Mystery (novel) 49, 60–61, 131–132, 140
Panek, Leroy Lad 8, 17, 59, 260
Panic Party (novel) 33
The Paper Bag (novel) 93–94, 134
Paradise Lost (epic poem) 194
Pares, Bip 181
Partridge, Eric 167, 263
Partridge, Ralph 41–42, 80, 82, 263–264
patent medicines 106, 115, 174
Paul the Apostle 237
Pearson, Edmund Lester 236
Pemberton, Noel 235
Pemberton-Billing Trial 234
Penguin Books 1, 42
Peril at Cranbury Hall (novel) 31, 90, 133, 268–269
Peril Bleu (novel) 234
Pilgrim's Progress (allegory) 148
Pinehurst (novel) 71
Pippett, Roger 22
The Pit-Prop Syndicate (novel) 153–154, 160, 163, 183, 186, 272
Plain, Gill 259
The Platinum Cat (novel) 106–107, 131
Playfair Cipher 267
Poe, Edgar Allan 219, 233–234
Poirot, Hercule (character) 11, 25, 72, 232, 260, 268, 276
Poison for One (novel) 38, 71–72, 74, 83, 121
Poison in the Parish (novel) 34
The Poisoned Chocolates Case (novel) 32
Polna ritual murder trials 52, 55–56
The Ponson Case (novel) 149–153, 160, 163, 186
Porter, Dennis 12, 17
Portugal 153
Priestley, April (character) 60
Priestley, Joseph 60
Priestley, Dr. Lancelot (character) 42–43, 45, 49, 56, 59, 60–63, 65–72, 74–80, 82–85, 91, 93–98, 101, 124, 130–131, 133–135, 138, 141, 143–144, 261, 265
Priestman, Martin 259
Princeton University 26
Proceed with Caution (novel) 71, 85–86, 144
Procter, Maurice 267

"The Professor and the Detective" (essay) 258
Pronzini, Bill 1, 3, 152
Pullein-Thompson, Josephine 25
pulp fiction 226
Punshon, E.R. 7, 33, 72, 80, 105
The Puritan Pleasures of the Detective Story (critical study) 146
The Pursuit of Crime (critical study) 12, 17

Queen's University Belfast 10, 193, 232, 237–238

Railways and Culture in Modern Britain (critical study) 259
Read, Sir Herbert 26, 28–29, 261–262
The Red Thumbmark (novel) 241
Released for Death (novel) 34
Rendell, Ruth 8, 258
Rhineland and Ruhr (political analysis) 55
Rhode, John (pseudonym of Cecil John Charles Street) 57–97 passim; origin of pseudonym 57; *see also* Street, Cecil John Charles
Rickard, Mrs. Victor 89
Rinehart, Mary Roberts 187
Rising Tide (journal) 177
The Robthorne Mystery (novel) 71, 93, 143
Rodell, Marie F. 266
Roger Sheringham and the Vane Mystery (novel) 32
Rohmer, Sax (Arthur Henry Sarsfield Ward) 30, 260
Rollo, Sergeant (character) 185
Root, R.K. 26
Ross, Inspector (character) 155
Ross, Superintendent (character) 203, 214–215, 276
Roughead, William 271, 277
Rouse, Alfred 232
Routley, Eric 146–147
Rowland, Susan A. 9, 259, 272
Rowley, George 26
Royal Air Force (R.A.F.) 116, 210
Royal Military College, Woolwich 48
Rubinstein, W.D. 269
Ruddick, Nicholas 195–196, 275
Rzepka, Charles 258

Sadleir, Michael 29
Saint—with Red Hands? (true crime study) 271
Saint-Saens, Camille 75

Salome (play) 235
Sapper (H.C. McNeile) 30, 58
Saturday Review of Literature 27
Sayers, Dorothy L. 1–3, 6, 8, 9–10, 17, 22, 24–25, 27–28, 30, 33, 34–36, 40, 43, 47, 87–90, 101–102, 108, 117, 125, 141, 159, 162, 164, 177, 233, 240, 253–254, 258–263, 274, 279; praise of "Humdrum" authors 18, 37–38, 72, 76, 78, 81–82, 228, 263; role in transformation of detective novel 34–37, 262–263; *see also* Crime Queens; Crofts, Freeman Wills; detective fiction; "Humdrums"; Street, Cecil John Charles
Scaggs, John 257, 259
Scarlatti, Domenico 28
Scotland 195, 230, 232–233, 237, 239
Scottish Baptist College 237
The Sea Mystery (novel) 20–21, 146, 158–161, 170, 185, 188
The Second Shot (novel) 32–33
The Secret Adversary (novel) 260
The Secret Meeting (novel) 93, 131, 140, 270
The Secret of Chimneys (novel) 11, 260
The Secret of High Eldersham (novel) 98, 100, 102, 105–106, 278
Selassie, Emperor Haile 237
Shakespeare, William 29
Shanks, Edward 125
shell shock 169
Sheringham, Roger (character) 31–32
Shiel, M.P. 233
Shifting Gears (critical study) 16–17
Shot at Dawn (novel) 22–23, 71, 80–82, 133, 144, 270
Sic Transit Gloria (novel) 34
Silence for the Murderer (novel) 148, 172
The Silk Stocking Murders (novel) 32
"The Simple Art of Murder" (essay) 167
Simpson, Paula 127, 267
Sinclair, May 233
Sir John Magill's Last Journey (novel) 29–30, 105, 146, 159–163, 170, 172–173, 184, 188, 273
Situation Vacant (novel) 114, 268–269
Smith, E. Baldwin 26
Smith, Erin A. 9–10
Smith, Nancy Hough 26

Snobbery with Violence (critical study) 11, 128, 142, 184; *see also* Watson, Colin
Snow, C.P. 24
Social Decay and Regeneration (social theory) 195
Society of Authors 177
Somerville, Vice-Admiral Henry Boyle Townshend 235
Somerville College (Oxford) 9
Soviet Union 182, 197, 274
Spectator (journal) 37, 41, 219
Spillane, Mickey 42
The Stabbing of George Henry Storrs (true crime study) 190
Stalin, Joseph 196–197
Stewart, Alfred Walter (J.J. Connington): academic pendanticism 238; alibis and timetables in novels of 223, 277; Arthur Conan Doyle 242; Aubrey Beardsley 240; and Auden's "The Guilty Vicarage" essay 275; authority and authoritarianism/totalitarianism 194–203; blood sports and torture 225, 235, 278; business and capitalism 198–199, 223–224, 236; as chemistry professor and scientist 193, 277; children's literature 234; cinema 240; class 197–199, 204–206, 210–216, 225–226, 231, 277; classical literature 194, 239–240; clue tabulations in novels of 226, 231; commercialism 236; and "The Counsellor" detective series 231; cynicism concerning humanity of 195–199, 203–204, 215–216, 222, 233, 236–237, 239, 276; decline in quality of work of 231–232; detective fiction 240–245; dispute with elder brother 277; Edgar Allan Poe and Mark Twain 233–234; epistolary friendship with Rupert Thomas Gould 194, 233–245; essays of 232; and family 194, 230, 237, 239–241, 277; France and Germany 236–237; Guy de Maupassant 234; health problems and death of 229–230, 232, 279; homosexuality 208–209, 235; ingenuity of his detective novels 193–194, 216–224, 225–233, 279; Ireland and the I.R.A. 195, 213, 235, 275; James Joyce and *Ulysses* 234; Japan 229, 275, 277; Jews 197, 199; landed

gentry 199, 216; League of Nations 237; Loch Ness Monster 233, 278; Lord Alfred Douglas and Oscar Wilde 235; modern novels 234; monarchy 196, 275; morality and religion 194, 196, 237, 240; practical joke devices 236; praise for books of 21–23, 38–39, 193–194, 216–217, 219–220, 222–224, 227–230, 260; R. Austin Freeman 195, 241–242, 279; race and ethnicity 195, 197–198, 201–202, 215, 276; relationships with professional colleagues and students 237–238; resemblance to series detective Sir Clinton Driffield 233–234; Second Italo-Abyssinian War 237; secularist outlook of 194; "self-expression" 204; sense of humor of 193–194, 228–229, 233; servants 213–215, 276–277; sex 194, 202, 204–210, 222, 224, 234–235, 276, 278; speedy writing of 277; spiritualism 242; supernatural literature 233–234; thrillers 226; the Titanic 233; United States 237, 275; Versailles Peace Treaty 237; women 197–198, 204–210, 224, 231, 275, 278; Woodrow Wilson and Edward M. House 278; *see also* detective novels; Humdrums; individual book and story titles

Stewart, Charles (brother) 277

Stewart, Frederick (brother) 277

Stewart, Irene (daughter) 198, 213, 230, 232, 237, 239–241, 276–279

Stewart, Lily Coats (wife) 237, 239–240, 276

Stewart, William (father) 195

Storrs, George Henry (murder case) 189–190

Storthes Hall (Yorkshire) 53

Strachey, John 40, 263

Strachey, Lytton 41, 263

Strangeways, Nigel (character) 80

Street, Caroline Bill (mother) 53

Street, Cecil John Charles: agrarianism 47, 118–119, 121–123; alibis and timetables in novels of 85–86, 108, 223, 268; ancestry and family of 48, 53, 123, 141–142; and Anthony Gilbert (Lucy Beatrice Malleson) 50, 87, 89, 267; as army artillery officer 48, 53, 122–123; as army intelligence officer 48, 57; artistic temperament and Bohemianism 141, 271; authority 47, 51, 53, 59, 125, 131–132; in Black and Tan War 48; British imperialism 55; business 47, 59, 66–67, 69–70, 82, 84–85, 119, 121, 123–124, 269; cars, machinery and technology 47, 87–88, 119–121, 269; cats 75–76, 87, 112–113; and Christianna Brand 90; class 47, 54, 57, 76–77, 95–97, 107–108, 110–112, 117–119, 121–132, 137–139, 143–144, 265, 269; Communism 54, 58–59, 85, 131; conviviality and storytelling of 89, 264; The Cottage, Swanton Novers, Norfolk 50, 86–87, 127; Crime Queen influence on 100–101, 141; David Lloyd George 265; declining health and death of 50, 55; detailed topography of novels 95–96, 267; in Detection Club 50, 57, 88–90, 138; as *Detection Medley* editor 89–90; detective story morals 81–81; Dictaphone use by 57, 91; and Dorothy L. Sayers 88–90; and drink 89; education of 48; as electrical engineer 48, 53, 88–89, 107–108, 116, 123; and Eric the Skull 88; Firlands, Woking, Surrey 53, 265; and food 87, 143; France 278; generosity to other writers 90; handwriting 89; as heir to R. Austin Freeman 45, 85; homosexuality 133; influence of Crime Queens on 100–101, 141; influence of Margaret Murray on when writing *The Secret of High Eldersham* 278; ingenuity of his detective novels (murder means/mechanics) 45–47, 66, 71–72, 79–85, 101–103, 105, 107–108; Inspector/Superintendent Hanslet modeled after 130, 270; as inspiration for John Dickson Carr's Colonel March character 90; the Irish 140, 271; Jews 47, 55–57, 59, 140; and John Dickson Carr 45, 49–50, 88–90; landed gentry 107–108, 121–124, 269, 271; and Lilian V. Neale and Paula Simpson 87; as literary stylist (allusions, characterization, settings and pure writing) 47, 51, 65–66, 70, 101–102, 104–106, 112–113, 130–131, 140–144, 265; local philanthropy of 127–129, 267, 269; and locked room plot device by 85, 104, 107, 112–113; London 267, 269; loss of creative inspiration and decline in quality of work 47, 71, 91, 93; marriage and sex 47, 51–52, 65, 70, 132–136, 141, 265, 270; mechanical interests of 53, 88–89, 265; the military 123, 132, 269; murder 62, 67, 69–71; nostalgia in his books 91; The Orchards, Laddingford, Kent 49–50, 128; peripatetic life of 50; philanthropic organizations 107–108, 114, 268; plutocrats 127–128; poison use in books 72–79, 93–95, 105–106, 114; police 62, 93, 130–131, 137–139, 271; politics 49, 54–57, 59, 84–85, 97, 114–118, 265; post–WW2 Labour government 97, 114–118, 269, 274; praise for novels of 17–18, 23–25, 38–39, 264; productivity of 47, 49, 57, 71, 90–92, 98; as "Public Brain-Tester No. 1" 18, 46–47; pubs 50, 95–97, 129, 131, 143–144, 269; as puzzle constructor 108–110, 112; race/ethnicity 52, 55, 70, 118; railroad detail in his books 104–106; rejection of literary Gothicism 142; religious Puritanism and ministers of religion 114–116, 132, 137, 270; sales of and income from novels 63; satire in novels of and sense of humor of 51–53, 101, 103, 105–108, 114, 268–269; servants 118, 128–130; social impact of World War II 135–136; Summerhill, Lyme Regis, Dorset 48; thrillers of 57–60, 98–100, 102–103; translations from French by 49; travel by 50, 118; true crime writing 47, 93, 136–140; Uplands, Woking, Surrey 53; Utopianism 54; Victorian architecture 265; Victorian patriarchy 137; village settings of his novels 50, 102, 109, 118–119, 125, 143; warfare 54–55, 265; wealth of 65; women 47, 65, 70–71, 111, 134–136, 265, 268; work 53–54, 110, 112,

116, 121, 123–128; in World War I 48–55, 82, 122; in World War II 86, 108; *see also* detective novels; Dodd, Mead and Company; Doubleday, Doran and Company; Humdrums; individual book and story titles; Kent, Constance (murder case); Wallace, Julia (murder case)
Street, Eileen Waller (second wife) 48, 50, 57, 86–87, 113, 128, 134, 264, 268, 271
Street, Hyacinth Maud Kirwan (first wife) 48, 141, 268, 270–271
Street, John Alfred (father) 53, 264–265
Street, Louisa May (half sister) 264–265
Street, Sophia Catherine (half sister) 264–265
Street, Verena Hyacinth Iris (daughter from first marriage) 48, 141–142
Sudden Death (novel) 22, 168, 172, 187–188, 273
Summerscale, Kate 136, 139, 271
Sunday Times (newspaper) 18, 34, 37, 166, 227, 229–230
Suspicion (film) 262
The Suspicions of Mr. Whicher (true crime study) 47, 136, 271
Swanton Novers (Norfolk) 50, 86–87, 127
The Sweepstake Murders (novel) 22, 194, 216, 222–224, 243, 244, 278
Swinburne, Algernon Charles 144
Switzerland 157
Symons, Julian 2, 6–8, 11, 13, 15–16, 18, 24–25, 29, 32, 37, 42–43, 47, 140, 153, 156–158, 167, 171, 180, 183, 190–191, 194, 232–233, 257, 262–264, 272, 274–275; role in development of "Humdrum" paradigm, 2, 6–7, 15–16; *see also Bloody Murder*; detective fiction; "Humdrums"

Tales of Detection (Everyman's Library) (short story collection) 34, 36
Talking About Detective Fiction (critical study) 11, 24, 28, 258; *see also* James, P.D.
Tanner, Inspector (character) 150–153, 155, 186, 272
Taylor, Bernard 139, 271
Taylor, Wendell Hertig 1, 3, 8, 13, 43, 78, 80, 91, 103, 106, 110, 180–181, 223–224, 257; *see also* Barzun, Jacques; *A Catalogue of Crime*
tea-party parsons 270
Tees Valley (England) 238
The Telephone Call (novel) 91–92, 133
Tennyson, Alfred 144
Terminal Visions (critical study) 195
Tey, Josephine 257–258; see also Crime Queens
Thackeray, William Makepeace 270
They Watched by Night (novel) 41, 71, 79–80, 91, 135–136
This Undesirable Residence (novel) 268
Thompson, Emma 41
Thompson, Laura 5, 9
Thompson-Bywaters murder case 31
Thomson, Basil 267
Thomson, H. Douglas 3, 17, 25, 30, 163, 261
Thorndyke, Dr. John (character) 3, 27, 45, 232, 241, 265, 272
The Three Corpse Trick (novel) 112, 114, 140, 267
Three Cousins Die (novel) 91
Tichi, Cecilia 16–17 ?
Time to Be in Earnest (autobiography) 10; see also James, P.D.
"The Titanic" 233
To Catch a Thief (novel) 4, 102–103, 126, 132, 134
Tom Tiddler's Island (novel() 210–211, 276, 278
Top Storey Murder (novel) 33
"Torquemada" (Edward Powys Mathers) 159
Tragedy at Ravensthorpe (novel) 194, 212–213, 216–217, 219
Tragedy at the Unicorn (novel) 61, 63, 269–270
Tragedy on the Line (novel) 90–91, 133–135, 184
The Treachery of France (political analysis) 49
Trent's Last Case (novel) 35, 180, 227
triolet 263
Troy, Agatha 141
Les Troyens (opera) 149
Truman, Harry S 274
Truth Comes Limping (novel) 42, 215–216, 231, 244, 276
Tryhorn, Frederick Gerald 232
Twain, Mark 233–234
Twelve Good Men (film) 66
The 12.30 from Croydon (novel) 38, 159, 166, 169–170

The Twenty-One Clues (novel) 206, 209–210
"The Two Cultures" (lecture) 24
The Two Graphs (novel) 93, 134, 144
The Two Tickets Puzzle (novel) 21–22, 276

Ultimate Island (critical study) 195–196
Ulysses (novel) 234
Under the Greenwood Tree (novel) 269
University League Book Club, Detective Group (Princeton) 26, 261
University of Glasgow 10, 194
University of Leeds 26
University of Toronto 27
Up the Garden Path (*The Fatal Garden*) (novel) 134
Upfield, Arthur 16
Utilitarianism 169

Vance, Philo (character) 260, 262
Vandam, Inspector (character) 154–155, 157, 187
Van de Water, Frederic F. 219
Van Dine, S.S. 159, 257, 260, 262
Vane, Harriet (character) 28, 141
The Vanishing Diary (novel) 91
Vegetable Duck (novel) 71–72, 78–79, 93, 128, 131, 266
The Venner Crime (novel) 71, 141
Victor Gollancz (publishing company) 35, 222, 253

Wade, Henry (Henry Lancelot Aubrey-Fletcher) 1–2, 7, 117, 257, 267, 273–274; role in transformation of detective novel 33–34
Wagar, W. Warren 195
Waghorn, Diana Morpeth 128, 134, 141
Waghorn, Inspector/Superintendent James (Jimmy) (character) 42, 61–62, 77–80, 84–85, 91, 93–97, 101, 125, 128, 130–131, 134–135, 140–142
Wakefield, H.R. 233
Wall Street Stock Market Crash of 1929 164, 170
Wallace, Edgar 30–31, 57, 65, 98, 226, 260, 262
Wallace, Julia (murder case) 93
Waller, John Francis 264
Walling, R.A.J. 7

Walpole, Hugh 89
Watson, Colin 11, 128, 132, 142, 184, 259, 270; misreading of sexual element in *Tragedy at the Unicorn*, 270; *see also* detective fiction; *Snobbery with Violence*
Watson, Dr. John (character) 219–220
Watteau's Shepherds (critical study) 8
Waugh, Hillary 267
Waye, Cecil (pseudonym of Cecil John Charles Street) 16, 98, 268; *see also* Street, Cecil John Charles
Webb, Mary 121
Weekly Standard (newspaper) 29
The Weight of the Evidence (novel) 27
Wellington College 48
Wells, H.G. 143, 204
Wendover, Squire (character) 201, 203, 208, 210, 212, 215–216, 218–219, 223–224, 226, 228, 231, 276
Wentworth, Patricia 279
Werewolf of London (film) 240

Wharton, Edith 5
Wheatley, Dennis 278
Where Is Barbara Prentice? (novel) 102–103, 105, 133, 136, 143
Whicher, Inspector Jonathan 136–137, 139
Whitbread & Co., Ltd. 125
Wilde, Oscar 235, 270
Wilhelm, Richard H. 26
Wilkinson, Stella 266
Williams, Charles 20–21, 159, 164, 170
Williams, Valentine 253
Willis, Inspector (character) 153–155, 157–158, 186–187, 272
Wilson, Edmund 259
Wilson, Woodrow 278
Wimsey, Lord Peter (character) 25, 28, 100, 141, 164, 232
"Wireless" (Rudyard Kipling short story) 66, 144
Wise, Berkeley Deane 147
The Witch-cult in Western Europe (historical monograph) 278
witchcraft 100, 105, 234, 278

Wodehouse, P.G. 260
Woking (Surrey) 53, 265
Wolfe, Nero (character) 261
Wood, Dave 264
Woode, Teak (character) 264
Woodthorpe, R.C. 89
World War I 9, 15, 17, 48–55, 82, 122, 222, 265; *see also* Street, Cecil John Charles
World War II 12, 15, 33, 42, 79–80, 86, 108, 267
WO2 (novel) 272
Wray, Fay 240
Wright, Richard 22
Wright, S. Fowler 235
Wrong, E.M. 17, 25
The Wychford Poisoning Case (novel) 31–32

Young, Inspector (character) 100
Young Robin Brand, Detective (novel) 155, 182, 184, 186, 190

The Zeal of the House (radio play) 177

www.ingramcontent.com/pod-product-compliance
Lightning Source LLC
Chambersburg PA
CBHW081540300426
44116CB00015B/2706